Moebius Anthropology

MOEBIUS ANTHROPOLOGY

Essays on the Forming of Form

Don Handelman

Edited by
Matan Shapiro and Jackie Feldman

berghahn
NEW YORK • OXFORD
www.berghahnbooks.com

First published in 2021 by
Berghahn Books
www.berghahnbooks.com

© 2021, 2024, 2026 Don Handelman
Open access ebook edition published in 2024
First paperback edition published in 2026

All rights reserved. Except for the quotation of short passages
for the purposes of criticism and review, no part of this book
may be reproduced in any form or by any means, electronic or
mechanical, including photocopying, recording, or any information
storage and retrieval system now known or to be invented,
without written permission of the publisher.

Library of Congress Cataloging-in-Publication Data

Names: Handelman, Don, author. | Shapiro, Matan, editor. | Feldman, Jackie, editor.
Title: Moebius Anthropology: Essays on the Forming of Form / Don Handelman; edited by
  Matan Shapiro and Jackie Feldman.
Description: New York: Berghahn Books, 2021. | Includes bibliographical references and
  index.
Identifiers: LCCN 2020035474 (print) | LCCN 2020035475 (ebook) |
  ISBN 9781789208542 (hardback) | ISBN 9781789208559 (epub)
Subjects: LCSH: Anthropology—Philosophy. | Form (Philosophy) | Phenomenology.
Classification: LCC GN33 .H255 2020 (print) | LCC GN33 (ebook) |
  DDC 301.01—dc23
LC record available at https://lccn.loc.gov/2020035474
LC ebook record available at https://lccn.loc.gov/2020035475

British Library Cataloguing in Publication Data
A catalogue record for this book is available from the British Library

EU GPSR Authorized Representative

LOGOS EUROPE, 9 rue Nicolas Poussin, 17000, LA ROCHELLE, France
Email: Contact@logoseurope.eu

ISBN 978-1-78920-854-2 hardback
ISBN 978-1-83695-115-5 paperback
ISBN 978-1-78920-855-9 epub
ISBN 978-1-80539-668-0 web pdf

https://doi.org/10.3167/9781789208542

This work is published subject to a Creative Commons Attribution
Noncommercial No Derivatives 4.0 License. The terms of the license
can be found at https://creativecommons.org/licenses/by-nc-nd/4.0/.
For uses beyond those covered in the license contact Berghahn Books.

For Bruce Kapferer

and

his cornucopia of wonderful ideas

warmed by a half century

of

heartfelt friendship

Contents

List of Illustrations ix

Acknowledgments x

Introduction 1
Matan Shapiro

Part I. Some Significant Formative Influences

Chapter 1. Henry Rupert, Washo Shaman 17

Chapter 2. Tracing Bureaucratic Logic through Surprise and Abduction 40

Part II. Forming Form: Ritual and Bureaucratic Logic

Chapter 3. Why Ritual in Its Own Right? How So? 63

Chapter 4. Bureaucratic Logic 93

Chapter 5. Bureaucratic Logic, Bureaucratic Aesthetics: The Opening Event of Holocaust Martyrs and Heroes Remembrance Day in Israel 126

Part III. Cosmological Trajectories

Chapter 6. Passages to Play: Paradox and Process 151

Chapter 7. Framing Hierarchically, Framing Moebiusly 171

Chapter 8. Inter-gration and Intra-gration in Cosmology 191

Part IV. Deleuzian Conjunctions

Chapter 9. Self-Exploders, Self-Sacrifice, and the Rhizomic Organization of Terrorism 213

Chapter 10. Thinking Moebiusly: Can We Learn about Ritual from Cinema with *Mulholland Drive*? 242

Chapter 11. Folding and Enfolding Walls: Statist Imperatives and Bureaucratic Aesthetics in Divided Jerusalem 269

Epilogue. Forming Form, Folding Time (Toward Dynamics through an Anthropology of Form)   289

Index   346

Illustrations

3.1. Calvin and Hobbes cartoon.   64

11.1. The Calatrava pylon-parabola at the western entrance to Jerusalem.   273

11.2. The Yad Vashem memorial complex with the old Holocaust museum in the background and the new Holocaust museum in the foreground.   275

11.3. The Avenue of the Righteous passing through the new Holocaust museum.   276

11.4. The mall-wall from the Old City wall, looking toward West Jerusalem.   280

11.5. The security wall chopping through Palestinian Abu Dis.   282

Acknowledgments

Were it not for Jackie Feldman and Matan Shapiro this book would not exist. Nearing eighty, I wanted to let go of asking about and contemplating the world as I saw it through my own parallax perspectives. I ceased university lecturing years ago, mainly due to increasingly severe chronic illness, yet also to release myself from institutional strictures that always had pressed and compressed. Jackie and Matan persuaded me to make another effort—arguing that compiling a volume something like this one was worth doing. I hope this is so. During the journey of sensing, feeling, and forming this book, Matan was a welcome sojourner, often offering critique and encouragement. Matan himself is indeed a brilliant brainstormer of paradoxes that provoke and complement the idea of moebius movement. My warm thanks to him and to Jackie.

This book is dedicated to Bruce Kapferer. More words would only dim my profound appreciation for the brilliance of his scholarship and the warmth of my comradely feeling toward him, now for over half a century.

Einat Bar-On Cohen has held me together for, by now, so many years. She is a wonderful friend and a fine anthropologist whose embodied and incisive thinking inspires me. Without her more than willing assistance in so many, many ways I would not be here to write these acknowledgements. Bless you, Einat.

Yaron Ezrahi, beloved friend, profound theorist of democracy, science, and the imagination, was my mage during the writing of the Epilogue to this book. And that took me a long time. Yaron was ready to discuss matters of the mind and heart at the drop of an intellectual hat (his, mine fits less well); and our talks were full of thought, reflection, and revelation. Yaron passed in 2019.

My dear friend, David Shulman, polymath that he is, deepened my feeling mind as we worked together on South Asian materials. And, when long ago he persuaded me that in south India the footprint of the elephant precedes the elephant itself, he gave me an inkling of what it is to think moebiusly.

Nita Schechet, a dear friend and an insightful scholar of literature, often joined me in our neighborhood coffee house for lengthy discussions on the art of the impossible. Her thoughts helped to inform my own on moebius. Nita passed in 2016.

I much appreciate younger colleagues who fill me in on their research and remind me that there is so much work to be done by talented scholars. In particular I want to mention Eyal Ben-Ari, Khaled Furani, Tova Gamliel, Lydia Ginzburg, Asaf Hazani, Nadeem Karkabi, Carol Kidron, Mina Meir-Dviri, Nitzan Rotem, Limor Samimian-Darash, Esther Schely-Newman, Avi Shoshana, Nurit Stadler.

A word on the cover art created by the manga artist, Shiriagari Kotobuki. Mr. Shiriagari was commissioned by the Hokusai Museum in Tokyo to do his take of a print of the ukiyo-e artist, Hokusai (1760–1849), from the latter's series, *Thirty-six Views of Mount Fuji*. Mr. Shiriagari took the large barrel being made by a cooper and turned it into a moebius surface. Making the barrel becomes a (perhaps infinitely) recursive task, if not a paradoxical endeavor since the cooper no longer can know whether he is inside or outside the barrel he is forming. To think moebiusly is to be seamlessly inside and outside the forming of form with near simultaneity. My thanks to both Mr. Shiriagari and the Hokusai Museum for enabling me to use this artwork.

Don Handelman
Jerusalem, June 2020

Introduction

Matan Shapiro

Know Your Feeling

In 1998, when he visited his friend the shamanic healer Jonathan Horwitz in Denmark, Don Handelman saw a ghost. He was lying on his back, his eyes closed as Horwitz chanted, directing energies into and away from the room. Handelman then felt an urge in him, a sort of presence, and opened his eyes. His pupils expanded as he found himself gazing at Henry Rupert, the Native American shaman with whom he had worked as a young student thirty-four years earlier near Carson City, Nevada. While Handelman was stunned to see Rupert—in flesh and blood although he had been among the dead since 1973—Rupert was casual and self-assured as he had been decades before, when they first met. Rupert bent over, putting his mouth on Handelman's mouth, breathing air into him. He then looked at Handelman intensely and uttered: "Know through your feelings, but know!" As he said that, he dissipated into thin air.

Contemplating on this close encounter in 2018 during a conversation with Jackie Feldman and myself, Handelman interpreted Rupert's message as a reaffirmation of his own intellectual trajectory in anthropology. "Henry," he said, "was the master of fusing together analytical thinking about the world and a deep feeling for some kind of sensory connectivity with everything in it. Washo cosmology was all about the cohesion of the fixed and the free, and you can decide for yourself where to locate emotions and where to locate epistemic knowledge in this equation." He continued:

> But the very possibility of this cohesion, the perception of reality as multiple, the idea that the free and the fixed can be fused in creative ways to inspire some kind of transformation in the world, countermanded everything I had learned in academia as an anthropologist in the '50s and '60s, which was all about making order out of movement by bringing it to a halt and putting it under control.

That encounter with Rupert in 1998 inspired in Don Handelman a sense of emotional integration combined with lucid conceptualization of something new. As Handelman understood this in hindsight, Rupert thus intimated that Handelman himself was capable of realizing empirically that same simultaneous duality of thinking and feeling in his ongoing intellectual work. Henry Rupert's resurgence from the dead in 1998 in that sense reignited Handelman's own quest to live an intellectual life in the shaman way, a *creative* intellectualism of sort. "One only knows in a fuller, perhaps in a more holistic sense, by knowing that feeling is integral to the existence and movement of organic worlds," Handelman explained.

The chapters in this book will serve as an index to decipher these somewhat confusing words. They express Don Handelman's unique intellectual stance with regard to the nature of human social phenomena. While supplying massive theoretical insights, Handelman's approach to the social—especially to its structuring—is primarily methodological, a systematic tool for cross-cultural analysis, which he has been developing over the last five decades. "My best moments and relationships," writes Handelman (2014: xv) in a short preface to his book on South Indian cosmology, "arrive . . . unannounced, quiet presences that sometimes are life-changing. My anthropology then and now is to grab onto a strange line of flight and then to hold on for dear life. To wherever." He continues, poetically:

> India fills the senses with imaginings, yet these are imaginings within imaginings, fractal imaginings that are borderless and, for me at least, that curve mind-work inward, involuting, yet involution that is emergent, always re-emerging elsewhere into another angle of an expanding cosmos to which I had not had access before. (Ibid.: xv)

Involution, convolution, imaginings, curving, cosmos: Don Handelman does not use these terms merely as poetical metaphors nor does he refer to them as rudimentary writing techniques used to sidestep intricate logical conundrums. Rather, he employs these terms directly and straight-forwardly as analytic "razors" (Handelman 2004) by which it becomes possible to capture social phenomena in their incessant dynamic, a dynamic which he refers to as the process of forming of social forms. Here, the often paradoxical and self-contradictory processes of formulating distinct types of feeling and knowing, in their creative localized formations, are not only objects of study but also conceptual-affective experimentations in their own right, which for him, as I now turn to explicate, must remain at the center of any anthropological analysis of what Handelman sees as the *logic* of forming of form.

The Logic of Forming of Forms

Don Handelman was born in Quebec, Canada, in 1939 to a working-class Jewish family. His parents had emigrated separately from the Ukraine to Canada, where they met and married. Until the age of fourteen, Handelman grew up in a remote rural hotel resort his father, uncle, and friends had bought and operated in the small town of Ste. Agathe des Monts. While it is difficult to assess what drove Handelman to turn to anthropology, he has stated in a biographical interview from the end of the 1990s (Handelman [1998–99] 2017) that living in the hotel provided him with a very dynamic perception of the social world at a very young age, as he was able to observe and feel the transformations between total emptiness off-season and the hustle and bustle of guests who kept coming and going during the busy periods. He studied in a tiny Protestant school in the town, and after graduation—he and one girl were the only students who had not dropped out of high school—moved to Montreal to study at McGill University. Handelman did poorly in most of his classes, excluding the Introduction to Anthropology course, which he says was less strange to him due to his teenage passion for reading science fiction novels. He then applied and was accepted into the MA program in anthropology at McGill (MA 1964), initiating a prolific research career in anthropology that included two years as a PhD candidate at the University of Pittsburgh (1964–66) and a doctoral degree under the supervision of Max Gluckman at the University of Manchester (1966–71), followed by numerous publications during thirty-three years of work as a professor at the Hebrew University of Jerusalem (1972–2005).[1]

From his MA days and throughout his long career, Handelman was deeply interested in social organization, a concept he understands not so much in sociological terms as rules, norms, and conventions, but rather in terms derived from theoretical physics of the David Bohm variety (e.g., Bohm 1980). For Handelman, "organization" consists of spontaneous becoming, a generative emergence of micro-structures that are ephemeral, albeit orderly, like climatic storms, with their own density and pace, depth and intensity and duration. It is from this basic interest in small-scale human interactions and their tendency to form something larger than the sum of their parts—three people working in a factory (1998: 104–12), a healing ritual involving Henry Rupert and a young girl (1967), a game in a workplace for the elderly in Jerusalem (1998: 86–101) that he called "the donkey game"—which stands at the heart of Handelman's lifelong fascination with "forming." "Whatever these people were generating together, even in a short span of time," Handelman states in the aforementioned biographical interview ([1998–99] 2017: 203), "would probably have its own forms, its own rules, which were then impacting on the participants and shaping their interaction." He continues:

> So you couldn't say about interaction, if you had two people beginning to interact, that one person plus one person would equal two, whatever their interaction was, however long it lasted. They'd always be generating something potentially new in their interaction. They were creating this kind of structure to their interaction, and that structure was also creating them as interactors, as they continued to interact. So I tried to think about it like that.

For Handelman, then, a dynamic of "forming" exists in all things, natural and social alike, at all times. In its social manifestation, this dynamic is generated by the ongoing fusion of epistemological and experiential/phenomenological aspects of Being. Social phenomena are never fully at rest. Yet, at the same time, as they are incessantly forming and un-forming, social processes are temporarily stabilized in concrete forms. Cultural practice, to use a widespread anthropological concept, keeps collapsing into itself as it is enacted, always fragmenting into variants of itself. In this process, culture becomes multiple independent forms with finite boundaries, i.e., density, specific gravity, and volume. Yet, at the same time Culture is flowing, a comprehensive, holistic totality, smooth as waves gushing in the ocean of History.

Although he had used the notion of "forming" in many texts and manuscripts, Handelman himself never formulated what "the logic of forming form" might be. Tentatively, in the gist of the argument developed so far, and while avoiding a fixed definition as such, I suggest that the logic of forming can be seen as plural and singular at the same time. It is both primordially self-energizing and a determinist creation, that is, depending on whether you experience forming authentically as it is happening or whether you choose an arbitrary point of emergence for the analysis of the process of forming.[2] The origin of ethnography, in this view, which is also the origin of analysis and its driving force, is a sort of sudden crystallization, which gains momentum and flight as it evolves within itself to bend space-time; but as it moves it also becomes a lever that gravitates to create concrete anthropomorphic figures, frameworks, and dwellings. While the logic of forming of form moves all the time, it sometimes indeed creates the illusion of motionless, passive, eternal presence. The logic(s) of forming of form thereby inhabit human minds, everywhere and always, which means that they are abstract and tangible at the same time. A vignette from that short preface on South Indian cosmology (Handelman 2014: xvi–xvii) will elucidate this (see Chapter Eight in this volume):

> One twilight I was relaxing on the balcony of a small hotel looking out at the waters of Big Lake, within which the goddess, Paiditalli, had been born, the Old City of Vizianagaram on the far side. The liquid depth of the waters. Porous mountains reflecting in the waters. The conjuncture of so much transformation and continuation in the lengthy association of Paiditalli with Vizianagaram, within which she emerges annually through her own interior fluidity, from her own liquid depths that are her cosmos, in order to grow anew the fruitfulness and vitality of the city. And I felt, indeed felt, an inkling, a momentary shadowy glimpse of just how recursive this cosmos is. Of how the depth of a mountain fits into the depth of a lake, while the porous interior of a mountain (with its swirling caves and twisting tunnels) can take in the sea. Of how in a plowed field the space between one furrow and another is a high mountain ridge, while the furrow itself filled with water is a deep lake. Of how, if the spheroid cosmos is turned on its head, the waters of the lake fall on the land like rain; as rainwater flows down the mountains into the fields and their furrows. Of

how all of these surfaces that are depths fit fluidly into one another, and of how this fullness of cosmos becomes immanent as Paiditalli appears in the human world. I went to sleep feeling deepened.

This vignette moves from an immobile and immutable setting—a hotel by the lake near an eternal mountain—to the fluid convulsion of the goddess in the water, which makes up the depth of the cosmos in the lake and under the mountain and ultimately within Handelman's own mind. From the tangible into the abstract and back again, the cosmos being at once a real, everlasting space for the living, and an exercise of the mind, a reflection, a thought process. It is precisely this simultaneity of one thing being another, and therefore neither (cf. Handelman 1998: 68), a nuance located between binary oppositions and clearly defined categorizations, which Handelman develops analytically as the space of and for the generation of meaningful social scientific iterations about knowing and feeling the world. This space is of course paradoxical, or at the very least obscure. Where does the lake begin and the sky end? When does the furrow distinguish itself from the mountain? Or, to use a famous example from Bateson (1977: 246), which Handelman himself has once used (2004: 12–13), what differentiates the swirling of a smoke ring from the air around it?

Don Handelman has consistently and systematically constructed methods to transform such paradoxical observations into heuristic devices for the cross-cultural comparison of social, cultural, and behavioral intensities. Handelman's method begins by identifying the processual emergence of otherness in mindful feelings and their convoluting, ongoing, motile dynamics. It continues with a description of how this dynamic consistently forms precarious, ever-changing social forms—a multiplicity of the conceptual and experiential structures inherent to human interactions in their localized manifestations. Within these terms the social thereby keeps twisting, turning, torqueing and bending, folding and unfolding, incessantly shaping new possibilities for being otherwise in cosmos.

Yet, as Handelman insists, that very image of a stable "whole" (cosmos, or indeed, society, culture, etc.) is always simultaneously shaped by flow, trajectory, and movement, the potentiality of change, which continues to recur in human practice as a result of these unfolding possibilities for transgression (or, if you prefer, immersion with otherness). The logic(s) of forming of form consequently prevail(s) as multiple dimensions of a single, infinitely complex, socio-natural universe, which inhabits people's minds as much as they imagine themselves to be elemental aspects "in" it.

For Handelman, then, the object of study of anthropology is the logic(s) of forming form. As with "curving" (Handelman 2004) or "involutions" (Handelman 2014), Handelman does not conceive of forming as a metaphor, a representation, or an allegory, but rather as a natural phenomenon whose tangible manifestation in the world is felt and known ontologically in body, mind, and soul. Moreover, this is not a "logic" in a semiotic sense, nor is it a socially produced discipline, common sense, or "discourse," as these are understood in traditional cultural constructionism. Rather, for Handelman, the logic of forming of form is an independent process that is fused with the social, but also one that manifests in the natural world separately from collective human phenomena. Its uniqueness as a "logic" is that it somehow knows itself *as* distinct from other logics, and hence it becomes a form in and of itself, which both emanates from and results in human experience while organizing humanly possible worlds in the making of concrete social dramas.

The logic of forming of form, to put this in yet other terms, is a system that emulates itself, but in so doing changes the conditions of its own reproduction. Humans cannot be said to produce or "create" the logic because, in Handelman's understanding of reality, there is no cause and effect. Rather, the logic of forming is in itself a continuous phenomenological instability, whose consequences sometimes gravitate toward structural rest or constancy, and sometimes not. Human beings in that sense are the vehicles through which the logic of forming of form manifests, while at the same time they are active agents that enhance that logic, divert it, and make their world through it. The logic of forming of form in that sense is inherent to a process of repetition that enfolds through itself to shape the precise dispositions that allow, as they transform, for the coming into being of something else. And this is true to the same extent for Vizianagaram, Jerusalem, and London.

Forming of Form in Ethnographic Analysis

In order to exemplify the logic of forming of form as the fusion of phenomenological and structural processes, Handelman has repeatedly used the image of the Moebius Strip, a single surface that has no inside and an outside, top or bottom, but rather, smooth continuity across regular distinctions. It is easy to make a Moebius by cutting a narrow strip of paper, twisting it 180 degrees and then connecting the two edges to form a continuous loop. If a tiny dragon were to walk on the surface of that loop it would be treading sometimes "on top" and sometimes "below," crossing from the "internal" to the "external" side effortlessly and unselfconsciously, as it would not be transgressing any threshold or boundary at any given time. For Handelman, this is the most crystalized experimentation of the paradox of "knowing and feeling," as Rupert has taught him. He claims (Handelman 2012: 68):

> The moebius [*sic*] surface is paradoxical because mathematical logic demands this, and the phenomenological acquiesces: topologically the surface has one side; phenomenally it is a binary, an outside and an in-side. "Out" and "in" relate to one another such that phenomenally they are separate and distinct yet topologically they are one another. Here logical paradox generates dynamism in every crossing of the boundary which also reproduces the boundary as paradox.

Hallmarking the paradox as a crucial topic of intellectual contemplation in the cross-cultural study of the logic of forming of form, Handelman thus suggests that it is not enough to focus on framing on the one hand and experience on the other. Rather, for Handelman, as amorphous as it sounds, the logic of forming of form is the infinite complexity inherent in the paradoxical fusion of these distinct human qualities of perception and conceptualization. What is new about Handelman's approach, as this compares with other contemporary theoreticians in anthropology, is that it treats affect as a property of the universe, an interdimensional quality of cosmological ontology in any of its localized manifestations everywhere in the world, which circulates simply because it needs to circulate. This Handelmanian "logic" is opposed to the classical Kantian idea that flow, or the transfer of affect, is initiated into the world through the power of various types of agents, who are themselves separated from the energy they produce.

Handelman thus characteristically insists that the very process of observing and then capturing in writing the infinitely complex localized ways by which people learn to "know their feelings" is *already* a form of analysis. When we focus on the paradox of the forming of form, we also understand something about the inherent dynamic of our own universe as humans, as members of society and as scholars. In that aspect Handelman's scholarship differs from Georg Simmel's (1972) famous depiction of social forms as objects of analysis; for Handelman, unlike Simmel, there are no external boundaries that define these forms as finite or stable. Handelman strives to move away from monistic terms—that is, away from dialectical processes—because for him these latter dialectical processes oblige us to include in our analysis rigid, categorical definitions, which thereby enforce stable and distinct binaries at the very core of our own interpretation. For Handelman these binaries are teleological because they force us to look at almost every social phenomenon through the back-and-forth movement of the dialectic ping-pong happening between them. Contrarily, Handelman reinvents the work of conceptualization itself through an emphasis on the inherently motile quality of social phenomena (cf. Holbraad 2012). He identifies the thingness of the social, that which is distinctively it—the phenomenality of phenomena, as he calls that "thing" in some of the chapters of this book—in such ongoing motility. For him, this is the crucial difference between a dynamic theory of the *forming* of forms and Simmel's theory of fully acknowledgeable and finalized forms.[3]

While seeking to describe the process by which research interlocutors cross-culturally conceive and practice their own ethnographic theories, Handelman's analyses nonetheless also refer to the scholarly efforts required for any anthropological extrapolation of meaning. While he has not been preoccupied with cross-cultural comparison in and of itself, he has nonetheless provided insights into a wide variety of ethnographic realities taking place in such distinct locations as Israel-Palestine, South India, Nevada, Newfoundland, and Northern Uganda. In a career lasting five decades, Don Handelman has thus striven to phrase a theory of social dynamics that would be flexible enough to account both for its own motility and for the spots in which it finds rest, a self-referential, double-edged method of observation that captures "the logic of forming of form" both as a phenomenon of nature and as a repetitive iteration of meaning in different social universes. I now turn to explicate how each of the essays selected for this volume expresses these efforts while contributing to the task of their crystallization into a coherent analytical framework.

The Book

Moebius Anthropology is an anthology of Don Handelman's major critical engagements with some of the ongoing debates in contemporary anthropology on the poetics and politics of ritual, play, cosmology, and power; widely defined. Don Handelman, Jackie Feldman, and I collaboratively handpicked the different essays out of a life-work portfolio consisting of dozens of published articles and several books, while also including three new chapters that have not yet been published. Each of these essays presents ethnographic insights on the logic of forming of form as this relates to the everyday subtleties of paradox and the self-perpetuating energy inherent in the structured dynamics of social action. The book is divided into four sections, followed by an Epilogue.

The first section, "Some Significant Formative Influences," includes Handelman's foundational ethnographic insights from the 1960s, which later informed much of his later writings and theoretical extrapolations. "The Development of a Washo Shaman" (on which Chapter One is based) is Don Handelman's first major published work, from 1967, in which he traces the life history of Henry Rupert, the Washo Shaman from near Carson City, Nevada, with whom he spoke at length in 1964. The essay takes a creative and unusual look not only at Rupert himself but also at the art of magic-making at large and how it is understood as a creative, processual forming and unforming of cosmological knowledge. In "Tracing Bureaucratic Logic through Surprise and Abduction," a previously unpublished essay, Handelman traces how his own personal life story has (almost accidentally) become entangled with Israeli society. In this chapter Handelman also lays the foundations for his theory of "bureaucratic logic," which receives wider attention in the second section of the book.

The second section, "Forming Form: Ritual and Bureaucratic Logic," focuses on the cosmological frameworks underlying the celebration of rituals as form-making social tools. The section moves from a highly analytic chapter aimed at exploring the very phenomenality of rituals as "forms that form forms," through to an analysis of how such forms manifest in different bureaucratic events. "Why Ritual in Its Own Right? How So?"—a revised version of an essay originally prepared as an introduction and epilogue for a special issue of *Social Analysis* (2004)—develops a unique method to analyze rituals. Rather than look at ritual from the perspective of the kinds of transformations it evokes in wider society, Handelman suggests we focus on that which the ritual does in and of itself, within itself. In this view, ritual is no longer primarily seen as a vehicle for the enactment of certain processes outside itself but rather as a self-reflexive system with a particular dynamic that must be studied first and foremost on its own terms. Only after we understand what these internal processes are, and how they do that which they are supposed to be doing, will we be able to reconnect the ritual to its external social surround and examine it in its wider holistic sense (cf. Shapiro 2015).[4] In "Bureaucratic Logic," Handelman meticulously describes the history of a form of "linear" classification brought into Palestine by the early Zionists, which became the main organizing "logic of forming of form" in the pre-State-of-Israel years. This form, as Handelman understands it, is premised on the assumption that different social categories can fit only into a well-demarcated "box" rather than overlap or interact in a non–mutually-exclusive way. Bureaucratic logic in the Israeli case is the linear schemes Israeli Jews put to work in order to capture and act on the phenomenality of social life marred by an ongoing political conflict with Palestinians, a conflict which is not merely a struggle over land or access to resources but also a debate over the very inclusion and exclusion of individuals and communities in the national body. In "Bureaucratic Logic, Bureaucratic Aesthetics: The Opening Event of Holocaust Martyrs and Heroes Remembrance Day in Israel," Handelman demonstrates the utility of the notion of bureaucratic logic in the analysis of an annual ritual enactment in contemporary Israel. Touching upon the morally charged issue of the memorialization of the Holocaust in the Israeli public sphere, Handelman shows how Zionist cosmology endorsed Jewish cosmological framing of time to generate a ritualized "high peak" in which the entire Zionist narrative can be experienced as a phenomenological ascension from the depth of the death pits to the heights of national liberation and independence.

The third section, "Cosmological Trajectories," includes some of Handelman's most innovative theoretical extrapolations of the notion of Moebius and paradox, which he sees as credible analytical tools for social analysis, especially as this relates to the comparative study of ethnographically grounded cosmologies. In "Passages to Play: Paradox and Process," Handelman analyzes two different kinds of play, one taking place top-down in the assertion of hierarchy and another taking place bottom-up through the implementation of paradox in everyday life. The chapter is based ethnographically on the analysis of Hindu myths and it remains one of the most influential turns in play theory in anthropology. The next chapter, "Framing Hierarchically, Framing Moebiusly," is in fact an elaborate debate with Gregory Bateson's theory of play and fantasy, in which Handelman meticulously explicates why "framing" is an insufficient analytical tool for the understanding of play. Instead, Handelman offers a re-analysis of Bateson, suggesting that play must be understood as both the conceptual framing of the action at hand *as well as* its phenomenological or experiential manifestation at the grassroots level. Remaining with the image of Moebius, Handelman insists that a unified theory of play, fantasy, myth, and paradox must include the ever-changing dynamic of the forming of form that is at once external and internal to individual minds. In the chapter concluding this section, "Inter-gration and Intra-gration in Cosmology," Handelman elaborates these ideas further to suggest a new methodology for the investigation of the social world. In this framework, we must primarily pay attention to local conceptualizations of boundaries that are taken to organize the shape of the universe, as well as to the types of movement that living beings take within it. In what Handelman calls an "organic" or pantheistic cosmos, humans and entities constantly interpenetrate one another's domains. This creates a particular social dynamic, which is premised on intuitive inclusion and syncretic fusion. Contrarily, in a "monothetic" or monotheistic cosmos, the boundary between humans and the divine *is* set, given, and predisposed, so that only God (and His armies) can intervene in the human domain. Consequently, argues Handelman, the social dynamic typical in these cases is that of exclusion and rigid classification, which coincides with the idea of bureaucratic logic as an underlying cosmological common sense in the Global North.

The fourth section, "Deleuzian Conjunctions," exposes Don Handelman's deep immersion in and substantial development of the innovative theories of Gilles Deleuze and Félix Guattari. All three chapters in this section implement the notions of the rhizome dynamic and the curving of social space-time in truly innovative ways, playing creatively with the tension between inside and outside as if along an imaginary Moebius Strip that appears in different forms. "Self-Exploders, Self-Sacrifice, and the Rhizomic Organization of Terrorism" explores the intersubjective nature of self-destructive acts in suicidal terror, wherein the internality of one's self literally becomes the shattering, shredding rage that devastates external realities. Taking an unusual (and often unpopular) philosophical approach toward this very charged political issue, Handelman analyzes in this chapter what kinds of cosmic worlds (rather than political goals) are created by this act of self-sacrifice. In this approach the rhizomic dynamic of terrorism—its complete disregard for commonsensical distinctions between combatants and civilians as well as its affront to the idea of citizenship as something that is contained "within" well-defined external borders—defines a cosmology of forming contrary to the linear formation of boundaries between self and other. In "Thinking Moebiusly: Can We Learn about Ritual from Cinema with *Mulholland Drive*?" Handelman elaborates the notion of rhizome into and through the notion of Moebius. He analyzes David Lynch's masterpiece as an emblem of transformation dynamics in the incessant forming and unforming of social form, as if it implodes from within as we watch the movie (or read the chapter) but also explodes forward and away from us into the screen, or page, and back. Handelman ultimately argues that the film "visualizes liminality from within itself" (Chapter Ten, this volume) and that this may give some insight on how rituals work elsewhere and beyond interactive media, making cinema itself a form of postmodern ritual process (cf. Kapferer 2014). In the third chapter of this section, "Folding and Enfolding Walls: Statist Imperatives and Bureaucratic Aesthetics in Divided Jerusalem," Handelman continues in the same direction, this time analyzing the spatiality of the city of Jerusalem through an innovative discussion of boundaries and walls that dissect the city on the one hand and circumscribe it on the other hand. He argues that the dynamic of "folding" is essential for the understanding of realpolitik in the city as much as it can illuminate our analytical imagination with regard to the role of boundaries and barriers in the making and unmaking of geopolitical realities.

In the Epilogue, Handelman adds the notion of time as elemental to his theory of the forming of social form, moving from a phenomenological perception of time as dimension—which is thus external to social life—to the idea that time is a duration, an ontological quality in and of itself, which *is* in fact the actual process of forming of social form. He uses this framework to analyze anew some of his earlier ideas about forming, curving and cosmology, as well as a re-examination of some of his own experiences in anthropology and of anthropology, from when he met Henry Rupert to the present day. As he unfolds the analysis, which draws on complexity theory and popular physics (especially Ilya Prigogine's famous argument about "time as arrow"), Handelman also frames knowledge as process, not a "thing" that can be stored and classified but rather an ongoing iteration of experience existing beyond epistemology, an intellectual ontology of the flow of internal and external time dynamics, by which what is knowable substantiates itself within and through social encounters. It is the structure of this encounter that is at the center of this book, an encounter between readers and Don Handelman's grand theoretical project in anthropology.

The Anthropology of Don Handelman

The anthropology of Don Handelman is paradoxical, but at the same time it is lucid and coherent in its ongoing effort to produce a dynamic rather than static interpretation of social processes.[5] It focuses on the organization of movement, the stable ephemerality of encounters, a rest in flow, curving, knowing, and feeling. Much like the knowledge of Washo cosmology, which Handelman acquired from Henry Rupert in the mid-1960s, it inherently includes a creative touch and a sparkle of brilliance that is always required for the stabilization of movement. Prophetically, almost, Handelman (1967: 462) concluded his first major publication, which analyzed Henry Rupert's life history, with the following words:

> We have good evidence of both social disorganization and psychological disturbance among acculturating peoples, and we can tentatively suggest that in many ways cultural processes have overwhelmed individual defenses in these cases by destroying traditional alternatives and failing to provide new ones. But what of the creative individual? What of the individual with great ego strength who is able to choose and combine traditional and new alternatives, not merely integrating them but developing new syntheses, which may be both personally satisfying and socially transmissible? Of such persons, and the roles they play, we know little.

Although he probably never planned it, Handelman's intellectual persona through the years has begun mirroring Henry Rupert's own image: a person with great ego strength able to create new alternatives to existing structures. As he sought to analyze the situated fusion of knowing and feeling across diverse fields of scholarly thought and inquiry, Handelman has systematically been advancing Rupert's own "Native American" cosmological assertion that holistic predicaments of culture are inscribed simultaneously and holistically in phenomenological *and* structural (indeed, conceptual) human landscapes. These landscapes, Handelman reminds us, in themselves always contain an infinite complexity of muses and therefore they are always inherently contradictory and paradoxical both as appearances in the individual mind and as collective symbols or reifications. As Handelman told me and Jackie Feldman in a private conversation about Henry Rupert, with which we began this introduction:

> What Henry told me was imperative: "Know through your feelings, but know." This was the crux of his wisdom. Structure is movement, interior movement, so is feeling, interior movement. Disciplines like anthropology are still suffering the divides created by Cartesian dualisms; but movement goes wherever it goes, as does the formation of local times.

Handelman's reading of social phenomena thereby attempts to break away from the Cartesian divide in endlessly creative ways (see Handelman 2007: 119–40). Here, both earthly and divine entities always look at themselves from the outside in order to validate their internal truths. Observable, situated, social phenomena, in other words, do not circumscribe stable or fixed identities but rather are always already indicating the emergence of possible realities, lines of flight, which *are* the structured organization of the encounter that is the business of anthropology. The intellectual effort required in order to dissect and understand this ongoing movement, as well as the moments in which it stabilizes into more-or-less finite forms, necessitates by default a creative force that engages paradox as intrinsic to the process of analysis.

In its comparative scope—that is, as a methodology—Handelman's analytic insights have also been developing slowly throughout his professional trajectory. It is a convoluted methodology, which Handelman kept adjusting and twisting and changing while working on different subjects, never actually aiming at the composition of a comprehensive theory of the social. Yet, as this book suggests, under the general framing of a Theory of the Forming of Form, Handelman has, after all, cumulatively produced over the years a consistent and lasting theory, which puts him side by side with the most sophisticated thinkers of our discipline in recent decades, from Marshall Sahlins through Bruce Kapferer and Victor Turner to Eduardo Viveiros de Castro, Bruno Latour and Marilyn Strathern.[6] It is worth mentioning here that Handelman has worked very closely with Bruce Kapferer and Victor Turner, with both of whom he maintained intimate friendships and fruitful professional cooperation throughout the years.

While some of the analytical terms and methods of argumentation presented in this book may sound cryptic at first for readers yet unfamiliar with the anthropology of Don Handelman, they will become clear as you progress through the chapters. As a unified collection, the chapters represent Don Handelman's major contribution to theoretical anthropology over a period of five decades. This books thus aims at bringing into the limelight one of the most original thinkers in theoretical anthropology of our generation, and, by way of doing this, making a significant contribution to contemporary anthropological knowledge production and intellectual critique more generally.

Notes

I thank Jackie Feldman for his useful comments on earlier drafts of this introduction. I also thank Don Handelman for his eye-opening responses to some of the arguments raised herein.

1. Soon after he arrived in Israel in February 1967 Don Handelman met his future wife, the sociologist Lea Shamgar, who through the years cowrote with him several important texts. Sadly, Lea died from cancer in 1995.
2. Handelman's comment to this assertion: "Why determinist? Or is the determinism an illusion created by lengthy durations of slow movement?"
3. Handelman himself rarely mentioned Simmel in his work. The comparison is my own.
4. Handelman's formulation of "ritual in its own right" was stimulated by the anthropologist, Galina Lindquist, whom Handelman describes as his muse of the intellect and emotion during a decade of intensive interaction. Sadly, Galina Lindquist died of cancer in 2008.
5. Handelman's comment to this assertion: "Where you use 'structure' I would use the 'organization' of movement rather than the sometimes 'more processual' sometimes 'more static.'"
6. Handelman's comment to this assertion: "That is not explicitly stated anywhere—a name as a theorist is given primarily to those who explicitly call their work theory."

References

Bateson, Gregory. 1977. "Afterword." In *About Bateson*, ed. John Brockman, 235–47. New York: E. P. Dutton.
Bohm, David. 1980. *Wholeness and the Implicate Order*. London: Routledge.
Handelman, Don. 1967. "The Development of a Washo Shaman." *Ethnology* 6: 444–64.
———. 1998. *Models and Mirrors: Towards an Anthropology of Public Events*. New York: Berghahn Books. First edition published 1990, Cambridge University Press.
———. (1998–99) 2017. "Surprised by Persistence: Ethnographers Among the Washoe, 1937–1965." Interview with Don Handelman. University of Nevada Oral History Program, 155–220. Retrieved January 2019 from https://archive.org/details/WashoeEthnographers.
———. 2004. "Introduction: Why Ritual in its Own Right? How so?" *Social Analysis* 48: 1–32.
———. 2007. "The Cartesian Divide of the Nation State: Emotion and Bureaucratic Logic." In *The Emotions: A Cultural Reader*, ed. Helena Wulff, 119–40. Oxford: Berg.
———. 2012. "Postlude: Framing Hierarchy, Framing Moebiusly." *Journal of Ritual Studies* 26: 65–77.
———. 2014. *One God, Two Goddesses, Three Studies of South Indian Cosmology*. Leiden: Brill.
Holbraad, Martin. 2012. *Truth in Motion: The Recursive Anthropology of Cuban Divination*. Chicago: University of Chicago Press.
Kafrerer, Bruce. 2014. *2001 and Counting: Kubrick, Nietzsche, and Anthropology*. Chicago: Prickly Paradigm Press.
Shapiro, Matan. 2015. "Curving the Social, or, Why Antagonistic Rituals in Brazil are Variations on a Theme." *Journal of the Royal Anthropological Institute* 22: 47–66.
Simmel, Georg. 1972. *On Individuality and Social Forms*. Edited by Donald N. Levine. Chicago: University of Chicago Press.

Part I
Some Significant Formative Influences

CHAPTER 1
HENRY RUPERT, WASHO SHAMAN

Author's Note

In 1964 I received an MA in Anthropology from McGill University for a thesis entitled, *West Indian Voluntary Associations in Montreal* (see Handelman 1967). A workmanlike job, brick on brick, uninspired and uninspiring, enabled mainly by the caring intelligence of my supervisor, the late Richard ("Dick") Salisbury, a Papua New Guinea specialist, himself the student of S. F. Nadel. On my way to the University of Pittsburgh to begin PhD studies in anthropology I passed that summer in a field training program in Nevada. There I met the shaman, Henry Rupert, and, through Henry, I began to learn to perceive and, so, to learn. And to learn through serendipity, accident, surprise, and abduction. Elsewhere (see Chapter Two, this volume, and Handelman 1993) I've described how it happened that Henry (who literally had declared himself dead to anthropologists) agreed to tell me about his shamanism. That summer with Henry and his family changed my sense of selfness and through this my sense of what anthropology might become for me. Henry opened my horizons, expanded my vision. Above all, my discussions with Henry whetted my imagination (that until then had been devoted mainly to reading science fiction). Put simply, Henry opened to me a life in anthropology. I left Nevada a different anthropologist.

And there were resonances and reverberations. Matan Shapiro mentions at the outset of the Introduction to this volume that Henry came to me in 1998 while I was being healed in Copenhagen by the shaman, Jonathan Horwitz. At that time, while we were visiting Copenhagen, my beloved friend, the late Galina Lindquist, brought me to Jonathan. Galina had studied with Jonathan in preparation for her doctoral fieldwork on neo-shamanism in Sweden (Lindquist 1997, Handelman 1999). Jonathan and his partner at the time, Anette Host, greeted me as an old friend, though we had never met. Jonathan told me something of his own story. When he returned from soldiering in Vietnam, Jonathan decided to study anthropology and enrolled in the graduate program at Columbia University. There he read the essay on Henry, published in 1967, that is reprinted below. Jonathan told me that this text had had a powerful effect on him and helped him decide to switch from anthropology to becoming a healing shaman, the healer I met in 1998. Then and there, Henry recursively returned to me, breathing life into me (once again) and telling me, "Know through your feelings, but know." The injunction, its synergistic synthesis, penetrated me through and through. The Cartesian divide took its leave.

Yet Henry's appearance did not close the circle. There were resonances and reverberations. His injunction pervaded the last fieldwork that I was able to participate in, in Andhra Pradesh together with M. V. Krishnayya and David Shulman (see Handelman 2014: 115–213) and, too, it has nudged me on and off, and perhaps is most prominent in this volume in Chapter Two on tracing bureaucratic logic and in Chapter Ten on the David Lynch film, *Mulholland Drive*. Too, I also should mention that while he was healing me in 1998, Jonathan had a vision, one that at the time made no sense whatsoever to me, and that I will not go into here. But over a year later that vision filled with significance . . .

This chapter presents the life history of the last shaman among the Washo Indians of western Nevada and eastern California. This man, Henry Rupert, presents us with a unique case of the development of a shamanic worldview through time. More specifically, he offers us an opportunity to examine the shaman as an innovator and potential innovator, especially with respect to the curing techniques and personal ideology relating him to the supernatural, the natural environment, and other men. While the anthropological literature is replete with descriptions of shamanic rituals and cultural configurations of shamanism in particular societies, as well as functional explanations purporting to explain the existence of shamanic institutions, little attention has been paid to the shaman as an innovator, although the idea was presented by Nadel (1946), exemplified by Voget (1950) in a somewhat different religious context, and briefly touched upon by Murphy (1964: 77). Henry Rupert exemplifies the shaman as a creative innovator and potential "cultural broker," and his life history will be presented as an essentially chronological sequence of events, situations, and ideas.

In the period before White contact, the Washo occupied territory between Lake Tahoe, on the border of present-day California and Nevada, and the Pine Nut Mountains east of Reno and Carson City; in the north their territory extended to Honey Lake, and in the south to Antelope Valley (Merriam and d'Azevedo 1957; Downs 1963: 117). In terms of social organization, the Washo were composed of three bands, although the family, sometimes nuclear and sometimes extended, was the primary unit of social organization; and the family unit decided the yearly round of hunting and gathering activities, sometimes under the leadership of antelope shamans and rabbit "bosses." A high prevalence of witches and sorcerers has also been reported among the aboriginal Washo (Leis 1963; Siskin 1941) in much the same configuration as has been reported for the neighboring Northern Paiute (Park 1939; Whiting 1950), with all shamans suspect as potential sorcerers. With increasing

White occupation of their territory during the late nineteenth century, their seasonal round was disrupted, and the Washo settled around White habitations and ranches, working as seasonal laborers, ranch hands, lumberjacks, and domestic servants. It was into this disrupted cultural milieu, and disorganized social situation, that Henry Rupert was born.

The Becoming and Being of a Shaman

Henry Rupert was born in 1885, the son of Pete Duncan and Susie John, both Washo, in Genoa, Nevada. Genoa was an area of lush farm- and ranch-land amidst the arid Nevada semi-desert which had been first settled by Mormon emigrants from Utah. In the shadows of Job's Peak, a 9,000-foot mountain in the Sierra Nevada range, the Mormons had farmed the desert and transformed it into the rich grassland it still is today. When Henry Rupert was still very young, about two to three years old, his father deserted the family. Henry did not meet his father again until he was twenty years old and his father, a complete stranger, was working as a handyman in a Chinese restaurant in Carson City. By this time Pete Duncan had remarried; and father and son remained strangers until Pete Duncan died.

Henry's mother, Susie John, worked as a domestic servant for a ranch in Genoa. Most of her time was taken up with her domestic chores, and Annie Rube, Henry's older sister, organized and managed the family household and acted as the family disciplinarian. Her husband, Charley Rube, worked as a ranch hand and fisherman, but he was also an antelope shaman, a man who in aboriginal times was entrusted with the task of "singing" antelope to sleep during the annual Washo antelope drives. Near the encampment of Henry Rupert's family lived Henry's mother's sister's husband, Welewkushkush, and his wife. Until the age of eight, when he was taken to school, Henry divided most of his time between Genoa during the winter and the shores of Lake Tahoe during the summer, usually in the company of either Charley Rube or Welewkushkush.

During his early years, Henry had a series of dreams which he still remembers with clarity, and which probably marked him early as having shamanic and mystic potential. As he describes the situation, he would go to sleep on the ground inside the family lean-to and dream of a bear who came and stood in the lean-to opening and stared at him. When he looked at the bear, it would vanish, and then Henry would fly up into the sky toward the moon. This dream recurred frequently over a fairly long period. As a youngster, Henry was also subject to spells of dizziness and fainting. These spells also occurred at bedtime, and both the lean-to and ground would whirl around in a circular motion. Henry would then tell his family to go outside the lean-to and build large fires to stop the ground from whirling about. However, no one paid any attention to his demands, and after a while he would recover.[1]

Welewkushkush, a well-known shaman among the Washo, was already between sixty and seventy years old when Henry was born, and on a number of occasions

Henry was able to watch him healing. During one of these curing sessions, Henry observed Welewkushkush dance barefoot in a lean-to fire and emerge unscathed. Not surprisingly, the youngster respected his uncle greatly both for his curing feats and for his generous, kind attitude and demeanor toward his patients, relatives, and acquaintances. Henry maintains that he harbored similar feelings of respect toward his brother-in-law, Charley Rube, and that the same general attitudes prevailed in his family relationships. He was never severely disciplined at any time, and only his sister, Annie Rube, scolded him. Nevertheless, even within this milieu, Henry exhibited strong feelings of hostility and aggression as well as independence, as exemplified by the following incident, quoted verbatim:

> Someone, I don't remember who, gave me a little puppy. I liked it very much. One evening that puppy made lots of noise, and he stealed [sic] some of the food we were going to have for supper. My elder sister gave me hell about it. She said: "You don't need that puppy in here; it's no good; get rid of it." I made up my mind to kill that puppy. I took it to a fence made out of rocks and I threw a big rock on top of the puppy and killed it. My mind was made up. When I make up my mind, I don't change it. The next evening they asked me where the puppy was. I told them I killed it, because they told me it had been no good.

During these early years Henry had few friends. He spent much time by himself wandering over desert and mountain for days at a time, living off the land when he could, and going hungry when he could not. Given the laissez-faire attitude within his family, he had to report to no one, nor did he even have to be home at regular intervals. While not self-sufficient, he was able and independent. On one occasion, he "hopped" a freight train to Sacramento to see what lay on the other side of the Sierra Nevada Mountains. He also exhibited a boundless curiosity about the natural world around him, a world filled with strange forces and beings, and their existence was often manifested to him. He still remembers sleeping in an abandoned campsite one night and seeing a strange object resembling a cloud pass close by his body while he was awake, and wondering what it represented. On another occasion, while walking down a deserted path at dusk, he saw a white object ahead of him. As he walked forward, it moved. When he stopped, the object also halted. He began to sweat heavily and was extremely frightened. Finally he gathered his courage, walked up to the object, and found an old nightshirt flapping in the evening breeze. Yet he wondered that the object flapped only when he walked forward and stopped when he desisted. Such incidents were not simple coincidences; they suggested an importance and significance that he was not yet able to unravel.

In 1892, at the age of seven, Henry received the first conscious intimation of what his future powers might be. A relative of his mother died; his mother was deep in mourning and quite despondent. Henry dreamt of the event which would follow, and the event came to pass during that winter. His mother went from the family encampment to a slue on the frozen Carson River, and there she attempted suicide by trying to break through the ice and drown herself. But the ice was too thick, and her attempt failed. This was the first time that Henry began to feel that he too might be gifted in the manner of his beloved uncle, Welewkushkush.

Without becoming unduly analytic at this point, it is pertinent to indicate that during these first eight years of Henry Rupert's life many of the elements which resulted in his becoming a shaman were already present. During these early years Henry was a Washo, but a Washo who camped on the fringes of the dominant White society upon whom his mother depended for her livelihood. He spoke no English, only Washo; his mother worked as a menial, a domestic servant; and his father had forever deserted the family encampment. There is little doubt that these factors engendered much hostility in Henry. Yet, because of the great degree of freedom allowed him, much of this hostility was dissipated in his extensive and lengthy wanderings, which at times almost take on the attributes of a rudimentary vision quest. As a child of a culturally disrupted and socially disorganized Indian group, he differed little from many other Indian children in the area, but even at this early age his dreams, visions, and fantasy world were beginning to coalesce around the conception that he might have unusual abilities. Also, he had no peers with whom to identify. His models of socialization and learning were much older and more important; they included a shaman and an antelope shaman, both very well versed in Washo lore and tradition. Both of these men, and in fact his whole family, presented him with models of behavior based on kindness and sympathy, and to a lesser extent, understanding. The aforementioned incident involving the puppy was apparently the one occasion in which Henry's hostility was expressed within the family milieu, and even here it was met with sympathy. Up to the present time, Henry Rupert exhibits strong loyalties and deep affection toward his immediate family, their children, and grandchildren.

In the phase of his life just described, Henry had models of behavior, models of affect, that he admired and respected, and on the whole, this outweighed his aggressive and hostile sentiments. But even more important in the long run were the personal qualities that he exhibited at an early age—his curiosity, independence, and perseverance, which overcame his strongest fears. We shall find these themes recurring again and again throughout his life.

Some ten miles north of Genoa and two miles south of Carson City is the Stewart Indian School. Today it is a boarding school primarily for Indian children from the Southwest, but in 1893 it was a center for the "forced acculturation" of Indian children from the Great Basin under the supervision and control of the United States Army. As part of its pacification program in the area, the Army required all Indian children to attend and board at Stewart until they had completed the equivalent of an eighth-grade education. Children held back by their parents were forcibly removed from their families by the cavalry. At the age of eight, Henry Rupert was taken from Genoa to Stewart, where he lived until the age of eighteen. It was here that he received the "power dream" which marked him as a potential shaman; here, too, he met his future wife, and here he began to formulate the basis of his philosophy of healing and his rationale for becoming a shaman, both of which were to be greatly expanded in later life.

At Stewart, Henry experienced an environment vastly different from that of his years of freedom and independence. Stewart was highly regimented and often brutal. This was Henry Rupert's first sustained contact with White society. Discipline was harsh, and every effort was made at forced acculturation. Order was maintained with a rawhide whip and detention cells. Children were not allowed to return home for short respites until they had completed three full years at Stewart. Classes were held in the mornings and in the evenings. In the afternoons the children were taught a trade. If a child was late for meals, he did not eat. Here also, Henry was introduced to White religion through a profusion of Catholic, Baptist, Methodist, and Anglican proselytizers. All the children were forcibly baptized. Every morning, before breakfast, the children attended services. At breakfast, prayers were sung in Latin. On Sundays the children went to church in the morning, and in the evening, they attended Bible classes and sang hymns. Some proselytizers even came on Saturdays and preached all afternoon.

The day after Henry arrived, he ran away, but he was quickly returned. All told he ran away three times. The second time he was severely whipped on his bare back. However, Henry did well in school, and he learned to set newspaper type. He found a friend in the school cook, who often gave him extra food to supplement the bare school rations. He also developed his own techniques for maintaining some symbolic degree of independence. On one occasion he accidentally broke a spoon and in consequence was forbidden to eat with a spoon for the next month; he then stole a spoon and used it. He resisted the blandishments of his schoolmates with regard to alcohol. The temptation was probably great, since his schoolmates went so far as to place a bottle of liquor under his pillow. At Stewart, Henry made his first close friend, Frank Rivers, another Washo; only to Frank did Henry confide his potential powers. It was also at Stewart that Henry first came to know intimately Indians from other tribes in the Great Basin—Northern Paiute and Shoshone—and his first girlfriend was a Paiute. One of Henry's strongest assets was his ability to absorb selectively those aspects of White culture which he felt were beneficial to him; thus he was able to master academic subjects, notably reading and writing, and learn an occupation, while resisting Christianity, regimentation, and alcohol.

In 1902, at the age of seventeen, Henry experienced his power dream, the event which marked him with certainty as shamanic material and which conferred certain abilities upon him. He described it to me as follows:

> I was sleeping in the school dormitory. I had a dream. I saw a buck in the west. It was a horned buck. It looked east. A voice said to me: "Don't kill my babies any more." I woke up, and it was raining outside, and I had a nosebleed in bed.

Henry interpreted the dream in the following way. The conjunction of buck and rain suggested that he could control the weather, since the buck was the "boss of the rain." The buck was standing in the west but looking east. The Washo believed that the souls of the recently dead travel south but that, soon after, the souls of those who have been evil turn east. The buck looking east was interpreted as a warning against developing certain potentialities which could become evil. The voice in the dream was that of a snake warning against the indiscriminate taking of life; previously Henry had killed wildlife, insects, and snakes without much concern. The rain, to which he had awakened, indicated that his major spirit power would be water. Awakening with a nosebleed placed the stamp of legitimacy upon the whole experience, since the Washo believed that this kind of physical reaction is necessary if the dream is to confer power. The fact that his spirit power was to be water was unusual, since most Washo shamans had animate rather than inanimate objects as their spirit helpers. Thus, while water baby was a fairly common spirit helper, water was not. In addition, weather control was highly unusual among the Washo, being more prevalent among both the Northern Paiute and the Shoshone.

The dream stressed certain potentials, specifically a Washo calling, that of shaman. It also confirmed the validity of Henry's early behavioral role models, Welewkushkush and Charley Rube, and their philosophy of living in harmony with the natural world. In so doing, it de-emphasized those aspects of White society and culture which contradicted Washo values and behavioral expectations, but it did not forbid Henry the continuation of his quest for knowledge in the White world. Rather, it suggested that he pick and choose his way in relation to earlier models, thus serving as both a warning and a promise of greatness. That it was a power dream was congruent with Henry's aspirations and expectations concerning himself and his future.

At this transition point in Henry's life, shortly before he left the Stewart School, the dream served as a guidepost which integrated both his childhood years and his years at the school. His indecisions regarding the future were resolved, and his aspirations of becoming a shaman were crystallized. But his ideology of healing remained inchoate, for he had not yet acquired the requisite shamanic techniques. He felt the need to help his people when they were ill, but he knew not how. Nevertheless, he was aware and insightful, and in learning through what he called the "law of nature" he set the stage for years of thought and introspection, aware also that discoveries came slowly: "One little thing may come every eight or ten years; you can't grab it in one bunch."

When Henry graduated from Stewart, he took a job as a typesetter with the Reno Evening Gazette, and he lived in Reno for most of the next ten years. During this period, he mastered hypnotic techniques and began curing. But the most immediate power conferred on him by his power dream was control of the weather, and in 1906 he exercised this power for the first time. During that summer, Henry went to visit his family in Genoa. While there, he used to hang his pocket watch over his bed. One evening, before retiring, he had a vision in which snow slowly, but completely, covered the face of the watch. That winter the snowfall was very heavy and too deep to enable him to cut firewood. One day, Henry concentrated on removing the snow. That night and all the next day it rained, resulting in fairly widespread flooding. Although he had told no one of what he had done, his older sister, Annie Rube, accused him of causing the floods.[2]

In the winter of 1908 he once again called down the rain, but in doing so he lost this power forever. The winter was again difficult, and one day he constructed a medicine bundle and dropped it into the Truckee River, which flows through Reno. That evening the weather turned warm and it rained. However, in tying his medicine bundle, Henry had used the buckskin from his shamanic rattle and replaced the buckskin on the rattle with a length of thread. This offended the spirit of the buck, the "boss of the rain," and Henry was never again able to control the weather.

During this time, Henry attended an exhibition of hypnotism at the Grand Theater in Reno. He was greatly impressed but thought the performance had been rehearsed. He told his friend, Frank Rivers, that he, too, could master the requisite techniques, and he ordered from Chicago a book entitled *The Art of Attention and the Science of Suggestion*. In the evenings, and on Sundays, Henry would go into the sandy hills surrounding Reno where he would practice his techniques on the stumps and rocks "as if they were human beings; I imagined they were alive; if somebody caught me at that they would put me in the crazy house." He mastered hypnotic techniques and held regular monthly sessions in the Reno Press Club, where he hypnotized people to the amusement and enjoyment of the assembled reporters. Interestingly, he felt no contradiction between acquiring power in a dream visitation and acquiring it from a book.

In 1907, Welewkushkush suggested that Henry hire another shaman to help him train and control his powers. The Washo believed that when the power, or spirit helper, first comes to a shaman he becomes ill, and that the novice shaman then hires an older experienced shaman to teach him how to extrude and control the intrusive spirit-power. Although Henry had experienced only a nosebleed in 1902 and did not consider this to be a "sickness," he followed his uncle's advice and hired the well-known Washo shaman Beleliwe, also known as Monkey Peter. The experienced shaman could also help the novice to renounce his power, if such was the latter's desire.[3] I do not know what the customary period of time was between the power dream and the hiring of another shaman to control the power, but in Henry's case some five years elapsed.

Beleliwe, instead of giving Henry specific advice, told him what he could accomplish with his power. He spoke of the two old women who had first brought the power of healing to the Washo, and he warned that the power of blood is evil. He also described some of the feats which shamans could accomplish, citing the cases of an old woman who had walked up the perpendicular side of a cliff, of Welewkushkush who had walked under the waters of Lake Tahoe without drowning, and of Southern Washo who danced in campfires. Then he told Henry: "All kinds of sickness will look pretty tough, but it will melt; it seems like you can't do anything with it, but it will melt." However, the actual content of the shamanic ritual had to be learned by observing other shamans at work. Significantly, Henry's attitudes toward Beleliwe were very similar to his attitudes toward Welewkushkush—respect and admiration for both their personal attributes and their work. He told me, "Beleliwe was a great man; he knew more than the rest put together." While Henry's feelings toward Welewkushkush changed somewhat during the next few years, Beleliwe's stature continued to grow. And when Robert Lowie, the distinguished anthropologist from the University of California at Berkeley, visited the Washo in 1926, Henry not only wished him to meet Beleliwe, but referred to him as a philosopher (Lowie 1939: 321).[4]

Henry performed his first successful cure in 1907. A brother of Frank Rivers had died of alcohol poisoning. His mother was deeply grieved and became very depressed. A White doctor was called in but was unable to calm the woman. A few days later Henry, as he was passing by, heard the old woman crying. He went in, washed her face, and prayed for her. She recovered. It is significant that this first cure was performed on the mother of his best friend—within a milieu where his confidence would be bolstered. It is also significant that Henry's family, with the exception of Welewkushkush, knew nothing of his shamanic power or his achievements with weather control until after this first cure. His reticence is an example of the self-doubt that always plagued him—doubt in his abilities and fear that he would not find the answers his curiosity demanded—but which drove him to greater efforts.

In his first cure, Henry used techniques generally similar to those utilized by other Washo shamans. Traditional Washo curing rituals required a shaman to work for three consecutive nights from dusk to midnight, and a fourth night until dawn. In the course of the ritual, repeated every night, Henry used tobacco, water, a rattle, a whistle, and eagle feathers. He began by smoking, praying, washing the patient's face with cold water, and sprinkling all his paraphernalia with cold water. He then blew smoke on the patient and prayed to come in contact with water. A peace offering followed, in which he paid for the health of the patient by scattering grey and yellow seeds mixed with pieces of abalone shell around the body of the patient; the seeds symbolized food, and the shells symbolized money. Next, he chanted, prayed, and again blew smoke on the patient and sprinkled his paraphernalia with cold water. Arising, he walked about blowing his whistle, attempting to attract the disease object or germ from the body of the patient and into his own body, whence it might be repulsed and captured by the whistle. Then he sat down again and blew a fine spray of cold water over the body of the patient. This ended the first half of the curing ritual, which was repeated each night.

At some time during the course of the ritual, Henry would receive visions relating both to the cause of the illness and the prognosis. They usually involved either the presence or absence of water. Thus, a vision of damp ground suggested that the patient was ill but would live a short while; muddy water suggested that the patient would live but would not recover completely; ice suggested that Henry must break through the ice and find water; burning sagebrush suggested that the patient would die quickly unless Henry could stamp out the fire. Over the four-night period the content of these visions, or occasionally dreams, tended to change. Thus, Henry might see a fire or a burned-over hillside on the first night, damp ground on the second, muddy water on the third, and on the fourth night a stream of clear, cold water or the Pacific Ocean rolling over the Sierra Nevada. The portent of the vision of the fourth night overrode those of the visions seen on the previous nights.

During 1907–08, Henry Rupert acquired his second spirit helper, a young Hindu male. At infrequent intervals, he used to visit a high school in Carson City which contained the skeleton of a Hindu, and on one of these visits the spirit of the Hindu "got on" Henry. Since the Hindu was a "White power," this precipitated a major conflict in Henry's fantasy world and in the most important area of his life, his healing. As a spirit helper, the Hindu demanded to be used in curing sessions. Henry's problem was how to reconcile the opposing demands of his Washo and Hindu spirit helpers. The confrontation and its resolution came in a dream:

> I saw this in a dream. The Hindu's work says: "You will do great things if you make us the leader in this kind of work." The two Indian women say no: "We started this with Henry Rupert; we were the first. He (the Hindu) has no right here; this work belongs to us." I didn't know what to make of it. I pondered on it for a long time. Finally I decided, and I told them what I decided: "We all do the same work; let's help each other and be partners." And that is the way it works today; nobody is the leader. The Hindu wanted to be the leader in this kind of work. The two women said no. I fixed it.

This dream dramatically illustrates the basic conflict between opposing themes in Henry Rupert's life: his desire to expand his potentials for learning and healing by utilizing non-Indian resources and his desire to follow the childhood models he loved and respected. His resolution of this conflict was highly sophisticated; he utilized a more complex level of conceptualization and synthesis in which both opposing themes were subsumed under a common rubric, that of healing, which applied to both categories of spirit helpers. This rubric was neither Washo nor "White" but constituted an ethic which cross-cut different ethnic and racial categories. I prefer the term "ethic" to "principle" because the synthesis had definite moral connotations of aiding and succoring others, and because to Henry the fact that he had become a healer was more important than either his being born a Washo or his forays into non-Indian knowledge. It was the Hindu who first gave Henry his insights into the components of the "law of nature" and offered him the code of living which he has since followed: to be honest, discreet, and faithful; to be kind and do no harm. These conceptions often ran counter to the behavior of traditional Washo shamans, but they were consistent with the models of Welewkushkush, Charley Rube, and Beleliwe. The ethic of healing which Henry developed was an integrated and complete synthesis; he was never troubled again by this kind of acculturative conflict.

After Henry acquired the Hindu spirit helper, a number of changes occurred in his curing techniques—the first of his innovations of which I am aware. Before beginning a cure, he would now place a handkerchief on his head to represent the Hindu's turban, and when he blew water on the patient, he prayed to the Hindu to come and rid the patient of his illness. He also began to place his hands on the patient's head, chest, and legs in a symbolic attempt to encompass the whole being of the patient with his power. He also began to envision himself differently while curing; while sitting by the side of the patient he saw himself as a skeleton with a turban on its head moving quickly around the body of the patient.

Henry did not perform his second cure until 1909, two years later. It was this cure which established him as a legitimate shaman among the Washo. The patient was a Washo whose family was camping on the Carson River near Minden, Nevada. This man had been treated by both shamans and White doctors without success, although the doctors had diagnosed his case as typhoid fever. Henry, although a novice shaman, had been consulted as a last resort and was successful in curing the patient.

In 1910, when Henry was working as a gardener and general handyman for a banker in Reno, he suffered from rheumatism and from broken ribs which had never healed properly. He went to his uncle, Welewkushkush, to be cured, but the latter merely presented him with a warning:

> He didn't work on me long. He just blew smoke on me, and we talked. He said: "The thing that is causing it is right here in your head, and you will forget all about your stiff joint; you don't have rheumatism. You might be very sick and your mind will go into the White people's world, and I can't go there and bring you back." He blew smoke on my forehead; that thing traveled in the smoke out of me, and I got well. The thing he drew out was a piece of printed matter. I didn't see it; he wouldn't show it to me. It was what I had in my head from studying books. He took out the Hindu's works. The printed matter belonged to the White people's world.

Welewkushkush suggested that Henry would receive no aid if he pursued his interest in the knowledge of White society and implied that he would become ill if he continued; the two worlds, Indian and non-Indian, must remain separate in terms of both intellect and affect. But the ethic of curing which Henry had synthesized from Indian and non-Indian elements prevailed over Welewkushkush's thinly veiled warning. His independence established Henry as a mature adult prepared to continue to develop his own philosophy of living and ultimately to restructure Washo cosmogony.

In October 1910, Henry married Lizzie, a Northern Paiute woman whom he had first met at the Stewart Indian School. Her father, Buckeroo John, a ranch hand and maker of rawhide lariats, had been a devotee of Jack Wilson, the apostle of the 1890 Ghost Dance. Buckeroo John did not approve of Henry as a prospective bridegroom, nor did he think highly of Henry's curing abilities. It was, nevertheless, significant that Henry should take a Paiute wife at a time when intermarriage was infrequent and generally viewed with disfavor, especially by shamans and other conservative Washo. The union produced four children, three of whom today live with their offspring in the same community as Henry. After his marriage, Henry returned to work with the Reno Evening Gazette, melting linotypes. But he soon came to suspect that the lead fumes were poisoning him, and he returned with his family to Genoa, where he worked as a ranch hand until 1924. During this period, he continued his healing, becoming increasingly well known.

In 1924, with all their children away at school in Stewart, by now operated by the Bureau of Indian Affairs, Henry and Lizzie decided to leave Genoa. Rather than choosing Dresslerville, the major Washo community of that time, Henry decided on Carson Colony, forty acres of land bought for the Washo in 1916 but unoccupied except for a few transient Northern Paiute and Shoshone families. In making this move, Henry isolated himself physically, and later also socially, when Lizzie died of tuberculosis in 1933 despite Henry's attempts to cure her. He became more of a recluse with greater opportunity to meditate upon the problems of healing. "Rupert, the sophisticated young Washo . . . was a mystic credited with shamanistic ambitions," says Lowie (1939: 321) of him at this time.

Henry also worked hard, planting and raising an acre of strawberries as well as a flock of turkeys. In the Depression years he earned as much as $100 a week during the summer months, and his flock of turkeys was later sold for $5,000. He also spent many evenings digging a large irrigation pond, which he later filled with goldfish.

But these were essentially years of thought, introspection, and self-examination. As a child, and later as a novice shaman, Henry had learned the tenets of traditional Washo religion. This included a conception of a spirit world populated by the departed souls of all animate beings which had populated the natural world. The spirit world resembled the natural world; it had the same people and a comparable round of activities. The age of a person in the spirit world was that at which he had died. The spirits of evil persons were segregated in one section of the spirit world, but they underwent no particular punishments because of their earthly transgressions. The spirits or ghosts of animate beings were feared as potential causes of illness because of their ability to intrude into the bodies of the living or to project inanimate disease-producing objects into them. When an individual died, consequently, his dwelling and possessions were burnt so that his ghost would be unable to retrace his path to the natural world.

The Washo had no coherent religious philosophy or theology, but they did have a number of creation myths and creator figures. Among the latter were the two old women who fought the Hindu in Henry's dream. However, these creator figures played but little part in the placation of the supernatural. In this respect the Washo dealt with the ghosts of animate beings, and these had the same motivations as living Washo, including revenge for present or past misdeeds and curiosity which brought them back to the world of the living. Hence, for example, parents avoided striking or spanking a child for fear of angering a dead relative, whose ghost might kill the child to punish the parents (Downs 1966: 60).

In the process of evolving a general ethic of healing, Henry Rupert reformulated some of the traditional conceptions of Washo cosmology. According to his new formulation, the substance and composition of the spirit world is very similar to electric waves or pulses of energy. These are everlasting and ever-present, and all objects in the natural world are also partially composed of them. To Henry, therefore, spirit and mind are the same, both being composed of what he called "ethereal waves." When an individual dreams, his "mind-power" travels to the spirit world, remaining connected to his material body by a thin lifeline of energy. If this thin thread of energy breaks, the individual's mind-power is unable to return to its material shell, and death results. According to Henry, when a person dies his departing spirit or "ego" remains temporarily encased in a weak body shell, the "astral body," but within one month the "astral body" falls away and the "pure" ego or spirit returns to the spirit world.

The spirit world itself has three planes—the first is a coarse level, the second a finer level, and the third was the finest or purest level. Normally, when a person dreams, his spirit or mind-power travels to the first level. Passage into the second level, either in dreams or death, is impossible unless the individual has been pure in mind and heart and has followed "the law of nature." The third level is the domain of "God," "creator," and "omnipotent life." All spiritual life from the highest to the lowest is a manifestation of some kind of energy, which has its ultimate source in the third level of the spirit world. This energy is an essence found in all animate life and inanimate objects in the natural world and may, in Henry's terms, be called "soul," "ego," "spirit," or "mind-power." The same energy is also the essence of all spirits, in which it coalesces into certain forms found in the natural world, thereby forming a connecting link between the natural and spirit worlds. While there is no actual separation of good and evil spirits in the hereafter, only those spirits which are "purer" in essence can reach the second level. No spirits, however, can reach the third level, the ultimate energy source.

We thus find, in conjunction with Henry's general ethic of healing, a general conception of "power" or "energy" which is the basis of healing. Henry makes no distinction between the miracles performed by the Old Testament prophets, those performed by Christ and his disciples, the healing powers of shamans, and his own work, since the basis of the power is the same in every case, though manifested at different times and in different social situations. All these people learned to tap the same source of energy and to channel it for purposes of curing and miracle-working. This power or energy is not, however, ethically neutral. It is positive and "good," and this accounts for Henry's disavowal of witchcraft and sorcery, which will be described later. Henry is aware that his conceptions are an act of faith. As he stated to me: "In my line of work I see it that way. Nobody told me this. Nobody can prove it. That is what I believe . . . the power is ever-present; it never wears out."

Because Henry's ethic of curing was based on contact with the supernatural or paranatural, it was necessary for him to develop some conception of a general source of power for curing. His personal restructuring of the spirit world did not rest on a dichotomy of good and evil but rather on a conception of differing degrees of "good." In his ideology, no person or spirit could be completely evil, thus precluding belief in active malevolent supernatural agencies. It was no longer conceivable that ghosts, for example, could cause illness by intruding their spirit essence into humans. All mind-power derived from the same source, and both the source and the power it represented were beneficent and could not be utilized for malevolent designs. Consequently, traditional Washo beliefs in malevolent ghosts, witchcraft, and sorcery no longer had a place in Henry's worldview. However, while human ghosts could not cause illness, the spirits of animal life and inanimate objects could and did.

How did Henry explain this possible contradiction? Everything, animate and inanimate, has some form of life, "ego," or "soul." All living things require water as a minimal basis for existence. So, for example, when feathers are not sprinkled with water at regular intervals, they take water from the person owning them, "drying" him out and making him ill. Henry did not consider this a malevolent action, but he held that a person who transgressed, consciously or unwittingly, was accountable, since if the feathers were given water, the patient would recover. In one case I recorded, that of an old man who could neither speak nor eat, Henry had the following diagnostic vision on the fourth night of the curing session. He was sitting at the eastern end of a valley hiding from a whirlwind. Seeing it coming straight toward him, he was frightened and hid in the willows. The whirlwind stopped in front of him, and a magpie flew out and lit on a nearby willow. After he emerged from the trance state, Henry was told by relatives that the patient had at one time made feather headdresses and that he still kept a trunk of them in a deserted cabin. Henry said to me:

> The trunk of feathers made him sick. I prayed to the feathers and the birds not to be angry; he thought he was doing right, but he didn't give them water. I said: "I will give you water; don't dry this fellow up." Next day he spoke and was okay.

Although the Washo attributed rattlesnake power, the power to sorcerize, to Welewkushkush, Henry maintained that Welewkushkush had been taught to handle rattlesnakes without personal harm, and that the Washo feared and mistrusted phenomena which they did not understand. In another case, an old female shaman was accused of killing both a Washo political figure and a promising young shaman because she coveted their positions of leadership. According to Henry, however, she was a fine old woman who understood "the law of nature" and lived according to it, and she could not be evil since her power was derived from a beneficent source. "They said she was a witch, but it was just coincidence. They blamed her for heart failure when she passed by. They couldn't prove it."

As Henry's fame as a healer spread, he began to receive patients from a wide variety of ethnic groups. Though not common, it was not unknown for Washo shamans to treat Northern Paiute and Shoshone patients, but Henry treated these and Hawaiian, Filipino, Mexican, and White patients as well. In this transcultural healing he was successful, doubtless because his ethic of healing gave him increased confidence in dealing with non-Indians. His status as a healer grew continuously, and he became known and respected as a successful shaman from the Shoshone Yomba reservation in central Nevada to Mexican enclaves in Sacramento. His increasing renown attracted non-Indian patients who had exhausted other alternatives. A number of cases will illustrate the diversity of his clientele.

In curing a Protestant minister, who came to him with severe headaches, Henry received the following diagnostic vision. He saw a large auditorium in which were seated on one side a group of Whites and the minister, and on the other a group of Indians representing various tribes. Between the two was a large stage on which dressed steers were falling, forming a large pile of meat ready to eat. Everyone in the auditorium ate of the meat, except for the minister. Henry told the latter that he would lose his headaches, but that he had made one mistake. The minister had been in the habit of serving tea and cake after his sermons, but while his congregation ate, he did not. This, said Henry, was the cause of his headaches, and the minister admitted the correctness of the assessment. The vision was a sophisticated reflection of the interrelationship between Henry's ethic of curing and his restructured cosmology. As he explained to the minister, the latter's abstention, in a congregation of both Whites and Indians who broke bread together, was inconsistent with both Henry's ethic of curing and the minister's status as a servant of God.

In 1942, Henry journeyed to Sacramento to treat an old Mexican woman who had been diagnosed as having a malignant tumor of the abdomen. On the first night, Henry was unable to find water. On the second night he saw a burned-over hillside of which a section had remained untouched. On the third night he saw a small lake between two hills, and on the fourth, a stream of running water. On the morning of the fifth day the lump had disappeared from the woman's abdomen, and she later recovered completely.

A number of other cases dealt with psychosomatic disorders. In one of these, a Shoshone boy from Austin, in central Nevada, was brought to Carson Colony to be treated by Henry. The boy had auditory hallucinations in which he heard three men, who were following him, constantly threatening to kill him. The cause of the illness was discovered to be a tooth of a spirit which had projected into the boy's head. At the end of the curing session the boy no longer heard voices. In another case, an ex-soldier who had fought in World War II was brought to Henry with severe lacerations around his neck. This man had visual hallucinations in which two German soldiers were attempting to strangle him with barbed wire, so that he tore continuously at his neck in the attempt to remove the wire. Henry treated him successfully. In the case of a White storekeeper from Fallon, Nevada, with an apparent history of heart trouble,

Henry found a butterfly in the man's chest and removed it. This man states to this day that he will not be treated by any other doctor than Henry.[5]

In 1942, at the age of fifty-seven, when Henry Rupert was working as a general handyman and night watchman at the Stewart Indian Agency, he decided to retire to Carson Colony and devote himself full-time to healing. He was acutely aware that "reality" in healing and living is a matter of relative perception, psychological set, and social situation. The Hindu spirit helper had told him: "What appertaineth unto one, another knoweth not." And on one occasion Henry stated to me: "You don't know what I am talking about, and the same is true for anybody who reads this thing you write. What is real for me is not real for you." As an example, he cited an occasion when he was walking across a bridge over the Truckee River in Reno. He saw a woman who wailed to him that her son had fallen into the river and pleaded with him to save the boy. Henry was about to plunge into the water when the woman's daughter appeared and told him that her mother had periodic hallucinations and there was no one in the water. Henry concluded: "It was real for that woman; she thought her son was in the water; but it isn't real for me. What I know is real for me, but it isn't real for anybody else."

We must remember, in considering the phenomenological basis of Henry's conception of "reality," that he was an adept hypnotist cognizant of the importance of gaining and holding a patient's attention during a curing session by the use of such instruments as a rattle and eagle feathers. "I use them," he told me, "only to gain the attention of the sick person, nothing more." When Henry was treating a sick old Washo woman in Woodfords, California, his Hindu spirit helper told him that her illness was being caused by the spirit of a dead mole which the woman kept as a gambling charm; the mole spirit wanted repayment for having been killed. The Hindu came to an agreement with the mole spirit: the woman would have to lose the sight of one eye, but she would live. Henry described what followed:

> As I prayed, I looked to the mountains. One of my eyes started to get dim. It started to close. I couldn't see out of it. At the same time, one of her eyes started to close and started to dim, and that's the way she left. She could only see out of one eye for the rest of her life, but she lived a long time . . . Funny things happen in my line of work, but it's true.

"Suggestions" made by the shaman in the context of the curing session are clearly an important factor in the efficacy of certain cures. A case in point was that of a young Washo who was brought to Henry. He had been unable to walk for a week and believed that he was stricken with polio. Henry worked on him for a few hours and then, during a rest period, told the young man that he did not have polio. He cited a personal experience of his own as an example. When he was working in Reno he had attended a medicine show, where he was examined and told that he had "heart trouble due to indigestion." Henry bought a bottle of medicine and drank some of it, after which his heart began to beat quickly and his breathing became irregular, but he then threw the bottle away and felt normal. After this illustration he again told his patient that he did not have polio, that his muscles were simply overworked, and that he should forget the matter. A week later the patient returned, saying that he had followed Henry's advice and felt fine.

In the course of his meditations and his dialogues with the spirit world, Henry also consciously restructured traditional Washo conceptions about the acquisition of shamanic power. The traditional Washo belief system required that an individual receive shamanic power involuntarily, through a dream or vision, after which he had the choice of either accepting or rejecting the power. While shamanic power tended to run in particular families, where children were socialized in an environment charged with the importance of dreams and the supernatural interpretations of events, shamanic power was never consciously transmitted from one person to another. Only after receiving power did a novice shaman hire an experienced practitioner to help him master and control it.

To Henry, however, living by "the law of nature" meant being closely attuned to the forces that created and controlled all beings and things of the world. Since power derived from a common pool of "energy," anyone who could tap this pool could use the resultant power for purposes of healing. In order to accomplish this, however, an individual had to possess certain personal qualities; he had to be honest, faithful, and discreet and live a pure life. It is significant that Henry first learned this possibility of the transmission of power from the Hindu, a non-Washo and non-Indian spirit helper. According to Henry:

> Anybody could learn it, but you have to come under these three things, and be like a recluse, and follow the law of nature. You can't be happy-go-lucky. If you live by nature, you can understand a little of nature and help nature do her work. I had to live just so to get what I was looking for. You can't get it by being foolish. I got it just by thinking. It took me over sixty years to learn that. If I had a teacher, I could have learned that in a month.

Even if a person was not pure enough to tap the power source himself, he might still borrow another's power for the purpose of effecting minor cures. Henry lent his power at least twice, once to a sister and once to a daughter-in-law, with the clear understanding that their use of the power was only temporary.

During the years when Henry was developing his own philosophy of healing and conceptions of cosmology he also continued patiently to search for new techniques and more efficacious curing methods. But he had little success until 1956, when, at the age of seventy, he undertook to cure George Robinson, a Hawaiian, who had married a distant relative of his and was living in Hayward, California. Robinson was also a curer and had been a personal friend for a number of years. Henry regarded him with much the same affection and respect with which he had earlier held Welewkushkush and Beleliwe.

George Robinson had asserted that nothing was impossible and that nothing could hurt him, and he paid the price of hubris. He gave a large feast for his children, but he did not invite a daughter of his wife Juanita by a previous marriage. Juanita, furious at this slight, decided not to live with George any longer. She began to fast and said she would die. She told George not to give her an elaborate funeral but to dispose of her body in the hills for the animals and birds to devour. He tried to cure her with all the methods at his disposal, but he failed, and she died. Henry attended the funeral. George buried Juanita with a gold ring, erected a headstone, and had a cement curbing built around her grave. He did not follow Juanita's instructions, and he fell seriously ill. Henry described his condition as follows:

> He was dying; he was like a block of wood. Kids jumped on his belly and he didn't feel it. He couldn't pass food; he couldn't feel pain.

On the first night of the cure Henry was unable to receive any visions of either diagnosis or prognosis. On the second night he saw the cement curbing around the grave. On the third night he saw the brass medal on the headstone bearing Juanita's name. On the fourth night he saw the gold ring and received the following vision of prognosis. He was walking along the bottom of a deep gulch and saw coming toward him a herd of stampeding cattle. Frightened, he labored to climb the steep hillside. He saw one clump of sagebrush, grasped it, and sat down beside it. One steer galloped up the hill, jumped over the sagebrush, and said: "Tomorrow you gonna eat meat." George Robinson recovered, and on the following day he was again able to feel pain and eat. Henry warned him to stay away from Juanita's grave for four years, lest the grave dry out the water in his body and again make him ill.

In return for being cured, Robinson made Henry a gift of some of his power, in the form of a Hawaiian spirit helper named George. Although George lived in a volcano in Hawaii, his power was at its maximum in the vicinity of Henry Rupert's home. Consequently, Henry now preferred to cure at home and would no longer journey to visit patients except in emergency cases. Henry received from George a new set of instructions. The most important of these—"Everything comes quick and goes away quick"—emphasized the speed and efficacy of the new Hawaiian techniques. The content of Henry's dream themes also changed. He saw a dead and desiccated chicken which returned to life, and the skeletal remains of a horse which also came alive. Robinson had claimed that he could bring the dead back to life, and these dreams showed Henry knew that this ability might also be his.

A curing session utilizing the techniques now took place in daylight, and it lasted no longer than four hours and sometimes as little as a few minutes, depending on the nature of the ailment. Henry no longer needed visions of diagnosis or prognosis, and he could also eliminate chants, the blowing of smoke and water on the patient, and the use of the whistle to capture disease objects. Instead the patient was asked the location of the pain or swelling and was seated in a chair facing west, the direction of the Hawaiian Islands. Standing behind the chair, Henry twice called upon George for help, each time placing his fingers on the patient's neck, with thumbs on spine, for about ten seconds. Then, with his hands again on the patient's neck, he called out: "Wake up my body, wake up my nerves and circulate my blood; let my whole body be normal; let my heart beat, my speech, my eyesight, and my breathing be normal; and give me strength." Next, standing in front of the patient, he stated: "This person says he was sick here; he had pains here; it's not there now; it's gone." Then he placed his hand on the "pain spot" for some five seconds and asked the patient to take a deep breath and move his head from side to side. Usually the pain departed, but sometimes it moved to a different part of the body, in which case Henry again invoked George and repeated the procedure three or four times. Then, placing his left hand on top of the patient's head and his right hand at the patient's feet, he called to George: "Please mend this." Finally, he removed his hands and said: "We will close this."

According to Henry, the key to these techniques is contained in the following statement by his Hawaiian spirit helper: "We help nature, and nature does the rest." The above is a description of "Hawaiian curing" in its simplest form, as applied by Henry to ailments which he regarded as easy to cure.

Henry did not discard his previous techniques completely. Though he worked for briefer periods in his cures, for severe ailments he would use both the Hindu and George, and he would search for visions of prognosis involving the presence or absence of water, as well as employing his newer methods. In effect, he had developed a set of functionally streamlined curing techniques, involving less reliance on ceremonial artifacts, from which he could pick and choose according to the nature of the ailment. At the advanced age of seventy, Henry relinquished willingly, without personal conflict, techniques that he had used for almost fifty years.

George posed no problems of integration for Henry. As a spirit helper, his power derived from the same general source as that of the Hindu, of water, and of the two old Indian women, and George's curing functions were incorporated into Henry's general ethic of healing, which overrode ethnic, racial, and cultural differences. The potential for innovation had not ended. From George he learned of a new way to stop bleeding in serious wounds quickly by placing his hands on the wound. However, the occasion to test this technique has not yet arisen, and Henry has doubts, not unreasonable or neurotic, as to his capacity to utilize it:

> I am kind of afraid of it; I don't have enough confidence. I have the idea it can't be done. I don't try it because I don't have enough confidence.

Today, Henry Rupert lives quietly in Carson Colony, continuing to cure, meditate, and tend a flourishing orchard in the desert. The Washo, despite their traditional fear and mistrust of shamans, regard Henry in a different light, recognizing, perhaps indirectly, the changes he represents. Leis (1963: 60) states:

> Only one [shaman] remained when we studied the Washo . . . and he was trusted and not feared by anyone. In other words, the sole remaining

shaman was "good" as opposed to the "bad" Indian doctors who practiced witchcraft.

My own experiences confirm this completely.

Exactly what the social consequences of Henry's personal innovations are likely to be is uncertain. It is clear that the Washo have little knowledge of either the extent or content of these innovations, although they recognize that he does not doctor in the traditional Washo manner. At present there are no budding young shamans among the Washo, and it is unlikely that future shamans will take the traditional path to gaining supernatural power. Although Henry does not proselytize, he offers an alternative, but the regimen and qualities required are either unappealing or rare. Nevertheless, the potentiality exists, and this could open a fascinating new chapter on shamanic healing among the Washo.

Conclusion

The most striking fact in this life history, to me, is the coherence and integration of the innovations considered. The conceptions, both of an ethic of healing and of a coherent cosmology, are congruent with one another. Within this framework, Henry has been able to incorporate heterocultural spirit helpers, new techniques of curing, and proficiency in transcultural curing, as well as to explore the possibility of transmitting and teaching his healing abilities. Although his childhood models have greatly influenced his development, he has been able to resist their strictures and to reconceptualize his thinking on sorcery and witchcraft as causes of illness in terms of his reinterpretation of Washo cosmology. Throughout the material presented run themes of curiosity, experimentation, and perseverance, balanced by uncertainty of success. Henry's personality unfolds, through the years, slowly and positively, with few contradictions. It takes the form of learning, testing, and integration, of working for maximal organization of all potentials within the framework of sophisticated general principles flexible enough to admit defeat in areas where spirit helpers are unable to operate. Thus, Henry has recognized, through experience, the illnesses he cannot treat, and has accepted these limitations while delving into potentially more fruitful areas.

It is highly inadequate to suggest that Henry Rupert adopted shamanism as a neurotic defense against personal aggression and instability, or simply that he made a successful adjustment to the acculturative situation in which he lived. The shaman has often been analyzed and typed as a neurotic or borderline psychotic who performs valuable social functions in a deviant role to which he is shunted to meet his own neurotic needs (cf. Kroeber 1940; Radin 1937: 108; Spencer and Jennings 1965: 151; Boyer 1962: 233; Lands 1960: 164; Devereux 1956, 1957: 1043, 1961a: 1088, 1961b: 63–64).[6] The neurotic defense of the shaman is conceptualized as unstable, transitory, and inadequate; the experience of becoming a shaman is also often described as a revitalization experience.

These conceptions are not applicable in the case described. Henry Rupert presents us with a case of continuous psychological development, growth, and innovation throughout his individual life span. His first innovations included both a complex philosophical statement about the nature of the supernatural and natural worlds and a sophisticated approach to transcultural curing. All his other innovations were integrated into this psychological matrix, and this has remained stable through time and space. While his uncertainties and fears are considerable, Henry knows that one cannot face the unknown with certainty, unless it is rooted in rigidity. While man is fallible, Henry believes that the only path to knowledge is through experimentation, and his fears have never stopped him from experimenting.

Unfortunately, in anthropology, we have few ways of describing or analyzing the ego strength or ego integrity of individuals in the cultures we deal with, and ordinarily this does not concern us. We have good evidence of both social disorganization and psychological disturbance among acculturating peoples, and we can tentatively suggest that, in many ways, cultural processes have overwhelmed individual defenses in these cases by destroying traditional alternatives and failing to provide new ones. But what of the creative individual? What of the individual with great ego strength who is able to choose and combine traditional and new alternatives, not merely integrating them but developing new syntheses which may be both personally satisfying and socially transmissible? Of such persons and the roles they play we know little. And the same is true of the shaman who, as Nadel has suggested, can play a creative and innovative role. In the case of Henry Rupert, we gain a glimpse of what the quality and content of such a synthesis can be in an acculturative situation.

Notes

First published in 1967 as "The Development of a Washo Shaman," *Ethnology* 6: 444–64. Reprinted with permission.

I did this fieldwork in Nevada during the summer of 1964. All materials presented in this chapter were originally recorded verbatim through the cooperation of Henry Rupert and, unless otherwise cited, are based on that record.

1. In this account there is an interesting conjunction of elements of bear, flying, and fire, which Eliade (1964) maintains are basic to the shamanistic complex, especially in North America.
2. This may be indirect evidence that his family expected Henry to gain power and were quite ready to attribute the cause of unusual events to him.
3. According to Welewkushkush, the recipient of a power dream who wished to reject the power covered himself with ashes, prayed to the intrusive spirit to leave him, and then washed the ashes off with clear water. This ritual was repeated daily over a four-month period under the direction of an experienced shaman. It should be noted that Henry did not become ill after his power dream and that he waited five years before hiring Beleliwe at the suggestion of Welewkushkush. This may suggest that Henry performed the Washo ritual mainly to appease his family and not because he believed it to be necessary.

4. Beleliwe died as the result of curing a tubercular patient in Carson City. He was able to take the tuberculosis "germ" out of the patient's body and into his own, but the germ lodged in the back of his neck, affecting his speech and bodily movements, and finally killing him. I do not know how Welewkushkush died, but he told Henry that he could cure anything but the common cold and that it would be the common cold which would finally kill him.
5. An interesting conclusion emerges from these and other cases. It seems possible that in a situation of culture change the doctor-patient relationship depends more on the faith inherent in the relationship than it does on common cultural background, cultural context, or cultural symbolism. In none of these cases did the patient know what Henry was doing; they accepted his efficaciousness as a matter of faith. It also seems likely that such doctor-patient relationships would not have been countenanced in traditional Washo society, where patients and their relatives were generally familiar at least with the techniques used, the paraphernalia required of a shaman, and the length of time required for a cure.
6. There are, of course, anthropologists who disagree with this formulation, e.g., Opler (1959, 1961), Honigmann (1960), Murdock (1965). Possibly the anthropologists' often ungenerous view of the shaman as a person is related to the way in which they often tend to identify and sympathize with a whole culture, and thus with the attitudes the majority have toward the shaman, rather than treating the shaman as a legitimate subcultural variant. It is ironic that these anthropologists can then return to their own culture and their own subcultural niches and complain about how society treats the "egghead" and the artist.

References

Boyer, L. Bruce. 1962. "Remarks on the Personality of Shamans." In *The Psychoanalytic Study of Society*, ed. Werner Muensterberger and Sidney Axelrad, 233–54. New York: International Universities Press.

Devereux, George. 1956. "Normal and Abnormal: The Key Problem of Psychiatric Anthropology." In *Some Uses of Anthropology, Theoretical and Applied*, ed. Joseph B. Casagrande and Thomas Gladwin, 30–48. Washington, DC: Anthropological Society of Washington.

———. 1957. "Dream Learning and Individual Ritual Differences in Mohave Shamanism." *American Anthropologist* 59: 1036–45.

———. 1961a. "Shamans as Neurotics." *American Anthropologist* 63: 1088–90.

———. 1961b. "Mohave Ethnopsychiatry and Suicide: The Psychiatric Knowledge and the Psychic Disturbances of an Indian Tribe." *Bulletins of the Bureau of American Ethnology* 175: 1–586.

Downs, James F. 1961. "Washo Religion." *Anthropological Records* 16: 365–85.

———. 1963. "Differential Response to White Contact: Paiute and Washo." In *The Washo Indians of California and Nevada*, ed. Warren L. d'Azevedo. Anthropological Papers, no. 67. Salt Lake City: University of Utah.

———. 1966. *The Two Worlds of the Washo*. New York: Holt, Rinehart & Winston.

Eliade, Mircea. 1964. *Shamanism: Archaic Techniques of Ecstasy*. New York: Princeton University Press.

Handelman, Don. 1967. "Leadership, Solidarity and Conflict in West Indian Immigrant Associations." *Human Organization* 26: 118–25.

———. 1993. "The Absence of Others, the Presence of Texts." In *Creativity/Anthropology*, ed. Smadar Lavie, Kirin Narayan, and Renato Rosaldo, 133–52. Ithaca: Cornell University Press.

———. 1999. "The Playful Seductions of Neo-Shamanic Ritual." *History of Religions* 39: 65–72.

———. 2014. *One God, Two Goddesses, Three Studies of South Indian Cosmology*. Leiden: Brill.

Honigmann, John J. 1960. "Review of *Culture and Mental Health*, Marvin K. Opler, ed." *American Anthropologist* 62: 920–23.

Kroeber, Alfred L. 1952. "Psychosis or Social Sanction." In his *The Nature of Culture*, 310–19. Chicago.

Lantis, Margaret. 1960. *Eskimo Childhood and Interpersonal Relations*. Seattle.
Leis, Philip E. 1963. "Washo Witchcraft: A Test of the Frustration-Aggression Hypothesis." In *The Washo Indians of California and Nevada*, ed. Warren L. d'Azevedo, 57–68. Anthropological Papers, no. 67. Salt Lake City: University of Utah.
Lindquist, Galina. 1997. *Shamanic Performances on the Urban Scene: Neo-Shamanism in Contemporary Sweden*. Stockholm Studies in Social Anthropology, no. 39. Stockholm.
Lowie, Robert. H. 1939. "Ethnographic Notes on the Washo." *University of California Publications in American Archaeology and Ethnology* 36: 301–52.
Merriam, Alan, and Warren L. d'Azevedo. 1957. "Washo Peyote Songs." *American Anthropologist* 59: 615–41.
Murdock, George P. 1965. "Tenino Shamanism." *Ethnology* 4: 165–71.
Murphy, Jane M. 1964. "Psychotherapeutic Aspects of Shamanism on St. Lawrence Island." In *Magic, Faith, and Healing*, ed. A. Kiev, 53–83. New York: Free Press.
Nadel, Siegfried F. 1946. "A Study of Shamanism in the Nuba Mountains." *Journal of the Royal Anthropological Institute* 76: 25–37.
Opler, Marvin K. 1959. "Dream Analysis in Ute Indian Therapy." In *Culture and Mental Health*, ed. Marvin K. Opler, 97–118. New York.
———. 1961. "On Devereux's Discussion of Ute Shamanism." *American Anthropologist* 63: 1091–93.
Park, Willard Z. 1936. *Shamanism in Western North America*. Evanston: Northwestern University Press.
Radin, P. 1937. *Primitive Religion*. New York: Viking Press.
Siskin, E. 1941. "The Impact of the Peyote Cult Upon Shamanism Among the Washo Indians." PhD dissertation. New Haven, CT: Yale University.
Spencer, Robert F., and Jesse D. Jennings. 1965. *The Native Americans*. New York: Harper and Row.
Voget, Fred. 1950. "A Shoshone Innovator." *American Anthropologist* 52: 53–63.
Whiting, Beatrice B. 1950. "Paiute Sorcery." *Viking Fund Publications in Anthropology* 15: 1–110.

CHAPTER 2

TRACING BUREAUCRATIC LOGIC THROUGH SURPRISE AND ABDUCTION

Author's Note

About a decade ago I was asked to contribute to an edited volume on Israel. The book's editor told me to do the chapter in any way I chose. I decided to concentrate on how the idea of bureaucratic logic came into focus for me. The only way to do this, I concluded, was to follow myself through the awakening to how the world I experienced was organized through lineal classification and categorization, and how so much of this awareness happened through what C. S. Peirce had termed the logic of abduction, as distinct from logics of deduction and induction which I had learned as a student but to which I had never given much attention as a practicing anthropologist. The chapter meanders through glimpses of my early life and, later, of the locations in which I did fieldwork; nonetheless this was how my relationship to bureaucratic logic emerged. The anthropology editor of the press was displeased and gave me an ultimatum: include Israeli materials only; after all, this was the topic of the entire volume. Well, this was not how I had become aware of bureaucratic logic; my search joined Israel to other locations and experiences. Her demand was sheer poetism. Poetism? A theory or presentation whose only claim for consideration is that it is aesthetically pleasing. In this instance the anthropology editor indeed joined together poetism and her own use of bureaucratic logic. Slice and dice the essay until it fit aesthetically within the volume without any regard for the truth of my search, as I understood it. I was content to withdraw the chapter and wait. . . .

Surprise: "A taking unawares or unprepared . . . astonishment . . . shock . . ."

For instance, when discovering the border of a lineal category:
In 1949 my parents and a friend drove from rural Quebec to Miami Beach for a midwinter vacation and took me along. I was ten. In the southern sunshine my skin became darker, and darkened daily. One afternoon my mother and I went to a department store to look around. Mom went to the ladies' wear. I was thirsty. Looking about I spotted taps for drinking water. They were labeled strangely: White, Colored. During my short, northern country life I had seen hardly anyone "colored," and I simply felt that I was white. So I went over to the White tap, bent over, and felt a hard, painful clip to my head that staggered me as a bored male voice told me, "Over there, nigger." Shocked, in tears, I ran to find my mother.

Abduction

"The whole operation of reasoning begins with *Abduction* . . . Its occasion is a *surprise*. That is, some belief, active or passive, formulated or unformulated, has just been broken up . . . The mind seeks to bring the facts, as modified by the new discovery, into order; that is, to form a general conception embracing them" (C. S. Peirce 1903).

For instance, by beginning to fill in that lineal category, above:
Two years previously, in 1947, Uncle Joe, my mother's brother, had taken me to see the Montreal Royals baseball team play at the old Delormier stadium in the city. The Royals were the Triple A farm club of the Brooklyn Dodgers. The occasion was the opportunity to see Jackie Robinson play. Robinson soon after went up to the Dodgers to become the first African-American player in the, until then, White Only Major Leagues. I was told that seeing Robinson play, breaking the racist color barrier (as it was called then), was a great event. I was so excited even if I didn't know exactly why. Two years later I had a fuller, more mindful feeling of how a racist category worked and how this moved within me. Until today whenever I think of either of the incidents the other comes to mind and breath catches in my throat.

Anthropology is the art of making connections among unlikes, within social orderings, among social orderings, through the mindful feeling of the anthropologist. Empirical connections one would say, emerging from the doubleness of anthropological research, the empirical presence of the site of research and the sense of the empirical within the anthropologist, within and outside the research site. Mindful feeling is being mindful feelingly since all practice is infused with feeling which enables it to be the practice that it is (See the Introduction to this volume and Handelman 2004: 101–3). Given the sensuous, cognitive, and social complexities of feeling mindful, the making of connections among the unlike is neither deductive nor inductive, neither knowing and on that basis knowing more (deduction) nor supposing on the basis of knowing and checking whether this is indeed knowing (induction). The art of making connections among unlikes may be something else, something like C. S. Peirce's idea of abduction, and I turn to this shortly.

In relation to another project, I became mindful of how I thought of the idea of "bureaucratic logic." In this chapter I want to trace the emergence of this idea. In doing this I realized that I had to traverse the personal, the social, and the professional, in a line of flight that was anything but linear. Bureaucratic logic is a logic of classification that is lineal. In lineal classification the boundaries of categories are akin to straight lines (in three and often four dimensions) tending strongly toward the uninterrupted and the unbending. Lineal classification forms categories separated from one another by absolutist boundaries, thereby ensuring that the content of each category is inclusive and exclusive. Lineal classification has the capacity to rupture, divide, and separate the strands of any connectivity: thus, splitting persons from one another though they may be related through socially organic ties, whether of family and kinship or by other powerful connections. Bureaucratic logic is a mainstay (indeed, a weapon) of the organization of the modern state, its institutions, the governmentalities associated with the organization of social ordering, and the state's capacity to control its inhabitants as well as to wield warfare against other populations. Yet bureaucratic logic has a still wider cachet in the formation of realities of classification, and I have used it ethnographically, for example, to understand how certain kinds of "rituals" in Israel and elsewhere are constituted and practiced. Bureaucratic logic is a major modality of shaping and ordering social (and other) forms especially prominent in (yet certainly not restricted to) modern social orders.

To trace the emergence of the idea of bureaucratic logic I needed to follow myself thought-wise, feeling-wise, probably chronologically, through fieldwork sites in Nevada, Israel, Newfoundland, and South India, and through a motley clutch of seemingly unconnected ideas that included ritual, play, welfare practice, bureaucracy, and cosmology. I also realized that were I to write a fictional anthropology in a spirit apposite to that of Borges's story, "The Garden of Forking Paths," I would call it "The Art of Connecting Dissimilarities." The story would be about the recursive nature of the paths we take and those we don't, and, so, about the consequential character of the unplanned yet nonetheless inevitably recursive. Two dynamics are critical for me in connecting dissimilarities, thereby awakening more fully the anthropological imagination—abduction (mentioned above) and recursiveness. The effects of the first may be more immediate while those of the second likely have lengthier temporal trajectories.

The spirit of curiosity that has informed modern fieldwork anthropology since Malinowski has been less compatible both with empirically based inductive reasoning and with the deductive, yet much more compatible in practice with abductive reasoning. Few anthropologists knew this term, and few seem to do so today, yet this is what they did in practice and perhaps still do. Charles Sanders Peirce, the nineteenth-century American polymath, wrote of a third logic of inquiry (in addition to the deductive and inductive) that he called the abductive. Peirce understood the abductive as the form of inquiry best suited to discovery, scientific and otherwise. Unlike both mainstays of rigorous inquiry that in the first instance depend upon the making of order, the abductive appositely depends upon the disintegration of coherence, the questioning of cohesion, the disruption of integration, the valuing of the unexpected. This is so because the practice of the abductive emerges from the eruption of the unexpected, flowers through surprise, and is activated even by plain astonishment that puts to the question whatever has been surmised, accepted, expected.

The logic of abduction is not that of deconstruction. Deconstruction (in its own terms) interrogates the premises of the solidity and certainty of structure that antedate questioning and critique. Contrastingly, the surprise and uncertainty that enable the abductive response happen because they happen, and, so, they continuously rediscover that social life, social dynamics, emerge from ongoing conditions of indeterminacy, and not from pre-existing order. The practice of abduction, born from surprise, responds to its astonishment by searching within and through surprise for interpretation, explanation, and further wonder in relation to the unknown.

If the anthropologist is more or less attentive to and mindful of unknowns, of the vagaries and uncertainties of fieldwork, while alert to the counter-intuitiveness that otherness should encourage, then abduction is the design of mindfulness most suited. In fieldwork, surprises open before the anthropologist in all directions. In an engrossing way the anthropologist as anthropologist exists through the strangeness of others, and if she can't or won't discover this, then anthropology is all the poorer. There is a conundrum in this for the anthropologist. The surprises that might lead to discovery must themselves be discovered in practice through the doings of those others among whom the anthropologist lives. Nonetheless he must not reduce surprise to common-sense understanding, nor should he theorize surprise into understanding. The first deflates the potential for discovery through surprise; the second straightjackets surprise through the pretense that theory is the imagination at work. There is an intimacy within the mindfully feeling anthropologist that joins together surprise and curiosity as the sustenance of the anthropological imagination, awakening and arousing abductive feeling-thinking. As an old joke has it, after a month in the field the novice anthropologist thinks he know everything; and after a year in the field he knows that he knows next to nothing. I believe that the anthropologist who doesn't experience surprise (indeed many surprises) in fieldwork and, so, feeling-thinking abductively, is not likely to do interesting analytical ethnography.

Recursiveness begins with repetition (see also the discussion on time in the Epilogue to this volume). Most simply, repetition is something happening again, given common-sense perception that repetition is the same (often boring and numbing) thing over again ... over again ... over again ... over itself ... (and into itself). Repetition innocuously embeds the recursive within itself. Repetition conceals how repetition loops, and one can say that the loop is constituted by "information," yet information of all kinds. Looping carries the information of repetition within it, yet is it the same information that repeats, as we often insist? Or is looping (called feedback in elementary systems theory) always connecting dissimilarity? Gilles Deleuze (1994) argues persuasively that every repetition constitutes difference. Therefore every return is a new beginning, given that inside every repetition there is the germ of emerging difference. Nothing is ever exactly the same, and, so, what goes around comes around . . . yet . . . comes around as different. In this regard Deleuze (1994: 57) quotes the nineteenth-century American poet, Benjamin Paul Blood: "the same returns not, save to bring the different. The slow round of the engraver's lathe gains but the breadth of a hair, but the difference is distributed back over the whole curve, never an instant true—ever not quite."[1]

Within every repetition there is the potential of difference. Gregory Bateson's insistence (said somewhere) that a difference to be a difference must make a difference can be qualified by saying that recursivity creates powerful difference little by little, and that such difference may eventually generate the creative and the chaotic (the flutter of butterfly wings of chaos theory). Thus the scale of recursive loops may be tiny (the engraver's lathe) and may be grand; the existence of loopings (as we often experience them) may become noticeable only through duration; yet, in Jung's terms, they may also become synchronous, the utterly sudden conjoining of unlikes that immediately make a difference, one that we may call insight, illumination—the proverbial lightbulb lighting up in one's head.[2] The grander loops initially seem more like lineal trajectories that take off and disappear from one's ken. One feels that they are gone forever, over and done with, and yet after perhaps lengthy durations returning surprisingly, even shockingly with feeling, striking one suddenly in the back of the head not as a reminder of what was but as the potential of what may be, what may become. This too is integral to ethnography and of course to the life of the ethnographer, saturated with looping (and more often than not with kinds of loopiness that intensive interaction with otherness generates).

So, asking me to be mindful of how I came to think up the idea of bureaucratic logic in relation to Israeli social ordering is asking me no less to consider surprise and recursiveness that in no small measure shaped my becoming whatever I am as an anthropologist, and perhaps as the human being I am. This of course is beyond me in a short chapter, and likely improbable altogether. Yet perhaps I can give a sensuous sense of where this idea came from within myself by recursively joining some bits of personal history to surprises through anthropology in different places.

Growing This Way and That

On my way to the University of Pittsburgh to study for a PhD in anthropology I went to Reno in the summer of 1964 to participate in a field training program at the University of Nevada, and pretty much by happenstance went to live in a small community of Native Americans who (to summarize complexities) were mainly Washo (*Washiw*). In this place lived the aging shaman, Henry Moses Rupert, who during a brief period gave me lessons on constituting reality that much later became strangely apposite to the idea of bureaucratic logic. For me getting there, to Nevada, (and, so, getting here to wherever I am at present) took a personally arduous route.

I was raised in a small town, north of Montreal during the 1940s and 1950s. In a francophone and devotedly Roman Catholic social surround, my parents preferred to send me to the anglophone and low-profile Anglican school, a proverbial little red wooden schoolhouse (painted yellow), with each classroom containing a number of grades and dormice under the radiators. The school bus daily collected kids spread out over a twenty-mile radius. Rote learning predominated, education for its own sake was not valued, and by the age of twelve or so children already were dropping out to go to work. By the last year of high school only four of us were left, and of these but two sat for and passed the provincial high school leaving exams, enabling us to attend university. The other graduate tragically was murdered some years later together with her boyfriend, leaving me the sole surviving graduate of the class of '56. My own sardonic joke was that I could hold a class reunion whenever it moved me to do so.

McGill University in Montreal was an excellent institution of scholarship, yet to me a surprise in terms of learning and not a pleasant one. Studying for a general BA degree I discovered early on that I did not understand what the professors were telling me nor what I was reading. Well, that's not quite accurate: I could outline and schematize study materials yet not comprehend the logics of how they fit together, held together, or were made to do so by scholars. The significance of the interiority of materials escaped me: perhaps by a hair's breadth, perhaps by a country mile, but just about always out of sync and out of reach. The worst (over and again) was trying to relate to formal systems with their own organization of principled rules, to logics that were ruled and precise: grammars, numerics, mathematics, and the reasonings of philosophies. The four years of the BA passed in this way as I accumulated a collection of mediocre grades.

Imagining what to do, thinking of everything I didn't want to do, I decided with trepidation to try for an MA in anthropology. The reason—simple and obtuse—was absurd in terms of choosing (at least temporarily) a career path: during my years at the university the only grade of A I had received was in the introductory course to anthropology. Given my grades, the departmental chair of sociology and anthropology thought my application a joke, yet he suggested, indeed fairly, that I take a make-up year, a double load of courses. If I did well enough, I could enter the MA program. I did this, though with one close call in a small project I was assigned to do. The assignment was to design and carry out a questionnaire-based study in a seminar in social psychology taught by the departmental chair. In my naivete and ignorance I thought that I had to create the questionnaire instrument (and the ways in which to analyze its results) rather than using an instrument already well-tested for its validity and reliability (as, I learned later, all the others in the seminar had done just this). My little study attained incomprehensible results. Following the silence that greeted my presentation of this failed effort, the chair turned to the others, yelping in his yip-yip voice, "Well . . . some of us have it . . . and some of us don't!" There was no doubt as to who didn't have it. At worst I was seen as stupid, at best, as a stolid dolt. Later on I did my MA thesis which turned out alright yet without imagination. After I completed the MA one of the sociologists, a Harvard PhD, came up to me in the corridor, shook my hand and said with a smile, "We never thought you'd make it." That was the summation until then of my entry into academia.

I write the above neither for didactic nor cathartic purpose, nor to strike a triumphal pose in retrospect. Rather, to underline that I had to learn that which so many years later I would call bureaucratic logic, but to learn this "on my own flesh" (as the saying goes in Hebrew). I was surprised over and again and learning, yet more through feeling mindful than through analyzing what was happening to me. Feeling the academic categories; feeling how to fit into and use these while masking the rough edges; and feeling that the boundaries of these categories (despite their sometime appearance of flexibility and give-and-take) are quite sharply demarcated, separating those within from those without (with the full double meaning of this). Above all, naturalizing the feeling that academia (for all its stress on creative scholarship) was primarily about making order in knowledge, or, rather, of making knowledge *as* order, even in anthropology (with its often necessarily messy fieldwork). The academic categories and the academic work that fit into them were all about the orderliness of the lived-in world as it is lived by the peoples that anthropologists studied. The academic task above all was to uncover the cultural-social regularities that enable these lived worlds to exist, and largely calling for a neatness and exactness in doing this that I have rejected for quite some time now. Decades later the idea of bureaucratic logic emerged from this early commotion of surprise, feeling, and trying to survive (within) academia.

Nonetheless, decades later I had become so accustomed to the demands of my peers (and myself) for precision in definition and analysis ("Can you be more *precise*?"; "What *exactly* do you intend?"; "How *exactly* does this work?"; and, above all, "SAY IT" with precision and exactness, as if all phenomena of the world exist in just these ways of clarity above all else, for how else could anything be done and known to be done if not said to be done in this way?).

The years of university were my first sustained, precarious experience of a complex bureaucratic organization that processed all of us as bits of information to be evaluated, classified, and assigned to discrete categories of (direct) consequence to our lives. The little yellow schoolhouse didn't count in this regard. From the bureaucratic perspective of making and sustaining regularity, surprise (and its corollary of abduction) are unwelcome, since surprise (perhaps) opens toward the potential questioning and critiquing of whatever has not played itself out according to expectation. Yet feeling this and trying to adapt were so distant from reflexive, mindful feeling. Above all, I hadn't a clue that so much scholarship in the social sciences and humanities *precisely* practiced itself into existence in order to do that which academic institutions did. My Nevada experience, which came to focus on Henry Rupert, added something (inchoate) in this regard.

Nevada: Practical Lessons in Phenomenology

Being with Henry Rupert was as far from bureaucratic logic as one could get. As a young man he had taken his family and left the social orders organized and run by others. He had settled into solitude, raising his children and devoting much of his life to the development of his healing potentialities. In Chapter One of this volume and elsewhere I have discussed Henry's cosmology of healing (Handelman 1967a, 1972). Without going into this cosmology here, how he came to talk to me after some weeks of denying that he was a shaman is relevant here. Without realizing the implications, I confuted an academic anthropological category (the life-history) for one that was quintessentially Henry (his life, his selfness). Despairing of ever learning about his shamanism, I instead suggested to him that we do his life-history—family history, kinship, upbringing, schooling, the kinds of work he had done, and so forth.

The academic category of life-history, despite its pretensions to being open-ended, could not be other than a representation of aspects of a life, a pragmatic rendition of a life in parts existing for anthropological purpose, a categorical partiality that shapes human being as one kind of thingness, indeed as a creation of academic linear logic. To himself within his selfness, Henry was an entirety, a whole, within which boundaries were erased and differences were woven through one another. Especially so for him as I came to learn, since he had revolutionized traditional healing by, for example, bringing together spirit helpers of disparate logics while doing away with their opposition to one another (see Chapter One). After I suggested a life-history we drifted into a long silence. After many minutes he spoke without any preamble: "My life has always been concerned with psychology. I was never a happy-go-lucky man like other Indians. I was always something of a recluse. I always tried to follow the laws of nature." I was astounded. This moment was the severest jolt I have experienced as an anthropologist, until then and since. I was driven from my academic typifications, knocked out of the conceit that I had any entitlement to a privileged vantage point on the lives of others, out of the idea that I had any authoritative imprimatur on the creation of knowledge, out of the Other as object (Handelman 1993: 138–39; Handelman 2016).

I was conversing with a man who had lived his life abductively, not accepting traditional understandings but trying to come to grips with the surprises of his own explorations of cosmos, treating these experiences and upsets empirically, as facts to be apprehended within his own changing comprehensions of the cosmic. I emphasize that his explorations were neither "deductive" nor "inductive." They were what, indeed whatever, he encountered in the holism of his world in which every action was consequential (which separated him from the scientist who almost always distinguishes between his or her disciplinary work and the world as lived and experienced).

My trying to make some (anthropological, personal) sense of Henry's world was not a matter of how reality was defined—in other words, if defined as real it is real in its consequences, to paraphrase W. I. Thomas's succinct and incisive understanding of the social definition of the situation, a mainstay of social-science thinking with strong resonances of phenomenology. Henry told me clearly and concisely a number of times that his reality was not my reality. In doing so he recursively turned my academic learning back on itself. In his world, reality was not the outcome of social negotiation or of consensus, nor for that matter the outcome of relations of social power. Nor were differences in his reality a matter of arbitrary distinction that were naturalized through use into common-sense expectations (as the sociologist, Harold Garfinkel, and others argued).

There are profound differences in how definition is done that are not covered by theories of the definition of the situation or by present-day constructivism. Nor are these differences covered by anthropological perspectives on relativism. Henry's (changing) cosmos could not become linear without being destroyed. His cosmos was entirely alive in all its elements, without any necessary or clear distinction between beings and objects (e.g., Ingold 2006). His cosmos was consciously recursive, in that every action effected everything else. And his cosmos was held together from within itself, a kind of integration for which there is no word in the English language. A cosmos so unlike the monotheistic that is closed off and held together from its boundary by an omnipotent God (see Chapter Eight and Handelman and Lindquist 2011). I understood little of this then nor for many years afterward, yet in some ways the knowledge was within me. Surprise and the abductive propensity in the field sedimented in me as they never had during my academic learning. And indirectly I learned about academia and academic knowledge through Henry Rupert. As mindful feeling, I understood Henry Rupert better than I had the teachings of my professors.

The academic knowledge of arbitrary boundaries, of categorical typologies, of categories sharply and distinctly separated from one another is the kind of analytical thinking that makes a virtue of the fragmentation of knowledge, of being, of existence torn into distinct and manageable parts.[3] An academic world in which fuzziness is largely perceived as futile and as the result of lazy thinking.[4] After Nevada I tried to be careful not to confute academic-style classification with that of people I studied, though in my Israeli experiences the two not only crisscrossed but also became interlocked in varying degrees. Through my Nevada experience I also learned with some surprise that phenomena that began to interest me deeply as an anthropologist and a human being were ones that I met in the field and not in book or classroom learning—the concrete phenomenon absorbed me, not the abstract, yet I found myself consistently theorizing the concrete, thereby (abductively) entering into concrete abstraction. With Nevada began a lifelong interest in ritual, though I had yet to encounter directly the phenomenon of bureaucracy as part of fieldwork research.

Israel: Ubiquitous Bureaucracy, Taken for Granted

The Israel I encountered first in 1967 (nineteen years after its founding) prior to the war of that late spring was a highly centralized state, put together top-down in so many spheres of organization and living, espousing socialist ideals (or at least this rhetoric), proud of its revolutionary initiatives and its martial prowess, and engrossed in the "ingathering of the exiles," bringing together Jewish immigrants from all over the world. I had come from the University of Manchester (where I ultimately submitted my PhD) as a member of Max Gluckman's Bernstein Israeli Research Scheme. The project was intended for the study of what then was called the "absorption of immigrants," the ways in which the new state was taking in Jewish immigrants in very large numbers and their responses to these great upheavals in their lives. My colleagues on this project mainly studied "communities"—collectivist moshavim and kibbutzim and new towns established especially for recent immigrants. Underlying and informing all of these and just about everything else in this country was bureaucratic infrastructure (and so it had been from the first socialist-Zionist efforts here in the 1920s [Shapira 1976]). The great bulk of anthropological studies of Israel at the time had pages filled with the doings of bureaucratic institutions (the richest of these was Dorothy Willner's *Nation-Building and Community in Israel* [1969]), yet as a subject in itself little attention was given to bureaucracy in contrast to politics, ideology, economics, ethnicity, and so forth. Bureaucracy was ubiquitous, yet was treated either as the unproblematic, natural servant of all those other structures that were making the country what it was becoming or was handled as an institution to be studied mainly in the tradition of Max Weber. This was the perspective of the then master of Israeli sociology S. N. Eisenstadt and his students, and also pretty much that of my supervisor, Max Gluckman.

Initially I was no different in my Israeli research. Bureaucracy was treated either as a backdrop to other doings or was studied as an organization. Though when one encountered bureaucracy in fieldwork it might arouse more reflexive perceptions, as in the following instance I recollected from May 1967.

> After breakfast in the institute where I am living and studying Hebrew, I board the crowded, clanking bus to the bank, to change British pounds into Israeli *lirot* [currency]. The excitable to the stolid. Three clerks, a line of metal folding chairs, and forms, many of them. As the first client moves over to the second clerk, the first sitting in line goes to the first clerk and the rest of us stand, almost synchronized, and move over one seat. From clerk to clerk, each with mounds of paper and a host of stamps standing like chessmen, to be moved strategically from form to form, adding, deducting, checking, checkmating the client over to the next clerk. From seat to seat we stand, move over, sit. Endgame, toppling under paper, spewed onto the pavement melting in the sun. Where in heaven's name do

> they keep all that paper, tripled, quadrupled, stacked in packets, packed in racks, racked on shelves, shelved . . . somewhere, more likely under the earth. Huge underground storage vaults crowded to their metal ceilings with paper, silent, orderly, stamped into submission. The paper substrate of the Zionist State, the textual foundations of its pioneering subjects. . . . (Handelman 2007: 119)

For personal reasons (I had met my future wife two weeks after arriving in Israel) I went to live in Jerusalem and had to find a subject or site for my doctoral fieldwork. Quiet, introspective, I was intimidated by the ferment and fervor of Israel and by the interpersonal pushiness and aggressiveness of Israelis and came very close to quitting altogether the Manchester project, though I spent much time walking and wandering through both sides of the city, the Jewish west and the Palestinian east, learning many of its ins and outs and ways around.[5] I was also learning what I was not: not an anthropologist of projects, not one who conceived of and furthered research initiatives in the academic world that thrived on research-as-project (and the monies needed to carry this through). However, wherever I found myself, I would find something that became intrinsically fascinating and that initially was not recognizable to me through my book learning to that point. Indirectly this is related to my later formulation of bureaucratic logic. Bureaucratic logic is a pushy concept, an idea that acts forcefully in the world—as when I understood much later that, perceived through bureaucratic logic, bureaucracy itself ceases to be simply the staid and immoveable repository of piles of regulations and documents and instead becomes probably the most forceful agent of deliberately making change in the colonial and postcolonial worlds. This understanding would not have come to me had I not spent a good deal of time later on in the company of bureaucrats. Nor would this understanding have come without surprise and the logic of the abductive.

After dithering overlong I grounded (thanks to the help of Emanuel Marx) in a complex of workshops that employed aged, poverty-stricken men and women. The work was repetitious, often boring, very low paid and at times demeaning, given the domineering and patronizing control, attitudes, and interventions of the women who ran the organization. So it was on the surface of things. With the months, my looking interiorized into seeing, and seeing turned into mindful feeling. Stories, jokes, humor, songs, ridicule, sadness, tragedy, emerged mindfully into my purview. Erving Goffman, a seminal thinker on interaction whose work I had met at McGill through my excellent MA supervisor, Dick Salisbury, found me once more. My PhD thesis took Goffman's wonderful idea (quite ignored in anthropology) of the "encounter" and turned it into a basic unit of social organization, one that only comes into existence with the onset of interaction, emerges and takes shape as the interaction continues, its emergent form affecting and effecting how the interaction proceeds as it is ongoing, and folds up with the end of that segment of interaction, whether lengthy or brief (Handelman 2006a and the Epilogue to this volume).

That period of fieldwork closely seeing the *how* of practice served me well from then on. Surprise is traced abductively first and foremost through how events are done or practiced. Perhaps only in this way can surprise be traced socially into its surprising character for the anthropologist and the effects and consequences this has for him and his work. The greatest surprise I had during that period of research occurred when I witnessed the creation of a highly playful game in one of the workshops. It came into existence, into practice, silently, without comment, and after a month or so of being played intensively disappeared quietly, never commented upon yet fraught with local significance in that workshop and fragile in its constitution (Handelman 1998: 86–101). Something that had to be seen to be believed, yet something that could not be interrogated while in existence and something that was never responded to by players and others after it had disappeared. A transient phenomenon full of meaning, yet one that if I hadn't seen it could never have been recouped in retrospect. Play, one of the great unstudied phenomena of academia (even as, ironically, it is basic to virtually all imaginative scholarly work) had appeared to me, play that had to be felt mindfully. I spent periods of the next two decades tracing my way through play and through what Brian Sutton-Smith (1997) called the playful attitude, also bringing this into contrast with "ritual" and entering into phenomena of play-within-ritual.

Bureaucracy made its appearance as part of this workshop research, not as surprise but as an inevitability in the kind of state and society that constituted Israel. Since many of the workers had come to the workshops through the welfare system, trying to trace their bureaucratic biographies there was integral to understanding at least portions of their late life-trajectories.[6] I related to the organization of welfare—its social workers, its files—as an institution. I discovered that the people in the workshops were perceived as debris, as the detritus of Israeli society regardless of their past lives (Handelman 1976). In this I learned too of how merciless this society (socialist and not) was to anyone and everyone (unless they were wealthy, political, and/or otherwise connected) who was impaired, disabled, deviant, incarcerated (in all kinds of institutions), or who otherwise rejected societal norms. It was a basic lesson in Israeliness stemming from the brutality of its pioneer heritage and its constant struggle for progress and disdain for weakness, yet for all that not to be forgiven regardless of the sacrifices of those who were perceived (and perhaps perceived themselves) as worthy of being sacrificed. Again, ironically, this elementary lesson has been so overlooked in studies of Israel throughout the decades, shuffled into, hidden and lost in arguments over inequalities in gender and ethnicity (and submerged in social class difference, though the latter is conveniently overlooked by anthropologists). At any rate, I had by then acquired ideas of ritual, play, and a small sense of bureaucracy, and I began to position these in relation to one another in terms of what Gregory Bateson (1972) called metacommunication, communication about communication, metamessages that implicitly guide one's voyages through situations, contexts, places, times. In my thinking the metamessage of ritual bespoke, "This is truth"; that of "This is play" referred to the multiplicities and falsehoods of "reality"; while bureaucracy didn't yet have a metamessage name, for I hadn't realized just how arbitrary and brutal were its classifications. Yet I did begin to comprehend just how different were bureaucratic phenomena from those other modes of organizing reality (or so I thought then).

Newfoundland: Doing Lineal Classification

After I received the PhD my wife and I decided to spend most of a year in Newfoundland where I looked more closely at welfare bureaucracy. After some months of learning the nuts and bolts of welfare in a city (and province) of very high unemployment I discovered the child welfare department, something of a revelation to me. At that time, child welfare in North America largely was dominated by the emerging formation of the distinction between child abuse and child neglect, the former phenomenon more active in directly damaging the child, the latter more passive in damaging the child. It became clear to me that these categories highly complemented one another, in that areas not covered by one was covered by the other, together forming something of a hermeneutic world of damage to children. Part of the job of caseworkers was to form and practice cases that established whether or not particular children in particular families qualified for inclusion in one or the other of these broad categories.

Much of the information (a good deal communicated anonymously) that triggered investigations came from family members and neighbors. Settling scores could be prominent. The caseworkers often had to adopt an investigative stance toward case-building. In cases of hard-core abuse the evidence could well be unequivocal. Other instances of suspicion were much grayer. In these latter instances, caseworkers had to construct realities that fit the (often conflicting) evidence of a case. I am not saying that they manufactured realities to suit their tasks. Yet in order to make the phenomenon called a case, and to make it stick, caseworkers did shape the resources at their disposal to form a reality within which a person or persons could be held culpable, at times with harsh consequences. In other words, caseworkers formed cases within which they could function as caseworkers. I began to see that these were exercises in practical phenomenology on the part of caseworkers (Handelman 1978). In one of the instances that I was able to document in detail the caseworker succeeded in obtaining the incarceration of a mother for ninety days of psychiatric observation *in order to* remove her from her child so that then the child could be taken into foster care and not returned to the mother for some time, if at all (Handelman 1983: 22–31). This mother likely had neglected two of her children who were put into foster care, but the child in question she called her "love child" and the little girl was in fine health in all respects. Nonetheless, within the forming of the case-world the mother was suspect and the child she loved had to be removed from her in whatever way possible. Shaping bureaucratic reality through the case enabled the social worker to act on and in the client's world. Henry Rupert and his practical phenomenology looped into Newfoundland child-welfare case-formation. After the caseworker obtained the order of incarceration, she reflexively exclaimed, "I could put away my own husband if I wanted to!" A moment of surprise, yet without an abductive response.

Henry was always aware, especially aware, of his experiences. Shaping his reality he was self-aware of how he did this and simultaneously fully aware that he became integral to the innerness of this reality. As I noted, Henry's cosmos was organic, held together within itself, through itself, since everything was alive, intra-connected, intra-related. As such, like many other organic varieties of cosmos, this one had no exterior boundaries; nothing held it together from its outside (Handelman and Lindquist 2011; Chapter Eight, this volume). So Henry's practical phenomenology was no less organic, springing from this kind of cosmos. In the Newfoundland research I realized more clearly than I had in Israel just how different were the bureaucrats' forming of reality (and how like their reality was my own). Bureaucratic shaping was always piecemeal, always arbitrarily sliced and spliced in relation to bureaucratic categories into which they needed to fit.

This enabled me to be mindful of the effects of bureaucratic classification on all kinds of populations—communities, those populations occupied by military rule, kin groups, families, neighborhoods, work groups, the poor, the infirm, and on and on. Bureaucratic classification was abrupt and linear rather than organic and continuous. Bureaucratic classification dismantled, ripped apart, and dismembered the organic. Bureaucratic classification insisted in the main that these rips and ruptures were neat cuts, virtually surgical, clean, complete, absolute, turning continuities and continua into total and totalizing differences. Indeed nothing was sacred before such onslaughts. Bureaucratic classification put these parts, these bits and pieces, together in different ways, new ways, insisting that they clamp and clump together, holding them together by forcing them to do so. If all this were so, and I thought it was, then these dynamics were no less significant than understanding bureaucracy as organization, as institution. I was edging into a logic of organization that sprang from the lineal classification of categories of inclusion and exclusion—this is the logic I later called "bureaucratic."

"Rituals" and Bureaucratic Classification

After Newfoundland I no longer studied bureaucracy per se. I began to focus more on ritual (and play within ritual), though primarily through reanalyzing case studies written by others. I had no set goals in doing this; I read a lot of ethnography and would awaken into analysis when struck with surprise that the analysis I was reading could be understood quite differently in terms of itself, without importing another theory to make a different case (Evens and Handelman 2006: 162–63). For some years I did a variety of these reanalyses, relating to each one as a quite separate piece, without any urge to move them all in any particular direction. A kind of Deleuze and Guattari intellectual rhizome, moving this way and that. I had no qualms about spending many months (and sometimes an entire year or more) on one article and then beginning another that had no seeming connection to the previous or to others.

In 1979 we went to Sri Lanka to visit Bruce Kapferer, a most dear friend. This was my first introduction to South Asia and we ended up doing some fieldwork on aspects of a great ritual complex dedicated to the South Indian deity, Murugan (a son of Shiva). Back in Israel I met David Shulman soon after he had completed his PhD in Indology. Discussing with David was fun, informative, enlightening. My knowledge of anything South Asian is largely self-taught and David was always supportive and helpful, nurturing my fascination as only he can do, and redirecting me whenever unwittingly I veered off the paths of possibility. With David's encouragement I began to study a cosmology of Murugan (known in northern India as Skanda or Kartikeyya). Henry Rupert returned, cosmology once more, yet very different from anything I had experienced, and just how different I wasn't really to realize for years. Yet my experiences with Henry were strangely more in resonance with these materials of medieval South India than were what I had learned about Western classifications. A recursiveness I hadn't an inkling of until it pierced me, awakening thoughts dormant for a long time; Henry bounding through my life with his ancient vigor. My interests in cosmology and ritual strengthened one another, powerfully aided by an ongoing fascination with India (Handelman and Shulman 1997, 2004; Handelman 2014).

Thinking of ritual (and cosmology) in Israel of the early 1980s I drifted into studies of State and state-related "ritual." At that time this subject was a near *tabula rasa* in Israel. The sociologist of communication, Elihu Katz, and I studied the Israeli national, civil "rituals" of Memorial Day for the War Dead and Independence Day; and Lea Shamgar-Handelman and I studied how the national emblem of Israel was chosen and, at the tiny end of the social spectrum, holiday celebrations and birthdays in Jewish kindergartens, which we found to be strongly State-related in how they socialized little children. I began to comprehend two things, surprises indeed to me. One was that although State and children's state-related "rituals" were called ritual or ceremony and the like by anthropologists and other scholars, the interior logics of *how* these were organized were utterly different from the rituals of Henry Rupert or those of traditional India and elsewhere that I had read about. I mean that these modern civil and civic "rituals" and traditional ones had *nothing* in common as far as I was concerned; and so the roof concept of "ritual" lost its value for me since it utterly skewed any radical, comparative, understanding of "ritual" (Handelman 2006b). Another surprise was that the interior logic of State and state-related "rituals" actually resembled more the kinds of classification I had found in studying bureaucracy in Newfoundland and those I encountered and read about on a daily basis in Israel, a state founded in and continuously reproduced through bureaucratic infrastructures and their social classifications, something quite taken for granted and considered hardly worth studying by anthropologists here.

We know from many "rites" of tribal and traditional social orderings that their logics of organization do transformation—of person, of social order, of cosmos. By contrast, the state, civil, and civic "rituals" I was studying did nothing (in my terms) within and through themselves; they were more like "presentations" and "re-presentations" organized through clear-cut classifications of sets of categories, and at times these classifications were shuffled around as set pieces, like cards in a deck, like snapshots in a stack. Around this time my friend, Emiko Ohnuki-Tierney, told Sue Allen-Mills, then the anthropology editor at Cambridge University Press, who was going through universities in the US looking for new book manuscripts, that it was worth visiting me in Minneapolis where my wife and I were spending a sabbatical year. I told Sue about my ideas for a more comparative work on "ritual"; she was enthusiastic and supportive; and I spent the rest of that sabbatical thinking further through these ideas.

I had read a lot on simple cybernetic ideas of "system" through Gregory Bateson and others (see the Epilogue to this volume) and began to perceive abductively that one didn't need to think of large-scale (Radcliffe-Brownian or Parsonian) social systems in order to see that a social order could have particular domains that were organized systemically while others were not. So, what of these "rituals" that did transformation in tribal and traditional social orderings? One way of thinking through such a "ritual" was to think of it as a small, even tiny, system organized to create a specific outcome through its own interior relational workings, an outcome that would be quite different from when the "ritual" began. In these social orderings, it was through these "rituals" that controlled and directed change was made in social and moral orderings, and in cosmos. By contrast, the interior organizations of state and civic "rituals" did nothing apart from exhibiting bureaucratic-like taxonomies and classifications.

A theory of comparative "ritual" organization, based first and foremost on the organization of forms of "ritual" and their interior dynamics (and not on cultural or social contexts) took shape. I threw out the term, "ritual," and instead used a more neutral one, "event," which enabled events as logics of form and dynamics to be compared across cultural and social orderings—and without any kind of event having primacy or pride of place. One such form was the event-that-models the world (an event that is organized systemically); another was the event-that-presents the world (the event organized through the presentation of bureaucratic-like classifications); and a third was the event-that-re-presents the world (the event organized to do reversals, inversions, and the like, e.g., carnivals and many festivals). So, too, any particular event could have phases or aspects of any or all of these modalities and variations thereof.[7] And then, surprise once more.

If events-that-model the world were premier loci of making deliberate, focused change in tribal and traditional social orderings, then where would I find their equivalents in a modern social ordering like Israel, where I lived? To put this otherwise, *how* is deliberate, focused change made most routinely and mundanely in a modern social ordering like Israel? I felt the answer lay in the multitude of social taxonomies through which people and things are classified and organized. This is the domain of modern bureaucracy in its myriads of form doing great and tiny acts of classification according to existing taxonomies, but also routinely making changes in existing taxonomies, altering the categories of classifications, and indeed inventing entirely new taxonomies. The simple fact is that even a tiny alteration in an existing category speedily and causally effects (and often affects) the persons who are the objective of the change, and of course others who are related or connected in various ways to the former. I cannot emphasize enough just how routine is the making of change through bureaucracy in modern social orderings. Making change through events-that-model the world was (and likely still is) a special event, perhaps invoking cosmic forces, perhaps the sacred, involving careful preparation, and perhaps fraught with danger as participants enter into and alter the very lineaments of cosmos (Turner 1967; Kapferer 1997). By contrast, making change through bureaucratic classification and the altering of classification are often so mundane and matter of fact.

Israel was a treasure trove for this kind of thinking about classification. That is, Israel was good to think with about bureaucratic classification. A moral and social ordering that valued the initiator, the doer, the actualizer (summarized in Hebrew by the term, *bitzu'ist*), while to be passive was to be perceived as a patsy (*friyer*); Israeli Jews never ready to bite the bullet; a State continuing as highly centralized, awash with bureaucratic decision-making effecting virtually all domains of existence; a powerful armed forces that are deeply organized through bureaucracy; a military power occupying and grabbing Palestinian lands through endless and endlessly invented and modified regulations that are first and foremost bureaucratic edicts with the force and impact of military law.

Bureaucracy invents classifications and makes new distinctions and divisions within existing ones. In either case time-space is opened in order to contain people and things defined in certain ways, according to certain criteria specific to inclusion (and exclusion). In this way, forms of the bureaucratic expand through a kind of cellular division of difference yet sameness—the adding of more units of organization to itself (a new title, a new office, a new subcommittee). Claude Lefort (1986: 108) comments that, "it is essential to grasp the movement by which bureaucracy creates its order. The more that activities are fragmented, departments are diversified, specialized, and compartmentalized . . . the more instances of coordination and supervision proliferate, by virtue of this very dispersion, and the more bureaucracy flourishes . . . Bureaucracy loves bureaucrats, just as much as bureaucrats love bureaucracy."

Michael King's argument enables extending the impact of the bureaucratic making of order to that made by the law. King argues that, "in the legal system social events derive their meaning through the law's unique binary code of lawful/unlawful, legal/illegal . . . These categories are mutually exclusive." Then he adds a crucial point, "Any act or utterance that codes social acts according to this binary code of lawful/unlawful may be regarded as part of the legal system, no matter where it was made and no matter who made it" (1993: 223). King is saying that in modern social orderings the implementation of division and contrast in terms of absolute categories of inclusion and exclusion has something of the feel, force, and aesthetic qualities of legal decision and mandate (see also Gray 1978: 141). In my terms, the phenomenal forms created by bureaucracy have embedded within themselves the feeling of the force, impact, and aesthetics of the symmetries of law. These distinctions certainly need not be binary, in the sense of a choice between two and only two possibilities. The crucial point is the maintenance of the *logic* of form, the symmetrical, absolutist distinction between inclusion and exclusion, such that truth is necessarily made into a singularity, and is rarely if ever a multiplicity.

In the ways that they make intentional, directed change, bureaucracy and law have important commonalities. And in studying Israeli state and civic "rituals" I learned just how much these events did *not* make directed change, unlike "rituals of transformation" in tribal and traditional social orderings. As I said, "rituals of transformation" and state and civic "rituals" have nothing in common. But in their stress on linear classification, state and civic events and bureaucracy have a great deal in common; and I often thought of the former as masking the latter, making the logic of the latter more aesthetically presentable and palatable, indeed, making it seductive.

In Israel the loci of making directed change through inventing and altering social classifications lay and lie primarily in bureaucracies of all kinds, while the in-forming of this kind of ordering and change is widespread. For example, in studying Israeli Jewish kindergartens in the 1980s Lea Shamgar-Handelman and I (Handelman 2004: 77–90) discovered that birthday parties there consistently taught children to experience and to witness how, from a societal perspective, they themselves were constituted through a lineal taxonomy of exact age. Through this taxonomy every year another precise numerical slice was added—a sort of sliced-salami model of age. No less, children could be de-constituted by taking them apart into a collection of yearly slices. It seemed that wherever I looked in Israel—for example, the official opening "ritual" of Holocaust Remembrance Day (see Chapter Five, this volume) or a memorial "ritual" following a civil disaster (Handelman 2004: 3–18, 101–17)—I found widespread support for the thesis that this social ordering was constituted in large measure through the making and changing of taxonomies of lineal classification, even as within me surprise dissipated and the abductive response lessened. Then it was easy for me to slip into the more formal phrasing of bureaucratic logic, which brought together all the attributes I have discussed here.

Things come together, but not neatly, not cleanly, not evenly, not according to any protocol or schedule or research method. Things come together then immediately are beginning to unravel and open up because the worlds we live in and study are endless in their ongoing complexity. Things begin to unravel because we cannot do other than be surprised and surprise, I argue, opens to abductive, mindful feeling . . . and . . . during these years I also did fieldwork in Andhra Pradesh and through this discovered cosmologies of female deities that these rituals open from and into (Handelman 2014). The contrast between the organic cosmologies we find in South India and the arbitrariness and abruptness of bureaucratic logic that slices and forms much of Israeli ordering is so striking that surprise revives. Now the contrast is leading me toward the cosmology within which bureaucratic logic was formed (at least in part) very long ago, that of monotheism as a very broad Judeo-Christian sensibility. And this may open me again to Israel as a place in which Jewish ontologies and bureaucratic logic may thread through and knot with one another (see the Epilogue to this volume). To arbitrarily close off this ongoing connecting of seeming dissimilarities would be poetism—a presentation whose major claim for consideration is that it is aesthetically pleasing. Here, I render this as closing before its time. Time will do its closing when its time.

Notes

1. Looking on the net at graphics of computer-driven repetitions one realizes that through astronomical numbers (209 billion iterations in one instance) these become highly complex and fully support Blood's poetic reverberations.
2. In the 1930s Bateson (1972) developed his pathbreaking though schematic theory of schismogenesis, in which social difference is generated through the repetition of patterned behavior. In other words, he argued that recursiveness contains the potential for difference generated through repetitive, customary interaction.
3. Brought out beautifully through western literature in John Vernon's *The Garden and the Map* (1973).
4. See, for example, Timothy Fitzgerald (2009). Fitzgerald calls Saler's use of "family resemblance," Wittgenstein's logic of classification, lazy thinking. See also the debunking of "fuzzy logic" by the logician, Susan Haack ([1974] 1996).
5. I use the term, Israeli, as it should be used, as was once used, and is hardly used any more. Israeli refers to all who hold Israeli citizenship. Today the term is used almost exclusively to refer to Jews who hold Israeli citizenship and so to exclude Palestinians who have Israeli citizenship.
6. I was helped by my late wife, Lea Shamgar-Handelman, and this in turn contributed to her research on the life situations of widows of the 1967 War (Shamgar-Handelman 1986).
7. Later I added Deleuze's (1993) idea of the "fold" and Maturana and Varela's idea of self-organization. Folding and self-organization are discussed in the Epilogue to this volume.

References

Bateson, Gregory. 1972. *Steps to an Ecology of Mind*. New York: Ballantine.
Deleuze, Gilles. 1993. *The Fold: Leibniz and the Baroque*. London: Athlone Press.
———. 1994. *Difference & Repetition*. London: Athlone Press.
Evens, T. M. S., and Don Handelman, eds. 2006. *The Manchester School: Practice and Ethnographic Praxis in Anthropology*. New York: Berghahn Books.
Fitzgerald, Timothy. 2009. "Benson Saler: 'Conceptualizing Religion: Some Recent Reflections': A Response." *Religion* 39: 194–97.
Gray, Bennison. 1978. "The Semiotics of Taxonomy." *Semiotica* 22: 127–50.
Haack, Susan. (1974) 1996. *Deviant Logic, Fuzzy Logic: Beyond the Formalism*. Chicago: University of Chicago Press.
Handelman, Don. 1967a. "The Development of a Washo Shaman." *Ethnology* 6: 444–64.
———. 1967b. "Transcultural Shamanic Healing: A Washo Example." *Ethnos* 32: 149–66.
———. 1972. "Aspects of the Moral Compact of a Washo Shaman." *Anthropological Quarterly* 45: 84–101.

———. 1976. "Bureaucratic Transactions: The Development of Official-client Relationships in Israel." In *Transaction and Meaning: Directions in the Anthropology of Exchange and Symbolic Behavior*, ed. Bruce Kapferer, 223–75. Philadelphia: ISHI.
———. 1978. "Bureaucratic Interpretation: The Perception of Child Abuse in Urban Newfoundland." In *Bureaucracy and World View: Studies in the Logic of Official Interpretation*, ed. Don Handelman and Elliott Leyton, 15–69. St. John's: Institute for Social and Economic Research, Memorial University of Newfoundland.
———. 1983. "Shaping Phenomenal Reality: Dialectic and Disjunction in the Bureaucratic Synthesis of Child Abuse in Urban Newfoundland." *Social Analysis* 13: 3–36.
———. 1993. "The Absence of Others, the Presence of Texts." In *Creativity/Anthropology*, ed. Smadar Lavie, Kirin Narayan, and Renato Rosaldo, 133–52. Ithaca: Cornell University Press.
———. 1998. *Models and Mirrors: Towards an Anthropology of Public Events*. 2nd ed. New York: Berghahn Books.
———. 2004. *Nationalism and the Israeli State: Bureaucratic Logic in Public Events*. Oxford: Berg.
———. 2006a. "The Extended Case: Interactional Foundations and Prospective Dimensions." In *The Manchester School: Practice and Ethnographic Praxis in Anthropology*, ed. T. M. S. Evens and Don Handelman, 94–117. New York: Berghahn Books.
———. 2006b. "Conceptual Alternatives to Ritual." In *Theorizing Ritual*, ed. Jens Kreinath, Jan Snoek, and Michael Stausberg, 37–49. Leiden: Brill.
———. 2007. "The Cartesian Divide of the Nation-State: Emotion and Bureaucratic Logic." In *The Emotions: A Cultural Reader*, ed. Helena Wulff, 119–40. Oxford: Berg.
———. 2014. *One God, Two Goddesses, Three Studies of South Indian Cosmology*. Leiden: Brill.
———. 2016. "The Ethic of Being Wrong: Taking Levinas into the Field." In *Reflecting on Reflexivity: The Human Condition as an Ontological Surprise*, ed. Terry Evens, Don Handelman, and Christopher Roberts, 44–61. New York: Berghahn Books.
Handelman, Don, and Galina Lindquist. 2011. "Religion, Politics and Globalization: The Long Past Foregrounding the Short Present—Prologue and Introduction." In *Religion, Politics and Globalization: Anthropological Approaches*, ed. Galina Lindquist and Don Handelman, 1–66. New York: Berghahn Books.
Handelman, Don, and David Shulman. 1997. *God Inside Out: Siva's Game of Dice*. New York: Oxford University Press.
———. 2004. *Siva in the Forest of Pines: An Essay on Exorcism and Self-Knowledge*. Delhi: Oxford University Press.
Ingold, Tim. 2006. "Re-thinking the Animate, Re-animating Thought." *Ethnos* 71: 9–20.
Kapferer, Bruce. 1997. *The Feast of the Sorcerer*. Chicago: Chicago University Press.
King, Michael. 1993. "The 'Truth' about Autopoiesis." *Journal of Law and Society* 20: 218–36.
Lefort, Claude. 1986. *The Political Forms of Modern Society: Bureaucracy, Democracy, Totalitarianism*. Cambridge, MA: MIT Press.
Peirce, C. S. 1903. "Abduction." In *The Commens Dictionary: Peirce's Terms in His Own Words. New Edition*, ed. M. Bergman and S. Paavola. Retrieved 2 February 2019 from http://www.commens.org/dictionary/ter/abduction.
Shamgar-Handelman, Lea. 1986. *Israeli War Widows: Beyond the Glory of Heroism*. South Hadley, MA: Bergin & Garvey.
Shapira, Jonathan. 1976. *The Formative Years of the Israeli Labour Party: The Organization of Power, 1919–1930*. London: Sage.
Sutton-Smith, Brian. 1997. *The Ambiguity of Play*. Cambridge, MA: Harvard University Press.
Turner, Victor. 1967. *The Forest of Symbols*. Ithaca: Cornell University Press.
Willner, Dorothy. 1969. *Nation-Building and Community in Israel*. Princeton: Princeton University Press.

Part II
Forming Form
Ritual and Bureaucratic Logic

CHAPTER 3

WHY RITUAL IN ITS OWN RIGHT? HOW SO?

Author's Note

Models and Mirrors, first published by Cambridge University Press in 1990 (and reissued with an extended preface in a paperback edition by Berghahn Books in 1998), was my signature book, my break with the conventional wisdoms that ritual was a real, phenomenal category. The book argued that ritual was a false category in that it assumed that all events included within the category shared attributes in common. Thus the ritual category indexed a pan-human relationship with transcendence and its sacrality (of which there were many subsumed varieties). I suggested that once we took an interior perspective on events called "ritual" their differences became more significant than their commonalities. The perspective I took was to ask about the interior logics of organization of such events. I found that the more complexly organized interiors generated and controlled dynamics intended to do transformation within and through the operation of the events themselves. However the more simply organized interiors did little more than present and represent the world outside the event to itself. The two extremes of event had nothing in common once one discarded the functionalist assumption that "ritual" is necessary for existence in all human social orderings. I argued further that events with more complex interior logics of organization were more autonomous of their social surrounds than were those with simpler interior logics; the latter were simply edited reflections of their social surrounds. To call "ritual" both the transformative and the representative varieties was in my view non-sensical.

I offered a simple rule-of-thumb to summarize the difference, using Lloyd Warner's 1930s discussion of the two-hundredth anniversary procession in honor of the founding of Yankee City (Newburyport MA) and Audrey Richard's discussion of the East African, Bemba *Chisungu* that transformed immature girls into mature women. In Yankee City the procession of floats showing chronologically significant historical events began in the distant past and moved progressively into the present. Through Chisungu the girls moved from immaturity into maturity. My rule-of-thumb asked, what happens if each of these events is run backward? Running the historical procession from the present to the distant past produces another representation, another narrative, of Yankee City, yet one that is fully acceptable. Running the Bemba *rite de passage* backward becomes scary. What could this produce? Likely someone or something utterly unacceptable, perhaps akin to the outcome of an event of sorcery. In terms of their interior logics of organization these two events have nothing in common. Treating them together as "ritual" only makes sense from a perspective external to the events themselves, one that summarizes them in terms of their functions for social ordering, but one that ignores how these events work within and through themselves.

In 2001, the late Kingsley Garbett, then the editor of *Social Analysis*, asked me to edit an issue of the journal on the topic of ritual. I returned to the ideas that had generated *Models and Mirrors*, but with a major difference. Now, I suggested taking a "ritual" event out of its sociocultural surround, learning as much as possible from how it forms itself within itself, in other words how it does this in its own right, and then returning the event to its surround . . . Potentially this would enable the comparison of "ritual" events in terms of their relative autonomy from their social surrounds and, consequently, how these events effected and affected their surrounds. My formulations were distant indeed from the representational emphasis in Clifford Geertz's dominant paradigm of models of, models for (borrowed from the philosopher, Max Black). This chapter (much of which was the Introduction to the special issue) discusses how my formulation works and how it helps to understand the degrees of interior complexity of the organization of "rituals," and the consequences of this for the social surround.

Figure 3.1. Calvin and Hobbes cartoon. © 1993 Watterson. Reprinted with permission of Andrews Mcmeel syndication. All rights reserved.

Calvin understands ritual as well as many anthropologists. Calvin is dramatizing thematics that I am trying to avoid. Complaining about the peanut butter, spoiled because his mother did not observe the proper ritual for scooping it out, he is telling us: do the ritual correctly. It exists because it has a *function*—control. Perform control in your ritual, and you will have control in your life. The ritual of how to scoop out peanut butter is a *representation* of life. Living produces its own symbols, its own reflections, and these are the ritual, existing to enact themes of living—here, that of control. The ritual has *meaning*, otherwise why the argument between Calvin and his mother over its importance for living? For Calvin, scooping out peanut butter is akin to a Geertzian model of and model for living—you scoop peanut butter the way you live your life. One thing is certain: to understand the peanut butter ritual, one begins with life, not with a jar of peanut butter. First, though, let's have a look at the peanut butter in the jar. . .

Some four decades ago, Claude Levi-Strauss called for the study of ritual "in itself and for itself . . . in order to determine its specific characteristics" (Levi-Strauss 1981: 669). Levi-Strauss's concern was to distinguish ritual from myth, his overriding focus of study. He identified myth with mind and thinking, and ritual with living and the attempt to overcome any break or interruption in the continuity of lived experience, the discontinuous made continuous (ibid.: 674–75). Ritual, he wrote, "turns back towards reality" (ibid.: 680) in that "it is not a direct response to the world, or even to experience of the world; it is a response to the way man thinks of the world" (ibid.: 681). Levi-Strauss worried that ritual commonly is conflated with myth— in other words, that ritual, too, becomes a repository of beliefs and representations connected to cultural philosophies about the world. In a more Turnerian, Geertzian, or, for that matter, Leachian idiom, ritual is perceived and made into a storehouse of symbols and scripts originating in the world outside ritual, activated within ritual in prescribed ways on predicated occasions, in order to inform and to somaticize participants with appropriate meanings and feelings related directly to their cultural worlds outside ritual. In Geertz's terms, borrowed from the philosopher, Max Black, ritual acts as a model of and model for cultural worlds, yet never ritual in itself and for itself, but always ritual as *representation*—the hegemonic modality for the study of rite in anthropology. A second, powerful modality, whose logic parallels the first, is ritual understood as *functional of* and *functional for* social order, a line of inquiry whose interior logic is no different from that of ritual as representation. A third modality, close to the first two in its logic, is ritual understood as yet another arena for the playing out of social, economic, and political competition and conflict.

The way of thinking on ritual outlined in this chapter is not that of Levi-Strauss, nor does it pursue his quest for universals, yet it originates from a not entirely dissimilar premise: if one wants to think about what ritual is in relation to itself, how it is put together and organized within itself, then first and foremost ritual should be studied in its own right and not be presumed immediately to be constituted through representations of the sociocultural surround that give it life. William of Occam's Razor is apposite here. If one is interested in ritual as phenomenon—in itself, for itself—then be parsimonious, first exhausting what can be learned of ritual from ritual and only then turning to the connectivities between ritual and wider sociocultural orders. Attend first to what seems to exist within a particular ritual by, as Gregory Bateson (1977: 239) put it, declining to pay attention to other suppositions as to how the ritual is constituted. Nevertheless, as I indicate further on, this is not a hard and fast distinction but one predicated on degrees of momentary autonomy of ritual from social order.

Here, the Razor carves parsimoniously in the direction opposite to that which is near-canonical in anthropology—there, ritual is a treasure storehouse of culture and society, epiphenomenally shaped to reflect and to reflect on the latter. Though this may be so for particular rituals, it is a matter not of *a priori* theorizing but rather of the analysis of particular ritual forms (Gerholm 1988; Smith 1982). Put otherwise, what particular rituals are about, what they are organized to do, how they accomplish what they do, are all empirical questions whose prime locus of inquiry is initially within the rituals themselves. The Razor slices open vectors of studying ritual within itself and its doing, within its interior dynamics and practices, and not initially from within the wider sociocultural fields within which ritual is embedded. To begin the analysis of ritual as phenomenon in its own right, no assumptions need be made immediately about how sociocultural order and ritual are related, neither about the meaning of signs and symbols that appear within a ritual, nor about the functional relationships between a ritual and social order. It is the phenomenal of the ritual itself that is the problematic at issue—a question perhaps even more of the logos of the phenomenon than of the phenomenal. And, more broadly, this problematic may be phrased as that of the extent, if any, to which particular phenomena have degrees of autonomy from the worlds that create them; whether such qualities of autonomy are significant; and, if so, what such significance might be about. The sole way in which to address this problematic is to make ritual phenomena themselves the locus and focus of inquiry.

None of the above claims that ritual phenomena exist independently of cultural and social orders. But the issue is how phenomena do exist as such in the social world. Phenomena are thus only if they are perceived to exist. Phenomena exist because they are perceived to be imbued with the real. This immediately implies that phenomena have degrees of autonomous existence—in other words, though always to varying degrees and through various qualities, phenomena do exist in and of themselves. Nonetheless, these degrees and qualities of autonomy are profound, for they seem to relate to what may be called the interior complexity of how phenomena are organized. In turn, the interior complexities of phenomena likely are related to what persons can do within them, and how they act on those persons.

This discussion continues earlier arguments intended to forgo claims to the value of any universal, overarching definition or conception of ritual (Handelman 1998, 2006).[1] No theory based on representation or functionalism can open to the tremendous diversity of phenomena that are called "ritual," and to their kinds and degrees of interior complexity. Yet my argument does not support a simple cultural relativism of ritual phenomena, aiming instead for a more comparativist perspective toward the integrity of ritual phenomena as phenomenal. Nevertheless, this orientation also shifts from a *logos* of the phenomenal toward one of the phenomenon.

In general terms, I suggest thinking about ritual in its own right through two steps.[2] The first is to separate (to an extent, arbitrarily) the phenomenon from its sociocultural surround, from its "environment," in order to analyze it in and of itself. This analysis is not an end in itself, but it is intended to be taken heuristically as far as one can. The second step is to reinsert the ritual into its surround, with the added knowledge of what has been learned about the ritual, taken in and of itself. The first step is more phenomenological, the phenomenon existing in its own right, together with the attempt (necessarily impossible) to exhaust the significance of its forming. The second step is more hermeneutical, including, more broadly, significance and, more pointedly, meaning, that extend toward the phenomenon from its surround. These steps illuminate whether—and if so, how—the ritual can be said to have its own interior integrity, and therefore whether it exists more as a representation of sociocultural order or more through its own autonomy from such order. In turn, this may clarify how the ritual as phenomenon relates to sociocultural order, without necessarily slipping into an inherently functionalist understanding.[3] Consider these steps as a thought experiment, one that requires the suspension of disbelief—the anthropological disbelief that aspects of ritual may be understood with value, apart from their cultural and contextual positioning.

Toward Ritual as Self-Organization

It is self-evident that the phenomenal world is constituted by phenomena that are culturally perceived, if not socially composed. It is less a truism to say that social phenomena are made to have, or to acquire, different kinds and degrees of complexity *within* themselves and in relation to their surrounds or environments. Emphasizing the existential "within-ness" of phenomena points to their irreducibility to the intentions and desires of their makers or shapers. It is essential to underscore here that though phenomena are of course breakable, they are never reducible without doing violence to their self-constitution. Fragmenting phenomena leave traces of their self-constitution, but their reduction erases even these. Social phenomena exist as phenomena, and so they exist in their own right, however fragile and transient this existence may be. Social phenomena, then, have self-integrity, with its intimations of integration. But self-integrity, the interior capacity of phenomena to sustain themselves, varies in kind and degree.

What I am calling "ritual," however loosely, is treated here as a class of phenomena whose forms, in greatly differing kind and degree, are characterized by interior complexity, self-integrity, and irreducibility to agent and environment. Thinking of ritual in this way is attempting to recover aspects of its *phenomenality*, yet doing so in the domain of the micro, the domain in which ritual phenomena are practiced into their phenomenality. This is important because the ideas I am using here parallel to some extent macro-domain discourses—called, variously, autopoiesis, synergetics (Haken 1993; Knyazeva 2003), complexity theory (Turner 1997), self-organization, and so forth—coming from the physical and biological sciences but resonating or made to resonate, if somewhat crudely, with "social systems." The distinction here between ritual as a micro-domain of organization and the macro-domains of social systems is crucial, because the claims I make for the organization of micro-level phenomena differ markedly from the requirements needed to think about macro-domain systemics.[4]

Perhaps the most elementary premise informing all approaches to self-organization is that this is possible only when whatever is being organized is self-referential or self-reflexive (Baecker 2001)—in other words, when whatever is organizing begins to put itself into its own organizing, so that whatever is organized until then influences whatever continues to be organized. Autopoiesis, for example (the term, coined by the biologist Humberto Maturana, literally means "self-making"), refers to dynamics through which "realities" come into existence "only through interactive processes determined solely by the organism's own organization" (Hayles 1999: 138). In my terms, the phenomenon organizes (to varying degrees) the phenomenon. If autopoietic relationships become fully systemic, the system self-reproduces: "it produces the components that produce it" (Bailey 1997: 86). In terms of ritual, one may argue—again, always in degrees—that a ritual produces the persons that will produce the ritual as that ritual that produces them (see Hayles 1999: 139). Thus, social autopoiesis or self-organization generates degrees of *autonomy* of the social phenomenon from its social surround (Mingers 2002: 294). As such, the integrity of the phenomenon—the practices that hold it together—derives degrees from within itself and less from its social surround. In relation to social phenomena, I emphasize the subjunctive character of this condition. Nonetheless, some social phenomena, some rituals, likely approach this tightly knit condition of becoming. A very tight fit between self-production and the transformed self is exemplified by Piroska Nagy's (2005) conception of intimate ritual within medieval religious weepers, which I will discuss further on. Bruce Kapferer's (1997) analysis of the Sinhalese Suniyama exorcism as a virtuality is an instance of a high degree of self-integrity and self-organization in ritual.

Self-reference entails making a distinction (Kauffman 1987: 53), in the simplest yet critical instance for this discussion, a distinction that the self-referential phenomenon makes between itself, through the very practice of self-referencing, and what I am calling its environment or social surround. Niklas Luhmann (1997) argues that self-referential distinctions, such as those the phenomenon makes between itself and its social surround, are reintroduced within the phenomenon itself, as integral to its self-organizing properties (see also King and Thornhill 2003).[5] Then the social phenomenon may be said to "look" inward in order to "look" outward, and to re-enter its surround from within itself. In another terminology, the social phenomenon includes the other or otherness within itself—both differentiating itself from and relating to this. Again, this is a matter of degree, shifting between the possibilities of the other as representation and the other as the emerging grounds for the transformation of being within ritual. This is what enables some rituals (which I will call more complex in their organization) to act on their social surround: in the very practice of separating itself from its social surround, the ritual contains the surround, thereby acting on the surround through what is done within the ritual. Kapferer's conception of virtuality, for example, through which the creation of cosmos from within itself emerges during the Sinhalese Suniyama exorcism, speaks directly to these issues (Kapferer 1997).

I suggest, then, that within ritual forms, autopoietic qualities of self-organization and qualities of complexity go hand in hand. Perhaps the greater the degree of interior complexity within a ritual, the greater will be its tendency to self-organize. And, so, the greater the tendency for self-organizing, the greater the capacity of the ritual for temporary autonomy from its sociocultural surround. Then, one step further, the greater this relative autonomy, the greater the capacity of the ritual to interiorize the distinction between itself and its surround and so to act on the latter from within itself, through the dynamics of the ritual design. Numerous case studies (see, for example, Handelman and Lindquist 2004) demonstrate that many rituals have within themselves the intentionality to change one or more of their participants through the very practice of ritual designs.

Topology (in a loose, nonmathematical sense) is relevant here because of its concern with form as self-connectivity (McNeil 2004). The topological movement from lesser to greater self-organization can be likened to that from a straight line to that of a curve, though in social terms it may be more advantageous to speak entirely of degrees of curvature. The less the tendency of a ritual to self-organization, the more its interior operation is akin to a straight line, a "line," moreover, that continues from and is continuous with its sociocultural surround, its existence dependent on representing the latter. Such ritual derives directly from its surround, hence its linear relationship to the latter and, too, the lesser complexity of its interior organization.[6] Here "map" is close to, almost isomorphic with, "territory." By contrast, the more the tendency of a ritual toward self-organization, the more its interior organization is akin to curving that arcs away from the immediate embrace of its sociocultural surround and moves toward self-enclosing and increasing self-integrity.

The self-referencing existence of cultural forms, their degree of self-organizing and self-integrity, is intimately related to issues of recursion. Bateson gives a simple physical example of recursion: a smoke ring, a torus, turning in upon itself, giving itself a separable existence. "It is, after all," writes Bateson (1977: 246), "made up of nothing but air marked with a little smoke. It is of the same substance with its 'environment.' But it has duration and location and a certain degree of separation by virtue of its own in-turned motion." This torus is an in-curving form containing the beginning of elementary self-referencing, the hallmark of integrity, and so of self-organizing, itself existing through recursion (on the movements that characterize the mathematical form known as the torus, see McNeil 2004: 19–25).

The social torus is constituted through a double movement: curving inwards, torqueing outwards, through form recognizing itself within itself, and on the basis of this self-integrity moving outwards, driving into broader cosmic and social worlds.[7] This double movement, inwards and outwards, is crucial to the existence of any social form containing within itself the potential for self-organizing, the propensity for the forming of difference within itself and for exfoliating this, twisting it back into the broader sociocultural surround.[8] The double movement—simultaneously curving toward closure and twisting toward openness—baldly describes ritual in its own right, separable yet inseparable from its surround. As separable, ritual can be examined as such. As inseparable, ritual twists back into relations with the broader worlds within which it is embedded and from which it takes form.[9]

Through their self-curvature, social forms, enclosing themselves within themselves as vectors of action, give themselves intentionality, organization, depth, and direction—in other words, shape.[10] Recursivity in a sense gives to itself a push, a *phusis* (Castoriades 1997: 331), toward completing what has been set in movement—these are the pulling qualities of propensity embedded in self-organization. No social form has the autonomous existence of absolute difference, yet without minimal self-propelling difference, no social form exists as it does, for whatever duration, under whatever conditions. This *propensity* to self-organization is present in the most mundane of everyday behavior and interaction. Studying face-to-face interaction, I was struck by how, whenever two or more persons began to interact, the double movement of curving toward closure and twisting toward openness came into existence, taking phenomenal shape. I coined the adage that in social interaction between two persons, one plus one never equaled two. Persons interacting were never the sum of their parts, since their interacting was mediated by the emergence of ephemeral, organizing forms whose duration was that of the interaction itself and whose emergent structures influenced the character of interaction as it emerged. Reshaping Erving Goffman's (1961) concept, I called these transient, yet continually present, emergent forms "encounters" (Handelman 1973, 1977; see the Epilogue to this volume for further discussion of the encounter).[11]

Important again is the double movement—of an everyday encounter emerging into phenomenal form, curving toward self-closure, toward some degree of self-organization, however momentary, however transient, separating itself temporarily from the social field, existing in its own right, then ending, twisting back, torqueing into broader social fields, dissipating, its character influencing encounters to come. Interpersonal encounters have self-organizing propensities. In mundane life these properties are often emergent phenomena of interaction as it is occurring. Though these properties differ vastly in their degrees of complexity, they curve recursively as they emerge, shaping the ongoing interaction. Self-organizing phenomenal forms have variable capacities to generate new aspects of themselves, during their activity. Even in highly rule-governed contexts, social interaction contains the potential to generate creativity, which may (or may not) become part of the curve toward phenomenal self-closure.[12] Social form is always in movement within itself. Luhmann

(1999: 19) writes that "form is the simultaneity of sequentiality," the compression of its dynamics. Form exists through its dynamics of self-forming and dissipation.

Forming form—phenomenal form emerging through practice—does not necessitate any principled distinction between mundane living and ritual (Handelman 1979). Both domains exist through the forming through practice of temporary, interactive social units—of whatever duration, space, and significance—that rejoin the sociocultural fields from which they emerge. The signal difference between mundane encounters and ritual may be more in how they self-organize and less in any meta-definition of sameness and difference from which all else follows—a position that still dominates attempts in anthropology to define ritual.

The phrasing of this chapter addresses ritual as a curving toward self-closure and self-organization, and as whatever depth and innerness this enclosing opens. Witness the insistence of so many rituals that they go elsewhere, elsewhen, within and through themselves. The movement from the line to the curve is that of conditions of self-organization. Curving, the line becomes self-referential, opening space, acquiring depth. In relating to itself, the curve organizes itself in terms of itself, thereby enabling its existential and phenomenal self-organization as different from whatever exists outside the curve, while including this distinction within its own self-referentiality. As Bateson (1977: 242) implies, phenomenal forms "survive through time only if they are recursive. They 'survive'—i.e., *literally live upon themselves*—and some survive longer than others." In these terms, sociocultural phenomena differ in the resources they have to live on, within themselves. When self-organization becomes highly complex, a ritual has more to live on, or rather, to live through, and we may speak, rightly so, of a separate world of causation and action, one in which, perhaps, all tenses exist simultaneously within self-same space.[13]

These thoughts on phenomena as inwardly curving self-enclosures resonate with Deleuze's interpretation of Leibniz's "fold." The fold may be conceptualized as the forming of a pocket of social action, as a folding in of movements of living, articulating persons within these curving self-enclosures in certain ways, not in others. As it curves, the fold or pocket opens the depths of time/space when/where no opening had existed a moment before. The opening itself is a curving of time/space, since the movement of living is neither stopped nor blocked, but shifted into itself, enfolded, reorganized, and thereby made different—minimally, partially, utterly—from the movements of whose courses the opening is but a moment. The fold or pocket inflects and involutes (Deleuze 1993: 14–26), entailing variable and varying degrees of self-organization, the autopoietic propensity that follows from the self-closing that is the curve. Yet the pocket is partial because the fold twists back, torqueing into the movements of living, refolding again in similar and dissimilar ways. The fold curves recursively because its forming is anti-Cartesian, turning over and upending the monothetic, and so resonating with many of the traditional and tribal rituals for which we have substantive ethnographic evidence.

This is no small matter, since numerous indigenous claims and exegeses insist that ritual does something—often transformative, temporarily, permanently—to cosmos, to participants. The doing of transformation through ritual requires curvature, the opening of time/space within which cause and effect can be joined self-referentially, such that each embeds knowledge of its relation to the other, thereby together influencing one another recursively in predictive, controlled ways. Cause and effect find one another through self-referentiality. To do controlled transformation, a ritual form must "know" it is doing this, in order to recognize change as both property and product of its operation. Curvature creates the existential knowledge of *what* it is that is curving, as distinct from whatever realities the curve emerges from and returns into. Moreover, curvature creates the existential knowledge of how what it is that is curving is changing *as* it is curving; so that, for example, more interiorly complex ritual is continuously becoming other to *its-self* as it is practiced, since it necessarily is changing in relation to its-self.

Folding, curvature, recursivity, self-referentiality, all are elemental to the idea that some forms of ritual must be separated from the sociocultural orders that create them, and thereby that these ritual forms temporarily are made autonomous of these surrounds. This was an implicit insight of Van Gennep and Victor Turner on *rites de passage* as the organization of social and self-transformation. Liminality is a time/space of curvature, of renewal, rebirth, resurgence, reshaping, remaking, and so forth. But liminality also is the folding of time/space into itself, such that whatever enters, wherever, is made to relate to itself differently, coming out elsewhere, otherwise. Nonetheless, as noted, we should never forget that the relationship of lineality-curvature always is relative; thus degrees of curvature, degrees of lineality, are ratios of self-knowledge and self-organization of and within ritual forms.

Claims coming from anthropology often weigh in from extremes: arguing on the one hand that if ritual does something, then either this is done through representations within ritual of the broader sociocultural order, enabling ritual to reflect or radiate how values, ideals, and relationships should be shaped and resolved, symbolically, functionally; or, on the other, that ritual is organized to act directly, causally, on sociocultural order. Both positions are valid, since each is related to the kinds and degrees of self-closure of a given ritual. From this perspective, ritual becomes the self-organizing of kinds and degrees of closure and their consequences. Therefore, variation in parameters of self-organizing should be sought and explored within any given ritual. These parameters also become one guideline for a comparative study of ritual that focuses on ritual form and its doings.

The above points to the error in thinking that a singular conceptualization or definition of ritual can encompass, let alone index, all "ritual" phenomena. Though all social phenomena are interactive and so have some degree of curving self-closure, varying from the nearly flat to the near autopoietic, their variations in self-organization relate, as Bateson commented, to the degrees of self-sustainability of sociocultural forms in their surrounds. I relate these variations in self-organization to the capacity of rituals to make difference or change occur through their own operations. Put simply, the more a ritual curves into the foldedness of self-closure, the greater its self-organizing and self-sustaining capacity. And, so, the greater is the ritual's capacity to effect difference or change through its operations. Then, the more distinctive is the ritual's torqueing back into social order.

This discussion points to an experimental moment in the study of ritual, one that asks what, if anything, can be discovered about the operation of ritual in relation to itself, rather than worrying immediately about the truth-value of this exercise. The truth-value of this experimental moment is never complete without the second part of the movement, ritual's twisting back, torqueing into sociocultural order. Nonetheless, scholars who insist that canons of scientific validity and its truth-claims are always at the forefront of brainstorming are unlikely to respond with any enthusiasm to this exercise. Ritual in its own right is not an end in itself but rather a perspective, a way of inquiring into ritual forms, into how rituals are put together, into whether, how, and to what degree such in-turning compositions have self-integrity. Rather than, "anything goes," as Feyerabend (1978: 28) put it, one can say that what goes around, if it comes around, does so with difference. What comes around, then, is more toroidal than spheroidal.

Beginning with ritual in its own right turns the canonical study of ritual on its head, since it obviates representation. That is, the gambit of ritual in its own right does away with the entire thrust of models of and models for, including the reign of the symbolic as symbolic of, and the functional as functional for. The gambit nullifying representation also does away with this as an inherent (and oft-thought sufficient) condition for the existence of ritual phenomena (see, e.g., Bloch 1992; Geertz 1980). This obviation of the necessity of representation includes the idea that ritual should be cultural self-narration (Geertz 1973) or that it must be a working out of social relations (Gluckman 1962). Instead, I am arguing that a radical way through which to learn of the relationship of ritual to social order is to examine first and foremost what, if anything, can be gleaned about a given ritual in relation to itself. The initial intention is to explain ritual more as phenomenon, as form, and less so as social order. Therefore, my premise is one of the a-representativity of ritual phenomena, a position neither pro- nor anti-representation.

The degree to which the interior organization (and therefore dynamics) of particular ritual forms are dependent on their representation of sociocultural order becomes an issue for study. From the perspective of particular ritual forms, it is social order that may be perceived as radically other rather than as continuous with these rites (de Coppet 1990). Or, from Kapferer's perspective, the virtual has the potential to generate all possibilities that a ritual is capable of actualizing in particular conditions of practice, including its generation of the sociocultural surround.[14] So, too, the way opens to considering whether a particular ritual form has self-organizing qualities. If a particular ritual form has only minimal self-organizing properties, then in such instances the definitiveness of the distinction between ritual and not-ritual may turn out to be irrelevant (de Coppet 1992: 2–3), or at least much less definitive.

Thinking on Ritual in Its Own Right

To amplify the above discussion, I discuss three ethnographic instances, adding practice to my argument for the theoretical value of learning about ritual through ritual. Each instance is discussed in terms of the two dynamics raised earlier: the degree of self-closure in the rite, and its twisting back and torqueing into social order. In my understanding, the first instance discussed has hardly any self-closure or tendency toward self-organization, and so has little or no twisting back; the second has self-closure coming into existence, but this is not sustainable, and one cannot quite speak of its twisting back; the third has complex curvature, the highest degree of self-closure and tendency toward self-organization, and undoubtedly twists back, powerfully torqueing into social order. These two dynamics correspond to the two methodological steps outlined previously: first, separating the ethnography of the ritual from its social surround in order to discuss it in its own right, and, second, re-embedding the ritual in social order.

Minimal Self-Closure: Maria Antonia Crosses the Rhine

The first instance, from eighteenth-century Europe, is that of Maria Antonia, the fourteen-year-old daughter of Austrian Empress Maria Theresa, on her way to France to wed the Dauphin, the future king, Louis XVI. Stopping at the Rhine, she was turned from an Austrian princess into a French one. This exchange of one identity for another had been preceded by intensive pedagogy at the Austrian court: instruction to perfect her French; lessons in deportment and appearance suitable to Versailles; changes in hairstyle; learning the latest minuets and fashionable card games; practicing the variety of bows and curtseys required by court etiquette; discussing matters of state and polity, and so on. A series of rituals had been practiced, including the French ambassador's state entry into Vienna, Maria Antonia's renunciation of all her hereditary rights, and her marriage by proxy to the French Dauphin (Haslip 1987: 4–8).

Her exchange of identity took place in a pavilion on an uninhabited island in the Rhine. The pavilion had five rooms, two facing east (toward Austria), two facing west (toward France), and in the middle a large hall where she was to be given over to France. Prior to this, Maria Antonia shed her Austrian garments and was redressed

> in the embroidered shifts and petticoats of her French trousseau, the silk stockings from Lyons, the diamond-buckled shoes from the court shoemaker of Versailles. Her Austrian attendants, many of whom she had known from childhood, came forward to bid her a last tearful goodbye. . .
> As formally as in a minuet, in which every gesture had been carefully

rehearsed, Marie Antoinette was now handed over to her new country. Prince Starhemberg led her up to a raised dais in the central hall, in front of which was a long table representing the symbolic frontier between France and Germany. Here waiting for her were the French envoys with the official documents. (Haslip 1987: 9–10)

In France, Marie Antoinette was married again, and entered into a series of rituals in which she was continually on display, in accordance with the etiquette of Versailles. Architectonically, Versailles embodied the king, and Marin (referring to Louis XIV) describes the topography as a "perfect simulacrum" of his portrait (1991: 180–81). In a sense, then, these rituals were practiced within the encompassing body of the king, the simulacrum fully continuous and perhaps isomorphic with its surround. The rituals of display were continuous with their surround. These rituals included the royal card game, the wedding banquet (held in a new theatre), and the levee—Marie Antoinette's daily rising from bed through acts of dressing in which every piece of clothing proffered her indexed the (changing) status and prestige of the performer. The levee of the king was even more complicated in the number and variety of categories of person who had roles to play in his getting up from and going to bed. These and other royal rituals of etiquette were the stuff of court life, ongoing arenas for competition over status in which the slightest fluctuation in value was registered immediately by the participants (Elias 1983: 78–116).

The interior organization of the fold in mid-Rhine leads not more deeply into itself but immediately outside, toward the courts organizing this formal exchange. There is no double movement of curving interiorly and torqueing anteriorly in this rite of exchanging the archduchess for the dauphine. One act leads additively to the next, then to the next, and so on. The curvature of this pocket is nearly flat, its trajectory shallow, barely recursive, forging forward into the next ritual display, and then the one after, and the one after that. The princess is entirely a vehicle of the symbolic, exchanging one set of representations for another. The persona of an Austrian princess is exchanged for that of a French one.

Despite the intricacy of protocol, the demeanor of personae, the multivocal symbolism of dress, and the political maneuvering, the ritual in mid-Rhine has no self-organizing properties. The ritual lacks complexity in relation to itself. In its entirety, this ritual (and all the others of the series, perhaps with the exception of the marriage rite) is lineally continuous with royal social order on each side of the river and reflects this in its transfer of representations from one authority to another. The significance of this ritual is wholly in its representations, as symbolic of the social orders that gave it shape: a model *of* courtly form, a model *for* courtly form. This is clear when the rite is reinserted analytically within social order.

The ritual in mid-Rhine was isomorphic with the organization of court life outside the rite. The ritual was another piece of the broader social matrix and was not divisible from this. The action within the ritual was entirely a manifestation of the patterning of court life. Here, ritual in its own right tells us that Maria Antonia's change of persona did not exist in its own right. There likely was no experiencing from the world within the rite of the world without as radically different (Foucault 1993: 59)—as I would expect to be the case in rituals with more powerful properties of self-organization. In this instance, the distinction itself between ritual and not-ritual may be irrelevant, since both domains were organized according to the same principles of formal demeanor and deference, and to the centrality of public, privileged gaze.

Curving toward Self-Closure: The Dancing Regiment

The second instance provides a sense of how a curvature of social autopoiesis can come into existence, since the instance—one of dance—practices curving self-closure metonymically, through its own movement. The dance is that of a regiment in eighteenth-century Geneva, observed by Jean-Jacques Rousseau. Members of a local regiment, on completing their exercises, ate together as companies. Most then gathered in a nearby square "and started dancing all together, officers and soldiers, around the fountain [in the square], to the basin of which the drummers, the fifers, and the torch bearers had mounted . . . the harmony of five or six hundred men in uniform, holding one another by the hand and forming a long ribbon which wound around, serpent-like, in cadence and without confusion, with countless turns and returns, countless sorts of figured evolutions . . . the sound of the drums, the glare of the torches . . . all of this created a very lively sensation" (Rousseau 1982: 135). It was late, the women had retired. Yet soon the windows filled with female spectators, and then women came out, the wives to their husbands, the servants with wine, the children half-clothed, running between their parents. The dance was suspended and, instead, embraces, laughs, well-wishes, caresses—a mood of "universal gaiety"— prevailed. Rousseau's father, trembling with feeling, embraced him, saying, "Jean-Jacques, love your country. Do you see these good Genevans? They are all friends, they are all brothers; joy and concord reign in their midst." Rousseau commented that he himself still felt this trembling feeling, continuing, "They wanted to pick up the dance again, but it was impossible; they did not know what they were doing any more; all heads were spinning with a drunkenness sweeter than that of wine. [Later] they had to part, each withdrawing peaceably with his family" (ibid.: 135–36).

Ritual in its own right notes that in this instance the opening of time/space immediately curves, the serpentine line of dancers, officers and men together, holding hands, stepping in unison, winding round, through countless turns and returns, to the beat of drums, the puff of fifes. The ritual curves further and further into self-closure, into self-reference, organizing itself over and again through its practice. The more the ritual curves, the deeper its self-enfolding. The self-organization of this pocket taking shape through movement is more complex than it appears on its mobile surface. This little world exists through rhythm, and rhythm depends on tempo. Tempo organizes the dancers, enabling them to exist together through rhythm (You

1994: 362). The aesthetic recurrence of rhythmicity and its movement generate their own time/space. Effectively, the dancers and musicians momentarily existed in their own ritual reality, quite autonomous of the immediate surround.

By contrast, the transfer of Maria Antonia according to protocol, from one phase to the next, is more lineally additive than transformative. However, the organizing tempo and rhythm of the regimental dance contain within their forming the propensity to fold. The curvature curves recursively through itself, forming the fold that is the curve enfolding its curvature. Time/space becomes more that of the fold, rather than a representation of the wider world. The winding shaping of this enfolding takes form in relation to the habitat of the square, the positioning of its fountain and that of the musicians.[15] Without leaving the interior of this rite, we can say that the dancers, though in uniform, likely were in more of an egalitarian relationship to one another than they were in the regiment outside of the dance. The men were doing what McNeill (1995: 2) calls "muscular bonding"—"the euphoric fellow feeling that prolonged and rhythmic muscular movement arouses among nearly all participants in such exercises"—though to discuss this further requires more information than the rite in itself supplies.

I underscore that in Rousseau's description of this rite, the double movement of curving self-closure and torqueing into exteriority was present to a degree. However, the dance roused unanticipated, emergent action from its social surround. The womenfolk, initially spectators, rushed from their homes to embrace their menfolk. The self-sustaining fold of the dance did not withstand the social surround torqueing into the dancers: the uni-form regiment turned into a multitude of family groups, a microcosm of a family-based order, and the harmonics of the euphoric bonding of the fighting men passed into the family groups (witness also the responses of Rousseau and his father).[16]

Given Rousseau's description, this is about as far as one can go in discussing the dancing of the regiment as a ritual in its own right. Here, the movement of social life suddenly (perhaps spontaneously) forms into a powerful self-enclosing curve, a fold self-organizing and augmenting the rhythm and harmonics of muscular bonding. The second step, re-embedding the ritual into the broader surround, implicates other aspects of this event, though without radically altering the rudimentary analysis I have offered of the ritual in relation to itself.

In keeping with this second step, Rousseau wrote that, previous to the dance, the soldiers had done their exercises and then had supped together in companies. The sequencing is significant, since the dance may have been the emergent property of the men drilling and eating together. By the sixteenth century in Europe, drilling organized soldiers in systems, and the maneuver, called the "countermarch" by the Dutch, turned a body of men with firearms into "a unit of continuous production" (Feld 1975: 424–25), one that folded and self-organized into a group that fired continuously—one that, in its own way, danced continuously to the rhythm of serried ranks in movement from front to back, to the tempo of firearms discharging.

The men who danced as a regiment knew the steps, the music, and how to synchronize these, but the dancing at that time and place has the sense of a spontaneous celebration and self-organization of the feelings aroused by drilling and eating together, sustainable for a time through its own propensity to fold recursively (just as drilling instilled). McNeill (1995: 8) argues that drilling together produces boundary loss in the individual and a collective feeling of oneness. Eating together undoubtedly enhances such collective feelings, harmonizing people's interiors in concert. Sliding into dance changed the geometries, the topologies of movement of the preceding practices. The dancers joined to one another through the folding, flowing currents of rhythmic movement, synchronization, direction, entering further into the relationship between exterior and interior of individual and collectivity opened by drilling and eating together. The fragmenting of the dance by kin torqued the dancers back into the broader surround, into their families, into another topology through which the military practiced exteriority against the enemy in order to protect the interiority of family units, the core of societal reproduction.

Self-Closure and Complexity: Slovene Pig-Sticking (Furez)

The third instance, pig-sticking on Slovene farmsteads, demonstrates that greater curvature increases the self-organizing complexity of ritual and, furthermore, radically alters what ritual can do, in its own right. I use Robert Minnich's rich ethnography to discuss further ritual in relation to itself and then re-embedding ritual in its sociocultural surround.

The rite of pig-sticking (*Furez*) is the day on the Slovene farmstead when pigs are killed and made into sausage and other pork products. The head of the household (*gospodar*) invites a "head butcher" and others who will participate in the killing and prepare the meat. Arriving in early morning, the "guest" butchers assemble around the kitchen table together with the *gospodar*. The head butcher takes the *gospodar*'s seat at the head of the table, also giving the *gospodar*'s wife, the *gospodinja*, any special instructions he may have. The mood during the small breakfast is quiet, subdued, solemn, as it is among the women in the kitchen. The head butcher says a prayer, crosses himself, and takes out his dagger-like "sticking knife," kept separate from his other blades and used only for killing pigs. The knife is thought to have its own powers and to do the killing, rather than the one who wields it (Minnich 1979: 187, 190).

The head butcher takes the pig out of the sty, and the others pin it down. The women retreat into the house. Uttering, "with God's help," the head butcher thrusts the knife into the pig's jugular vein, stabbing the heart. The head butcher may then etch a cross in blood below the neck (ibid.: 111). Until the pig is dead, there is tense silence among the butchers. Before the butchering begins, or before the carcass is taken into the house, it is blessed, sprinkled with holy water at the threshold of the house, or sprinkled with blessed salt by the *gospodinja*. The body then is convertible for human consumption (ibid.: 114). Usually, both skinning and butchering are done outside, and once these tasks are completed, the body parts are taken inside, where the butchers take over space, though not in the kitchen. Many of the particular cuts of meat and the cured products from the *Furez* are designated especially for particular meals, ritual and other, throughout the calendar year of the household. These Slovenes say: "Each limb [of the pig] has its own nameday" (ibid.: 107).

With the body parts inside the home, the mood of the participants changes acutely, from withdrawn solemnity to sociability, joking, fun. After a jovial midday meal, the butchers make sausages: raw sausage for smoking, blood sausage, and *klobasa*, the meat sausage. They shape the first *klobasa* as a gigantic phallus, or as a double-segment circular sausage with a third segment attached and protruding through the circle, a pointed sign of sexual intercourse (ibid.: 117). Either a butcher brings the phallus into the kitchen or the *gospodinja* comes to take it. In their separate work areas, the men and women continue their ribald joking about this sausage, which remains unnamed.

As night falls, with the sausage-making and cooking completed, people arrive for the *Furez* supper. The guests include neighbors, kin, and the wives and children of the butchers. The table is decked in white, the best service is used, and seats of honor are given to the eldest present. The *gospodar* returns to prominence through his speechmaking. The meal itself is huge and lengthy, with many different sausages, cuts of pork, other dishes, and wine and brandy. Afterwards, the participants dance and sing, even until dawn.

The Rite in Its Own Right

These are the bare bones of the event. Most evident is the event's lineal sequencing. If we go by activity and mood, there are three segments. In the first, solemnity and religiosity prevail before and during the killing, and during the skinning and slicing up of the carcass, throughout all of which the head butcher displaces the *gospodar*. The second consists of bringing the body parts inside the home, with the subsequent sausage-making by the men and cooking by the women. This segment is characterized by fun, ribaldry, sexual joking, degrees of embarrassment, and greater sociability. The third is the festive meal—lengthy, convivial, replete with speeches by the reinstated *gospodar* and talk, stories, music, and song—embracing many guests.

The segments must take place in the lineal order they do. The pig cannot be killed before the guest butchers arrive and make their preparations. The body parts must not be taken inside the house before being blessed. Joking should not occur before sausage-making begins. The festive meal cannot be held until all of the pork products are ready and additional guests arrive. Each segment corresponds to periods of the day—morning, afternoon, evening.[17] Each segment has its own high point: in the first, the killing of the pig; in the second, the phallus-like *klobasa* made of the pig's intestine; in the third, the high conviviality of numerous people, many from outside the farmstead, joining together. The high degree of curving self-closure is immediately evident. The pig returns, but different, consecrated, sexualized. The butchers return, but different, their solemnity transformed into jovial ribaldry. The women return; the home returns. The second segment is a recurving of the first, and so forth. Each recursion increases the propensity of folding the rite deeper and more fully into itself, making it more complex, more a ritual existing phenomenally in relation to itself.[18]

In sequence, the three segments also have a sense of climax embedded within their movement. A high degree of recursion enables transformation. The movement may be glossed as that of death into procreation, procreation into an extended familial order, the fruits of procreation feasting on the death that promises life for the living. The segments are not modular (as those involving Maria Antonia were, to a high degree), in that their order cannot be switched about without utterly altering the integrity of the occasion's recursive folding. On the basis of what we know so far, there is an internal logic to the propensity of the temporal sequencing, one that appears lineal (segment moving to segment) yet that is self-closing. The movement of the sequencing is a widening gyre, taking off from the death of the pig and flowing around the farmstead, momentarily changing its interior and its relationship to its exterior. The farmstead is folded into itself but comes out somewhere else.

This is evident in analyzing movement through space, especially that between the interior and exterior of the farmstead. The household invites outsiders inside. The guest butchers enter farmstead and home, eating breakfast together, the head butcher displacing the *gospodar*, who, as Minnich comments, becomes a guest in his own home. The border—the distinction between interior and environment, in Luhmann's terms—between the farmstead and its exterior is stretched into the inside, into the home, especially by the head butcher, who is an analogue of the exterior plane of this border. Exterior becomes interior, a fold opening and containing this different order of things as its dynamics. Furthermore, the head butcher, the exterior made interior, moves toward the pig and its destruction. Yet on the basis of ritual in its own right, we cannot say anything directly about the pig and its possible relationship to bordering, since this information is lodged in the sociocultural surround of the ritual.

Nonetheless, we can say that the killing of the pig is marked by bordering signs. With a brief invocation, the killer crosses himself, separating himself from the pig he will kill. His pig-sticking knife has killing power of its own, separating it from the killer who wields it. The skinned corpse is sprinkled with blessed salt, separating it from what it was in life, enabling it to cross the home threshold, from outside to inside. All this suggests that there is something in the pig, perhaps related to its coming death, involving its separation from human beings. Perhaps because pig and human are somehow related, even intimately? When the pig, apparently associated with outside, comes inside, it does so in pieces. An analogue of the exterior, the pig has been taken apart, and it is the interiors of this analogue—especially intestines, stomach, blood—that come inside. Inside, the interiors of the pig are used to alter mood and relationships of the interior of the home.

The butchers coming back inside the home with the insides of the pig are not the same butchers who went outside to kill that pig. Their demeanor is different, and deep within the home they begin the intimate work of turning the pig's interiors into sustenance. The pig's insides, intestines and stomach, become the container, another recursive pocket within the complex fold, to be filled with the man-made mix of minced pork. Inside the home, the interior of the pig is made into the exterior of the sausage, shaped by the men into signs of sexuality and procreation, cooked by the women and later taken into the interiors of the people who will feast on it. One analogue of exteriority, the butchers, destroys and transforms another, the pig. One sign of the transformed pig, the transformed exterior (sexuality, procreation), is consumed and made interior by the participants, in the course of which they, too, are transformed. The self-organizing properties of *Furez* operate through this propensity of folding and enfolding the fold that continues to be folded recursively, thereby destroying exteriorities that function in the everyday. Folding within folding generates deep interiority. Thus, this ritual fold generates itself as more autonomous of the everyday, becoming in its own right a specialized context for change that will twist back, torqueing into the everyday, effecting this.

Inside the home, both butchers and women are preparing pork as food. This complementarity in work between "outside" men and "inside" women is one ground through which they relate to one another. The pig gives its interior to be made into a male sexual organ extruding from the outside male within the home of the inside female. Coming to the women, the penis is cooked, domesticated, perhaps with intimations of fertilization and procreation, perhaps with connotations of the "birth" of something else, something that will be the "offspring" of exterior within interior. If so, then this entire process depends upon making the domains of outside and inside, exterior and interior, bend and curve recursively into one another, segment into segment. Beginning with the coming of the guest butchers, the distinction between exterior and interior is enfolded, thereby self-enclosing the fold of the *Furez*.

What might this birthing be? We know from the ritual that the corpse of the pig is being made into sustenance, and that during its preparation and later as food this corpse is the basis for commensality, sociality, intimacy. We know that later on the festive supper opens the farmstead even further to outsiders, expanding in duration and number. Perhaps this social expansion is the birth of something else?

Everything said so far is accessible through analyzing the ritual in its own right and yet, more significantly, is integral to that ritual, in and of itself—all this without deriving the ritual form and dynamics from the broader order of things, the usual sequence of thinking in anthropological analysis. We see that this ritual has its own integrity of recursive self-organization, and, as such, this ritual form may have the propensity (indeed the interior capacity) to accomplish something that the farmstead cannot do on its own. To discuss this further, I take the second step of re-embedding the ritual within the broader order of things, as its recursion twists back, torqueing into the wider society.

The Rite Re-embedded

The Slovene peasant-farmers of this region place great value on the social and economic autonomy of their farmsteads and nuclear families. Autonomy is a bastion of their identity. Farmsteads (not family lines) signify to these peasant-farmers "the continuity and stability of a local social and economic universe" (Minnich 1979: 64). The all-important standing of the *gospodar* is identified with a place, the farmstead, his "home ground," and not with a family line. On the front stage (though not the backstage) of the farmstead, the *gospodar* appears as the sovereign of his immediate family. The relationship between *gospodars* is that of equals, while a *gospodar* entering the domain of another usually becomes "guest" in relation to "host," accepting the hospitality and authority of the latter.

These peasant-farmers say that *Furez* is a special occasion practiced annually, preferably close to but before Christmas. The *Furez* supper is the household's most festive and richest annual meal. The pig is the only animal raised here for slaughter. Its killing is given the special name of pig-sticking, while the infrequent killing of other farm animals is referred to as slaughtering. The pig has an unusual status among these peasant-farmers. More than any other farm animal, the pig is involved in the daily routines of its keepers (ibid.: 134). Swine food commonly is prepared on the kitchen hearth, and there is some sharing of kinds of food among people and swine—cabbage and potatoes, and, in the past, millet and corn. Pigs and farm people, writes Minnich (1979: 143), are close associates. Yet unlike other farm animals, pigs are not given names, are not personalized. Moreover, pigs proffer the most prolific referents for local obscenities and sexual joking, while the most powerful rhetorical abuse refers to pigs and their inhuman qualities: "swine lap up and wallow in their own excrement," and "sows devour their young" (ibid.: 138). On the one hand, the pig exists only to give its life, but on the other, only for the pig is an annual *Furez* held.

As a farmstead animal, the pig has a special status—close to people, distanced from people, the nonhuman refracting the human, its death ritualized, its flayed and dismembered corpse intimating sexuality, procreation, commensality. On the human side, the autonomous *gospodar* abdicates front-stage authority to the head butcher, a "stranger" to the ideologically independent farmstead. The *gospodar* thereby distances himself from the killing within his domain. In turn, the head butcher is distanced from the killing by the belief that his special dagger has the power to do the deed and kill. Nothing human, no one belonging to the farmstead, kills the pig. It is not an immaculate death, yet, moving in that direction—a death with qualities of an ordeal (witness the change of mood from prior to and then after the killing) in which the killer takes distance and the corpse is sanctified. Yet what is being killed? And by whom? As I asked earlier, what is being birthed?

On the basis of ritual in its own right, I argued that the butchers are analogues of the border between exterior and interior, the border thereby stretched into the farmstead, into the pigsty, into the pig, into the corpse, into the home, turning outside into inside, emerging through the pig's interior as the power of sexuality and procreation, penetrating the kitchen, the women's domain, there cooked into sustenance that sustains human beings and social relationships. Ritual in its own right identifies a dynamic of curving, of self-closing, forming a fold that itself is a border reorganizing itself with profound consequences for the farmstead. Yet if the butchers are the analogues of a moveable border, what is the pig, given the additional ethnography from the sociocultural surround?

The moveable border that is the butchers meets the pig. Given its cultural attributes, the pig also has qualities of a living border. The pig is something like the stranger, yet positioned deep within the farmstead rather than outside it, perhaps a border between the human and the un-human, the human and itself, an un-human other living in close proximity to humans, the distinction between un-human and human, between selfness and otherness within the farmstead. Yet it is a border to be effaced, if the pig is to die for humans so that they can become more fully human as social and sociable beings. As the head butcher kills the pig, one stranger destroys another, one (exterior) border destroys another (interior) one, opening the farmstead simultaneously from its outside and its inside, enabling numerous guests to move from the exterior to the deeply interior, toward the festive supper, and the pig to move toward becoming food for that repast. The cut-up pieces of this interior border (the pig), made into sausage, become the sustenance for a generative, procreative sociality of labor between strange men and household women, extending later in the day to the greater collectivity of the festive supper.

It is this opening of the farmstead— blossoming within the self-organizing time/space of the fold, its participants interacting through the night into the new day through joy, fun, good spirits, and fellowship—that is being birthed. Minnich (1979: 138–40) comments that the killing of the pig, of a close associate, is consecrated to a degree and has qualities of sacrifice (ibid.: 191), though there are difficulties in stating this baldly. Sacrifice destroys boundaries in order to create new ones, new forms. Killing the pig—destroying the implicit border, deeply interior within the farmstead, and domesticating this deep interiority that signifies otherness, the unnamed, obscenity, unbridled sexuality, and yet a kind of intimacy—is done by the head butcher, the exterior plane of that other, more explicit border separating the autonomous farmstead from social others. The exterior border destroys the interior border, changing both in the process, so that during the remainder of the fold's time/space, neither border exists. As I commented, the butchers re-entering the home are not the same ones who went out to kill the pig. Now they are more the intimates of the home, their own sexuality and procreative drive more open, especially brought home through ribaldry; and to a degree, the women respond in kind. Butchers and women cooperate in shaping sustenance from the sacrifice.

The corpse of the pig also is changed—blessed before its body parts move into the home. One border destroys the other, destroying itself in the process. Furthermore, this nullifying of borders enables whatever they excluded to flow together and to fill out into fruitful union. The *gospodar*—who, in his rightful standing as the head of the farmstead, would block these movements—stands down, stands aside, and is implicated neither in the killing nor in the changes in relationships within the household. The sustenance formed from the sacrifice has qualities of a sacrament, eaten in various forms during the festive meal by the solidary, though more amorphous, collectivity of kin, neighbors, friends.

This re-embedded analysis may also illuminate why *Furez* should be practiced before and close to the Catholic Christmas. If the pig is a sacrifice eaten as sacrament by the autonomous farmstead, itself "reborn" as a broad, solidary community without clear-cut borders and with little internal hierarchy, then in cosmic terms *Furez* resonates with Christmas as a preparation for the birth of the savior, whose sacrificial death is transformed into sacrament. I am not saying that *Furez* is an analogue of the birth and death of Christ, but I am saying that through the self-organizing closure of the *Furez* fold, one is made to resonate with the other. Prior to Christmas, the farmstead takes itself apart from within itself so that it is remade and delimited again, yet differently, by its exteriors turned into interiors.[19]

These interiors become recursive pockets in the curving fold of *Furez*. That is, *Furez* itself is a filling—and fillings within fillings—of the time/space opened through self-organization. The farmstead is filled with strangers (the butchers); the pig is filled with itself (the pork mix stuffed into its intestines); the home is filled with people (the guests); the people are filled with pork. The time/space of *Furez* is filled entirely with its own special mix. These fillings within fillings likely would not occur without the erasure of boundaries, enabling different substances with different values to enter one another. This also is a kind of filling of the world, a bringing of the world into fullness; perhaps this echoes practices of All Hallows, All Souls, and All Saints, in the Christian universe, filling the cosmos with an entirety of its presence, awaiting the coming presence of Christ.[20]

Complexity and Self-Organization

The three instances discussed here begin to show how "rituals," when treated analytically in their own right, demonstrate varying degrees of interior self-organization and complexity. Degrees of self-organization support the contention that the most complex kind of agency a ritual can have built into its design is that of making radical change through its own interior dynamics. The least complex is for a ritual to be quite continuous with the sociocultural surround, lineally reflecting and representing it in manifold ways of show and tell—telling it stories about itself; showing it to itself from various aspects; magnifying, miniaturizing, upending, celebrating, mourning, and so forth. In the latter instance, the connectivity between ritual and its surround passes through a border that hardly distinguishes, hardly differentiates, between one and the other, since the mandate of such ritual is more that of highlighting, embellishing, enhancing, and condensing than of creating difference and making change. Yet more complex agency depends upon greater curvature; curvature leads inevitably to self-reference and reification as a relatively autonomous phenomenon or event; and relative autonomy leads to self-organization that activates controlled causality to make change. In practice, the causality of curvature is circular (Haken 1993), through which distinctions such as those of "structure" and "process" are indivisible; through which structure as process bends through causality into itself, coming out elsewhere, differently, re-formed. Within the complexities of increasing self-organization, causality is not linear.

In the instance of Maria Antonia at the Rhine, her crossing as Marie Antoinette was one of a lineally continuous series of events, each event a module, such that the addition together of the modules constituted the entire passage. One may surmise that though integral to a culture of royal display and elaboration, many of these modules could have been done away with, should geopolitical and other conditions have required this.[21] The basic movement from Vienna to Versailles, from Maria Antonia to Marie Antoinette, would not have been effected, even if the status and esteem of the royal houses suffered. In the instance of the regiment, moving into dance embodied an explicit dynamic, away from the lineal into curving. The movement into dance immediately shaped some degree of more complex self-organization that sustained itself as distinct from its surround, if only for a short while. Of the three cases, *Furez* demonstrates that when a program for radical change is integral to ritual design, the ritual will be self-organizing to a high degree and relatively autonomous from its surround. These three instances suggest that studying ritual in its own right may be a useful strategy for thinking on ritual, one quite distinct from those usually encountered in anthropology and cognate disciplines, and in these terms opening toward a more comparative study of the phenomenality of ritual that is committed neither to the pursuit of universal definitions of ritual nor to cultural relativism.

Must Ritual Be Social?

Understandably, one would think, the social is the heartland of ritual studies. What is ritual, if not the Durkheimian effervescence of the social? Yet the premises of ritual in its own right try to free us from the so deeply embedded anthropological stricture that ritual is social because it must be attached to, relate to, or service some group. Ritual is created by groups and expressive of groups, otherwise it is insignificant. This complicity of ritual and groupness implicitly demands that rite have meaning or function for the social, the *raison d'être* of ritual's existence. Thus, the structures, dynamics, and processes of ritual are immediately oriented to the social. Rarely considered is that taking this tack eliminates other potentialities in which thinking on ritual ignores the borders of the social.

Nonetheless, if ritual is (though I am less than certain of this) *the* great generating ground of the human phantasmagoric, as I think Bruce Kapferer argues, then insisting that this ground must be utterly social denies (again) the essential *phenomenality* of ritual phenomena. I argued earlier that the constitution of phenomenon *qua* phenomenon should have a central place in ritual studies. Protecting the phenomenality of ritual insists, as I tried to show, that it should be possible to avoid committing the analysis of a particular ritual to meaning/function even before one grasps just what its shape implicates. Yet this requires that we begin analysis with the phenomenality of the phenomenon itself, and not with its surround. If form is to exist in and of itself, to whatever degree, minimally, maximally, with whatever qualities, it must have *integrity*—completeness or wholeness, as its Latin root intimates. The degrees and qualities of completeness of the ritual phenomenon constitute its phenomenality, giving to it textures and rhythms of phenomenal reality.

The emphasis that I put on the form and forming of phenomenality is an attempt to avoid prejudging what any given ritual is about (indeed if it is about anything that may be specified). Yet this also is to refrain deliberately from defining the term "ritual," since monothetic definition insists on exact distinctions of the either/or variety (see Chapter Four, this volume). Speaking of degrees of self-closure and integrity is a way of trying to avoid the over-reification of ritual phenomena while nonetheless insisting on their phenomenality.

Now, it is easy for me to write of degrees and qualities of curvature as indices of the complexity of self-organization that a given ritual develops or evolves, while claiming that complexity effects what participants are able to do through that ritual form, and, too, what ritual form is able to do through its own dynamics—yet, so what? In terms of their potential application, these ideas are vague, loose, seemingly bearing little relevance to the practice of ritual. Nonetheless, these ideas are terms of reference, a way of thinking that is distinct from those usually used to conceptualize and think about ritual. Whether this way of thinking makes any difference to the study of ritual is not for me to say. However, this perspective does tell anthropologists and others that unless they put aside the conventional tool kits of the ritual trade, they will continue to reproduce rituals as qualities of the known, and these may well be very distant from the potentialities generated by conceptualizing ritual as the creative grounds of the phantasmagoric.

If this is so then ritual becomes the imagining of the social, yet through ritual, not through the social. Thus a ritual imaginary comes to the fore—the capacities of rite to imagine otherness, other-where, other-when, through its own self-organizing media and their originary grounds. Ritual self-forming and the self-organizing of rite are done always through a ritual imaginary. Ritual in its own right recognizes that the comprehensiveness and usage of the imaginary vary with the integrity of self-organization that particular rites enable and accomplish. Simplistically (yet recognizing this), the greater this integrity, the greater the autopoietic autonomy of the rite from its social surround. It is these self-organizing qualities of phenomena that give them relative freedom toward the social. In turn, these qualities enable studies of ritual in its own right to border the social.

Yet how social must a ritual be in order to be ritual? Given that the grounds for a particular ritual will be social in some way, must its form be directly accountable to the social? I will venture that whether a given ritual form is accountable directly to the social is contingent upon its practice and whether this practice will have meaning and function for the social. Meaning/function, then, is not a given that follows directly from the fact that the ritual is practiced. Questioning whether particular ritual forms must be social in their phenomenality pushes the discussion of ritual beyond the usually acceptable.

The medievalist, Piroska Nagy, offers us a case in point through that which she calls "intimate ritual," that of religious weeping during the European High Middle Ages. During the High Medieval period religious weeping was called the "gift of tears." This was said to be given by God, indicating His presence within the weeper, the tears washing away the sins of the latter. Weeping affected the *homo interior*, the "inner person" of the weeper. In this way the soul of the weeper was cleansed and transformed. Some medieval authors drew a parallel between the baptism, the purification by exterior water, and weeping as the interior "water of tears," an internal "baptism of tears" that complemented and completed the exterior purification (Nagy 2004: 125).

Nagy emphasizes that the intimate ritual of weeping occurred entirely within the being of the weeper, such that the weeping could remain invisible, entirely within the interior of the weeper. Understood within its historical environment, this was not a solipsistic rite, simply between the person and herself. Instead, she opened her within-ness to the potentialities of cosmos, to God's penetration that reorganized her from within herself. The person embodied her ritual, taking it within her wherever she went, her body becoming the interface between ritual and social surround. Weepers took both sides of the distinction between self and the social into themselves, making the social subordinate to the self, thereby opening the way to personal mysticism.

For some three centuries, these persons limited the presence of the social within their intimate ritual or, perhaps more accurately, shut in the social within themselves. For people around her, the ritual dynamics within such a person were no less mysterious than are those of many other initiation rites. As such this ritual neither was formalized nor was under the control of church and social order. The efficacy of weeping "lay in the [very] act of weeping itself" (Nagy 2004: 128), the act induced by God through his hidden relationship with the individual, a relational dynamic that continued throughout the life course of the weeper. The occurrence of this ritual was directed neither by sociality nor by the formal theology of the church. Indeed through weeping the individual circumvented the social controls of church and community. Nonetheless, at its height the ritual was not perceived as anti-social, for weeping indexed God's presence within the weeper.[22] Nagy rightly writes of weeping as a lifelong intimate ritual of initiation into the mysteries of salvation of the soul. Her think-piece is a provocative challenge to the insistence of canonical anthropology that ritual be grounded in shared meaning and its social function.

Nagy's work intimates a problematic that in my view can hardly be solved through beginning the analysis of ritual with its social and cultural surround. At issue here is how ritual works when the participants do not share common understandings of cultural symbols, and when those who are being healed have at best only a sketchy sense of and limited feel for the cosmological premises that inform the existence of the ritual. I foundered on this problem some fifty years ago, and the halting explanation I offered then (Handelman 1967) really limped, to say the least. At issue for me was the latest healing ritual of the Washo shaman, Henry Rupert (see Chapter One and the Epilogue to this volume). Henry had transformed his healing so that its form, technics, and thematics were utterly foreign to everyone I knew or heard of whom he had treated in the recent past. Nonetheless, patients of great social and cultural diversity continued to come for treatment, and his reputation only gained in stature. One could not really speak of cultural meaning or of social function. He was a recluse, issues of power were irrelevant to him, and he resisted representation when anthropologists and others thrust this upon him (Handelman 1993). In anthropological terms my perception today of his transformed healing is as opaque as it was then. I can say that he represented nothing—nothing, that is, other than the actualization of potentiality, of an emerging strand of the phantasmagoric.

Ritual in more traditional social orders likely is a most prominent venue of phenomena privileged with cultural creation through the potentiation of the possible. In this sense, much traditional ritual is a vortex of the virtual, in the way Kapferer (2004) uses the virtual—as a vortex through which cosmoses are made, but no less *explored* in their making.[23] Yet traditional rituals as venues of creativity have hardly been explored as such, nor will they so long as there persist the obsessions with Durkheimian functionalism, with Geertzian stories that people tell themselves about themselves, with the Gluckmanian conception of ritual as social relations (Gluckman 1962), and with ritual reduced to arenas of politics and power (Bell 1992). *All* of these perspectives ironically deny the virtual capacities of ritual, closing the phenomenality of rite to the creative potentialities of the imaginary, of potentiality itself.

Ritual in its own right plainly says to take the very phenomenality of ritual seriously *if* you are interested in the phenomenon of ritual. Then study ritual through ritual, and see where this leads, especially as to whether these directions are worthwhile. Surprisingly (is it?), no existing avenues are shut by this approach—though they become more contingent and, thus, more open. And, after all, Calvin, the ritual expert, can always retort: "If you can't control your peanut butter, you can't expect to control your life."

Notes

First published in 2004 as "Introduction: Why Ritual in Its Own Right? How So?," *Social Analysis* 48: 1–32. Reprinted with permission.

1. Frits Staal (1996: 131–32) argues that ritual exists "for its own sake," constituting "its own aim or goal." Therefore, ritual does not have meaning within itself, for its own sake, since meaning indexes representation. My perspectives coincide to an extent, though I reject his speaking for "ritual" as a generic category, and so, too, his use of any specific ritual, in particular the Vedic *agnicayana*, as paradigmatic of all ritual. See Malamoud (2002: 25) on systemic aspects of the *agnicayana*.

2. The phrasing "ritual in its own right" was used by de Boeck and Devisch (1994) to develop a critique of studies of divinatory ritual in Central Africa, particularly those of Victor Turner, in which the dynamics of ritual transformation are reduced, in their words, to a script or text located in social order and not in the ritual moment.
3. The overall perspective resonates to a degree with the call by Castoriadis (1997: 339) to comprehend social and psychological forms and patterns from within themselves, from the perspective of their "self-constitution."
4. By shifting from the usual discussion of *levels* of macro/micro-organization to *domains* of organization, I am assuming that the existence of micro-domains, however they are organized, is not predicated on the existence of macro-systems. By beginning analysis with the micro-domain of ritual, I enable the relationship between ritual and its (more macro) surround to be guided by the ways in which the ritual is organized, without assuming that this is subordinated to or directly derived from the macro.
5. The reasoning likely depends on Spencer Brown's (1969) logical injunction that once a distinction is made, both sides of the distinction must be included in what follows.
6. Just how embedded lineality is in Western taken-for-granted perceiving and thinking is brilliantly discussed by Lee (1959).
7. On torsion, see Bunn (1981: 16–17) who argues that in torsion, or torque, as I use it, there is discontinuity rather than absolute fit in the joining of difference—here, the torqueing of ritual into social order.
8. On propensity in form, see Jullien (1995: 75–89).
9. Here I sidestep my own position (which I continue to hold) that the idea of ritual is utterly otiose (see Handelman 1998, 2006). On the development in Western thought of the phenomenal category of "ritual," see Boudewijnse (1995) and Asad (1993).
10. On the significance of "depth" for recursivity, see Rosen (2004).
11. Erving Goffman (1981: 63) wrote of his belief that "the way to study something is to start by taking a shot at treating the matter as a system in its own right . . . it is [this] bias which led me to try to treat face-to-face interaction as a domain in its own right . . . and to try to rescue the term 'interaction' from the place where the great social psychologists and their avowed followers seemed prepared to leave it."
12. The position for creativity in ritual action during ritual performance is argued by Csordas (1997: 250–65).
13. Deleuze's (1991: 58–59, 118) reading of Bergson moves in this direction. The curve may be said to create past and future simultaneously, folding them into one another, creating short cuts between them.
14. Thus, the greater the self-organizing and self-sustaining capacities of a ritual, the greater the degree of discontinuity in its torqueing back into social order. However, if ritual self-organization creates itself as the replacement of social order, so that the ritual is the simulacrum of the basic premises of social order, then there is no discontinuity between the two. The outcome of the ritual returns to its surround *as* that surround. Here there is no longer any distinction between the ideal and the real, between map and territory.
15. Unlike the lineal movement of Maria Antonia, the trajectory of the dancers likely moved through a recursive multistability of perspective, of dancers holding onto dancers moving past dancers holding onto dancers who were moving past them. Multistability refers to a fluidity of perception, a multiplicity of perspectives, opening pathways of possibility that nonetheless keep proportional relationships and ratios, thereby exploring variations of propensity within form and sense (see Friedson 1996: 139–44; Ihde 1983).
16. Rousseau's remembering may be called imagistic and episodic (Whitehouse 2000: 9–11, 92–93). The event likely was more a singular than a repetitive episode, though one with powerful, particularistic reverberations for the participants.
17. In the not distant past, *Furez* was held on three consecutive days, each day given over to one of the three segments.

18. There is the question, beyond the scope of this work, of whether the folding of a rite deeper and deeper into itself might not generate fractal-like qualities within the phenomenon. Today, this would be my understanding of my reanalysis (Handelman 1979) of Bateson's analysis of *naven* behavior among the Sepik River Iatmul—the fractal-like relationship between a single *utterance* that is fully *naven* behavior, on the one hand, and a complex *performance* that is fully *naven* behavior, on the other. Its fractal-like qualities would self-enclose the phenomenon within its own variations, expansions, contractions. See my comments on *naven* behavior in Chapter Seven of this volume.
19. This part of the re-embedded analysis may be understood as a modification of Zempleni's (1990: 208) argument that "what disintegrates the group periodically on the inside is converted in a force which delimits it continuously from the outside."
20. Might not these "fillings" be thought of, in relation to one another, as having fractal-like qualities?
21. On modularity in ritual organization, see Handelman 2004.
22. The sinologist, Kristofer Schipper, himself a Taoist priest, once told me that the Taoist priest could do, step by step, an entire ritual within his mind, and that the efficacy of the self-same rite would be the equivalent of its performance in the temple before an audience. The ritual was performed before an audience when it was paid for (personal communication, Netherlands Institute for Advanced Study, spring 1988). In the first instance the ritual was cosmological, yet was it social?
23. Here I emphasize traditional ritual as a venue of creativity, since I do not think that rituals associated with modern state orders have much of this capacity. See Handelman 2004.

References

Asad, Talal. 1993. *Genealogies of Religion: Discipline and Reasons of Power in Christianity and Islam.* Baltimore: Johns Hopkins University Press.
Baecker, Dirk. 2001. "Why Systems?" *Theory, Culture & Society* 18: 59–74.
Bailey, Kenneth D. 1997. "The Autopoiesis of Social Systems: Assessing Luhmann's Theory of Self-Reference." *Systems Research and Behavioral Science* 14: 83–100.
Bateson, Gregory. 1977. "Afterword." In *About Bateson*, ed. John Brockman, 235–47. New York: E. P. Dutton.
Bell, Catherine. 1992. *Ritual Theory, Ritual Practice.* New York: Oxford University Press.
Bloch, Maurice. 1992. *Prey into Hunter: The Politics of Religious Experience.* Cambridge, UK: Cambridge University Press.
Boudewijnse, Barbara. 1995. "The Conceptualization of Ritual: A History of Its Problematic Aspects." *Jaarboek voor Liturgie-Onderzoek* 11: 31–56.
Bunn, James H. 1981. *The Dimensionality of Signs, Tools, and Models.* Bloomington: Indiana University Press.
Castoriades, Cornelius. 1997. *World in Fragments.* Stanford: Stanford University Press.
Csordas, Thomas J. 1997. *Language, Charisma, and Creativity: The Ritual Life of a Religious Movement.* Berkeley: University of California Press.
Darnton, Robert. 1985. *The Great Cat Massacre and Other Episodes of French Cultural History.* New York: Vintage Books.
de Boeck, Filip, and Rene Devisch. 1994. "Ndembu, Luunda and Yaka Divination Compared: From Representation and Social Engineering to Embodiment and Worldmaking." *Journal of Religion in Africa* 24: 98–133.
de Coppet, Daniel. 1990. "The Society as an Ultimate Value and the Socio-Cosmic Configuration." *Ethnos* 55: 140–150.
———. 1992. "Introduction." In *Understanding Rituals*, ed. Daniel de Coppet, 1–10. London: Routledge.

Deleuze, Gilles. 1991. *Bergsonism*. New York: Zone Books.
———. 1993. *The Fold: Leibniz and the Baroque*. London: Athlone Press.
Elias, Norbert. 1983. *The Court Society*. New York: Pantheon Books.
Feld, M. D. 1975. "Middle-Class Society and the Rise of Military Professionalism: The Dutch Army 1589–1609." *Armed Forces and Society* 1: 419–42.
Feyerabend, Paul. 1978. *Against Method*. London: Verso.
Foucault, Michel. 1993. "Dream, Imagination and Existence," trans. Forrest Williams. In *Dream and Existence* by Michel Foucault and Ludwig Binswanger, ed. Keith Hoeller, 31–38. Atlantic Highlands: Humanities Press.
Friedson, Steven M. 1996. *Dancing Prophets: Musical Experience in Tumbuka Healing*. Chicago: University of Chicago Press.
Geertz, Clifford. 1973. *The Interpretation of Cultures*. New York: Basic Books.
———. 1980. *Negara: The Theatre State in Nineteenth-Century Bali*. Princeton: Princeton: University Press.
Gerholm, Tomas. 1988. "On Ritual: A Postmodernist View." *Ethnos* 53: 190–203.
Gluckman, Max, ed. 1962. *Rituals of Social Relations*. Manchester: Manchester University Press.
Goffman, Erving. 1961. *Encounters: Two Studies in the Sociology of Interaction*. Indianapolis: Bobbs-Merrill.
———. 1981. "A Reply to Denzin and Keller." *Contemporary Sociology* 10: 60–68.
Gurevich, Aaron. 1995. *The Origins of European Individualism*. Oxford: Blackwell.
Haken, Hermann. 1993. "Are Synergetic Systems (Including Brains) Machines?" In *The Machine as Metaphor and Tool*, ed. Hermann Haken, Anders Karlqvist, and Uno Svedin, 123–37. Berlin: Springer-Verlag.
Handelman, Don. 1967. "Transcultural Shamanic Healing: A Washo Example." *Ethnos* 32: 149–66.
———. 1973. "Gossip in Encounters: The Transmission of Information in a Bounded Social Setting." *Man* n.s.: 210–27.
———. 1977. *Work and Play Among the Aged: Interaction, Replication and Emergence in a Jerusalem Setting*. Assen: Van Gorcum.
———. 1979. "Is Naven Ludic? Paradox and the Communication of Identity." *Social Analysis* 1: 177–91.
———. 1993. "The Absence of Others, the Presence of Texts." In *Creativity/Anthropology*, ed. Smadar Lavie, Kirin Narayan, and Renato Rosaldo, 133–52. Ithaca: Cornell University Press.
———. 1998. *Models and Mirrors: Towards an Anthropology of Public Events*. 2nd ed. New York: Berghahn Books.
———. 1999. "The Playful Seductions of Neo-Shamanic Ritual." *History of Religions* 39: 65–72.
———. 2002. "Postlude: The Interior Sociality of Self-transformation." In *Self and Self-transformation in the History of Religions*, ed. David Shulman and Guy Stroumsa, 236–353. New York: Oxford University Press.
———. 2004. "Designs of Ritual: The City Dionysia in Fifth-Century Athens." In *Celebrations: Sanctuaries and the Vestiges of Cult Activity*. ed. Michael Wedde, 207–35. Athens: Norwegian Institute at Athens.
———. 2006. "Conceptual Alternatives to Ritual." In *Theorizing Ritual*, ed. Jens Kreinath, Jan Snoek, and Michael Stausberg, 37–49. Leiden: Brill.
Haslip, Joan. 1987. *Marie Antoinette*. London: Weidenfeld and Nicolson.
Hayles, N. Katherine. 1999. *How We Became Posthuman: Virtual Bodies in Cybernetics, Literature, and Informatics*. Chicago: University of Chicago Press.
Horgan, John. 1998. *The End of Science*. London: Abacus.
Ihde, Don. 1983. *Existential Technics*. Albany: State University of New York Press.
Innis, Robert E. 2001. "Perception, Interpretation, and the Signs of Art." *Journal of Speculative Philosophy* 15: 20–33.
Jullien, François. 1995. *The Propensity of Things: Towards a History of Efficacy in China*, trans. Janet Lloyd. New York: Zone Books.

Kapferer, Bruce. 1997. *The Feast of the Sorcerer*. Chicago: University of Chicago Press.
———. 2004. "Ritual Dynamics and Virtual Practice: Beyond Representation and Meaning." *Social Analysis* 48: 35–54.
Kauffman, Louis H. 1987. "Self-Reference and Recursive Forms." *Journal of Social and Biological Structures* 10: 53–72.
King, Michael, and Chris Thornhill. 2003. "'Will the Real Niklas Luhmann Stand Up, Please.' A Reply to John Mingers." *Sociological Review* 51: 276–85.
Knyazeva, Helena. 2003. "Self-Reflective Synergetics." *Systems Research and Behavioral Science* 20: 53–64.
Lee, Dorothy. 1959. *Freedom and Culture*. Englewood Cliffs: Prentice-Hall.
Levi-Strauss, Claude. 1981. *The Naked Man*. New York: Harper & Row.
Luhmann, Niklas. 1997. "The Control of Intransparency." *Systems Research and Behavioral Science* 14: 359–71.
———. 1999. "The Paradox of Form." In *Problems of Form*, ed. Dirk Baecker, 15–26. Writing Science Series. Stanford: Stanford University Press.
Malamoud, Charles. 2002. "A Body Made of Words and Poetic Meters." In *Self and Self-Transformation in the History of Religions*, ed. David Shulman and Guy G. Stroumsa, 19–28. New York: Oxford University Press.
Marin, Louis. 1991. "Classical, Baroque: Versailles, or the Architecture of the Prince." *Yale French Studies* 80: 167–82.
McNeil, Donald H. 2004. "What's going on with the topology of recursion?" *The SEED Journal* 4: 2–37. http://www.library.utoronto.ca/see/pages/SEED_Journal.html.
McNeill, William H. 1995. *Keeping Together in Time: Dance and Drill in Human History*. Cambridge, MA: Harvard University Press.
Mingers, John. 2002. "Can Social Systems Be Autopoietic? Assessing Luhmann's Social Theory." *Sociological Review* 50: 278–99.
Minnich, Robert Gary. 1979. *The Homemade World of Zagaj: An Interpretation of the "Practical Life" Among Traditional Peasant-Farmers in West Haloze-Slovenia, Yugoslavia* (Occasional Paper No. 18). Bergen: Sosialantropologisk Institut, Universitetet I Bergen.
Nagy, Piroska. 2004. "Religious Weeping as Ritual in the Medieval West." *Social Analysis* 48: 119–37.
Rosen, Steven M. 2004. "What Is Radical Recursion?" *The SEED Journal* 4: 38–57. http://www.library.utoronto.ca/see/pages/SEED_Journal.html.
Rousseau, Jean-Jacques. 1982. *Politics and the Arts: Letter to M. D'Alembert on the Theatre*. Ithaca: Cornell University Press.
Smith, Pierre. 1982. "Aspects of the Organization of Rites." In *Between Myth and Transgression: Structuralist Essays in Religion, History, and Myth*, ed. Michel Izard and Pierre Smith, 103–28. Chicago: University of Chicago Press.
Spencer Brown, G. 1969. *Laws of Form*. London: Allen and Unwin.
Staal, Frits. 1996. *Ritual and Mantras: Rules without Meaning*. Delhi: Motilal Banarsidass.
Sutton-Smith, Brian. 1997. *The Ambiguities of Play*. Cambridge, MA: Harvard University Press.
Turner, Frederick. 1997. "Foreword: Chaos and Social Science." In *Chaos, Complexity, and Sociology*, ed. Raymond A. Eve, Sara Horsfall, and Mary E. Lee, xi–xxvii. Thousand Oaks: Sage.
Whitehouse, Harvey. 2000. *Arguments and Icons: Divergent Modes of Religiosity*. Oxford: Oxford University Press.
You, Haili. 1994. "Defining Rhythm: Aspects of an Anthropology of Rhythm." *Culture, Medicine and Psychiatry* 18: 361–84.
Zempleni, Andras. 1990. "How Do Societies and 'Corporate' Groups Delimit Themselves? A Puzzle Common to Social and Medical Anthropology." *Culture, Medicine and Psychiatry* 14: 201–11.

CHAPTER 4

BUREAUCRATIC LOGIC

Author's Note

I began to think more formally about the logic of much bureaucratic endeavor some years after fieldwork in Newfoundland on welfare bureaucracy. I was dissatisfied with Weber's paradigm of bureaucracy as institution which was and continues to be dominant in the social sciences. In my view, missing from this paradigm is what I would call today the logic of the forming of form that bureaucracy creates. In 1981 I co-edited (with Jeff Collmann) a special issue of *Social Analysis* entitled "Administrative Frameworks and Clients." In thinking about the special issue, Michel Foucault's *The Order of Things: An Archeology of the Human Sciences*, was a blessing. Foucault understood profoundly how the creation of taxonomies and their organization was critical to the emergence of modernity in Europe and elsewhere.

I understood that the metier of bureaucracy could be understood in these terms; and I tried out an initial formulation of the idea in the Introduction (Handelman 1981). I suggested that bureaucracy produces and systemically organizes social categories that shape their contents, human and otherwise. Later on, in *Models and Mirrors* (1990: 77–78), I suggested that,

> The paradigmatic form of organization of the modern state is that of bureaucracy. The most elementary feature of bureaucracy is that it is a device for the ongoing generation of taxonomies—of ways of classifying aspects of the world, and of relating to these categories. The ideal practice of bureaucracy is that of orthopraxy . . . the metier of bureaucratic organization is the making of controlled change through the creation and manipulation of taxonomy . . . bureaucracy does all of this in the most mundane and routine of ways.

Chapter Four refines and expands these ideas. The chapter comes from my book, *Nationalism and the Israeli State: Bureaucratic Logic in Public Events* (2004). The upshot of my perspective is that the invention and application of systemically organized taxonomies is the most powerful device for making routine change (destructive and creative) ever invented by Human Being. Indeed, this may be approaching an apex as the digital age gains momentum and systemic depth and strength.

The forming of form through bureaucratic logic is discussed in depth in this chapter. The chapter proposes one trace through which this logic may have developed in Europe during the past few hundred years and follows one route through which the logic reached pre-state Palestine via socialists from Russia, where it was put to work in the building of the Zionist state-in-the-making.

Before continuing, let me remind about the kind of classification that bureaucratic logic generates. This classification is linear, with two intersecting axes, vertical and horizontal. The vertical axis is composed of levels of classification in a hierarchy of levels in which each higher level subsumes the lower, and is itself subsumed by the level above. The horizontal axis—a given level of classification—is composed of n number of categories, each of which contrasts with and excludes all others on the same level. All the categories on a given level of abstraction are the equivalents of one another. This logic does not produce dichotomous distinctions. A scheme of classification can have n number of levels of abstraction, and n number of categories on any given level. The classification does insist, however, that a given item be placed in one and only one of the existing categories on a given level of classification, and therefore that it be excluded from all the rest on that level. This is a highly prevalent mode of ordering, of sorting contents into categories, and of relating these categories and their levels to one another. This is a way of organizing a classification of individuals, groups, or things, grasped for purposes of classification as nuclear entities. The taxonomies produced may interface, interlock, and compete with one another, yet they discourage overlap and permeability among themselves. Bureaucratic logic is not a democratic dynamic, nor an egalitarian one.[1]

The development of bureaucratic logic comes fully into being when two conditions are satisfied: one condition is metaphysical, referring to the emergence of the conscious, systematic, classification of information that is made autonomous from the natural, God-given order of things. Through time the doing of classification gains conscious control over the means of classifying. Thus, second, a pragmatic science of classification comes fully into existence; and, this science of classification comes to be organized as a system in the self-correcting sense.

The Monothetic Forming of Form

Bowker and Star (1999: 10) define classification as, "a spatial, temporal, or spatio-temporal segmentation of the world." They add that a classification system is "a set of boxes (metaphorical or literal) into which things can be put to then do some kind of work—bureaucratic or knowledge production." This kind of lineal classification scheme is called monothetic and has been traced to Aristotle's *Organon* and to his *Metaphysics* (see Ellen 1979). Sokal (1974: 1116), writing of classification in science, emphasizes "the ordering or arrangement of objects into groups or sets on the basis of their relationships." If, in science, classification is intended to bring forth relationships that do exist in the natural world, but that may not be easy to grasp and delineate, in social life we are referring to invented schemas of categorization (though their invention may be ancient, their arbitrariness hidden in mythistory). Reified, these schemes are put to work to classify and act on phenomena. In monothetic or Aristotelian classification, precision always is preferred to no precision (Bowker and Star 1999: 103), regardless of the validity of the precise distinctions among categories at a given level of abstraction, or between levels of abstraction. This suggests that often it is more important to classify with preciseness for the sake of creating a world of precision, than it is to worry about how accurately this classification reflects the world it is made to act upon.

Invented schemes of lineal classification are intended to create facts; and C. Wright Mills (1959) commented long ago that to the bureaucrat the world is a (self-obvious) world of facts, to be treated according to firm rules. Undoubtedly there are frequent clashes of classifications invented at different times by different agencies for different purposes. Yet ideally these problems are intended to be resolved through monothetic distinctions. Bureaucratic logic is a procrustean practice—it cuts, shapes, and changes phenomena more with regard to its own hermeneutic of closure than in terms of how these phenomena otherwise exist in their worlds.[2] Though conflicts over particular classifications are continually generated, there is little argumentation over whether this kind of classifying is indeed the way to organize many aspects of public life, including the interface between public and private. Instead this kind of classifying is a self-obvious practicality in a world of facts (e.g., Haines 1990).

Monothetic classification builds closure into its own scheme since it is designed to enclose totally the world it describes, thereby exhausting the possibilities of that world in terms of the scheme. The scheme of classification folds into itself its own contingencies (cultural, social, legal) that are unfolded under various conditions. Both the folding and unfolding are symmetrical. Bureaucratic logic values symmetry in classification, in both its vertical and horizontal dimensions. Symmetry signifies boundedness, formality, order (Weyl 1952: 16). Exhausting a world of its contents through monothetic classification is the exercising of symmetrical order. Symmetry invokes the locating of every thing in its proper place, thereby enabling a monothetic taxonomy to be a simultaneity of all its categories.

Yet the practice of classification is necessarily a sequence of action, and therefore temporal. A form or scheme of classification is then also "the simultaneity of sequentiality" (Luhmann 1999: 19). By totalizing itself in these ways, a scheme of classification may be accorded relative autonomy from its social environment. This is especially so for law courts deciding on how to classify in matters of falsehood and truth, guilt and innocence; but it is also so for the multitudes of administrative decisions about classification, for examinations in education, and for a host of athletic contests and games, all of which are concerned with the classifying and re-classifying of candidates and competitors (Handelman 1998: xxxvii–xli; Hoskin 1996; Hoskin and Macve 1995).[3]

Monothetic classification is associated closely with counting in its simplest sense of adding and subtracting so that one number is not another, with making these kinds of counts in which an item goes into one category and not another nor in both. Stone (1988: 128) points to the act of this counting as categorizing, as a decision about what to include and exclude. Moreover, to categorize requires boundaries that inform whether something belongs or not. Such numbers, she argues, are like metaphors—they are "about how to count as . . . [so that] to categorize in counting or to analogize in metaphors is to select one feature of something, assert a likeness on the basis of that feature, and ignore all other features. To count is to form a category . . ." by emphasizing a feature of inclusion and excluding all else (ibid.: 129). Therefore monothetic classification has analogical qualities that can be rendered as inclusion, exclusion, the making of hierarchies. These qualities are symbolized with every act of counting of this kind. Every monothetic taxonomy not only totalizes itself but practices and symbolizes that very totalization in every act of its classifying. These properties are deeply embedded in bureaucratic logic.

Something of the same is so for the performance of an event of presentation. The performance comes into existence through the taxonomies that are integral to that event. The taxonomies contribute to shaping the performance. The logic of form that shaped the taxonomies shapes the performance.[4]

Tracing Bureaucratic Logic through Classification

Logics of the forming of form that are more linear and relatively autonomous from natural cosmos are ancient (e.g., Handelman 1995; Luhmann 1999: 22), and I will not try to account for their histories. However, in Europe there is one historical vector of the forming of linear classification that contributes to this discussion in two ways. It gives a sense of a bureaucratic logic coming to the fore and shows the broad spectrum of its influence. Through its European peregrination from the German principalities to Russia, this vector later left its traces in the early history of Zionist presence in pre-state Palestine, and the beginnings there of a highly centralized, bureaucratic proto-state, the precursor of the present State. This vector gathers strength and momentum during the period, roughly of the sixteenth through the eighteenth century, when the formation and practice of lineal taxonomic classification was understood to be under the conscious control and implementation of human agency, and was used deliberately to shape, discipline, and change social order. I break these developments into two overlapping segments: the first discusses changes in the cosmology of classification from which the monothetic emerged dominant; while the second takes up how the monothetic contributed to a sense of proto-bureaucratic community in central Europe. Toward the close of this discussion I bring out the resonances between bureaucratic logic and that which Deleuze and Guattari call the state-form. In my reading, the state-form is a logic of the forming of form, one that converges in modernity with bureaucratic logic, in a torsion of these logics that enseams together the dynamic of monothetic classification with those that Deleuze and Guattari call capture, containment, striation, smoothing.

The first segment of the historical vector traces the consequences of classifying knowledge of the world totally and quite monothetically. In *The Order of Things* (1973) Foucault provides an insightful, historicized perspective on the crystallization of monothetic classification in Europe.[5] He tells us that the sciences of the seventeenth century were informed by ways of seeing the world that can be glossed as "rationalism." Through these perceptions, "comparison became a function of order . . . progressing naturally from the simple to the complex . . . . The activity of the mind . . . will therefore no longer consist in drawing things together [through similarities] . . . but, on the contrary, in discriminating" (1973: 54). Rationalism used the idea of taxonomy to make monothetic order: to distinguish, to divide, to locate, to name, and to connect things living and dead according to their natural characteristics, in order to make these things clearly visible. The phenomenal world surrendered and made explicit what was thought to be its essences. Foucault (1973: 131–32, my emphasis) comments that:

> What came surreptitiously into being between the age of the theatre [the Renaissance] and that of the catalogue [the seventeenth century] was not the desire for knowledge, but *a new way of connecting things* both to the eye and to discourse . . . . The ever more complete preservation of what was written, the establishment of archives, then of filing systems for them, the reorganization of libraries, the drawing up of catalogues, indexes, and inventories, all these things represent . . . an order of the same type as that which was being established between living creatures.

Linnaeus began his new way of connecting things taxonomically by modifying but hardly rejecting the Great Chain of Being, the cosmos of God the Creator (Tillyard n.d.), which he enhanced through the precision of monothetic classification. Yet scientific taxonomies helped to shift classification further from the God-given toward the humanly constructed (Weinstock 1985; Frangsmyr 1994; Gould 1987). As an idea of science, the forming of monothetic taxonomy shaped perceptions of the physical world by opening time/space to the capture and containment of all things, living and inert, through their naming, itemization, placement. All things were classified exclusively and inclusively on vertical axes and horizontal planes in concordance with explicit rules that enabled the classified to enter the discourse of the classifier.

To construct a taxonomic scheme there had to be explicit rules for the delineation of categories, and for the inclusion of items within them; for the aggregation of categories at higher and lower planes, and for the resolution of anomalies when an item fit more than one category on the same plane of abstraction. Therefore there had to be rules also for the creation of new categories, through division and addition. The decision-rules of scientific, monothetic taxonomies were understood as conscious and secular constructions, without divine inspiration, yet mirroring its precision. This conception of classification resembled that of a static, monothetic form, rule-governed yet empty of content. More accurately, this dynamic of the forming of form moved relatively slowly, though with definitiveness and the need to assimilate new items uncovered in faraway places in this age of discovery. This slow dynamic was closer to movement in the divinely created and regulated natural cosmos. Yet, to the extent that the decision-rules of a taxonomic scheme did their work of comparison, contrast, attribution, and distribution, one could also speak of the "rationality" and "efficiency" of the taxonomy.

This idea of taxonomy as a totality of information was hardly restricted to science. Mapping and placing, naming and classifying, became pervasive to the practices of the period. Yet because the taxonomy was a slow-moving dynamic, to render social life visibly taxonomic required the application of considerable force. Force often took the form of power through presentation. In one of Foucault's striking examples, instructions to control an outbreak of plague in seventeenth-century France, the taxonomic map is the territory.

In response to the tendrils of infection, of disorder, death, chaos, the town is sealed. Within, it is divided into sections and streets, each under the authority of an official. Dwellers are locked within their homes, bread and wine reach their doorsteps via small wooden canals that branch out from more central ones. The only people to move between houses are the higher officials and the non-persons who carry the corpses and the sick from place to place, from category to category. The boundaries of this "frozen space" (Foucault 1979: 195) are controlled by officials, themselves fixed in place. Surveillance within the town is pervasive. Every day each of the inhabitants of a house appears before his allocated window, to answer the roll call of officials: name, age, sex, death, illness, irregularity, all are inscribed and recorded. In this way the totalization of information is emended. "The relation of each individual to his disease and to his death passes through representatives of power, the registration they make of it, the decisions they take on it" (ibid.: 197).

The application of such social taxonomies is proto-bureaucratic. The minute, visible, forceful application of classification is living presentational evidence of its validity: the town has become "[t]his enclosed, segmented space, observed at every point, in which individuals are inserted in a fixed place, in which the slightest movements are supervised, in which events are recorded . . ." (ibid.: 197). The vision is that of the perfectly governed polity in which: "power is mobilized; it makes itself everywhere present and visible . . . it separates, it immobilizes, it partitions; it constructs for a time what is both a counter-city and the perfect society . . ." (Foucault 1979: 205; Eliav-Feldon 1982: 45). The perfectly governed society is one in which every person is classified and catalogued, and, therefore, in principle is regulated.

The age of the theater and that of the catalogue collided and intersected in numerous public venues, as the following instance from Bologna indicates. There, for one hundred and fifty years during the seventeenth and eighteenth centuries, taxonomizing science was linked intimately to events of presentation. During this period a public anatomy course—the dissection of an entire human body with accompanying scholarly exegesis and learned debate—was held annually for ten to fifteen days during the carnival period (Ferrari 1987). The dissection was an exercise in monothetic precision and rigor in the naming and classifying of body parts, their functioning and function—a disciplined exercise of taking apart an individual whole, but under the total control of science. The public dissection was a spectacle infused with the scientific (and proto-bureaucratic) de-forming of form.

Of especial fascination here is how this monothetic de-formation emerges from the discourse of science and takes the form of spectacle, of a presentation of parts held up for inspection, one by one. And, that the anatomy course was held during carnival, and was attended also by anonymous masked revelers. Carnival de-formed the monothetic by raucously playing with the body, exposing hidden social innards, upending and jumbling social order, blurring boundaries among distinct categories and torqueing them into one another. As this occurred, the dissection and presentation of body parts simultaneously began to make monothetic order in this world of carnival, an order that formed scientific classification out of the de-formation of a human whole that concealed most of its body parts within itself. Here science took the aesthetic form of a proto-bureaucratic spectacle that laid out for didactic inspection that which was usually hidden within the body.

During the eighteenth century, Western perceptions turned the interior integration of the scientific taxonomy—the archive, the table, the catalogue—into one of organic relationships. Foucault (1973: 218) puts this shift in the following way: "the general area of knowledge is no longer that of identities and differences . . . of a general taxonomia . . . but an area made up of organic structures, that is, of internal relations between elements whose totality performs a function . . . the link between one organic structure and another . . . can no longer be the identity [in and of itself] of one or several elements, but must be the identity of the relation between the elements and of the function they perform . . . ." Rendered as components in organic relationships, classified items practiced functions for entire classifications. This more complex division of labor within and among monothetic taxonomies began to shift into that which we recognize as a functional system: a hierarchic assemblage of levels and categories, that are thought to belong more together than apart; each of which contribute specialized functions to the existence of the whole assemblage. The entire assemblage is dependent on the functions of each of its parts, as they are on one another.

Relationships of interdependence informed the taxonomy with a quicker dynamic of purpose and direction, and so provided social life with more proficient fulcrums of power: the ratio of force to social control changed, so that less force could achieve more powerful effects. The premises of monothetic classification were not disposed of; instead its forming was in-formed by a more "systemic"' organization. Systemic taxonomizing enabled one to influence in monothetic, totalistic ways whatever was reorganized. Should a part (and its specialized function) be altered, the repercussions would be felt throughout the entire system. As a depiction of organization, the table of contents was to be replaced by the flow chart, while the theorizing of Spencer and Maine, Tönnies and Durkheim, waited at the threshold.

The forming logic that shaped scientific and other taxonomies valued the visual above all other senses. The scientific gaze can be called "attestive," following Ezrahi (1990: 72–87), the gaze of knowledge that dispassionately uncovers, dissects, classifies, and displays the facts of phenomena. The attestive eye is no less integral to the bureaucratic ethos. Science and bureaucracy produce, preserve, and use texts without number. Classification commonly depends on the eye. Therefore, bureaucratic work is also hermeneutical; its practices and explanations follow from its own premises. Bureaucratic logic moves toward the self-exegetical and the contemplative. Nonetheless this hermeneutic continually implicates the gaze (Jay 1992).

The synthesis of the visual, the taxonomic, and the systemic was exemplified by innovative topological designs like that of Jeremy Bentham's late–eighteenth-century Panopticon, intended as a site for punishment and work. The Panopticon was a design of taxonomy as spectacle, made systemic. The name reflects Greek roots, meaning "all-seeing." The panopticon: a circular, tiered building composed of individual cells whose inmates cannot see one another, but all of whom are visible to supervisors in a central tower who, in turn, are hidden from the inmates. The supervisors themselves are visible to the director, who is hidden from everyone. Exterminated from the panoptic sort is sociality, the interconnectedness and interchange of human beings, their seeing and feeling one another as subjects. Present are the "clients" of the organization, each individual reduced to a body controlled by abstraction, by the geometric: separated, numbered, supervised, put to productive tasks, each within the isolation of his cell—and on continuous display. Who exercises power and why is of no immediate relevance: whoever occupies the tower, the center, the office, the apex of hierarchy, operates the classifying gaze of perfect taxonomy and its systemic control. Indeed, the Panopticon has been called a "materialized classification" (Jacques-Alain Miller, cited in Bozovic 1995: 24). The Panopticon is the dynamic of the bureaucratic forming of form gazing at the forming of its product, the client, who is enacting the ways in which he has come to be taxonomized. Here this forming logic gives shape and life to a living taxonomy that is in the ongoing performance of presentation.[6]

In the Panopticon, Bentham intended to create a perfectly symmetric cosmology of scopic supervision, its hierarchy analogous to that of God, angels, and humans; yet a secular microcosmos, one consciously invented, synthesizing surveillance, control, and the changing of individuals. In the entry of the prisoner into the Panopticon, Bentham joined bureaucratic logic to an event of presentation, to a show decidedly didactic in content, one to be staged by the "manager of a theatre" (Bentham 1995: 101). In this entry (Bentham called it a "masquerade.") the prisoner performed and attested to his own guilt and sentencing in order to persuade others not to transgress (Bozovic 1995: 5). The prisoner performed himself as a confession through which his hidden feelings were exteriorized, so that both his interior and exterior fit perfectly within the taxonomizing form he was in the process of becoming. This was similar to the anatomy dissection, except that in the Panopticon the corpse came alive. In performing himself, the prisoner embodied his guilt.[7] As the prisoner performed his entry, he formed himself into a spectacle pervaded by bureaucratic logic; then to be moved deeper into the prison, into his isolated cubicle, to live entirely by this logic of the forming of form, as an ongoing spectacle controlled by bureaucratic logic.[8]

The Panopticon entry contrasts decisively with the behavior of the prisoner in earlier times before his public execution. In Royal France the prisoner performed his own guilt in a great public spectacle of self-fragmentation that reflected and celebrated the holistic power of the King, embodied in the identity of his person and his kingdom (Foucault 1979; Ezrahi 1990: 72–74); while, within the panoptic forming of form, the prisoner performed in seclusion, before a committee of his sorters (including a theater manager), those who executed his shaping. Rather than his own dismemberment through execution, the panoptic prisoner was individuated, torn from his social integument of relationship and exchange, and put to work in a world itself detached, anonymous, autonomous. The panoptic vision brings together the taxonomic and a more modern sense of the systemic, so that the exercise of power could become "lighter, more rapid, more effective, a design of subtle coercion for a society to come" (Foucault 1979: 209). Such a design would require little fiscal expenditure; would be labor intensive; would be politically discreet; would be relatively invisible; would arouse little resistance; and would raise the effects of social power to maximum intensity and specificity.[9]

In the twentieth century, Weber's conception of rational-legal authority became the cornerstone of much modern thinking on bureaucracy. My concern here is not with the concept's current status, but with how this concept further developed the dynamics of the bureaucratic forming of form. Weber's understanding of bureaucracy implicitly depended on the premise of classification. The rational-legal bureaucratic type (Weber 1964: 329–40) has the following characteristics. It requires a classification of "offices." Offices are defined by "rules" ("a consistent system of abstract rules, intentionally established"). All offices are regulated by a "continuous organization" of rules that inform the overall scheme of classification. Thus the organization of offices can be understood as a taxonomy of categories of office, regulated by general principles of classification. The contents of a category of office are defined by the boundary rules of the taxonomy in relation to the particular category in question. (Such contents concern spheres of authority, competence, technical knowledge, procedures for making decisions, and so forth). Offices as categories are situated within a hierarchy of levels of superordination and subordination. The entire schema is understood as a secular construction, one whose practice is intended to exhaust the phenomenal domain to which it is applied. "Monothetic rationality" is embedded in this idea of bureaucracy; in its abstract, intentional principles of hierarchical organization and integration, and in its clean-cut definitions of categories (i.e., offices) that are exclusive and inclusive. Weber's conception of modern bureaucracy, which he termed "a power instrument of the first order—for the one who controls the bureaucratic apparatus" (Gerth and Mills 1958: 228), depends on premises both of taxonomy and of the systemic.[10]

The Weberian paradigm of bureaucracy bears a strong semblance to the organization of taxonomies, social and scientific, of the seventeenth century, yet now informed by systemic premises. The *raison d'être* of the bureaucratic form is systemic taxonomic practice. In the modern age, the shaping of form is purposive, directed, directional. The organization is shaped to intentionally accomplish some goal; and to accomplish this the relationship between means and ends is made explicit and rationalist. The functions of offices are specialized and specific in their complex interdependence. The entire system is infused with a social power whose focused intensity is evident on any of its levels, in any of its parts.

As a generalized system of processing information, this schema is in principle *devoid* of content, just as it is devoid of ethics. The bureaucratic schema can be filled with any content, to be processed in accordance with instructions. This is why it frightened Weber, though he was a German nationalist. This is why Bauman (1989: 106) argues that bureaucracy "is intrinsically capable of genocidal action," since its operators can target, select out, and seal off a social category from a multitude of others. Wyschogrod (1985: 39) contends that this may be done through a "sorting myth," a cosmogonic method of dividing off, excluding, and even destroying certain social categories, so as to remake others as organic, as essence, as foundational, as a purified people, as a united family. The monothetic bureaucratic logic that organizes this exclusion and seclusion of the selected category may become the only frame of reference for its victims, the members of the category (Bauman 1989: 123), and therefore their hope and death of hope.[11]

Underscored here over and again are the qualities of modern social organization and of the modern state that use bureaucratic logic to invent and modify taxonomies in the most commonsense and routine of ways. These classifications, often systemic, proliferate and flourish in the present as never before, dividing any and all social units—group, community, family, relationship—and fragmenting, classifying, and reshaping the humanity of human beings . . . but also destroying this. The inner vision of bureaucratic logic is that of a hermeneutical gaze of "viewpoints unaffected by standpoints" (Illich 1995: 52). The bureaucratic forming of form is capable of consciously and deliberately creating virtually any reality and of processing its contents.[12]

The development of the Science of Police had profound consequences for moral and social order in the emerging societies of Central and Eastern Europe, and eventually on the proto-bureaucratic state-in-the-making of the socialist Zionists in Palestine. The Science of Police depended on bureaucratic logic but moved this shaping more explicitly and firmly toward the political, toward the dynamics of organizing and administering community. I turn to discussing bureaucratic logic in the Science of Police.[13]

Bureaucratic Logic in the Science of Police

In Central Europe the religious conflicts of the Thirty Years' War (1618–48) were ended by the peace of Westphalia (1648). This began the end of the dominance of the Holy Roman Empire. In Foucault's (2007: 348) terms, that which then came into being was "a new rationality by . . . carving out the domain of the state in the great cosmo-theological world of medieval and Renaissance thought." The empire was characterized by a multitude of smaller and larger states and principalities whose existence was legitimated by the peace of Westphalia that emerged from "the strong conviction at the time in the virtues of a centralized and unified political authority as a guarantor of virtuous government" (Harding and Harding 2006: 411). Westphalia formally recognized the territorial integrity of the multitude of German-speaking principalities (which for a century many had been exercising in practice). Foucault (2007: 317) comments on these principalities, "We can think of these German states, which were constituted, reorganized, and sometimes even fabricated at the time of the treaty of Westphalia . . . as veritable small, micro-state laboratories that could serve both as models and sites of experiment."

During the seventeenth and eighteenth centuries these principalities practiced ways of ordering the state through a forming of form that has been called "Police," "the well-ordered police state," or "the science of police" (Raeff 1983; see also Oestreich 1982: 155–65). The science of police emerged fully from the domain of the political in the German micro-states. Coming out of the feudal structure of the Holy Roman Empire, these states had no tradition of specialized administrative personnel, though administrative specialization began to be developed and taught in the German universities. Foucault (2007: 318) calls this specialization "something with practically no equivalent in Europe . . . , an absolutely German specialty that spreads throughout Europe and exerts a crucial influence." With the shattering of the occidental Christian cosmos and empire and the rejection of ecclesiastical institutions, it was the secular authorities, the secular political domain, that stepped in with ordinances of the science of police (Raeff 1983: 56).

The science of police was neither the police nor the police state in today's sense of these terms. The practices of the science of police deliberately planned and administered the shape and substance of *Gemeinschaft* (community), such that people would behave as they should for the common good (*res publica*), the good that encompassed and included them all and that in this case specifically included the "set of means that serve the splendor of the entire state and the happiness of all its citizens" (Foucault 2007: 313–14), that is, the desirability of their living fruitful, productive, satisfying lives. This was to be accomplished by "establishing a closer connection between the moral realm and the life-style of the population . . . [the] acceptance of the duties of earthly existence for its own sake. It was imperative that the *same* norms and values inform every activity of the individual and group" (Raeff 1983: 88, my emphasis). In this the beliefs and teachings of the churches had a vital role; yet the churches were under the protection of the state, and in the Protestant states the ordinances of police regulated the proper performance of all aspects of church life, and amongst these, first and foremost, ritual (ibid.: 59).

To practice, and so to create the good of all—the state and its citizens—required the deliberate, rational, standardization and exactness in specifying similarity and difference in order to introduce uniform classifications; thereby to compare and to control persons in the most specific of ways (Kharkhordin 2001: 227). So, statistical information was collected, bearing on the capacities and resources of populations and their territories (rates of birth and death appeared; covert denunciation of neighbors was commended). New taxonomies based on age, sex, occupation, and health were invented, intended to increase wealth and population, but also to enable intervention in and to alleviate a wide variety of social problems. People would be enabled to live happier lives, as individuals and as groups, within the nexus of concerned regulation. Through correct practices, people were *naturalized*, one could say, into perceiving these ways of living *as best for the well-being of one and all*. These practices of togetherness effected the group-centered character of social order, the sense that good ways of living were integral to social relationships. Though the beginnings of the science of police had powerful qualities of imposition and coercion, with time these ways of living, and living together, came to be felt as naturally right for the interiority of collectivity, perhaps even as sprouting from values of Gemeinschaft and likely undergirded by values of holism.

Through what I call bureaucratic logic, the science of police was practiced by promulgating and applying standardized administrative ordinances and rules for behavior within very broad domains of intervention, yet in highly specific detail. So, in various places the science of police set rules for the use of the personal pronoun between parents and children, for the dimensions of saddles, for the enumeration of what should be drunk and consumed during wedding feasts, for the number of people permitted to attend a christening, and so forth. A rational science of endless, detailed listings of classification in the interests of the "good order of public matters" (Pasquino 1991: 111) in the interests of the forming and shaping of collectivity as a community of hardworking, industrious people for the good of the state (Raeff 1983: 87–88). Police regulations tried to organize everything that went unregulated, that lacked clear form in a society of the three estates—this was "a great effort of formation of the social body," one that demanded degrees of order that reached beyond law and encroached on domains new to becoming occupied by public ordering (Pasquino 1991: 111).[14] In terms of its institutions, the science of police in the German principalities was more proto-bureaucratic than bureaucratic, yet it established a "gridwork of order" (Gordon 1991: 20) that paid close, regulating attention to the itemization, movement, and flow of persons and goods.

Above all, the patterning of this gridwork of order and its taxonomies was symmetrical in its control of variance, variation, idiosyncrasy. Simmel ([1896] 1968: 72–73) argues that the "tendency to organize all of society symmetrically . . . according to general principles is shared by all despotic forms of social organization . . . . Symmetrical organizations facilitate the ruling of many from a single point. Norms can be imposed from above with less resistance and greater effectiveness in a symmetrical organization than in a system whose inner structure is irregular and fluctuating." This was so for the science of police, and more generally is so for all social forms shaped through bureaucratic logic. Bureaucratic logic generates the symmetries of monothetic taxonomizing. The science of police totalized the control of sameness and difference through taking responsibility for society and sociality (Foucault 2007: 326). Central to the ethos of living that was to be more than just living was the linking of the state's strength to the felicity of the individual, such that men's happiness was turned into the utility of the state, indeed into the very strength of the state (Foucault 2007: 327).

The same kind of link held for communities. Raeff points out that through compartmentalization (like the number of people permitted to attend a christening) the family was made more private, separated more from extended kin and social networks. The person was individualized (and expected to become a more productive and efficient worker) and individuated (and, so, accentuated as a unit of counting and governance). Yet together with this the community became solidary through its self-managing and self-policing, all for the common good; and persons felt the significance of the organizing community in their lives, as individuals and as group members. Thus the public sphere penetrated deeply within the private, so that the emergence of the private sphere (the family, the individual) incorporated powerful visions of the public good as a collective endeavor, one that contributed to making the private domain reliant on that of the public and its governance. Governance had opened points of entry into the private sphere, and the private sphere was imbued with values of the public.[15] Individuation in my usage refers to the categorical separation of person from person, making each into an individuate through administrative forces external to the person. Bureaucratic logic individuates when it generates taxonomies within which the person is made a member of an aggregate in a particular social category and is isolated in this way for administrative purposes. Individualization refers to the person perceived as a unique being in terms of psychologistic qualities. As Lemke (2001: 191) puts it, "Foucault endeavors to show how the modern sovereign state and the modern autonomous individual co-determine each other's emergence." The modern state shaped individual agency to fit the spread of pastoral power through bureaucratic institutions (Foucault 1982: 783–85). These institutions individuated the person and tended to the person so individuated. The individual exercised agency within the range of possibilities extended by individuating bureaucracies.

The powerful sense of solidary, organic groupness that came into existence in the German principalities emerged together with the power of this groupness to shape and discipline the person as an individual, yet as the exercise of power integral to the happiness of both community and individual. In Foucault's terms, the pastoral care of the state was joined to the care of selfhood. Thus in Foucault's view, individual agency is a modern, bureaucratic conception of that which I am calling both the individualization and the individuation of the person, in terms of which the individual participates in his or her own self-formation (Foucault 1980; Rose 1998).[16] Articulated together were the welfare of the group and the well-being of the individual who was managed in the first instance from outside himself, leading him to value his membership in and feelings for groupness and community, and his creative independence within groupness. Most intriguing, the enabling of both division (through classification) and unification eventually came to grow from the deeply organic sense of groupness, bottom-up, as it were—out of the well-being and happiness of community and not simply from the coercion of authority. The German sociologist, Ferdinand Tönnies, called this adhesion to the holism of Gemeinschaft, the "spontaneous will" (*Naturwille*), in our terms the utter naturalization of the individual into the social whole. Therefore this enablement did not alienate levels of social order from one another, for culturally they came to grow out of one another—their relationship was continuous with one another, with the individual and individualism firmly embedded within and integral to community. By the beginning of the nineteenth century the German philosopher, Johan Gottleib Fichte, could say that the goal of social order was "the complete unity and unanimity of all its members" (quoted in Hartman 1997: 123). In the Prussian state, which unified Germany politically in the nineteenth century, the top-down formation of absolutist statehood met the more bottom-up values of holistic community, the long-term effects of the Science of Police.[17]

The tsars of Russia, beginning with Peter I, brought ideas of the well-ordered police state into the very different grounds of eighteenth-century Russia. Unlike the more interior forming of community in the German principalities, Peter imposed the science of police top-down on Russian social and moral order. His project was to wrench into existence an abstract conception of the state, one that conceived of its policy in terms of rational efficiency in ordering and changing society through didactics, regulation, and prescription (Raeff 1983: 205). Instead of an incompact empire governed loosely from its center but with high degrees of local autonomy, he introduced centralized and centralizing administration, and built a new capital, Saint Petersburg, as the exemplar of rectilinear hierarchy and functional planning (Scott 1998: 194). The bureaucratic forming of form took shape through top-down coercion and compulsion, discipline, and regimentation (Raeff 1983: 237; Stites 1989: 19–24). Peter introduced bureaucratic institutions that formally separated government from other domains of life, that required written records, and that paid attention to the minutiae of office (inkwells, furniture, office hours) (Raeff 1983: 203). The terminology of the state, as an apparatus of government independent of ruler and ruled, appeared in Russian in the eighteenth century. The state—the bureaucracy and legal apparatus—was brought into existence in between ruler and ruled in the name of the common good but imposed from above as coercive form (Kharkhordin 2001). Catherine the Great made the administrative system introduced by Peter more efficient, in trying to shape a society that would reflect the practices of the well-ordered police state, and that would help rather than hinder the modernizing efforts of the state. Her reforms rationalized administration on lower levels of state organization, and effected ways of life on local levels. Nonetheless, Russian statutes continued to stress the repressive and punitive dimensions of police law (Raeff 1983: 224–54).

The science of police worked well in the closely-knit German principalities because the logic of its forming of form had resonated deeply and harmonically among groups, individuals, and moral order. By contrast, the Russian version of police continued to be imposed from above to hold together the vastness, heterogeneity, and locality of Russia as empire and as frontier state. One could argue that the top-down imposition of order in Russia continued to be a major force for societal control until the fall of the Soviet empire in 1989. Unlike the German case, the Russian case has continuously generated profound discontinuities and a lack of organic integration between different levels of social order.

The socialist Zionist leaders who rose to prominence in Palestine came there from Russia after 1905 and then again after the October Revolution. They were well inculcated in top-down social and moral order, but they were also deeply concerned that this turn into a powerful sense of organic community, one that would be felt to grow from the bottom up. They brought with them the shaping force and power of Russian (and then Soviet) bureaucratic organization, but also the more distant resonance of German organic groupness with its interior force of shaping moral and social order categorically, yet nonetheless felt to grow from within itself.[18]

The science of police is close to what Foucault (1991: 103) calls governmentality. The sensibilities of governmentality are important here because they relate directly to forms that constitute the state, and to public events that reflect what is felt to be significant in this state of being. Governmentality should be read as govern-mentality, or simply as government—the perceptions that the State should intervene systemically, however loosely articulated the systems, in the lives, relationships, networks, and enterprises of its own citizens, for its own good and for their well-being. Therefore governmentality can be understood as forms of activity that shape, guide, and affect the conduct of persons (Gordon 1991: 2). Paralleling my claim that bureaucratic logic is a logic of practice, the practice of forming in certain ways and not in others, Foucault (1991: 97) argues that governmentality is the practice of forming acts of governing—the reality of governmentality is its doing. Thus the shift into the Jewish nation-in-arms through national public events is a practice of governmentality through which distinctions between state and nation are erased, the heads of state become the heads of the nation, and the symmetries of inclusion and exclusion are practiced to a high degree.[19]

Governmentality in Foucault's usage is much more than the formal apparatus of state administration—it is closer to a composite reality put together by institutions, procedures, myths, analyses, reflections, strategies, and tactics that enable the shaping, effecting and affecting of populations (Foucault 1991: 102–3). The practices of governmentality may be totalistic, top-down, and all-embracing, or, as Rose (1996b: 57, 61) argues for advanced liberal democracies, these practices may exist at the "molecular level" of social orders, in relation to "micro-moral domains." Trouillot (2001: 130), echoing Foucault, points out that, "statelike processes and practices also obtain increasingly in nongovernmental sites such as NGOs or trans-state institutions such as the World Bank. These practices, in turn, produce effects as powerful as those of national governments."[20] Their effects are state-like. Public events of presentation in the modern state are no less the products of this governmental ensemble of the state and the state-like.

Yet much of the complexity in coordinating the mentalities of a governing ensemble depends on the use of the flexibility of bureaucratic logic in inventing and altering linear classification. Bureaucratic logic enables the tailoring of classification to the sorting and organizing of micro- and macro-levels, and to a wide variety of social units of heterogeneous composition. Bureaucratic logic gives to strategies of governmentality a tremendous range of adaptation in the face of complex, rapidly shifting social, political, and economic conditions.[21]

Bureaucratic Logic and the State-Form

Logics of the forming of form address the imagining and formation of phenomenal worlds. The forming of phenomenal worlds is ongoing, never-ending. In the case of bureaucratic logic, the métier of the forms of organization that this logic informs is that of change, acting on and altering phenomenal worlds continuously, by adding, subtracting, dividing, and re-dividing levels and categories of classification through which these worlds are put together and taken apart. Yet bureaucratic logic is hardly the sole logic of the forming of form we can identify. Most likely there is a vast field of logics of the forming of form—not universals for the shaping of particular social forms, but a fuzzy reservoir of human imaginaries, of potentials of logics of forming.

My reading of Deleuze and Guattari (1988) suggests that their concept of the state-form is a logic of forming. The logic of the state-form complements bureaucratic logic, and this relationship is discussed here. Deleuze and Guattari ask us to imagine how logics of form inevitably emerge from one another, changing themselves as they do. This is especially significant here because the forming logic of the state-form opens toward the state. Bureaucratic logic and the state-form share dynamics that enable them to interact synergistically, to provide together certain crucial attributes of the state in modernity.

The forming logic of the state-form is arboreal and spatial: the shaping is tree-like, deeply rooted, in-place, a fundament of origins and ancestry reaching unbroken from the distant past into the far future, centered stably around an *axis mundi* that opens in all directions and planes, unmoving, vertical, tall, hierarchical, protective under the cover of its shading; branching and reproducing clearly, exactly. This logic of forming expands by capture, by taking space, by reproducing its form in additional spaces, by making over these spaces into places. The state-form extends itself lineally, a design for quantitative growth of space and population (Patton 2000). The state-form gives especial attention to shaping and controlling its own interiority, as distinct from exteriority. Deleuze and Guattari (1986: 15) write that: "the law of the State is . . . that of interior and exterior. The State is sovereignty. But sovereignty only reigns over what it is capable of internalizing, of appropriating locally." Space is striated-smooth. The state-form striates the space it contains (Deleuze and Guattari 1988: 385). Striated space "closes a surface, divides it up at determinate intervals, establishes breaks . . ." (ibid.: 481). This is the lineal forming of measurable spaces, and of standardized measures to determine all similarities and differences within these spaces.

Deleuze and Guattari relate the state-form to (in my terms) the logic of forming that they call the rhizome. Each of these logics is interior to the other, such that in particular social, historical conditions, each generates the other, each emerging from the other; just as, under other conditions, each meets the other through the interface of exteriors that clash. The rhizome grows open-ended networks of indeterminate nexuses that are shifting, incompact, without centers, without hierarchy, so that any point of a rhizome can connect to any other without going through another. The rhizome is a multiplicity of dimensions, not of bounded linear categories. The lines of the rhizome are flat (not vertical) because these lines continually fill all of their dimensionality. Rhizomes that are broken, shattered, scattered, activate one or another line of movement and growth. The rhizomic has no deep structure, no foundational axis, nor the capacity to grow anything except itself, yet without knowing precisely what it is. So the rhizomic cannot trace itself: it has no capacity for self-organization through memory; no capacity to account, to locate, to specify, to count; and therefore no capacity to capture (even itself) (ibid.: 7–20). The rhizome is smooth space, the space of a patchwork of continuous variation without unity of direction (ibid.: 481). Yet where the rhizome shows nodes of massification, the logic of the state-form is emerging.

The Israeli state, Israeli-Jewish nationalism, the project of shaping Jews as national in their citizenship, have always been at war with the rhizomic logic of forming. From the perspective of governmentality, any felt fragmentation (ideological, ethnic, religious) among Israeli Jews is the subversive appearance of the rhizomic. In these terms, Palestinian citizens of Israel, perceived as the enemy from the founding of the state, should be excluded from the arboreal unity that characterizes the community of Israeli Jews. Jews should relate organically toward one another within their community-state; whereas, Palestinians are perceived by so many Jews as threatening, as a fifth-column.

Deleuze and Guattari take for granted that the state-form generates its own apparatus of self-regulation. Yet I am arguing that bureaucratic logic exists in its own right, and that it shapes without necessary reference to whatever forms of organization emerge from shaping by the state-form. Like the state-form, bureaucratic logic shapes and controls the social surfaces of its expanding space through the capture of new territory for the deployment of power. A classification creates space that simultaneously is captured, bounded, contained. Yet whatever lies beyond the boundary of this captured space becomes the basis for further extension. New classifications create their own *raison d'être* for expansion and self-totalization.[22]

The classifications invented through bureaucratic logic also open space within their containment by making new divisions within existing ones. Complementing the arboreal logic of the state-form, bureaucratic logic enables bureaucratic form to expand through a kind of cellular division of difference yet sameness—the adding of more units of organization to itself (a new title, a new office, a new subcommittee). Bureaucratic logic enables bureaucratic form to attend to finer and ever-increasing details (Lefort 1986: 95). Thus, Lefort (1986: 108) comments that, "it is essential to grasp the movement by which bureaucracy creates its order. The more that activities are fragmented, departments are diversified, specialized, and compartmentalized . . . the more instances of coordination and supervision proliferate, by virtue of this very dispersion, and the more bureaucracy flourishes . . . . Bureaucracy loves bureaucrats, just as much as bureaucrats love bureaucracy."

Given the powerful affinity between bureaucratic logic and monothetic classification, the former is continually implicated in the kind of counting that, as noted, is symbolic of inclusion, exclusion, hierarchy. Stone (1988: 128) points out that this language of counting sounds highly political. Inclusion and exclusion are terms that suggest community, boundaries, allies, enemies; selection implicates privilege and discrimination (and social triage and genocide); while the characteristics that define a class of categories or the category itself connote value judgement and hierarchy. Both bureaucratic logic and the state-form symbolize acts of counting and the arbitrary fragmentation or augmentation of numbers into yet other numbers. Every act of counting practices and regenerates this logic.

The dynamic of capture, containment, and taxonomic division within classification has the formidable impetus and coercion of law in modern society. King (1993: 223) argues that,

> in the legal system social events derive their meaning through the law's unique binary code of lawful/unlawful, legal/illegal. An event in the social environment cannot be interpreted simultaneously as lawful and unlawful or as falling both within and outside the scope of the law. These categories are mutually exclusive . . . . Any act or utterance that codes social acts according to this binary code of lawful unlawful may be regarded as part of the legal system, no matter where it was made and no matter who made it.

King is saying that in modern social orders the implementation of division and contrast in terms of absolute categories of inclusion and exclusion has something of the feel, force, and aesthetic qualities of legal mandate (see also Gray 1978: 141). In my terms, the phenomenal forms generated by bureaucratic logic have imbedded in them the feeling of the force impact, and aesthetics of the symmetries of law. These distinctions need not be binary, in the sense of a choice between two and only two possibilities. The crucial point is the maintenance of the logic of form, the symmetrical distinction between inclusion and exclusion. In monothetic terms, truth is necessarily a singularity, not a multiplicity.

Deleuze and Guattari emphasize that the relationship between the state-form and the rhizome is not dialectical, given that each of these imaginaries exists within the other. Their relationship to one another is that of the continual emergence of each within the other, while this process exteriorizes them into near-absolute distinctiveness only under extraordinary conditions. Bureaucratic logic, however, drives toward a perfect fit between the borders of categories, smoothing the interface between a subject to be counted and a category of classification, so that the category wholly contains the subject. This meeting is procrustean, territorializing the subject as a space of subjection, yet also smoothing, shaping the subject to the category, while smoothing each category to others of the taxonomy. As it striates form, bureaucratic logic simultaneously smooths form.

Bureaucratic logic de-territorializes, in the terms of Deleuze and Guattari, since its formings have the capacity to amputate any and all social relationships (whether of family, kin, community, friendship), thereby severing and separating persons from one another, from their locations in space (thus, imprisonment, transfer, ethnic cleansing, exile), from their usual trajectories of living, and even from their pasts (thus, social erasure and lobotomy) (Bogard 2000: 270). The social surface of the individual can be separated from any organic conception of the "person," amputating the social from the personal, making the social surfaces of individuals placed within the same category homogeneous with one another.

In Israel, this smoothing of social surfaces operates in the bringing together of nationality, ethnicity, and minority. The classification of nationality contributes to the taxonomy of Jewish ethnicity and Palestinian minority, a taxonomy organized so that minority is made inferior to ethnicity. In terms of this taxonomy, superior Jewish ethnicity should show the value of national feeling on its social surface, while this is forbidden to the Palestinian minority.

Through bureaucratic logic, taxonomized space is the smooth depending from the striated, the striated depending from the smooth. The space within taxonomy is made smooth, standardized, homogeneous, every category symmetrically comparable to and relating neatly to every other on the same level of abstraction, and between levels. Simultaneously, the very creation of the entire scheme of social classification depends on its internal borders between exclusive categories. Bureaucratic classification is striating; it is simultaneously smoothing. Bureaucratic classification is smoothing; it is simultaneously striating. The interface between categories in a classification schema is smoothed, so that their "edges" fit together; while the fitting together of categories is itself striating.

Bureaucratic logic re-territorializes, in that it generates taxonomies of containment, so that within a taxonomy each category is put into its proper place. Bureaucratic logic joins smoothing to classifying, enabling and enhancing the fit among surfaces. Yet in its capacity to generate form as de-territorialized, as striated and lineal, bureaucratic logic is itself highly mobile without the need for deep roots of the arboreal state-form. Thus, bureaucratic logic can be practiced as its own metaphysics. Unlike the state-form, bureaucratic logic easily shifts its coordinates to shape containment in any terrain. No less, this logic is infinitely expandable, unless ordered to stop. Bureaucratic logic is a near-perfect "machine" of capture, forming interiority that is always exterior to itself, preparing always to capture exteriorly and to interiorize whatever it grasps and contains. Given its lack of essentialism in forming classification, bureaucratic logic opens time-space for new phenomena, like hybrids, that combine or transgress categories. The hybrid is simply another phenomenon, one that in accordance with this logic requires classification, as hybrid, or as appendage to a taxonomy.[23]

Two examples from the early years of the Israeli state will give a sense of the arbitrary power of the directed use of bureaucratic logic, and of the flexibility of this apparatus of capture and containment. (This reasoning is ongoing, has not changed to this day, and is perhaps the most potent weapon in the ongoing confiscation of Palestinian lands in the occupied territories). The Absentee Property Law placed property abandoned by Palestinians during the 1948 War under the control of the Custodian of Absentee Property. Yet some thirty thousand Palestinians had fled from one place to another within Israel, and so had not left and were not refugees. Government bureaucracy applied the Absentee Property Law. To wit, any person who may have traveled to Beirut, Bethlehem, or elsewhere, even for a one-day visit, but outside borders that had not existed during the British Mandate, was classified as a "present absentee." Such a person, one who was absent in his very presence, a non-person in terms of his property rights, indeed had his property confiscated (Peretz 1991). Through this and other legislation, the State gained a goodly portion of agricultural land that had belonged to Palestinians who became Israeli citizens.

Under emergency regulations promulgated by the British Mandate, the military governor could declare any area closed for national security reasons. After the 1948 War the population of twelve Arab villages were not permitted to return to areas that had been closed, though they had not left the country. Under an ordinance of the Ministry of Agriculture, the land was classified as uncultivated. The owners were notified that if they did not immediately cultivate these lands, the areas would be confiscated. However, the villagers could not enter these lands because the area was closed by military order. So the lands were expropriated and leased to Jewish farmers; and the villagers were left homeless (Rouhana 1997: 61; see also, Drury and Winn 1992; Benvenisti 1990).[24]

In *A Thousand Plateaus*, Deleuze and Guattari are steadfast in their ahistoricism, resolute in their commitment to imagining and exploring dynamics of space, the skins of the imaginary. Yet, no less, the shaping of time—its smoothing and striating—is most relevant for the forms of the modern state, and for its public events of nationhood and nationalism. Many scholars have commented on the importance for governmentality of controlling a people's sense of time, of shaping or of adopting shapes of time within which people know themselves and others as historical beings (or as people without history, in Eric Wolf's phrasing) through national imaginings of duration and periodization (Gross 1985; Verdery 1996: 39–57).

In my terms, the smoothing of time refers to metaphysics of the temporal, within which time is made to flow continuously, such that any markers of time embedded in the flow do not impede its movement, but are integral to its continuity.[25] Smoothing does not mean that time is necessarily lineal, in the sense of having a flat temporal trajectory. Jewish time imparts its significance through rhythmic pulsation, as I argue in Part II of the Epilogue. The smoothing and planning of time, indeed the very capture of time, enables the modern state to have a national history—either an unbroken past through time or a past that strives through national activity in the present to mend hiatus and to reshape gaps of discontinuity. The senses of national pastness, upon which so-called "collective memory" often depends, themselves depend from some shaping of national history or mythistory. A paramount device for the smoothing of time in the modern state is the event of presentation, since such events show themselves as fact, without questions, without conundra. These qualities of presentation show the joining and smoothing of present to past as unbroken duration (without showing the joints of their joining).

Yet events of presentation (see, for example, Chapter Five), even as they smooth, also striate time. Most simply the striation of time is its division, especially its classification into intervals in a taxonomy of time, so that any phenomenon within this containment is locatable exactly in its time. Conversely, any group or individual is divisible into its own history as a sequence of time-parts, synchronized temporally yet detachable from one another, like the slices of a salami. State and person are composed of time-parts, whereby any of their durations—often reckoned in years—can be sliced off the salami for purposes of classification. Clock time striates however it is counted, as do schedules, timetables, and the like. So, too, their synchronizations with one another are themselves classifications whose function is to enable surfaces of categories to juxtapose smoothly with one another through time. Just as mythistorical time is smoothed, so, too, this time must be striated—divided, dated, made lineal and sequential—since our understanding of history requires its mapping, its capture and containment, made interior as national history (see Gell 1992). Generally, the smoothing of national time, national history, also generates its striation, its markings of prominent times; for these, like body markings and incisions of initiation, make a difference in the perception of national and biographical selves.

The Bureaucratization of Politics in Jewish Palestine

The dominant ideological narratives in pre-state Jewish society in Palestine and later in Israel have given primacy to one or another idealistic vision of a Jewish collectivity, equating individualism with the breakdown of their dreams (Ezrahi 1997: 81–89). All have diminished the individual as a person with agency. Zionist socialism, the dominant organizing force in Jewish Palestine, held a utopian vision of Jewish autonomy and Jewish statehood, to be attained through social engineering. As noted, virtually all of the founders of socialist Zionism in Palestine came from Russia between 1905 and 1926, the last group experiencing the first years of Soviet rule. They perceived themselves as socialists and nationalists, and where they came from influenced how they built Zionist presence in Palestine (Shapiro 1993: 66). Unlike western Europeans' concerns with liberal democracy and civil rights, the founders of Zionist socialism stressed the relationship between nation and nationalism, placing issues of rights squarely within the purview of the collectivity (Shapiro 1993: 79; Yanai 1996).

The vision of the Russian state as an administrative utopia lasted well into the nineteenth century. The few who held power arranged the lives of the others, to organize them for production, combat, or detention, through hierarchy, discipline, regimentation, rational planning, welfare planning, and a geometrical environment (Stites 1989: 19). Yet even as ideas of utopia declined, "the dream of state power refashioning the land and the people was too alluring to die, and it appealed even to the most radical social dreamers who hated the tsarist state and whose ultimate vision was a stateless society" (ibid.: 23). The October Revolution augmented obsessions with top-down reform and control, with increasing efficiency and machine-like systemic visions of social and economic production, with Taylorism and Fordism (ibid.: 146–49)—in other words, with the forming of form through capture, containment, striation. It is from this milieu of planned, administrative, systemic collectivism, with its Russian echoes of Police and the totalistic encompassment of the individual by the social order, that the founders of socialist Zionism arrived in Palestine.

So much attention has been given to the ideological dreams of these leaders, and so much less to the elementary fact that first and foremost they were attending to the building of bureaucratic infrastructure as the bedrock for their political and economic vision of a future state. Erecting bureaucracy was basic to their efforts, and this shaping had immense impact on their political and economic organization during the period of the *Yishuv*, the Zionist settler "community" of pre-state Palestine (Yuval-Davis1987: 77), and then on forms of organization after statehood. These people were imbued with Russian political culture—tsarist absolutism and government intervention in all spheres of living, dominated by a collectivist orientation (Shapiro 1976: 2). The *Histadrut* (General Federation of Labor) umbrella trade-union organization, was established in 1920, and by 1925, David Ben-Gurion, the leader of the major political party of the Yishuv, Akhdut Ha'avodah (and later the first prime minister of the State), claimed that, "The Histadrut has been built like a quasi-state with self-rule for the working class . . ." (Shapiro 1993: 70; see also Yanai 1996: 139; Shalev 1992). This quasi-state included trade unions, labor exchanges, workers' kitchens, schools, public works bureaus, settlement departments, and so forth.

The nascent bureaucracy was taken over by the dominant political party, using methods reflecting how the Communist Party in the Soviet Union had gained control of the state by establishing party cells in all important centers of power, leading to control by a powerful, centralized party machine. In Palestine the socialist Zionist leadership built a strong party machine with cells in all Histadrut organizations, and by 1927 their party received an absolute majority in Histadrut elections. The founders of the party became the heads of the Histadrut, while the members of the inner council of the party were mostly bureaucrats in the Histadrut. In the Soviet Union the political leadership that created the bureaucracy became the product of "an apotheosis of bureaucratic institutions, an ultra-bureaucracy" (Pintner and Rowney 1980: 11). Bruno Rizzi (1985) called this "bureaucratic collectivism," "the ascent of a new, bureaucratic ruling class and the conversion of the means of production into a new form of property, owned through the state in a nationalized . . . form" (Westoby 1985: 2). Something similar occurred in Palestine.

Ben-Gurion's desire to shape his political forces as a disciplined, obedient "army of labor" (a version of the nation-in-arms, modeled perhaps on Trotsky's idea of labor armies) was rejected by his party. Yet there was no disagreement that the issue was how to build a total organization, materially and spiritually, one that included party and Histadrut (Shapiro 1976: 60). One major Zionist figure called the Histadrut an "administrative democracy" (ibid.: 67)—a bureaucracy manned by politicians who used political practices to run organizations and bureaucratic practices to organize politics. Huntington and Brzezinski (cited in Shapiro 1976) called these leaders in Soviet Russia "bureaucratic-politicians," in that only those who were prepared to head the bureaucracy could hold onto political leadership. The Soviet bureaucrat first had to demonstrate his mastery over the operation of systems of bureaucratic classification, thereby passing "tests" of his expertise, before he moved into the role of politician. These features of the bureaucrat-politician seem to have been the case also in the Yishuv (and later in the State). Bureaucratic-political practices in Palestine, argues Shapiro, were closer to the bureaucratic politics of Soviet Russia than they were to the electoral politics of democratic states.

The dominant party, becoming Mapai in 1930 (and then the Labor Party in 1969), set out to persuade the other Zionist parties of the Yishuv to reorganize themselves as copies of itself. Mapai supplied these parties with resources—financial, material, territorial—in exchange for coalition support; and also encouraged them to develop their own bureaucratic infrastructures, which led to close ties between these apparatuses across party lines (Shapiro 1993: 74). Major private enterprises accommodated their practices to Zionist socialist and nationalist rhetoric, arguing that industry, too, was integral to the armature of Jewish nation-building (Frenkel, Shenhav, and Herzog 1997). The success of the Jewish national in Palestine depended to a high degree on the development of bureaucratic infrastructures. Though limited and embryonic in their resources, these infrastructures did their utmost to organize, control, plan, and totalize numerous spheres of living (including that of public events, largely planned and organized by committee). Though the scale of these activities (like the population) was relatively small, the solution to problems demanded greater centralization of activists, officials, and offices. As activities expanded and the structuring of living became more complex, new taxonomies and standards of classification had to be invented continually.[26]

There also were the distant resonances of Police, with its powerful stress on the embrace of collectivity by the community, in that whatever was demanded by its regulations should resonate deeply with the desires of its members. Ben-Eliezer (1998b) contends that even as their elders in the Yishuv were intent on shaping a societal infrastructure through bureaucratization, among the younger native-born generation of socialist-Zionists the distinction between coercion and consent often blurred, and the will of the collectivity (of its leaders) was intended to be identical with the desire of individual members. He quotes a youth movement speaker: "We have no state, we are a Yishuv and a movement that counts on volunteering, and we have no regime . . . [but] the movement can declare a regime of volunteering, with anyone who does not volunteer being removed from the group. Today this council should declare that we are a movement of collective volunteering" (Ben-Eliezer 1998b: 378). Ben-Eliezer maintains that these people were creating a system of domination through the practice of certain kinds of organization over a broad range of interpersonal relations.

On the other hand, the Jewish proto-state was thoroughly pervaded by bureaucratic logic, which organized numerous domains of living, connecting officials and clients through rules, regulations, their bending and breaking. Every act that applied a regulation, that categorized a person, population, or thing, and that argued over proper classification, necessarily practiced and regenerated the bureaucratic logic of the forming of form.

Nonetheless, in the Yishuv, persons had degrees of choice as to national affiliation, as to whether to join a political party, as to what sources of aid to turn to, as to which friends to associate with (especially across the Jewish/Arab interface). This proto-state still was closer to a "civil society," in the sense of a "free association, not under the tutelage of state power" (Taylor 1990: 98). During much of that period it was easier for individual Jews and Arabs to develop social relationships with one another.[27] After statehood, choices were narrowed, even pinched off. Bureaucratic logic was related indelibly to the laws of the land and to regulating its infrastructure.[28] This was a country in which ideas of liberal democracy, espousing the rights of the individual and of "minorities" against encroachment by the state, did not have and have not had much success. More and more strongly present is the use of the Holocaust as the foundational catastrophe that empowers nationalism and the nation-under-arms.[29] The ways in which these presences are formed depend to a high degree on bureaucratic logic.

Notes

First published in 2004 as "Bureaucratic Logic," in Don Handelman, *Nationalism and The Israeli State: Bureaucratic Logic in Public Events*, Oxford: Berg Press. Reprinted with permission from Berg Press.
 1. That bureaucratic logic is used endlessly in social orders that are to organize social life raises questions about the influence of the logic on democratic setups.
 2. Bowker and Star (1999: 98) write of how the virus is dealt with through biological classification: "there has been a deliberate effort to create something that looks and feels like other biological classifications, even though the virus itself transgresses basic categories (it jumps across hosts of different kinds, steals from its host, mutates rapidly, and so forth) . . . . Even in this most phenomenologically difficult of cases, the world must still be cut up into recognizable temporal and spatial units." The virus of course is unaffected by scientific classifications.
 3. Fuzzier forms of classification are also integral to the routine grounds of everyday living. These include polythetic classification (Sokal 1974; Needham 1975), Wittgenstein's (1953) idea of "family resemblance," and Kosko's (1993) notion of multivalence. In these fuzzy classifications, items are brought together through that which psychologists have called "complexive classes," or "chain complexes" (Vygotsky 1962). That is, members of a class of items are connected to one another by attributes not shared by all members of that class. Vygotsky described a child beginning with a small yellow triangle, then adding a red triangle, then a red circle, and so forth. When children used this kind of associative classification in school—classing a chair with a pencil because both are yellow, the pencil with a pointer because both are long and thin, and then regarding all three objects as constituting a class of objects, they were corrected by the teacher, who insisted on the recognition of a feature common to all members of the class: thus, pencil was classified with pen (as writing instruments), and so forth. In a series of pioneering experiments, Rosch (1975; Rosch et al. 1976) argued that family resemblances, a form of complexive groupings, are integral to how adults compose more abstract levels of classification, so that, for example, the class or level of "furniture" is arrived at by using complexive groupings of attributes. Note the close association between monothetic classification, racism, and eugenics, in official thinking, and the likely association between fuzzy classification, multiculturalism, and ideas of hybrid and cyborg. In anthropology, attention should be drawn to Strathern's (1988) studies of gender in Melanesia, and to gender's fluid character, such that female is an accentuated version of male, male of female, and which is which may quite depend on context. See also Roy Wagner's recent formulation of a holographic worldview; Handelman and Shulman (1997: 194–97) on the Hindu deity, Siva, as a holographic god; and Handelman (1995b). Yet note Atran's (1996) argument that all biological taxonomies of living kinds seem to have universal properties that accord more or less with monothetic classification.
 4. Yet, too, those who put a classification to work also feed their own values into the scheme, and this needs to be taken into account in how classification impacts on that which it classifies. So, the bureaucratic innocence in census-taking can be turned easily to horrendous purpose. The Nazis used the Dutch comprehensive population registration system, set up to enable more accurate social science research, to identify Jews and Gypsies in The Netherlands (Seltzer and Anderson 2001). In 1988 the Iraqi war against the Kurds used the 1987 national census to define the target group of Kurds against whom to practice extermination (Salih 1996).
 5. I use Foucault here, despite critiques of his historicism (e.g., Patey 1984: 266–69), given that his formulations offer a useful point of start for tracing this vector of bureaucratic logic.
 6. The panopticon is a distant modification of the earlier *Kunstkammer*, the form of museum that in the interests of science brought together greatly disparate objects, natural and artifactual, ahistorical and historical, encouraging the playful forging of metaphoric relationships between unlike objects. Connectivity through metaphor illuminated the ongoing creation and creative potential of the world (Bredekamp 1995: 69ff.). Unlike the Panopticon world, the holism

of the *Kunstkammer* world was predicated on degrees of asymmetry. Utilitarian thought later broke down the playful asymmetries of the *Kunstkammer* world into units that were combinable through monothetic logic, valuing the resulting symmetries in classification, whether in science or bureaucracy. On symmetries in modern science see Wechsler (1988) and McAllister (1996: 39–44).

7. In Kafka's short story, "In the penal colony," the prisoner learns of his guilt and punishment as they are inscribed on (and in) his body by a writing machine, thereby forming him into a bureaucratic text—the human being as the embodied, sensuous spectacle of bureaucratic order, not unlike the tattooed arm number invented for prisoners in Auschwitz, one that soon developed its own taxonomic distinctions (numbers for women on the inside of the forearm, for men on the outside).

8. Through the monothetic forming of form, surveillance of the individual comes decisively to the fore through total access to his isolation and display. A century earlier, Leibniz, in his, "An Odd Thought Concerning a New Sort of Exhibition (or rather, an Academy of Sciences)," written in September 1675, had proposed a series of "academies" for the public exhibition of scientific inventions, as well as "academies" of games and pleasures. Surveillance was important to the covert functioning of the latter, yet here the scopic still was hidden: "These [. . .] [academies of pleasure] would be built in such a way that the director of the house could hear and see everything said and done without any one perceiving him, by means of mirrors and openings, something that would be very important for the state [. . .]." (The translation of this passage is in Wiener 1957: 465.)

9. Such renditions are the visionary forerunners of the organizational forms we know today as total institutions, service organizations, people-processing organizations, and so forth. Such administrative frameworks use techniques of social, psychologistic, educational, and bureaucratic intervention in the lives of persons defined as their "clients" (see, among others, Scott 1969; Dandekar 1990; Rose 1998; Bogard 1996; Handelman 1976, 1978).

10. Weber, however, never used the metaphor of the "iron cage," but rather the "shell as hard as steel," which has quite different connotations; nor did he metaphorize bureaucracy as this "shell" (Baehr 2001).

11. Bourdieu (1998: 52) maintains that through its "molding power" the modern state "wields a genuinely creative quasi-divine power" (see also Calhoun 1997: 76). Yet the logic of this creativity is that of the bureaucratic, the quasi-divine power emanating from the capacity of this logic to change social worlds by altering their classifications.

12. For example, though the powerful connections during the nineteenth and twentieth centuries among science, statistics, eugenics, and racism are well documented, ideas like that of bureaucratic logic, as the forming of form, are rarely if ever referred to. Thus Evans (1997: 295), writing on the Department of Native Affairs in mid-twentieth-century South Africa, clearly joins together science and racism to that which I am calling bureaucratic logic, but his approach goes no deeper than the study of institutions as such.

13. The forming of bureaucratic logic received impetus from other developments: from European colonialism and colonial administration (Arendt 1958), from the science of statistics, literally, the science of the state (Desrosieres 1998; Gigerenzer et al. 1989), from the embracing of numeration (Cohen 1982), and from individualism and its freedoms inherent in ideas of social contract, but also from the revolutionary reorganization of the military, and from shifts of education toward more universal criteria.

14. Foucault (2007: 338) thus likens police to a "permanent *coup d'Etat*," one that "is exercised and functions in the name of and in terms of the principles of its own rationality, without having to mold or model itself on the otherwise given rules of justice." In this formulation, Foucault comes close to those of Carl Schmitt, and then Agamben in "the state of exception." Yet, in certain ways, Foucault's formulation is the more profound because he is referring to a state of *permanent* exception concerned with endless self-regulation and, so, continuously renewing itself.

15. Rose (1998: 99–115) argues that in liberal, democratic societies the intention of governmentality is to produce, shape, and regulate the moral order within the psychological individual, rather than to suppress individuality, as is the case under totalitarian regimes.
16. This self-formation may take the shape of the "individual as enterprise," the management of personal identity through which one is employed in this enterprise of living throughout one's lifetime (Gordon 1991: 44). This perspective on self-identity dovetails well with the individual internalization of bureaucratic logic, and with the current emphasis on the importance of psychologies of self-actualization, self-autonomy, and the performance of self, raising the issue of how these psychologies contribute to the grounding of bureaucratic logic within the individual. See also Rieff (1966).
17. Here I do not follow developments in Prussia and the shaping of the bureaucratic-military absolutist state, this attempt to construct "a huge human automaton" (Rosenberg 1958: 38). To no small degree, the model here for bureaucratic absolutism was military (Anderson 1996: 243–46). According to Oestreich (1982: 258–72), in Germany the formation of the absolutist state, of top-down bureaucratic and military order met the more localized, more bottom-up "science of police" in what became their common goal of shaping and disciplining social and moral order. The developments in the principalities likely have had very long-term effects through German idealism, linking, for example, with the ethnographic insight that German individualism develops best within organic groups (Norman 1991).
18. That group formation not only be imposed top-down but also, quite mysteriously, emerge from within the group has been an ongoing concern of Israeli Jews. In Hebrew this process is often called "crystallization" (*gibush*), and a group of people brought or thrown together does not have groupness, this sense of belonging together naturally, until they feel this crystallization of sentiment (see Katriel 1991a). I emphasize "feel," for there are no conscious, objective, social indices of how and when this sense of groupness comes into existence. People just feel when it has. In the Israeli case this crystallization is related to the coming into being of the nation-in-arms and the family-in-arms, and its existence has powerful commonsensical aesthetic qualities for many Israeli Jews.
19. The nation-in-arms is invoked with every declaration that Israel is "a Jewish and democratic state"—a sequence that privileges and empowers Jewish over democratic (see Kimmerling 2002). So, too, with the declaration that the character of Israeli society, and the future of the state, will be decided on only by Israeli Jews—a pronouncement of inclusion and exclusion, evoking an embattled people who must stand alone, together, otherwise they will lose their knowledge of who they are. Every such declaration is also a commemoration and a celebration of every other occasion when this was the case, or when it will be so.
20. Walby (1999) argues that the European Union is a new kind of state, a "regulatory state." A state in which the law, a most powerful generator and applier of linear classification, plays a central role. She argues that it is "the ability to deploy power through a regulatory framework, rather than through the monopolization of violence or the provision of welfare, which is the key to the distinctive nature of the regulatory state" (1999: 123).
21. Laumann and Knoke (1987: 382), in a large-scale study of American government bureaucracies, understand the state as "a complex entity spanning multiple policy domains, comprising both government organizations and those core private sector participants whose interests must be taken into account." They found that many of the classifications generated by government bureaucracies, which have major effects on the worlds beyond these organizations, are intended first and foremost for the internal purposes of these bureaucracies, in particular to conserve their own existence.
22. So, a Californian without a driver's license would not be able to use a credit card or cash a check. Such persons are issued with "non-driver" driving licenses (Herzfeld 1992: 46), thereby capturing them within the taxonomy through whose practice they are enabled to live like others.
23. Ironically, bureaucratic logic also reflects aspects of the rhizomic. For all their linearity, the trajectories of bureaucratic logic are often tangential, without set direction or set sequence of

movement in capturing, containing, and de-territorializing space and time. Because bureaucratic logic is arbitrary in its construction and motion, it moves easily, in any direction, through any vectors, in making over space/time as its own.

24. Since 1948, Israeli governments and the IDF have nurtured (in career terms) generations of military colonial bureaucrats. Military bureaucrats ruled Palestinian citizens of Israel from 1950 until 1966 in areas of concentrated Arab population (see Lustick 1980; Shammas 1991); and they rule, from 1967 through the present, all or part of the occupied territories. Military rule is by administrative order, and judicial proceedings are autarchic and often draconian. Human rights are irrelevant to making order through containment and classification. Estimates are that since 1967 (as of 7 April 2002) the military bureaucracy in the West Bank has issued 1500 administrative orders (as of 7 April 2002), each with the binding force of law, and together embracing virtually all domains of living and livelihood. The orders set in place a complex system of permits, through which permissions are required in order to carry out a very long list of activities. The granting and withholding of permits function to reward and punish applicants. Military government is the extreme shaping of form through bureaucratic logic. On the ambivalence of the Israeli Supreme Court toward the military government and its rulings in the occupied territories, see Kretzmer (2002), who argues strongly that the Court consistently finds in favor of the authorities because, in part, Israel is defined as the State of the Jewish People, and therefore that any action perceived as contrary to the interests of this national collectivity is regarded as a threat to the security of the state (Kretzmer 2002: 193).
25. However prevalent, this is but one metaphysics of temporal movement. See, for example, Briggs (1992) on Inuit, and Rosaldo (1980) on Ilongot.
26. Arguments over whether the people who did these tasks were "bureaucrats," or whether they were "functionaries" who behaved as bureaucrats (Carmi and Rosenfeld 1991), seem misplaced. First and foremost, they were people who invented and applied a wide range of taxonomies of classification, and who used bureaucratic logic to do so. After 1948 they moved without difficulty into new and renamed offices and positions within the state infrastructures.
27. Thus, an "Oriental" identity, one that sought common cause between Jews and Palestinians, may have been viable in the pre-state period, at least among some intellectuals (see Eyal 1996; Cordoba 1980). After 1948, governmental taxonomies and their practices made such alliances difficult and costly.
28. Carmi and Rosenfeld (1989) argue that there were limited parallels between the socialist organization of the Yishuv and the state bureaucracy after 1948; so that the State's total bureaucratization of the Arab national and refugee problems constituted a radical transformation in the organization of the social order. Though the scale of things changed drastically with statehood, bureaucratic logic clearly antedates formal statehood.
29. The first Israeli astronaut, who died in the disintegration of the space shuttle, Columbia, took with him into space a small Torah scroll that had survived the Holocaust and a drawing of the earth as seen from the moon, made by a small boy in Theresienstadt (*Ha'aretz*, 2 February 2003, English Edition). Echoing the author, Ka-tzetnik (Yehiel De-Nur), the Holocaust was becoming another planet.

References

Arendt, Hannah. 1958. *The Origins of Totalitarianism*. New York: Meridian.
Atran, Scott. 1996. "Modes of Thinking About Living Kinds: Science, Symbolism, and Common Sense." In *Modes of Thought: Explorations in Culture and Cognition*, ed. David. R. Olsen and Nancy Torrance, 216–60. Cambridge, UK: Cambridge University Press.
Baehr, Peter. 2001. "The 'Iron Cage' and the 'Shell as Hard as Steel': Parsons, Weber and the '*Stalhartes Gehause*' metaphor in *The Protestant Ethic and the Spirit of Capitalism*." *History and Theory* 40: 153–69.

Bauman, Zygmunt. 1989. *Modernity and the Holocaust.* Ithaca: Cornell University Press.
Ben-Eliezer, Uri. 1998. "State vs. Civil Society? A Non-Binary Model of Domination Through the Example of Israel." *Journal of Historical Sociology* 11: 370–96.
Bentham, Jeremy. 1995. *The Panopticon Writings,* ed. M. Bozovic. London: Verso.
Benvenisti, Eyal. 1990. *Legal Dualism: The Absorption of the Occupied Territories into Israel.* Boulder: Westview.
Bogard, William. 1996. *The Simulation of Surveillance: Hypercontrol in Telematic Societies.* Cambridge, UK: Cambridge University Press.
Bourdieu, Pierre. 1998. "Rethinking the State: Genesis and Structure of the Bureaucratic Field." In *Practical Reason,* 35–63. Cambridge, UK: Polity.
Bowker, Geoffrey C., and Susan Leigh Star. 1999. *Sorting Things Out: Classification and its Consequences.* Cambridge, MA: MIT Press.
Bozovic, Miran. 1995. "Introduction: 'An Utterly Dark Spot.'" In *The Panopticon Writings,* by Jeremy Bentham, ed. Miran Bozovic, 1–27. London: Verso.
Bredekamp, Horst. 1995. *The Lure of Antiquity and the Cult of the Machine: The Kunstkammer and the Evolution of Nature.* Princeton: Princeton University Press.
Briggs, Jean. 1992. "Lines, Cycles, and Transformations: Temporal Perspectives on Inuit Action." In *Contemporary Futures,* ed. Sandra Wallman, 83–108. London: Routledge.
Calhoun, Craig. 1997. "Nationalism and the Public Sphere." In *Public and Private Thought and Practice,* ed. Jeff Weintraub and Krishan Kumar, 75–102. Chicago: University of Chicago Press.
Carmi, Shulamit, and Henry Rosenfeld. 1989. "The Emergence of Militaristic Nationalism in Israel." *International Journal of Politics, Culture and Society* 3: 5–49.
———. 1991. "The Radical Change: From a Socialist Perspective to Militarism (rejoinder to Ben-Eliezer and Shamir)." *International Journal of Politics, Culture and Society* 4: 577–87.
Cohen, Patricia Cline. 1982. *A Calculating People: The Spread of Numeracy in Early America.* Chicago: University of Chicago Press.
Cordoba, Avraham. 1980. "The Institutionalization of a Cultural Center in Palestine: The Case of the Writers' Association." *Jewish Social Studies* 42: 37–62.
Dandekar, Christopher. 1990. *Surveillance, Power and Modernity: Bureaucracy and Discipline From 1700 to the Present Day.* Cambridge, UK: Polity.
Deleuze, Gilles, and Felix Guattari. 1986. *Nomadology: The War Machine.* New York: Semiotext(e).
———. 1988. *A Thousand Plateaus.* London: Athlone.
Desrosieres, Alain. 1998. *The Politics of Large Numbers: A History of Statistical Reasoning.* Cambridge, MA: Harvard University Press.
Drury, Richard Toshiyuki, and Robert C. Winn. 1992. *Plowshares and Swords: The Economics of Occupation on the West Bank.* Boston: Beacon.
Eliav-Feldon, Miriam. 1982. *Realistic Utopias: The Ideal Imaginary Societies of the Renaissance, 1516–1630.* Oxford: Oxford University Press.
Ellen, Roy. 1979. "Introductory Essay." In *Classifications in Their Social Context,* ed. Roy F. Ellen and David Reason, 1–32. London: Academic Press.
Evans, Ivan. 1997. *Bureaucracy and Race: Native Administration in South Africa.* Berkeley: University of California Press.
Eyal, Gil. 1996. "The Discursive Origins of Israeli Separatism: The Case of the Arab Village." *Theory and Society* 25: 389–429.
Ezrahi, Yaron. 1990. *The Descent of Icarus: Science and the Transformation of Contemporary Democracy.* Cambridge, MA: Harvard University Press.
———. 1997. *Rubber Bullets: Power and Conscience in Modern Israel.* New York: Farrar, Straus & Giroux.
Ferrari, Giovanna. 1987. "Public Anatomy Lessons and the Carnival: The Anatomy Theatre of Bologna." *Past and Present* 117: 50–106.
Foucault, Michel. 1973. *The Order of Things: An Archeology of the Human Sciences.* New York: Vintage.

———. 1979. *Discipline and Punish: The Birth of the Prison*. New York: Vintage.
———. 1980. *Power/Knowledge*. New York: Pantheon.
———. 1982. "The Subject and Power." *Critical Inquiry* 8: 775–95.
———. 1991. "Governmentality." In *The Foucault Effect: Studies in Governmentality*, ed. Graham Burchell, Colin Gordon, and Peter Miller, 87–104. Hemel Hempstead: Harvester Wheatsheaf.
———. 2007. *Security, Territory, Population: Lectures at the College de France, 1977–78*. Basingstoke: Palgrave Macmillan.
Frangsmyr, Tore, ed. 1994. *Linnaeus: The Man and His Work*. Canton, MA: Science History Publications/USA.
Frenkel, Michal, Yehouda Shenhav, and Hanna Herzog. 1997. "The Political Embeddedness of Managerial Ideologies in Pre-State Israel: The Case of PPL 1920–1948." *Journal of Management History* 3: 120–44.
Gell, Alfred. 1992. *The Anthropology of Time: Cultural Constructions of Cultural Maps and Images*. Oxford: Berg.
Gerth, Hans, and C. Wright Mills. 1958. *From Max Weber*. New York: Oxford University Press.
Gigerenzer, Gerd, Zeno Swijtink, Theodore Porter, Lorraine Daston, John Beatty, and Lorenze Kruger. 1989. *The Empire of Chance: How Probability Changed Science and Everyday Life*. Cambridge, UK: Cambridge University Press.
Gordon, Colin. 1991. "Governmental Rationality: An Introduction." In *The Foucault Effect: Studies in Governmentality*, ed. Graham Burchell, Colin Gordon, and Peter Miller, 1–51. Hemel Hempstead: Harvester Wheatsheaf.
Gould, Stephen Jay. 1987. *Time's Arrow, Time's Cycle: Myth and Metaphor in the Discovery of Geological Time*. Cambridge, MA: Harvard University Press.
Grey, Bennison. 1978. "The Semiotics of Taxonomy." *Semiotica* 22: 127–50.
Gross, David. 1985. "Temporality and the Modern State." *Theory and Society* 14: 53–82.
Haines, David W. 1990. "Conformity in the Face of Ambiguity: A Bureaucratic Dilemma." *Semiotica* 78 (3/4): 249–69.
Handelman, Don. 1976. "Bureaucratic Transactions: The Development of Official-Client Relationships in Israel." In *Transaction and Meaning*, ed. Bruce Kapferer, 223–75. Philadelphia: ISHI.
———. 1978. "Bureaucratic Interpretation: The Perception of Child Abuse in Urban Newfoundland." In *Bureaucracy and World View: Studies in the Logic of Official Interpretation*, ed. Don Handelman and Elliott Leyton, 15–69. St. John's: Institute of Social and Economic Research, Memorial University of Newfoundland.
———. 1981. "Introduction: The Idea of Bureaucratic Organization." *Social Analysis* 9: 5–23.
———. 1990. *Model and Mirrors: Towards an Anthropology of Public Events*. Cambridge: Cambridge University Press.
———. 1995. "Cultural Taxonomy and Bureaucracy in Ancient China: The Book of Lord Shang." *International Journal of Politics, Culture and Society* 9: 263–93.
———. 1998. 'Preface to Second Edition: Theorizing Through Models and Mirrors." In *Models and Mirrors: Towards an Anthropology of Public Events*, x–lii. New York: Berghahn Books.
Handelman, Don, and David Shulman. 1997. *God Inside Out: Siva's Game of Dice*. New York: Oxford University Press.
Harding, Christopher, and Nicola Harding. 2006. "Who Designed the Westphalian System? Probing the Epistemology of the Westphalian Debates: Moses Was but a Juggler and King James the New Solomon." *Law, Culture and the Humanities* 2: 399–419.
Hartman, Geoffrey H. 1997. *The Fateful Question of Culture*. New York: Columbia University Press.
Herzfeld, Michael. 1992. *The Social Production of Indifference: Exploring the Symbolic Roots of Western Bureaucracy*. Oxford: Berg.
Horgan, John. 1998. *The End of Science*. London: Abacus.
Hoskin, Keith. 1996. "The 'Awful Idea of Accountability': Inscribing People into the Measurement of Objects." In *Accountability: Power, Ethos and the Technologies of Managing*, ed. Rolland Munro and Jan Mouritsen, 265–82. London: International Thomson Business Press.

Hoskin, Keith, and Richard H. Macve. 1995. "Accounting and the Examination: A Genealogy of Disciplinary Power." In *Michel Foucault (2): Critical Assessments*, ed. Barry Smart, 99–138. London: Routledge.
Illich, Ivan. 1995. "Guarding the Eye in the Age of Show." *Res* 28: 47–61.
Jay, Martin. 1992. "Scopic Regimes of Modernity." In *Modernity and Identity*, ed. Scott Lash and Jonathan Friedman, 178–95. Oxford: Blackwell.
Katriel, Tamar. 1991. "Gibush: The Crystallization Metaphor in Israeli Cultural Semantics." In *Communal Webs: Communication and Culture in Contemporary Israel*, 11–34. Albany: State University of New York Press.
Kharkhordin, Oleg. 2001. "What is the State? The Russian Concept of *Gosudarstvo* in the European Context." *History and Theory* 40: 206–40.
Kimmerling, Baruch. 2002. "Jurisdiction in an Immigrant Settler Society: The 'Jewish and Democratic State.'" *Comparative Political Studies* 35: 1119–44.
King, Michael. 1993. "The 'Truth' About Autopoiesis." *Journal of Law and Society* 20: 218–36.
Kosko, Bart. 1993. *Fuzzy Thinking: The New Science of Fuzzy Logic*. New York: Hyperion.
Kretzmer, David. 2002. *The Occupation of Justice: The Supreme Court of Israel and the Occupied Territories*. Albany: State University of New York Press.
Laumann, Edward O., and David Knoke. 1987. *The Organizational State: Social Choice in National Policy Domains*. Madison: University of Wisconsin Press.
Lee, Dorothy. 1959. "Codifications of Reality: Lineal and Nonlineal." In *Freedom and Culture*, 89–120. Englewood Cliffs: Prentice-Hall.
Lefort, Claude. 1986. *The Political Forms of Modern Society: Bureaucracy, Democracy, Totalitarianism*. Cambridge, MA: MIT Press.
Lemke, Thomas. 2001. "'The Birth of Bio-politics': Michel Foucault's Lecture at the College de France on Neo-Liberal Governmentality." *Economy and Society* 30: 190–207.
Luhmann, Niklas. 1999. "The Paradox of Form." In *Problems of Form*, ed. Dirk Baecker, 15–26. Writing Science Series. Stanford: Stanford University Press.
Lustick, Ian. 1980. *Arabs in the Jewish State: Israel's Control of a National Minority*. Austin: University of Texas Press.
Mills, C. Wright. 1959. *The Sociological Imagination*. New York: Oxford University Press.
Needham, Rodney. 1975. "Polythetic Classification: Convergence and Consequences." *Man* n.s. (10): 349–369.
Norman, Karin. 1991. *A Sound Family Makes a Sound State: Ideology and Upbringing in a German Village*. Stockholm Studies in Social Anthropology, No. 24. Stockholm: Almqvist and Wiksell.
Oestreich, Gerhard. 1982. *Neostoicism and the Early Modern State*. Cambridge, UK: Cambridge University Press.
Pasquino, Pasquale. 1991. "Theatrum Politicum: The Genealogy of Capital—Police and the State of Prosperity." In *The Foucault Effect: Studies in Governmentality*, ed. Graham Burchell, Colin Gordon, and Peter Miller, 105–18. Hemel Hempstead: Harvester Wheatsheaf.
Patey, Douglas Lane. 1984. *Probability and Literary Form*. Cambridge, UK: Cambridge University Press.
Patton, Paul. 2000. *Deleuze and the Political*. London: Routledge.
Peretz, Don. 1991. "Early State Policy Towards the Arab Population, 1948–1955." In *New Perspectives on Israeli History*, ed. Laurence J. Silberstein, 82–102. New York: New York University Press.
Pintner, Walter M., and Don K. Rowney. 1980. "Officialdom and Bureaucratization: An Introduction." In *Russian Officialdom*, ed. Walter M. Pintner and Don K. Rowney, 3–18. Chapel Hill: University of North Carolina Press.
Raeff, Marc. 1983. *The Well-Ordered Police State: Social and Institutional Change Through Law in the Germanies and Russia, 1600–1800*. New Haven: Yale University Press.
Rieff, Philip. 1966. *The Triumph of the Therapeutic: Uses of Faith After Freud*. New York: Harper and Row.

Rizzi, Bruno. 1985. *The Bureaucratization of the World: The USSR: Bureaucratic Collectivism.* London: Tavistock.
Rosaldo, Renato. *Ilongot Headhunting.* Stanford: Stanford University Press.
Rosch, Eleanor. 1975. "Cognitive Representations of Semantic Categories," *Journal of Experimental Psychology* 104: 192–233.
Rosch, Eleanor, Carolyn B. Mervis, Wayne D. Gray, David M. Johnson, and Penny Boyes-Bream. 1976. "Basic Objects in Natural Categories." *Cognitive Psychology* 8: 382–439.
Rose, Nikolas. 1989. *Governing the Soul: The Shaping of the Private Self.* London: Routledge.
———. 1996a. "The Death of the Social? Re-figuring the Territory of Government." *Economy and Society* 25: 327–56.
———. 1996b. "Governing 'Advanced' Liberal Democracies." In *Foucault and Political Reason: Liberalism, Neo-Liberalism and Rationalities of Government*, ed. A. Barry, T. Osborne, and Nikolas Rose, 37–64. Chicago: University of Chicago Press.
———. 1998. *Inventing Our Selves: Psychology, Power, Personhood.* Cambridge, UK: Cambridge University Press.
Rosenberg, Hans. 1958. *Bureaucracy, Aristocracy and Autocracy: The Prussian Experience, 1660–1815.* Boston: Beacon.
Rouhana, Nadim N. 1997. *Palestinian Citizens in an Ethnic Jewish State: Identities in Conflict.* New Haven: Yale University Press.
Salih, Khaled. 1996. "Demonizing a Minority: The Case of the Kurds in Iraq." In *National Minorities and Diasporas: Identities and Rights in the Middle East*, ed. Kirsten E. Schulze, Martin Stokes, and Colm Campbell, 81–94. London: I.B. Tauris.
Scott, James C. 1998. *Seeing Like a State.* New Haven: Yale University Press.
Scott, Robert. 1969. *The Making of Blind Men.* New York: Russell Sage Foundation.
Seltzer, William, and Margo Anderson. 2001. "The Dark Side of Numbers: The Role of Population Data Systems in Human Rights Abuses." *Social Research* 68: 481–513.
Shammas, Anton. 1991. "At Half-mast—Myths, Symbols, and Rituals of the Emerging State: A Personal Testimony of an 'Israeli Arab.'" In *New Perspectives on Israeli History*, ed. Laurence J. Silberstein, 216–24. New York: New York University Press.
Shapiro, Jonathan. 1993. "The Historical Origins of Israeli Democracy." In *Israeli Democracy under Stress*, ed. Ehud Sprinzak and Larry Diamond, 65–80. Boulder: Lynne Rienner Publishers.
Simmel, Georg. (1896) 1968. "Sociological Aesthetics." In *The Conflict in Modern Culture and Other Essays*, 68–80. New York: Teachers College Press.
Sokal, Robert R. 1974. "Classification: Principles, Purposes, Progress, Prospects." *Science* 185: 1115–23.
Stites, Richard. 1989. *Revolutionary Dreams: Utopian Vision and Experimental Life in the Russian Revolution.* New York: Oxford University Press.
Stone, Deborah. 1988. *Policy Paradox and Political Reason.* Glenview: Scott, Foresman & Co.
Strathern, Marilyn. 1988. *The Gender of the Gift.* Berkeley: University of California Press.
Taylor, Charles. 1990. "Modes of Civil Society." *Public Culture* 3: 95–118.
Tillyard, Eustace M.W. n.d. *The Elizabethan World Picture.* New York: Vintage.
Trouillot, Michel-Rolph. 2001. "The Anthropology of the State in the Age of Globalization: Close Encounters of the Deceptive Kind." *Current Anthropology* 42: 125–33.
Verdery, Katherine. 1996. *What Was Socialism and What Comes Next?* Princeton: Princeton University Press.
Vishvanathan, Shiv. 1990. "On the Annals of the Laboratory State." In *Science, Hegemony and Violence*, ed. Ashis Nandy, 257–88. Delhi: Oxford University Press.
Vygotsky, Lev S. 1962. *Thought and Language.* Cambridge, MA: MIT Press.
Walby, Sylvia. 1999. "The New Regulatory State: The Social Powers of the European Union." *British Journal of Sociology* 50: 118–40.
Weber, Max. 1964. *Theory of Social and Economic Organization.* Glencoe: Free Press.
Wechsler, Judith, ed. 1988. *On Aesthetics in Science.* Boston: Birkhauser.

Weinstock, John, ed. 1985. *Contemporary Perspectives on Linnaeus*. Lanham: University Press of America.
Westoby, Adam. 1985. "Introduction." In *The Bureaucratization of the World* by Bruno Rizzi, 1–33. London: Tavistock.
Weyl, Hermann. 1952. *Symmetry*. Princeton: Princeton University Press.
Wiener, Philip P. 1957. "Leibniz's project of a Public Exhibition of Scientific Inventions." In *Roots of Scientific Thought: A Cultural Perspective*, ed. Philip P. Wiener and Aaron Noland, 460–68. New York: Basic Books.
Wittgenstein, Ludwig. 1953. *Philosophical Investigations*. Oxford: Blackwell.
Wyschograd, Edith. 1985. *Spirit in Ashes: Hegel, Heidegger, and Man-Made Mass Death*. New Haven: Yale University Press.
Yanai, Nathan. 1996. "The Citizen as Pioneer: Ben-Gurion's Concept of Citizenship." *Israel Studies* 1: 127–43.
Yuval-Davis, Nira. 1987. "The Jewish Collectivity and National Reproduction in Israel." *Khamsin* 13: 60–93.

CHAPTER 5

BUREAUCRATIC LOGIC, BUREAUCRATIC AESTHETICS
THE OPENING EVENT OF HOLOCAUST MARTYRS AND HEROES REMEMBRANCE DAY IN ISRAEL

Author's Note

This chapter was prepared first in 2001 for a workshop on Performance Genres and Comparative Aesthetics, organized by Angela Hobart and Bruce Kapferer. It is offered here as a case study of how bureaucratic logic organizes a major public event in Israel, one that annually commemorates the Holocaust dead. Though in more recent years technology has been put to good effect in this event, its logic of organization has not changed. Throughout the emphasis is on representation through the presentation, one after another, of linearly and precisely defined social categories. The murderous events that constituted the core of the Holocaust were dynamic in the extreme, killing upon killing upon killing . . . Yet its commemoration here abuts on the static. In this there are lessons for the kind of aesthetics that bureaucratic logic enables and promotes. I return to bureaucratic aesthetics in Chapter Eleven.

My concern here is with logics and aesthetics that organize rituals. I will argue that the logics of ritual organization are intimately related to practice, informing practice with its shaping of goals, action, movement, direction. So, too, are aesthetics crucial to practice; for that matter, perhaps practice works best, if I can put it like this, when given its senses by aesthetics. Aesthetics are crucial to practice; while logics of organization hardly exist without practice. Logics, in the terms used here, are the ways that inform how the practices of connecting, of fitting together—people, things, worlds—are done. Aesthetics, on the other hand, enable the very connecting, the fitting together, to be done in practice. Aesthetics are informed, obviously, by cultural logics. The logic of ritual organization and the aesthetics of practice form a set without which there is no such phenomenon that might be called ritual. However, I do not intend that there be any clean-cut conceptual distinction between "logic" and "aesthetics." Perhaps because through practice, logic and aesthetics mesh together epistemology and the sensuous, their relationship is vague. In my view, the relationship between logic and aesthetics is teleological rather than lineal—if logic is present so are aesthetics. Perhaps logic generates its own aesthetic as it is practiced into being by that aesthetic.

I want to argue more generally that aesthetics are crucial to all practice—to the very practice of practice—in the regularities of mundane living; and that in this sense the aesthetics of ritual practice may not be radically distinct from those of everyday practice. To make these arguments relatively straightforward, I will discuss aspects of the state ritual that officially opens Holocaust Martyrs and Heroes Remembrance Day in Israel (*Yom HaShoah v'HaGvura*), a day popularly if facetiously known as Holocaust Day. Officially, the ritual is called a Memorial Gathering (*atzeret zikaron*). The logic of organization of this event I will call bureaucratic logic, and its aesthetics, bureaucratic aesthetics. I will argue that this ritual, despite its empathic and emotive sacralization in Israeli society, is an extension of the logic and aesthetics of mundane bureaucratic order. The military logic of organization is continuous with the logic that organizes the performance of the Holocaust Memorial Gathering. Here the logic and aesthetics of ritual are organized as a continuation of mundane, bureaucratic practice.

Underlying my argument is the claim that in the history of modern Western thought, the conceptualization and treatment of "aesthetics," as a higher-order condition of value and knowledge, took a terribly wrong turn, in its thorough and unrelenting identification with beauty, art, truth, reflection, and so forth. To save the significance and the inestimable value of aesthetics in the mundane, and in the ritual living of lives, aesthetics should not be severed and parted from the grounding of social and personal practice.

The Aesthetic "Feel" of Practice

My understanding of the aesthetic in mundane living is quite rough and ready—for that matter, murky—and again is not given to any neat definition. My sense of the aesthetic is something like the "feel" that one has for that which one is doing; the feel for that which can only be called the "rightness" of how one is doing what one is doing, or how this is done in concert. The aesthetic in mundane living is related to Bergson's idea of "habit memory," which is a way of attending kinesthetically to one's own body, monitoring that which one is doing. As Sheets-Johnstone (2000: 360) points out for the individual, "this is memory etched in movement," providing unconscious ways of behaving that "engender a *felt sense of rightness* in doing what one does . . . we feel at home in our bodies . . . because we resonate with a familiar dynamics, a tactile-kinesthetic dynamics that we have come to establish as our own way of doing something, whether brushing our teeth, throwing a ball, playing the violin, or walking" (Sheets-Johnstone 2000: 360–61, my emphasis). This sense of rightness or "fitness" (Hardin 1993: 12)—kinesthetic, sensuous, interpersonal—indexes the aesthetics of living unselfconsciously, in the main. No less, this sense of rightness is one of feeling—unselfconsciously, one monitors affectively. This is a sense of rightness not in moral terms but in the sense of how one does that which one is doing.[1] The aesthetics of mundane living are forms of autopoiesis, of self-organization, that produce and conserve personal and intercorporeal awareness through feeling the rightness of action, of practice, inside oneself, outside oneself, and between oneself and others (see also Inglis and Hughson 2000: 289). To put this otherwise, the everyday aesthetics of practice are feelings of rightness-in-doing, of feeling that which feels right in doing that which we are doing. In Michael Polanyi's (1966: 17–23) terms, one could say that mundane aesthetics are a kind of "indwelling" of tacit knowing, a knowing that, as he puts it, always relates to or includes more than we can tell, were we able to relate this knowingly. Paraphrasing Polanyi, Jack Katz (1999: 314) argues that "effective action requires that we disattend our body as we act, focusing away from the point at which our body intersects with the world." In my view, tacit knowing is the feeling of disattending/attending that enables the exterior world of practice and the interior world of experience to be united as the exterior world of experience and the interior world of practice (see also Dufrenne 1973: 446). Mikel Dufrenne (1973: 377) argues that to feel is to transcend. The aesthetics of practice transcend practice by enabling practice to communicate "more than we can tell," while feeling the rightness of not needing to, or not being able to, tell this. The aesthetics of practice integrate us with that which we do, in ways that self-produce and self-organize this integration as more than we can tell and as feeling the rightness of this.

This positioning, as Katz (1999: 314) points out, "leads quickly to an appreciation of the essential place of aesthetics in all behaviors, however mundane or esoteric." In mundane living, it is the aesthetics of practice, in my terms, that enable people and social orders to naturalize their own arbitrariness, to know their worlds tacitly as "natural," as "taken for granted" (see Bourdieu 1977: 164; Garfinkel 1967; Geertz 1983: 86–91). Without the aesthetics of practice/experience there is no feel of rightness in practice, no feel that this is how doing is doing, how doing is done, how done continues on into doing.

Aesthetics, then, are crucial to the naturalness of the feel of mundane practice as more than we can tell, indeed, as more than we can know, self-consciously, self-reflexively. Practice is inevitably the fitting together of person and world, person and person, person and action, action and action—their fitting into, yet through one another. Aesthetics—the synesthetic, sensuous feel of things fitting together (and not fitting together)—is that which enables us to proceed coherently, perspectively, and prospectively in the hereness of nowness, as it were. Simmel (1994a: 10) wrote that "the human being is . . . the bordering creature who has no border." I would add that the bordering creature in kinesthetic movement is always on the edge of coming into being, and so is always creating borders in order to cross them, in order to move. The aesthetics of practice have something intimate to do with the creation and crossing of borders, and how these are done. It is by creating and crossing borders, the sites at which exosmosis and endosmosis (Simmel 1994b: 11) of the fluidity of selfness and otherness occur, that fitting together is accomplished. To put this yet more emphatically, without the mundane aesthetics of practice, there likely would not be self-integrating individuals nor, for that matter, social life. The aesthetics of practice not only enable practice—they are the persuasive grounds, the grounds that persuade us that practice is in the process of being done as the kind of practice it is (or is becoming). Perhaps this could be called the persuasive self-embodiment of the truth-claims of practice. Aesthetics may be more like an ongoing *gestalt*, in the sense of a "coherent entity" (Polanyi 1966), or an entity whose coherence is continuously coming into being, fitting itself together self-persuasively, even as that which it fits together ruptures and breaks.

Since we must know ourselves indirectly, through interaction, through others and their mediation, through what might be called the "practice of betweenness," there is always a break (perhaps an ongoing break) in any aesthetics of mundane practice. The very feel or sense of rightness also constitutes a temporal lag, however small; a lack of synchronization with oneself and with others. As Katz (1999: 315) puts it, "I see, hear, feel, and express myself through actions that in part always remain behind myself, always just beyond the reach of my self-awareness." In this regard, we are always trying to catch up with ourselves and with others. This is integral to the sense of mundane aesthetics as more than one can tell. But this is also the break between a ritual and mundane social order—the possible shift from an aesthetics of mundane practice to something else; the world catching up with its rituals and their visions (and dynamics) of order; the break that may open toward radical shifts in aesthetics of performance or that may continue to hone its aesthetics, but in different venues.[2] Here, my concern is with the latter, as it organizes the opening ritual of Holocaust Remembrance Day.

Bureaucratic Logic and the Event of Presentation

Earlier I said that cultural logics inform us as to how practice fits together people, things, and worlds. Bureaucratic logic indexes how certain kinds of cultural taxonomies are organized and practiced. Recent studies of modern bureaucracy and its origins recognize clearly that it is constructed of premises about how worlds are put together, how they work, and how this knowledge may be known (Brown 1978: 373; Morgan 1986; Astley 1985; Melossi and Pavarini 1981). Nonetheless, not recognized is the premise that the epistemology of bureaucratic logic is to intimately engage in the invention and practice of taxonomy that is lineal, exclusivist, and hierarchical in character. Bureaucratic logic is a mentality of the modern world that consciously invents and deploys lineal taxonomy to create, to control, and to change order. The conscious control over processes of classification is a most powerful means through which to shape social order (Handelman 1995; Shamgar-Handelman and Handelman 1991: 308).

The use of bureaucratic logic encourages the invention of forms of classification that are hierarchical and exclusivist. In true Linnean fashion, the boundaries of categories of classification on the same level of abstraction are mutually exclusive and are organized in hierarchies of subsumation and exclusion. This lineal logic of classification—of membership that is permitted, exclusively, in one and only one category on the same level of abstraction within a given taxonomic scheme—is powerfully implicated in the making of "difference" in modern life. That is, it is implicated in our mechanistic capacities to make infinitesimal and infinite distinctions of difference that mutually exclude whatever they fragment, while insisting on the significance of these divisions. (On this logic, see Wyschogrod 1985.) In hierarchical terms, we perceive levels of difference as nesting quite neatly and naturally within one another, thereby encompassing difference within yet more subsuming difference.

Bureaucratic logic informs institutions as to how to continually invent and implement new taxonomies by reimagining and reorganizing the social categories of everyday life. This logic consciously informs how to consciously create social categories that can be made to divide, to fragment, to reclassify, and to reshape members of any social unit—group, community, family, relationship. This logic informs how to perceive that the making of division through the creation of a boundary is also the demarcation of differences that are naturalized on either side of this border. Therefore, bureaucratic logic foregrounds the significance of boundaries that separate mutually exclusive categories from one another.

No less than any other mode of informing the organization of realities, bureaucratic logic is enabled by its own aesthetics of practice that give to its use the feel of rightness. In keeping with the significance of ocular centrism and the gaze in the modern epoch (Foucault 1973, 1979; Jay 1992a), these, one may say, are the aesthetics of anatomization—of laying out, defining, classifying, specifying, inspecting, and enumerating all of the parts that constitute some totality. In modern bureaucratic society, in the modern bureaucratic state, these aesthetics of bureaucratic logic are performed in public most explicitly in rituals that I call events of presentation (Handelman 1998). The organization of performance in the public event of presentation often (but not necessarily always) is pervaded by aesthetics of bureaucratic logic. Again, I am arguing that it is aesthetics that enable us to sense the rightness of organization and practice; and so, too, of performance (which, as noted, I understand as the heightened consciousness, and perhaps the morphogenesis, of practice). In other words, the logic and aesthetics of events of presentation are strongly continuous with the logic and aesthetics that organize so many domains of mundane life. There is no radical shift in logic and aesthetic from the mundane to this kind of ritual.[3]

The event of presentation often shapes, puts into place, and demonstratively shows social taxonomies. To a high degree, taxonomies are put on view, their categories filled, and members of these categories are used to perform a repertoire of symbolic actions. Perhaps there are here taxonomies in motion, a spectacle of bureaucratic logic whose aesthetic feel of rightness enables their performance. Events of presentation may be societal icons, fully open to the inspection of the public gaze. These rituals rarely conceal any mysteries, nor is their atmosphere particularly mysterious. Their purpose may be to assert the determinacy of the significance that they enclose within themselves. Such rituals are ocular-centric, their symbolism arranged often in the form of a relatively static tableau, or a tableau in motion. The actions of performers (like the categories they embody) rarely overlap and are carefully allocated, measured, and often synchronized. Order is continually seen to be practiced during the event.

The opening ceremony of Holocaust Martyrs and Heroes Remembrance Day is held in Jerusalem at Yad Vashem, the Holocaust Memorial Authority, which is the national site of Holocaust memorialism in Israel. The ceremony, televised in its entirety, is a major ritual occasion of the state, the first of the three major "ritual days" legislated after Israel's declaration of independence.

I have chosen this Holocaust occasion to press my arguments on bureaucratic logic and bureaucratic aesthetics in statist public events especially because the Holocaust is a highly emotional and volatile subject (and increasingly so) in Jewish-Israeli everyday life (Friedlander and Seligman 1994; Young 1990; Handelman and Shamgar-Handelman 1996; Handelman 2004: 171–99; Feldman 2000; Kidron 2000). In Israeli discourse, popular and academic alike, the ritualization of the Holocaust is attended to primarily (and often solely) in terms of moral, philosophical, theological, historical, and political valences and their consequences, as if the logic and aesthetics of ritualism and commemoration are irrelevant to how these valences are expressed and conveyed. Yet it is the logic of ritual organization that in no small measure is shaping the significance of the Holocaust in Israeli society.[4] And in no small measure it is the practiced aesthetics of this logic that enable such events to take, naturalistically, the presentational, taxonomic form that they do, and to be appreciated as such.

The Military Envelopment of the Memorial Gathering

Like all Israeli state events, the Memorial Gathering is enclosed by a cocoon shaped by military classification. The Israel Defense Forces (IDF) has a major presence in this opening event, described in the next section. Yet the explicit participation of the IDF is but the tip of the military presence—the Gathering exists as it does by being enveloped by the military. The presence of the military envelope serves a practical and functional purpose—to ensure monothetic order in keeping with the forming capacities of bureaucratic logic and the state-form. The differences between military and bureaucratic logic are more matters of content and direction than of premises of classification. Therefore my discussion is of the military as the exercise of bureaucratic logic. Both the Gathering and the IDF are metonymic with bureaucratic logic. In terms of a logic and aesthetics of classification and its practice, the military instructions to protect the occasion cannot be separated from the performance itself of that occasion. I turn now to these instructions and their monothetic logic.

The overall responsibility for planning and enacting the event lies with Yad Vashem. Nonetheless the Army's instructions to secure and to protect the site of the Gathering envelop and ultimately control Yad Vashem's roles. Though Yad Vashem appears in official control of the Gathering, there are points at which this institution is dependent upon or subordinate to the IDF. At times there is a struggle between the overt and hidden enactments—one example will suffice here. The Army's concern is to secure the Gathering against terrorist attacks. The President and Prime Minister of the State attend, as do official representatives of foreign states. Yad Vashem wants the event enacted according to its script. Both Yad Vashem and the IDF are deeply committed to the vision of the State and nation-in-arms as the protective bastions against any future Holocaust. The final rehearsal takes place in the late afternoon, before the Gathering begins. Some hours before, the IDF seals off Yad Vashem as a closed military area, under the Emergency Regulations. The Army controls all access and movement within this area.

In 1988 the Gathering took place some months after the outbreak of the first Intifada, and the local IDF Commander decided to seal off the site (itself distant from any actual clashes) earlier than usual, in what Yad Vashem personnel described as a fit of "security hysteria." Consequently the announcers and members of the choir and orchestra were either unable to enter the site or to rehearse properly there. This could have affected the performance adversely, and led to discussions between Yad Vashem administrators and Army officers. A compromise was hammered out, but the Army's ultimate control of the site was uncontested.

Both sides in this dispute are organized through bureaucratic logic. At issue is not only a division of labor and spheres of authority, but the very forming and application of taxonomic categories—the relentless creation and invocation of arbitrary, categorical difference. Yad Vashem orders the presentation of the Holocaust in monothetic terms, and the Army does the same to Yad Vashem. Yad Vashem, open to the public six days a week, and receiving in the neighborhood of a million visitors a year, is redefined categorically by the IDF, and on this basis is turned into a fortress, into another order of ordering.

The significance of the IDF's act of closure may be lost on the parties concerned, yet it must be stressed. The official Holocaust memorial is itself remade—ghettoized—within the national landscape intended ideologically to be open. The fortress is besieged within itself, granted the status of a protected species, and placed apart. As the participants commemorate the Holocaust, they themselves are set apart as the potential victims of another Holocaust (thereby encouraging their self-classification as such). This irony is foreign to the bureaucratic logic used. At issue is whose taxonomic ordering of reality will prevail. The Army has the advantage, since it envelops Yad Vashem in its timescape. The military vision of order puts in place and territorializes a taxonomy of control and discipline hidden in the main from the Gathering's participants, yet intended to embed them all within its surveillance. The classified territory becomes the mirror image peering within itself in a panopticon-like way. The Army creates an event within which order is made yet is not to be seen, complementing the order made to be seen in the Gathering itself. The Army relentlessly and symmetrically divides and classifies time, space, people, and function. There is no ambiguity in classification. Everyone and everything connected with the Gathering is placed in one or another category. The focus here is on Army planning for a Gathering in the 1990s. After this I discuss relevant aspects of the Gathering enacted at that time.

Time was sliced cleanly into two consecutive phases. The first phase spanned four days, from the 7th to the 10th of April, during which preparations and rehearsals were done. The second stage began at 15:00 hours on the 10th of April, when military forces secured the area, and lasted until the end of the Gathering at approximately 21:00 hours. The list of Army goals was lengthy and exhaustive: to control all approaches to the ceremonial plaza where the Gathering would be held; to secure the entire area of Yad Vashem and its roads and byways, using foot patrols on the near and distant peripheries, motorized patrols on the roads, as well as positioning bomb disposal personnel; to establish observation points at controlling locations; to use military police to secure the parking lots; to use civil defense reservists and soldiers of the Women's Corps to search the bags (and where necessary, the person) of all entering the ceremonial area; to use bomb disposal personnel to check all vehicles entering the area; to have in readiness Medical Corps personnel to treat and evacuate, according to need; and to coordinate with bodyguards of the Security Services (*Sherutei Bitakhon*, aka *Shabak*) who safeguard the seating of Israeli dignitaries. Safeguarding the ceremonial plaza itself was also the responsibility of the Security Services from the moment the dignitaries entered.

To implement these goals, the IDF used several hundred military personnel belonging to the regular army, the Military Police, the Border Police, the sappers, the Medical Corps, the Women's Corps, and the Civil Defense Guard. Military personnel were divided into eleven units: these included a regional command center with communication specialists; forces to secure and to safeguard the approaches to Yad Vashem; a preventive force on a rooftop overlooking the plaza; an assault force for more incisive intervention; and patrols on axes triangulating the entire area of the memorial complex.

This relentless classifying shapes discrete, modular, monothetic categories. Taken together, these categories are organized vertically (those ranked higher control those ranked lower) and horizontally (categories on the same level do not overlap in their contents and functions). The dimensions of each category are measured: the kind and number of personnel, the kind and number of weapons and other artifacts. Together, these categories totalize space and time—they suck in, subsume, and make order among all the phenomena toward which their taxonomy is aimed. Nothing, no one, is left outside the monothetic classifying of space, time, people. The taxonomy includes itself, and so is self-sealing. All are under control and discipline, whether they know this or not. Since the categories are modular, they can be altered, shifted, redesigned, added to or subtracted from the taxonomy without changing the operational efficiency of the classifications.

The effect of having all the categories of the military taxonomy in position on the ground, enveloping and surveilling everyone and everything within the Holocaust memorial, is something like a public event in its own right. An event of presentation, but organized as a concealed scopic system controlling itself and aimed at the Memorial Gathering. This systemic apparatus is hidden from outsiders who do not hold the code to the military taxonomy. Nonetheless the hidden military classification is present and piercingly scopic, in place and space, reshaping the landscape into vectors of force, moving according to preset instructions, holding everything within its gaze. An event that itself is the gaze of control, a symmetric, systemic, covert tableau, the embodiment of bureaucratic logic and aesthetics in systemic motion—a lookout precisely here, a roadblock directly there, a patrol moving through a specified axis, an assault force held in instant readiness.

The military event is an analogue of the state-form, capturing and containing through the forming enabled by bureaucratic logic and aesthetics. The covert military event surveils the entire site of the Memorial complex, enveloping this and the Gathering performed there. The military apparatus cocoons the memorial site in its taxonomic closure, gazing at the displayed tableau of the past, at the practice of Holocaust memorialism. The hidden present (the military) disciplines and orders the visible past (the Holocaust event) that is made to appear as if it controls the visible present. The tableau of the Memorial Gathering is immobile and static, in contrast to that of the military, mobile, flexible, systemic.

The Memorial Gathering

My concern here is to show how the Memorial Gathering is performed as a taxonomic tableau of categories, one that embodies in its organization ideas of bureaucratic logic and aesthetics, as discussed earlier. I do not closely interpret the symbolism of this event (as I have done elsewhere for the opening ceremonies of Israeli Remembrance Day for the War Dead and Independence Day; see Handelman 1998: 191–233).

The gathering lasts approximately one hour. The setting is the Warsaw Ghetto Plaza (dedicated to the revolt staged in the ghetto) at Yad Vashem, dominated on one side by a high brick wall (called the Wall of Remembrance; hereafter, the Wall), within which are embedded reproductions of Nathan Rapoport's original sculpture and bas-relief that stand on the site of the razed Warsaw Ghetto (see Young 1989). The sculpture and bas-relief effectively divide the Wall into sections, two categories; and during the ceremony itself attention is shifted from one to the other (from right to left, facing the Wall, the direction in which Hebrew and Yiddish are written).

The Taxonomy of the Wall of Remembrance

The large bronze bas-relief of the Last March is embedded within the right side of the Wall. The bas-relief depends through a horizontal, longitudinal axis that depicts Jews—all older men, women, and children who look like they are from a ghetto or *shtetl*—clustered together, eyes averted from the viewer, bent beneath the burdens they carry, appearing to walk into a strong wind, sorrowfully marching to some unknown destination. Whatever this destination, it leads to their annihilation. To the left of the bas-relief is a sculpture of the fighters of the Warsaw Ghetto uprising, one that emphasizes verticality and height. Recessed within the Wall, these fighters, most of whom are young, stand tall and strong at the ready, grasping rifles and grenades, facing the viewer and looking straight ahead at a distant horizon. In the Warsaw original, the bas-relief is placed on the reverse side of the ghetto uprising sculpture, so that bas-relief and sculpture cannot be seen together. At Yad Vashem, the bas-relief and the sculpture are placed in a lineal relationship of two scenes. The bas-relief (given this genre of art) has less depth of figuration and more sketchiness than does the more fully formed sculpture.

These two scenes constitute a taxonomy of the sequencing of narrative history, one that more cleanly divides Jewish perceptions of history into a before and an after, into categories of destruction and ascension, and that shifts one into the other. As I noted above, at Yad Vashem these two scenes should be looked at from right to left—from the driven despair of the breaking edges of generations of Jews, of the very young and the old on the bas-relief, to the fierce determination of the ghetto fighters, the maturing of embattled but powerful strength. The scenes move from the horizontal stretch of the bas-relief, an even plane of suffering that extends indefinitely without relief, to the unbending verticality of the sculpture, which stops movement through posture, gesture, and positioning (even bending the lineality of the Wall), communicating a message of this-far-and-no-further. These are all themes of the dominant narrative of the Holocaust in present-day Zionist Israel, and, so too, of Yad Vashem. It is this narrative framing that dominates the taxonomic shift from catastrophe to regeneration that is enacted within the ritual gathering. I first discuss the visual placement of social categories along the Wall, and then their performative sequencing during the ritual.

Since its inception, the plaza has been used as the venue for the ritual gathering. The Wall itself is made to frame the performance. The major social categories of the performance are laid out, in lineal fashion, along the breadth of the Wall. The vertical, recessed sculpture of the ghetto fighters is used to break this tableau into two segments. To the right (facing the Wall) of the vertical sculpture, the area of the bas-relief, the catastrophe and sorrow of the Holocaust dominate the performance tableau. To the left, the fighting response dominates.

For the ritual, a central memorial beacon is placed between the bas-relief and the ghetto fighters sculpture—but more to the right side, identified with the Holocaust catastrophe. In 1991, the gas flame of this beacon reached to the very top of the Wall. The flame emerged from a cone set atop a squared base, rising high through a spiral of barbed wire, searing and transcending the barbs that tore the flesh, heart, and the very life of the Jewish people. To the right of this central beacon are two podia that are used by the announcers of the ceremony (who also perform the memorial readings) and by those who deliver speeches and prayers. Still further to the right are situated the choir and orchestra. The right side, then, is identified more with what could be called civil/religious (as opposed to military) order, as well as with Holocaust suffering.

By contrast, the categories of the left side are identified primarily with military order. Immediately to the left of the central beacon stands the Honor Guard of the IDF, with naked bayonets fixed to automatic weapons. Further left, atop a lower extension of the Wall, are placed six memorial beacons in memory of the six million Jews who perished in the Holocaust. During the ritual the beacons are lit ceremoniously by persons chosen by the Yad Vashem administration. The beacon lighters are assisted by Gadna paramilitary youth in uniform who hand them the lit torches with which they kindle the beacons. Framing the entire tableau at its extreme left is the flag of the state. Thus, the fighting response to the Holocaust—the IDF Honor Guard, the beacon lighters, the paramilitary youth—is itself framed, enclosed on its right by the ghetto fighters sculpture and on its left by the state flag. The sequencing of the ritual shifts from stateless Holocaust victims driven fatedly, to Jews standing their ground, focused for battle, intergenerational, national.

Thus, during the performance, the narrative—or, more accurately, the visual sequence of taxonomy, of bas-relief and sculpture—is extended from World War II into the present. This sequencing of categories shifts the Jews from that of uprising (signified by the sculpture) to that of the State of Israel (signified by the national flag). The fighting response extends into the present, within the state. During the ritual, the entire Zionist version of recent history is taxonomized as a classification of historical events laid bare and explicated before the gaze of the audience.[5] The audience sits facing the Wall, dignitaries and speakers in the first row.[6]

In terms of the sequencing of the ritual, the initial focus of activity tends to cluster around the bas-relief, with its figures bent beneath tribulation—the unredeemable tragic side of the Holocaust tableau. However, with the lighting of the six beacons, the focus of activity is shifted to the fighting response. The beacon lighters are often living heroes and heroines of the Holocaust—the living embodiments of the Warsaw Ghetto sculpture—who stand above the level of the audience, on the low wall of beacons, to the very left of the tableau. By contrast, the Jews depicted in the bas-relief no longer exist in this version of history—either they have been turned into survivors and perhaps fighters (who live in Israel), or they are dead "martyrs," in the language of this day of remembrance. In any case, there is no mimetic embodiment of the category of martyr within the performance of the ritual—only the ghostly outlines of figures long past, frozen in the bronze of the bas-relief. When all the taxonomic categories are added together, category by category, they constitute a version of history that connects the annihilation of the Holocaust to the fighting response in the face of oppression, and connects the fighting response to the active, armed protection offered to Jews by the State of Israel (which is embodied by the Honor Guard and paramilitary youth, who protect the beacon-lighter survivors, all of them grasped within the protective envelope of the IDF, which safeguards the entire site).

Taxonomy and the Three Generations

The section of the performative tableau that I am calling "the fighting response" is embodied in three distinct categories that are no less metaphysical and historical in their temporal linkage. These categories are those of three generations of fighters, which can be likened to the grandparental, the parental, and their offspring. The beacon lighters are analogous to the grandparental generation who, born in Europe, survived the Holocaust (often heroically), and made the decision to "ascend" to Israel, thereby making this their future, through which they aligned themselves with the generation of founders and pioneers.[7] They light the beacons of remembrance, which are also flames of destruction and sacrifice, rising and transcending, as it were, their own pasts. The Honor Guard of the IDF, standing near the beacon lighters, fixed bayonets at the ready, is composed of young soldiers who are doing their compulsory military service. They are analogous to the generation of children of the survivors, who have grown to maturity within Israel. They serve the state directly, in its uniform modality, honoring and protecting the generation of Holocaust survivors who themselves pioneered the Jewish fighting response in Europe and who later joined their efforts to those of the pioneers in Israel. The beacon lighters are handed their torches by the uniformed (but unarmed) paramilitary youth. The youth are analogous to the generation of Israeli Jewish grandchildren to whom belongs the more distant future. As they hand over the lit torches, the paramilitary youth (the still-unformed future) enable the beacon lighters (the past) to remember and to commemorate, all the while protected by the Honor Guard (the fighting present).

The narrative structures and the three-generational paradigm of remembrance are at the heart of the symbolism of the gathering; and they are encoded through the aesthetics of temporal rhythmicity, of low to high. I emphasize the aesthetics of temporality because, in terms of my earlier argument, it is aesthetics that enable the natural feel of the rightness of practice. The experiencing of the organization of categories in sequence as temporal—in a relationship of low to high—feels right in a fully natural sense in monotheistic cosmologies.

Neither the rhythmicity of Jewish time nor the paradigm of three generations is explicitly recognized in the ritual. The bureaucratic logic for the composition of symbolic meaning seems to require the specification and description of discrete taxonomic elements and categories. But beyond this, bureaucratic logic should enable the arbitrary combining or joining of categories to one another, in somewhat arithmetical ways, by bringing them into conjunction—added to, subtracted from, or mixed together. Yet, aesthetically, these taxonomic elements and categories are enabled to be practiced, felt, and experienced as moral rhythmics of time. And, though in practice we recognize the rightness of these rhythms of temporality, they are also "more than we can know," and therefore they encompass us aesthetically in ways that in their fullness of becoming are beyond our ken.

Bureaucratic Logic and the Planning of the Ritual

The presence of bureaucratic logic is plainly evident in the comments of a planner and organizer of the early opening ceremonies of remembrance at Yad Vashem, which first used the Wall of Remembrance. He stated that the arrangement of taxonomic categories, in my terms, along the length of the Wall was primarily a matter of practicality, of a somewhat arbitrary positioning according to available space. Thus, one listed the elements needing to be included, without particular attention to the consequences of their particular positioning in relation to one another. So, once the decision was taken to use the Wall and the taxonomic categories I have mentioned, the only space sufficient for the six beacons was on the left side. Therefore, since the national Honor Guard defended/celebrated the beacon lighters, it too went to the left side. The national flag, then, also went to the left side, as did, of course, the paramilitary youth whose task it was to hand a lit torch to the beacon lighters. But then, all space on the left side was taken up, and the choir had to go to the right side, and so, too, did the orchestra. This disposition, said the organizer, "has no meaning."[8]

The distribution along the Wall of categories of participation was done, approximately, according to the following thinking: first, decide which elements should be included in the ritual; second, arrange them in relation to one another so that they all fit into the available space/time. In this there is the arbitrary character of bureaucratic logic, yet also the tacit aesthetic perception (which accords with this logic) that like goes together with like. Once the beacons were positioned arbitrarily, the beacon lighters, Honor Guard, paramilitary youth, and flag also joined the beacons. All these elements fit together naturally; they belong together without much thought. Once they were brought into conjunction, their positioning in relation to one another—their symbolic interaction—immediately began to make emergent, perhaps even unintended, meaning (see Handelman and Shamgar-Handelman 1993). One result of this interactive making of meaning was the structuring of the doubled visual narrative; another was that which I am calling the paradigm of the three generations, clustered about the flames of sacrifice, remembrance, and freedom. Relatively unrelated symbols brought serendipitously near to one another within contexts officially defined as symbolic are likely to be felt symbolically related to one another—they are felt, aesthetically, to fit together even if this remains implicit.

The organizers of the first Holocaust memorial ceremonies decided that a proper ritual of remembrance should include at least three discrete, taxonomic categories of symbolic activities, without specifying their relationship to one another. These categories were the following: (1) a category of actions mandatory for a religious memorial (the reciting of the mourner's prayer [*kaddish*], and of "God full of mercy" [*El maleh rahamim*]); (2) an "artistic" category (consisting of appropriate music and song); and (3) a category of speeches and readings. Music and songs, readings and speeches, were then mixed together and synchronized through alternation: a song followed a speech or reading, and so forth; while the religious practices were clustered toward the end of the ritual. In keeping with bureaucratic logic, these three categories were defined arbitrarily, yet their conjunction produced an aesthetically clean-cut alternation between words and song that felt right—perhaps in that it maintained the discreteness of speech and music, even as it brought them into conjunction. Furthermore, these secular practices were kept together in a broader category, separated from the category of religious practices, most of which were used to close the ritual.

Bureaucratic Aesthetics: Exactitude, Itemization, Modularity

Bureaucratic aesthetics insist on the exactitude of definitions of categories, their borders cleanly demarcated in relation to one another, demonstrating their differences. In keeping with the aesthetics of exactness in division, the sequence of ritual action was divided into segments of measured time, to produce as perfect a synchronization as possible between these parts within ritual space. This aesthetics of exact division and combination, of parts fitting together as if in a machine, are what, above all, enabled the performers to be in the right place at the right time. In a way, this exactness of synchronization was the primary integrating force in this ritual, holding together pieces that otherwise might have little or no sense of connectivity with one another. Much of the logic of integration of this ritual is in the construction of time and space as formats, without which many of the parts marshaled for the ritual might well fly off symbolically in all directions, or trip over one another.

Crucial to this construction of integration is the role of the announcer. In the performance itself, one of the tasks of the announcers is to report the condition of synchronization in the ritual, by telling the audience which segment will perform next. This fully expresses the bureaucratic logic that informs the event, since the announcing of each segment is simultaneously an enunciation of the demarcation of its bounded modularity. The announcer does coordinate the ritual from within its own enactment—but, since the ritual is not organized systemically, the announcer (unlike the commander of the military envelope) has no capacity to modify its course. The announcer may be more a representation of integration within the ritual, than a generating force that produces integration.

In this kind of event it is the extreme modularity of the contents or parts of the ritual that enables its construction and integration as a whole; and, so too, the capacity of its organizers to add and subtract modules almost at will. This is true, of course, for the arbitrariness of much of the practice of everyday life in social orders organized by bureaucratic logic, aesthetics, and apparatuses. There are, then, powerful continuities and similarities between the organization of the gathering and the organization of the everyday.

The 1991 Memorial Gathering: Sequencing

In the 1991 gathering, there were twenty discrete segments. Their sequencing (and the time of each in minutes) was as follows:

1. entry of the Honor Guard (five minutes before the start of the ritual)
2. entry of the president of the state (2:00)
3. lowering the state flag to half-mast (2:30)
4. lighting the central memorial beacon by the president (3:00)
5. song by choir (2:00)
6. speech by the chairman of the Yad Vashem directorate (2:00)
7. song by choir (2:00)
8. speech by the director of Yad Vashem (2:00)
9. song by cantor, "God, God, why did you forsake us?" accompanied by the choir (3:00)
10. speech by the representative of partisans' organizations (3:00)
11. speech by the prime minister (5:00)
12. reading of poem by an announcer (2:30)
13. song by choir (2:00)
14. lighting the six beacons (8:00, including the introductions of the announcer and accompanying music)
15. reading by an announcer of a text of the "live witnessing" (*edut haia*) of the massacre of Jews in the area of Pinsk, during World War II (3:00)
16. readings of psalms by the Sephardic chief rabbi of the state (2:00)
17. recitation of *Kaddish*, the mourner's prayer for the dead (2:00)
18. song by cantor, *Yizkor*, the prayer of remembrance (6:00)
19. songs by choir (2:00)
20. singing of the national anthem, *Ha-Tikvah* (The Hope) (2:00)[9]

The total time formally allocated to the ritual is one hour and thirty seconds.

Like the tableau placed through space along the Wall, the sequence of acts through time is categorical, segmentary, and modular. Parts or segments can be inserted or extracted with ease. The logic of connectivity among these modules and the sense of rightness of their performance apparently must be external to the ritual itself. That is, the ritual has no internal dynamics that are organic to it. Most segments have been rehearsed, and it is through this that participants learn about their roles in connection to other segments; but they have no mandate, say, for ad hoc improvisation if something should go wrong with the organization of time/space in performance. The bureaucratic logic and aesthetics of performance seems to require that, in their entirety, segments be externally administered by a director or organizer—in a functional sense, by bureaucrats who ensure that the performers of every category be in the right place at the right time for the correct duration.

Especially notable in the tableau of categories of persons and segments of practice is just how little kinesic movement there is by the performers and when there is motion, just how contained and restricted it is. Some categories of persons are glued in place throughout the event (Honor Guard, choir, orchestra). Others move very short distances (from the front row of the audience) to take fixed positions temporarily on the podia and behind the beacons. The contents of the taxonomic categories take up their assigned positions and remain rigidly in place. At all times the entire tableau is overt and visible to the gaze of the audience—and, of course, to the television camera that need hardly shift position in order to telecast the performance.[10] The performer is the (near) perfect embodiment of his category of membership in the performance—he neither expands nor restricts this, nor plays with this. Instead he always contributes to the vision of overall perfected taxonomic ordering. All of this speaks to a regime of discipline in aesthetic presentation that is beyond the nationalist and the statist but is closest to the bureaucratic ordering of people and things.

Framing

Despite the segmented character of performance modules, there is some framing of sequence at the beginning and the end of the ritual. Yet this framing, too, is highly categorical and modular. As the representation of the protective might of the state, the IDF Honor Guard takes up position first, to await the entry of the president and prime minister, the ranking citizens of the state. Within the ritual, the Honor Guard, the military, anticipates the arrival of the civil state. The state flag is lowered to half-mast, signifying the entry of state and citizenry into mourning. The central memorial beacon is lit, signifying the entry of the people into remembrance. Though none of these symbolic acts are essential to such an event, their sequencing demonstrates the logic of the state's protective encompassment of the performance.

Thus, the people do not enter into remembrance until the state first enters into mourning. In these terms, the state controls, coordinates, and synchronizes the remembrance of the Holocaust. State control is practiced through the presentation, in sequence, of a taxonomy of categories of power (the Honor Guard), of authority (the president and prime minister), and of peoplehood (the central beacon). So, too, the end of the event is practiced by the collective singing (by performers and audience members) of the national anthem—the ritual does not end until the state grants it closure. Though this framing signifies the control and power of the state throughout the ritual, the logic of categorization and connection in presentation is that of the bureaucratic. In other words, it is the way in which the bureaucratic mindset organizes the event as it does that enables the ritual to signify the control and power of the state as it does.

In these aesthetics of presentation the taxonomic categories are displayed and activated, one by one—each is a segment, discrete and quite self-contained, lacking dynamics of design that generate any organic momentum of performance. Just as each category of controlled and constrained formulaic action is added to the next, so, too, can the event be deconstructed into these segments without doing much violence to the event as a whole. Despite the variety of physical postures of the different categories of performers—standing on guard, sitting and holding musical instruments, standing and lighting a beacon, standing and orating, standing and singing—the very immobility and functionality of their embodiments, their movements, suggest that like proper functionaries they could all be seated behind a desk or stood behind a wicket. This ceremonial montage points to the resonance generated by bureaucratic logic in modern social orders like that of Israel with the ordering of society beyond the ritual site, almost without needing any inflection, let alone transformation.

Lighting the Memorial Beacons

The taxonomics of bureaucratic logic and aesthetics organize the lengthiest segment of the ritual, its dramatic highlight, the lighting of the six memorial beacons. Each year a Yad Vashem committee chooses one or more themes to commemorate in the Memorial Gathering, the categories of persons who will represent this theme, and the actual persons who will embody these categories by igniting the beacons in the name of the theme. In 1991 the theme chosen was the fiftieth anniversary of the destruction of the Jewries of the Soviet Union, Yugoslavia, and Bukovina. In its deliberations, the committee emphasized that the Holocaust lives of those chosen had to be unique and striking, so as to attract the media. In the 1991 ritual, the beacon lighters numbered eleven (three beacons were each lit by two persons in unison, and another by three in unison). They had been military heroes, partisans, survivors of ghettos and escapees from concentration camps, children during the Holocaust (one, now a Supreme Court justice, hidden by a "peasant savior of souls"), the mother of a young child slaughtered at Babi Yar whose own mother had been murdered there, and a "righteous gentile" who made his home in Israel.[11] Each of these represented a particular segment of the destroyed Jewries of the themes, and each segment was declared as such by the announcers.

Despite the qualifications of heroism and suffering of the beacon lighters, and despite the death and pain they commemorated, this was enunciated in the announcers' texts as the enumeration of a precise anatomy of horror and as a trait list of its attributes and locations.[12] Thus, the first beacon lighter was introduced by the following text (given here in part):

> A full fifty years after the extermination of the Jews in the Soviet territories conquered by the Nazis, in memory of the Jews of Lithuania, Latvia, Estonia, and Byelorussia who were murdered . . . the murder of Ponar—near Vilna, the nine in Kovno, Rumbala—near Riga, Maly Trostinets—near Minsk, and many other places, ascending first to light the beacon is a new immigrant from the Soviet Union who was in a prisoner camp in the Minsk Ghetto, escaped and joined the partisans in the forests, one of the survivors of the concentration camp, Skarzysko.

This trait listing, together with those of other texts, seems to practice the premise that an enumeration of details at the microlevel of Nazi actions will produce a comprehensive vision of the multitude of catastrophes that today we call the Holocaust. (In this regard, see the critical comment by Jay [1992b: 103].) This kind of listing by categories that are cross-indexed, as it were, with other categories, is precisely one of the attitudes of bureaucratic logic, enabled by a bureaucratic aesthetic, which equates the addition and enumeration of mass with a holistic totality. This logic and its aesthetic of every detail in its proper place are commonplace in the organization of our lifeworlds.

Conclusion

If events like the Memorial Gathering are organized through bureaucratic logic and the aesthetics of practice, then this makes a difference in the kinds of messages that the event can communicate. From the perspectives of the state, the organizers, and the audience, the Memorial Gathering is a moral project of the state, carried out in the name of the Jewish people. Given that the state is a Jewish one, the moral duty of its representatives is to remember the evils of the past—evils that fragmented and threatened the Jewish people—and to protect these fragments, as a whole, from threats in the present. This whole is, of course, more than the sum of its values. Crucial to this moral project is the practice of remembering the past. Here, remembering is cast as an itemization, an accounting of the past, occurrence by occurrence, point by point—perhaps an aesthetic double-entry bookkeeping of remembrance. Nonetheless, holism in turn requires ways of communicating its totalistic and comprehensive visions, ones that encompass the discrete itemizations of remembering.

I have argued throughout this chapter (and elsewhere) that bureaucratic logic is pervasive in the modern world and that it dominates what I call events of presentation. The practice of bureaucratic logic is enabled by the bureaucratic aesthetics of lineal organization, arithmetic modularity, exclusivist classification, and exactitude in itemization; and, for that matter, the invention of all these modalities. Thus, these logical and aesthetic qualities of taxonomization dominate public events that are organized in ways similar to the Memorial Gathering. In the case of the gathering, the power of taxonomizing is brought home more clearly by the ways in which the military envelops the event through its own taxonomies. But the premises of taxonomy used by the military are no different from those used to organize the gathering, and, for that matter, both are quite similar to ones that are powerful, if more camouflaged, in the practice of daily life in social orders with prominent bureaucratic infrastructures. To no small degree, in keeping with taxonomic logic and aesthetics, the relationships between the practices of the ritual and the practices of daily life are fractal.

The elements used in the gathering are without a doubt highly symbolic—nevertheless, the practice of this kind of event depends on connections within and among taxonomies rather than on relationships that are organic, dynamic, and transforming. The bureaucratic message is made explicit in the visible tableau of the gathering. This message stresses the practice of exclusivist classification, fragmentation, and itemization, at the expense of the holism of the vision of remembrance. The state's holistic, moral project is shaped, modified, and fragmented by its passage through the organizing media of bureaucratic logic and aesthetics. The vision and feeling of the Holocaust stand rigidly at attention, open to minute inspection, petrified in place. The vision shifts toward the totalitarian in its presentation.

Ironically, bureaucratic logic and aesthetics contribute to separating the Jewish Holocaust from all other atrocities and to classifying it as the unique, historical occurrence of the planned extermination of an entire people—a category with a single member (indeed, a category that paradoxically is a member of itself and is therefore self-sealing and quite resistant to surrendering its self-referentiality, which augments its power exponentially). This exclusivist patterning, with all its inherent dangers (see, for example, Ophir 1987) resonates with the taxonomic treatment of profound tragedy that characterizes the Memorial Gathering. In this instance, bureaucratic logic and aesthetics support (indeed, nourish) the exclusivist state, nationalism, and remembrance that recursively gather themselves within themselves, an in-gathering that separates the Holocaust from too many other instances of human catastrophe.

In Israel, many persons both identify with and feel alienated from these state rituals. Part of our identification (even as this may repel us) is because we ourselves often are both the practitioners and the targets of bureaucratic logic and aesthetics in everyday life. The kinds of classification used, and the practice of their enabling, are common-sensically obvious to us in the way we live much of our lives. We are not reflexive about our practice of this logic nor about its aesthetic enablement—about our practice of practice. Another reason for our lack of reflexivity is the way in which scholars, in particular, philosophers and art historians, have framed off, classified, and separated aesthetics from its role in the practice of everyday life. It is this separation of aesthetics as a realm apart, one dominated by values of beauty and truth, by genres of art, literature, music, and so forth, that has focused scholarly and elitist reflexivity almost exclusively on aesthetics per se, as a discrete domain of culture. In so doing, the intimate enabling of virtually all practice that aesthetics does, is lost.

The final point I will make points to intimations of lawfulness in the use of bureaucratic logic and aesthetics. One scholar, Michael King, has argued that in Western legal systems, law depends for its ontology on a binary code of lawful/unlawful, legal/illegal, and the like. To carry this a step further, law is a prime way of classifying everyday acts within exclusivist taxonomies, with great authority, and with powerful social and personal consequences. Legal systems operate to generate decisions that clarify conditions of vagueness, overlapping rights, allocations of responsibility, and so forth; and legal systems underwrite these decisions with lineal, ontological sanctification. King (1993: 223) suggests further that "any act or utterance that codes social acts according to this binary code of lawful/unlawful may be regarded as part of the legal system." In other words, this logic of the legal system is much more embracing and totalizing than the formal system as such. Yet even more than this, the binary meets the criteria of exclusivist taxonomic classification. Therefore, this kind of taxonomic classification, which has a much broader range than the binary as such, can be substituted for the latter. Now, I have argued that the operation of such exclusivist logic points to the presence of bureaucratic logic. In my terms, then, the operation of bureaucratic logic in Western societies continually implicates the presence of lawfulness. Indeed, bureaucratic logic is itself authorized ontologically to a degree by a sense or feeling of lawfulness in producing and practicing the kind of lineal, taxonomic classification that it does. There is then an aesthetics, itself imbued with a sense of lawfulness, indeed, of rightness, that enables the practice of bureaucratic logic in everyday life. This is one modern version of aesthetics that enables practice—and one, I think, that helps to explain why the bureaucratic logic of classification used in the Memorial Gathering and in everyday life works on so many of us aesthetically. However, it might also explain why we may be so ambivalent to the practice of such classification, yet without knowing exactly and precisely why.

Notes

First published in 2005 as "Bureaucratic Logic, Bureaucratic Aesthetics: The Opening Event of Holocaust Martyrs and Heroes Remembrance Day in Israel," in *Aesthetics in Performance: Formations of Symbolic Construction and Experience*, ed. Angela Hobart and Bruce Kapferer, 196–215. New York: Berghahn Books. Reprinted with permission.

1. In other words, it is done like this because it is done like this—this is how it is felt to be done when one does it.
2. For my purposes here the difference between mundane practice and performance is that the latter is that of practice writ large, consciously and self-reflexively. Therefore, mundane practice slips in and out of performance, apart from the conscious shift into ritual, in which performance becomes the mundane.
3. This is so despite claims for the sacralizing qualities of all manners of ritual, including, for example, "secular ritual" (Moore and Myerhoff 1977). Not a few of the studies in that volume,

with their focus on "ritual," would have benefited from being analyzed in terms of bureaucratic logic.
4. The ethos of bureaucratic framing conditions all statist rituals in Israel. For an example of the collision between bureaucratic logic and popular sentiment, see the discussion of the funeral of the Israeli Prime Minister, Menachem Begin, in Bilu and Levy (1993).
5. In later years, a second state flag has been placed atop the Wall, above the bas-relief, as a symbol of the statist, national encompassment and transcendence of the sorrow symbolized by the suffering Jews, beneath.
6. In later years, a large video screen has been hung on the Wall, above the Honor Guard, and is used for audiovisual contextualizations, for example, to personalize the introductions of the beacon lighters through autobiographical narratives of these persons, which were taped beforehand.
7. The Hebrew term for Jewish immigration to Israel is *aliyah*, literally, ascent.
8. Binyamin Arnon, interviewed at Yad Vashem by Noemi Lerner, 24 July 1991.
9. By 1995, some of the speeches by functionaries had been taken out of the program.
10. One may argue that the stronger sense of movement, of dynamics—archetypal, historicist—is located in the poetics of rhetoric, song, and prayer, which I do not discuss here. Nonetheless, the speeches are stilted; the songs, often old favorites; and the psalms and prayers, generic insertions into ritual.
11. The honor of "righteous gentile" is bestowed by Yad Vashem (in the name of the state) on non-Jews who endangered their own lives by rescuing Jews during World War II.
12. In this respect, the form of these introductions resembled the *Yizkor* prayer of remembrance that can be expanded to include a limitless listing of attributes to be remembered.

References

Astley, W. Graham. 1985. "Administrative Science as Socially Constructed Truth." *Administrative Science Quarterly* 30: 497–513.
Ben-Amos, Avner, and Eyal Ben-Ari. 1995. "Resonance and Reverberation: Ritual and Bureaucracy in the State Funerals of the French Third Republic." *Theory and Society* 24: 163–91.
Bilu, Yoram, and Andre Levy. 1993. "The Elusive Sanctification of Menachem Begin." *International Journal of Politics, Culture and Society* 7: 297–328.
Bourdieu, Pierre. 1977. *Outline of a Theory of Practice*. Cambridge, UK: Cambridge University Press.
Brown, Richard Harvey. 1978. "Bureaucracy as Praxis: Toward a Political Phenomenology of Formal Organizations." *Administrative Science Quarterly* 23: 365–82.
Dufrenne, Mikel. 1973. *The Phenomenology of Aesthetic Experience*. Evanston: Northwestern University Press.
Feldman, Jackie. 2000. "'It Is My Brothers Whom I Am Seeking': Israeli Youth Voyages to Holocaust Poland." PhD dissertation. Hebrew University of Jerusalem.
Foucault, Michel. 1973. *The Order of Things*. New York: Vintage.
———. 1979. *Discipline and Punish*. New York: Vintage.
Friedlander, Saul, and Adam Seligman. 1994. "*The Israeli Memory of the Shoah: On Symbols, Rituals, and Ideological Polarization.*" In *HereNow: Space, Time and Modernity*, ed. Roger Friedland and Deirdre Boden, 356–71. Berkeley: University of California Press.
Garfinkel, Harold. 1967. *Studies in Ethnomethodology*. Englewood Cliffs: Prentice-Hall.
Geertz, Clifford. 1983. *Local Knowledge*. New York: Harper Colophon.
Handelman, Don. 1995. "Cultural Taxonomy and Bureaucracy in Ancient China: *The Book of Lord Shang*." *International Journal of Politics, Culture and Society* 9: 263–93.
———. 1998. *Models and Mirrors: Towards an Anthropology of Public Events*. New York: Berghahn Books.
———. 2004. *Nationalism and the Israeli State: Bureaucratic Logic in Public Events*. Oxford: Berg.

Handelman, Don, and Lea Shamgar-Handelman. 1993. "Aesthetics versus Ideology in National Symbolism: The Creation of the Emblem of Israel." *Public Culture* 5: 431–49.

———. 1996. "The Presence of Absence: The Memorialism of National Death in Israel." In *Grasping Land: Space and Place in Contemporary Israeli Discourse and Experience*, ed. Eyal Ben-Ari and Yoram Bilu, 85–128. Albany: SUNY Press.

Hardin, Kris L. 1993. *The Aesthetics of Action: Continuity and Change in a West African Town*. Washington, DC: Smithsonian Institution Press.

Inglis, David, and John Hughson. 2000. "The Beautiful Game and the Proto-aesthetics of the Everyday." *Cultural Values* 4: 279–97.

Jay, Martin. 1992a. "Scopic Regimes of Modernity." In *Modernity and Identity*, ed. S. Lash and J. Friedman, 178–95. Oxford: Blackwell.

———. 1992b. "Of Plots, Witnesses, and Judgements." In *Probing the Limits of Representation*, ed. Saul Friedlander, 97–107. Cambridge, MA: Harvard University Press.

Katz, Jack. 1999. *How Emotions Work*. Chicago: University of Chicago Press.

Kidron, Carol. 2000. "Amcha's Second Generation Holocaust Survivors: A Recursive Journey into the Past to Construct Wounded Carriers of Memory." MA thesis. Hebrew University of Jerusalem.

Kimmerling, Baruch, in collaboration with Irit Backer. 1985. *The Interrupted System: Israeli Civilians in War and Routine Times*. New Brunswick: Transaction Books.

King, Michael. 1993. "The 'Truth' about Autopoeisis." *Journal of Law and Society* 20: 218–36.

Melossi, Dario, and Massimo Pavarini. 1981. *The Prison and the Factory*. London: Macmillan.

Moore, Sally F., and Barbara Myerhoff, eds. 1977. *Secular Ritual*. Assen, Netherlands: Van Gorcum.

Morgan, Gareth. 1986. *Images of Organization*. Beverly Hills: Sage.

Ophir, Adi. 1987. "On Sanctifying the Holocaust: An Anti-theological Treatise." *Tikkun* 2: 61–67.

Polanyi, Michael. 1962. *Personal Knowledge: Towards a Post-Critical Philosophy*. New York: Harper Torchbooks.

———. 1967. *The Tacit Dimension*. London: Routledge & Kegan Paul.

Shamgar-Handelman, Lea, and Don Handelman. 1991. "Celebrations of Bureaucracy: Birthday Parties in Israeli Kindergartens." *Ethnology* 30: 293–312.

Sheets-Johnstone, Maxine. 2000. "Kinetic Tactile-Kinesthetic Bodies: Ontogenetical Foundations of Apprenticeship Learning." *Human Studies* 23: 343–70.

Simmel, Georg. 1994a. "Bridge and Door." *Theory, Culture and Society* 11: 5–10.

———. 1994b. "The Picture Frame: An Aesthetic Study." *Theory, Culture and Society* 11: 11–17.

Wyschogrod, Edith. 1985. *Spirit in Ashes: Hegel, Heidegger, and Man-Made Mass Death*. New Haven: Yale University Press.

Young, James. 1989. "The Biography of a Memorial Icon: Nathan Rapoport's Warsaw Ghetto Monument." *Representations* 26: 69–106.

———. 1990. "When a Day Remembers: A Performative History of Yom Ha-Shoah." *History and Memory* 2: 54–75.

Part III
Cosmological Trajectories

Chapter 6

Passages to Play
Paradox and Process

Author's Note

I hadn't given any attention to play and the playful prior to 1969. Unsurprisingly, my interest in play was triggered by surprise. In 1969 I was observing interaction among aged workers in workshops in Jerusalem. This eventually turned into the study of encounters discussed in the Epilogue to this volume. While I was there something extraordinary, at least for me, occurred in one of the workshops which employed both women and men. Without prologue or comment the men stealthily began to hang the untwisted metal from a hangar onto the backs of the trousers of one another. When the "butt" discovered his "tail" the other men in the shop would call out loudly, "Donkey! Donkey!," accompanied by the laughter of both men and women. This developed into turn-taking among the men, and only among the men. This activity went on throughout working hours, day after day for about a month. I emphasize that all of this was done without any comments or discussions about who had the right to participate, about how to behave on the parts of men and women, about what the rules were, and so forth. This activity ended as it had begun—silently, without comment—and was not resurrected while I was there. I realized during the period of this activity that I myself could not comment or ask questions about it since it moved almost as if it didn't exist, and I feared drawing attention to this fragility. Yet, when I did so after its disappearance no one remembered any of the details, as if it had been utterly inconsequential, indeed had not existed. And, had I not seen it in practice, it indeed would not have existed anywhere. My abductive understanding of this organized activity is available in Chapter Four of *Models and Mirrors*, and I won't go into it here. Suffice to say that during that month I had encountered spontaneous play that emerged into a game; and, moreover, that this was fraught with significance for any understanding of local life within the shop. An alternative reality that again and again slipped through the social crevices of the shop and that momentarily overturned the dominant daily reality of the workplace.

The dynamic, flexible, and reflexive qualities of play have been on my horizons ever since I read Gregory Bateson's brilliant essays on play, its framing, and the paradoxical passage between serious reality and that of play ("The Message, 'This Is Play,'" and "A Theory of Play and Fantasy"). Bateson's ideas were critical in developing my thoughts. His thinking enabled me to bring the framing of play into conjunction with those of ritual, bureaucracy, and charisma (Handelman 1977, 1981). In 1991 I gave the Distinguished Lecture of The Anthropological Association for the Study of Play (TAASP, which later became TASP, The Association for the Study of Play). Here I brought together thinking on play and cosmology, recognizing that there are cosmoses that embed play at a high level of abstraction. In these cosmos qualities of play are integral to the very organization of cosmos. Here play is a top-down idea. And here the qualities of play lend fluid dynamism to the organization of cosmos, resonating throughout its entirety. For a closer look at this thesis, see Handelman and Shulman's *God Inside Out: Siva's Game of Dice* (1997). By contrast, in cosmoses in which play is not embedded at a high level of organization its qualities tend to erupt from below, bottom-up. Then play is perceived as momentary, unserious, ephemeral, yet subversive. The lecture was published in 1992 in the TAASP journal, *Play and Culture*. The journal died after that year, though I take no responsibility for its demise.

> If you're going to study play you've got to carry in the forefront of your mind what sort of logical type this class is. What is the level of classification, what does it enclose, what are the messages that label it, if any, and so on?
> —Gregory Bateson, "Play and Paradigm"

The concept of cosmos refers to the order of a cultural universe in its broadest, most comprehensive sense (Long 1987). Whether ideas of play can be related substantially to conceptions of cosmos is one major test of the power of play, of its forceful influence on the organization of the human imagination that we call culture. Are there grounds to support the view that ideas of play may influence the ways traditional cosmologies are put together, the ways they work? If so, what does this say about the structuring of cosmologies in which ideas of play have little or no role? The implications of these questions are far reaching, and there is more than a little hubris in raising them in such an unadorned fashion, without numerous scholarly qualifications and emendations. Nonetheless, I believe that such questions go to the heart of play in the human universe, whether play is our invention or whether it is a biological disposition. Therefore, these questions should be addressed even though our efforts, indeed my efforts, fumble, stumble, and trip over only a tiny outcrop of these cosmic puzzles.

I haven't any clear-cut answers. The route I would like to take you through is circuitous and, at the outset, seems to have little direct relevance to the questions posed. But, as scholars of play, I hope you agree that the shortest distance is often roundabout.

The route I've planned goes through a passage to a way station. This passage is from what may be called, rather awkwardly, not-play (or non-play), to play. My premise is that play, and ideas that can be understood to resonate with play, are given some autonomous recognition in virtually all cultures; therefore, cultures make some ideational distinction between not-play and play. Given that these are distinct ideational domains, they are related by the passage from one to the other. So, too, this passage occurs through what may be called, heuristically, a boundary or a frame—the nexus where messages of not-play and play interact. This meeting place is strange, for it is constituted from paradox. Yet paradox contains qualities that help us to understand the power of play in human cosmology.

The way station I mentioned is inside the boundary itself, the boundary in between not-play and play, the boundary composed of paradox. By peering within this boundary, we may find qualities of play that help to explain its effect on boundaries and its potential influence on the organization of cosmos.

On the basis of these arguments, I will suggest the following relationship between play and cosmos and will reformulate this further on. If qualities of play found within the boundary between not-play and play are present in a particular cosmos, then where these qualities of play are located in that cosmic scheme will influence the ways that cosmos is conceived to exist and to operate. To put this more straightforwardly, a cosmic scheme that is influenced by premises of play seems to operate quite differently from one that is less so.

I will apply this approach in a rudimentary manner by taking up a few aspects of Hindu cosmology, within which an idea of play seems to be embedded at a high level of abstraction. In this respect, mythic and religious cosmologies are more amenable to these preliminary formulations because metaphysical conceptions are often made more forthright. In closing, I will touch on questions of comparison by distinguishing between what I call top-down play and bottom-up play.

Passages to Play: Extending Bateson's Problem of Play as Paradox

In his seminal essay "A Theory of Play and Fantasy," first published in 1955, Bateson (1972) made three basic points. First, the invocation of play creates a boundary in between not-play and play. Second, this boundary is paradoxical. Third, this same invocation of play also overcomes the paradox it creates, enabling passage into the reality of play. For my purposes, it is important to understand how his analysis proceeded. Bateson problematized the relationship of not-play to play by using Whitehead and Russell's (1927) theory of logical types. This enabled Bateson to posit play as an abstraction different from that of not-play. The logic of play, he seemed to argue, frames it differently from that of not-play.

Let me emphasize at the outset that Bateson's problem was epistemological—that is, his concern was the character of the relationship of not-play to play, as a puzzle in adaptive communication. In his view, this relationship privileged neither not-play nor play. Neither was inferior to the other. Not-play and play were organized according to premises that were different. But more than this, their respective premises radically contradicted one another to create what Hofstadter (1980) has called a tangled hierarchy. At issue was not the contents of these domains (e.g., whether one was real and serious and the other, illusory and pretend). Instead, the problem of their difference was located in the very nexus of their interaction, in the logic of the frame (in the logic of what I call the boundary) in between not-play and play.

Bateson recognized that this kind of frame has a peculiar, paradoxical character. He wrote, "it is our hypothesis that the message 'This is play' establishes a paradoxical frame comparable to Epimenides's paradox" (Bateson 1972: 184). As I noted, this invocation or metamessage of play—which Bateson called "This is play"—does three things simultaneously: it creates the frame; it creates the paradox of the frame; and it overrides this paradox, opening the way into play. The paradox referred to is of the self-referential variety. So, Epimenides, the Cretan, stated that all Cretans were liars. A more compact version of this kind of paradox would simply say "This statement is false." If the statement is true, then it is false; but if the statement is false, then it falsifies itself. Playfully, we could replace the period that ends this sentence with the sign for infinity, at least for a time.

Among the examples that Bateson used to illustrate this paradox is one closer in substance to the issue of play—the example of the bite and the playful nip. The playful nip looks like a bite, but it signifies something quite different. It is a bite, and it is not a bite, at one and the same time. It is a different bite, perhaps an imaginary bite, a bite that does not exist, yet does, for it is consequential as a bite that wasn't (Handelman 1990: 69). Or, one may say that the playful nip is a bite on its way to becoming what it isn't. Simultaneously, the playful nip is not only a bite and a nonbite, not only one thing and another, but also a bite in process, in transformation to something else. Something looks like what it isn't (Napier 1986: 1), and indeed it is that. This kind of formulation has significant implications for the boundary between not-play and play, and I will get to this shortly.

In his 1955 essay, Bateson addressed the logic of self-referential paradox as structure and process (and therefore also as temporal). Bateson depicted a self-referential paradox in terms of a rectangular frame within which was written, "All statements within this frame are untrue," followed by two alternatives within the rectangle, "I love you" and "I hate you." This rectangular frame may be misleading if one thinks that it models a paradoxical reality that one enters into, on the other side of the boundary. Quite the contrary, this depiction models the interior logic of the frame itself. In other words, it models the boundary, or the threshold between realities. Likewise, the depiction models the paradoxical interior of the boundary in between not-play and play.[1] Let me emphasize that the realities of play are not necessarily paradoxical in relation to themselves, but play is paradoxical in relation to not-play.

Bateson barely addressed the interior features of play worlds themselves—of how these realities are put together and experienced, subjects that have been the focus of so much thought and research. However, he did demonstrate imaginatively and incisively the problematic character of the paradoxical passage from not-play to play.

Nevertheless, he speedily disregarded the significance of this paradoxical passage for an epistemology of play by invoking the metamessage "This is play." This metamessage enables us, with speed and ease, to override the paradox of passage from one kind of abstraction, one kind of reality, to another, on a routine and mundane basis, without paying heed to the magnitude of our accomplishment.

This is where Bateson stopped. Having found the way out of paradox, Bateson didn't look into paradox, yet there he would have found hints of how play works and what play can do. Instead, with the solution for the passage to play in hand, Bateson pursued no further that which paradox, and paradox as boundary, intimate about play and about the effects of play on boundaries. Nonetheless, my reading of Bateson is of an implicit invitation to peer into the paradoxical composition of this kind of boundary in order to consider the relevance of paradox for play. I would like to turn to this now.

Peering into Boundaries

Most boundaries with which we are familiar in daily life either are traversed routinely or close off special domains of experience. Both are commonly marked by thresholds, whether these are thresholds of space (physical and visible), of time (counted and felt), or of sociality (known and normative). For my purposes, the presence of all such boundaries can be summarized as shifts in social definition, from some segment of continuity to its discontinuity, where this discontinuity is the location of boundary. Here the sides of the boundary are adjacent to and contiguous with one another. Regardless of how forceful these boundaries are, whether because of their pervasiveness or because of the hegemonies of power they signify, there is nothing inherently problematic about them. They separate alternatives in an either/or fashion. These boundaries are constructs that retain their shape through either consensus or imposition. They are always subject to redefinition and change. These boundaries are not relevant to the themes pursued here.

Boundaries that are made out of self-referential paradox are quite distinct and are especially significant for my purposes. More generally, such boundaries probably symbolize locations of potential crossing between different realities. In this regard, the passage to play is analogous to the classic problem of paradoxical movement between contrasting levels or domains of cosmos, from one reality to another, movement that Eliade (1964: 483–86) called paradoxical passage (e.g., the necessity to go where night and day meet, to find a gate in a blank wall, or to pass between two boulders that constantly clash together). In other words, it is to simultaneously do one thing and its contrary, to do the impossible.

Such points of passage are made out of paradox. The interior of the boundary in between not-play and play is constituted as a severely restricted and highly redundant world, one that is formed through self-reference, contradiction, and infinite regress and that encloses itself within itself (Hughes and Brecht 1984: 1). This tiny world of paradox is itself a simulation of the passage between realities. In its most rudimentary form, this miniscule world consists of two alternatives (I love you / I hate you; this is not-play / this is play; and so on). These alternatives are governed by self-contradiction such that each leads to and negates the other, which leads to and negates the other, and so forth. According to Bateson (1980: 130), "Norbert Weiner used to point out that if you present the Epimenides paradox to a computer, the answer will come out yes . . . no . . . yes . . . no . . . until the computer runs out of ink or energy."

Paradox is generated because each alternative exists on the same level of abstraction, where each is given the same value as the other and is without the capacity to dominate or to cancel the other. The paradox seems like an impassable trap. On the other hand, the very conjunction and interaction of these contradictory alternatives makes this kind of paradox a nexus of potential crossing between levels of abstraction or between alternative realities.

In her fascinating book, *Paradoxia Epidemica: The Renaissance Tradition of Paradox*, Colie (1966) pointed to several premises of self-referential paradox that are especially relevant to the interior of the paradoxical boundary of neither/nor. She noted, first, the closed structure of this sort of paradox. "The perfect self-contradiction," she wrote, "is a perfect equivocation" (Colie 1966: 6). She continued, "It tells the truth and it doesn't . . . its negative and positive meanings are so balanced that one meaning can never outweigh the other, though weighed to eternity." Indeed, such paradox has no formal ending (ibid.: 21).

Not only is this sort of paradox totalistic, but inside itself it breaks down and re-synthesizes the contradictions that are the basis for its very existence. Thus, not only does such paradox deal with itself both as form and as content, as subject and object, but it also collapses these distinctions. Subject turns into object, object into subject. So too, the means of paradox are always its ends as it turns endlessly in and upon itself (ibid.: 518). Phrased otherwise, this kind of paradox transforms itself continually and continuously; its structure is also its process, its process its very structure. The stability of paradox is change. The internal collapse of categories and their resynthesis are evidence for Colie that paradox ultimately insists upon a unity of being. Paradox, she commented, folds "all its parts into one unbroken [whole] . . . paradox is self-regarding, self-contained, and self-confirming; it attempts to give the appearance of ontological wholeness" (ibid.: 518). Given its powerful momentum toward wholeness and totality, toward seamlessness and self-separation, this kind of paradox creates a powerful demarcation, a forceful boundary.

Yet inside this special boundary, there is another aspect of importance. Colie (1966: 7) wrote that the self-referential paradox is "profoundly self-critical," for within its narrow strictures it is continually calling itself into question, making itself problematic. She commented that it operates at the "limits of discourse" (ibid.: 10), calling into question those categories that are thought out in order to express human thought. Playing on the Latin term for mirror, *speculum*, she added that the self-referential paradox is "literally, speculative, its meanings infinitely mirrored, infinitely reflected, in each other" (ibid.: 6). Infinite regress, but it is also an imaginative search for the parameters of the in-between condition of boundariness—that is, of being in-between. Reflecting further, Colie insisted that, "like a tight spring, the implications of any particular paradox impel that paradox beyond its own limitation to defy its own categories" (ibid.: 11). Self-limited, it denies limitation. Here she intimated that just as paradox bounds itself off and closes itself in, so, too, does it have the potential to open itself, to become a nexus of passage, of crossing through the impassable. Paradox may function as a gateway (Yusa 1987: 191).

These premises of self-referential paradox compose the boundary between not-play and play. In turn, the paradox generates qualities that are of direct relevance to ideas of play and to how play can act on other boundaries.

Thus, paradox is not only full of movement but is constituted wholly and only through movement. Once set into operation, it seems to go on forever, nearing a metaphor of perpetual motion. It is a fiercely dynamic medium, one that is highly processual (cf. Slaate 1968). Its being is always a becoming, to paraphrase Gadamer (1988: 110), and it is conducive to spherical thinking rather than to lineal thought (Yusa 1987: 194). Just as it contains and collapses distinctions—between ends and means, structure and function—so it actualizes the perfect praxis of idea and action.[2] There seems to be no such phenomenon as a static paradox, or one that is stable without being continually unstable. Indeed, the paradox of self-reference is highly systemic in its self-reproduction through self-transformation.

The only way out of this sort of paradox (aside from waiting for entropy to degenerate the structure) is to make a choice. The passage through paradox is a matter of agency. In this, the self-criticism of paradox is significant because it spells out alternatives even as it attributes equal values to these alternatives. Self-doubt evokes a reflexive stance that may break the dynamic deadlock of the paradoxical boundary.

Choice requires a hierarchy of value, the preference of one alternative to others. This preference is an index of change in value, one that breaks the dynamic deadlock. Passage through this kind of boundary is always a discourse on change in values. Phrased differently, there is no movement between realities without a change in values. The capacity to change values is a prerequisite of moving between levels of abstraction, whether this is seemingly as simple as an act of imagination, as in the case of play, or as complex as training in self-transcendence. The passage through paradox demands this capacity. This is the significance of Bateson's metamessage, "This is play." It is a message of passage through paradox because it makes a choice—it puts the value of play above that of not-play. One cannot play without changing values, without changing the value of reality, without changing realities.

These qualities of paradox have strong affinities to qualities of play. The paradoxical boundary, the passage from not-play to play through neither/nor, cryptically prefigures many of the qualities of play realities. Especially important is the powerful thrust of processuality. The passage to play makes a structural difference, but one that is related intimately to processuality. Processuality speaks to the flexibility and malleability, the fluidity and changeability, that pervade so many contexts of play.[3] At the same time, the paradoxical passage from not-play to play creates self-transformation through two degrees of abstraction. One is the level of the paradox itself, the level of neither/nor, where not-play and play interact, lead to, and turn into the other. The second is the movement between levels or realities, through the metamessage that enables choice, and so enables exit from the paradox and entry into play.

Let me reformulate the relationship between play and cosmos that I put forward at the beginning of this lecture. Every invocation of play demonstrates the immediate presence of the impassable yet fluid boundary that is passed through. Every invocation of play demonstrates the immediate presence of premises of self-transformation. Every invocation of play puts things in motion. Every invocation of play demonstrates the immediate presence of qualities that enable passage through this boundary—and once more I especially emphasize qualities of movement and change.[4]

This formulation suggests the following kind of correspondence: the higher, the more abstract, the level of cosmos at which these qualities of play are embedded and legitimated, the greater the influence of these qualities on the organization of that cosmos. Therefore, where the invocation of play is embedded in cosmos at a high level of abstraction, its fluid, transformational qualities reappear also at lower levels of abstraction, permeating their influence there. The boundaries throughout such a cosmos are more malleable, and the entire cosmos may approximate more closely a system of self-transformation.

Play and Self-Transforming Cosmology: Lila and Maya

I return now to the question of relationships between play and cosmos. I'd like to address (with great brevity) two ideas that have been prominent in Indian cosmologies. One is called *lila*,[5] and the other, *maya*.[6] Like their more recent counterparts, the ancient cosmologies within which these ideas were invented and flourished made the continuing existence of cosmos contingent on perpetual change. Cosmos continually transformed itself continuously, reproducing itself as phenomenal form.[7]

In the ancient Sanskrit text, the *Rig Veda*, the cosmic Self (*Brahman*) is the undifferentiated, unreflective unity that "breathes or pulsates by itself, though without breath" (Miller 1985: 53). At some moment it began the directional process of differentiating itself, thereby creating the level of gods, who in turn gave shape to human agency. One may argue that a paradox of self-reference is embedded in that initial moment of differentiation when the cosmic Self became to itself simultaneously one thing and another, Self and Other. I will return to this shortly.

Following the first movement of the cosmic Self, evolution continued ceaselessly through extremely lengthy durations. Yet all evolution was entropic. Eventually the process would reverse itself, destroying the phenomenal cosmos and returning to the sentient but undifferentiated and unreflective cosmic Self, then to begin another cosmic cycle.

The order of this world was never at rest, never static—it was one of an ongoing "becoming." The fundamental rhythms of these cosmic processes were analogous to those of expansion and contraction, construction and destruction, or, in the language of the *Rig Veda*, weave forth, weave back (Miller 1985: 58). Expansion and construction connote descent and devolution through the creation of a hierarchy of increasingly material levels of phenomenal reality. Contraction and destruction refer to contrary processes that ascend to a condition of cosmic holism, one without difference. In this cosmos, "everything is in constant motion . . . but this constancy of movement is itself the stability of cosmic order" (ibid.: 289).

Ideas of play were given cosmic significance, especially in relation to the puzzle of why the cosmic Self, utterly without desire or need, bothered to create the phenomenal cosmos. The concept of lila answered this. Lila is a Sanskrit noun that means play or sport—in the sense of diversion, amusement, fun. It also connotes effortless, rapid movement (Huizinga 1970: 51). The highly influential text, the *Vedanta Sutra* of the third century CE, states that the creative activity of the Divine is mere lila, "such as we see in ordinary life" (Thibault 1962, pt. 1, bk. 2, sect. 1, verse 33). The great religious teacher, Shankara (ninth century CE), commented on this passage:

> The process of inhalation and exhalation is going on without reference to any extraneous purpose, merely following the law of its own nature. Analogously, the activity of the Lord also may be supposed to be mere sport, proceeding from his own nature, without reference to any purpose. (Thibault 1962: 356–57)

Lila is the motive that is without motive: spontaneous action wholly for its own sake (cf. O'Flaherty 1984: 230). The Divine makes and regulates the cosmos out of neither need nor necessity, "but by a free and joyous creativity that is integral to his own nature. He acts in a state of rapt absorption comparable to that of an artist possessed by his creative vision" (Hein 1987: 550). In lila, in play, the Divine takes spontaneous delight in his own self-transformation and, therefore, in that of the cosmos with which he is homologous (Zimmer 1984: 24). By providing the motive, as it were, for the ongoing creation of the phenomenal cosmos, lila embeds the metamessage "This is play" at a high, abstract level of cosmic organization.

Earlier, I said that a paradox of self-reference was embedded in the initial movement, the first moment of differentiation within the cosmic Self. Through that movement, the cosmic Self became to itself simultaneously one thing and another, self and other, through lila. Let me emphasize that in this cosmos, this paradox was integral to the beginning of self-definition, to the very creation of Self through the division between Self and Other. Moreover, this also was the creation of self-alienation, of estrangement from Self, of knowing oneself otherwise, because this was inherent in the creation of Other from Self, Self from Other.[8]

Therefore, this paradox of self-reference also constituted the very first boundary, that between Self and Other. This boundary also was created in lila—that is, by the equivalent of the metamessage "This is play." Indeed, this is the boundary in between not-play (the undifferentiated cosmic Self) and play (the creation of the Other, and the definition of the Self through the Other). Likewise, lila signified the first passage through this boundary, just as this passage signified the creation of cosmos. In this cosmology, lila (play) is implicated in many rudiments of the creation of being and cosmos—of Self and Other, of the boundary in between them, and of self-alienation.

In the terms I have outlined, the metamessage "This is play" imputes to the comprehensive organization of this cosmos all of the qualities of play that are embedded in the paradoxical passage from not-play to play. These are the qualities of malleability and fluidity, movement and change. As I noted, in the cosmology under discussion, the paradoxical passage from not-play to play is embedded in the very first movement of the cosmic Self as it began the creation of the phenomenal cosmos. Movement, one may say, is the mysterious choice of the cosmic Self. It is the passage from inaction to action, from immobility to mobility. Processuality is encoded in this paradoxical passage, and cosmic action and movement are identified with play. These qualities of play are attached to all differences among levels, to all boundaries, putting them in play in the cosmic system.

In all Indian cosmologies, cosmic process is cosmic regulation. Divine play (lila) was identified not only with creation but also with its ongoing processuality. For example, in numerous classical myths, the god Shiva and his wife play dice. The dice are named after the great eons of time in Hinduism. One scholar (Hiltebeitel 1987: 473) has commented that "The dice play of the divine couple thus represents the continuity of the universe and their absorption with and within it."

The character of play (lila) was also embedded within certain great deities of later Hinduism. Here lila is related to their capacity to manifest themselves within the human world. Their shifts among levels, and their abrupt appearances among humankind, are the embodied effects of cosmic processes in the world. Their appearances are paradoxical. Prominent among these puzzles is the paradox of the infinite god who is "embedded in finite form," at the human level of cosmos (Dimock 1989: 164). This paradox plays on the simultaneous difference yet non-difference between god and humankind and on their simultaneous separation and non-separation from one another. Therefore, to humankind, deity is at one and the same time transcendent and immanent, unknowable and knowable (*bheda/abheda*) (Dimock 1989: 162; Handelman 1987a).

For example, the god Krishna is a human form (*avatara*) of the god Vishnu. Krishna contains the entire cosmos within himself. He is a child, full of spontaneous, mischievous fun, playing with his own shadow, stealing butter, and eating dirt. He is a beautiful youth who plays the flute, frolics, and seduces the village girls (see Hawley 1981; Kinsley 1975). He is the misshapen, monstrous, primeval, Jagganath. One Indologist (Dimock 1989: 165) commented that all of these Krishnas are real, and all are really Krishna—each form is the infinite, essential godhead (Dimock 1976: 113). These forms are his play, his lilas, because "the full deity [who is the cosmos] is in constant motion and therefore of everchanging form" (Dimock 1989: 164; Handelman 1987a).[9]

As I discussed in relation to the cosmic Self, the motion of lila intimates motive in the creation of the phenomenal universe. Moreover, the appearance of lila is that of the Divine, the manifestation of cosmic process on different levels of the universe. In both instances, this presence of play is also the presence of boundaries. In the first instance—that of creation—lila points to the making of boundaries, that is, the making of those differences among phenomena that define and constitute the world.[10] In the second—the transformative manifestation of deity—lila demonstrates passage through boundaries. Embedded at a high level of cosmic organization, the idea of play influences the fluidity and permeability of boundaries. Barriers to passage are transmuted more into waystations or signposts; the continual, playful movement of cosmic forces among levels relates directly to the transformative character of the entire cosmos.[11]

A few remarks now on maya, a crucial idea in Indian cosmologies. Although it has no linguistic link to play, the qualities of maya complement to a high degree those of lila. Lila and maya have a good deal of functional resonance with one another in their implications for the organization of cosmos. The authoritative, etymological study of maya (Burrow 1980: 319) stated that the word, by itself, meant craft or skill, but when the word was used in connection with deities, it connoted their mysterious "management or manipulation of the forces of nature" and, less frequently, their acts of creation.[12] Metaphors of maya often emphasize its elusive force for continuing change (Lannoy 1971: 290).[13] Later it acquired the meaning of the power of illusion.

A most enigmatic concept, maya is full of the powers that move the phenomenal cosmos and keep it in motion, in accordance with its own nature (Miller 1985: 114); that nature is of "something constantly being made" (O'Flaherty 1984: 119). Maya, one may say, is the management of motion. So, for example, in the following verse from the *Rig Veda* (10.85.18–19a, cited in Johnson 1980: 92), maya refers to the power that moves sun and moon and, by implication, the cosmos in its entirety:

> One after another the two turn, by maya,
> Two children playing, going round a sacrifice.
> One, regards all creatures,
> The other, establishing the seasons, is born again.
> Ever anew and anew being born, he comes [repeatedly]
> into existence.

Possessed in differing degrees by deities, demons, and humans, maya is the faculty by which they weave changes into the continually shifting fabric of the phenomenal cosmos. Maya alters the cosmic warp and weft, transmuting its balances and imbalances such that the entire cosmic system continues to operate according to its own nature. In this regard, maya is something like the miraculous means for the manipulation of cosmic order, by which the cosmic system produces the phenomenal effects of and for its own continuing existence (cf. Shastri 1911: 31).

These sidelong glances into Indian cosmology can do no more than give a rhetorical thrust to the claim that this cosmos is organized according to premises of self-transformation. Yet this argument is significant for an appreciation of the powers of play in different cosmologies. In using the phrasing of self-transformation, I want to stress the following. This cosmos is in a condition of continual and continuous change. Less obvious, perhaps, is that this change is total. The parts, as it were, of this cosmic system have no inherent shape, no integral stability, in their own right. Everything, everyone, is in process, undergoing change all the time. At issue, then, is not the changing of relationships among the stable parts of this system, but instead how everything is thought to change within itself through its relations to everything else.[14]

Indian cosmologies totalize change through various theories of creation and destruction, from the smallest to the grandest of scales, and through brief periods and extremely lengthy temporal cycles. These are cosmologies in which the cosmos totally absorbs its own changes within itself just as it makes all these changes within its own totality. From top to bottom, these cosmic hierarchies resonate with those qualities of play that exemplify fluidity and malleability, movement and change.

Homeostasis is not especially desirable in these cosmologies because this signifies a balanced state that slows down or ends the processes of transformation, the natural condition of the cosmos. When there are tendencies toward homeostasis in this kind of cosmos, it responds by teetering and slipping—indeed, by imbalancing itself toward continuing processuality. This is like saying that the self-transforming system subverts itself in order to function.

I'd like to illustrate this point with an incident from perhaps the greatest of Indian epics, the *Mahabharata*. The power implicated in this story is that of maya, not lila, but it is maya resonating with the powers of play. The *Mahabharata* is extremely long and convoluted, and the incident I have in mind is considered quite minor, as more of an embellishment to the weighty ideas and strenuous action of the epic. But I think of this little incident in terms of what chaos theory calls the "butterfly effect"—the idea, for example, that "a butterfly stirring the air today in Peking can transform storm systems next month in New York," to quote Gleick (1988: 8).

The *Mahabharata* is set in the seam between two great eons of time as the universe moves into the lowest, the most entropic of these (the *Kaliyuga*), with its increased strife and disintegration of the cosmic weave (Hiltebeitel 1987: 473). The stories of the epic tell of the struggles between two great families of cousins, the five Pandava brothers and their rivals, the Kauravas. The eldest of the five brothers, Yudhisthira, is to be consecrated as a great monarch, the height of majesty, the upholder of moral boundaries, laws, and duties (*dharmaraja*). He is to be the perfect ruler, the perfect regulator of the natural order of the kingdom.

He decides to build a magnificent palace, worthy of his title, and commissions the most eminent of architects to do this.[15] The architect is greatly indebted to the

Pandava brothers. Previously, they had saved his life, and he strives to the utmost to carry out the commission. Indeed, he succeeds. The palace is perfection and rivals those of the lesser gods. For that matter, the palace is a model, a microcosm of the cosmos over which the king rules. There is only one little flaw. The architect is a demon (*asura*), and demons, like deities, are heavy with the powers of maya. Although doing his very best for the Pandavas, the demon nonetheless is true to his own transformative nature, and so he cannot help but build a few illusions into the structure of the palace.

The king invites his cousins, the Kauravas to visit the palace. All wonder in admiration at its beauty. But one Kaurava, Duryodhana, keeps tripping over the little glitches in this perfection. Where there is a pool, he sees solid floor and falls into the water. Where he sees an entryway, there is only solid surface on which he cracks his head. At each mishap he is mocked, the butt of laughter. His anger grows; his hatred festers. He goes home, schemes revenge, and comes up with a plan to invite the king to play dice. The king loses everything in this game, including himself. The five brothers are forced into lengthy exile. And entropy, the fragmentation and destruction of social and cosmic order, gathers direction and momentum to end eventually in utter holocaust and the annihilation of all. A minor error of perspective, seemingly no more than a prop, contributes to gigantic effects. But whose is the error?

During this era of increasing entropy, the consecration of the perfect ruler is an act of stability, perhaps a striving for homeostasis. It runs counter to, perhaps even blocks, the progressive degeneration of the cosmos during this phase of its devolution. The demon builds illusion into the palace, into this microcosm of the kingdom. For that matter, he builds change into this stable perfection. Things are not as they seem. Illusion is something that looks like one thing yet is another.

Perhaps it is one thing that not only masks something else but is on its way to becoming that other thing. Illusion is something in process, undergoing change. Illusion is transforming. The architect, true to his own nature and to that of the cosmos, builds imbalance within homeostasis and transforms this seeming stability, tipping it over, setting it into movement that cannot be reversed. Maya, the power of cosmic management and therefore of change, resonating with the messages of play, of lila, keeps the cosmos true to itself, perpetually self-transforming.

Play and Cosmos: Top-Down or Bottom-Up?

I have argued that the locations of play, of where play is perceived to be embedded in the cosmic order of things, effects its influence. This focus on the locations of play in conceptions of cosmos also opens the way to comparison. Therefore I will conclude by contrasting, in a most preliminary way, play that is top-down and play that is bottom-up.

In Indian cosmology, play is a top-down idea. Passages to play and their premises are embedded at a high level of abstraction and generality. The qualities of play resonate and resound throughout the whole. But more than this, qualities of play are integral to the very operation of the cosmos. In this regard, to be in play, to partake of the qualities of play, is to be attuned to cosmic processes and their ideals of self-transformation. To be in play is to reproduce time and again the very premises that inform the existence of this kind of cosmos.[16]

Cosmologies are related to cultural ideologies. So too, the processual qualities of play that I have emphasized—fluidity and malleability, movement and change—are deeply embedded in Indian cultural ideologies under a variety of rubrics. As one commentator has noted, "The most striking aspect of play activity in India . . . is its tendency to set in motion, to propel the society forwards by an incessant circulation" (Lannoy 1971: 195).[17]

Now, in cosmologies where premises of play are *not* embedded at a high level, and are *not* integral to the organization of cosmos, the phenomena of play seem to erupt more from the bottom. By bottom-up play I mean that play often is phrased in opposition to, or as a negation of, the order of things. This is the perception of play as unserious, illusory, and ephemeral, but it is also the perception of play as subversive and as resisting the order of things.

To my mind, these descriptions apply to the roles of play in, for example, mainstream monotheistic cosmologies. There, relationships between God and humankind are organized generally in terms of rupture, of absolute difference and hardened boundaries, and of opposites. Frye (1980: 11) once commented that the encounter of the God of creation and man as a creative being "seems to be rather like what some of the great poets of nuclear physics have described as the encounter of matter with anti-matter: each annihilates the other." There the premises of play have a role neither in cosmogony nor in the organization of cosmos. Historically, play has survived and at times flourished in these contexts—but almost always from the bottom up.

Bottom-up play has deep roots in monotheistic cosmologies. It has dominated play phenomena even in periods and places, like those of medieval and Renaissance Europe, that scholars hold out as exemplars of the near-cosmic presence of play. For example, the medieval grotesque discussed by Gurevich (1988: 176–210), the Feast of Fools (Gilhus 1990), and carnival and the carnivalesque (Bakhtin 1968; Burke 1978: 178–205; Camporesi 1988: 47, 51, 208–20; Handelman 1990; Le Roy Ladurie 1979) were all perceived to combine qualities of the unserious and the comic, and of confrontation and resistance. Undoubtedly, these instances qualify as bottom-up play, and numerous other examples from these and other periods can be adduced.[18]

In this regard, the subsequent influences of the Reformation, and the emergence of pronounced contrasts between work and play, were not a radical break with the Western past but construed its heritages of play in other rhetorics, other forms.[19] So it is in the present: theologians of play at the postmodern edge must know that if they desire a dominant metaphysic to emerge from Western heritages of play then they will have to invent it.[20] In the historical developments of monotheistic frameworks, the thrusts of play are strongly from the bottom up.

The bottom-up entry of play into routine living is often a battle for presence, a struggle over space and time devoted to other practices, and a confrontation over legitimacy, apart from special occasions and places that indeed are set apart. So play is often perceived to lurk within the interstices and to spill over from the margins. The effortless, quicksilver qualities of play are always the same, but the epistemological status of these qualities differs radically between cosmologies that embed such qualities at the top of cosmic hierarchy and cosmologies that locate such qualities nearer the bottom.[21]

Top-down or bottom-up? I am arguing that there are *essential* qualities of play that make it different from not-play and that these qualities are encoded within passages to play and are reproduced continually with each crossing. Nonetheless, I am insisting that those aspects of play closer to cultural sensibilities are *contextual*. Thus, the interpretations of play, the meanings of play, the significance of play, and the powers of play are contextual, reflecting the valuations others and ourselves put on essential qualities of play. Play seems rarely to be a neutral idea, as Mechling (1989: 308–10) has reminded us. Top-down or bottom-up? The vision is crude, yet the implications may be telling. Top-down or bottom-up? Find the passages to play.

Notes

First published in 1992 as "Passages to Play: Paradox and Process," *Play & Culture* 5: 1–19. Reprinted with permission.
1. Some scholars make paradoxical boundaries, like that in between not-play and play, unproblematical. Three examples will suffice. Goffman (1974: 40–46) supposedly built on Bateson's idea of the play frame in order to analyze the shift from not-play to play. Goffman grotesquely turned this into a problem of mechanics: strips of play, made to mimic strips of not-play, were laid like lumber, strip on strip, through simple alterations in social conventions. Buckley (1983: 389) conflated the contents of play realities with the paradox of the play frame and thereby argued that Bateson considered the realities of play to be paradoxical from within. Goffman and Buckley reduced play to forms of not-play, making each *continuous* with the other. Schechner (1988: 16) argued that the "Batesonian play frame is a rationalist attempt to stabilize and localize playing, to contain it safely within definable borders." Schechner complemented Buckley by conflating Bateson's argument on passages to play with the substance of play within play frames. All three ignored the logic of passages to play.
2. Here paradox is similar to Csikzentmihalyi's (1974) notion of flow. On the perfect praxis of idea and action, see Handelman (1991).
3. Elsewhere (Handelman 1990: 63–72) I point to the affinities between play and uncertainty. In this regard, uncertainty is a mode of processuality. Thus the presence of play within ritual signifies changes that the ritual is undergoing, often as part of its structure of intentionality.
4. Relationships between play and boundary are discussed in Handelman (1981; 1990: 236–65).
5. Diacritical marks of transliterated Sanskrit terms are omitted in order to ease printing. So too, only the first use of each term is italicized.
6. Schechner (1988) addressed lila and maya in his own fashion, in a previous address to The Association for the Study of Play.
7. Ancient Indo-European cosmologies (including those of ancient India) made change integral to their operation. Lincoln (1986) discussed two complementary Indo-European visions of cosmic creation. In one, the body of a primordial being became the raw material from which

cosmos was made. In the other, the elements that composed the phenomenal cosmos became the material from which the body of the first man was made. Lincoln (1986: 33) argued that each vision was a phase in an encompassing process whereby "whenever the cosmos is created, the body is destroyed, and . . . whenever the body is created, the cosmos is destroyed." Cosmos and body, macrocosm and microcosm were alternative forms of one another, each broken down and transformed into the other (ibid.: 40). In this kind of cosmos, the only constancy was that of change. Cosmos operated by transforming itself and even by absorbing itself. It constituted a cultural milieu within which ideas of play as a cosmic process gained prominence.

8. Thus, play is integral to the dynamic relationship between integration and fragmentation that is characteristic of many Indian cosmologies.

9. Just so, the god Shiva simultaneously is higher and lower, transcendent and immanent in his play, his lilas (see Dessigane, Pattabiramin, and Filliozat 1960). Thus, "All the time that Shiva made love with Sati [his wife], it was just his divine play, for he was entirely self-controlled and without emotional excitement the whole time [. . .] when Sati died, Shiva, the great Yogi, wept like a lover in agony, but this is just his divine play, to act like a lover, for in fact he is unconquered and without emotional excitement" (Shiva Purana, quoted in O'Flaherty 1973: 147).

10. Finding the correct balance in the character of boundaries was an important feature of ancient Indian cosmogonies. There was an emphasis on fluidity and change in the necessity to make adjustments in the quality of boundaries because their creator was imperfect in his creations. Thus the parts of the cosmos might be insufficiently differentiated from one another and, therefore, too similar to one another (*jami*). These boundaries were overly soft and shapeless, so the parts they bounded became joined indiscriminately, losing their distinctiveness and producing cosmic chaos. Or, the parts might be excessively differentiated from one another, thereby lacking all connectivity, and therefore separated and dispersed, without any cohesion (*prthak*). These boundaries were overly rigid, preventing all interaction between parts and producing cosmic chaos. See Smith (1989: 50–69) for an extensive exposition of these ideas.

11. Just as deities descend through levels and boundaries of cosmos, transforming their shapes and their relevance to cosmic process, so in theory can humans transform themselves into lesser deities in their own right (cf. Parry 1985).

12. The Sanskrit term maya derives from the same Indo-European root as the Greek term *metis* (Burrow 1980). These terms have much resonance. Metis refers to cunning intelligence. In versions of cosmology, Metis was a primordial female deity. Among the connotations of metis are fast or incessant movement, swiftness, mobility, shimmering sheen, the power of metamorphosis, and multiplicity. Gods and humans endowed with metis were able to dominate (perhaps manage?) uncertain, fluid, rapidly changing situations (see Detienne and Vernant 1978: 5–23). In varieties of Hinduism (for example, Shaivism), maya is understood as female.

13. More so than lila, maya enables the existence of the paradoxical relationships between the transcendent and the immanent deity, who is simultaneously one thing and another. Thus, a Sanskrit text (*Brhadaranyaka Upanisad*, 2.1.20) metaphorizes creation as the spider who weaves the world out of and around itself. Shulman (1985: 167) commented, "the god is both the source and the victim of the creative process of weaving a world, maya, in all its beauty and its entangling danger."

14. The Durkheimian legacy has left two powerful analogies of systemic functioning: the machine and the living organism. Both are misleading if used in conjunction with the concept of the self-transforming system. Machine and organism both depend on functional relationships between parts or organs that exist as permanently defined, autonomous entities. The variability of relationships among parts or organs constitutes the dynamism of these systems. Needham (1965: 540) compared the Hindu universe to a perpetual-motion machine. The analogy is partial. Despite the prominence of the body as a microcosm in Indian thought, the self-transforming system must break itself down in order to reconstitute and endure. The equiva-

lent, in terms of machine and organism, would be of one part turning into another—something like a wheel turning into a lever, a heart into a stomach.
15. The architect's name is transliterated as Maya, meaning *maker*. This is not related etymologically to the transformative power that is transliterated as maya.
16. In this kind of self-transformative cosmic framework, experiential contrasts between ritual and play begin to break down. In varieties of Hinduism, ritual as the repair of the world may be infused with playful moments or may be framed playfully. In abstract terms, these playful moments signify more the operation of cosmic processes and less their subversion. I would add these emendations to my own contrasting of play and ritual (Handelman 1977; 1987b); and I would emend Henricks (1980) in a similar vein, arguing that his position has more validity in relation to Western perspectives but requires modification in relation to play in self-transforming cosmologies.
17. During the past two decades, an increasing number of scholars have pointed to the significance of ideas of processuality in Indian life. Thus, stasis is undesirable (Das 1985; Kapferer 1983 [on Sri Lanka]; Ostor 1980); personhood, relationships, and matter itself are all perceived as fluid, shifting, and mutable (Daniels 1984; Marriott 1989: 17–18) while relationships between humans and gods are more continuous (Parry 1985). Even Dumont's (1970) seemingly rigid structuralism is relevant here, given his great insight that a hierarchical system based on difference (he discussed caste) is extremely flexible, elastic, and internally expandable, so long as hierarchical relationships are maintained continuously throughout the system. None of these studies conceptualize processuality as play, yet qualities of play are very close to an ethos of processuality that informs much of the recent scholarship on India. Process as play, and play as process, are embedded deeply not only in cosmology but also more indirectly in Indian cultural ideologies.
18. Even within the carnivalesque world created by Rabelais, the most playfully subversive is more a bottom-up phenomenon. Thus, although both Gargantua and his son Pantagruel are bottom-up characters, the circumstances of their respective births point to the production of the playfully subversive as more bottom-up. Gargantua cannot exit naturally through his mother's birth canal and must find another aperture. Forced higher (against his will, one might say), he emerges through her left ear (Putnam 1955: 69)—in other words, through her head. For all his excesses, he becomes a scholar and subsidizer of a utopian, humanistic community. Covered in fur, Pantagruel is born from his mother's belly, killing her in childbirth (Putnam 1955: 237). Pantagruel is even more subversive than his father. Within the entirety of this carnivalesque world, the playful is graduated in increasing degrees of subversion, from top to bottom—in keeping therefore with Western monotheisms. I am indebted to John McClelland for pointing me to these births.
19. I take issue with the view that the development of Protestantism was a necessary condition for the emergence of play as subversion and resistance in Western cosmologies (cf. Norbeck 1971; Turner 1974). Though this was a significant contributing factor, such conceptions of play are associated more with cosmologies that are not self-transformative and that include Western monotheisms, as these developed long before the Reformation.
20. See Miller (1970). This is no less so for scholars of performance who endow play with universal meanings of seduction (see Schechner 1988).
21. In discussion, Beverly Stoeltje raised the question of whether top-down and bottom-up play could be related to the gender of cosmic principles or deities. Though the issue is important, I can only offer some brief thoughts. I associated top-down play with self-transformative cosmic systems, which are approximated by varieties of Hinduism. Hinduism has highly elaborated goddess traditions in which the female may be understood as ultimate reality. In the post-Vedic *Markandeya Purana* (fifth to sixth centuries CE), the male deity is described on occasion as an emanation of the female (Coburn 1985: 80). More radically, the goddess is described as encompassing her own female principle (Coburn 1985: 137, 147) and, one may add, as being complete in herself. This suggests that there may be greater interchangeability of male and female

in self-transformative cosmic systems (this seems to be so in varieties of classical Hinduism; cf. Zimmer 1972: 123). If play is integral to such systems, this will be activated as easily by female principles as by male, and top-down cosmic play need not be gender specific.

Compare this to the ruptures in Western monotheisms between creativity and cosmogenesis (the preserve of male deity) on the one hand, and procreativity and reproduction (a female preserve) on the other (Weigle 1989: 60–61). This division of labor is hierarchical (high/low, spiritual/earthy), and there is little interchangeability of deity in terms of gender. One should ask whether there is any tendency to identify bottom-up play with female figures (or with inversions of the male). Consider, too, the thirteenth-century Gugliemites who envisioned salvation through the female—with female cardinals under a female pope, the vicaress of a female Holy Spirit, incarnated in order to establish a new Church. The sect was exterminated by the inquisition (Wessley 1978).

References

Bakhtin, Mikhail. 1968. *Rabelais and His World*. Cambridge, MA: MIT Press.
Bateson, Gregory. 1972. "A Theory of Play and Fantasy." In *Steps to an Ecology of Mind*, 177–93. New York: Ballantine.
———. 1980. *Mind and Nature: A Necessary Unity*. New York: Bantam.
———. 1988. "Play and Paradigm." *Play & Culture* 1: 20–27.
Buckley, Anthony D. 1983. "Playful Rebellion: Social Control and the Framing of Experience in an Ulster Community." *Man* n.s.: 383–95.
Burke, Peter. 1978. *Popular Culture in Early Modern Europe*. London: Temple Smith.
Burrow, Thomas. 1980. "Sanskrit MA—'To Make, Produce, Create.'" *Bulletin of the School of Oriental and African Studies* 43: 311–28.
Camporesi, Piero. 1988. *The Incorruptible Flesh: Bodily Mutation and Mortification in Religion and Folklore*. Cambridge, UK: Cambridge University Press.
Coburn, Thomas B. 1985. *Devi-Mahatmya: The Crystallization of the Goddess Tradition*. Columbia, MO: South Asia Books.
Colie, Rosalie L. 1966. *Paradoxia Epidemica: The Renaissance Tradition of Paradox*. Princeton: Princeton University Press.
Czikszentmihalyi, Mihaly. 1974. *Beyond Boredom and Anxiety*. San Francisco: Jossey-Bass.
Daniels, Valentine. 1984. *Fluid Signs: Being a Person the Tamil Way*. Berkeley: University of California Press.
Das, Veena. 1985. "Paradigms of Body Symbolism: An Analysis of Selected Themes in Hindu Culture." In *Indian Religion*, ed. Richard Burghart and Audrey Cantlie, 180–207. London: Centre of South Asian Studies, School of Oriental and African Studies.
Dessigane, R., P. Z. Pattabiramin, and Jean Filliozat. 1960. *La Legende des Jeux de Civa a Madurai*. Pondichery: Institut Francais d'Indologie.
Detienne, Marcel, and Jean-Pierre Vernant. 1978. *Cunning Intelligence in Greek Culture and Society*. Sussex: Harvester Press.
Dimock, Edward C. 1976. "Religious Biography in India: The Nectar of the Acts of Caitanya." In *The Biographical Process: Studies in the History and Psychology of Religion*, ed. Frank E. Reynolds and Donald Capps, 109–17. The Hague: Mouton.
———. 1989. "Lila." *History of Religions* 29: 159–73.
Dumont, Louis. 1970. *Homo Hierarchicus*. London: Paladin.
Eliade, Mircea. 1964. *Shamanism: Archaic Techniques of Ecstasy*. New York: Pantheon.
Frye, Northrop. 1980. *Creation and Recreation*. Toronto: University of Toronto Press.
Gadamer, Hans-Georg. 1988. *Truth and Method*. New York: Crossroad.
Gilhus, Ingvild Salid. 1990. "Carnival in Religion: The Feast of Fools in France." *Numen* 37: 24–52.
Gleick, James. 1988. *Chaos: The Making of a New Science*. London: Cardinal.

Goffman, Erving. 1974. *Frame Analysis*. New York: Harper and Row.
Gurevich, Aron. 1988. *Medieval Popular Culture: Problems of Belief and Perception*. Cambridge, UK: Cambridge University Press.
Handelman, Don. 1977. "Play and Ritual: Complementary Frames of Meta-communication." In *It's a Funny Thing, Humour*, ed. Antony J. Chapman and Hugh C. Foot, 185–92. London: Pergamon.
———. 1981. "The Ritual-clown: Attributes and Affinities." *Anthropos* 76: 321–70.
———. 1987a. "Myths of Murugan: Asymmetry and Hierarchy in a South Indian Puranic Cosmology." *History of Religions* 27: 133–70.
———. 1987b. "Play." *Encyclopedia of Religion* 11: 363–68.
———. 1990. *Models and Mirrors: Towards an Anthropology of Public Events*. Cambridge, UK: Cambridge University Press.
———. 1991. "Symbolic Types, the Body, and Circus." *Semiotica* 85: 205–25.
Hawley, John S. 1981. *At Play with Krishna: Pilgrimage Dramas from Brindavan*. Princeton: Princeton University Press.
Hein, Norbert. 1987. "Lila." *Encyclopedia of Religion* 8: 550–54.
Henricks, Thomas S. 1980. "Ascending and Descending Meaning: A Theoretical Inquiry into Play and Ritual." *Sociological Inquiry* 50: 25–37.
Hiltebeitel, Alf. 1987. "Gambling." *Encyclopedia of Religion* 5: 468–74.
Hofstadter, Douglas R. 1980. *Godel, Escher, Bach: An Eternal Golden Braid*. New York: Vintage.
Hughes, Patrick, and George Brecht. 1984. *Vicious Circles and Infinity: An Anthology of Paradoxes*. Harmondsworth: Penguin.
Huizinga, Johan. 1970. *Homo Ludens: A Study of the Play Element in Culture*. London: Paladin.
Johnson, Willard L. 1980. *Poetry and Speculation of the Rg Veda*. Berkeley: University of California Press.
Kapferer, Bruce. 1983. *A Celebration of Demons: Exorcism and the Aesthetics of Healing in Sri Lanka*. Bloomington: Indiana University Press.
Kinsley, David R. 1975. *The Sword and the Flute: Kali and Krsna, Dark Visions of the Terrible and the Sublime in Hindu Mythology*. Berkeley: University of California Press.
Lannoy, Richard. 1971. *The Speaking Tree: A Study of Indian Culture and Society*. London: Oxford University Press.
Le Roy Ladurie, Emmanuel. 1979. *Carnival: A People's Uprising at Romans, 1579–1580*. New York: George Braziller.
Lincoln, Bruce. 1986. *Myth, Cosmos, and Society: Indo-European Themes of Creation and Destruction*. Cambridge, MA: Harvard University Press.
Long, Charles H. 1987. "Cosmogony." *Encyclopedia of Religion* 4: 94–100.
Marriott, McKim. 1989. "Constructing an Indian Ethnosociology." *Contributions to Indian Sociology* n.s.: 1–39.
Mechling, Jay. 1989. "Morality Play." *Play & Culture* 2: 304–16.
Miller, David L. 1970. *Gods and Games: Toward a Theology of Play*. New York: Harper Colophon.
Miller, Jeanine. 1985. *The Vision of Cosmic Order in the Vedas*. London: Routledge & Kegan Paul.
Napier, A. David. 1986. *Masks, Transformation, and Paradox*. Berkeley: University of California Press.
Needham, Joseph. 1965. *Science and Civilization in China*. Vol. 4, Part 2. Cambridge, UK: Cambridge University Press.
Norbeck, Edward. 1971. "Man at Play." *Play, a Natural History Magazine Supplement* (December): 48–53.
O'Flaherty, Wendy Doniger. 1973. *Asceticism and Eroticism in the Mythology of Siva*. London: Oxford University Press.
———. 1984. *Dreams, Illusions, and Other Realities*. Chicago: University of Chicago Press.
Ostor, Akos. 1980. *The Play of the Gods: Locality, Ideology, Structure, and Time in the Festivals of a Bengali Town*. Chicago: University of Chicago Press.

Parry, Jonathan. 1985. "The Aghori Ascetics of Benares." In *Indian Religion*, ed. Richard Burghart and Audrey Cantlie, 51–78. London: Centre of South Asian Studies, School of Oriental and African Studies.
Putnam, Samuel, ed. and trans. 1955. *The Portable Rabelais*. New York: Viking Press.
Schechner, Richard. 1988. "Playing." *Play & Culture* 1: 3–19.
Shastri, Prabhu Dutt. 1911. *The Doctrine of Maya in the Philosophy of the Vedanta*. London: Luzac.
Shulman, David D. 1985. *The King and the Clown in South Indian Myth and Poetry*. Princeton: Princeton University Press.
Slaate, Howard A. 1968. *The Pertinence of Paradox*. New York: Humanities Press.
Smith, Brian K. 1989. *Reflections on Resemblance, Ritual, and Religion*. New York: Oxford University Press.
Thibault, George, trans. 1962. *The Vedanta Sutras of Badarayana, with the commentary by Sankara*. New York: Dover.
Turner, Victor W. 1974. "Liminal to Liminoid, in Play, Flow, and Ritual: An Essay in Comparative Symbology." *Rice University Studies* 60: 53–92.
Weigle, Marta. 1989. *Creation and Procreation: Feminist Reflections on Mythologies of Cosmogony and Parturition*. Philadelphia: University of Pennsylvania Press.
Wessley, Stephen E. 1978. "The Thirteenth-Century Guglielmites: Salvation Through Women." In *Medieval Women*, ed. Derek Baker, 289–303. Oxford: Blackwell.
Whitehead, Alfred North, and Bertrand Russell. 1927. *Principia Mathematica*. Cambridge, UK: Cambridge University Press.
Yusa, Michiko. 1987. "Paradox and Riddles." *Encyclopedia of Religion* 11: 189–95.
Zimmer, Heinrich. 1972. *Myths and Symbols in Indian Art and Civilization*. Princeton: Princeton University Press.
———. 1984. *Artistic Form and Yoga in the Sacred Images of India*. Princeton: Princeton University Press.

CHAPTER 7

FRAMING HIERARCHICALLY, FRAMING MOEBIUSLY

Author's Note

A preliminary version of this chapter was prepared as a response to the presentations of a panel on "Reframing *Naven*" at the Annual Meeting of the American Academy of Religion in 2009. This was an opportunity to rethink lineal framing. Lineal framing, to which we are so accustomed in the most mundane of ways, separates absolutely and definitively between one side of the frame or boundary and the other, for example, between outside and inside. Whereas in Chapter Six, I argued for examining the interior of the frame itself in order to find clues to passage through the boundary, in this chapter I suggest that in certain, perhaps in many instances, the idea of lineal framing and its making of neat order should be put aside entirely. I was invigorated by the thinking of Steven Rosen (a polymath in his own right) in his *Science, Paradox, and the Moebius Principle* (1994) which gave me the impetus to think moebiusly on framing. To think with what Rosen (2006) calls post-mathematical topology. Thus I understood that if a frame is constituted through self-entering moebius movement then one can do away with the ideas (that deeply informed Bateson's thinking) that a frame must be lineal; that passage through a frame must require metacommunication and meta-organization; and, so, that the organization of framing must be hierarchical. This opens to framing that is interactive, and, as such, to more fuzziness and indeed messiness in how framing relates to realities.

More than twenty years earlier I used a more structural approach to understanding what the appearance of sacred clowns within ritual accomplished. I suggested then that the paradoxical interior of the sacred clown resonated with the interior of the boundary, foretelling the argument that is Chapter Six of this volume. In the earlier study I understood that sacred clowns were intimately involved in moving ritual within itself through itself, thereby shifting ritual from one phase into another by themselves revolving within themselves through their own contradictory and oppositional attributes (Handelman 1981). However, thinking moebiusly, I later concluded (Handelman 2009) that rather than the interior of the sacred clown being composed of structural oppositions this self-same interior of the clown was more fluid and dynamic. Thus it was this fluidity that was homologous with the fluidity of the moebius-like boundaries within the ritual. And, so, it was this homology of fluidness that enabled the sacred clowns to pull one phase after another into and out of the ritual. In Chapter Seven I extend this thinking to the interior organization of cosmos, contrasting cosmos that is intra-grated within itself more through fluid moebius-like movement and interior transformation to cosmos that is more inter-grated by monothetic hierarchies whose ultimate ordering is actually outside cosmos itself. I expand on this argument in Chapter Eight of this volume.

Prelude

I am taking a roundabout way in thinking about Gregory Bateson's theory of framing. This enables me to foreground certain of my own positions. Bateson's approach to framing had great personal impact on me in the late 1960s. Doing my PhD thesis in anthropology on face-to-face interaction in small work groups, I discovered that emerging realities of play and game were crucial to comprehending the daily goings-on in these settings. Bateson's idea of metacommunication gave me insight into how realities like play and ritual could be entered because they were constituted sometimes as radically different within everyday realities, Bateson gave to the idea of framing a complexity that had not existed beforehand and that (apart from Erving Goffman [1974]) has hardly existed since, yet who could have expected Bateson to be simply commonsensical and matter-of-fact? In anthropology at the time, framing was hardly mentioned analytically.

I eventually realized that Bateson's play frame, and his framing as this could be applied to ritual, is itself composed of logical paradox. Indeed, the paradox *is* the frame (see Chapter Six), and without the paradox there is no such frame. Or, we can say that the metacommunication of paradox is itself the frame. For Bateson, metacommunication is critical to the organization of framing, and the metalevel necessarily operates hierarchically and more abstractly. This is clear in the theory of schizophrenia he developed with Jackson, Haley, and Weakland (Bateson 1972: 203–78). The lack of a hierarchical metamessage develops in the victim a kind of terminal chaos within which communication is all "noise," all self-disrupting, all self-negating. The celebrated idea of the double bind results from oscillation between opposing values that are destructive because they are not organized hierarchically and that therefore are self-negating (I love you / I hate you). If this oscillation were hierarchized, then one of these values would become the metamessage, subordinating the other, and, so, the system of self-other communication could stabilize.

In Bateson's (1972: 184) diagram of the play frame, the metacommunication "All statements within this frame are untrue," should not be (as he places it) inside the rectangular frame. More accurately, "All statements within this frame, etc." should be written as the frame itself, because it is this (truth) claim that invokes the paradox that is the framing. "This is play" is a further direction in which the frame may be taken, given the paradox of crossing into this kind of reality. Perhaps there are others. If the metacommunication itself is the frame, then the frame must be in hierarchical relationship to its "sides," to what it frames on the one hand and to what it leaves outside on the other. Logical paradox—the higher level in this instance—acts as a block to passage through itself (Colie 1966). The paradox both creates and separates realities. The solution to passage is to change values (perceptions, emotions) that belong to one side to those that are regnant on the other side. With this shift, the paradox-as-block disappears and/or one finds oneself on the other side (though I'm not so certain of this).

In Bateson's pathbreaking cybernetic analysis of *naven* behavior in the epilogue to the 1958 edition of *Naven,* his use of feedback to analyze social setups gave me a tool to think on rituals that do radical change within and through their own interior organization, and to separate these out from events that could be discussed straightforwardly as presentations and representations of sociocultural orderings. In turn this made me realize that basically collecting together all "ritual" events under the rubric of RITUAL, even when they had little or nothing in common, is not just pointless but indeed detrimental to comprehending these occasions (Handelman 2006a). This was the impetus for writing *Models and Mirrors* (Handelman [1990] 1998), which argued that there will be no progress toward a general theory of ritual until the term "ritual" itself is thrown out and other ways of thinking are encouraged. I mention this here because at the time that I took to the idea of metacommunication as a universal property of framing and interactivity, basic to analyzing play and ritual, I began to think on South Indian Hindu cosmologies with my colleague, the Indologist David Shulman, and to do fieldwork in South India on goddess rituals. Then my perspective changed little by little.

For one thing, the status of logical paradox of the Epimenides variety came into question as did, together with this, the premises of linear framing. Logical paradox abounds in India, yet mostly as something perhaps to be noted as curiosity and largely disregarded. My own understanding of logical paradox as blocking passage, as acting as a trap for mind and perception (Colie 1966), seems to have little or no cachet in India. While such paradox blocks Westerners from moving through to elsewhere, for Indians paradox itself is a forming or shaping of potential reality to be played with and perhaps appreciated (O'Flaherty 1984). Through India the idea of metacommunication also came into question, sometimes. David Shulman is fond of saying that in

India the elephant does not precede the footprint that it leaves behind. Rather, first the footprint appears, followed by the elephant, coming into being and presence—in Western terms, the effect appears before the cause. To put this another way, cause and effect exist simultaneously, and entireties appear entirely, together, so that distinguishing between signifier and signified, and thereby addressing their relationship (which is at the heart of the idea of symbol, of representation and of symbolic analysis), just doesn't play. Of course this relationship can be forced to cooperate, but this is indeed just that, forced, and somehow not true to the rituals I observed and had a hand in discussing, in which the symbolic as representation loses its authenticity (Handelman 2014). So, too, in the cosmic logics which historically influenced these and other rituals (i.e., Handelman and Shulman 1997, 2004). This is not simply to relativize these matters but rather to insist that great variabilities and uncertainties open up, that I doubt can be addressed deeply and profoundly in terms of existing theories of ritual, so long as the habit of, the convenience of, and the investment in this rubric of RITUAL, with its great biases (especially those of representation), hold sway.

I also began to doubt the universality of metacommunication that, as I understand it in terms of Bateson, must be in a hierarchical relationship to the "content" of frames like those of play and ritual. My critique of Batesonian framing recognizes that levels are related recursively, reciprocally, though I may do this too implicitly. After all, Bateson thought with systems that were constituted through levels, through the reflexivity of second-order thinking, and so forth, and there is no Batesonian system without recursiveness and reciprocity among levels. Yet these are levels of increasing abstraction, and I had doubts about the neat hierarchical nesting of these levels of communication within one another in Batesonian formulations.

For Bateson, recursive cybernetic-like feedback loops (positive and negative) were critical to understanding how systemic or systemic-like properties organize cosmic and social orderings. In these terms, a feedback loop cannot describe itself, that is, it cannot be reflexive toward what it is and what it is doing, and therefore requires a higher-order feedback loop (above, and, so, external to the first loop) to do this, thereby correcting the activity of the lower loop, which communicates this to the higher loop. I will return to this in a moment. I also began to question the universalizing proposition that our understanding of reflexivity requires a perspective of externality or otherness which itself tends toward a clear-cut distinction between inside/outside, self/other. This claim, I venture to say, is basic to understanding reflexivity through the academic disciplines. In human setups and systems, reflexivity is critical, because on it depends the capacity to self-correct, to alter direction, to return and repeat, and so forth. Therefore reflexivity is central to Batesonian framing. Norbert Wiley (in Harries-Jones 1995: 250) puts reflexive organization in the following way (which Bateson himself accepted): "A reflexive hierarchy is an inter-relation between communicators and the same interrelation looked back at itself from an 'outside' vantage point. The notion of reflexivity always entails an ability of an intelligent being, or group, to 'get out' of itself in order to attend to itself."

At issue for me became whether there are alternative ways of conceiving framing that do not require the premise of meta-organization and its hierarchical, linear order, and that alter the relationship of framing to reflexivity.[1] It was in this spirit that I suggested moebius framing as a stimulus to thought, one that would not simply make order neatly between realities by separating them cleanly and meta-organizing the inside of the frame.[2] Rather, one that would open the way for mess and fuzziness in organization. This in the spirit of Bateson's first metalogue ("Why Do Things Get in a Muddle?") in *Steps to an Ecology of Mind* (1972: 3–8), appreciating "noise" in the setup that Bateson understood as desirable (unlike the cyberneticians), as "playful and creative"—as novelty that could lead to the creation of new patterns (Harries-Jones 1995: 113–14). Alternative dynamics of framing should bring forth the flexibility of organization and not simply its capacity to make linear order.

Moebius qualities helped me to understand just how taken-for-granted in Western thinking is lineal hierarchy and the role of the meta in this logic of organizing; and, so, just how significant logical paradox could be in such setups. Let me illustrate this in the following manner, which, in my view, has cosmic implications. Say we begin with a feedback loop. A feedback loop is relational. Common to Russell's Theory of Logical Types (if this is used as the basis for a cybernetic system) and to Batesonian thinking is that such a loop does what it does yet cannot describe itself or what it does. It is not self-reflexive. So, needed is a higher-order loop which encompasses the lower and describes what the latter does. This more abstract loop is necessarily both relational and reflexive about the setup. It is a relationship about a relationship. Yet, though the second loop does what it does, it cannot describe itself and what it does. Therefore a still higher loop is needed, and this third encompasses and describes reflexively what the two lower ones do, but it cannot describe itself. Even if we drop the transitive character of Russell's levels (as Jens Kreinath [2012] argues) and accept that the levels in Bateson's hierarchy are intransitive, interactive, and reciprocal (Harries-Jones 1995: 248), this emerging "system" contains the following problem: will it become self-limiting, as metalevels are piled atop one another? Moreover, will it become self-limiting yet not fully self-knowing (which would enable it to consciously change itself in systemic ways)? One way of self-closing and self-limiting is to create a metalevel as logical paradox. As such, the paradox itself becomes an impassable boundary that closes and turns the entire system back on itself.

Then it struck me that, looking from the opposite direction, top down, this is the elementary logic of organization of the surviving monotheistic cosmoses. The ancient Hebrew cosmos, the first of the surviving monotheisms, during a lengthy period came to postulate an absolute rupture, an utter discontinuity between God the creator and human beings, creating a binary of absolute difference yet similarity (God first created man in his image and then changed this similitude). God, the cosmic encompassment, is outside His cosmos, holding the entirety of cosmos together from outside itself. Human beings cannot penetrate the paradox that separates him/her from God. Within itself, cosmos is held together through *integration*, the relationships *between* its parts. The other surviving monotheisms modified this paradigm but basically remained within it. But the important point is that the monotheisms shattered the logic of cosmic organization that was (and still is in many respects) prominent among traditional and tribal peoples.

The late Galina Lindquist and I argue that so many of these tribal and traditional cosmoses are held together from within themselves, through the dense, intense, multiple, and overlapping connectivities of their interiorities. These cosmoses are held together through what I call *intra-gration*; they are quite continuous within themselves (absolutist binary distinctions are rare), organizing through multiple domains or planes rather than more discrete, clearly hierarchical levels. Indeed they may have no closure at all, no external boundaries, since they are held together from within themselves; and in these cosmoses logical paradox does not play the roles it has in the surviving monotheistic cosmoses. The creation and operation of these tribal and traditional cosmoses are more akin to autopoiesis (i.e., self-creation) and self-organization than they are to the metalevels of encompassment and disjunction of the surviving monotheisms.[3] (These arguments are developed in Handelman and Lindquist 2011.) Yet these traditional and tribal cosmoses are no less reflexive than are the surviving monotheistic ones, but the former are continuously self-entering, *and their reflexivity derives from this*, from their ongoing entering within their own interiorities. Self-entering moebius movement can be understood to *fold* into itself, to self-connect through itself, thereby describing itself self-referentially, yet without creating levels or binary distinctions between inside and outside. This actually relates to the potentiality for fractal organization in such cosmoses, but fractals that entangle or braid with one another rather than nesting neatly within one another on different scales.

An intra-grated cosmos invokes a holism quite different from a cosmos that is integrated through encompassment, one which continues to have binary distinction at its core, metaphysically and historically. Altogether, however, binary structure (*pace* Levi-Strauss) may be a limited case of organization through recursiveness. In the surviving monotheisms, binaries are foundational, and logical paradox that derives from binary organization has powerful stopping power when it becomes a hard-and-fast boundary that in the first instance is impenetrable to human being's attempts to interact directly with God (though of course there are both historical and present-day modifications to this). Yet, as I pointed out, in India what looks like a logical paradox and may be recognized as such *is* more a curiosity than a block to movement. There, in cosmoses and in many areas of ritual, binaries are irrelevant and symbolism as representation makes no sense.

This description of a cosmos that is intra-grated through the density and intensity of its self-entering recursivities and infra-connectivities, has moebius-like qualities, but this moebiusness goes deep, way inside and through and through. Unlike Yair Neuman (2003), I do not see that the self-entering self-enfolding dynamics of moebiusness, which may characterize setups that are held together by themselves, through themselves, are paradoxical. If we keep in mind that moebius dynamics are neither hierarchical nor structural, then they are not characterized by movement that . . . starts . . . stops . . . starts. . . . There is no "make a distinction" that creates sides, that creates a binary (the first step in G. Spencer Brown's [1969] influential treatise on a logic of emerging space), and that enabled, for example, Hegel's theory of the dialectic, and Louis Dumont's (1970, 1986) theory of holism as encompassment. Take away the binary and moebius movement that has one side that turns or twists into itself, and so that has two sides that are never two, becomes illuminating. More generally, the use of chaos theory by anthropologists (Mosko and Damon 2005) and other social scientists needs to recognize that the stop . . . start . . . stop . . . mentality of analysis which continues to distinguish between "structure" and "process" (and other similar distinctions) simply retards recognition of the dynamics that are the social and the cultural (Handelman 2007). The interior potentiality of moebiusness is relevant as well to how certain rituals may be framed, and to how deeply this framing goes. Linear framing may be shallow by comparison, lending itself more to distinctions between a frame and its content. The potentially deep framing of moebiusness may plumb interiority to depths that emerge elsewhere and differently, and in this sense their *raison d'être* may be metaphysical, as is that of numerous rituals that are intended to do transformation within and through themselves.

Moebius Qualities of Ritual Framing: Or Is Moebius Necessarily Paradoxical?

Jens Kreinath (2012) has done an exhaustive and stimulating rethinking of *naven*, arguing that Bateson's conception of framing is compatible with that of moebius framing, and adding the idea of fractal dynamics to discuss framing in the Iatmul *naven* "ritual." Kreinath opts for a universal logic of the phenomenon of boundary (as apparently did Bateson) and for the mathematical reasoning that enables this. Just about all discussions of "boundary" agree that it has two sides, one outside and one inside (see for example, Zerubavel 1991). In Bateson's terms the movement from outside to inside requires a higher, hierarchical level of abstraction, an encompassing metalevel, to accomplish passage. Recursively, the metalevel informs and is informed by the lower level. Kreinath agrees with Yair Neuman that the boundary (in Bateson's evocative phrasing) is a difference that makes a difference, "a paradoxical event." Bateson's thinking on the frame, "This is play," implies the paradoxicalness and dynamism of boundaries more generally.

Neuman introduces moebius-as-boundary in order to highlight the self-referencing paradoxical nature of the boundary generating difference. The moebius surface is paradoxical because mathematical logic demands this, and the phenomenological acquiesces: topologically the surface has one side; phenomenally it is a binary, an outside and an in-side. "Out" and "in" relate to one another such that phenomenally they are separate and distinct yet topologically they are one another. Here logical paradox generates dynamism in every crossing of the boundary which also reproduces the boundary as paradox.

Does the moebius surface necessarily have the qualities that Neuman and Kreinath ascribe to it? Must the moebius surface be a paradoxical form? For Neuman the phenomenological is cultural, and the topological, mathematical. Yet whose phenomenological culture axiomatically established the ever-presentness of a binary distinction resulting from the postulation of a linear boundary, and, so, its two sides (after all, Spencer Brown was a mathematician and a logician)? Is the phenomenological culturally subordinate to the topological, given that the latter claims the truth of its universalism, which the former cannot do (despite Merleau-Ponty)? I do not think that the moebius form must be paradoxical in relation to itself, despite mathematically being both one-sided and two-sided, two-dimensional and three-dimensional. If one looks at the surface from the outside, it curves into itself. Yet if one moves along the moebius surface from its inside, it appears flat and never seems to curve self-referentially, even as it goes elsewhere. Moving on this surface, one doesn't know if one is outside or inside since the surface is continuous within itself. We can say of the moebius surface that what goes around comes around . . . only differently.[4] One can argue that the moebius surface is relatively autonomous of its environment precisely because it is continuously self-entering, self-referencing, self-reflexive, self-processing. Yet it is *because* of these qualities that this surface is not paradoxical in relation to itself. The loops of the moebius surface are not hierarchical, higher abstractions of one another.[5] So they may be described as braiding with one another, thereby making their relationships both stronger and more complex, since they all hold together from within, through one another. Therefore moebius framing likely is more resilient in its self-integration than is lineal framing.

Moebius framing comes closer to opening into forms within ritual that entangle and braid with one another (Handelman 2006c). Consider the sequencing of phases within ritual. Is an act or event coming before or after another a matter of norm, program, and script, as such positioning is commonly described in ritual studies? Or is it the very practice of an act that brings into phenomenal presence an act that "comes after," as it were, yet that is already present (perhaps as potential) in the former as it emerges? An act shaping that which will come after itself even as it shapes itself into practice? An act that "hooks" itself into a future that becomes possible because the former is phenomenally actualizing itself? Those self-entering reflexive moebius qualities that enable passage into ritual—going around and coming around . . . but differently—may be no less the properties that enable the ritual to move into itself and through itself, shaping itself into its future so that what is "coming around" is no less present in what is "going around." The boundary between one phase and another *within* a ritual may be no less moebius in its dynamics than the boundary between the environment and the ritual. One can envisage some rituals as braids of moebius surfaces that self-enter and emerge further along or deeper into the braid. This kind of movement of the ritual through itself—this deeply interior quality of dynamism—generates the ritual and abjures the shift of one ritual phase into another as something like stop . . . start . . . stop. This entangling and braiding of ritual within and through itself is closer to what I called (in the previous section) intra-gration rather than in-tegration, to ritual creating and holding itself together from within itself through its own emerging phenomenal *integrity*, the very quality that makes a particular ritual the kind of phenomenon that it is. This is the significance of thinking of ritual as self-organizing. The idea of braiding, if it is ever developed, may well offer a very different take on classification through ritual, one closer to the polythetic and to Wittgenstein's (1953; see especially Saler 2008) idea of "family resemblance" and Vygotsky's (1962) of "chain complexes."

Kreinath (and Neuman) argue that there is a universal logic of framing that will be based in mathematical logic, itself a universal method of reasoning. I am of mixed mind though more doubtful than not. Moebius framing and lineal framing seem to be radical extremes, yet in a *field* of framings we hardly have begun to think on. Jadran Mimica (1988), who studies the Iqwaye people of Papua New Guinea, once said during discussion (in 1999 at the Israel Institute for Advanced Studies) that among them ritual is something like a "swelling" of aspects of everyday life, hardly an occasion on the other side of a binary set apart in order to act on social life, yet also not an event with the recursive complexities of moebius framing. Perhaps among the Iqwaye, ritual does what social life does, only more intensely (and densely) so? So perhaps the boundary of ritual among the Iqwaye is neither a linear frame nor a moebius one, but one located elsewhere in the field of framings? Bruce Kapferer argues in *The Feast of the Sorcerer* (1997) that the Sinhalese *Suniyama* exorcism creates the cosmos entirely out of itself since it contains the basic premises and the dynamics of the cultural order, which created the ritual, which creates the cultural order and its cosmos. A ritual intensely recursive, hardly lineal, possibly moebius in its framing, yet perhaps not, again located elsewhere in the field of framings.

Today I would think twice and more about turning play and ritual into a binary whose two sides complement one another, with play metacommunicating make-believe and ritual, truth. In Batesonian terms, as Engler and Gardiner (2012) point out, the binary would be organized hierarchically, with that of truth subordinating make-believe, which in turn subverts the former, especially when play (which I un-derstand more abstractly as indeterminacy) is located within ritual. The binary of play and ritual has an explanatory capacity, but it also is too overburdened. In the 1970s an ongoing issue in thinking on play was its relevance to sociocultural orders; and, for a few, the relevance of play to ritual phenomena. As it turned out, two major books (Spariosu 1989; Sutton-Smith 1997) marked the apex of play studies, which since then has turned primarily to Internet play (Danet 2001) and video games.[6]

The Fractal *Wau* in *Naven*

My understanding of *naven* behavior changes accordingly in the wake of Roy Wag-ner's (2001) discussion of the fractal person in Melanesia and Jens Kreinath's (2012) discussion of fractals. Previously I had argued that the *wau* (the classificatory mother's brother) playfully inverted himself in relation to his *laua* (the classificatory sister's son) and through this rebalanced this relationship which had been thrown out of kilter by the increase in status of the *laua* in relationship to his *wau*, because of the achievements of the *laua*. A neat solution through play to the instantaneous destabilizing of a crucial Iatmul social relationship. Today I would try to argue something like the following: faced with the accomplishment of his *laua*, the *wau* goes into himself and finds a fractal part of his distributed personhood which is entangled and shared with female kin, and in the full-blown dramatization of *naven* the *wau* acts out to others this aspect of his fractal being. This fractal part is him and it is also others. He does not turn himself inside-out or upside-down (both standard forms of inversion), but rather interiorly finds a part or part of others that is also part of his selfness and that is directly relevant to the *naven* context. In this sense, *naven* opens interiorly to others and this may be a movement that is more moebius-like yet closer to Melanesia. What looks like a binary inversion on the part of the *wau* is more like a non-linear re-assemblage of his person in relation to that of the *laua* and others. This could be understood through play as make-believe, yet this is no longer necessary since *the wau is not pretending to be other than he fractally is.*[7]

Though he alludes to this, Kreinath (2012) does not mention a fascinating fractal-like aspect of *naven* behavior—the way its forms condense and expand one another. This is the feature of *naven* behavior that persuaded me in the first instance that the fractal is relevant here. The most compact form of *naven* behavior is a single sentence—"Husband thou indeed" —which the *wau* utters (on hearing of the *laua's* accomplishment) in the absence of the latter, yet which condenses the core significance of what the *wau* is doing in *naven*. If the *laua is* present then the *wau* says the sentence, throws lime powder on his *laua*, and recites a list of his own descent group's genealogical names. I note here that these two forms are the least social in terms of the number of participants and in the spread of relationships that are affected by *naven* behavior, and this may be why Kreinath does not dwell on them, given his insistence that ritual must be social.[8] The third form is the fully fledged, with the *wau* constituted in evident detail through both male and female attributes, with the participation of multiple others (Bateson 1958: 84–85, 109, 111, 119, 259, 288). Bateson wrote that he did not really understand the first two forms until he had witnessed the full-blown one. The fractal-like nesting of scale here is hard to ignore, yet with the following proviso—the social fractal is two-way, it both condenses and expands into and out of itself. In this regard these fractal forms also may be thought of as entangled with one another, their choice dependent on social and contextual forms.

It is worth noting here that Wagner's conception of the fractal person in Melanesia is paralleled in another radical rethinking of cultural personhood, that of McKim Marriott's (1989: 1–39; Babb 1990) ethnosociology of India. Marriott thinks of the interior entirety of the person as continually reformed, reorganized, and nuanced through what I call intra-action with many others—persons, the earth he/she was born on, one's home, the constellations, and so forth. The substances of person, of all persons, move from the interior of one to the interior of another without necessarily becoming exterior (see, for example, Bar-On Cohen 2009 for a temporary setup of this sort). All of these beings (they are all alive) continually exchange elementary substances, thereby continuously altering their being in relation to one another (see Daniels 1984). They are deeply in-tangled with one another. Entireties here are first and foremost intra-grated rather than integrated, and the entirety of the person is, in a sense, cosmic, without going outside of itself. Though the fractal *wau* is unlike Marriott's understanding of Indian personhood, the former may be just as intra-active as interactive in *naven* behavior.

Kreinath (in press) uses the mathematical idea of random fractal dynamics to conceptualize the emergence of indeterminate factors emanating from unpredictable decisions of individual participants, which introduces uncertainty and contingency into *naven* interaction. The problem of emergence in social life is crucial to understanding the appearance of change in any social setup and is the key to one of Bateson's originary and brilliant concepts, schismogenesis, through which similarities, indeed identities in interaction, generate the emergence of difference, and differences in interaction generate similarity. Potentially, schismogenetic dynamics are open-ended and so do not surrender to the academic temptation and comfort to slip into a Hegelian dialectical mode whose processes generate the very parameters which self-constrain and limit the dynamics of emergence. Yet, apart from the value in thinking experimentally with such ideas, do we need random fractal dynamics to think about the indeterminacy of and the appearance in social life of emergent and unexpected properties? All interaction generates "noise" in Batesonian terms. Novel elements (regardless of how tiny) continuously appear, even as the great majority are disregarded and discarded, while a few are focused on and elaborated (Handelman 1977, 2006b; see too the Epilogue to this volume). Indeterminacy and the potential for change are always present. This brings us back to "ritual" and the making of change.

Naven as Social Ritual

Let's say for the sake of argument that all rituals are social, and so are relational. For example, for the anthropologist, Michael Houseman (and, I surmise, for Kreinath), ritual must be social, put together through the sociocultural and producing and altering social arrangements and social relationships. I think there is basic agreement on this among anthropologists.[9] Houseman's (2005) illuminating experimental ritual, "The Red and the Black," is very convincing in this respect. Houseman built into the design of his invented ritual the kinds of social changes he wanted it to produce among his students, and the design persuaded the students and did just this. Does Houseman's ritual do *trans-formation*, that is, the changing of one form of being into another, or does it more directly move that being from one category to another within a setup of classification? Changing a person from ill-health to improved health, or reviving an entropic cosmos, may not be only a matter of persuasion and performance, but of metaphysical alterations. The Jewish bar-mitzvah is a social ritual which confirms shifting a thirteen-year-old male from the social category of a child to that of an adult who is competent to fully participate in religious ritual. The change in category, in status, is profound, yet the ritual is a performance that only confirms what is already known; it does not directly trans-form the inner being of the youngster. On the other hand, the circumcision ritual—the cut that binds—done to a tiny male infant is trans-formative, since through a blood sacrifice (of a perfect form) the tiny male is de-formed by the cutting of the foreskin, de-created from God's image in which he was created, and re-formed in his de-creation as one forever bound as fully and only human to the Almighty, as one of His chosen people, a status he can never be fully rid of. The infant is related to socially as a Jew, yet elemental qualities in his self-constitution are understood to change unalterably through the ritual. He is potentiated for the future in a radically different way. The act of sacrifice is one of trans-formation, with the infant perhaps aware of this as shock and pain.

Naven behavior is social ritual first and foremost, and perhaps entirely so. It is ritual behavior that is wholly continuous with social life (perhaps as something like a "swelling," an accentuation and intensification of the social, as Mimica mentioned for the Iqwaye people).[10] This is emphasized even more if we accept that *naven* in its different forms is constituted at least in part through social fractals. The fractal is powerfully recursive and reproductive in its self-similarity, yet it is not trans-formative. *Naven* does rearrangement and recalibration of social relationships, but I do not consider these transformations since in them there is no radical change of one being or form into another. The fractal character of *naven* points to the continuousness of the *wau* with and among the fractal parts of his person. Random fractal dynamics may open ways to indeterminate change and perhaps to unplanned trans-forms, yet this is strongly discouraged in rituals whose phenomenal integrity depends on their interior design (nonetheless, see Kreinath n.d.). However, here is one example of what may be a random fractal dynamic in an unusual setting in which fractal-like forms seem to be prominent, taken from Sundar Kaali (2006).

In the region of Tanjavur in South India there are ritual enactments of the story of the demon-king, Hiranya, and his slaying at the claws of Visnu's avatara, the man-lion Narasimha. In one village these performances have taken an unusual turn in that all of the characters in the performance arena, with the exception of Narasimha/Vishnu, are doubled. There may be one cosmos in this performance or two, or perhaps a second is coming into existence; yet in any case something new has or is developing and the doubles seem to be fractals of one another, even as Narasimha/Vishnu holds all cosmos together from inside himself/itself. Because of a special boon, the demon-king cannot be killed under ordinary circumstances and he threatens the integrity of Vishnu's cosmos. Nonetheless the man-lion triumphs and cosmic entropy is reversed.

Especially interesting here is what did indeed happen during one performance. The defeat of the demon-king is usually demonstrated in performance by removing his crown and giving it to the man-lion. On this occasion, as Kaali notes, a performer of high status who was enacting Narasimha removed the man-lion's mask—his face, his being—at the climactic moment and brought it to the demon-king (apparently without knowing consciously why he did so), thereby announcing (but also in a way, generating) the victory of the demon-king over the god. This ending should never have happened, and it was corrected ritually; nonetheless the ending seemed a possible outcome, emotionally and logically, and one that, within the ritual enactment, had of course profound cosmic implications. In this ritual performance, within which a (perhaps random) fractal-like organization had developed, a random fractal suddenly emerged that threatened to entirely upset the logic of the cosmos being enacted ritually.

Framing and Depth

One of these issues is the depth of the frame. If for Bateson the metamessage constitutes the frame, then the depth of the frame is "thin" (as it especially would be in using set theory to discuss this). However, if the frame has moebius, braiding, or fractal qualities, the issue of depth becomes complex. For example, if a frame is constituted through self-entering moebius qualities, where do these "end" as it were? They may enter deeper into the ritual, connecting to, braiding with, boundaries and thematics within. There may be no clear-cut distinction between a metacommunicational feedback loop and information that is keyed to this, especially if the self-entering qualities of moebius also begin to self-organize. Thus it is worth considering the topology of homotopy.

Homotopy refers to two paths (or lines) that have the same points of start and the same endpoints but different ways of going from one to the other. The homotope contains different forms that coalesce between these points of start and the endpoints. Then there is smooth passage among these forms even though they are quite different in form and purpose. Put otherwise, two forms are homotopic if the deformation from one to the other is continuous (Armstrong 1979). A *common* example is the cup with a round handle that can morph into a doughnut, a torus, and back or likely elsewhere. These forms are quite different even though their smooth passages into and out of one another are related to their sharing only one hole in each, as do all the forms "in between," as it were.[11]

If one thinks that this idea is simply distant from anthropology and social organization, consider the pioneering study of Edmund Leach, *Political Systems of Highland Burma* (1954: 8–9). Leach argues that the Kachin peoples have two contradictory political modes of organization. One is the *shan* form, which is something like feudal hierarchy. The other is the *gumlao* form which is anarchistic and egalitarian. Most Kachin communities are neither one or the other, but rather that which Leach calls the *gumsa* form. *Gumsa* communities are unstable in their political organization: with favorable economic circumstances they shift toward the Shan form; with unfavorable ones, toward the *gumlao*. Despite the profound differences between *shan* and *gumlao*, Leach understands each Kachin community as a variant turning within itself toward one or the other; in homotopic terms, as paths or planes that have the same starting points and endpoints but that move on different lines between the two.[12]

Cleaning Up Bateson's Framing

In an enlightening essay, Steven Engler and Mark Gardiner (2012) are owed a debt for disentangling Bateson's framing from Russell's set theory; for emphasizing that the frame need not be paradoxical in Russell's sense; for explicating that there is no necessary hierarchy of frame that distinguishes "outside" from "inside"; and for arguing that "something" framed differently (i.e., play) should be considered in its own right and not as a "not-something," which reduces its truth value and makes it hierarchically subordinate to whatever that "something" is. As I see it now, that Batesonian frames can be confused with Russellian sets is a good reason to rethink framing. Their introduction of Frege and denotation in place of Russell and hierarchical Logical Types enables the nuancing of framings and their graduated entering into one another, or indeed their entanglements with one another. Undoubtedly, we can think of social life as constituted through numerous framings with persons *moving* through these frames in the courses of living. This was Goffman's (1974) later understanding of social life, in which experience of the interpersonal became laminated into its framings.

Engler and Gardiner's critique of the centrality that Bateson gives to Korzybski's map-territory distinction is important since again for Bateson this is the relationship between representation that lacks truth and reality that is truth. A character in the noir thriller, *Blindside* (Bayer 1990), says, "Photographs lie; diagrams tell the truth." Diagrams make no claims to truth, as photos (in the pre-digital photo age) often do. Diagrams can neither be real nor unreal since they purport to be nothing other than that which they are, selective abstractions that have no significance outside themselves (i.e., the diagram of the London Underground cannot be used to move around London outside of the Underground). Lewis Carroll (1893: 169) showed the absurdity in confuting the map-as-representation with the territory-as-real (the idea later was adopted by Borges). In *Bruno and Sylvie Concluded*, the interlocutor converses with Mein Herr on the value of maps. The interlocutor tells Mein Herr that the largest map considered useful is on the scale of six inches to the mile. Mein Herr responds with amazement, telling how in his country people tried a scale of six yards to the mile, then a hundred yards to the mile, and "then came the grandest idea of all! We actually made a map of the country, on the scale of *a mile to the mile!*" Asked whether this map has been used much, Mein Herr responds: "It has never been spread out yet . . . . the farmers objected: they said it would cover the whole country, and shut out the sunlight! So now we use the country itself, as its own map, and I assure you it does nearly as well." The absurdity is one of trying to do the representation (the map) of a normal territory which will be no different than the territory, yet which will be the not-territory because it is a representation which is intended to replace the territory but cannot because it is not the territory, but a representation of this. When the territory is used within itself as a guide to itself it does quite well, even if it is not an abstraction of itself.

Engler and Gardiner argue that if Batesonian framing is treated in Fregian terms as a denotative guide, then relationships within the frame are sense-making, relativistically, but not, or not necessarily so, outside the frame. In this regard, ritual as itself does not necessarily denote truth outside itself but makes sense within itself to itself—thus the Catholic priest, the wafer, and the body of Christ come together. This may be another way of arguing (though from very different premises than mine) that ritual is worth studying in its own right, in and of itself—that ritual should make sense to itself (see Chapter Three, this volume).[13] The denotative, guiding function of the frame is metacommunicative, but this too is relativistic—more or less distinctive, more or less explicit, more or less powerful, and so forth. In this regard, ritual need not be set apart from the everyday in a hard-and-fast way, but may be similar, for example, to what Mimica called "swelling." For that matter, "swelling" may well describe all the forms of *naven*, understood fractally.

For Engler and Gardiner, framing-as-map denotes where ritual is positioned in the world. They do not relate to the interiors of frames, of rituals. If I understood them correctly, they would argue that frames within ritual also are marked and guided by further denotative shifts into context. Yet missing from their formulations is any attention to *practice*, apart from the semantic (implying that rituals are context-sensitive grammars?). Perhaps too much reliance has been placed on the cognitive (and semantic) constitution of framing? Which in a way is "thin" framing, unlike the "thick" framing of moebius qualities of self-entering, which is that which rituals of trans-formation do? And that not enough reliance has been given to practices that bring a ritual into being and shape its self-forming and self-organization that may separate it from the everyday?

Conclusion

Bateson's holistic vision was cosmic and all-embracing. He proposed a universal logic of framing that was consonant with his understanding of the systemic organization of cosmos in its fullest sense. If we accept that cosmoses differed in their organization (and likely continue to do so, to various degrees) then it is not that Bateson's universalism fails in the face of relativism, but that human beings have created great variability in the metaphysics of their cosmoses, and of their rituals. There is no universal frame for "ritual." Generally speaking, there is not even a single more advantageous theoretical perspective to take on the framing of ritual. While this reflects the weaknesses of the category of "ritual," it nonetheless highlights the need to think empirically, abductively (in C. S. Peirce's sense; see Chapter Two), through a case-by-case approach to ritual framing. At present this is the intuitive way to go, since it is more likely to open to fruitful ideas for analyses of framing.

Utterly evident is that the understanding of framing as first and foremost cognitive is wrong-headed. Sensuousness and aesthetics (in the sense of practice, not beauty, [see Chapter Five, this volume]) are integral to ritual framing. To complicate this, if one takes a framing approach to ritual (and this is not self-evident or given), should one relate only to the frame as it relates ritual to the world around it? Or should one ask whether framing is no less important within a given ritual, whether it is constituted through phases, whether these, too, should be considered framed, and how it is that the ritual moves through them, frame after frame, frame within frame, frame entangled with frame? If so, we would have to ask whether the same kind of frame is consonant throughout the ritual.

Issues of framing within ritual come to the fore when rituals that do trans-formation within and through themselves are distinguished from rituals that are continuous throughout themselves. In the former, trans-formation may be predicated on making a kind of being or condition of being discontinuous while using cultural dynamics to create this form or condition differently, indeed perhaps as another form or condition of being. In the latter, rituals that are wholly social tend to rearrange, conform, and confirm social relations through representation rather than transformation. In *Models and Mirrors* (Handelman 1998: 47–48) I suggested a simple rule of thumb to check the distinction in ritual between trans-formation and representation: run the ritual backward (hypothetically, of course). In a ritual that does representation, running it backward may well produce a different cultural narrative, yet one that is viable. In a ritual that does trans-formation, say one of healing, running it backward is likely to produce the unviable, perhaps the deleterious, perhaps sorcery in place of healing. If framing is to be of increased value in studying "ritual," then we need to expand our sense of the multiplicity of framings that shape ritual phenomena from without and from within.

Notes

First published in 2012 as "Postlude: Framing Hierarchically, Framing Moebiusly," *Journal of Ritual Studies* 26: 65–77. Reprinted with permission of co-editors of *Journal of Ritual Studies*, Professor Pamela J. Stewart and Professor Andrew Strathern.

1. Making framing looser and more flexible is not a new issue. Framing in art is a case in point. The sixteenth-century portrait painter, Jan Gossaert, painted subjects with an empty picture frame behind them. He took them out of the picture frame and painted them more realistically, perhaps more true-to-life, warts and all. See his *A Young Princess (Dorothea of Denmark?)*, c. 1530. (The National Gallery, London), and his *The Children of Christian II of Denmark*, c. 1526. (The Royal Collection). Metaframing does not work for Picasso's cubist *Portrait of Jaime Sabartes as a Spanish Nobleman*, 1939. The portrait is usually understood as bringing together multiple external perspectives of vision as a simultaneity of the same face. I think that in this

work (and in many others) Picasso paints the face as it is in mundane motion, showing the dynamism of expressive movement that is within itself as face.
2. The moebius strip is a mathematical construct, yet its form and (perhaps its dynamic) are found in nature, for example in the circulation of the earth's warmer and cooler ocean currents. On the nano-scale, the moebius form has been created at Arizona State University ("DNA art imitates life: Construction of a nanoscale Mobius strip") using a variant of origami DNA, measuring less than a thousandth of the width of a human hair, and thought to have a variety of applications (Science Daily, accessed 16 August 2020 <https://www.sciencedaily.com/releases/2010/10/101004101530.htm>). At the opposite extreme of scale, astrophysicists using the Herschel telescope have identified a twisted ring of gas and dust at the center of the Milky Way galaxy, measuring something like six-hundred light years across. Called a twisted ellipse by the scientists, the ring includes some of the most active areas of star formation in the galaxy. At the center of the ellipse is a massive black hole. And, who knows, perhaps this gigantic twisted ellipse will turn out to have moebius properties ("Herschel telescope discovered twisted ring of gas and dust at the centre of our galaxy," World Socialist Web Site, accessed 16 July 2020 <https://www.wsws.org/en/articles/2011/08/ring-a05.html>).
3. Niklas Luhmann postulates that social autopoiesis refers to systems that differentiate themselves from their environments through their recursive operations, through their self-organization. Phillip Guddemi (2007: 914) dubs as "sympoietic" those recursive systems that do not bound themselves from their environment. In the case of cosmos, which is self-creating, intensely recursive, yet without boundaries, sympoietic organization might be relevant. In the case of rituals of transformation that do enclose themselves recursively, the autopoietic self-organizing sense is more relevant.
4. David Lynch uses this quality in his films, *Lost Highway* and *Mulholland Drive* (see Chapter Ten).
5. Perhaps it is because Kreinath takes Bateson's universal framing to be paradoxical and hierarchical that he does not understand why I did not so much abandon this formulation as look for alternatives that related with greater congruence to a variety of the empirical materials.
6. In this book, Sutton-Smith introduced the idea of "playfulness" with the intention of modifying emphasis on the abrupt discontinuity between "play" and the serious. In this respect, Engler and Gardiner are close to his position.
7. Gil Daryn's (2006) ethnographic analysis of a community of Nepalese Brahmins is one of the few detailed works in anthropology that actively uses the idea of the fractal.
8. Elsewhere I address the issue of "how social must ritual be?" (Handelman 2005b; and Chapter Three, this volume).
9. Houseman's approach to ritual has strong resonances with that of the social anthropologists of the Manchester School (founded by Max Gluckman) during the 1950s and 1960s (see Evens and Handelman 2006). The Manchester School utterly eschewed metaphysics in the understanding of ritual, concentrating entirely on social arrangements and relationships. One need only compare Gluckman's essay, *Les rites de passage* (1962) with his student, Victor Turner's discussion of rites of passage in his *The Ritual Process* (1969), after he broke with the Manchester insistence that all ritual was solely social.
10. Communication to the colloquium of the Research Group, "Narratives of Ritual," The Israel Institute for Advanced Studies, May 1999.
11. http://en.wikipedia.org/wiki/homotopy. Accessed 14 August 2020.
12. It is worth noting that Leach (1961: 7) was an early proponent in anthropology of thinking topologically.
13. The eighteenth-century empiricist philosopher, Bishop George Berkeley, felt fully the complete identity of the Father, the Son, and the Holy Ghost within the Mass and simultaneously the absence of this identity, indeed the distinctiveness of each from the others. Outside the Mass, as philosopher rather than believer, he concluded that the simultaneous presence of identity and non-identity was impossible.

References

Armstrong, M. A. 1979. *Basic Topology*. Maidenhead: McGraw-Hill.
Babb, L. A. 1990. "Social Science Inside Out." *Contributions to Indian Sociology* 24: 201–13.
Bar-On Cohen, Einat. 2009. "*Kibadachi* in Karate: Pain and Crossing Boundaries Within the 'Lived Body' and Within Sociality." *Journal of the Royal Anthropological Institute* n.s. 15: 610–29.
Bateson, Gregory. 1958. *Naven*. 2nd ed. Stanford: Stanford University Press.
———. 1972. *Steps to an Ecology of Mind*. New York: Ballantine.
Bayer, William. 1990. *Blindside*. New York: Signet.
Carroll, Lewis. 1893. *Sylvie and Bruno Concluded*. London: Macmillan.
Colie, Rosalie L. 1966. *Paradoxia Epidemica: The Renaissance Tradition of Paradox*. Princeton: Princeton University Press.
Danet, Brenda. 2001. *Cyberpl@y*. Oxford: Berg.
Daniels, Valentine. 1984. *Being a Person the Tamil Way*. Berkeley: University of California Press.
Dumont, Louis. 1970. *Homo Hierarchicus: The Caste System and its Implications*. London: Abacus.
———. 1986. *Essays on Individualism: Modern Ideology in Anthropological Perspective*. Chicago: University of Chicago Press.
Daryn, Gil. 2006. *Encompassing a Fractal World: The Energetic Female Core in Myth and Everyday Life—A Few Lessons Drawn from the Nepalese Himalaya*. New York: Lexington Books.
Evens, T. M. S., and Don Handelman, eds. 2006. *The Manchester School: Practice and Ethnographic Praxis in Anthropology*. New York: Berghahn Books.
Gluckman, Max. 1962. "Les rites de passage." In *Essays on the Ritual of Social Relations*, ed. Max Gluckman, 1–52. Manchester: Manchester University Press.
Goffman, Erving. 1974. *Frame Analysis: An Essay on the Organization of Experience*. New York: Harper Colophon.
Guddemi, Phillip. 2007. "Toward Batesonian Sociocybernetics: From *Naven* to the Mind Beyond the Skin." *Kybernetes* 36: 905–14.
Handelman, Don. 1977. *Work and Play Among the Aged: Interaction, Replication and Emergence in a Jerusalem Setting*. Assen: Van Gorcum.
———. 1981. "The Ritual Clown: Attributes and Affinities." *Anthropos* 76: 321–70.
———. (1990) 1998. *Models and Mirrors: Towards an Anthropology of Public Events*. New York: Berghahn Books.
———. 1992. "Passages to Play: Paradox and Process." *Play and Culture* 5: 1–19.
———. 1995. "The Guises of the Goddess and the Transformation of the Male: Gangamma's Visit to Tirupati and the Continuum of Gender." In *Syllables of Sky: Studies in the Civilization of South India in Honor of Velcheru Narayana Rao*, ed. David Shulman, 281–335. Delhi: Oxford University Press.
———. 2004. *Nationalism and the Israeli State: Bureaucratic Logic in Public Events*. Oxford: Berg.
———. 2005a. "Introduction: Why Ritual in its Own Right? How So?" In *Ritual in its Own Right: Explorations in the Dynamics of Transformation*, ed. Don Handelman and Galina Lindquist, 1–32. New York: Berghahn Books.
———. 2005b. "Epilogue: Toing and Froing the Social." In *Ritual in its Own Right: Explorations in the Dynamics of Transformation*, ed. Don Handelman and Galina Lindquist, 213–22. New York: Berghahn Books.
———. 2006a. "Conceptual Alternatives to Ritual." In *Theorizing Ritual*, ed. Jens Kreinath, J. Snoek, and M. Stausberg, 37–49. Leiden: Brill.
———. 2006b. "The Extended Case: Interactional Foundations and Prospective Dimensions." In *The Manchester School*, ed. T. M. S. Evens and Don Handelman, 94–117. New York: Berghahn Books.
———. 2006c. "Postlude: Toward a Braiding of Frame." In *Behind the Mask: Dance, Healing, and Possession in South India*, ed. David Shulman and Deborah Thiagarajan, 248–64. South and Southeast Asian Series. Ann Arbor: University of Michigan.

———. 2007. "How Dynamic is the Anthropology of Chaos?" *Focaal: European Journal of Anthropology* 50: 155–65.

———. 2009. "Clowns in Ritual: Are Ritual Boundaries Lineal? Moebius-like?" In *Risus Sacer—Sacrum Risibile*, ed. Katja Gvozdeva and Werner Rocke, 307–25. Berlin: Peter Lang.

———. 2010. "Folding and Enfolding Walls: Statist Imperatives and Bureaucratic Aesthetics in Divided Jerusalem." *Social Analysis* 54: 60–79.

Handelman, Don, M. V. Krishnayya, and David Shulman. 2014. "Growing a Kingdom: The Goddess of Depth in Vizianagaram." In *One God, Two Goddesses, Three Studies of South Indian Cosmology* by Don Handelman. Leiden: Brill.

Handelman, Don, and Galina Lindquist. 2011. "Religion, Politics, and Globalization: The Long Past Foregrounding the Short Present—Prologue and Introduction." In *Religion, Politics, and Globalization: Anthropological Approaches*, ed. Galina Lindquist and Don Handelman, 1–66. New York: Berghahn Books.

Handelman, Don, and David Shulman. 1997. *God Inside Out: Siva's Game of Dice*. New York: Oxford University Press.

———. 2004. *Siva in the Forest of Pines: An Essay on Sorcery and Self Knowledge*. Delhi: Oxford University Press.

Harries-Jones, Peter. 1995. *A Recursive Vision: Ecological Understanding and Gregory Bateson*. Toronto: University of Toronto Press.

Houseman, Michael. 2005. "The Red and the Black: A Practical Experiment for Thinking about Ritual." In *Ritual in its Own Right Explorations in the Dynamics of Transformation*, ed. Don Handelman and Galina Lindquist, 75–97. New York: Berghahn Books.

Kaali, Sundar. 2006. "Masquerading Death: Aspects of Ritual Masking in the Community Theaters of Tanjavur." In *Masked Ritual and Performance in South India*, ed. David Shulman and Deborah Thiagarajan, 89–106. South and Southeast Asian Series. Ann Arbor: University of Michigan.

Kapferer, Bruce. 1997. *The Feast of the Sorcerer*. Chicago: University of Chicago Press.

Kreinath, Jens. 2012. "Naven, Moebius Strip, and Random Fractal Dynamics: Reframing Bateson's Play Frame and the Use of Mathematical Models for the Study of Ritual." *Journal of Ritual Studies* 26: 39–64.

———. In press. "Playing with Frames of Reference in Muslim Rituals of Saint Veneration: Random Fractals in Encounters and Interactions with Non-Human Agents Among Arab Alawites in Hatay." *Anthropological Theory*.

Leach, Edmund. 1954. *Political Systems of Highland Burma*. London: G. Bell and Sons.

Marriott, McKim. 1989. "Constructing an Indian Ethnosociology." *Contributions to Indian Sociology* 23: 1–39.

Mimica, Jadran. 1988. *Intimations of Infinity*. Oxford: Berg.

Mosko, Mark S., and Frederick H. Damon, eds. 2005. *On the Order of Chaos: Social Anthropology and the Science of Chaos*. New York: Berghahn Books.

Neuman, Yair. 2003. "Mobius and Paradox: On the Abstract Structure of Boundary Events in Semiotic Systems." *Semiotica* 147: 135–78.

O'Flaherty, Wendy Doniger. 1984. *Dreams, Illusions, and Other Realities*. Chicago: University of Chicago Press.

Rosen, Steven M. 1994. *Science, Paradox, and the Moebius Principle*. Albany: SUNY Press.

———. 2006. *Topologies of the Flesh: A Multidimensional Exploration of the Lifeworld*. Athens: Ohio University Press.

Saler, Benson. 2008. "Conceptualizing Religion: Some Recent Reflections." *Religion* 38: 219–25.

Spariosu, Mihai I. 1989. *Dionysus Reborn: Play and the Aesthetic Dimension in Modern Philosophical and Scientific Discourse*. Ithaca: Cornell University Press.

Spencer Brown, G. 1969. *Laws of Form*. London: Allen & Unwin.

Sutton-Smith, Brian. 1997. *The Ambiguities of Play*. Cambridge, MA: Harvard University Press.

Turner, Victor. 1969. *The Ritual Process: Structure and Anti-Structure*. Chicago: Aldine.

Vygotsky, Lev S. 1962. *Thought and Language*. Cambridge, MA: MIT Press.
Wagner, Roy. 2001. *An Anthropology of the Subject: Holographic Worldview in New Guinea and its Meaning and Significance for the World of Anthropology*. Berkeley: University of California Press.
Wittgenstein, Ludwig. 1953. *Philosophical Investigations*. Oxford: Blackwell.

Chapter 8

Inter-gration and Intra-gration in Cosmology

Author's Note

This chapter was prepared initially for a discussion on contemporary cosmologies at University College London in 2011. This discussion was an opportunity to expand further on the idea of an intra-grated cosmos, one that is held together more from within itself through itself, and that of an inter-grated cosmos that is held together from outside itself. I associate the first kind of cosmos more with tribal and traditional cultural orderings and the second more with monotheistic social orderings.

I argue counterintuitively that in cosmoses of the more open kind—held together within themselves, through themselves—there is less emphasis on the external boundaries of cosmos. On the other hand, monotheistic cosmoses are of the more closed kind, since they are held together from outside themselves by their creator God, all-knowing and surviving any destruction of the world He created. Here great attention is given to how cosmos is closed, separating human beings from the creator God who in large measure dictates rules for living a moral existence (perhaps especially so in Judaism). I go into some detail of a goddess cosmos in South India that is intra-grated (and analyzed in greater detail in Chapter Four of Handelman 2014). Moreover, I argue that cosmos should not be reduced to the social, and that this should be at the heart of cosmology and metaphysics, in a sense, to cosmology in its own right. This approach is largely abandoned by anthropologies which perceive, wrongly in my view, that by definition cosmos is closed and therefore out of sync especially with the movements of modernization and globalization.

Introduction

At the roots of what we call "religion" are values of *holism* (Handelman and Lindquist 2011). The late Galina Lindquist and I contended that such values were never extinguished during very lengthy periods in ancient and traditional worlds in which holism related first and foremost to cosmos, indeed to cosmos that hold itself together from within itself, through itself—as *intra-gration*.[1] This kind of cosmos was shattered primarily by the historical emergence of the monotheisms that shaped cosmoses that were "encompassed"—that were held together from outside themselves. These developments are associated with a lengthy period that Karl Jaspers called the Axial Age (See Bellah and Joas 2012; Robbins 2009; Thomassen 2010). Lindquist and I call this shattering of cosmos, in areas of the ancient world, the First Great Rupture of Cosmos.

Nonetheless, values of holism continued through modern Western worlds, as these values were lodged in what came to be called "religion," and still later in peoplehood, nationhood, statism, ethnicity, and not least in the individual (culminating in Foucault's idea of the care of the self).[2] In Part I, I explore relationships among holism and cosmos, stopping with the First Great Rupture. Following this, in Part II, I outline, through its rituals, a goddess cosmos in South India that, in emerging from itself as an ongoing dynamic, holds itself together from its interior. This exemplifies the idea of cosmos intra-grating holistically. I close with a discussion of this cosmic logic.

Part I: Holism and Cosmos

Louis Dumont understands holism (and individualism) as value through which the social is organized. Dumont (1986: 279) gives the following succinct definition of holism: "We call holist [holistic] an ideology [which he understands as 'value"] that valorizes the social whole and neglects or subordinates [the value of] the human individual."

I modify Dumont's formulation as follows: holism entails the *integrity* of the *entirety*, where the "entirety" may be any kind of human unit, and where these units are not necessarily bounded clearly (in the sense of being contained from their boundaries inward). The emphasis within an entirety is on *integrity*, which there are many different ways of accomplishing. I use integrity here in the sense of entireness, completeness, soundness. Integrity is related to integration. Integration refers more to parts added together to constitute a whole—so that in the first instance the connection between parts is additive—thus, an inter-gration through connections of betweenness. By contrast, my intention for integrity refers more to the synergistic relationships within and through the parts of a whole—thus, the connections between parts must be intra-relational, held together through their entirety. My interest is in how worlds are holding together through the metaphysics of the human, through the imaginaries of the human, where "world" may vary from the cosmic to the individual, even as, say, in modernity, religion becomes civil, political, national, secular, individualized, yet forming and re-forming around the globe, carrying their seeds of holism (Handelman and Lindquist 2011: 42–45). *Cosmos* here refers to the entirety of the phenomenal lived-space of all entities—human and other-than-human—the entirety of a world of all dimensions of existence.

Beginnings—Holistic Cosmos Held Together from within Itself

As noted, cosmoses may be distinguished broadly if crudely in terms of their logics of organization, between (1) those held together *largely* from within themselves and (2) those held together *largely* from their boundaries, from outside themselves. Cosmos held together from within and through itself applies primarily to a wide variety of archaic, traditional, and tribal cosmoses. Cosmos held together from outside itself is pertinent particularly to the surviving monotheisms.

In the English language there is no word I can find to describe how something is intra-grated from within itself through the self-integrity of its interiority, rather than from outside itself—an excellent monotheistic understanding of integration. In English (translated from the French) the word made prominent by Louis Dumont (1981) to describe how something—social, cultural—is held together from *outside* itself is "encompassment." My dictionary defines "encompass" (and "incompass") as, "to surround, to encircle, to include, to contain, to get in one's power." This kind of being-held-together is crucial to monotheistic cosmoses.

Yet consider the following dynamics of an ancient holistic cosmos of Mahayana Buddhism, that of the cosmos of the Chinese Hua-yen school of Buddhism from the seventh century CE (Cook 1972: 2):

> Far away in the heavenly abode of the great god Indra, there is a wonderful net which has been hung by some cunning artificer in such a manner that it stretches out infinitely in all directions. In accordance with the extravagant tastes of deities, the artificer has hung a single glittering jewel in each "eye" of the net, and since the net itself is infinite in dimensions, the jewels are infinite in number. There hang the jewels glittering like stars of the first magnitude, a wonderful sight to behold. If we now arbitrarily select one of these jewels for inspection and look closely at it, we will discover that in its polished surface there are reflected all the other jewels in the net, infinite in number. Not only that, but each of the jewels reflected in this one jewel is also reflecting all the other jewels, so that there is an infinite reflecting process occurring . . . . This is a cosmos in which there is an infinitely repeated interrelationship among all the members of the cosmos.

This relationship is said to be one of simultaneous . . . mutual inter-causality (which I read as mutually relational or indeed intra-relational).

Every jewel is the sole cause for the infinity of jewels, but simultaneously the infinite whole of jewels is the cause for every single jewel. In terms of beings, each . . . is at once the cause for the whole and is caused by the whole, and what is called existence is a vast body made up of an infinity of [beings] all sustaining each other and defining each other. The cosmos is, in short, a self-creating, self-maintaining, and self-defining organism . . . what affects one item in the vast inventory of the cosmos affects every other individual therein. (Cook 1972: 3–4)

The Hua-yen cosmos has no center, or, if there is a center, "it is everywhere. Man certainly is not the center, nor is some god" (ibid.: 4). Note that the Hua-yen cosmos has no external boundaries, unlike the absolute, virtually impassable boundary between God and human beings to which the surviving monotheisms have accustomed us to as natural and commonsensical. The Hua-yen cosmos is not enclosed from outside itself, in contrast to our understanding of the kind of holism suggested by Dumont's idea of "encompassment."

The absence of boundaries in the Hua-yen cosmos is attested to by the emphasis on the infinity of intra-relationships that in a strong sense *are* this cosmos. This cosmos holds itself together through its intra-relationalities, the very densities and textures of these connections creating a thick mesh of intensities of mutual being. This kind of cosmos lives wholly through itself—within which human being and other-than-human are thought to be alive and interactive.

The Hua-yen cosmos is *continuous within itself*. Continuousness here is graduated between levels and among domains without necessarily abrupt shifts or ruptures between human beings and other-than-human. Cosmos is hierarchical yet flowing, with an utter abhorrence of *stasis*. I contend that a continuousness of cosmos is generally immanent, *not* transcendent, since continuousness is primarily self-referential, referring to nothing outside itself (See Jacobsen [1976] on ancient Mesopotamia), without implying in the least that cosmic continuousness indexes harmony and an absence of fragmentation (though it may index ongoing self-creation—autopoiesis and self-repair from within itself).

Analogous descriptions of organic cosmos with the qualities I ascribe to this abound for a host of tribal cosmologies. Without romanticizing this, tribal cosmologies had integrity: these were and are cosmoses that were true to themselves within themselves, held together from within themselves through the densities, intensities, and textures of the fullness of intra-acting connectivities with deep resonances between deities, human beings, other beings, and the continuousness of their shared cosmos. In my terms, in such cosmologies *holism is only sometimes dependent on cosmic closure*. Indeed, much of the historical and ethnographic evidence points to holistic cosmologies that are open.

With regard to the eventual emergence of Western cosmology, two great ruptures of holistic cosmoses developed historically. The first emerged during what is often called the Axial Age; while the second, the separation of politics from religion, sometimes referred to as the Great Separation (Lilia 2007), formed through the deep rupture in Western European Christian culture provoked, in particular, by the Protestant Reformation, beginning in the sixteenth century. Monotheistic cosmos, forming through the first rupture, contained the beginnings of a foundational break with itself, within itself.

The First Great Rupture: The Axial Age

The cultural loci of these radical ruptures in cosmic organization are usually given as Greece (of the philosophers), Palestine (of the Hebrew prophets), Iran (of Zoroaster), China (of Lao-tse), and India (of the Buddha). The most persuasive instances are those of ancient Israel and Greece (but only of the *philosophes*). The rupture of cosmic holism severed the graduated continuousness of cosmos, such that the other-than-human separated from the human. This separation enabled that which scholars call "transcendence" to emerge within cosmos. On the other side of the rupture, Deity became unknowable to human being, positioned way beyond the capability, capacity, and knowability of the latter. How were human beings able to relate to the now transcendent divine?

The rupture created the other-worldly transcendence of the gods. God and gods were no longer of this world, even of this cosmos. God and gods become the absolute creators of cosmos rather than living within and integral to it, no longer sharing with human beings the substances from which cosmos was constituted. This is where the idea of encompassment comes in.

My Axial Age concern here is with what the historian of religion Jan Assman (2008: 75) calls the "revolutionary monotheism" of ancient Israel, and how this indelibly changed the logics through which cosmos was held together. The emergence of monotheism eventually came to posit the absolute separation of God the transcendent Creator from humankind. God crossed this chasm at will; yet, human beings might cross it only through prayer and sacrifice. Frankfort and Frankfort (1963: 241–44) argue that, "The God of the Hebrews is pure being, unqualified, ineffable. He is *holy*. That means he is *sui generis* . . . . It means that all values are ultimately attributes of God alone . . . . Only a God who transcends every phenomenon . . . can be the one and only ground of all existence." Herewith and underlined is the contrast between a cosmos that holds together from within itself through itself, and the emerging monotheistic cosmos of the Hebrew God who is boundless, infinite, unnameable, unfathomable, creating His finite cosmos as one ruptured from himself.

Given the absolute boundary between God and the human, the ancient Hebrew cosmos became held together from its exterior by the transcendent God whose eternal existence did not depend on that of his finite cosmos. The integration of this cosmos depended on its being *encompassed* by God, by his moral injunctions. As noted, cosmos acquires exteriority through the cosmic rupture, and so the capacity to be encompassed by transcendent deity. The rupture of the intra-grated holistic cosmos led to the creation of another kind of holism, that of the monotheistic, in which

God holds his cosmos together from its boundaries, while his primary positioning is outside his creation. Basically, he is independent of the cosmos of his creation whose parts are inter-grated. The monotheistic cosmos turned the perfection of the human being into the divine purpose of the universe, while setting before human being the goal of organizing the world into one that was truly, exclusively, and solely human. For as various scholars (e.g., Bruno Latour) have commented, in the worlds that eventually derived from monotheism, most living beings who were other-than-human were either killed off, reduced in their communicative capacities with humans, or, treated as inert, were no longer perceived as living.

So far, I have referred in the abstract to cosmos that holds itself together through the densities and intensities of its own interiority. Now I turn to a goddess cosmos in South India to introduce one variety of how such a holistic cosmos might work. I do this in brief using ritual events through which the goddess—Paiditalli, the Golden Lady—forms and re-forms as she changes herself and her cosmos.[3]

Part II: The Fluid Cosmic Logic of the Goddess Paiditalli

The venue of the following discussion is the small city and former kingdom of Vizianagaram in northeastern Andhra Pradesh. Culturally, Vizianagaram is in the region called Kalinga, and Vizianagaram shared cultural themes with other previously extant little kingdoms (e.g., neighboring Bobilli), some of whose kingship-related rituals have been studied by anthropologists in Puri (Apffel-Marglin 1981, 2008) and Jeypore in Orissa (Schnepel 1996, 2002), and Bastar in Madhya Pradesh (Gell 1997). With all the hubris entailed, I will attempt here to take something of the perspective of the goddess.

Paiditalli's story and her relationship to the kingdom of Vizianagaram begins in the eighteenth century. In January 1757, Vijaya Rama Raju, the Raja of Vizianagaram, aided by French irregulars led by the adventurer Charles de Bussy (who held a *farman* from the Padshah in Delhi to collect taxes in the Kalinga region), set out to war with Bobilli.[4] In the foundational myth of Paiditalli, the younger sister of the Raja, Paidimamba, pleaded with him not to go to battle, saying nothing good would come of it. Vizianagaram was victorious, Bobilli destroyed, and yet that very night the Raja was killed in his tent by the greatest hero of Bobilli. Hearing of his death, overcome with grief, Paidimamba hurled herself into a lake close to Vizianagaram and drowned. Before entering the waters, she said she would return, and her death was self-sacrificial. Later she appeared to fishermen and told them to dive and find her image. She emerged from the depths as the goddess, Paiditalli, onto the hard, flat surfaces of the land. Her shrine, called the Wilderness Temple, was erected close to the lake. Later, a second shrine, called the Square Temple (echoing the square mandala according to which the old city was built), was located in the vicinity of the palace-fort of the Raja. Paiditalli had returned with the explicit aim of protecting and aiding kingdom and kingship. She resides roughly half the year in the Wilderness

Temple and half in the Square Temple. The climax of her yearly return is a great Jatra (festival; literally, movement)—the Sirimanu—through which a people's version of kingship is renewed.

The cosmos of Paiditalli is radically different in its logics of organization from those of most other South Indian deities as they are discussed in the literature. This goddess cosmos is characterized by dynamism, by interiority, by depth, by fluidity, and by hardness, yet by a somewhat different sense of hierarchy than that which one might expect in India.

Paidimamba, the Raja's sister, left the brittle flatness of the land and went into depths of water. The fluid is replete with itself, extremely dense, leaving no interior emptiness, no holes, without boundaries in itself, and in continuous movement within itself. The sister rose from the depths of fluidity as the goddess, Paiditalli, emerged onto the surface that she had left. The land of the surface is dry and thin, its features fixed in form and perhaps in place, organized by the linearity of rule, of law, rectilinear (its spaces cultivated and ordered in different ways), and constituted in terms of temporal distinctions and movement that are formed through starts and stops, often through counted durations. Yet surface must have the fluid (water) to survive. This hardened surface is that of the animate and human world which of course is integral to Paiditalli's cosmos. Yet this world is that of the surface of Paiditalli's interior fluidity. Surface, then, exists because it is the flattened, hardened, rigid, encrusted portions of Paiditalli's cosmos. And these rigid portions are fragile (Handelman and Shulman 2004). When fluid rises on this surface, the latter becomes softer, more malleable, and more tensile, amenable to being shaped to awaken fertility and growth upon which humankind depends.

Though Paiditalli desires to help humankind in its struggle on the inhospitable surface of her cosmos (though humanity can exist nowhere else) this is not the location where she is most at home to herself, most fully herself. Her fluidity, her deep interiority, is self–intra-grating through its never-ceasing dynamic movement which continuously permeates itself. Deep within herself is where she is most true to herself as herself. Thus, as she approaches the surface of her cosmos, one can say that her transition is severe (though likely not abrupt—her cosmos is continuous, as is she within herself). And it is here, on her hardened, fixed surface of selfness (so unlike her true selfness) that human beings use ritual to affect and effect this transition as gently as they can, to bring her once more to perceive human needs, to re-awaken her desire to aid the people of Vizianagaram, their kingship and king.

The highest degree of *intra-gration* in Paiditalli's cosmos is deep within herself, within her infinite depths (which have no center) where she is most fully herself, uninterrupted, undivided, wholly dynamic. The lowest degree of intra-gration is near or on the surface of her cosmos, in the animate world. Here rituals aid or enable the presence of the goddess to become form, phase by phase. In doing so she quickens life in the encrustation, infusing this with the dynamism of reviving growth. Rituals are the primary if indirect source of thinking on Paiditalli's cosmos.[5]

I turn briefly to the ritual phases through which Paiditalli annually emerges into form, moving from formlessness within her own deep interiority into her own shallows, from which she wades ashore to where the human dwells, and where shaping and self-shaping through ritual begins and continues, until and then after its climax.

Devara Pandaga Ritual: The Birth of the Goddess on Her Cosmic Surface

This ritual cycle begins near the end of the hot season (usually in May), broken by the coming of the monsoon. The hot season is blazing and extremely dry. In the past this was the primary period of disease and epidemic, and goddesses in South India are often the bringers both of the extreme heating of disease and its healing, its blessed cooling. The *devara pandaga* ritual takes place on the shore of the lake where in 1757 the king's sister drowned herself and emerged as Paiditalli. In the stillness of the deep night, her priest and his two helpers enter the waters. On shore, in clusters here and there, are gathered devotees of the goddess. The priest and his helpers address the goddess, pleading with her to come, cajoling her, yet also as time passes cursing and insulting Paiditalli in efforts to arouse her from her depths. Sometimes this is a difficult birth, taking hours; yet sometimes it is easier and quicker. Nonetheless Paiditalli often resists coming, and then when she does appear it is with force, in anger at being disturbed deep within her fluid depths.

All await a sign of fire in the dark sky. Eventually a spark appears, perhaps heat lightning, which is seen as falling into the water. The priest and his helpers grasp handfuls of mud from the lake bottom even as they fall unconscious with the force of the anger of the goddess's coming, and they immediately are dragged ashore, their fists clenched around oozing mud. The priest sees in the mud the two colors that are the essence of the Goddess (and of the female in general). One is gold, the color of turmeric (*pasuppu*), and the other, vermilion, the redness of *kunkum*. In her coming, Paiditalli joins together the basic elements of cosmos: fire (the lightning), air (through which she passes), water (the lake from which she emerges), and earth (the mud within which her essence rests). She comes as an infant re-born. Women on the shore immediately feed her and ritually protect her in her openness and helplessness in the animate world. I call the goddess in this form, Mud-Paiditalli; within the mud she is relatively labile, fluid, amorphous, perhaps still closer to her own depths. Nonetheless the initial shaping and hardening into form is occurring, and her fluidity lessens as she takes on form. Simultaneously, Paiditalli brings the depth and density of cosmic interiority and fluidity to the hardness, dryness, and brittleness of the human world, softening this, making this more malleable to reshaping, and, so, more suitable for the deeper potential of fertility and growth, as the monsoon rains come.

Mud-Paiditalli is placed in a *jangidi*, a winnowing basket. The basket's concave inner surface has been rubbed intensively with golden-colored turmeric. In the center of the basket is a largish circular bed of vermilion *kunkum* surrounded by white flowers. On the bed of *kunkum* is a circular lamp filled with camphor, in which is a lit, long wick and a raw mango. The whole basket is formed as female. The winnowing basket is rubbed with turmeric as is the face of an auspicious married woman after her morning bath. This intensifies her femaleness and gives this greater depth, greater density and self-resonance. The basket is marked with a dot of vermilion *kunkum*, as is the female forehead—intended to ward off any untoward forces in the vicinity. In Andhra the winnowing basket is strongly associated with the womb and female fertility (Handelman 2014), and the mango with the vagina and the birth of goddesses.

Thus: face within the womb, vagina within the face, a lit lamp on the forehead, a mark of respect and worship. The newborn amorphous infant is placed simultaneously deep within the female form (the *jangidi*) yet also on its intensified (and therefore deeper) surface, from which she will continue to emerge and mature in the human world. The female turns into and through herself, interior becoming more exterior, exterior becoming more interior. Autopoietically, the goddess gives birth to herself, first in the lake and then on shore, at the water's edge, in the winnowing basket. Coming from deep within herself, she is placed deep within herself on the shore of the hardness of the human world, into an exterior womb on the surface of the human world, an exterior womb that is no less a cradle, one designed for the human forming of the female—which is how the winnowing basket has been prepared here. The goddess gives birth to herself without ever leaving herself, which speaks to the depth and density of her cosmos. In this sense she is permitting human beings to shape her for their need to create depth and life within the flatness of civilization. She is quiet now, a slumbering infant.

Dawn breaks, and the winnowing basket is carried in procession from the lake into the city, to the Square Temple some hundreds of meters from the palace-fort of the Raja. In the climactic ritual of this renewal of kingship, the goddess will move between her Square Temple and the palace-fort.

The Goddess Becomes Womb

Within the inner sanctum (*garbha griha*) of the Square Temple, Mud-Paiditalli is divided into clumps which rejuvenate metal pots of the goddess that have been taken out of storage. Fifteen days later the dried mud is carefully put back into the lake, and two, new, spheroidal pots (made from lake-bottom clay) are placed in the inner sanctum where for the next months (through August) they absorb the energies and female qualities (turmeric and *kunkum*) of the infant from her permanent metal pots. Her amorphousness is curved, the energies are curving, the curvature enclosing itself with her energies within this: Paiditalli enclosing herself within herself. The two clay pots are a virginal womb for and of the goddess, her own form within which she matures and evolves. Mud-Paiditalli turns herself into Pot-Paiditalli. She herself is described as "innocent," as prepubescent. In effect, the goddess is moving from womb to womb, from the lake of her origins to infancy in the wicker basket to her own pre-existing metal pots to her own clay pots shaped especially for her on this occasion. Each womb is a locus of depth on the superficial surface of the human world. Even as her form acquires a measure of solid presence, she continues flowing within herself. She is the Golden Goddess and in South India gold is the solid that is the closest to the fluid.

Just as Paiditalli's movement from womb to womb opens depth and softness in the hard, shallow surface of the human world, so, too, does the growing of rice, the food staple. The maturing of the goddess within the Square Temple parallels the growing of rice in the rural fields outside the city. Farmers perceive powerful parallels between the growth of the rice plant and female pregnancy. The paddy is planted in a rice-plot (*aku-madi*), a corner of the larger field. Around the end of July, the sprouts are removed and transplanted into the larger field. Around this time, Paiditalli transplants herself from the mud into the metal pots. Inside the plant the pannicle buds begin forming, shaping what is called the "little stomach," akin to the first signs of pregnancy. By late August, as the rice stomach grows very visibly, the two, empty, clay pots that are Pot-Paiditalli, daily begin leaving the Square Temple, going into the Old City of Vizianagaram. While the rice-plant flowers, its female and male reproductive organs are pollinated together by the wind. The flower turns into seed and develops a quasi-protective hull that fills with liquid (starch and protein). As the flower falls away, this milky fluid is visible. Farmers say that "the flower becomes pregnant with milk," proof that the soft, green seed is a viable offspring. The plant is successfully pregnant within itself as the seeds develop and is heavy with rice as it bends back and down, ready for harvesting.

The annual rice cycle in the region of Vizianagaram is related intimately to the opening of space and depth—in seeding, in the extrusion of shoots, in the ploughing of furrows and filling them with water, in the transplanting, in the protrusion of the stomach in the extruding plant, in the forming of the milk-pregnancy, and in the birth of the mature turmeric-colored rice. The dynamics are those of interiority exteriorizing itself and emerging onto the softened, now receptive, indeed welcoming, surface that is the human world. The dynamics of exteriorization are primarily female, generating new life from within life. This is Paiditalli's purpose on the surface of her cosmos.

Pot-Paiditalli Furrows and Sows

During the period that stomach, flower, and milk pregnancy appear in the rice plant, the clay pots of Pot-Paiditalli leave the Square Temple most evenings during August and September and go through Old Vizianagaram, street by street, alley by alley. This is the first phase of Paiditalli's evolution that is marked less by her interiorization within womb-like structures and more by her bringing her fertility, her womb, to human beings. Now she is actively moving into the thin hardness of a kingdom in need of softening, depth, fertilization, and healing. As she goes from home to home, Pot-Paiditalli is met by family members, especially women, who place their offerings in the pots and ask for the goddess's blessing. This worship, night after night, street after street, is akin to *furrowing* the surfaces of the city, opening space for the depth of presence of the goddess within home after home. So, too, one can think of these movements of the goddess as sowing the coming of kingship in every corner of the *furrowed* mandala of the Old City. The climactic harvesting will occur during the Sirimanu, as the king is brought anew to his palace-fort, renewing this intra-grative core of the kingdom.

The Tevadam Rite: Paiditalli Sprouts from the Earth

As the sowing of the city nears completion during the second half of September, Paiditalli reappears, now growing in a Tamarind tree (*cinta cettu*) some 40–45 feet high, in the midst of paddy fields.[6] At the beginning of October, Tree-Paiditalli is carefully, ritually, taken out of the earth, and on to the city where she rests quietly in a street close to her priest's home until the Sirimanu Jatra some ten days later. In contrast to Mud-Paiditalli, Tree-Paiditalli demands to enter the human plane of her cosmos, to sacrifice herself once more (being cut, severed, injured). This is her most prominent exteriorization of herself within her cosmos as she forms herself as thoroughly solid and lineal in shape, with powerful linear directionality (unlike the recursiveness of the pot). She is the goddess evolving further, her cosmos preparing to harvest and deliver kingship within the Old City, energized and prepared by Pot-Paiditalli. Unlike her precursors, she is her own shrine, independent of any fixed location. Utterly self-aware, she extrudes and protrudes into the human world within herself.

From her top, four slender pieces are sliced away, with one given a crude visage. Three are the head-body of Paiditalli and her arms, yet no less the head-body of her younger brother, Potu Raju (the Buffalo King). The fourth is also Paiditalli. In the priest's yard the vehicles for the Jatra are being assembled. Foremost is the Sirimanu carriage (*ratham*) itself which will carry Tree-Paiditalli, enabling her to swivel up and down or to rotate. To her top will be slotted, and in this way fixed there, a seat and footrest. As the Jatra nears, Tree-Paiditalli is intensified and self-intensifies through offerings and sacrifices, her tree-body rubbed with turmeric, red rings of vermilion traced round her girth, camphor lamps placed along her entire length which is caressed over and over.

In other rituals the night before the Jatra, the Potu Raju qualities of Paiditalli (the three-piece) are nurtured (indeed treated as an infant) even as she becomes more she-he, her-him. Potu Raju is the generic younger brother of the goddess in South India. Where the Goddess is present, his presence is ubiquitous (Biardeau 2004), considered her guardian and protector. Yet now the goddess, her cosmos, contains him, and he emerges from, is cut from her so that their relationship and presence is fuzzy-minded (and likely felt fuzzily in ways that people cannot articulate), and they infra-lap (rather than overlap) even as they separate. Both are one and the one is the goddess within herself. In effect, Paiditalli gives birth to her younger brother as she does to the entirety of the cosmos.

The Surimanu Jatra: Tree-Paiditalli Carries the King Home

A small city bursting with visitors: perhaps three to four hundred thousand persons have come to Vizianagaram to see the Sirimanu. Tree-Paiditalli's length is again rubbed with turmeric and she is taken by ox cart to the Square Temple and there mounted on her carriage. Her priest wears the white, silken finery of a raja (and given to him by the son of the last Raja of Vizianagaram), the raja's turban on his head. He is garlanded and receives turmeric and vermilion. Tied with new saris into the seat, with one hand he holds tightly onto the fourth sliver cut from her head even as she carries him throughout the journey. In his lap, wrapped in a silk cloth, is the three-piece, the other three slivers cut from her head, who are Paiditalli—Potu Raju, the goddess, and her younger brother.

With a great cry, a wave-like sigh from the assembled, Tree-Paiditalli lifts her priest high in the air at a 45-degree angle and swings him in an arc of 180 degrees. This great raising and heightening of space is the opening of the *depth* of the kingdom by Tree-Paiditalli, harvesting its capacities for creativity and growth sowed and rejuvenated by the goddess. King and kingship *sprout* from Tree-Paiditalli into her priest, the receptacle formed to receive them within the human world. Tree-Paiditalli and her entourage make three journeys from the Square Temple to the palace-fort and back. The first is climactic, carried high on the surging waves of the crowd's emotions. During each successive round there is less overt excitement, the waves subsiding, becoming gentler, gentler. Yet there is no lessening of enthusiasm and more a sense of increasing fullness, repletion, and quietude as a difficult, lengthy journey nears its completion. As the sun sets with the third return of Tree-Paiditalli to the Temple, the Sirimanu ends.

From the human perspective the priest is possessed by Paiditalli. From Paiditalli's perspective—if I may be allowed the hubris of this extrapolation—she absorbs him fully into her interiority so that he becomes part of her greater depths. The new saris are her, tying him into her, dressing him, enclosing him so that he is held next to her as a mother would carry an infant in front of her. From this perspective the world of Vizianagaram is an exteriorization from within the cosmos during this period when Paiditalli comes closest to exteriorizing herself in this way. And it is within herself that the king sprouts into the priest becoming the raja, the priest who *is* the raja, just as the raja is no less the slain brother of the younger sister who drowned herself and became a goddess and who has a younger brother who emerges from her. The priest-turned-king sprouts from within the interior of the goddess as she brings him to his palace-fort, the sovereign center of the kingdom. In this sense the autopoietic goddess brings the king out of herself into her own exterior, *into an extension of herself* that is still herself and, within this, into the kingdom of Vizianagaram that she has sown and grown with her blessings. In a profound sense, within herself she gives birth to the king, her brother—or to her brother, the king. Put otherwise, the king slips out from the goddess just as Potu Raju emerges from his sister. Now older sisters both, younger brothers both.

The Uyyala Kambulu Ritual: Paiditalli Swings Away to the Wilderness Temple

All post-Sirimanu rituals are intended to quiet, soothe, and please Paiditalli, to make her softly sleepy. The two weeks after the Sirimanu are felt as a spooky period of betwixt and between, a post-harvest lull, perhaps a time of cosmic dissipation. A swing is erected outside the Square Temple. Some parts are from an old Sirimanu carriage. In effect the swing is another vehicle (*ratham*) for Paiditalli, yet a fluid, modulating version of the Sirimanu carriage. After these two weeks, aspects of the goddess are placed on the swing which is referred to as a cradle. From the apex of her maturity in the human world during the Sirimanu, Paiditalli again moves toward infanthood, moving deeper into herself, involuting, withdrawing from the encrusted, superficial, human part of her cosmos into her fruitful depths. Her priest speaks of Paiditalli now as a young girl, and of the swinging as a lullaby. In the past the swinging away was more explicitly a *pavalimpu seva* ritual, one of putting the goddess to bed as is done every evening in her temples. Now she is swung away to her Wilderness Temple next to the lake, there going deeper into herself, into her intra-grated cosmos where she is said to sleep, to rest—into the fluid, dense, continuous, flowing depths of herself, where she remains from mid-October to mid-May, far from the thin, brittle, divided, and bounded world of humans, the world of kingdom and kingship.

Conclusion: Reflections on a South Indian Cosmic Logic

I suggested in Part I that, in an intra-grated cosmos, holism is only sometimes dependent on cosmic closure. Instead, these holistic cosmoses are open, rather than enclosed from their exteriors. So, how does Paiditalli's cosmos hold together—sort of topologically (and unrelated to the mathematics of topology)? This is something like trying to visualize the first nano-moments of the Big Bang before anything existed externally to whatever expands from, as it were, its inside.

Paiditalli's cosmos emerges from deep within herself, from fluid bottomless depths, from her autopoietic beginnings in the lake. Visualized, this is something like an inverted conus without a cap, which rises through itself to protrude above itself without leaving itself. The dynamic is from an inside without end toward a non-existent outside, without ever fully surfacing outside because everything continues to be inside, and then moving from the direction of a non-existent outside into inside, the cone-without-cap going into itself without end—while the actual shaping of these movements is done through ritual. Were I to look for boundedness to this intra-grated cosmos, where would I look? The liquid depths of innerness have no bottom. Neither does the cosmos have an exterior, an outside. Instead, in moving further outward from the deep innerness of great densities and intensities of ever-flowing fluidity, there is a hardening, a rigidifying, through which depth turns into encrustation. This may be called a surface, yet it is inside cosmos. This dynamic is cosmic process—the less deep slows and in slowing becomes encrusted with itself.

Thus cosmos is held together by shifts in concentrations of gravity from deep-within to less deep-within. As the intensity of deeper fluidity rises outward, the positioning of densities, of qualities of energy and fruitfulness, shift, softening the less-deep encrustations of the fluid that are the animate world of human beings. This dynamic reaches the apex of its own interiority in a concentration of gravity in the least deep-within during the Sirimanu in the merging of Potu Raju, king, and brother within the goddess at the very top of Tree-Paiditalli.

In Paiditalli's cosmos the encrustations of the fluid are entropic, a senescence of cosmos: these are the regions in which fluidity slows, encounters obstacles, dries out, losing the energy of the fertile and the fruitful, and, so, withers and dies. The rituals I have discussed drive this melting of crusted fluids of the as-if surface, the less-deep. Understood in this way, there are no boundaries to this cosmos, and even their formation toward outer-ness, into encrustation which is decay, cries out for their softening and dissolution.

This cosmos is fluid yet without boundedness, without encompassment, seemingly an impossibility, yet not so since existence-as-fluid is what there is, and this existence discovers its own currents within itself, the goddess within herself, the human within the goddess. Nonetheless this cosmos is not a closed system since it is unbounded, yet neither is it open since it includes everything there is. Similarly, calling this a porous system merely begs the question. One can say of course that this is merely a cosmos constructed through ritual and therefore illusory, and, so, minimally related to the realities of daily existence of human being. This leads into fruitless discussion on religion and social order (see Handelman and Lindquist 2011), and in the case of Vizianagaram also denies the profoundly fluid, involutional, cultural currents that emerged in the kingdom of Vizianagaram during the nineteenth century.[7]

The cosmos discussed here has powerful resonances with a medieval South Indian cosmos of Siva (Handelman and Shulman 2004). I briefly draw attention to this cosmos, thereby stipulating that it is worth thinking again on other South Indian cosmoses through time.

Siva, the great god, the creator of cosmos and its interior depths, is told that in the Forest of Pines there are sages who have forgotten him and instead seek enlightenment through severe ascetic practices. Siva goes to the faraway Forest where the sages practice their asceticism, accompanied by Visnu in his female form as Mohini. While naked ash-strewn Siva seduces the sages' chaste wives, ravishing Mohini arouses the sages from their asceticism with her sexual allure. When the sages become aware of what has befallen them and their wives, they curse Siva (whom they do not recognize) as a wicked, lascivious magician and plan to kill him. From their great sacrificial fire appear weapons one by one to attack Siva, yet he catches and tames each one and makes it part of himself (tiger, axe, elephant, deer, snakes, two-headed drum, the bleached skull of Brahma, etc.). Defeated, the sages recognize him as the great god and worship him once more. Then in the Forest he dances (as Nataraja, Lord of the

Dance) for the first time, desisting only as the cosmos, nearing collapse, terrifies all the assembled.

Siva is the all-knowing cosmos of his creation and he is affected by what transpires within it. He does not encompass his cosmos—this has no boundary—but he is anywhere and everywhere within it. He is the life principle of cosmos. His cosmos, though not liquid, nonetheless flows continually just as he does. The alternative—entropy, stasis—is the destruction of cosmos, of himself. Evident at the outset is that his quality of knowing has deteriorated, for he is unaware that the sages deny his existence and have become autonomous of him. In effect, part of his cosmos has congealed, hardened, fragmented, leaving cosmos, himself, diminished, less whole. After Siva and Mohini destroy the self-contemplation of the sages, the latter practice sorcery against Siva. Through this he discovers that he had lost significant attributes of his being, for the weapons they send against him are aspects of himself that fragmented from him as did the Forest—and he takes them back, completing himself again, softening the Forest back into himself, into cosmos as the sages worship him. Fully himself once more, he dances, and the dynamic is both that of destruction and creation, for the two are inseparable. Implicit in this is that Siva, like Paiditalli, must continually conserve his cosmos from its interior, finding those loci that are losing dynamism, freeing them from senescence that is entropy, so that again they are intra-related, held together from within. In both Vizianagaram and the Pine Forest there are powerful continuities though separated by hundreds of years, and in both instances cosmic work is directed to reviving human beings and their surround.

Paiditalli's cosmos (and that of the medieval Siva) are flowing, full of currents and shifting volumes of density, without boundedness. These cosmoses are highly systemic. Yet how can fluidity without boundaries be systemic? Would the question itself arise without one or another perspective that insisted on intra-gration rather than inte(r)gration, or without a perspective that eschews cosmos as container,[8] instead seeking dynamics? One interesting idea that emerges from thinking on "primitive" cosmos as intra-grating is that, without external containment (in the monotheistic sense), cosmos is not necessarily self-limiting but potentially can go on and on. If cosmos is characterized by fluid dynamics (which to my knowledge no monotheistic cosmos is) then the problematic of holding itself together is even more acute. However, if cosmos is less exteriorizing than it is interiorizing, plumbing depths rather than expanding through space (as, for example, encompassment and other ideas of hierarchical meta-organization stress), then holding together may be a problem of movement through other dimensions of which we are unaware or do not recognize. Consider that which transpires at the top of Tree-Paiditalli during the Sirimanu Jatra as the balance of fluid densities shifts toward lesser depth and sister, brother, king, and goddess all come together through the priest, or, more accurately, all go through one another so that they cannot be distinguished from one another.

So, perhaps, Paiditalli's fluid cosmos is held together through recursiveness, and this recursiveness is activated primarily by ritual. Paiditalli's essential being is fluid depth without end. Her natural condition of being is going deep into her own depths, becoming denser as she goes, distant from the congelation in her lesser depths. Left to her own nature, she would stay in her own depths and her human world would dry, harden, fragment. Ritual activates the recursiveness to shift the intensities of her densities toward the human world. Recursivity braids cosmos together through movement, though not through structure, unless one argues that structure itself is movement (i.e., Prigogine and Stengers [1984] on every thing existing through the movement of its own time because this is basic to its interior existence—and time, of whatever variety, is movement). Yet saying that recursiveness braids together a fluid cosmos through the very movement of recursiveness is nonetheless arguing that cosmos intra-grates itself from within since the entirety, fluidity, is recursive through and through.

In anthropology, studies like that of Paiditalli's cosmos demand rethinking movement, be it called process or dynamics. Victor Turner (1977) called for this long ago. There are attempts, for example, Daryn's (2006) use of fractals to discuss in stimulating ways a Nepalese Brahmin world, Roy Wagner's (2001) maddeningly creative use of the holographic worldview, and the worthy attempts to apply chaos theory in the chapters of Mosko and Damon (2005).[9] The latter volume would have been more potent had the contributors rethought "structure" as varieties of the temporal—perhaps "structure" as slow or very slow temporal processes—thereby avoiding the division of "structure" and "process" that inevitably demands "stops" ("structure") and "starts" ("process") which subvert the very dynamics proposed by chaos theory (Handelman 2007). Temporality (though less so linear time) may accomplish unification in a way that space (and structure) are less capable of, given that the latter tend to segregate and separate (Rosen 1994: 203–4).[10]

I said at the outset of Part II that my intention regarding the cosmos of Paiditalli is metaphysical. In sociocultural anthropology the usual approach to cosmology is to begin with the social, the cultural, and construct cosmos on these bases. What happens then is that the limning of cosmos tends strongly to *reflect* the social, the cultural, and rarely goes beyond this. Otherwise, fears of theology take over, and Western philosophies of the ontological, especially phenomenology, may be invoked to sidestep these worries. In his late, great work, *The Elementary Forms of Religious Life,* Durkheim came to the idea of effervescence to recognize that something critical to human existence is shaped by people together that cannot be reduced to the social (or the cultural), just as the social cannot be reduced to the individual. In my view, this kind of recognition is at the heart of the study of cosmology and its metaphysics. One can enter into cosmos in its own right and fruitfully discover different kinds of entirety.[11]

Notes

First published in 2014 as "Inter-gration and intra-gration in Cosmology," in *Framing Cosmologies: The Anthropology of Worlds*, ed. Allen Abramson and Martin Holbraad, 95–115. Manchester: University of Manchester Press. Reprinted with permission.

1. A neologism is necessary since the conception that informs it is foreign to standard English language usage.
2. In the perspective offered here, values of individualism are not antithetical to values of holism. Rather, more at issue are differences and shifts in scale that reorganize values of holism, rather than radical changes in value. In the Western individual (yet obviously not only) there continues the sense of an entity that holds together rather than fragments. My response to postmodern claims for the fragmentation of a unified self is that it has always been preferable, analytically, to speak of qualities of selfness rather than of the self (Handelman 2002).
3. For the fuller ethnography, see Handelman, Krishnayya, and Shulman (2014).
4. Narratives of this war are discussed in Narayana Rao, Shulman, and Subrahmanyam (2001: 24–92).
5. The surface is not uniformly hard. Lakes, springs, caves in the mountains, are all softer areas within the hardness. The human beings in these locales—fishers, hunters—resonate more naturally with the fluidity of the goddess. So, too, healers in their healing soften the rigidity of the surface.
6. The tamarind can grow beyond sixty feet. Its wood is hard and dense; its heartwood colored dark red, its sapwood yellowish.
7. After the 1757 debacle at Bobilli, Vizianagaram ceased being an expansionist kingdom and turned inward. In the nineteenth century this social involution produced a cultural florescence in the Telugu country. Under royal patronage, Vizianagaram became the most vibrant cultural center between Calcutta and Madras through creativities that engaged intensive introspection in language, tantric yoga, ayurvedic healing, and more. The cosmos of Paiditalli and the ritual cycle that activated this in the human world may have been another post-1757 shaping of this involution through popular ritual rather than through royal rites of renewal.
8. Leading to the oft misguided notion of linear framing and content within the frame (Handelman 2012; see also Chapter Seven).
9. My interpretation of McKim Marriott's (e.g., 1989) perspective on the exchange of substances in India among what I could call sentient cosmic particles (human and other) which continuously alter each other's interiority, influences the idea of intra-gration in everyday life. For example, the inter-action among persons in the West is understood—through phenomenology, self-theory, symbolic interactionism and the like—as an utterance or action that comes from one's interior self, moving to one's (often facial) exterior and is absorbed through alter's (often facial) exterior, entering alter's interior self, back and forth. What is related to goes outside of one and enters into another from the exterior, and so forth. With Marriott's general perspective on the exchange of substances in India, a quite different constellation emerges. Persons, the earth, one's home, are related through depths of movement (Daniels 1984), such that, rather than moving from depth (of self) to surface and over to another surface and into depth (of the self of another), the exchange of substances in India moves from the depths of the person directly to the depths of another, yet not only between persons but between person and house, between person and natal earth, and so forth (see Bar-On Cohen [2009] on accomplishing a related condition of being in karate). Extrapolating further, all of these cosmic particles are somehow related to one another through their insides, their depths, and the changing densities and intensities of these intra-relationships. Indeed, this is an intra-gration of cosmos in the everyday. As Babb (1990: 202) writes on Marriott's theory, "This is surely a possible world. Whether it (or something like it) is an actual world, a world conceptually and perceptually dwelt in by Hindus, is one of the most interesting questions yet raised in the anthropology of India."

10. Interestingly, as Allen Abramson notes, this connects to the late-modern physics of quantum theory (see Rosen 1994: 203–4, and, among quantum physicists, especially Bohm 1981). Abramson comments (personal communication) that the quantum cosmos goes on and on without closure and perhaps without reversing itself. In the case of a human cosmos like that of Paiditalli, recursive braiding (rather than closure) is accomplished through made ritual.
11. Or as the late Roy Wagner (2001) might have said, be discovered by cosmos in its own right.

References

Apffel-Marglin, Frederique. 1981. "Kings and Wives: The Separation of Status and Royal Power." *Contributions to Indian Sociology* 15: 155–81.
———. 2008. *Rhythms of Life: Enacting the World with the Goddesses of Orissa*. New Delhi: Oxford University Press.
Assman, Jan. 2008. *Gods and Men: Egypt, Israel, and the Rise of Monotheism*. Madison: University of Wisconsin Press.
Babb, Lawrence A. 1990. "Social Science Inside Out." *Contributions to Indian Sociology* 24: 201–13.
Bar-On Cohen, Einat. 2009. "*Kibadachi* in Karate: Pain and Crossing Boundaries Within the 'Lived Body' and Within Sociality." *Journal of the Royal Anthropological Institute* n.s.: 610–29.
Bellah, Robert N., and Hans Joas, eds. 2012. *The Axial Age and its Consequences*. Cambridge, MA: Harvard University Press.
Biardeau, Madeleine. 2004. *Stories about Posts: Vedic Variations around the Hindu Goddess*. Chicago: University of Chicago Press.
Bohm, David. 1981. *Wholeness and the Implicate Order*. London: Routledge.
Cook, Francis H. 1972. *Hua-yen Buddhism: The Jewel Net of Indra*. University Park: Pennsylvania State University.
Daniels, Valentine. 1984. *Fluid Signs: Being a Person the Tamil Way*. Berkeley: University of California Press.
Daryn, Gil. 2006. *Encompassing a Fractal World: The Energetic Female Core in Myth and Everyday Life: A Few Lessons Drawn from the Nepalese Himalaya*. New York: Lexington Books.
Dumont, Louis. 1981. *Homo Hierarchicus*. Rev. ed. Chicago: University of Chicago Press.
———. 1986. *Essays on Individualism: Modem Ideology in Anthropological Perspective*. Chicago: University of Chicago Press.
Frankfort, Henry, and Henriette A. Frankfort. 1963. "The Emancipation of Thought from Myth." In *Before Philosophy: An Essay on Speculative Thought in the Ancient Near East*, ed. Henri Frankfort, H. A. Frankfort, John A. Wilson, and Thorkild Jacobsen, 237–63. Harmonsdworth: Penguin Books.
Gell, Alfred. 1997. "Exalting the King and Obstructing the State: A Political Interpretation of Royal Ritual in Bastar District, Central India." *Journal of the Royal Anthropological Institute* n.s. 3: 433–50.
Handelman, Don. 2002. "The Interior Sociality of Self-transformation." In *Self and Self-Transformation in the History of Religions*, ed. David Shulman and Guy G. Stroumsa, 236–53. New York: Oxford University Press.
———. 2005. "Introduction: Why Ritual in its Own Right? How So?" In *Ritual in its Own Right: Exploring the Dynamics of Transformation*, ed. Don Handelman and Galina Lindquist, 1–32. New York: Berghahn Books.
———. 2007. "How Dynamic is the Anthropology of Chaos?" *Focaal: European Journal of Anthropology* 50: 155–65.
———. 2012. "Postlude: Framing Hierarchically, Framing Moebiusly." *Journal of Ritual Studies* 26: 65–77.

———. 2014. "The Guises of the Goddess and the Transformation of the Male: Gangamma's Visit to Tirupati and the Continuum of Gender." In *One God, Two Goddesses, Three Studies of South Indian Cosmology*, 63–113. Leiden: Brill.

Handelman, Don, M. V. Krishnayya, and David Shulman. 2014. "Growing a Kingdom: The Goddess of Depth in Vizianagaram." In *One God, Two Goddesses, Three Studies of South Indian Cosmology* by Don Handelman, 115–213. Leiden: Brill.

Handelman, Don, and Galina Lindquist. 2011. "Religion, Politics, and Globalization: The Long Past Foregrounding the Short Present—Prologue and Introduction." In *Religion, Politics, and Globalization: Anthropological Approaches*, ed. Galina Lindquist and Don Handelman, 1–66. New York: Berghahn Books.

Handelman, Don, and David Shulman. 2004. *Siva in the Forest of Pine: An Essay on Sorcery and Self-Knowledge*. New Delhi: Oxford University Press.

Jacobsen, Thorkild. 1976. *The Treasures of Darkness: A History of Mesopotamian Religion*. New Haven: Yale University Press.

Lilla, Mark. 2007. *The Stillborn God: Religion, Politics, and the Modern West*. New York: Knopf.

Marriott, McKim. 1989. "Constructing an Indian Ethnosociology." *Contributions to Indian Sociology* n.s. 23: 1–39.

Mosko, Mark S., and Frederick H. Damon, eds. 2008. *On the Order of Chaos: Social Anthropology and the Science of Chaos*. New York: Berghahn Books.

Narayana Rao, Velcheru, David Shulman, and Sanjay Subrahmanyam. 2001. *Textures of Time: Writing History in South India 1600–1800*. Delhi: Permanent Black.

Prigogine, Ilya, and Isabelle Stengers. 1984. *Order Out of Chaos*. New York: Bantam Books.

Robbins, Joel. 2009. "Is the Trans- in Transnational the Trans- in Transcendent?" In *Transnational Transcendence: Essays on Religion and Globalization*, ed. Thomas J. Csordas, 55–72. Berkeley: University of California Press.

Rosen, Steven M. 1994. *Science, Paradox, and the Moebius Principle: The Evolution of a "Transcultural" Approach to Wholeness*. Albany: SUNY Press.

Schnepel, Burkhard. 1996. "The Hindu King's Authority Reconsidered: Durga-Puja and Dasara in a South Orissan Jungle Kingdom." In *Political Ritual*, ed. Asa Boholm,126–57. Goteberg: Institute for Advanced Studies in Social Anthropology.

———. 2002. *The Jungle Kings: Ethnohistorical Aspects of Politics and Ritual in Orissa*. New Delhi: Manohar.

Thomassen, Bjorn. 2010. "Anthropology, Multiple Modernities and the Axial Age Debate." *Anthropological Theory* 10: 321–42.

Turner, Victor. 1977. "Process, System, and Symbol: A New Anthropological Synthesis." *Daedalus* 106: 61–80.

Wagner, Roy. 2001. *An Anthropology of the Subject*. Berkeley: University of California Press.

Part IV
Deleuzian Conjunctions

CHAPTER 9

SELF-EXPLODERS, SELF-SACRIFICE, AND THE RHIZOMIC ORGANIZATION OF TERRORISM

Author's Note

In January 1996 the Harry Frank Guggenheim Foundation and Bruce Kapferer brought together a small group of anthropologists of whom I was one to critique his manuscript of *The Feast of the Sorcerer* so that Bruce could make final alterations if he so wished before the final manuscript was sent to press. To my knowledge, through this magnificent book Bruce was the first anthropologist to introduce Deleuzian thinking to an anthropological readership. This, too, was my introduction to Deleuze, especially to his and Guattari's *A Thousand Plateaus*, a primer, perhaps *the* primer, for counterintuitive thinking. For me, Deleuze and Guattari were a blessing of the imagination. I am not a Deleuzian, for wedding myself to a particular conceptual perspective has always felt wrongheaded, while imagining potentialities certainly was the fun in what I did. When I was younger the science fiction of Cordwainer Smith, Theodore Sturgeon, Ursula LeGuin, Frank Herbert, Philip K. Dick, Joanna Russ, Samuel Delaney, and others, gave me that opportunity. Meeting the writings of Deleuze (and, of course, Guattari) so much later restored to me something of the enthusiasm for wakeful dreaming, hence they were a blessing to my imagination, indeed blessing mine own imagination.

I wrote "Self-Exploders . . ." for a lecture series at Stockholm University in 2005 organized by Galina Lindquist. The literature on terrorism was replete with discussions of terrorist networks, yet I didn't find a single mention of the Deleuze and Guattari idea of the rhizome. In explaining the tremendous adaptive potential of today's terrorism, using the rhizome was so much more powerful than that of the network, and showed me the value of practicing Deleuzian thinking.

The human bombs of today's terrorism are self-exploders. I do not refer to *self-exploder* lightly. Exploding the self is the self-destruction of one's intimate interior being, one's own journeys of becoming, the existential being-ness through which each of us (in manifoldly different cultural ways) experiences and knows worlds, inside one's self, outside one's self. Since self comes into existence and is formed and forming through relating to otherness, the self is a social being. To self-explode self is then a social act, a social practice, one intended to act on the world through one's own self-destruction. As social practice, self-explosion radiates outwards, into sociality, into its fragmentation, disruption, dismemberment. As social practice, self-exploding leads directly to the potentiality of self-sacrifice in today's world. Self-sacrifice indexes the voluntary giving of one's life for otherness—protecting this, saving this, bringing this into existence through self-destruction. The giving of one's self to otherness no less indexes altruism (Gambetta 2005b: 259), the gift of devotion—to a cause, to a belief, to others, and on. Therefore, and I emphasize this connectivity, the social giving of one's self to otherness as self-sacrifice often has *cosmic* implications when selfness and otherness in relation to one another are comprehended as integral to world-making. The creation of worlds through the destruction of worlds. This is the linkage I want to explore through the practice of self-exploding in and from the Middle East by considering, toward the end of this chapter, the self-exploder as a double sacrifice—of the enemy other and of the (purified and consecrated) self, and the implications of this for cosmic destruction and creation.

Self-exploding and the organization of today's terrorism both have qualities of a nomadic, rhizomic dynamic, in the terms created by Deleuze and Guattari. The rhizomic dynamic of movement has qualities of asymmetry, speed, intensity, laterality, and penetration (Deleuze and Guattari 1983, 1986, 1988). As far as I can tell, self-exploder terrorism adopted these qualities for practical reasons, for putting together (again in Deleuzian terms) assemblages that worked, especially within globalizing, transnational, and urban ecologies. To a high degree, these dynamic, rhizomic qualities potentiate and enable the organization of terrorism to culminate eventfully in self-explosion. Though the rhizomic organization of terrorism and self-explosion have not been brought to conjoin one another in any deliberate, conscious way, they evolved together through practice, coming powerfully to complement one another. The rhizomic organization of terrorism foregrounds self-explosion as sacrifice, and the rhizomic is discussed here prior to addressing the latter.

Following this brief introduction, the chapter continues with the section "Terrorism in Modernity," considering thinking on terrorism that situates human bombs as a more "civilian" (though not noncombatant) response to perceived, felt, grievance. I then take up "The Rhizome and the Self-Organization of Terrorism," afterwards turning to that which I am calling self-exploding, its sacrificial qualities, and its implications for cosmic order. I close by thinking on the attacks of 9/11 as ritual sacrifice and cosmic (re)origination. The logic of my argument moves from the phenomenon of terrorism more generally, to the organization of terrorism, to the terrorist act (that itself has rhizomic qualities). I do not discuss any psychology of self-exploders—so far this has been discussed primarily and often only in universal terms of suiciding and suicide. This I regard as of little or no aid in comprehending much of the significance of self-exploders in today's world.[1]

Self-exploders appeared in the Near East in 1983, during the civil war in Lebanon, when attacks by the Shi'a movement Hezbollah against American and French military peacekeeping forces and against Israeli military targets caused major casualties. The departure of the peacekeepers from Lebanon was linked to these attacks. Major training grounds at the time were in the Sudan, and in Afghanistan during the occupation by and battles against the Soviet armies there. That war in Afghanistan attracted and exported Muslim fighters from and to a broad swath of North Africa, the Balkans, the Caucasus, the Near East, Pakistan, and Southeast Asia. The success of Hezbollah with self-exploders in Lebanon may have influenced their use by the Liberation Tigers of Tamil Eelam (LTTE) beginning in the late 1980s (see Roberts n.d., 2005a, 2005b) and likely had an effect on al-Qaida (Gunaratna 2002: 147).

Human bombs appeared in Israel/Palestine during the 1990s, when Hamas and Palestinian Islamic Jihad (and later, during the Second Intifada, Fatah) adopted the Hezbollah initiative. The first Hamas self-exploders blew themselves up following the massacre in the Cave of the Patriarchs/Ibrahimi Mosque in Hebron, where according to Jewish and Muslim traditions Abraham/Ibrahim is buried (Beinin 2003: 15). On Purim, 25 February 1994, an annual holiday unusual in Judaism in that it is given over to inversion, license, and the blurring of boundaries between good and bad, a physician and settler, Baruch Goldstein entered the mosque in his army reserve fatigues and shot well over a hundred and fifty Muslim worshipers, of whom twenty-nine died. He was torn to pieces by the survivors. Goldstein the terrorist undoubtedly perceived himself as a self-sacrifice for the greater Jewish good in the biblical Land of Israel. His remains were buried in Rabbi Meir Kahane Park, and his tomb has become a pilgrimage site for West Bank settlers and their sympathizers. The inscription on his tomb reads: "Here lies the *saint*, Dr. Baruch Kappel Goldstein, blessed be the memory of the *righteous* and *holy* man, may the Lord avenge his blood, who devoted his soul to the Jews, Jewish religion and Jewish land. His hands are innocent and his heart is pure. He was killed as a *martyr of G-d*." (my emphases)

Attackers have detonated themselves or their bombs in numerous locations in the Middle East and Asia and, more recently in European capitals (Madrid, London). Their greatest success has been, of course, 9/11, the 2001 attacks on the Twin Towers and the Pentagon, in which the brilliance of a rhizomic attack and the catastrophe of its aftermath were magnified for all to see, as were the severity of the American bureaucratic responses through law, classification, and regulation.[2] Self-exploding terrorism appears as an apparently new means of mass violence (but see, too, Dale 1988; Andriolo 2002), joining in the savagery of the twentieth and now the twenty-first centuries, on the edge of the uncomfortably incomprehensible in the religiousness of its self-destructiveness, in its indiscriminate massacring, and in its seemingly tenuous and diffuse social organization.

Responses to terrorism by intellectuals and university academics are commonly moralistic, outraged at the butchering of innocent noncombatants; at the destruction of peaceful, law-abiding civilian sectors; and at the transnational influx into Western states of archaics or primitives in a globalizing world. Scholarly and political thinking join in perceiving terrorism in grandiose terms—a war of civilizations, a war among the so-called universal Abrahamic religions of Islam, Christianity, and Judaism, a theophany of Gog and Magog. With few exceptions, there is consensus that suicide bombers are terrorists, though there is no agreement as to what entails terror nor how to define this. Obviously, terror can be defined categorically, legalistically, normatively—but whether this can be a substantive rendition of the phenomenal in its social, existential, and eschatological dimensions is quite another matter, one hardly addressed. This affects how liberal scholarship is relating to terrorist phenomena.

The following premises infuse much scholarly thinking about these human precision bombs (as Michael Roberts calls them), about the contexts that shape them, and about the ways in which they organize. First, the perpetrators are suiciders, often mentally unstable or impressionable, trapped in the unstable flux of modernity, unable to find their footings, alienated and frustrated human detritus (e.g., Moghaddam 2005). In Durkheimian terms, their lives are underintegrated, insufficiently moored in a societal matrix, and they drift into what he called egoistical suicide, killing themselves for their own sake. Or, their lives are overintegrated within an authoritarian religious matrix, and so they are driven to give their lives to the cause in acts that Durkheim called altruistic suicide (Durkheim 1952: 152–240).[3] I return to this theme, briefly, further on.

Second, commonsensical and scholarly thinking concur that there is a clear-cut ethical and functional distinction between the civilian and the combatant—combatants are borderers, protecting civilians who live within borders and who are not complicit in the oppressions that are perpetrated by their states, officials, and armies. Therefore attacks on civilians violate this categorical distinction: these attacks treat noncombatants as fully complicit in the oppression and devastation carried through by states of which they are members. Whatever else it is, terrorism is understood as deviant violence against innocent civilians.[4] Today's terrorism, with its colonial and neocolonial legacies, puts this to the question.

Terrorism in Modernity

During the twentieth century, warfare between states turned from battles primarily between armies to violence aimed deliberately at civilian populations. No less, states attacked their own subject populations (the Armenian genocide, the Herero genocide [e.g., Hull 2005: 7–90], the Holocaust of European Jewry). The bulk of casualties during World War I were those of combatants. Poison gas was used by military against military. In World War II this completely turned about: Auschwitz, *Einsatzgruppen*, Hiroshima and Nagasaki, Dresden and London, and on and on.[5] States deliberately attacking one another's civilian populations and their own, making them prime targets for mass slaughter. Western states terrorizing Western noncombatants, thereby making them no longer quite that, no longer innocent noncombatants but integral to strategizing the weakening of enemy capacities and capabilities, if not the very extermination of that enemy. If in the more distant past, "The law of nations held that war was a contest between states, waged by official, uniformed, armed forces," in more recent times, "as entire economies and societies have been conscripted to the war effort and military and nonmilitary work have converged, [there has been] a gradual loosening of what constitutes a legitimate military target" (Smith 2002: 361). Civilian targets that also contribute to war use increasingly are treated as unambiguous military targets. "The vogue today is the 'Strategic Ring Theory' of striking critical nodes of infrastructure in order to induce 'strategic paralysis' in one's enemy" (Smith 2002: 362).

The massacring, killing, and brutalizing of subject populations that had flourished during centuries of colonial rule surfaced within the motherlands and fatherlands, internally and in relation to one another. Despite numerous international treaties against the manufacture and proliferation of weapons of mass destruction, against war crimes, and so forth, during the twentieth century it became more and more acceptable to attack civilians and civilian targets. In Edith Wyschogrod's (1985) momentous phrasing, the *logic* of manmade mass death became fully formed during the twentieth century.

Sociologist of law Donald Black argues that "terrorism in its purest form is *self-help* by organized civilians who covertly inflict mass violence on other civilians" (2004: 16, my emphasis).[6] Terrorism, he argues, is highly moralistic, often utopian, and intended to exert social control by responding to grievance with aggression, especially when there is no other redress, or when redress does not work.[7] Religious international terrorists may well resemble millenarian mystical Christian movements of medieval Europe (Black 2004: 18) whose utopian orientation, wrote Karl Mannheim (1936: 220), "tends at every moment to turn into hostility towards the world, its culture, and all its works and earthly achievements" (see also Cohn [1970]*).

Black (2004: 15) contends, "Violence occurs when a conflict structure is violent.... Every form of violence," he writes, "has its own structure.... Structures kill and maim, not individuals or collectivities." The conflict structure of "pure terrorism" (Black uses this as a Weberian ideal type), like some of its organization and strategies, resembles that of the Deleuzian rhizome in relation to the state. Pure terrorism whose aim is the mass killing and maiming of civilians by civilians takes shape on behalf of one collectivity against another that is perceived as culturally and socially foreign, and as superior in military, political, and economic power. Hence the Madrid rush-hour commuter train bombings in 2004, and the London Underground bombings in 2005. Two decades ago, Rapoport (1984: 675) could (perhaps) argue that terrorists tend "to choose methods that minimize the terrorist's risks; the targets, accordingly, are increasingly defenseless victims who have less and less value as symbols and less responsibility for any condition that the terrorists say they want to alter." If this was ever the case, it ceased to be so in the age of the self-exploder, when boundaries between the military and the civilian, between combatant and noncombatant, are blurred and even effaced, and when terrorism extends self-exploding and other opportunities to civilians, both male and female (Gambetta 2005b: 283).

In 2003 there were ninety-eight self-exploder attacks around the world (Atran 2004a). Not only are most of the targets of these attacks civilian, but civilians are perceived to be complicit in the oppressive enterprises of the offending states because they do not oppose these states. Of no less significance, implicit in the complicit is the intentional. Complicity is a declaration of intentionality—civilians thereby are intentional accomplices of the oppressive states they are members in and shelter within. The deeper implication is that the distinction between the officially designated armed forces of the state and its civilian citizens no longer holds. Civilians are held responsible for their government and its practices. Civilians, then, should take responsibility for their governments just as Islamist terrorists take responsibility for the well-being of Islam. There are no longer any innocents, only perpetrators and the complicit. This has more than a little prominence in America, for example, in the bombing of the federal office building in Oklahoma City, yet no less in the Columbine high school massacre and in similar mass murders.[8] I will discuss intentionality further, in relation to sacrifice.

However, the brutal converse of all this is that in the name of national security, indeed security even more broadly conceived as Total (and Totalizing) Security, there are no longer civilian innocents in the eyes of the State either (see Bajc 2007).[9] All are at least under suspicion unless cleared for the moment. Thus every stop at a security portal where ID is demanded, every passage through a metal detector, is a form of *interrogation* into whether passage will be permitted, an interrogation into that which is not evident on the surface of being, an interrogation that can be highly condensed in time and act, even left entirely to machines, or stretched out to include questioning, body search, and even incarceration. CCTV systems in civic spaces, and the monitoring of private phone conversations and email no less attest to the fact that all are under suspicion until shown not to be. So too does the current official enthusiasm for simplistic behavior profiling in public spaces: "The authorities at about a dozen US airports now monitor passengers' involuntary actions in hopes of nabbing potential terrorists, and Miami officials are so impressed with such behavior recognition techniques that they plan to have janitors, coffee-shop workers and skycaps trained to detect dangerous fliers."[10] A hostile environment for the unwary traveler who is unaware of his own subtle behavioral habits.

The practice of terrorism is a phenomenon of late modernity, of the last century and this one, as technology has enabled transnational strike trajectories across lengthy distances, separating, for example, a colonial power from those whom it oppresses or oppressed (Atran 2004b). Violent civilians fighting back, attacking the oppressive state through its civilians who are perceived as complicit, rejecting the distinct classification of civilian and military (e.g., Asad 2007: 17, 22).[11] Violent civilians or quasi-civilians (those with limited martial training) in small groups are systematic wild cards, mutating, developing, emerging in their own ways with less of or quite without the external strictures imposed by bureaucratic states, as was the case with terrorism during the Cold War (Ackerman 2006). But the ways in which this is coming to be done, if al-Qaida is any example, are through rhizomic transformations of state organization.

The Rhizome and the Self-Organization of Terrorism

Much of (pure) terrorism is organized through forms of organization that are antithetical to the modern state. The infrastructure of the modern Western state is highly bureaucratic, its institutions organized around clearly defined offices and tasks, a clear-cut division of labor, hierarchies of officials, and chains of command. This holds no less for the armed forces, the intelligence agencies, and the secret police. The modern state is deeply rooted in clearly bounded territories whose borders are inviolate and within which its sovereignty is supreme. State systems work best when pitted against other states with the same logic of organization or under conditions of colonization when conquering or grabbing territory and economic resources, or controlling these, are often primary goals. So, too, during the Cold War the Soviet Union and the United States sponsored and used terrorist activities as arms of state to further national goals, but also kept the scope and intensity of these activities tempered (Raufer 2003: 392).

The organization of transnational terrorism that has blossomed during the past two decades is different. Consider the following scenario recently posed by a researcher:

> Now, imagine a company, or agency, with global markets, or an international mission, say IBM or the CIA. If their offices have been raided worldwide, or bombarded, tens of millions of dollars confiscated from them, all their known bank accounts blocked, their computers seized, their electronic communication systems destroyed, thousands of their employees and part of their leadership arrested—even killed sometimes—could these organizations still function? No, of course not. (Ibid.: 395)

He is referring to al-Qaida, though whether there is a unified organization (like a corporation, say IBM, or a bureaucracy, say the CIA) that can be called "al-Qaida" is unlikely. If not this, then what manner of entity is working here? No one seems to know the overall state of affairs—al-Qaida, and probably other terrorist entities, like the anarchists of the late nineteenth century, constitute an "inscrutable case" (Gambetta 2005a), one about which there is no stable truth to find out. This is so not only because terrorist formation may be quite loosely held together, but also because it is in ongoing change. So the forming of terrorist entities varies within a field of potentialities, enabling (indeed, potentiating) the simultaneous emergence of more hierarchical formations, more network-like formations, and more rhizome-like formations, perhaps shifting through these different modalities. I will turn to the rhizome shortly.

In the case of al-Qaida, the best documented of these organizations, these forms mutate, radically changing their formations. In its early years in Afghanistan, al-Qaida was a highly structured, more guerilla-like hierarchical formation run from the top by Osama bin Laden and dedicated to fighting the Soviet occupation there. Bin Laden was reputed to own or control eighty companies around the world (Hoffman 2003: 434). In the Sudan alone he owned construction, manufacturing, currency trading, import-export, and agricultural businesses (Bergen 2001: 47–49), and he had established a set of valuable Islamic charities in Saudi Arabia with international sections. Following the defeat of the Soviets in Afghanistan, bin Laden turned al-Qaida toward more transnational terror operations (while continuing more of a conventional war against the Northern Alliance). Bin Laden in part reoriented the organization toward more network-like formations that enabled making decisions and carrying out operations to be done locally, without referring to an apex or center. This was the case with the first World Trade Center bombing in 1992; with Ramzi Ahmed Yousef's plan, developed in the Philippines in 1994–95, to simultaneously bomb twelve American commercial airliners in midflight over the Pacific (Hoffman 2003: 436); and with the plan to assassinate the Pope in Manila in 1995, using an assassin dressed as a priest who was to explode himself while kissing the papal ring (Hassan 2001; Gunaratna 2002: 175).

More network-like formations strongly contributed to the planning and putting together of the cells for the 9/11 attacks. The terrorists trained in al-Qaida facilities in Afghanistan, and later received logistical support from sleeper cells in Europe and Southeast Asia in order to enter the United States (Mishal and Rosenthal 2005: 279). The attackers themselves were divided into a number of cells that were unknown to one another, except through operators or cut-outs (in Cold War espionage language)—the pilots met the other attackers only on the morning of 9/11. Moreover, it is likely that not all members of the same cell knew one another. Meetings were held to synchronize distant segments or cells of the network and to discuss progress, but then these ties went dormant.[12] The 9/11 attacks are estimated to have cost under 500,000 USD (Basile 2004: 172).[13]

An important attribute of this shift in organization is that terrorism becomes more of a bottom-up phenomenon, with local initiatives and local cells whose destruction have limited effects on the viability of larger transnational terrorist networks. Bottom-up formation is highly emergent, spawning a multitude of directions, but also recursiveness and numerous loci of leadership.[14] These are indeed qualities of rhizomic formation. Following the American invasion of Afghanistan and the destruction of al-Qaida infrastructure—its bases of operation and training camps—al-Qaida ceased holding to two tenets of conventional organizations: first, attachment to territory—apart from the religious-political imaginary of the first Islamic State shaped by Muhammad after he was driven from Mecca to Medina—and, second, permanent institutional presence (Mishal and Rosenthal 2005: 279).[15]

Thus the networks and cells of al-Qaida decentralized further, becoming weakly coupled in their connections to one another, though tightly coupled within themselves. Weak coupling allows greater agency, enabling cells to adapt less abstractly and more directly and immediately to their environments, while setting their own agendas. Maksim Tsvetovat and Kathleen Farley (2003) who modeled covert (terrorist) networks found that attacking them as one would a hierarchical organization, for example by targeted assassinations of network or cell leaders (a major Israeli weapon)—thereby "beheading" and fragmenting such entities—was not effective. Cells are highly adaptive and heal themselves, either by finding ways to reconnect to the network, by operating on their own, or by becoming dormant and waiting. Al-Qaida's cells have been likened to clusters of grapes, such that a grape plucked does not affect the viability of others of the bunch (Gunaratna 2002: 97). Since cells tend toward the autopoietic in interaction with local ecologies, they also tend not to replicate one another in their organization (Knorr Cetina 2005: 230).

Tight coupling within cells gives them *esprit de corps* and a sense of fictive kinship.[16] Entities that come into existence in bottom-up ways generate more complex behavior and action than is produced by top-down, deliberate planning according to a hierarchical chain of command (Marion and Uhl-Bien 2003: 70). Bottom-up forming encourages experimentation and learning from experience. Marion and Uhl-Bien (2003: 71) contend that "al-Qaida leadership provided models of creativity, dropped seeds of innovation, encouraged innovative initiatives, stimulated the growth of supporting resources and largely stayed out of the way of spontaneous growth and innovation." So, al-Qaida can create or help to create ad hoc cells to carry out local missions of their own choice, specifications, and modes of operation. The March 2004 attack on commuter trains in Madrid is an example. The attack was coordinated by a Tunisian who created an ad hoc cell by connecting to a local group of immigrants called the Moroccan Islamic Combat Group, without direct links to al-Qaida (Mishal and Rosenthal 2005: 288). The elimination of the Madrid attackers did little or no damage to the nets of al-Qaida, which probably proceeded to set up other local ad hoc cells elsewhere. The cell that carried out the 2005 London Underground bombings was autopoietic, obtaining most if not all of its bomb-making information from the Internet. Many of these cells "are not durable units but changing implementations of short-term projects sequentially replaced by new projects—they are units that their creators plan from the outset to abolish, abandon and recreate as non-identical units at a different location" (Knorr Cetina 2005: 229).

A further adaptive or mutating form, emerging from nets of loosely coupled terrorist cells, is what is called *swarming*—terrorists from different groups come together from scattered locations to hone in on multiple targets and then disperse, perhaps to form other swarms (Atran 2004a).[17]

The economics of al-Qaida are especially instructive in relation to the emergent bottom-up forming of cells and nets. Though American bureaucracies have shut down many channels of al-Qaida monies in the United States, its devolving character makes it extremely difficult to track money sources globally. Al-Qaida seems not to benefit from state funding. Monies raised by Islamic charities, in Saudi Arabia, for example, may be moved through Islamic banks (governed by Shari'a law) that are subjected to little bureaucratic regulation and oversight, and through *hawala* ("transfer," "exchange," "change") networks, long institutionalized in South Asia and the Middle East. In *hawala*, there are no transfers between money traders; instead, one *hawaldar* will fax or phone another, telling him to give a sum of cash to a particular recipient. Particular transactions are not recorded; instead *hawaldara* keep track of the balance of their accounts with one another, the outstanding balance eventually to be settled in various ways (cf. Berkowitz, Woodward, and Woodward 2005). Al-Qaida separates monies for its operational cells from its sources of funding. Until now, every successful operation sponsored by al-Qaida has used different money sources, the funds for any given operation arriving through multiple routes. According to al-Qaida's training manual, the commander of a cell is to divide finances into monies to be invested and monies to be saved for operations (Basile 2004: 171–76). Cells are intended to be as financially self-sufficient as possible, in keeping with their loose coupling and agency in choosing targets and organizing attacks.

Transnational terrorism has emerged from the mass killing of civilians characterizing much bloodletting among and within states especially from World War II on, becoming matter-of-course. These terrorist networks and groupings often are more civilian-terrorists, or at most quasi-military, than they are military. They are, in the main, civilians taking up or turning themselves into weapons against civilians, directly reaching civilian populations whom they hold complicit in the perduring existence of regimes that have or that are oppressing them. Attacks by civilians upon civilians are not only strategic decisions to damage easier "soft" targets—these attacks in their own ways are uprisings that go directly to those held most responsible; those sheltering behind the violent bureaucracies that are the military.

Discussing the history of warfare, Lind et al. (1989) suggest that a fourth generation of forms of war is emerging, and that terrorism is integral to this: terrorism "attempts to bypass the enemy's military entirely and strike directly at his homeland at civilian targets. Ideally, the enemy's military is simply irrelevant to the terrorist." Military culture remains a culture of order even as the battlefields are ones of disorder. Military culture, they point out, "has become contradictory to the battlefield" (but see endnote 18). Both the forming of cells and the trajectories of attack are becoming more rhizomic. The International Institute for Strategic Studies states that the

Iraq War is generating "an already decentralized and evasive transnational terrorist network to become more 'virtual' and protean and, therefore, harder to identify and neutralize" (2003). Knorr Cetina (2005: 214) maintains that today's terrorism is not only global but constitutes "the emergence of global microstructures; of forms of connectivity and coordination that combine global reach with microstructural mechanisms that instantiate self-organizing principles and patterns."

Little by little, terrorist attackers, their cells and nets, are becoming more deterritorialized, more mobile, more *nomadic* in a transnational, globalizing world—they are becoming rhizomic in their forming. In a topological sense, terrorist attackers *are* their movement, and the dynamic of this movement is rhizomic. Deleuze and Guattari (1988) distinguish the rhizomic from the state form, that form of organizing that captures, incorporates, and stabilizes whatever it takes in within its boundaries. Yet as Deleuze and Guattari intend, the state form and the rhizome are metamorphs of one another. Every subversion, uprising, insurrection within the state is a node of the rhizomic, of an unpredictable dynamic that undermines the verticality of the deeply rooted, the beginnings of a line of flight, a trajectory that will destroy distinctions between interior and exterior, erasing borders. No less, every swelling within a rhizome, every shift toward hierarchical self-organization is a node of a potential state form in the making, of the emergence of boundaries, of distinctions between interior and exterior, of verticality, of the deeply rooted. Many transnational terrorists are migrants moving from one state to another, settling in new places yet becoming nomadic, fluid cysts within the weightiness of statist territorial positioning.

What is rhizomic forming, according to Deleuze and Guattari's sense of this vegetal dynamic? The rhizome is not a root, but rather a tuber or bulb that ramifies growth in all directions, on, over, and under the ground, a multiplicity of diversities without clear boundaries, or perhaps whose boundaries are densities of connectedness, with shallow tendrils without any natural points of closure, with multiple entrances and ongoing, spreading movement. Within this dynamic maze of movement any point can be connected to any other, and this making of connection never ceases. Rhizomic organization has no fixed points in its lines of flight (as Deleuze and Guattari call its movements), and therefore has only potentialities to emerge vertically, to grow hierarchy and stratification with differences in status, authority, gatekeepers, and specialized guardians of order sign-posted by the uniform—in other words, to becoming top-down organization, the bureaucratic state in miniature. "A rhizome," they write, "can be cracked and broken at any point; it starts off again following one or another of its lines, or even other lines" (Deleuze and Guattari 1983: 17–18). A crucial dynamic of the rhizomic is *speed*. The bureaucratic state form exists through the stability of its territorialism, the portentousness of its deep-rootedness, the weightiness of its regulations, the density of its institutions. The rhizome turns a point—the potential node of swelling into verticality—into an intense line of flight through the speed with which it moves. Speed vanishes the boundary, its blockage and stoppage disappearing with it.[18]

Deleuze and Guattari (1983: 49) write: "In opposition to centered systems (even multi-centered), with hierarchical communication and pre-established connections, the rhizome is an a-centered system, non-hierarchical and nonsignifying, without a General, without an organizing memory or central autonomy." The rhizome cannot answer to a structural or generative model, for there is no grammar through which to generate a rhizome. Therefore the rhizome makes and morphs itself as it moves.[19] Here, in a strange yet powerful way, rhizome and self-exploder join in the same line of flight. In the emergence of its manifold evolution, al-Qaida has developed qualities of the rhizomic—loosely organized, decentralized, flexible in practice (Gunaratna 2002: 11, 57–58, 95), penetrating fluidly from multiple directions, while encouraging if only by example, the sprouting of autonomous rhizomes, terror cells with potentially these sorts of capacities.[20] Moreover, speed and intensity are the dynamic of the self-exploder, as they are of the rhizome. A founder of Palestinian Islamic Jihad wrote in 1988 on the importance of penetrating the territory of the enemy, in making the case for what he called "exceptional martyrdom," aimed at countering objections by Islamic religious figures to suicide bombing. "We cannot achieve the goal of these operations if our *mujahid* [holy warrior] is not able to create an explosion within seconds and is unable to prevent the enemy from blocking the operation. All these results can be achieved through the explosion" (Hassan 2001). A leader of Hamas commented to Nasra Hassan (2001): "The main thing is to guarantee that a large number of the enemy will be affected. With an explosive belt or bag, the bomber has control over vision, location, and timing." And al-Zawahiri of al-Qaida, in his post-9/11 book, wrote on "the need to concentrate on the method of martyrdom operations as the most successful way of inflicting damage against the opponent and the least costly to the *mujahidin* in terms of casualties" (Gunaratna 2002: 224).

It is crucial to recognize here that the individual self-exploder is himself/herself a tiny rhizome in its asymmetric movement and speed, intensity and depth of penetration, a tiny rhizome that is a small piece or segment of a larger rhizome, a cell in self-organization and line of flight, itself perhaps part of a larger rhizomic agglomerate. A recent case in point of the above was the self-exploder Abdullah al-Asiri, who flew from Yemen to Jeddah in Saudi Arabia with half a kilo of explosive secreted in "a bodily orifice" (perhaps in his rectum, since he refrained from eating or drinking for forty hours), and who then succeeded in getting into close proximity to the Saudi interior minister, whereupon the explosives were detonated by a call from his controllers to a cell phone.[21]

Just as some terrorist cells are rhizomic in their dynamics, putting down no permanent roots, deterritorializing their networks, weapons, and finances, combining local conditions and religious-mythic abstraction into practice, so, too, they accomplish the complete synthesis of idea and action, of *perfect praxis*, through the act of self-explosion. Moving in emerging lines of horizontal flight, shifting direction, communicating through cyberspace, cells connect to other cells or to members of these.

And so the emerging phenomenon of swarming for a particular operation, gathering together a multiplicity and diversity of persons and resources into what Deleuze and Guattari (1988) call an "assemblage," here a transient proliferation of the dimensions of the phenomenon that also changes its nature. So, too, just as the ruptured rhizome starts up again, cells show adaptability in self-healing after parts of cells or networks are destroyed. And, the cell or cells act at speed, refusing to accentuate any point of potential stability, sometimes choosing the objective at the last moment, often angularly penetrating to the target, controlling the line of flight, of access, to a high degree. It is the rhizomic qualities of the terrorist cell and network, the rhizomic qualities of the individual self-exploder, that make them so effective against weighty structures, solidified ponderously in place in the bureaucratic state, making it so difficult for the state to trace the activities of the rhizomic. The terrorist rhizome may become a perduring threat to the promise of the state that total security is the right of civilians and the belief of the latter (who are no less True Believers) in this promise.[22] I return to the response of the state in the conclusion.[23]

Rhizomic terrorism is also complemented powerfully by the character of Islam that is emerging through the jihad declared by al-Qaida and other Islamist agglomerates. The usual analyses done on the Islamic roots of jihad and their influence on al-Qaida and others is to classify and pigeonhole according to traditional social movements—Salafi, Wahabi, and so forth (e.g., Sageman 2004)—such that these movements are made to exist historically and currently as the neatly compartmentalized progenitors of today's jihad and as the ideological motivators of Islamic self-exploders. In a much more penetrating analysis, Faisal Devji (2005: 50) argues that, for al-Qaida and associates, "Islamic history and authority has been completely disaggregated and is no longer clustered within more or less distinct lineages of doctrine or ideology that can be identified with particular groups." Devji (2005: 51) contends: "In effect all traditional forms of intellectual and political grouping or identification have been fragmented, their elements scattered like debris for the picking, to be recycled in ever more temporary constructions." One result of this is what he calls the "democratization of authority in the Muslim world" (ibid.: 51), and so the "radical individuation of Islam" through which many Muslims become related much more tenuously to traditional modes of collective solidarity "based on some common history of needs, interests or ideas" (Devji 2005: 31; see also Brown 2001: 110). This perspective of global dynamics enables understanding of how today's Muslim self-exploders and other terrorists constitute such heterogeneous agglomerations, and, so, too, the flexibility, mobility, and tensile strength of their rhizomic self-organization (putting to the question, for example, studies that evaluate the enabling of extremism in jihad in terms of the selective inaccuracy with which bin Laden and other terrorist leaders and ideologues use the Qur'an and Hadith (e.g., Gwynne 2006). The individuation of the self-exploder, and the self-exploder as a rhizomic segment or piece of a rhizome, are directly relevant to self-exploding sacrifice.

Self-Exploding Sacrifice

The rhizome is a metamorph, transforming itself through its own dynamics of ongoing movement, through its assemblages and lines of flight. In this respect the rhizomic form of terrorism and self-exploder is complemented by the very act of self-explosion and the preparation leading to this, once we understand that the act is one of self-sacrifice, and that sacrifice is a practice of transformation. To get at this, the interior logic of sacrifice needs discussion.

In the most influential work on suicide written in the modern era, Emile Durkheim (1951: 152–240) distinguished between *egoistic suicide*, the intention to kill oneself for oneself, and *altruistic suicide*, the preparedness to kill oneself for others, as in warfare. In either instance, Durkheim abhorred the taking of one's own life. This is the canonical attitude of all three monotheistic universal religions—God gives life and only God has the right to take life. The modern state claims a monopoly on doing violence, primarily through its violent bureaucracies (within which I include military, judiciary, and police). Suicide transgresses both the monotheisms and the states that developed from them.

Though no general theory of sacrifice will satisfy all the phenomena that anthropologists and historians of religion call sacrifice, a few general points are relevant here. Whatever else it is, sacrifice is an act of violence—a violence done to natural form, natural in the sense of form existing in the integrity of its created shape in the cosmos. Kapferer (1997: 189) argues that sacrifice is "a primordial act . . . a total act [. . . in which] the force of sacrifice [is] constitutive both of the being of the person at the center of sacrifice and of the person as himself or herself [as] a being who constitutes. . . . The violence of sacrifice underlines sacrifice as the total act: an act that can have immanent within its process the entire potential and process of human being." He (1997: 190) continues:

> Violence is quintessentially the form of totalizing action, the explosion of possibility and of possibility exploded. . . . The act of killing in sacrifice is a conjunction of the force of life with death, and of the separation of life from death. This conjunctive/disjunctive energy is the vital force of sacrifice. The motion towards killing is the conjunction . . . of death with life. The moment of killing, the peak of the death-life conjunction, is also the radical separation, the disjunction of life from death.

In sacrifice, natural form is taken apart—cut, rent, torn, split, burnt—so that something else can come into existence.[24] The violence of sacrifice is originary (Kapferer 1997: 190). Put differently, the violence done to form through sacrifice is violence that is done to the boundary, perhaps to the origination of boundary and being that no less is that of cosmos. The violence done to the sacrifice alters, opens, momentarily destroys the boundary between levels, domains, or realms of cosmos. Thus sacrifice, as Kapferer argues, is an act of primordial transformation, of radical change.

Through this something unseen will take shape or have consequential effects in the world.

Sacrifice is a foundational practice in the three monotheisms (in Judaism, the *aqedah*—Abraham's preparedness to sacrifice Isaac, and God's acceptance of an animal substitution; in Islam, Ishmael's *willingness* to be sacrificed by Ibrahim for Allah, the willingness that nears, that perhaps is, self-sacrifice; in Christianity, the self-sacrifice of Christ). In Islam, self-sacrifice must be death in the service of God's plan but is first and foremost *active* struggle with correct *intention* in the service of God's plan (Lewinstein 2001: 78–81). Self-sacrifice may differ from sacrifice in the degree of its closure and in the totalization of its intensity and dynamic of movement. Its explosion is no less its implosion. The sacrificer is no less the sacrificed—as one dies for an exterior goal or cause, one's self or soul is transformed interiorly, perhaps the purification or release of an authentic self (Verkaaik 2005: 141), perhaps the instantaneous transference of the soul to paradise (Hassan 2001). A Hamas self-exploder whose bomb failed to explode described to Nasra Hassan (2001) how he felt when chosen for martyrdom: "It's as if a very high impenetrable wall separated you from Paradise or Hell. . . . Allah has promised one or the other to his creatures. So, by pressing the detonator, you can immediately open the door to Paradise—it is the shortest path to Heaven." Another described the immediacy of paradise as: "It is very, very near—right in front of our eyes. It lies beneath the thumb. On the other side of the detonator."

If the victim is made holy or sacred in the act of sacrifice (Hubert and Mauss 1964: 9)—a *sacrificium*—this is because the violence of its destruction momentarily destroys the boundary between cosmic levels, this destruction becoming an originary locus of the reconstitution of cosmos. In Israel/Palestine in the name of jihad, the Islamist self-exploder simultaneously kills himself as a self-sacrifice that transports him to paradise and kills enemies, others, thereby offering them as a sacrifice to Allah to open the way to the creation of the Palestinian nation-state, as part of the *ummah*, the universal Islamic religious polity (Strenski 2003: 4; Hage 2003: 69) that in its making is perforce fragmentary and transnational.[25] I return in a moment to this theme. In the warfare of the modern state, the ethos of heroic death in battle acquires the status of self-sacrifice (Greenhouse 1989; Marvin and Ingle 1999; Handelman 2004; Zerubavel 1995).

Sacrifice is originary; suicide is abhorred. Suicide is a sin, self-sacrifice is not. Sacrifice is transformative; suicide is merely self-destructive. Under what conditions in monotheistic traditions and in modern states does self-destruction become transformative, and so is turned into sacrifice?[26] The question lies at the heart of the emerging conundra of self-exploders. The matter of *intentionality* is crucial here.[27] Intentionality establishes a conscious relationship of consequence between sacrificer and sacrificed, between destroyer and offering (see Kapferer 1997: 192–98). In the case of the self-exploder, much of this relationship is within the self, thereby fusing and totalizing commitment and outcome. Closed into itself—into selfness—the locus of sacrifice becomes absolute. Commitment predicated on the direction of dying, of transformation, exploding exteriorly, transforming interiorly. The idea of "exceptional martyrdom," mentioned above, depends on this embodiment of intentionality. So, too, a Muslim cleric making the case for martyrdom argues, "while both suicide and acts of martyrdom require the express act of will of the perpetrator, what matters is not the act, but the intention [*niyya*] of the martyr" (Israeli 2002: 35).[28]

Shaping the Ritual Sacrifice

Sacrifice is the perfect praxis—the perfect synthesis—of idea, intention, action. The inner logic of self-exploders—in Israel/Palestine and those of 9/11—configures how this praxis of self-sacrifice is accomplished through the ritual shaping of self. Central to this is an agency different from that of individualism made free for itself, the individual for himself. Devji's argument on the spreading of individuation in today's Islam, mentioned earlier, is especially relevant here. Devji (2005: 34) contends that today's jihad largely rejects "the classical doctrine of holy war as a collective or political obligation [*farzkifaya*]." Instead, holy war becomes "an individual and ethical obligation [*farz ayn*] like prayer. . . . [Holy war] becomes spiritualized and finally puts the jihad beyond the pragmatism of political life. . . . So, whereas liberals as well as fundamentalist Muslims tried to instrumentalize Islam by attributing social, political or economic functions to its beliefs or practices, the jihad does just the opposite—its task is to de-instrumentalize Islam and make it part of everyday ethics" (2005: 34; see also Gwynne 2006: 14, 16; Brown 2001: 110–11). Today's jihad, like previous movements, develops in the peripheries of the Muslim world, with practices that braid together the charismatic, the heretical, the experiential, the mystical—the Muslim content of which "draws upon the flotsam and jetsam of received wisdoms and remembered histories [. . . denying] the existence of distinct orders or genealogies of Islamic authority" (Devji 2005: 41–42). Instead, personal faith, repentance, and the quest for salvation rise to the fore together with the democratization of authority in which prophecy, dream, and messianism are prominent, rather than the traditional, even canonical knowledge of texts (ibid.: 42, 48). If this jihad emerged out of oppression of Muslim populations, it has become a metaphysical war, "an effort to define the terms of global social relations outside the language of state and citizenship" (ibid.: 76)—and it is through this that self-explosion and self-sacrifice become sacred practice intended to transform cosmos through individual intentionality and action.[29]

Relevant thinking on individual agency, self-discipline, and ethics in present-day Islam comes, appositely, from a study of putting on the veil by Muslim women. Saba Mahmood discusses how women in Egypt take on veiling through *docility*, though this is not the docility of the passive abandoning of agency—rather, it refers literally to the *malleability* needed to be taught particular skills, and this demands "struggle, effort, exertion, and achievement" (Mahmood 2001: 210). This is an internal struggle within and against one's self, one not distant from the struggle demanded by jihad (see Euben 2002: 12). Putting on the veil is the preparedness to respond positively to shaping oneself, in relation to self and others, as one is being shaped. Thus, "while wearing the veil at first serves as a means to tutor oneself in the attributes of shyness, it is also simultaneously integral to the practice of shyness. . . . One veils," argue these women, "not to *express* [my emphasis] an identity but as a necessary, if insufficient condition for attaining the goal internal to that practice—namely, the creation of a shy and modest self. The veil in this sense is the means of both *being* and *becoming* a certain kind of person" (Mahmood 2001: 214–15, emphasis in original). Putting on the veil is a bi-directional self-declaring practice of ascetic intent—interior and exterior.

Taking on the veil is an exterior practice that develops interior qualities that, in turn, "comes to regulate and govern one's behavior without conscious deliberation" (Mahmood 2001: 216). The practice of shyness, modesty, and patience become inseparable from one's interior intentionality and desire, as both are inseparable from the significance of the theology and eschatology that inspire these. The veil becomes integral to the face, not as covering but as an embodiment of synthesizing interiority and exteriority, of showing one's authentic interior selfness on one's exterior. One's holism, within and without. The distance from face to veil is, at it were, the absence of distance between re-formed self and the practice of self-transcendence, between an ethics of self-accountability and an ethics of self-responsibility, embodied by the veil-face. So, too, when the bomber puts the bomb on himself and becomes a self-exploder, the distance between self and self-transcendence diminishes and then disappears if he self-explodes successfully. Both in the instances of women veiling and in jihad there is the dynamic of making Islam universal. Devji (2005: 94) puts it this way for the forming of the self-exploder: "the forging of a generic Muslim, one who loses all cultural and historical particularity by his or her destruction in an act of martyrdom."

There are three hand-written copies of a four-page document in Arabic that the 9/11 self-exploders left behind. The document can be called a spiritual manual (Kippenberg 2005).[30] If we accept it as a guide to the preparation of the self-exploders (we have no way of knowing whether they followed this), then it gives an inkling of how the self-exploders ritualized and shaped themselves in spirit and body (Mneimneh and Makiya 2002) before attacking and transforming themselves through the total and totalizing act of martyring self-sacrifice.

In Arabic, to be martyred, to have one's martyrdom seen and witnessed, to witness one's own martyrdom, are all highly complementary through the term *shahadat*—"Witnessing means martyrdom. . . . There is a close link between seeing and dying in the etymology of martyrdom" (Devji 2005: 94).[31] But the significance of shahadat is much greater than that of the individual martyr's self-experiencing—the term resonates powerfully with medieval and modern understandings of enduring habitus (Nederman 1989; Bourdieu 1977) and too with the Deleuze and Guattari

(1988) understanding of dynamic assemblage constituted to momentarily reshape and act on realities. Devji (2005: 94–95) comments that:

> *Shahadat* involves not only the person whose life is voluntarily sacrificed for the cause of God, but *everyone* [my emphasis] annihilated in this cause whether willingly or not. Not only people, but animals, buildings and other inanimate objects as well may participate in the rite, including even those who witness the martyrdom of others without themselves being killed. . . . *Shahadat* is a fundamentally social and therefore inclusive act, the pity and compassion it excites among witnesses forming part of its classical as much as contemporary definition . . . perpetrators, victims, bystanders, other animate and inanimate witnesses, near or far, all of whom constitute by their very seeing the landscape of the jihad as a site of sociability.

The total act of self-exploding brings into one another habitus in its more enduring reality and assemblage in its more immediate configuration, through where and when the self explodes. Self-sacrifice in these terms is always an act of *cosmogenesis* that ultimately is social, while the scale and grandeur of the self-sacrifice expands its sociability.

The transitory assemblage that enables the explosion totalizes habitus through the sacrifice, a total act that is intended to be one of cosmic (re)creation. The sacrifice and martyrdom are shaped as their own proof, utterly self-contained (Devji 2005: 102, 104), supremely interior even as they effect the exteriority of habitus. Implicitly or explicitly, this shaping of the 9/11 sacrifice likely speaks to its ritual forming through preparation, even though this aspect of the totality of the act has been quite ignored by scholars and other interpreters.[32]

In the spiritual manual, the attack is called a raid (*ghazwa*) for the sake of God, one whose intention is voluntary and whose preparation is ascetic—in classical Arabic literature, like all wars against infidels, "a kind of worship" (Kippenberg 2005: 36). The term "*raid*" also referred to each of the groups or cells that came together on the morning of 9/11 to do the attack. The manual orientates the conditions of being of the attackers, toward one another and individually. It opens with "a mutual pledge (*bai'a*) to die and the renewal of intent (*niyya*)" (Kippenberg 2005: 37).[33] Intention and action must braid together, both in worship and in battle and in battle as worship. Intention must be such that the attacker is purified of all personal emotion, such as a desire for personal vengeance, so that the sacrifice is selfless. Selfless, yet self-responsible and the outcome of free choice, the (self-)sacrificial total and totalizing act is turned into the practice of ethics, argues Devji (2005: 102, 120). Only when the action is for the sake of God alone, can violence be turned into sacred act (Kippenberg 2005: 39). In my terms, the sacrificer prepares himself as a vehicle of self-transformation through violence, the pure gift (Kapferer 1997), the self-sacrifice of the selfless self, the sacrifice of other. Through their pledge of mutuality, the self-sacrificers form or re-form themselves as a community. As a microcosm, the entire (male) religious polity goes to a battle of self-sacrifice for the sake of God.[34]

The manual divides the raid into a three-part sequence: the first part, the night before, during which the attacker struggles with his own soul; the second part, the following morning at the airport, when the attacker struggles with the satanic forces all about him, all of the unbelievers and their institutions; and the third part, the battle against the unbelievers inside the airplane. The sequencing of these three parts is significant. First, the purification of deepest interiority within the person, as he takes into himself and embodies the ascetic state of being of the sacrificer for God (Euben 2002: 19). Second, the exteriorization of this condition of being, as the intentionality of the sacrificer's line of flight moves into the world, meeting the first ranks of the enemy face-to-face, yet needing to elude these in order to penetrate the target and close with his victims. Third, the violence of sacrifice.

The manual prescribes fifteen exercises for the night before the attack. These include recitals, prayers, meditations, and purifications.[35] Cook (2002: 25) contends that "during the period of time covered by 'The Last Night' the attackers would consider themselves to be dead." Kippenberg (2005: 39) comments that the Arabic word for "recital" (*dhikr*) means "remembering" in a broad sense; and that the manual chooses Suras 8 and 9 from the Qur'an, both originating when Muhammad the persecuted prophet had turned into the warrior and had begun establishing the Islamic State in Medina, breaking off all contact with non-Muslims except that of attack, kill, or convert. Following the recital of the Suras, the manual prescribes Sufi practices of self-forming. The carnal self wants to live, not die. Yet the ascetic, denying the world, must persuade, tame, awaken, and drive the self to action through self-purification. Not unlike the woman who puts on the veil, the self-sacrificer must become patient and modest, with honed will and dedication. Thus Mohamed Atta, thought to be the leader of the four cells, left instructions long before the 9/11 attack that whosoever washed his corpse should wear gloves so that his genitals would not be touched; and asked that pregnant women and unclean persons not be allowed to see his body, attend his funeral, or go to his grave (Gole 2002). There follow instructions on sharpening the sacrificial knife and the wearing of proper clothing for the attack. In the morning, prayers, a ritual washing, the shaving of excess hair from the body and the application of perfume (Mneimneh and Makiya 2002). Cook argues that the attention to preparation of their bodies by the attackers is related to the preparation of a corpse for burial. Thus, "One should note that in Islam, although normally corpses are prepared after death [*sic*], the body of a *shahid* is deemed to have been purified by the act of martyrdom, and the body is buried in the state in which the person died" (Cook 2002: 25). With all of these purifying acts—spiritual, physical—the first part of the manual ends.

Mneimneh and Makiya (2002) argue that the attackers enter a great sacred drama and the heroic deeds of the Companions of the Prophet of the Seventh Century. Probably so, yet the attackers are preparing themselves both as sacrifices and as sacrificed. For this they ritualize themselves as warriors, re-forming self and body through inner discipline and purification, so that these will awaken with agency, as one. So, too, they prepare themselves as the perfect sacrifice to God, selfless, honed, aimed, totally committed, their intentionality utterly willed and joined to their task. They re-create themselves as the very capacity to deliver both *other* (the infidel) and *self* (the true believer) as the totalizing of sacrificial violence, the entirety of cosmos in the process of transformation.[36]

In the second part of this ritual, the warrior ventures forth from within himself on the way to the airport, advancing his being into a world ruled by satanic powers, yet protected from them, undetected by them. So long as he is in a condition of worship, of living truth, reminding himself repeatedly of God, he can deceive those who live in a world of lies as to his identity (Kippenberg 2005: 42–43). At each point in the journey he silently invokes God's blessing. He wears his purified intentional interiority on his exterior, and this mask or shield cannot be pierced by his enemies, by "Western Civilization," as the manual says, with all its technological might.

In the third part of the ritual, quietly reciting Qur'an and prayers, the attacker enters the plane, and self-sacrifice, martyrdom, dominates, yet as always, this can only be granted by God, by His divinely authorized plan, to which martyrdom is submission (Euben 2002: 26). The manual tells the attackers to "Clench your teeth as did [your] predecessors . . . before engaging in battle. Hit as would heroes who desire not to return to the World" (Mneimneh and Makiya 2002; Kippenberg 2005: 45). If there is resistance to the hijacking, those persons should be killed as a "ritual slaughter" (*dhabaha*, rather than *qatala*, to kill), as an act of grace conferred by God and an offering made to God, through filial devotion on behalf of the attacker's parents. According to Mneimneh and Makiya, dictionaries of classical Arabic give the meaning of *dhabaha* as "to cleave, slit, or rip something open. This is the word used for slitting the two external jugular veins in the throat of an animal. It is quick, direct, and always *physically intimate:* one does not slaughter with a gun, or a bomb, from afar. . . . *Dhabaha* is also that which Abraham was prepared to do to his son on God's instructions." And, as the sacrificer enters his own death, the manual says, "When the moment of truth comes near, and zero hour is upon you, open your chest welcoming death on the path of God" (Kippenberg 2005: 46). "Opening his chest," his interior, the sacrificer is himself the perfect sacrifice, selflessly welcoming self-death, self-sacrifice. Devji (2005: 120) argues that this moment of martyrdom is "the purest and therefore the most ethical of acts, because in destroying himself its soldier becomes fully human by assuming complete responsibility for his fate beyond the reach of any need, interest or idea."[37]

I have suggested that the logic of this moment is one of transformation, the totalizing of a microcosmos constituted of self and other in which self dedicates the sacrifice of other and, simultaneously, dedicates his own death by sacrifice, all by the grace of God, in the name of martyrdom and the generation of the transcendent Islamic polity. The entire sequence—which I understand as a ritual sequence

(Handelman 2005)—shapes a line of flight through which the self of the sacrificer is first made malleable within itself and shaped through purification and dedication of intent. This self is a self among fellow selves, filiated selves, a band of warrior brothers who selflessly are no longer other to one another among themselves. Self-dedicated, they know one another intimately, indeed a condition of *communitas*. This interior self (and selves) then emerges from within itself, thrusting rhizomically with speed and intensity deep within the world of the alien enemy other, until it penetrates the interior of the selfness of this other (within the aircraft, outside the aircraft). The interior self of the sacrificer kills that of the other, thereby destroying its existence in this microcosmos. The sacrificer, self-witnessing, self-sacrifices, and this microcosmos with its presence of the alien enemy other utterly ceases to exist. In its own way, this is a primordial act of transformation at the very heart of creation; perhaps, as Agamben (1998: 105) puts it, this is the "survival of the state of nature at the very heart of the state."

Sacrifice, as we understand this in traditional moral orders, is an *economy of violence*, of violence calibrated to accomplish transformations necessary for dynamics of survival of person, group, social order, in a self-creating cosmos.[38] The "state of nature" at the very heart of moral order was calibrated to destroy in ongoing relationship to that which would be created within social orders. The manmade mass death of the twentieth century has exploded through the massive deaths of trench warfare, through the military killings of civilians in World War II, and now through mutations of civilians massacring civilians augmented by rhizomic terrorism. The economy of sacrificial violence inflated in modernity and blew up, as sacrifice already joined to military death and the military slaughter of civilians became joined to civilians slaughtering civilians, and to terrorism. *Sacrifice itself becomes rhizomic*, braided into speed, penetration, and small-scale acts amplified into massive uncertainty by state and global responses. Terrorism and self-sacrificial terrorism target the very complexities upon which modern infrastructures depend, demonstrating the fragility of their jointing, of their coordination and synchronization. Potential targets move toward the infinite in number (Simon and Benjamin 2001–02: 14), certainly a lesson of today's Iraq, and the state mobilizes "to wage infinite war on an indefinite enemy" (Dillon 2002: 77).

The outcome of these amplifications may be what Beck (2002: 41) calls the world risk society, "a world of uncontrollable risk" in which rhizomic terrorism and self-exploders join together with vectors of ecological deterioration, disease, starvation, population movement, mass slaughter, financial crises, all of which overflow the borders of particular states, fill interstices in fuzzy areas among and amidst fuzzy states (Mbembe 2000), and are transnational in differing configurations of presence and effect, amplifying threat, fear, and its administration (e.g., Virilio 2007: 17–18).

State response to rhizomic terrorism is to reify borders; to exact the marking and identification of persons; to slow down, stop, and freeze movement (e.g., Bajc 2007); to increase surveillance in public spaces and private lives—to shape an increasingly gated, exclusionary state. In general to adopt what Virilio (2007: 43) calls the myth of "a precautionary principle," which seems to promise absolute security to everyone selected for inclusion within state bastions manned by fear against exterior threat, demanding what Beck (2002: 41) calls the feigning of control over the uncontrollable. Without a doubt, the terrorism I am discussing and state initiatives are intimately complicit and powerfully self-fulfilling (Zulaika 2003). To a serious degree, states contribute to the shaping of terror for their own purposes (American support for al-Qaida in Afghanistan against the Soviets; Israeli support for the early Hamas as a counterweight to Fatah).

Yet this relationship between terrorism and state cannot be reduced to the methodological rationalism of economistic calculations of the political. Metaphysics stirs just beneath the surface in its world-breaking and world-making capacities. Through rhizomic violence, Muslim self-exploders seek an end to violence in the creation of the goodness of a transcendent polity, even as the destruction they do engenders further violence that denies the realization of this or any other utopia. Americans dote on the badness of rhizomic violence within their borders and elsewhere, even as they erect more and higher walls of the good to imprison this—always failing, always convinced of the utopic righteousness of their cause (see Duclos 1998). Responding to the rhizomic through its trans-form, the state form, in order to destroy the former, just augments and accelerates the rhizome-state form dynamic. Yet in the present day the forming and destroying dynamic of rhizome and state form, each within the other, each growing the other, are increasingly amplified by technological means of control and destruction, threatening life more than any "war of civilizations."

Notes

First published in 2011 as "Self-Exploders, Self-Sacrifice, and the Rhizomic Organization of Terrorism," in *Religion, Politics and Globalization: Anthropological Approaches*, ed. Galina Lindquist and Don Handelman, 231–62. New York: Berghahn Books. Reprinted with permission. Though not deliberately, this work emerged contrapuntally to my *Nationalism and the Israeli State: Bureaucratic Logic in Public Events* (2004). That book focuses on the forming power of the bureaucratic logic of the state. This chapter was given in seminars at the University of Bergen, the University of Capetown, and Stockholm University. My thanks to the participants for their responses. For their comments I am indebted especially to Smadar Lavie, the late Galina Lindquist, Limor Samimian Darash, and Liora Sion.

1. The term *suicide bomber* is an oxymoron. The intention of this bomber is, first and foremost, purposefully to kill other people. (The point is made by Israeli [2002] and others, though I reached this position independently). The formative dynamic of the act is that the bomber dies in killing others; and this conjoining of self and other may index the logic of sacrifice permeating many of these acts. Nasra Hassan (2001) reports that Hamas self-exploders are called "sacred exploders."
2. One should not forget that a terrorist cell on 9/11 also intended the hijacking of a flight from Heathrow to Manchester in order to crash the aircraft into the British Houses of Parliament. By the time the cell members reached Heathrow, the attacks in America already had occurred and the airport was closed to flight traffic (Gunaratna 2002: 119).

3. Durkheim himself was offended by suicide. This may have reflected the deeply rooted monotheism of the modern Western state, and the value given to the individual as an autonomous social unit in France and elsewhere. If the individual is understood as an autonomous microunit, then it is a holistic entirety, even if in a limited sense. Then self-killing makes the microunit extinct, the death of no value to social order. However, for the individual to die for group bonds and values is to create death as sacrifice, death that is of value to social order.
4. Thus most scholars and theologians of Islam whom we hear of distinguish between canonical religion that eschews suicide, whatever the cause and intention, and sects that deviate from the canon.
5. See W. G. Sebald's (2004) discussions of the allied bombing of Hamburg, and John Hersey's ([1946] 1989) all but forgotten classic description of Hiroshima nuclearized, as told by survivors.
6. Contrast this with the definition of terrorism given by the US State Department in 1983: "Terrorism is premeditated, politically motivated violence perpetrated against non-combatant targets by sub-national groups or clandestine agents, usually intended to influence an audience" (Kippenberg 2005: 55).
7. Philosophers differ, in their own terms, as to whether terror is a moral act. Compare with Primoratz's (1997) contention that terrorism is morally impermissible, and Held's (1991) claim that terrorism is justified in terms of human rights and distributive justice. See also Devji's (2005: 120) argument that martyrdom entails an ethical act.
8. Pure terrorism seems to be quite absent from conflicts within relatively homogeneous social orders; there, riots, assassinations, and guerrilla warfare will be more prominent (Black 2004: 20).
9. Neocleous (2006: 374–76) charts how, in the United States, the idea of "national security" developed from that of "social security." Social security policies, designed in the main to protect the citizenry against rapacious capitalism, also spawned the idea of national security after World War II. Neocleous (2006: 378–80) argues that the "national security state" was intended first and foremost not for military purposes as such, but to further economic security, in other words to make the world safe for capital expansion and accumulation.
10. *International Herald Tribune*, 9–10 September 2006. See also, "Judging Evil Intent: It's All in the Body Language—A New Squad at Dulles Airport Is Scrutinizing Travelers for Behavioral Signs of Bad Intentions," *International Herald Tribune*, 18 August 2006.
11. This schematic portrait is much more complex than I have space for here. As Mbembe (2003: 31–33) notes, military operations and the right to killing practices are no longer the monopoly of states—thus mercenaries, child soldiers, citizen soldiers, and privateers abound in different combinations in Africa, in spaces that are "a patchwork of overlapping and incomplete rights to rule . . . inextricably superimposed and tangled, in which different de facto juridical instances are geographically interwoven and plural allegiances, asymmetrical suzerainties, and enclaves abound" (Mbembe 2003: 31).
12. Krebs, http://www.firstmonday.org/issues/issue7_/krebs/.
13. Before 9/11, al-Qaida operatives returned over 20,000 USD in unused funds to leaders in the Middle East (Basile 2004: 172). Hassan (2001) reports that the cost of organizing an armed self-exploder to enter Israel was about 150 USD. The ingredients are of the order of nails, gunpowder, a light switch and cable, mercury, acetone. The most expensive item is transportation. For that matter, the bombs exploded in London in 2005 cost only a few hundred pounds sterling (*Observer*, 9 April 2006).
14. Researchers of organizations sometimes speak of "autocatalysis"—"a tendency of recursive systems to self-generate catalysts that speed up or enable the emergence and evolution of forms" (Marion and Uhl-Bien 2003: 61).
15. These qualities are why some analysts compare al-Qaida to a modern corporation whose existence is primarily through the flow of capital, investment, and production, rather than through any permanent physical presence in particular places.

16. According to Scott Atran (2003), al-Qaida, Hamas, Palestinian Islamic Jihad, and Hezbollah use small cells of three to eight members who are brought to feel the cell as a family of fictive kin "for whom they are as willing to die as a mother for her child or a soldier for his buddies." http://www.interdisciplines.org/terrorism/papers/1. See also Sageman (2004). A rich source of information on self-exploders in Gaza, especially during the First Intifada, is Oliver and Steinberg (2005).
17. Thus Iraq's Ansar al-Islam and Pakistan's Lashkar-e-Jhangvi and Jaish-e-Muhammed may be coordinating operations, following al-Qaida's example and swarming through their own impetus (Atran 2004b). Swarming in warfare is said to have powerful historical antecedents (Edwards 2005: 13–52), and the language and ideas of swarming are used by strategic planners to describe future warfare built through highly mobile and flexible units that join together for particular operations and then disperse, no longer using fixed weapons platforms as bases from which to launch operations, adapting to continuously changing battlescapes that are related to as ecosystems (Arquilla and Ronfeldt 2000; Dillon 2002: 72). Such imaginaries seem to be rejected by American military brass. See also Dillon (2002: 74). Nonetheless, there is evidence that the initial (and successful) American attacks on Afghanistan and Iraq used swarming tactics. Some Israeli military strategists in low-intensity urban warfare on the West Bank explicitly adapt the rhizome of Deleuze and Guattari to develop strategies of "infestation" in attack (Weizman 2006a) and "necrotactics" (Weizman 2006b). From a military perspective, necrotactics reverse traditional goals of warfare by temporarily entering strategic ground *solely* in order to kill enemies (Weizman 2006b: 81). The last Israeli army offensive into Gaza, called *Operation Cast Lead*, used necrotactics. Asaf Hazani (personal communication) tells me that Israeli Army "infestation strategies" were taken from those used by the French paras in the battle for the Casbah of Algiers. Especially interesting are the rhizomic parallels in movement between self-exploders and some military units. Likely they learn from one another. In response to the Israeli Army's practice of low-density urban warfare, its ethicist, a professor of analytic philosophy, is defining neat moral distinctions (similar to those formulated to cover "ticking bombs") between "preventive killing" and assassination. In other words, as to when murder is moral (see Kasher and Yadlin 2005a, 2005b).
18. Implicit within, though especially germane to the Deleuze and Guattari argument is that the deeply rooted state-form is especially vulnerable where its lines of movement slow down, becoming densely constricted with limited lines of flight. For the self-exploder, such concentrations, approaching stasis in the restricted movement within them, are excellent targets. Perhaps for al-Qaida the Twin Towers were a lure hard to resist, a gigantic trap of limited, clumsy, machinic, vertical movement, existing (like all skyscrapers) ethereally, seemingly unconnected to their own grounding in the world of human beings, with no ethical responsibility to the earthy struggling "ants" way below. Exploded, the Twin Towers were revealed as ponderous trees deeply rooted in earth masquerading as sky.
19. Consider the implications of the rhizomic dynamic when it is propelled by a universal religion.
20. In differing degrees, Hezbollah (in Lebanon) and now Hamas (in Gaza) are evolving in counterpoint to al-Qaida, from more rhizomic to more centralized, deeply rooted organizations. The point is that these are various potentialities actualizing; and so far, these organizations have shown high capacities for altering their self-organization in relation to changing circumstance and ecology.
21. *Ha'aretz* (English edition), 13 September 2009.
22. Despite the relevance of rhizomic dynamics to understanding terrorist cells and networks in relation to state structures, I found no such connections in the literature I read, apart from one essay by a historian (Griffin 2003). He, however, uses *rhizome* as an ideal type, while Deleuze and Guattari understand the dynamic as entirely relational.
23. *Rhizome* should be differentiated from *network*. The rhizome is its own dynamic, obviating distinctions of the order of "structure" and "process" or "structure" and "content." The rhizomic point is itself dynamic, swelling into verticality, receding into the snaking lateral movement of

another rhizome in the making. The conception of network, as this usually is understood, including its application to terrorism (Knorr Cetina 2005; Sageman 2004), depends on relatively fixed points (the individuals in the net) whose relatedness to one another is analyzed through how the structural properties of these points connect these individuals to one another. Network, then, is first and foremost a structure to which the content of relatedness between points is imputed. This relatedness (through structural properties of points, and through the content of relatedness that connects these points) is confounded with dynamics. On the other hand, network could also be understood as an emergent property of the rhizomic dynamic, one driving toward structuration and verticality.

24. Violence can be done equally well to vegetal form as to animal or human. The ancient Greeks called the "dismemberment" of form *sparagmos*, and the term was used extensively by Victor Turner to denote social order taken apart ritually.
25. From its outset Islam was a political religion, aimed at the creation of an Islamic State, the intention of the Prophet during the last decade of his life, after he left Mecca for Medina. Muhammad can also be cast, in the present era, "as the chief example of both self-sacrificial death and self-sacrifice (*tad'hia*') that is linked essentially with jihad" (Strenski 2003: 14). Such positions are criticized by Ahmad (2009: 148) who argues that, "it is [only] during the early twentieth century that a fully developed political theory of the Islamic state emerged in the discourse of Islamism."
26. Israeli (2002: 25–26) traces the Hezbollah innovation of what he calls "islamikaze" to the Shi'a reversal of the tragic mourning of the suffering and martyrdom of Imam Hussein at Karbala into the celebratory attacking martyrdom of the bombers, in which Hussein becomes not someone to be mourned but a heroic model of the battling warrior. Israeli's neologism is based on the similarities he perceives between Islamic human bombers and the Japanese kamikaze of World War II. On kamikaze see Ohnuki-Tierney (2002).
27. As Friedman (2002: 108) comments, intellectuals tend to take intentionality away from the bombers, turning them into representations or embodiments of social problems. Intellectuals thereby miss the workings of praxis that they so often extol.
28. The ultimate decision as to the intentionality of the self-exploder is that of heaven, of Allah.
29. If the appellation of *suicide bomber* is accepted without critique, as Asad (2007) does, this obviates the transformative dynamic of self-sacrifice. Indeed, this is a signal weakness in Asad's analysis. Thus, "Suicide [in the Abrahamic religions] is a sin because it is a unique act of freedom, a right that neither the religious authorities nor the nation-state allows" (Asad 2007: 67). Yet, the self-sacrificer in Islam cannot know beforehand how God will judge his intentionality and whether God will accept his self-sacrifice.
30. Kippenberg (2005: 56–57) notes that *The 9/11 Commission Report* (2004) reconstructs the sequence of events leading to the attack yet utterly ignores the manual. The American "concept of a war against evil portrays the attackers as devoid of religious faith." The faithless cannot have morality in a state that, after all, is one of Christian believers.
31. Lewinstein (2001: 79) comments on early Islam that *shahid* likely acquired its sense as "martyr" as "a reflex of late antique Christian usage."
32. Neria et al. (2005: 7–8) argue that this document presents an "as if" reality, in effect, ritual-as-pretense of ritual that enabled the attackers to dissociate themselves from the real, violent consequences of their action. In my view this demonstrates a complete lack of comprehension of the relationship between sacrifice, violence, and transformation. To date, psychologists have contributed little to comprehending self-exploders (for example, Guss, Tuason, and Teixeira 2007).
33. For Hasan al-Bana, the founder of the Muslim Brotherhood, "death is the very goal of *jihad*, and willingness to die is the key to its success" (Brown 2001: 113).
34. I am not concerned with whether or not such formations accord with "canonical" Islamic traditions. My premise is that in all moral and social orders, religious life, like all other domains of living, goes through innovation and emergence, most of which is disregarded and discarded,

though each has its own history, were we able to trace this. This has been a prominent theme of my thinking for the past four decades. As I have discussed this here, the entire phenomenon of terrorism as we are experiencing this is innovative, as is, to a degree, the rhizomic forming this takes, in movement, changing shapes. Must religious forming accord always with Durkheimian genealogical foundationalism? My position here accords in more general substantial terms with that of Faisal Devji (2005).

35. When the practices of the manual are referred to, too often this offers "rational" explanation of the order of: "prayer is ritual designed to block thought, to prevent the spontaneous upsurge of disobedient impulses and inclinations. Prayer is anesthesia" (Holmes 2005: 151–52). For a psychologistic rationalization of the manual, see Neria et al. (2005).

36. Hassan (2001) quotes Palestinian bombers (whose explosives failed to detonate) as saying, "We were in a constant state of worship. . . . Those were the happiest days of my life," and "We were floating, swimming, in the feeling that we were about to enter eternity."

37. This argument gives us an idea of just why it is so important on the part of Western media, scholars, publicists, and politicians to demean and denigrate the terrorist self-sacrificer by labeling him or her mentally ill, mentally retarded, lost in despair and hopelessness, brainwashed, and, not least, without true religious belief. Devji (2005: 120) writes that "the Islam of the suicide bomber is an absolutely personal quality, as distant from the group identity of the traditional cleric as it is from the state ideology of the fundamentalist."

38. This is lost sight of too often by scholars of the logic of "sacrificial violence" in modernity, in which violence and sacrifice are nearly equated. As Martel (2006: 819) puts it, "if everything is sacrifice, then nothing is sacrifice."

References

Ackerman, Bruce. 2006. *Before the Next Attack: Preserving Civil Liberties in an Age of Terrorism*. New Haven: Yale University Press.
Agamben, Giorgio. 1998. *Homo Sacer: Sovereign Power and Bare Life*. Stanford: Stanford University Press.
Ahmad, Irfan. 2009. "Genealogy of the Islamic State: Reflections on Maududi's Political Thought and Islam." *Journal of the Royal Anthropological Institute* n.s.: S145–S162.
Andriolo, Karin. 2002. "Murder by Suicide: Episodes from Muslim History." *American Anthropologist* 104: 736–42.
Arquilla, John, and David Ronfeldt. 2000. *Swarming and the Future of Conflict*. Santa Monica: Rand Corporation.
Asad, Talal. 2007. *On Suicide Bombing*. New York: Columbia University Press.
Atran, Scott. 2003. "Genesis and Future of Suicide Terrorism." *Science* 299: 1534–39.
———. 2004a. "Trends in Suicide Terrorism: Sense and Nonsense." World Federation of Scientists Permanent Monitoring Panel on Terrorism, Erice, Sicily.
———. 2004b. "The Jihadist Mutation." Retrieved 21 December 2005 from http://www.jamestown.org/publications_details.php?volume_id=400&&issue_id = 2929.
Bajc, Vida. 2007. "Surveillance in Public Rituals: Security Meta-ritual and the 2005 US Presidential Inauguration." *American Behavioral Scientist* 50: 1648–73.
Basile, Mark. 2004. "Going to the Source: Why Al Qaeda's Financial Network Is Likely to Withstand the Current War on Terrorist Financing." *Studies in Conflict and Terrorism* 27: 169–85.
Beck, Ulrich. 2002. "The Terrorist Threat: World Risk Society Revisited." *Theory, Culture & Society* 19: 39–55.
Beinin, Joel. 2003. "Is Terrorism a Useful Term in Understanding the Middle East and the Palestinian-Israel Conflict?" *Radical History Review* 85: 12–23.
Bergen, Peter. 2001. *Holy Terror, Inc.: Inside the Secret World of Osama bin Laden*. New York: Free Press.

Berkowitz, Steven D., Lloyd H. Woodward, and Caitlin Woodward. 2005. "The Use of Formal Methods to Map, Analyze and Interpret *Hawala* and Terrorist-Related Remittance Systems." *Structure and Dynamics: eJournal of Anthropological and Related Sciences*. Retrieved 10 May 2006 from http://repositories cdlib.org/imbs/socdyn/sdeas/vol1/iss2/artc.

Black, Donald. 2004. "The Geometry of Terrorism." *Sociological Theory* 22: 14–25.

Bourdieu, Pierre. 1977. *Outline of a Theory of Practice*. Cambridge, UK: Cambridge University Press.

Brown, Daniel. 2001. "Martyrdom in Sunni Revivalist Thought." In *Sacrificing the Self: Perspectives on Martyrdom and Religion*, ed. Margaret Cormack, 107–17. New York: Oxford University Press.

Cohn, Norman. 1970. *Pursuit of the Millennium: Revolutionary Millenarians and Mystical Anarchists in the Middle Ages*. New York: Oxford University Press.

Cook, David. 2002. "Suicide Attacks or 'Martyrdom Operations' in Contemporary Jihad Literature." *Nova Religio: The Journal of Alternative and Emergent Religions* 6: 7–43.

Dale, Stephen Frederic. 1988. "Religious Suicide in Islamic Asia: Anticolonial Terrorism in India, Indonesia, and the Philippines." *Journal of Conflict Resolution* 32: 37–59.

Deleuze, Gilles, and Felix Guattari. 1983. *On the Line*. New York: Semiotext(e).

———. 1986. *Nomadology: The War Machine*. New York: Semiotext(e).

———. 1988. A *Thousand Plateaus*. London: Athlone Press.

Devji, Faisal. 2005. *Landscapes of the Jihad: Militancy, Morality, Modernity*. London: Hurst.

Dillon, Michael. 2002. "Network Society, Network-centric Warfare and the State of Emergency." *Theory, Culture & Society* 19: 71–79.

Duclos, Denis. 1998. *The Werewolf Complex: America's Fascination with Violence*. Oxford: Berg.

Durkheim, Emile. 1952. *Suicide*. London: Routledge & Kegan Paul.

Edwards, Sean J. A. 2005. *Swarming and the Future of Warfare*. Rand Corporation, Document No.: RGSD-189. Retrieved 14 April 2006 from http://www.rand.org/pubs/rgs_dissertations/RGSD189.

Euben, Roxanne L. 2002. "Killing (for) Politics: *Jihad*, Martyrdom and Political Action." *Political Theory* 30: 4–35.

Friedman, Jonathan. 2002. "From Nine-Eleven to Seven-Eleven: The Poverty of Interpretation." *Social Analysis: The International Journal of Social and Cultural Practice* 46: 104–9.

Gambetta, Diego. 2005a. "Reason and Terror: Has 9/11 Made It Hard to Think Straight?" *Boston Review*. Retrieved 30 January 2006 from http://bostonreview.net/BR29.2/gambetta.html.

———. 2005b. "Can We Make Sense of Suicide Missions?" In *Making Sense of Suicide Missions*, ed. Diego Gambetta, 259–99. Oxford: Oxford University Press.

Gole, Nilufer. 2002. "Close Encounters: Islam, Modernity and Violence." In *Understanding September 11*, ed. Craig J. Calhoun, Paul Price, and Ashley S. Timmer. New York: New West Press.

Greenhouse, Carol. 1989. "Fighting for Peace." In *Peace and War: Cross-Cultural Perspectives*, ed. Mary LeCron Foster and Robert A. Rubinstein, 49–60. New Brunswick: Transaction Books.

Griffin, Roger. 2003. "From Slime Mould to Rhizome: An Introduction to the Groupuscular Right." *Patterns of Prejudice* 37: 27–50.

Gunaratna, Rohan. 2002. *Inside Al Qaeda: Global Network of Terror*. New York: Columbia University Press.

Guss, C. Dominik, Ma. Teresa Tuason, and Vanessa B. Teixeira. 2007. "A Cultural-Psychological Theory of Contemporary Islamic Martyrdom." *Journal for the Theory of Social Behavior* 37: 415–45.

Gwynne, Rosalind W. 2006. "Usama bin Laden, the Qu'ran and Jihad." *Religion* 36: 61–90.

Hage, Ghassan. 2003. "'Comes a time we are all enthusiasm': Understanding Palestinian Suicide Bombers in Times of Exighophobia." *Public Culture* 15: 65–89.

Handelman, Don. 2004. *Nationalism and the Israeli State: Bureaucratic Logic in Public Events*. Oxford: Berg.

———. 2005. "Introduction: Why Ritual in Its Own Right? How So?" In *Ritual in its Own Right: Exploring the Dynamics of Transformation*, ed. Don Handelman and Galina Lindquist, 1–32. New York: Berghahn Books.

Hassan, Nasra. 2001. "An Arsenal of Believers: Talking to the 'Human Bombs.'" *New Yorker*, 11 November.
Held, Virginia. 1991. "Terrorism, Rights, and Political Goals." In *Violence, Terrorism, and Justice*, ed. Raymond G. Frey and Cristopher W. Morris, 59–85. Cambridge, UK: Cambridge University Press.
Hersey, John. (1946) 1989. *Hiroshima*. New York: Vintage.
Hoffman, Bruce. 2003. "Al Qaeda, Trends in Terrorism, and Future Potentialities: An Assessment." *Studies in Conflict and Terrorism* 26: 429–42.
Holmes, Stephen. 2005. "Al-Qaeda, September 11, 2001." In *Making Sense of Suicide Missions*, ed. Diego Gambetta, 131–72. Oxford: Oxford University Press.
Hubert, Henri, and Marcel Mauss. 1964. *Sacrifice: Its Nature and Function*. Chicago: University of Chicago Press.
Hull, Isabel V. 2005. *Absolute Destruction: Military Culture and the Practices of War in Imperial Germany*. Ithaca: Cornell University Press.
International Institute for Strategic Studies. 2003. *The Military Balance 2003–2004*. London: Arundel House.
Israeli, Raphael. 2002. "A Manual of Islamic Fundamentalist Terrorism." *Terrorism and Political Violence* 14: 23–40.
Kapferer, Bruce. 1997. *The Feast of the Sorcerer*. Chicago: University of Chicago Press.
Kasher, Asa, and Amos Yadlin. 2005a. "Assassination and Preventive Killing." *SAIS Review* 25: 41–57.
———. 2005b. "Military Ethics of Fighting Terror: An Israeli Perspective." *Journal of Military Ethics* 4: 3–32.
Kippenberg, Hans G. 2005. "'Consider that it is a raid on the path of God': The Spiritual Manual of the Attackers of 9/11." *Numen* 52: 29–58.
Knorr Cetina, Karin. 2005. "Complex Global Microstructures: The New Terrorist Societies." *Theory, Culture & Society* 22: 213–34.
Krebs, Valdis E. n.d. "Uncloaking Terrorist Networks." Retrieved 11 September 2005 from http://www.firstmonday.org/ issues/issue7_4/krebs/.
Lewinstein, Keith. 2001. "The Revaluation of Martyrdom in Early Islam." In *Sacrificing the Self: Perspectives on Martyrdom and Religion*, ed. Margaret Cormack. New York: Oxford University Press, 78–91.
Lind, William S., Keith Nightengale, John F. Schmitt, Joseph W. Sutton, and Gary I. Wilson. 1989. "The Changing Face of War: Into the Fourth Generation." *Marine Corps Gazette*, 22–26 October. http://www.d-n-i.net/fcs/4th_gen_war_gazette.htm.
Mahmood, Saba. 2001. "Feminist Theory, Embodiment, and the Docile Agent: Some Reflections on the Egyptian Islamic Revival." *Cultural Anthropology* 16: 202–36.
Mannheim, Karl. 1936. *Ideology and Utopia*. London: Routledge & Kegan Paul.
Marion, Russ, and Mary Uhl-Bien. 2003. "Complexity Theory and Al-Qaeda: Examining Complex Leadership." *Emergence* 5: 54–76.
Martel, James R. 2006. "Can we do away with sacrifice?" *Political Theory* 34: 814–20.
Marvin, Carolyn, and David W. Ingle. 1999. *Blood Sacrifice and the Nation: Totem Rituals and the American Flag*. Cambridge, UK: Cambridge University Press.
Mbembe, Achille. 2000. "At the Edge of the World: Boundaries, Territoriality, and Sovereignty in Africa." *Public Culture* 12: 259–84.
———. 2003. "Necropolitics." *Public Culture* 15: 11–40.
Mishal, Shaul, and Maoz Rosenthal. 2005. "Al-Qaeda as a Dune Organization: Toward a Typology of Islamic Terrorist Organizations." *Studies in Conflict and Terrorism* 28: 275–93.
Mneimneh, Hassan, and Kanan Makiya. 2002. "Manual for a 'Raid.'" *New York Review of Books* 49 (January 17).
Moghaddam, Fathali M. 2005. "The Staircase to Terrorism: A Psychological Exploration." *American Psychologist* 60: 161–69.

NAACSOS Conference, Day 3, Pittsburgh, PA. Retrieved 5 July 2005 from http://casos.cs.cmu.edu/events/conferences/2003/proceedings.html.

Nederman, Cary J. 1989. "Nature, Ethics, and the Doctrine of 'Habitus': Aristotelian Moral Psychology in the Twelfth Century." *Traditio* 45: 87–110.

Neocleous, Mark. 2006. "From Social to National Security: On the Fabrication of Economic Order." *Security Dialogue* 37: 363–84.

Neria, Yuval, David Roe, Benjamin Beit-Hallahmi, Hassan Mneimneh, Alana Balaban, and Randall Marshall. 2005. "The Al Qaeda 9/11 Instructions: A Study in the Construction of Religious Martyrdom." *Religion* 35: 1–11.

Ohnuki-Tierney, Emiko. 2002. *Kamikaze, Cherry Blossoms, and Nationalisms: The Militarization of Aesthetics in Japanese History*. Chicago: University of Chicago Press.

Oliver, Anne Marie, and Paul Steinberg. 2005. *The Road to Martyrs' Square: A Journey into the World of the Suicide Bomber*. New York: Oxford University Press.

Primoratz, Igor. 1997. "The Morality of Terrorism." *Journal of Applied Philosophy* 14: 221–33.

Rapoport, David C. 1984. "Fear and Trembling: Terrorism in Three Religious Traditions." *American Political Science Review* 78: 658–77.

Raufer, Xavier. 2003. "Al Qaeda: A Different Diagnosis." *Studies in Conflict and Terrorism* 26: 391–98.

Roberts, Michael. n.d. "Blunders in Tigerland: Pape's Muddles on 'Suicide Bombers' in Sri Lanka." Unpublished manuscript.

———. 2005a. "Tamil Tiger 'Martyrs': Regenerating Divine Potency?" *Studies in Conflict and Terrorism* 28: 493–514.

———. 2005b. "Saivite Symbolism, Sacrifice and Tamil Tiger Rites." *Social Analysis* 59: 67–93.

Sageman, Marc. 2004. *Understanding Terror Networks*. Philadelphia: University of Pennsylvania Press.

Simon, Steven, and Daniel Benjamin. 2001–2. "The Terror." *Survival* 43: 5–18.

Smith, Thomas W. 2002. "The New Law of War: Legitimizing Hi-tech and Infrastructural Violence." *International Studies Quarterly* 46: 355–74.

Strenski, Ivan. 2003. "Sacrifice, Gift and the Social Logic of Muslim 'Human Bombers.'" *Terrorism and Political Violence* 15: 1–34.

Tsvetovat, Maksim, and Kathleen M. Carley. 2003. "Bouncing Back: Recovery Mechanisms of Covert Networks." NAACSOS conference proceedings, Pittsburgh, PA.

Verkaaik, Oskar. 2005. "Purity and Transgression: Sacred Violence and the Quest for Authenticity." In *MESS—Mediterranean Ethnological Summer School*, vol. 6, ed. B. Kravanja and M. Vranjes, 139–54. Ljubljana: Department of Ethnology and Cultural Anthropology, Faculty of Arts, University of Ljubljana.

Virilio, Paul. 2007. *The Original Accident*. Cambridge, UK: Polity Press.

Weizman, Eyal. 2006a. "Walking through Walls: Soldiers as Architects in the Israeli-Palestinian Conflict." *Radical Philosophy* 136: 8–22.

———. 2006b. "Introduction to Shimon Naveh, Between the Striated and the Smooth." *Cabinet* 22: 81–88.

Wyschogrod, Edith. 1985. *Spirit in Ashes: Hegel, Heidegger and Man-Made Mass Death*. New Haven: Yale University Press.

Zerubavel, Yael. 1995. *Recovered Roots: Collective Memory and the Making of Israeli National Tradition*. Chicago: University of Chicago Press.

Zulaika, Joseba. 2003. "The Self-Fulfilling Prophecies of Counterterrorism." *Radical History Review* 85: 191–99.

CHAPTER 10

THINKING MOEBIUSLY

CAN WE LEARN ABOUT RITUAL FROM CINEMA WITH MULHOLLAND DRIVE?

Author's Note

In 2001 I saw David Lynch's extraordinary film *Mulholland Drive* in Stockholm. The next evening I returned with Galina Lindquist, and she was equally enthusiastic. We discussed the film over and again, imagining its implications beyond representation. I perceived *MD* as a moebius movie, as a moebius surface in action. Not as evident a moebius movie as Lynch's *Lost Highway*, yet so much more complex in its turning-into-itself-coming-out-elsewhere in order to return to itself, differently. In 2005 I participated in a discussion on "The Interface Between Ritual, Theatre and Film," in Ascona, Switzerland. Out of this came a draft of this chapter. I had never formally studied film as a medium, though in the late 1970s and early 1980s I had co-taught a course with Elihu Katz on public events and media events, which also was beneficial for the creation of *Models and Mirrors*. Elihu is a founder of the sociology of communication, and the course rehearsed many of the televised media occasions that formulated the argument of *Media Events: The Live Broadcasting of History* (1992), that he coauthored with the semiotician of communication, Daniel Dayan. So I was not completely unfamiliar with thinking on screen images, sequences, and their narratives.

In perceiving MD as a cosmos in difficulty, I was influenced by Deleuze's brilliant thinking on cinema. Interestingly, his ideas moved extremely well through the moebius movement of *Mulholland Drive*.

> Regularity is easier to represent than chaos.
> If one were to say: I want to represent chaos
> using a handful of mud, it's quite hard to show
> the viewer that it's mud. Such things only work
> when they're still recognizable.
> —M. C. Escher

> There are new things coming up every second . . . but
> the present is the most elusive, because it's going real fast.
> —David Lynch in *Lynch on Lynch*

Prolapse

Recently the following happens to me, or, more moebiusly, happens to me as I am happening to me: before me the light of the television screen implodes, a whiteness spiraling inward within the screen, swallowing itself. I am elsewhere, perhaps in another room; perhaps I go through the screen, imploding. Startled, I am facing myself, self to self. The I facing I, a quizzical smile on his tight lips, holds up his hands in loose fists and waggles them toward me. Whatever else is happening here, I am opening space—perhaps within my self—that has not existed, and this space is interactive, open-ended, emergent, reflexive. However it is that I and I arrive together within this opened space (as the TV screen seems to enter within itself), the movement is not linear. Perhaps in a moebius-like dynamic I curve into my self and divide, so that I both repeat myself and produce myself as different, permutating my self through its transmutations. Though I am the I that I am, I have no doubt that the I facing I is I. Yet two. Yet different. I *in-flect* myself into *re-flection* that enables the two-ness to be recognized as different from the one-ness, and so to relate to this in an embryonically nonlinear way (I am startled; I smile and waggle fists toward my surprise; I stare at my waggling fists). A generative dynamic, a creative process, in which I, momentarily a micro-world unto myself, become a site of cosmogenesis, somewhere within-through the *interval* opening between one-ness and two-ness, sliding into and out of myself, involuting, evolving. Moebius movement, one-ness curving through its own space, through its own time, repeating its own space-time yet creating this as different, as two-ness, as two-ness that then is both inside and outside itself, yet where/when inside is no less outside, and outside no less inside.

Borges (1994: 15), in his brief meditation, *Borges and I*, opens with the inflecting line, "It is to my other self, to Borges, that things happen," and closes with, "I cannot tell which one of us is writing this page," Borges relating moebiusly to Borges, curving through one another. The inflection opens a site of cosmogenesis, an interval for a two-ness of Borges through which Borges is taking over Borges until they merge, becoming one but different, each inside-outside the other.[1] In my experience and in Borges's imaginary, mimesis, the creation of difference from sameness, is no less moebius, a dynamic that permutes our singularities, such that the permutations transmute sites of cosmogenesis without destroying their elasticity.

Moebius Dynamics

The moebius dynamic is a *self-entering form* (Neuman 2003: 143, 145) such that each re-entry, each curving through itself, is no less a folding in the Deleuzian sense (Deleuze 1993: 8) than it is an opening of interiority, recursively opening space/time where, again, none had existed.[2] As it exits itself it re-enters itself; in re-entering itself it re-exits itself. It has no stable exteriority or interiority, no ground on which to rest, only changing perspectives through movement. This kind of self-organization is pivotal to the film, *Mulholland Drive*, which I discuss in detail below, and which I use to ask whether the study of rituals of transformation can learn from cinema.

As I will stress throughout this chapter, moebius dynamics bring disparate levels or domains into conjunction, yet relate to them as *existing on a single plane of continuous movement*. In this regard, the moebius dynamic is implicated in rituals that transform within and through themselves (see Chapter Three; Handelman 1998; Kapferer 1997) by generating, operating, and moving through multiple actualities, enabling them to turn into one another. Too, this dynamic is implicated in films that bring multiple actualities into existence, blurring their boundaries and traversing them. I discuss actuality (and virtuality) further on.

Moebius dynamics, curving, folding recursively, and, no less, virtuality and actuality, are all entangled in my question of, can we learn about ritual from cinema? In these dynamics of curving and folding there is something that speaks to many rituals that in their self-organizing propensities have the capacities to do transformation within and through themselves. Rituals that do trans-formation seem to have properties of self-organization, of forming themselves through themselves within themselves, in ways that enable complex changes to be done through them. Thus, shaped into their plan, their design, is the future to be actualized.[3] Furthermore, these rituals are reflexive, such that in being cognizant of themselves as they are practiced, they include themselves within themselves. In this regard, no less than the doer practicing the doing of ritual, the ritual that is being done becomes aware of the doer (see Baudrillard 2000: 76), incorporating the doer within itself, thereby further effecting what is being done. Can we learn about ritual from cinema? If so, then thinking on their respective movements within and through themselves may well be the axis of their relatedness.

These nonlinear dynamics—from the point of inflection, through more complex folding and moebius movement, to degrees of self-organization—often are submerged in ritual forms. These dynamics sometimes are intertwined and overlaid with masses of detail and elaboration, sometimes coded so that only ritual specialists enter these hidden or disguised space-times of ritual, sometimes highly schematized so that what is present to the senses is powerfully minimalist yet enclosing (as may be the case with the activity of ritual texts within rite). More simply, ritual worlds commonly interpolate, interpenetrate, and fold together the visible and not-visible, the unseen and seen as the *um-felt* of the *umwelt*, and this conjoining of here-not-here often is understood by natives (whoever they are) as locus or nexus of trans-formation.

Film is hyper-real because it is hyper-visual, magnifying, reducing, changing proportions, altering angles of perception, giving shape to the seemingly shapeless, speeding up, slowing down, superimposing, fading and zooming, reversing time, inverting space, through shot, cut, and montage, and, for that matter, hyper-moving, for even if stilled, its images are coiled into and tense with motion. Paraphrasing Claude Levi-Strauss, film is good to imagine with.[4] It is our crooking medium, a misshaping medium for imagining the visual—for enabling visuality to fill and overflow the imaginary, visuality as the great enlightenment sensory adventure (see Jay 1993, Levin 1993). And, so, also a medium for imagining how trans-formings might look-like-they-are-happening-even-though-we-cannot-know-they-are-happening.[5]

I have tried elsewhere to identify how dynamics of trans-formation are done through ritual, approaching this problematic from various perspectives (Handelman 1998, 2005, 2006), and regarding all of these attempts as failures, albeit, perhaps, interesting ones. I fully expect to fail over and again—dynamics of transformation in themselves are indeed elusive within rituals that make change happen through themselves, and these dynamics slip away from discourse that cannot address their very fullness of existence in multiple planes, dimensions, vectors, circumferences, that Deleuze calls virtuality—regardless of whether such discourse is symbolic, semiotic, structuralist, hermeneutic, phenomenological, and perhaps systemic. Transformation is elusive because it is dynamic rather than a ritual recipe; shapeless, fluid, trajecting, vectoring, rather than moving between static points of start . . . stop . . . start. And I am neither a Renaissance alchemist nor a modern scientist.

Thinking on Ritual through Filmic Dynamics

I thought to attempt here to learn something about visualizing ritual transformation through film, trying to open an *interval* between them,[6] a space-time for reflection, from which to move in the direction of both without denying either.[7] I do not mean documentary film on ritual, which, like the anthropologist strives for realism and authenticity in reporting and representation, nor film that uses "ritual" as such in its plot or narration; rather, I mean film that permutes its own inflections, its moebius-movements and their shapings. Film that in a filmic sense may have qualities of self-organization built into its forming; film that perhaps can be *seen* and through this *felt* to do trans-formation through its self-organizing qualities. Film that imagines all of this and that tries to give visual shape to its imaginings, encouraging trajectories of desire for the just-out-of-sight.[8] Thereby (wittingly or not) trying to make these dynamics visible. I will try to see some of these thoughts through *Mulholland Drive*.

Consider the following, in which Larisa Kingston-Mann has a *filmic* response to actuality, one that permutes another potential actuality by imagining this through the virtual film medium which plays with time/space in the creation of actualities:

> While reading my economic history, I came across this information: that the engineers at Ford and Co. had gotten some of their ideas about an assembly line from seeing the Chicago slaughterhouses, the way the carcasses swung down a line on chains, being disassembled piece by piece.
>
> And I thought: such a rich image, and whose idea was it to reverse that image, so that it was one of assembly, of adding-together, instead of taking-apart? Such a *filmic response*, is it not, to run the slaughterhouse in reverse [my emphasis]? It's happening at the same time as the rise of the movies: the early "teens" [of the Twentieth Century], and I can't help thinking there's something so timely about it, the way early films were constantly playing with the ability to thread it backwards and have people miraculously un-eat food, buildings spring to life and be kissed by the wrecking ball, the hero unsticks from the ground and flies up to the top of the tall building. And here is someone who runs the slaughterhouse backwards, building cows. And from that takes inspiration, that you can have a moving line which accumulates parts until voila, a finished product, an automobile, a model T-for-time-runs-backwards. I love synchronicity.[9]

A model T-for-time-runs-backwards, a dynamic that imagines one mode of production, one actuality, into another, so that cars emerge from cows, one form of movement turning into another, permuting the same dynamic of motion.[10] To look at a film in this way pushes to discard baggage from anthropology that imposes formal strictures on ideas of ritual, and, no less, baggage from film studies that take their theoretical impetus from varieties of textual criticism and cultural critique. The sorts of constraints that anthropologists commonly impose on "ritual" as a global integument, giving to it hardness, rigidity, and inflexibility, for example, between its exterior and interior, a framing that makes digital the relatedness of ritual to not-ritual, an either/or distinctiveness that accords with the classic Durkheimian separation of sacred and profane realities. Then, formal properties posited for ritual naturalistically mimic this framing, giving to ritual qualities of repetition, stylized behavior, order (Moore and Myerhoff 1977: 7), and Rappaport's (1999: 24) influential definition of ritual as: "The performance of more or less invariant sequences of formal acts and utterances not entirely encoded by the performers." Such formal qualities, argues Rappaport (1999: 53), establish the bedrock messages of ritual as canonical.

Much thinking on ritual in anthropology reduces transformation done through ritual to narrative, to, in Geertz's phrasing, stories that people tell themselves about themselves, thereby recuperating values, identity, group boundaries, and so forth—another version of Durkheimian group solidarity without effervescence. Transformation is reduced to narrative and plot, and how change occurs through ritual contexts becomes a matter of how narrative is put together and performed. Analysis of cinema, following on approaches of cultural studies and literary criticism, so often understand films as narrative, as dramatic psychologies of personae, as representations of social order, as surrealistic and parodic reflections of all of these—as metacommentaries on social life.

Given that so many rituals are organized to act on and to trans-form aspects of social orders, we must consider dynamics that are interior to such rituals as their own worlds of self-organization, put together to do transformation. Worlds unto themselves, such rituals contain the dynamics of permutating themselves within themselves, thereby transforming whatever is within them, the intention of their attention. Such rituals enfold and permutate actualities of cosmos, health, maturity, life-passage, and so forth. Rituals that do transformation produce "the shock of the real immanence of the metaphysical" (Murphie 2002: 192). Film in its own right is an assemblage that includes the imagination, with the capacity to play with *showing* the actualization of potentials of the metaphysical, the metaphysical understood as existence forming and re-forming through potentialities becoming actualities. Film can *show* how actualities intersect and collide, changing and effecting one another.

Film paradoxically is a flat medium that peers into *depths* and their interior workings (Stephenson and Debrix 1970: 55). Nonetheless, in order to try to think on ritual through film, the usual baggage of plot, narrative and representation needs to be put aside as much as possible, thereby highlighting dynamics that enable certain films to have the strange processes and coherences that they do, dynamics that should not be reduced to technology and filming techniques. Ideas of Deleuze—singularity, actuality, virtuality, crystallization—resonate with and hone my desire to focus on moebius-like dynamics, and I will make intensive use of them in discussing the film, following the synopsis, below.

Mulholland Drive

> Moments lost in time,
> like tears in rain.
> —*Blade Runner*

Mulholland Drive, (henceforth *MD*) written and directed by David Lynch, attracts scholars of cinema. Their studies treat the film as a whole, as a unity, and so as one that contains mystery, and puzzles to unravel. Most cut to the perspective that Sinnerbrink (2005: 3) calls "reductive" rationalism—"the tendency to treat films as illustrations of theoretical concepts or ideological perspectives that can be properly deciphered only once submitted to conceptual analysis or subsumed within a philosophical metalanguage."[11] These studies agree that *MD* has no conventional linear narrative, but do find linear logic by arguing that *MD* combines dream (the first four-fifths of the film) together with hallucination and flashback, all of which are explained by the final one-fifth that is the reality, the authentic, exposing the dream character of the first four-fifths, thereby straightening and stiffening the former (Hayles and Gessler 2004; Sinnerbrink 2005; Nochimson 2002).[12]

MD is unsettling not because it divides into dream positioned before reality, but because the film is constructed as an entirety within itself, never leaving itself, providing an entirely interior optic on/in itself without any exterior perspective whatsoever for the viewer who is drawn within, disoriented, unable to take an Archimedean standpoint, confused by the multiple actualities that Borges (1998) summarized as the garden of forking paths.[13] A film that swallows itself, a form re-entering itself moebiusly, aligning the strange relations among its actualities on the same plane, transforming itself from within itself, without positing to itself any exterior perspective—in this sense a world without exteriority. Thus, the autopoiesis of a world permutating itself into worlds, and, perhaps in this aiding another look at ritual, though the film on its face has no relation to ritual. This is what I will want to scratch at a bit in the concluding section.

Despite the above Disclaimers, a Practical Need for a (Somewhat Skewed) Synopsis of the Plot

The opening shot is of young couples jitterbugging without background except for the shadows they cast, then overlaid dreamily through a rising mist by the happy face of a young blonde woman, and then by a grandparental-looking couple, one on either side of her.

A beautiful young brunette with hair to her shoulders, wearing a black dress, is being driven at night in a dark-colored car up winding, wooded, dark Mulholland Drive in Hollywood. Above and out of sight, two cars full of raucous youngsters are drag-racing downhill. The dark car suddenly stops, the brunette is alarmed, the driver (another man sitting next to him, both in dark suit and tie) turns, a silenced pistol aimed at the brunette. At that moment the drag-racers crash into the parked car. The brunette alone staggers away from the accident, through the woods, downhill, falling asleep under bushes next to an apartment complex, the Havenhurst. She awakens to a middle-aged woman directing a taxi-driver to load her bags; the brunette then slips inside the woman's well-to-do apartment before the latter locks the door.

[I][14] Two men are sitting in Winkies diner during daytime. One tells the other of a dream he's had for the second time—it is half-night, he is sitting in Winkies, and he is terrified. His friend is standing by the counter, next to the cash register, and he too is frightened. The sitting man sees through the wall of the diner, sees a horrific face outside, at the back of the diner. He tells his friend, in the present, "He's doing it." And wants to know whether that man is outside now. His friend goes to the counter to pay, standing exactly where he did in the dream. They go outside, around to the back of Winkies. As they near the backyard area, a face slides out from behind the wall of the diner—a face blackened with dirt, perhaps with fungus, with long, dark, matted hair, a derelict's face with gleaming eyes and teeth. The dreamer clutches his heart, collapsing. The Derelict's face slides back, out of sight.

A young woman arrives in Hollywood, (apparently) accompanied by a warm older couple, Irene and her partner, who address the young woman as Betty, treating her gently, gravely, and tenderly, then leaving in a limousine, **[II]** grinning and laughing together with glee, somewhat unpleasantly. Both are most pleased. Betty takes a taxi to the Havenhurst apartment complex, where she will stay while her aunt Ruth is traveling. She meets Coco, the manager who gives her the key. Inside she finds the brunette who says she's been in a car accident and has lost her memory. Asked her name, she takes that of Rita, from a movie poster of Rita Hayworth in the bathroom.

Cut to a depth-shot of a room painted red (the Red Room) **[III]**, lengthened beyond ordinary proportions, a foreshortened microphone hanging on the wall. Deep within the narrow room sits a small man in a wheelchair, Mr. Roque, who hears reports through the microphone and issues orders by implication. He says that *the girl is still missing.*

Betty tells Rita to look in her purse for ID. A close-up of the black purse, the loud sound of the zipper opening. Inside are bundles of cash and a large, triangular blue key. **[IV]** At that moment Rita remembers she had been going to Mulholland Drive. Betty wants to investigate the accident. Betty and Rita are sitting in Winkies Diner, checking the newspaper for information about the accident. Rita sees the name Diane on the wall (the name of the waitress on duty), and Rita remembers the name, Diane Selwyn, and wonders if its hers. Outside Winkies, Betty calls Diane Selwyn's number. Though the voice on the answering machine is not Rita's, Betty knows the voice.

Adam Kesher is casting the female lead for his film, *The Sylvia North Story*. At a boardroom meeting, Kesher, the director, is told bluntly by two mafia types to hire Camilla Rhodes by saying while Camilla is auditioning, "This is the one." They show him the photo of a young blonde with upswept hair and pouty lips. Kesher refuses. One of the mafia types yells, "This is the girl. It is no longer your film. *This is the girl.*" Cut to the Red Room. **[V]** Mr. Roque is listening to the boardroom discussion through the microphone. The film producer comes from the meeting to report to Mr. Roque, who implies that the entire production should be shut down.

Kesher's credit cards are canceled; his bank account emptied. He receives a message to go to a corral at the very top of Beechwood Canyon, there to meet the Cowboy. That night he drives to the wilderness at the road's end, going through the crude gateway, a steer skull at its apex together with a light flashing red as he enters, emitting a droning sound. **[VI]** The corral is empty, but Kesher turns and there is the Cowboy, a medium-sized trim figure, with a kerchief around his neck and a white six-gallon hat on his head. The Cowboy warns Kesher about his attitude, telling him to take Camilla Rhodes during the auditions, saying "This is the girl." He adds, "You will see me one more time if you do good; you will see me two more times if you do bad."

Betty goes to her own audition for a lead role while Rita stays in the apartment. The director, Bob Brooker, tells Betty and the actor with whom she is playing the scene, "Don't play it for real until it gets real." The audition goes extremely well, and Betty is taken to the casting audition for the *The Sylvia North Story*, where Kesher says, "This is the girl" when blonde Camilla Rhodes (the woman in the photo) is auditioning. Betty and Adam exchange looks of longing, but Betty runs off to help Rita find her identity.

The two women go to the address they found for the name, Diane Selwyn. A female neighbor who knows Diane Selwyn does not recognize Rita, so she is not Diane. There is no response to the knocking on Diane's door. Betty finds a smallish window that opens and enters. The front door opens from within, Betty reappears, one hand over her mouth and nose. Going through the dark apartment the women enter the bedroom. On the bed, lying on its side away from the doorway, knees bent, is a decomposing woman's corpse. A close up of her distorted face, but she is unrecognizable, perhaps with dark blonde hair. Both women flee in panic. A close up of their faces—they are terrified—rippling in-and-out of phase, here-and-not-here, shattering. **[VII]**

Back in the apartment, Betty cuts Rita's hair, disguising her with a shortish blonde wig. Standing side-by-side before a full-length mirror, both blonde, they shift toward one another, though their features are strikingly different. Sleeping together in the same large bed, they make love, Betty saying she is in love with Rita. Betty's profile (she is on her back) and Rita's full face (she is on her side, facing Betty's profile) seem to have a common integument. Later, Rita mutters in her sleep, "Silencio, silencio, no hay banda [there is no band], no orchestra, silencio, silencio . . ." Rita opens her eyes, saying, "It's not okay." She's terrified. Yet now she knows where to go (apparently to find her lost identity). Though it is 2 a.m., she asks Betty to accompany her—to the Club Silencio, at the dead end of a broad, deserted alley.

Inside is a small auditorium with plush seats but few occupants. A few box seats overlook the stage, only one of which is occupied, by a stately, gowned women, her blue hair piled atop her head. Onstage is a magician, saying, "This is all a tape recording. There is no band, yet we hear the music . . . It's all recorded . . . It is an illusion . . . ." "Listen," he intones, raising his arms as violent thunder echoes throughout the Club, suffused in blue light. **[VIII]** Betty, terrified, shudders uncontrollably and Rita holds her. Onstage, the magician disappears in a cloud of smoke. An MC in a red suit presents the singer, Rebekah Del Rio.[15] With close-ups of her heavily made-up face, she sings Roy Orbison's country-and-western song, "Crying," in Spanish with great pathos. Rita and Betty weep together. Del Rio collapses onstage and is dragged off. Her voice continues the song. Betty opens her purse and finds a square blue box with a small triangular opening. The lovers look at each other with dread; they rush to the apartment.

Rita goes to the bedroom closet for her purse, the cash and triangular key inside. Suddenly she realizes Betty is gone. She opens the blue box with the blue key and peers inside. A closeup of indigo darkness fills vision totally, the box heard falling with a thud to the carpet. **[IX]** The doorway to the bedroom looms, the dark corridor beyond. Aunt Ruth appears in the doorway, looks into the room, but it is empty, no purse, no box, no clothes on the bed. She looks puzzled, as if she heard something and had come to check, shrugs and leaves.

The doorway looms and the dark hallway within, rippling and shuddering in-and-out-of-phase moving into still greater darkness, opening into a dark room, a figure lying on her side on the bed, face hidden, knees bent. The sound of a door opening—standing in the doorway the Cowboy says, "Hey pretty girl, time to wake up." Darkness. **[X]** Again the woman on her side, the Cowboy in the doorway closing the door carefully, and again the girl on her side. Darkness again.[16] The sound of knocking, the woman turning over, awakening, putting on a worn robe. Its Betty, though looking slovenly, disheveled, dull. The apartment resembles the one in which Betty and Rita found the rotting corpse.

At the door is the female neighbor who addresses Betty as Diane, asking where she's been. An ordinary blue key lies at the edge of the coffee table. She says, leaving, "Oh, by the way, those two detectives came by again looking for you." Cut to Diane at the kitchen sink, looking through the window. She turns suddenly and there is Rita, though Diane calls her Camilla. Then Diane is shivering, scared. Cut to Diane in the bare kitchen, making coffee. She takes her cup toward the sofa. Camilla is lying there, bare-breasted as Diane, also bare-breasted, climbs over the back of the sofa onto Camilla, and they caress. There is no blue key on the coffee table. Camilla pushes Diane away, saying "We shouldn't do this anymore." (Here [wherever this is] Camilla Rhodes is the lead in Adam Kesher's film, *The Sylvia North Story*, and is having an affair with Kesher). Raging, Diane throws out Camilla. Diane in shorts sits on the sofa, crying with fury, masturbating, as the phone rings in the bedroom. Answering the phone, Diane is wearing a black dress. Camilla is calling—the car is waiting to take Diane to an address on Mulholland Drive.

A dark car driving through the night up winding Mulholland Drive, stopping unexpectedly. Diane is alarmed; but Camilla appears, taking her by the hand up through the woods to Adam Kesher's home where a party is underway. Here Coco (the Havenhurst manager) is Kesher's mother. Diane tells that she won a jitterbug contest; her aunt died, leaving her some money, so she came to Hollywood, meeting Camilla on the movie set of *The Sylvia North Story*, where Camilla was the star. Diane hoped for the part, but the director, Bob Brooker was not impressed with her. A blonde woman whispers in Camilla's ear at the dinner table. They kiss intimately. Camilla is "This is the girl," the Camilla Rhodes whom the mafia men were adamant would receive the lead in the film. Camilla/Rita enjoys Diane's pain and discomfort. The Cowboy passes in the far background, going elsewhere. Kesher, laughing, is announcing to everyone his and Camilla's . . . the sound of a crash . . . .

Cut to Winkies and a fallen tray. Diane is hiring a killer to murder Camilla. The waitress is named Betty. Diane pays cash, pushing a photo of Camilla across the table, saying "This is the girl." The killer gives her an ordinary blue key, saying "When it's finished, you'll find this where I told you." At this moment, standing at the cash register is the man who accompanied the dreamer who saw the Derelict through the wall, behind Winkies.

Night. Alongside a dumpster behind Winkies the Derelict sits next to a small fire, turning the blue box in his hands. He puts the box into a paper bag and drops it to the ground. A close up of the open bag, an edge of the box visible. Two tiny figures, Irene and her partner, emerge screeching maniacally with laughter, their arms outstretched, reaching. [**XI**]

Cut to a close-up of the ordinary blue key on the coffee table, Diane sitting in her tawdry robe on the sofa, staring at it. A loud rapping on the door, the tiny figures of Irene and her partner crawling under it into the apartment. Diane hears the laughter, the knocking continues, the laughter wild and screechy and the old couple, now full-sized, arms outstretched reaching for Diane are upon her, as she turns and runs into the bedroom, flinging herself onto the bed, scrabbling in a drawer, frantically pulling out a pistol, shooting herself in the mouth, lying on her side, knees bent.

Heavy mist forms in the bedroom, entirely obscuring the scene. The mysterious visage of the Derelict, full-face, appears in the mist. Then the dreamy face of Betty/Diane, happy and vital as she is as Betty, and next to her the face of Rita/Camilla, but blonde and warm as she is as Rita.

Cut to the empty stage of Club Silencio, and to the regal woman in the box seat who quietly but sibilantly declares, "Silencio."

Transformative Moments

Analysis lives by and largely through map-making (and its cartesian, geometric origins), and the map, as John Vernon (1973: 10) comments, "Relates the whole to its parts as an addition of discrete entities rather than as a fluid unity of transformations." Map-like, *MD* becomes a container with at least one neat compartmentalization: most of the film is fantasy, the last minutes, reality. Fantasy contrasted to reality—the former unreal, inauthentic, subjective; the latter, real, authentic, objective. Ultimately, any ruler-edged contrast between fantasy and reality recuperates a linear logic of progression in which reality is the benchmark, the touchstone, the foundation, whose stability (indeed, its reality-testing) gives the lie to fantasy. Anyone who embraces fantasy rather than reality verges on the psychotic or disappears within this miasma, in keeping with the map-like dualism between sanity and insanity (Vernon 1973). In keeping with these analyses, most of *MD* is the interior vision of a sick mind.

From this perspective the logic of *MD* is not that different from, say, the film, *The Night of the Following Day* (1968), a straightforwardly chilling tale of kidnapping, torture, and murder, in which only the very last minutes reveal the entire film until then to have been a dream whose horrific reality is only just beginning in earnest as the film closes. . . In keeping with the fantasy/reality dualism, *MD*'s numerous strange-looking and strange-sounding characters and scenes are intended as entertaining curlicues, making a fairly mundane plot very mysterious. Is this it? A film cluttered with red herrings harboring clues in a fantasy re-arranging reality, enabling the dreamer to momentarily escape her lonely, miserable existence and its furies? As I commented, *MD* is good to imagine with for students of transformation, once we put aside the dualism of fantasy/reality and try to avoid using the film either as representation or as an illustration of theory. Then we can ask how this film imagines transformation, and whether this is helpful in opening space for imagining dynamics of transformation in ritual.

The Opening and Closing of *Mulholland Drive*

Before turning to the moments I indicated in the synopsis, orientating toward and preparing for transformation and then actualizing this, I discuss briefly the opening and closing of *MD*, for together these demonstrate the powerfully recursive self-organizing in the film. The opening shot is of acrobatic jitterbugging couples, against a bluish background that has no dimensionality or orientation apart from that given by the dancing figures and the shadows they cast. The figures dancing in space, without flooring, without ceiling, without horizon. Some are dancing higher than others, some are huge, others quite small, while some are indistinct, parts here and there, disappearing into one another. On closer look, there are only a few couples, their foregrounding and size changing, overlapping—dancers permutating. Moreover the dancing is without beginning or ending—it is happening; it is a present—its only temporality that of the tempo and rhythm of the music and the movement of the dancers. But a present full of potentiality, a Deleuzian virtuality, complete, full, real, within itself.

Whitish mist billows, partly obscuring the dancers, and the dreamy, upraised, exalted face of Betty appears in the mist, joyous, exhilarated, then joined on either side by that of Irene and her partner. As long as it lasts (for over one minute) the dancing scene is self-reproducing. It is Klee's site of cosmogenesis, his nondimensional point, "an event that awaits an event," as Deleuze (1993: 15) puts it, an event that awaits in-flection, curvature, the folding of reality into itself—the formation of complexity. Cosmic form begins to take shape quickly—the mist obscuring the frenetic dancers as the faces of Betty and the old couple appear, a meta-presence that is launching this filmic micro-universe in which Betty is a major protagonist and the old couple have a significant role in her fate. Yet these faces are, like the dancers, still a nondimensional point, though in-flection has begun. Unlike the dancers, the faces clearly have identity, albeit virtual. Shortly, this virtuality of the filmic micro-cosmos will generate actuality—horizons of being and becoming, dimensionality, character, and trajectories of action becoming vectors of consequence.

MD closes immediately following Diane's suicide. Mist forms in the bedroom, swirling, gathering, entirely obscuring space. From within the mist the dark, mysterious visage of the Derelict appears, full-face. Then Betty/Diane's visage appears in silhouette, a happy, sparkling Betty, followed by the faces, side by side, of Betty/Diane and Rita/Camilla, both as blondes, intimately warming one another. Cut to the empty stage of Club Silencio and the blue-haired regal woman in the box seat, almost whispering, "Silencio." The close is just that, a closure, not an ending as such.[17] The closure of actualities, the return to cosmic nondimensionality, to de-flection, awaiting an event, awaiting an actuality.

The opening and closing mirror one another, a doubling of a sort, the near largest circuit or envelope of the film, in Deleuzian terms. The mists of space/time fold into the mists of space/time, though differently, for Betty is Betty/Diane, joined by Rita/Camilla, their potentialities of being multiplied, expanded, amplified. Their microcosmos is changed, for it has *per-mutated*, literally going through itself and altering, though not ending. Both the Old Couple who appear with Betty in the opening and the Derelict who appears just prior to the two women in the closing have crucial purposes, as I discuss below, in the forming of actualities between opening and closing. And beyond this fold, another yet more encompassing circuit, the opening of swerving, swooping, arcing, exuberant jitterbug dancing and music utterly stilled and folded into the unmoving, upright woman in the box seat at Club Silencio, with her emphatic whisper, "Silencio." The microcosmos re-entering itself moebiusly, quietening, stilling, awaiting . . . not ending.[18] Within these two great recursivities of "encompassing space" (Deleuze 1992: 218) is the entirety of the film's existence, of its presents and pasts, but no less the potentialities of its futures, yet unscreened (or screening interactively within viewers).[19] In this regard the film is ritual-like, a site of cosmogenesis, in-flection, closure . . . poised to begin the dynamic once again, yet responding to conditions that will generate other actualities.

The Accident

The drag-racers crashing into the car in which the brunette is a moment from being murdered is an accident in the fullest sense—an unexpected happening in an unpredictable world that destroys an intended action, the murder. The accident is a Deleuzian *singularity*, a point or event from which divergences begin to occur as ordinaries are disrupted and re-form differently. An event resonating with the in-flected point of cosmogenesis. This is still the same world, yet altering itself within itself, as Deleuze (1993: 60) comments, "because a singular point is only the coincidence of two ordinary points from different vectors." One vector, the dragsters, collides with another, the-murder-in-process, and a new inflection appears as the brunette staggers away from the crash. Singularities, argues Deleuze (1990: 52), "are turning points . . . bottlenecks, knots . . . points of fusion and boiling." But the singularity "is quite *indifferent* to the individual and the collective, the personal and the impersonal . . . singularity is neutral," in the sense that it happens because it happens, yet it makes sense as such in the cosmos of its occurrence (De Landa 2002: 15, 35).

The trajectory the brunette develops is neutral—wandering downhill, perhaps because of the city lights below, perhaps downhill is easier going—but its accumulations are not. For her this singularity is also her re-birth from certain death. Her trajectory into life is creating *another actuality*. The singularity is a great rupture in the ordinaries of cosmic continuity, its effects akin to the damage wreaked by terrible illness or a natural disaster, a tiny yet cosmic occurrence.

Without her memory, the brunette is out-of-place in this actuality. She experiences her sensual reality, its immediacy, yet there only is this immediacy, for she has lost actuality, the present-ness of tense, the very relationality that moves her within present-past-future, the potentialities of relationality that are virtuality. Looking at herself in the bathroom mirror in the Havenhurst apartment, in the mirror of her potential knowledge of self, she begins recreating herself, forming and entering another actuality, another present that cannot pass into past because this is so foreshortened as to hardly exist as yet. As the brunette's virtuality re-forms, the actuality that emerges into being does so moebiusly, reorganizing her through an attractor itself coming into existence through the singularity of the accident—the powerful feelings she and Betty have for one another, the solidity of this second actuality.

Deleuze (1989: 81), following Bergson, argues that, "the past is constituted not after the present that it was but at the same time, time has to split itself in two at each moment as present and past . . . it has to split the present in two heterogeneous directions, one of which is launched toward the future while the other falls into the past." Time is this split, Borges's garden of forking paths. The singularity of the accident blocks this dynamic of time splitting simultaneously in its actuality. In the singularity's wake, strange characters and weird forces appear, with moebius-like transformative effects on actuality.

For the brunette the singularity blocks the past, her virtuality, so that time in a sense is post-singular, time in which she has such an emotional effect on Betty who was on quite a different life-trajectory. As time re-forms again for the brunette, now Rita, the second actuality is forming, relating moebiusly to the one before as the women search for the brunette. So, too, do strange and menacing characters for whom the existence of "the girl" (still missing; this is the girl) is troubling. Something in the forming of this second actuality is aberrant, perhaps related to the continuing existence of the brunette, and to her becoming an attractor for Betty.

Deleuze (1989: 79) contends that "the image has to be present and past, still present and already past, at once and at the same time. The past does not follow the present that it is no longer, it coexists with the present it was. The present is the actual image and its contemporaneous past is the virtual image, the image in a mirror." The image in the mirror, the ideal image, perfect in that it is the very idea of the image, is past, yet changing in its present, its actuality which comes into existence because of the potentiality of its virtuality, the idea of image.[20] The virtual and the actual, coupled together in what Deleuze refers to as the tightest of circuits, the tightest of recursivities, are what he calls an *image-crystal*, an image of present-ness continually grounding itself in its own past-ness, its own tense-ness, of form moebiusly re-entering itself, the image of form re-entering the idea of form, the idea of form re-entering the image of form.

Every actuality is simultaneously and partially within its own virtuality, as the qualities of each pass into the other, refracting one another so that actuality and virtuality become indistinguishable within the image-crystal. The image-crystal that in my terms is form re-entering the image of form (witness Da Vinci, note 20) and emerging from this, is prominent in cinema *and* in certain rituals (Bruce Kapferer [1997, 2013] has argued these points, in his own way, for the virtuality-actuality of the Sinhalese Suniyama exorcism rite). The image-crystal, I add, is itself a focus of trans-formation, since potentiality enters actuality through virtuality; potentiality shaped to become actual (as we know is the case in ritual). Nonetheless, the dynamic of movement within the image-crystal is then moebius-like, a dynamic of connecting and relating planes of existing (and imagining) that, even if they are in conjunction (and they may well not be), are not continuous with one another. The first actuality (of which there is only a bare hint) turns into the second through a moebius-like dynamic in which terror turns into desire tinged with fear (Rita's emotions do bleed into the second actuality from the first). The great image-crystals of *MD* are the two that relate opening and closing: the opening dancers and the closing lady of Club Silencio, and the opening Betty and Old Couple and the closing Derelict, Betty and Rita.

Yet the brunette is memoryless, without past, with bare virtuality, without grounds from which to speak of her very existence (apart from her name, Rita, from a film poster of Rita Hayworth).[21] Her search for her memory, her identity, driven by Betty, is no less a search for the actuality she has lost. No less, menacing characters of whom she is unaware also want her back in that actuality within which she dies. These two trajectories, or "lines of the universe" (Deleuze 1992: 218), moebiusly join together moments that prepare the way for and do transformation, from one actuality to another. This is transformation that emerges from cosmic design, from the virtuality of the cosmos of the film (regardless of how limited this is), rather than from the shocks of singularity itself.

Moments Preparing for Transformation

The first moment of preparation takes place at Winkies diner [I]. The diner reveals itself as moebius-space, an interiority full of curvature through which memory is refracted from one actuality to another. Here the dreamer recounts his vision of the horrific face he saw through the diner wall, the wall itself becoming mirror-like, another curve through which the dreamer faces a still deeper space, one that shortly will change his life. In the dumpster zone of detritus, the face slides out from behind the wall as the dreamer approaches, and the dreamer is struck down by the face as its power (his memory of his dream) enters him. The Derelict is interstitial, a homeless nomad, an urban forager curving to and fro, a creature of the interval which suddenly opens for the dreamer. Like other creatures of the interval, he is a figure of great power, a shamanic shifter who moebiusly relates and changes the planes of actuality.[22] The dreamer enters a curve as he goes out the front door of the diner and around the side toward the back, the Derelict sliding out, conjoining the dreamer's gaze, completing the curvature, both suddenly on the same plane, both curving together despite the great disparity in their trajectories.

Like the first, the second moment introduces figures of power. As the Old Couple accompanying Betty sit in the back seat of the vehicle taking them away, they are grinning with glee, the sweetness they showed Betty becoming something else, perhaps malevolent **[II]**. They seem to know something she does not. Their very presence bodes apprehension. They too are shaping this actuality in which Betty shortly will meet Rita.

The third moment is the presence of the enigmatic, omnipotent Mr. Roque within the distorted dimensions of the Red Room **[III]**, wherein he receives and coordinates reports about the missing girl—yet *where* is she missing from? Just missing from the accident scene? Missing from the actuality within which the accident happened and where she will be murdered? Missing from her own memory, thereby further rupturing plans for her elimination in the actuality of the accident? Beginning an actuality in which Rita-without-virtuality will meet Betty? An actuality in which Rita's presence will destroy Betty, yet perhaps will save herself elsewhere? If Rita recovers her memory, her past-ness, indeed her virtual selfness, will this resituate her in the actuality from which she has gone missing, or will she go elsewhere?

The fourth moment of preparation reminds that all the locations mentioned so far—the diner dumpster zone, the back of a car, the Red Room—are *intervals*, all in their own way the opening of space/time that had not existed a moment before, treacherous passages into interiorities, where things happen that are threatening to the ordinaries of mundane lives. The fourth is simply the close-up of Rita's black purse and the magnified sound as she unzips it, looking for her identity. *Riiip*—an interval opening. Inside she finds cash (which never makes sense in the actuality she now is helping to create) and the triangular blue key **[IV]**, the key of virtuality which will open a perilous passage into the transformation of actuality. The key that already is forming another actuality within this second one. The very presence of the key suggests that some sort of *cosmic correction* to the effects of the singularity is being put in position.

The fifth moment is again in the Red Room, demonstrating Mr. Roque's power as the producer of *The Sylvia North Story* stands fearfully at the room's threshold **[V]**, receiving indirect instructions to shut the film down, to pressure Adam Kesher into hiring Camilla Rhodes for the lead. In this actuality these forces will not permit Rita to become a star, and they are acting to drive her into the actuality of her death. The sixth moment is Kesher's meeting with the threatening Cowboy **[VI]**, after he traverses the menacing archway into the metaspace of the corral. Like Mr. Roque, the Cowboy, a shamanic shifter, is shaping actuality to effect Rita.

Betty enters Diane Selwyn's apartment through a narrow aperture, a perilous passage into a dark interior of space/time that suddenly opens, of death and bodily corruption **[VII]**. Betty unknowingly sees her own rotting corpse. Or does she? Her corpse in this actuality? *This is the only point where I have to go outside the interiority of the film* to note that the actress who plays Betty does not play this corpse. Roche (2004: 46) comments insightfully that

> the decomposition of Rita's and Betty's image occurs *after* they have been confronted with an image-crystal that functions as a bridge between the Betty/Rita part of the movie and the Diane/Camilla part, both parts reflecting each other without defining which is the reflected and which is the reflection . . . the image-crystal contains two films . . . the second image is *almost* identical to the first, so that one can't tell Diane apart from her reflection.

The transformation of actuality is almost done here; the women see and smell another potential actuality in virtuality, one not yet formed and determined in their own actuality (though on its way); and this shakes the stability of their own. As the women flee, their actuality begins to disintegrate—a closeup of their faces as they run forward shows them in terror, rippling and shuddering in-and-out-of-focus, here-and-not-here, shattering. An aperture seems to be opening around them even as they flee, sucking them in. Two films, in filmic terms, or the dynamic of one actuality transforming into another?

The two women twin, almost becoming one: Betty cuts Rita's hair, fitting her with a blonde wig—they look like one another, make love, fitting into one another. Made two, the two permutate toward becoming one as the solidity of actuality disintegrates around them, their love the powerful bond holding the second actuality together, protecting Rita from the destruction prevented by the singularity of the accident. Rita dreaming, mutters in her sleep—there is no band, there is no orchestra, it's not okay. She awakens distraught, but now knows exactly where to go to trace her lost identity—the Club Silencio. As memory returns and her virtuality deepens, she is being driven from this second actuality, as it is collapsing around her.

Club Silencio is an *interval* within which this actuality is deliberately made to disintegrate **[A]**.[23] Perhaps another singularity is opening within actuality, yet this one is designed deliberately to take actuality apart in particular ways. I call this a planned, cosmic singularity because though the singularity is intended, no one is able to predict what manner of attractors will influence trajectories emerging from this maelstrom of inflection. Onstage, the magician, the MC in the red suit, and Rebekah Del Rio, all drive actuality to implode, losing its self-referents, a chasm opening between idea and action, signifier and signified, indeed between Actuality and Virtuality—there is no orchestra but there is music; there is thunder but no storm; the voice of Del Rio continues its pathos after she collapses. All sound is *now* a recording but *once* it was real. Actuality is detached from virtuality within this *interval* suddenly opening in space/time, the continuousness of its moebius relation to virtuality rupturing. Just as Rita lost her memory and so her virtuality, creating a new actuality, now this entire actuality is losing its virtuality, its metaphysical grounding in what Deleuze calls grains of time, imploding within the inflecting singularity of Club Silencio. The visible, the actual, has no past nor future. And Betty in the depth of her purse finds the Blue Box, the aperture again of a moebius dynamic that will permutate actualities (perhaps as an infinite series) transforming this one into another. With the appearance of the Blue Box the second actuality stands forth as a circuit of key (its outset) and box (its close), an image crystal of actuality (the key) entering virtuality (the box), emerging moebiusly as actuality re-aligned and transmuted.

The collapse of actuality continues back in the apartment. Betty disappears, winking out behind Rita's back, and Rita herself and the remainder of this actuality implode within the Blue Box **[B]**. Vision enters the doorway, traveling a dark hallway rippling and shuddering, becoming still darker, opening into a darkened bedroom, a figure lying on her side on the bed, knees bent. This actuality is activated by the Cowboy **[C]** in the doorway, telling the woman it's time to wake up—in this actuality. Club Silencio, the Blue Box, the bedroom, the Cowboy, all are aligned moebiusly on the same plane, and one actuality crystallizes from within another, through the virtuality of the Blue Box.

Some of the characters in this third actuality are the same as they were in the second, while others are present but are other persons. This third actuality seems stable, every character has its memory and so its virtual potentiality. The cosmic attempts to stop Rita, now Camilla Rhodes, from becoming a star have failed, yet she will be destroyed, as will her destroyer, Betty, who is now Diane. That is, there is a greater dynamic driving the third actuality into virtual relations with the other two, a grand time-crystal of permutative actualities forming virtually through one another, moving toward the outer envelope that moebiusly joins together the opening and closing of the film, folding them into one another.

Thus, though the fate of Rita/Camilla may have been sealed in the first actuality, her moebius-like passage to the second and then the third, created an anomaly, the survival of "Rita," which this micro-cosmos eliminates. And, just as Diane and Camilla become so similar to and synchronized with one another in the second actuality, so they share the same fate in the third. The second actuality makes of them women twinned in love;[24] the third separates them agonistically, so that they destroy one another. The third erases all traces of the contamination created by the anomaly of the survival of "Rita" in the first actuality and the strengthening of this anomaly in the second.

The closing phase of the transformation of actuality **[D]** gathers together a great concentration of forces to destroy the permutating anomaly created by "Rita's" survival and, as a consequence, her life-giving relationship with Betty—this destruction includes the self-killing of the latter as Diane, after she has killed Rita. Coming together are the Cowboy activating the third actuality; the Derelict in the interval-space behind Winkies; the Blue Box, aligning actualities on the same plane; the Old Couple, emerging from the Blue Box at the Derelict's feet, who attack Betty/Diane, driving her to self-death. In its own way, *MD* is a highly self-organizing micro-cosmos; and, again in its own way, mirrored through the refractions of modernity and cinematics, *MD* is a simple filmic form of a "primitive" cosmic logic of organization.

On the "surface" of the film none of this is evident, and hence the recourse among scholars and others to the cartesian dichotomy of fantasy/reality and the like. In my moebius-like visualizing of *Mulholland Drive*, I see the film creating a micro-cosmos within which there are dynamic permutations of actuality, in which the absence of virtuality is shown to be consequential for actuality, and in which modes of transformation are crucial to keeping this cosmos stable through permutations of actuality.

Interval

> The man who can't visualize a horse galloping on a tomato is an idiot.
> —Andre Breton

Sergei Eisenstein's pioneer thinking on montage is apposite here. Eisenstein (1975: 4) wrote that "while playing with pieces of film, they [the 'leftists of montage'] discovered a certain property in the toy . . . two film pieces of any kind, placed together, inevitably combine into a new concept, a new quality, arising out of that juxtaposition."[25] He (1975: 7; see also Eisenstein 1949: 254) continued, "The juxtaposition of two separate shots by splicing them together resemble not so much a simple sum of one shot plus another shot—as it does a creation . . . in every such juxtaposition *the result is qualitatively distinguishable* from each component element viewed separately."

The interval is a break that may expand into a gap, an intermediate space, a zone of difference, through which the film necessarily passes, and which may be used to alter it, ordinarily as sequence, but also radically, in its dynamic composition. Deleuze (1989: 276–79) discusses the interval in terms of *rational* and *irrational* cuts. The rational cut respects the integrity of images and sequences of image such that "the limit as interval is included as the end of the one [sequence of images] or as the beginning of the other [the next sequence]" (ibid.: 277). The intervals that are rational cuts construct a continuous world of images in which the interval itself serves the continuousness of the series. The irrational cut on the other hand slices through, divides, and thereby fragments images, image from sound, continuousness. "Euclidean coordinates" are lost (ibid.: 278).[26]

The irrational cut, however, *sets the interval free*, since it no longer has an integral relationship to the image by setting its limit, by maintaining the integrity of the unity of image and sound. In a way the interval exists in its own right, with its own permutative effects. The irrational cut enables the expansion, elaboration, and involution of the interval. The interval may become its own self-entering and self-exiting form, evolving its own virtuality-actuality.

Mulholland Drive shows just how powerful such intervals can be, figuring in its transformations, dissolving one actuality, ramifying another. In *MD* the intervals are the moments when virtual preparations are made for transforming actuality—often through characters I have called shamanic shifters—and in locations where transformation is done, in the Club Silencio and immediately after in the Havenhurst apartment, and in the third actuality, behind Winkie's. The interval freed by the irrational cut is *chiasmic*, in Merleau-Ponty's (1968) terms—a zone of cross-over through which one actuality transmutes or torques into another, perhaps bringing the latter into existence. This speaks to, perhaps even visualizes aspects of rituals of transformation, highlighting just how crucial the interval may be in such rites.

It is its irrational cuts (though I prefer a-rational) and its recursive involution and elaboration of the interval that make *MD* a film with an entirely interior view—so that any exterior Archimedean perspective is always subverted by moebius movement. The experience may be akin to being inside one's own body, entirely *in-bodied sensuously*, trying to make sense of a myriad of pulsating, throbbing, dripping, evacuating shapes and contours of flesh, connected by conduits of all sorts transporting fluids in many dimensions and directions, all composed of tiny en-walled bits with their own lives, utterly dynamic, impossible to comprehend, indubitably real.

This may also be the condition of participants in numerous rituals of transformation and in their intervals that are re-entering self-entering forms. From within the interval set free, without exteriority, there may be loss of balance, uncertainty, sometimes apprehension, as actuality forms but is not neatly accessible to literal description, or to enumeration of a series of acts, musical scores, utterances, commands, sacrifices, symbols . . . symbols. The interval of transformation can be itemized, yet I wonder whether it can be fully grasped as an entirety within itself—moebiusly, it is swallowing itself and whoever enters it. The interiority of much ritual dynamics is less amenable to academic *meta*-level discourse because it is so profoundly an *infra*-processual dynamic. A film like *MD* may give us some sense of how this might be visualized. It is a film that plays with in-between-ness, in-between the infinite seedbed of virtuality and potential actualities coming into existence, a film that visualizes liminality from within itself. A film whose interior dynamics are never exhausted, never ending, perhaps only abating, slowing, curving moebiusly into themselves; and so, in Deleuzian terms, always "starting again in the middle rather than moving from a beginning to an end" (Rajchman 2000: 58). Transformative ritual, too, never ends despite its linear cause-and-effect appearance. Such ritual enters abeyance or abatement, existing in its virtual cosmos as an ever-present on-going dynamic of cosmic self-organization even when not activated; so that, once activated again, it begins "in the middle" of its own ongoing relationship to cosmic process.

I said earlier that Victor Turner's theory of transformative ritual—the single most influential theory of ritual in modern anthropology—is one of the interval. In his theory, transformation depends on the freeing of the interval.[27] The liminal phase in *rites de passage* is an interval that, in Deleuze's filmic terms, has been freed by irrational cut from the serial character of the mundane—the liminal phase is not sacred, rather it is *a-serial*, independent, a self-entering form of virtual space/time, moebiusly recursive as it generates actualities. Transformative ritual then can be understood as an assemblage for the generation of permutating actualities emerging from virtuality, within intervals. It is within intervals that powers meet humans. And I would not be surprised if, in cosmic terms, the interval in ritual which may look like a crack, a narrow aperture, opens interiorly, within itself, to swallow the compass of cosmos from within itself; as happens in the transformative moments of *Mulholland Drive*. Yet this would be a cosmos that throws up singularities. Not a legalistic, bureaucratic cosmos that turns singularities into exceptions—in which the accident, the illness, the earthquake, the desire, are exceptional in that they should never happen, and so they are to be dealt with and effaced through normative rules and regulations as exceptions to the rule, rather than as singularities. However, the cosmos that throws up singularities is often a traditional one, in which the singularity is unexpected but not unusual or exceptional; and, so, the cosmos which generates singularity is always in its own middle, as are the rituals resonating with this cosmos that are also in their own middle, even as they begin.

An interval theory of rituals of transformation would try to address the virtual-actual conundrum (as Kapferer 1997, 2013 has begun to do). I would think on the following. Rituals that do transformation through their own operations emerge through an irrational or a-rational cut that is elaborated into an interval. Whether this is predicated on dualisms of the order of sacred-profane or canonical-indexical (Rappaport 1999) is of less significance than that it is done. The interval is a virtuality, utterly real in its cosmic potentialities that generate and permutate actualities, and that themselves become the outcomes of ritual. Thus Kapferer (1997) argues for the Sinhalese Suniyama exorcism that, through the virtual-actual relationship, actuality can be slowed, acted upon, mended, changed.

Within the interval, actuality is formed through recursiveness, through curvature and folding. Folding invokes the moebius movement of self-entering and self-exiting form, that of a highly interior perspective on ritual. Folding perhaps also *crumples* time, in Michel Serres's (1995: 81–122; Ma 2000) terms, and I think space as well, so that any time, any space, can touch and torque into any other. The crumpling of time/space injects reflexivity into the interiority of ritual; reflexivity of the kind that I sometimes describe as *the eye seeing itself seeing*—again, not a metaperspective on interiority but rather an infra-sensuousness through which senses are utterly attuned to themselves.[28] Within this virtuality of ritual, actuality is formed, formed so as to permutate itself once the moebius dynamic self-exits, the folding turning inside-out, the new actuality returned to or torqueing into the social surround of the ritual.

A brief example reported by Sundar Kaali (2006) shows the value of thinking through cinema about ritual. The ritual play, *Hiranya Natakam* is performed widely in South India. The play enacts the story of the demon king, Hiranya, whose son Prahlada was a great devotee of the god, Vishnu, and for this was persecuted by his father who belittled Vishnu and challenged the deity to appear. In the climax to the play the *avatara* of Vishnu, Narasimha the man-lion, appears from within a solid pillar and disembowels Hiranya. In a number of villages that are geographically contiguous in the Tanjavur region the performance is varied in the following way: almost all of the characters are doubled in the performance area, each a mimetic of the other. Narasimha himself, the cosmic encompassment who, one may argue, contains all the other characters, is not doubled. For whatever the reasons that the characters appear in twos, this doubling seems to be a historically emergent property of the enactment of this ritual play in this locale. An emergent property that is an a-rational cut, opening an interval within each character.

Though this apparently cannot be seen, I believe that the doubles are *expansions* of one another, opening space/time that had not existed before—not so unlike the Handelmans and Borgeses with whom I opened this excursus. Within the performance zone the doubles may be bringing something else into being beyond the mimetic production of their similarity. The doubles create an interval between them, a singular interval of virtuality within the performance area itself. Moebiusly, the doubles interact amongst themselves through this interval with all its potentiality, moving the action inside and outside, permutating toward diverging performances, diverging outcomes. Put otherwise, within the performance area there are two, overlapping, ritual plays going on simultaneously, both articulated especially by the encompassing Narasimha. Yet, within the emerging embryonic space between them, these parallel mimetic performances are on their way to throwing up a variant of *Hiranya Natakam* in which each play, each set of actors, may diverge substantially from the other, thereby potentially creating a new storyline. Whatever the local conditions, the virtuality of the *Hiranya Natakam* cosmos is generating an actuality significantly different from the usual, an actuality taking shape through its own virtuality; an actuality generating further divergence through the interaction of its own doubling forms.

Especially interesting here is what did indeed happen during one performance. The defeat of the demon-king is usually marked by removing his crown and giving it to Narasimha. On this occasion, as Sundar Kaali notes, a performer of high status removed Narasimha's mask at the climactic moment and brought it to Hiranya (apparently without knowing consciously why he did so), thereby marking the victory of the demon-king over the god. Though this ending was corrected by doing the ritual-play over again (ridding the enactment of its unexpected singularity), the singularity itself was a potential outcome formed from virtuality, one with its own emotional and logical satisfactions. Moreover, given Narasimha's encompassment of the cosmos, this was an outcome with profound implications.

Can we learn from cinema about ritual? This may depend, for instance, on our theorizing the interval toward a theory of virtuality in ritual. The kinds of dynamics I have pointed to in discussing *Mulholland Drive* are not prominent in anthropological studies of ritual whose primary concern is the relationship between ritual and social order, with primacy in explaining the former accorded to the latter. Little attention is given to how, as I put it in Chapter Three, ritual works in its own right through dynamics that belong to ritual, rather than those that are exterior to and apart from this. In its own ways, *Mulholland Drive* shows how the ritual imaginary may benefit from thinking with a theory of rite that draws together singularity and actuality within virtuality, and their alignment within interval through a self-entering self-exiting dynamic like that of moebius.

Notes

My thanks to Ruth HaCohen, Lydia Ginzburg, Bruce Kapferer, and Galina Lindquist for their critical comments.

1. The phrasing, site of cosmogenesis, or "between dimensions," is that of Deleuze (1993: 15), following Paul Klee, referring to the world itself, its beginning between Idea and inflection, an *elastic* point, becoming what it is but different, a permutative dynamic of the ways the elastic can be stretched, shaped in space, through time, through itself, as Klee demonstrates over and again. The Kleeian point is a particular event, a singularity in Deleuzian terms, attracting elements to itself, just as the canvas, the lines, the brush and hand, are attracted to and from that point, creating an image unlike any other yet entirely in the world of others, related genetically to them.
2. The moebius surface is traversed from one of its sides to the other without crossing an edge or border. Rosen (1994: 9) comments that, "points on opposite sides are intimately connected—they can be thought of as 'twisting' or 'dissolving' into each other, as being bound together internally." So, "in the moebius transformation, reflexive self-reference and reference to the other are thoroughly blended . . . the moebius aspect turns back upon itself and, at the same time, upholds what is different" (ibid.: 14).
3. See this argument in Helm (2005: 78–79).
4. The influence of film on scholarly imaginations has hardly been broached. Algazi (2004) argues that Norbert Elias in 1935 thought in filmic terms while conceptualizing historical change. Zischler (2003) traces the films Franz Kafka (an inveterate filmgoer) went to see, and quotes Theodor Adorno to wit, "Kafka's novels are not prompt books for the experimental theater . . . . Rather, they are the last, disappearing textual links to silent film (which, not coincidently, disappeared nearly simultaneously with Kafka's death)" (Zischler 2003: 58).
5. Egginton argues that theatre, as distinct from ritual, came into existence in its own right in fifteenth-century Spain with the invention of the stage, separating audience from actors. This created "the experience of fiction," an alternative, viable imaginary reality that had not existed before, since during the Middle Ages the performance of a story was ontologically part of the entirety of the world, the only world in existence (Egginton 1996: 402; see also Egginton 2003). "Once the screen is in place, following Lacan, the gaze is never merely a position to be taken up, but rather an object to be desired" (Egginton 1996: 404). What the spectator cannot see, then, becomes the trajectory of desire. There, somehow, yet invisible; there, somehow, perhaps traceable through its traces. This brings us back to dynamics of transformation in ritual: whatever the goal of transformation, this is the desired—yet unseen, invisible, out of sight, distant, just around the corner, in front of our noses—toward which the trajectory of intentionality soars and burrows. Not the invisibility of separate worlds, distinct realities, but rather one cosmos, perhaps curving, folding, twisting, through whose virtualities one moves to reach or create other actualities.
6. The interval, to which I return in the closing section, is crucial to transformation through ritual.
7. Elsewhere, I argue adamantly that there is no over-arching idea, rubric, or phenomenon that can be called "ritual" around the world (Handelman 1998, 2006). Not because "ritual" is a Christian cultural formation (Asad 1993) not applicable elsewhere, but because there are perva-

sive differences in self-organization between events or rituals that trans-form and those that do representation (Handelman 1998, 2004).
8. Andrey Tarkovsky (1989: 116), the singular director, writes that, "a self-organising structure takes shape during editing because of the distinctive properties given the material during shooting." The logic of self-organization comes together when the "distinctive properties" of a rhythm of time, the "time-thrust within the frames" (ibid.: 119), comes through and then the entire film comes together through its rhythm of time. Tarkovsky (1989: 117) insists that, "time courses through the picture despite editing rather than because of it." The film, then, is reaching beyond itself toward that which is out of sight, beyond the frame, beyond itself. See also, Frampton (2006) on the idea that (logics of) film *think* into existence their composition, movement, and characters. When watching a film we are embraced by a process of thinking embedded within the picture.
9. From an email sent by Larisa Kingston-Mann to her mother, Esther Kingston-Mann (13 October 1998). Used with the permission of Larissa Mann, given in an email, 17 August 2005.
10. Beller (2003: 95) shifts this kind of imaginary into a Marxist mode by arguing that the "cut" of assembly line work later shifts to the work of cinema spectators following the "cuts" through which film is constituted. "Cinema," he argues, "took the formal properties of the assembly line and introjected them as consciousness."
11. Thus Zizek's (2000) Lacanian analysis of a previous Lynch film, *Lost Highway* (1997); and a study of Lynch's TV series, *Twin Peaks*, as media poetry that re-mediates the mythic character of American middle-class social order (O'Connor 2004).
12. Hayles and Gessler (2004) argue that their solution to *MD* meets the ten clues that Lynch provided to enable viewers to make sense of the film. For Lynch's ten clues, see <www.mulholland-drive.net>, and for his attitude to them, see Rodley (2005: 289). Gessler, <www.sscnet.ucla.edu/geoeg/gessler/topics/mulholland-drive>, provides a minute summary of the chronology of *MD*. Buckland (2003) tells the production history of *MD* and its multiple threads.
13. In this regard, the viewer becomes part of the systemic organization of the film, yet of its second-order systemics. The viewer then is organized by the reflexive self-organization of the film, and has difficulty seeing whether the film is purposive and goal-directed (see Glanville 2004: 1384). One consequence seems to be that a system of this kind "will always expand beyond the frames of reference adopted by observers . . . ," and therefore is in principle unpredictable (Scott 2004: 1370). This is my understanding of *MD*—to some degree *the film is unpredictable to itself*, and struggles with its own uncertainty, sucking the viewer into this.
14. Square brackets indicate the points in the film that are loci in which different dimensions are aligned on the same plane, junctures of potential transformation—of one dimension entering into and effecting another.
15. Del Rio is a female vocalist in present-day Los Angeles, playing herself in the film. She has a website.
16. By this point close to two hours of the film have elapsed. The remainder takes some twenty-five minutes.
17. Claude Lanzmann, who directed the epic nine-hour film, *Shoah*, asked: "When does the Holocaust really end?" replying: "When I really had to conclude [the film] [. . .] I decided that the last image of the film would be [. . .] an endlessly rolling [. . .] train" (quoted in Felman 1992: 242). An actuality train rolling back into the potentiality of its virtuality.
18. Thain (2004: 3, 7), in a Deleuzian analysis, notes how the close of *Lost Highway* curves, in my terms, into its opening. Buckland comments that the narrative of *Lost Highway* "is literally organized like a moebius strip." (Posting to Film-Philosophy Salon <film-philosophy@jismail.ac.uk>, 8 January 2006).
19. On interactivity between viewer and (TV) screen, see Handelman (2000, 2003).
20. Da Vinci (2002: 79) caught this Deleuzian understanding of virtuality/actuality in the fifteenth century: "To see whether your painting as a whole corresponds to the thing represented, take a mirror and set it so that it reflects the model [which the painting represents], and compare

this reflection with your picture, and carefully examine the whole surface to see whether the two images of the object are similar . . . . And since the mirror can create the illusion of relief by means of lines and of light and shadow, you, who have among your colors more powerful shadows and lights than those of the mirror, if you know how to combine them as you should, will also be able to make your work seem like the reality seen in a great mirror."

21. Rita Hayworth suffered from Alzheimer's and likely lost her memory and virtual existence within herself; so the poster itself is a perfect node for the brunette to search for her own identity, the two Ritas in themselves an image-crystal.
22. See Rodley (2005: 277) for the origins of Winkies and the Derelict.
23. Transformative moments are shown by capital letters.
24. Lynch (Rodley 2005: 289) calls *Mulholland Drive* "a love story."
25. Without knowing Eisenstein's writings, I argued this for ritual (Handelman 2004: 112), and more generally for the positioning in close proximity to one another of unrelated symbols that, as it were, magnetize a relationship between them and give to this the potentiality of significance, if not meaning (Handelman and Shamgar-Handelman 1993).
26. More recently I have begun to wonder how Deleuze's distinction between irrational and rational cuts can be brought into planar conjunction with Andrey Tarkovsky's adamantine sense that frame and film are filled with "time-thrust" (1989: 119) that pulsates and moves the entirety of the film from outset to closure. The task of editing a film is discovering the time-thrusts of frames and allowing these to come together, indeed to "link together" (1989: 117). Tarkovsky continues, "The distinctive time running through the shots makes the rhythm of the picture; and rhythm is determined not by the length of edited pieces, but by the pressure of the time that runs through them. Editing cannot determine rhythm [. . .] time courses through the picture despite editing rather than because of it [. . .] The course of time, recorded in the frame, is what the director has to catch in the pieces laid out on the editing table" (1989: 117).
27. Turner's predecessor, Arnold Van Gennep, likely was influenced by the nineteenth-century interest in the *limen*, the threshold of perception, which also so effected impressionist painting, especially that of Seurat and other pointillists (Prendeville 1999: 377).
28. Picasso depicts this wonderfully in some of his cubist faces—one eye looking outward, the other trying to look at the face doing the looking, yet from within that face—a self-other perspective that is interior to a single figure. I'm thinking, for example, of *Der gelbe pullover* (1939) and *Der maler und sein modell* (1971), both in the Berggruen Museum in Berlin.

References

Algazi, Gadi. 2004. "Making Invisible Movement Visible: Norbert Elias's Motion Pictures." Workshop on *Science and the Changing Sense of Reality circa 1900*, Max Planck Institute for the History of Science, Berlin, 11–14 November.
Asad, Talal. 1993. *Genealogies of Religion*. Baltimore: Johns Hopkins University Press.
Baudrillard, Jean. 2000. *The Vital Illusion*. New York: Columbia University Press.
Beller, Jonathan. 2003. "The Cinematic Mode of Production: Towards a Political Economy of the Postmodern." *Culture, Theory and Critique* 44: 91–106.
Borges, Jorge Luis. 1994. "Borges and I." *Antaeus* 73/74: 5.
———. 1998. "The Garden of Forking Paths." In *Collected Fictions*, 119–28. London: Allen Lane.
Buckland, Warren. 2003. "'A Sad, Bad Traffic Accident': The Televisual Prehistory of David Lynch's Film *Mulholland Drive*.'" *New Review of Film and Television Studies* 1: 131–47.
Da Vinci, Leonardo. 2002. *Leonardo on Art and the Artist*. Mineola: Dover.
Dayan, Daniel, and Elihu Katz. 1992. *Media Events: The Live Broadcasting of History*. Cambridge, MA: Harvard University Press.
De Landa, Manuel. 2002. *Intensive Science and Virtual Philosophy*. London: Continuum.
Deleuze, Gilles. 1989. *Cinema 2: The Time-Image*. London: Athlone Press.

———. 1990. *The Logic of Sense*. New York: Columbia University Press.
———. 1992. *Cinema 1: The Movement-Image*. London: Athlone Press.
———. 1993. *The Fold: Leibniz and the Baroque*. London: Athlone Press.
Eisenstein, Sergei. 1949. *Film Form: Essays in Film Theory*. New York: Harcourt, Brace & World.
———. 1975. *The Film Sense*. New York: Harcourt, Brace, Jovanovich.
Egginton, William. 1996. "An Epistemology of the Stage: Theatricality and Subjectivity in Early Modern Spain." *New Literary History* 27: 391–413.
———. 2003. *How the World Became a Stage: Presence, Theatricality, and the Question of Modernity*. Albany: SUNY Press.
Felman, Shoshana. 1992. "The Return of the Voice: Claude Lanzmann's *Shoah*." In *Testimony: Crises of Witnessing in Literature, Psychoanalysis and History*, ed. Shoshana Fellman and Dori Laub, 204–83. New York: Routledge.
Frampton, Daniel. 2006. *Filmosophy*. London: Wallflower Press.
Glanville, Ranulph. 2004. "The Purpose of Second-order Cybernetics." *Kybernetes* 33: 1379–86.
Handelman, Don. 1998. *Models and Mirrors: Towards an Anthropology of Public Events*. 2nd ed. New York: Berghahn Books.
———. 2000. "Into the Television Screen: The Individual Viewer as a Locus of Creativity?" ("In den Fernsehbildschirm hinein. Der einzelne Zuschauer als ein Ort der Kreativitat?"). In *Religiose Funktionen des Fernsehens?* ed. Gunter Thomas, 247–58. Wiesbaden: Westdeutscher Verlag.
———. 2003. "Towards the Virtual Encounter: Horton and Wohl's 'Mass Communication and Para-social Interaction." In *Canonic Texts in Media Research*, ed. Elihu Katz, John Durham Peters, Tamar Liebes, and Avril Orloff, 137–51. London: Polity.
———. 2004. *Nationalism and the Israeli State: Bureaucratic Logic in Public Events*. Oxford: Berg.
———. 2006. "Conceptual Alternatives to Ritual." In *Theorizing Ritual*, ed. Jens Kreinath, Jan Snoek, and Michael Stausberg, 37–49. Leiden: Brill.
Handelman, Don, and Lea Shamgar-Handelman. 1993. "Aesthetics Versus Ideology in National Symbolism: The Creation of the Emblem of Israel." *Public Culture* 5: 431–49.
Hayles, N. Katherine, and Nicholas Gessler. 2004. "The Slipstream of Mixed Reality: Unstable Ontologies and Semiotic Markers in *The Thirteenth Floor*, *Dark City*, and *Mulholland Drive*." *Publications of the Modern Language Association* 119: 482–99.
Helm, Bertrand P. 2005. "Borges's Elimination of Past and Future: A Paradox." *KronoScope* 5: 73–82.
Jay, Martin. 1993. *Downcast Eyes: The Denigration of Vision in Twentieth-Century French Thought*. Berkeley: University of California Press.
Kaali, Sundar. 2006. "Masquerading Death: Aspects of Ritual Masking in the Community Theaters of Tanjavur." In *Behind the Mask: Dance, Healing, and Possession in South Asia*, ed. David Shulman and Deborah Thiagarajan, 89–106. Ann Arbor: South and Southeast Asian Series, University of Michigan.
Kapferer, Bruce. 1997. *The Feast of the Sorcerer*. Chicago: University of Chicago Press.
———. 2013. "Montage and Time: Deleuze, Cinema, and a Buddhist Sorcery Rite." In *Transcultural Montage*, ed. Christian Suhr and Rane Willerslev, 20–39. New York: Berghahn Books.
Levin, David Michael, ed. 1993. *Modernity and the Hegemony of Vision*. Berkeley: University of California Press.
Ma, Ming-Qian. 2000. "'The Past is No Longer Out-of-date': Topological Time and its Foldable Nearness in Michel Serres's Philosophy." *Configurations* 8: 235–44.
Merleau-Ponty, Maurice. 1968. *The Visible and the Invisible*. Evanston: Northwestern University Press.
Moore, Sally Falk, and Barbara Myerhoff. 1977. "Introduction: Secular Ritual: Forms and Meaning." In *Secular Ritual*, ed. Sally F. Moore and Barbara Myerhoff, 3–24. Assen: Van Gorcum.
Murphie, Andrew. 2002. "Putting the Virtual Back into VR." In *A Shock to Thought: Expression After Deleuze and Guattari*, ed. Brian Massumi, 188–214. New York: Routledge.
Neuman, Yair. 2003. "Mobius and Paradox: On the Abstract Structure of Boundary Events in Semiotic Systems." *Semiotica* 147: 135–48.

Nochimson, Martha P. 2002. "*Mulholland Drive*." *Film Quarterly* 56: 37–55.
O'Connor, Tom. 2004. "Bourgeois Myth Versus Media Poetry in Prime-Time: Re-visiting Mark Frost and David Lynch's *Twin Peaks*." *Social Semiotics* 14: 309–33.
Prendeville, Brendan. 1999. "Merleau-Ponty, Realism and Painting: Psychophysical Space and the Space of Exchange." *Art History* 33: 364–88.
Rajchman, John. 2000. *The Deleuze Connections*. Cambridge, MA: MIT Press.
Rappaport, Roy. 1999. *Religion and the Making of Humanity*. Cambridge, UK: Cambridge University Press.
Roche, David. 2004. "The Death of the Subject in David Lynch's *Lost Highway* and *Mulholland Drive*." *EREA* 2: 42–52. http://www.e-rea.org.
Rodley, Chris. 2005. *Lynch on Lynch*. Rev. ed. London: Faber and Faber.
Rosen, Steven M. 1994. *Science, Paradox, and the Moebius Principle: The Evolution of a "Transcultural" Approach to Holism*. Albany: SUNY Press.
Scott, Bernard. 2004. "Second-order Cybernetics: An Historical Introduction." *Kybernetes* 33: 1365–78.
Serres, Michel. 1995. *Genesis*. Ann Arbor: University of Michigan Press.
Sinnerbrink, Robert. 2005. "Cinematic Ideas: David Lynch's *Mulholland Drive*." *Film Philosophy: International Salon-Journal* 9. http://www.film-philosophy.com
Stephenson, Ralph, and J. R. Debrix. 1970. *The Cinema as Art*. Harmondsworth: Penguin.
Tarkovsky, Andrey. 1989. *Sculpting in Time*. Austin: University of Texas Press.
Thain, Alanna. 2004. "Funny how secrets travel: David Lynch's *Lost Highway*." *Invisible Culture: An Electronic Journal for Visual Culture* 8. http://www.rochester.edu/in_visible_culture/Issue_8/thain.html
Vernon, John. 1973. *The Garden and the Map: Schizophrenia in Twentieth-Century Literature and Culture*. Bloomington: Indiana University Press.
Zischler, Hanns. 2003. *Kafka Goes to the Movies*. Chicago: University of Chicago Press.
Zizek, Slavoj. 2000. *The Art of the Ridiculous Sublime: On David Lynch's* Lost Highway. Seattle: Walter Chapin Simpson Center for the Humanities, University of Washington.

Chapter 11

Folding and Enfolding Walls
Statist Imperatives and Bureaucratic Aesthetics in Divided Jerusalem

Author's Note

Deleuze's proposition for inquiry in the epigraph to this chapter jump-started my thinking on how to make significant connections between the seemingly unlike, yet connections that would be dynamic rather than simply structural. In this chapter on the cityscape of today's Jerusalem I connect places that turn into spaces that relate to one another as a vector of force that contributes to shaping and controlling the cityscape through bureaucratic aesthetics of the Israeli State. I find the spaces of this vector through a post-mathematical topology which can only be dynamic in its movement, thereby jettisoning topography which can only be static, without movement, without dynamic.

> You should not try to find whether an idea is just or correct. You should look for a completely different idea, elsewhere, in another area, so that something passes between the two which is neither in one nor the other . . . You don't have to be learned, to know or be familiar with a particular area, but to pick up this or that in areas which are very different.
> —Gilles Deleuze, *Dialogues II*

After the 1948 Arab-Israeli War, the armistice line ran through Jerusalem on a roughly north-south axis. That line developed into a dilapidated no man's land, with ongoing back-and-forth sniper fire. The ancient Old City remained in Jordan, its western Ottoman walls lying alongside the armistice line. After the 1967 June War, the Israeli government annexed an area that included Jordanian Jerusalem, together with a large area of the adjacent West Bank, all of which was made part of a single municipal territory. The Israeli state declared this new entity to be "United Jerusalem, the Eternal Capital of Israel" (Klein 2005: 55). Ever since, actualizing a single Jerusalem, united through conquest under Israeli rule (although quite divided in mundane life), has been a statist imperative. In this state project, architecture has a prominent role. According to Nitzan-Shiftan (2005: 231), architecture "as a technique of execution . . . is not transparent—it is neither devoid of ideology, nor is it readily accessible to political dictates, particularly not in sites saturated with national and religious symbolism. On the contrary, politicians are largely dependent on professionals who have privileged access to the spatial tools of architecture." Given the powerful presence of Jerusalem in the symbolism of each of the monotheisms and in the religious and secular cultures that emerged from these religions—and, no less, the prominence of Jerusalem in the Arab-Israeli conflict—the making and shaping of built forms there are often perceived through synecdoche, that is, the parts are seen as standing for the whole. Often changes in built form are a felt aesthetic presence that is immediately plumbed, analytically, common-sensically, for its significance in relation to the city-as-whole.

Since 1967, after seizing the heights surrounding the Palestinian city, Israel has been building a wide, dense arc of housing for Israeli Jews, without giving building permits to Palestinians. Residential building has been accompanied by a variety of physical barriers. The most recent, dubbed officially the "separation fence," is intended to wall off much of the Palestinian city from its hinterland in the occupied West Bank, territory that might be given to the Palestinian-state-in-the-making, should this ever be actualized. Israel controls the Palestinian city with a bureaucratic and militaristic iron hand, while minimally investing in infrastructure for its Palestinian inhabitants, even as Israeli governance insists that the entire city is a seamless unity (Benvenisti 1995).

It is in this Israel-controlled cityscape that I discuss one vector of statist-related physical forms that have qualities of walls. Although here I consider only official and quasi-official forming of space, my intention is to bring out the dynamic of folding and enfolding space through the shaping of walls as a transforming vector of control. The term "vector" comes from the Latin *vehere*, to carry. The vector as carrier refers to a line in space that has both the magnitude and direction of a quantity. Since I use the word "vector" in a loosely topological way, the line of space becomes one of connectivities that need not be linear and may well be recursive. In my usage, the vector carries value through space, value that is enhanced, augmented, made more powerful as it moves into and through the enfoldings I discuss. In traversing these enfoldings, value turns into force, that of the state and its imperatives.

The architectural forms I discuss are new, ostensibly without relation to one another, yet together they create this vector of force, as the cityscape shifts from west to east. The first is a bridge pylon, while the others I refer to as walls, although only the last ordinarily would be understood as such. The first of these walls is a new historical museum of the Holocaust (the "museum-wall"). The second is a massive continuous stretch of new buildings (the "mall-wall") that crosses the former no man's land between Jewish West Jerusalem and the southwestern walls of the Old City. The third is the "separation barrier" between Palestinian East Jerusalem and its hinterland. Together, these four constructions are one topological vector shaping the cityscape. Using the idea of topology in a broad way enables all four constructions to be implicated together in how the city is being shaped and practiced in accordance with statist imperatives. Crucially, this vector is self-referential. Therefore, what I will call its "beginning" (the bridge pylon) and its "end" (the separation fence) fold into one another, transforming the force of directionality into the totalizing of recursive energy.

I return to topological thinking in relation to that which Gilles Deleuze referred to as "folding," a dynamic especially relevant to discussing the forming of form, in both social and material terms (Handelman 2005). By describing three of the constructions as walls, I imply that they partake of an aesthetics that I regard as bureaucratic, a topic that will be addressed in the concluding remarks.

In terms of their aesthetic form, cityscapes are usually analyzed by social scientists in terms of topography—the ways in which forms are situated on surfaces and through the lines on these surfaces that connect the forms. Topography relates more to material and social positioning in four-dimensional space. It is less concerned with the dynamics that actively shape forms and relations among forms through different scales and intensities, through vectors that come into being as forms are being formed, and that give direction and impetus to these vectorial thrusts. Topography is passive in that it can be presented as a given of things, natural or human-made. This sense of passivity easily enables social scientists to use features of topography as containers of representations of social and historical formations. Representation reflects, presents, reflects—but does nothing through itself. Topographies are representations; they, too, do nothing through themselves. They reflect forces (political, economic, ideological, architectural) that originate elsewhere. Thus, sites in the cityscape may be perceived as dense mappings of meaning, yet these are passive receptacles whose significance is to be deciphered.[1] As Deleuze (1994: 67) comments, "Representation has only a single centre, a unique and receding perspective, and in consequence a false depth. It mediates everything, but mobilises and moves nothing."[2]

The dominant use of aesthetics continues to link this to representation. For the pre-Socratic Greeks, *aisthesis*, or sense perception, was not separated from *logos*, and "physical sensory perception was trusted as knowledge" (Kane 2007: 83). The metaphysical project of the Age of Reason was to separate *aisthesis* from *logos* and to tie aesthetics to representation. I use aesthetics in a somewhat combined way as "sensuous knowledge" (Goldman 2001: 255), as knowledge that is trusted but largely tacit and taken for granted. My usage of the aesthetic refers to something more like the "feel" that one has for what one is doing or seeing or moving through kinesthetically (or perceiving through other of the senses)—the feel for the "rightness" of how one is doing what one is doing, or how this is done in concert, the feel of the senses forming form through practice. The aesthetic in mundane living is related to Bergson's notion of "habit memory," of attending kinesthetically to one's own body, monitoring what one is doing; but, I add, attending kinesthetically no less to the surround, including of course the built environment. In this regard, movement itself is a sense, as the body continuously changes position, revising the information it takes in from the environment, as do other of the senses in their own ways. Therefore, this is also a haptic aesthetics of practicing formed and forming space, of "memory etched in movement," of the body, of the surround.[3]

These mundane aesthetics are an indwelling of largely tacit knowledge that always seems to include more than we can tell, were we able to relate this knowingly (Polanyi 1962: 314; idem 1966: 17–23). Tacit knowing is the feeling of disattending to ourselves, which moves us beyond ourselves, enabling the exterior world of practice and the interior world of experience to be unified as the exterior world of experience and the interior world of practice (see Dufrenne 1973: 446; Katz 1999: 314). Indeed, the aesthetics of practice lead us to "an appreciation of the essential place of aesthetics in all behaviors, however mundane or esoteric" (Katz 1999: 314). No less, the aesthetics of practice lead us to all surrounds and, I emphasize, to vectors of force that connect through these surrounds in and during multiple dimensions.

In trying to consider how an aesthetics of statist practice forms the constructions to be addressed in this chapter, I will perhaps escape to a degree from the passive receptacles of representational symbolism, away from topographical thinking and more toward the topological, toward a dynamic of the relational among forms. Each of the four new constructions is, in its own right, a separate venue of statist imperatives for Jerusalem. Nonetheless, each is a variation of the dynamic of folding, and the vector of these variations intensifies its wall-ish qualities as it thrusts from west to east.

The Beginning—the Calatrava Pylon-Parabola

Driving up to Jerusalem (to a height of some 800 meters) from the coast in the west, the highway enters the lip of the city at a busy intersection and continues into the west-east axis that begins the major thoroughfare, Jaffa Road, which runs through the city all the way to the Ottoman-period walls of the Old City, the border of the Palestinian city. Traversing the intersection, roughly from north to south, is a cable-stayed bridge, some 360 meters in length, designed by Spanish architect Santiago Calatrava (see Fig. 11.1). When it became fully operational in 2011, the bridge was also adjusted to carry light-rail lines above the intersection. Part of the support system of the bridge is a slender steel pylon, some 118 meters in height, inclining toward the east. From either side of the pylon, steel cables in the shape of a parabola hold the bridge in place.[4] The parabolic imparts a sense of three-dimensionality to the pylon and its steel cables. Inaugurated in June 2008, the pylon is considered by Israeli authorities

Figure 11.1. The Calatrava pylon-parabola at the western entrance to Jerusalem. Photograph by the author.

to be the major visual landmark at the entry to the Jewish city. The pylon-parabola quickly acquired a biblical referent, the harp of King David (the mythical founder of the Israelite city) and is referred to as the Chords Bridge or the Bridge of (musical) Strings—a giant harp embedded in the city's western entrance.

Since the founding of the State of Israel in 1948 with Jerusalem as the capital, the Jewish city has welcomed Jews to its precincts from the westerly direction with its dense concentration of finance, business, and industry on the coastal plain. The most striking feature of this pylon positioned at the edge of the mountain is its openness in multiple dimensions. It is quite transparent, concealing nothing, as it were, yet with quite extensive presence, visible from numerous points on the ridges around the city. The pylon leans into the city, opening the way, beginning an enfoldment. It soars into the heaven from different perspectives, sometimes shaping a great bird with outstretched wings, sometimes a feathery embracing cloak, sometimes the mythical harp of the love poetry and psalms of the ancient David.

The parabolic form of the pylon imparts a complexity to the open air, to open space through which it moves. In his discussion of Leibniz and the Baroque, Deleuze takes in the fold, the folding of space-time that is the opening of a different forming, a forming of difference that had not existed before in that space and time. Folding may be conceptualized as the forming of a pocket (of space, of time, of social action, and of their intersections)—a folding in of structures, of movements of living, articulating persons within these curving self-enclosures in certain ways and not in others. As it curves, the fold or pocket opens the depths of space-time where/when no opening had existed a moment before. The opening itself is a curving of space-time, since the movement of living is neither stopped nor blocked, but shifted into itself, enfolded, reorganized, and thereby made different, minimally, partially, utterly, from the movements in whose courses the opening is but a moment (Handelman 2005: 14). The fold or pocket inflects and involutes (Deleuze 1993: 14–26), entailing variable degrees of the emergence of autopoietic propensities for self-organization that follow from the self-closing that is the curve. The fold curves recursively because its forming in itself is anti-lineal, anti-Cartesian, turning over, upending. Of especial interest here is that Deleuze (ibid.: 16) cites Paul Klee as calling a point—the (pure) event that is a point of inflection—"'a site of cosmogenesis' . . . 'between dimensions.'"[5]

Consider the parabolic pylon. It begins a curve, soaring as its curve leans and swerves into the city. This curvature has an axis, the pylon, yet it does not have a center that is centering itself, since its movement is upward, outward, reaching beyond the physical extension of the cables themselves. It is a folding dynamic, but one just beginning, the folding reaching toward, into the city even as it soars into the heavens, gently, openly, enfolding both together. The point of inflection, the beginning, is the point of cosmogenesis for the vector (continuously emerging into being, here, elsewhere) that I am beginning to discuss—a point of cosmogenesis whose parabolic extension seems to modulate space harmonically (resonating with the metaphor of David's harp), imparting a rhythm to the ether.[6] Looked at this way, the pylon-parabola begins to take on the forming of a net, one that is in movement, leaning transparently, benignly, into its catchment area.

A net, not yet a wall. I problematize this beginning by shifting to the new Holocaust History Museum at the national Holocaust memorial, Yad Vashem (which means "A Place and a Name"). As I noted at the outset, the relationality of spaces that I am connecting is more topological, less topographical. So, although Yad Vashem is not quite on the west-east trajectory that begins here with the pylon-parabola, it is undoubtedly on that trajectory once temporality is added to the vector.

The Museum-Wall—Folding History into the State

Today the Israeli state is sieved through the Holocaust. During the state's early years, its representatives rarely raised the likelihood that its foundation emerged from the Holocaust or that the United Nations vote in 1947 in favor of this founding was a response to genocide. Israel's political leadership presented the establishment of the state as its own accomplishment. Nonetheless, statist imperative demanded commemoration of the Holocaust. Yet the end of European Jewry and the beginning of the new Jews of Palestine and then Israel were presented as two separate narrative trajectories—one buried into near extinction as the other was rising into prominence. In these narratives the fate of European Jewry was the inevitable dead-ended outcome of Diaspora living. Only as an independent nation-state could Jews have a future in a world of states.

In the present-day political realities of Israel, which have powerfully revived the presence of the religious Judaic as the cultural grounds for the existence of the Jewish people inside and outside the state, these two historical narratives have merged to the point that the state is now the direct consequence of the Holocaust. This causal relationship must be honored and sanctified continuously with respect and vigilance, since the conditions of the Holocaust are everywhere anew.[7] Most immediately, the Israeli people and state are threatened by the enmity of Palestinians and, more generally, of Muslims (perceived independently of Israeli occupation and settlement of the territories). It is in these senses that the trajectory of beginning (the open, although directional, folding of the pylon-parabola) has on its existential horizon the historical museum of Yad Vashem, through which it must pass.

The old Holocaust museum was located in a squarish, nondescript building, one of the cluster that makes up the core of the Yad Vashem memorial complex (see Fig. 11.2, the building in the left background). All of the buildings in this complex offer a blank exterior visage, the horrific realities of the genocide being hidden from external view (Handelman and Shamgar-Handelman 1997). Despite being concealed deep inside and far away, those horrors are immediately here and now. The exhibition in the old museum, which had been in place for about thirty years, was designed by historians and resembled a musty illustrated book of Holocaust history. Over the years since it opened, the Israeli political leadership had begun to emphasize Israel's role as the natural leader in Holocaust commemoration. The new Holocaust History Museum is a response to the tremendous rise in Holocaust commemoration among world Jewry, especially in the United States, culminating in the political success of placing the United States Holocaust Memorial Museum on the National Mall

Figure 11.2. The Yad Vashem memorial complex with the old Holocaust museum in the background and the new Holocaust museum in the foreground. Photograph by the author.

in Washington, DC, in the heart of American national symbolism. The new commemorative sites use innovative designs and aesthetics that had left Yad Vashem in their wake. The new Holocaust museum is intended to rectify this—or so its leaders imagine.

My focus here is only on the exterior of this building and its positioning within the national Holocaust memorial. The Yad Vashem complex is built along the top of a ridge, with most of the buildings fronting along its southern exposure. The outermost walkway along the circumference of the ridge is named the Avenue of the Righteous Among the Nations. On either side of the long walkway are carob trees dedicated to particular Gentiles who, at risk to their own lives, saved Jews during the Holocaust (see Fig. 11.3). These trees, these dedications, are an outer bulwark, protective of the memories of elsewhen, elsewhere that are lodged within the complex. The three largest free-standing monuments of the complex are dedicated to the resistance and heroism of Jews during World War II. Open to the elements, they thrust abruptly upward from the land, dominating the perspective. The symmetric triangulation of these three monuments corresponds to the shape of the ridge and forms another bulwark within that of the Avenue of the Righteous. Within these two bulwarks are the major memorial buildings, protected by righteous Gentiles and by Jewish resistance and heroism (see Handelman and Shamgar-Handelman 1997: 101–10).

The positioning of the new museum reverses this patterning. The shape of the building is a long triangle, some 200 meters in length, positioned to intersect at a right angle with the Avenue of the Righteous. There are two openings set into the sloping wall of the building, facing outward toward the beginning of the complex.

Figure 11.3. The Avenue of the Righteous passing through the new Holocaust museum. Photograph by the author.

One is the entrance to the museum. The other opening is a larger rectangle the width of the Avenue of the Righteous, continuing this walkway through the wall of the museum into the larger territory of the complex beyond. There are no windows or other apertures in the sloping side of the museum. But where the two sloping walls meet at their apex, there is a triangular skylight, a prism that runs the length of the building. On the northerly side of the Avenue, the museum triangle plunges into the mountain ridge of the complex, with the skylight above ground. At its northerly end the museum triangle emerges from the ridge, its sloping sides folding back and cantilevered to open into the space of large windows that frame an expansive view of the city below.

The exhibits of the museum's interior roughly correspond to the tripartition of the exterior walls. The first section of the exterior walls, including the entrance, corresponds to the first portion of the standard Israeli narrative of the Holocaust—the prologue, the rise to power of the Nazis, the setting of the trap, the condition of no exit. The second section of the exterior walls, buried in the earth of the ridge, corresponds to the second portion of the narrative—the extermination of European Jewry in concentration and death camps. Often these deaths are understood in religious terms as self-sacrifice, as dying in the name of God (*al Kiddush HaShem*). The third section of the exterior walls, emerging ("exploding," in the words of the architect [Safdie 2006: 94]) from their burial, opening into the light toward the vista of the living city below, corresponds to the narrative's third part—the liberation from the camps and emigration to the Israeli state-in-the-making, the pinnacle of freedom achieved through war and sacrifice (Handelman 2004: 171–99). Along the entire length of the museum its triangular skylight prism remains above ground, a honed, cutting-edge slicing-open of the earth that exposes the sacrifices of the Holocaust beneath the ground to the redemption that illuminates this history with the light of the heavens over the State of Israel. One perceptive interpreter comments that "the architect's act of violence in slitting open the ground is felt viscerally, expressing itself as an archeological scar symbolically healed by the landscape itself" (Ockman 2006a: 21; see also Bennett 2005: 35).

The vector that begins with the ethereal innocence of the pylon-parabola breaks (explodes) out of the historical museum as a *topos* of enfolded force that has been transformed through sacrifice into the violence and redemption of war and destruction.[8] The motto "never forget" is no less that of "always remember," and nowadays the force of national remembering drives primarily eastward, striving to incorporate whatever it penetrates.

Astride the Avenue of the Righteous, the new historical museum becomes an integral part of the protective bulwarks around the other buildings and sites of the memorial complex. As noted previously, the old museum, huddled amid and deep within the configuration of Holocaust remembrance buildings, was enfolded by the protective bulwarks around it. The new museum comes forth, directly confronting the visitor, in his or her face, as it were. Its forming is a wall, severe in its absolutism of controlling passage. The building's exterior walls repel the climbing gaze, except through the permitted apertures. The architect of the new museum writes: "I was determined to cast the entire museum monolithically, jointless, unadorned—without any exterior waterproofing or cladding . . . I wanted just the basic structure" (Safdie 2006: 98). Elsewhere he says, "I wanted something so primeval and archeological that you don't think about the architecture" (Dean 2005: 113). Yet the new museum is no less a fold. All buildings of course are folded materials and spaces that are enclosed and closed to varying degrees. Used banally in relation to material constructions, this could reduce Deleuzian folding to a *non sequitur*. Nonetheless, the Deleuzian fold is always a dynamic, constituted through other dynamics—the ways in which folding is done, the interactivity of exteriors and interiors, how folds are lived, the degrees of self-organizing within the fold, the contents that are shaped and shape. All these enable distinguishing among many varieties of folds and folds within folds (Deleuze 1999: 97). Moreover, from this perspective even folds in solids may become more textured rather than given as is, once and for all.

This site is a museum engulfed by a wall, a museum within a wall, a museum embedded in a wall, a museum-wall, a front-line enfolding of horrific history folded into itself, unlike the old museum, where the horrific was enfolded away anonymously, its vulnerability protected amid a cluster of memorial buildings. The new museum enfolds horrific memory on its very front line, thrusting it in the face of mundane life. This folding itself is powerful, since the fold in its forming regenerates the historical narrative of that which it enfolds. Thus, the standard Holocaust narrative of Israel is now on the front line (facing eastward toward the most immediate enemy) as it buttresses Holocaust memorialism. Simultaneously interiorizing/introverting and exteriorizing/extroverting, the museum-wall practices itself into existence from its outside and its inside—the self-fortifying wall of memory that unfolds history and memory within itself, even as it zealously guards yet opens the way to the parceling out of this history and memory through other buildings and sites in the memorial complex. No less, the museum-wall is dedicated to consumption—the consuming of history and memory.

The museum-wall is a fold in time-space of the topological variety that scientists refer to as "rubber sheet geometry" (Asad 1999: 41)—a fold through which any point in time-space may touch any other. The folding of the pylon-parabola touches the museum-wall—the embryonic openness of the parabola folding closes itself into the unyielding history of Holocaust that today enfolds and interiorizes so much memory work in Jewish Israel. In present-day Jewish Jerusalem, many journeys that meander eastward will touch Holocaust time, will pass into Holocaust time, into the time of the great sacrifice, becoming locked into the self-fortification of memory that the Holocaust has become, thereby emerging transformed, more self-protective, more defensive, more aggressive, more warlike. Today, this front line moves eastward. In the culture of the Jewish nation-state, in which memory and history are always on the way and always in the way, there is little choice but to go through memory and history and take them on the way, take them along, as our vector develops, involutes, expands, armoring itself with walls that are no less spears as it gathers force. This vector acquires the pointed desire to spear consumption as it moves eastward.

The Mall-Wall—Vector Becomes Vortex

Jaffa Road, with the pylon-parabola at its western end, runs eastward until it meets the Ottoman walls of the Old City and then runs alongside these in a southwesterly direction, along the 1949 armistice lines. After the 1967 war, much thought and argument went into planning how to relate architectonically to captured East Jerusalem and just what to build in this former no man's land between the Israeli and the Palestinian cities (Nitzan-Shiftan 2005).[9] It was unthinkable for the Jewish-Israeli politicians, the army, and the general Jewish public to leave this as a (memory) scar running through the middle of the now joined city. Forty-three years later, the most dominant presence in this interstitial zone is almost complete, ramming across the former no man's land to the Old City. This project (designed by the architect who also did the new Holocaust history museum) stretches for about a quarter of a kilometer (likely longer) along the length of the slope of a hill, meeting Jaffa Road and the Old City walls at the Jaffa Gate, the only entry point into the Old City along the entirety of its southwesterly walls.

Perhaps the most striking feature of this project is that its entire length is uninterrupted, building abutting building, one after another (indeed reminiscent of the new Holocaust history museum). No less striking, the entire length of this built presence is bisected by a broad walkway with shops and restaurants on both sides,[10] intended for solidly upscale shoppers. Many stores are chain outlets, selling trendy brand-name clothes and shoes that fill shopping malls. Others sell jewelry a cut above the average, and one is a pipe and tobacco shop, a rarity in a country in which the imagery of the pipe harks back to a time perceived as more thoughtful, more intellectual. This mall, encased all the way to the Jaffa Gate, is almost entirely without perspectives to the outside environment.

At its Jewish city western end, this project is bulkier, with apartment buildings and a hotel reaching eight stories on both sides of the walkway. Farther east, the buildings are lower but still utterly obscure any view from the walkway of the nearby Old City walls (see Fig. 11.4), unless one climbs out of the walkway on its northerly side onto an open promenade that runs alongside the walls.[11] Yet there is only one set of stairs on that side along the walkway's entire length. Along the other, southerly side of the walkway, there are nine flights of stairs that go downslope to the street below (called Valley [*HaEmek*] Road), where the entrances to the parking garages are located. At this lower level, these entrances run almost the full length of the project. Walking the mall toward the Jaffa Gate, the horizon of ancient city walls is constricted to a single image, that of the Tower of David next to the Jaffa Gate, since the nineteenth century a popular icon of Jerusalem for Jews. The rest of the vista is completely effaced. So,

Figure 11.4. The mall-wall from the Old City wall, looking toward West Jerusalem. Photograph by the author.

too, as one approaches the end of this shopping street, the elegant presence of the Jaffa Gate itself is blocked from view until one climbs the steep thirty or so steps to surface above the mall's encasing.

From the western end of the project, looking down Valley Road toward the Old City walls, the entrance to this street itself looks like a huge gateway. To one's left there are the buildings of the mall, and to one's right is a bulky, relatively new hotel, David's Citadel. With massive pillars supporting its entranceway (an example of what I call "Third Temple" architecture), it is a near parody of the modest symmetric proportions of the Ottoman period Jaffa Gate all the way at the far Old City end. When walking on Valley Road along the base of the mall-wall toward the Jaffa Gate, to one's left the Old City's southwesterly walls are completely obscured from view by the massive wall of continuous construction, with the linearity and instrumentality of its buying deeply embedded within.[12]

What does the mall-wall signify in terms of this discussion? This Jewish wall, a massive presence, blocks from view a section of the uninterrupted perspective of the Old City walls, which are integral to the grand presence of this ancient city and its history. Indeed, the mall-wall substitutes itself, a modern Jewish wall, one devoted to consumption, for a portion of the Old City Ottoman wall. Today, this is the only length of the Old City walls whose vista is obscured. Moreover, this meeting of the Jewish mall-wall and the largely Palestinian Old City is now the only location along the walls where the Jewish city threatens to penetrate the latter. Thus, I see the mall-wall driving toward the Old City, a bulwark of Jewish West Jerusalem that is no less a spear, or, more aptly, a battering ram, aimed at the Arab Jaffa Gate.

The mall-wall as a line of mass, as a projectile of the might of the Jewish state, propels itself at the ancient, deeply textured Old City walls and beyond.[13] No less, this projectile is the accelerating mass of consumer consumption and Israeli economic domination; indeed, the entirety of this line of force is justified in terms of, and is dedicated to, consumption. The mall-wall enfolds the capacity to consume—the long line of stores on either side, their windows full of separate items, the passers-by caught in the seductive gaze of objects-for-sale, one by one, all available to the desires of the buyer. The eye passes from item to item, from shop window to shop window, each of which has the potential to offer shoppers whatever they wish in order to stimulate their fantasies. These exchanges are embedded within the wall-mall, enclosed into itself without external perspectives—a closed single-purpose vessel with tunnel vision *en route* to the Old City. Within itself the mall-wall turns the vector into a vortical funnel, a vortex generated by and for desires of consumption, funnelled through the recursive self-enclosure. Within this, the desire to acquire, to own, to consume, is reified, accentuated, expanded, whirling through itself, augmenting itself as it is aimed at the Old City, which the state acquires, owns, and desires to consume over and over, altering its particular goals and strategies from time to time, yet never altering its need to make it its own. In this vector, the violence of sacrifice is whirled into another variety of absolutist violence—that of the commodity fetishism of ownership, certainly a prominent form of nationalist consumption.

The Impenetrable Block—the End Folding Back, into the Beginning

Beyond the Old City, on the eastern edges of Jerusalem, is the yet unfinished security barrier that Israel calls the separation fence, but which is intended to practice absolute division, domination, and sovereignty (Ben-Eliezer and Feinstein 2008). Planned during the Second Intifada, the entire length of the separation barrier, if completed, will span some 800 kilometers. Constituted in the main by networks of fences and trenches, with watchtowers, roadblocks, and gates distributed along its length, the barrier is legitimized in the name of "security needs" (see Sorkin 2005; Weizman 2007: 161–82).[14] In the Jerusalem area, the barrier (see Fig. 11.5) snakes up and down its ridges for some 170 kilometers, cutting off much of East Jerusalem from its Palestinian hinterlands. In neighborhoods of densely built housing, the fences become a wall of concrete slabs some 8 meters in height, splitting streets, chopping apart houses and social relations, separating farmers from their agricultural lands. The path of the fence/wall is quite arbitrary, based on army evaluations of security, but no less routed by the military, bureaucratic, and political establishments to include much additional land for settlements that will then be on the Israeli side of the barrier.[15]

Tens of thousands of Palestinians, official residents of "united" Jerusalem, now find themselves on the other side of the barrier, unable to enter the city by any direct route, their neighborhoods receiving no municipal services (health, education,

Figure 11.5. The security wall chopping through Palestinian Abu Dis. Photograph by the author.

welfare, garbage collection, ambulance service, repairs to the water and electricity systems, etc.). The effect of the security barrier will be to destroy Palestinian metropolitan Jerusalem "and control it without annexing it" (Klein 2005: 71). In the words of Ehud Barak, a former Israeli prime minister and the current minister of defense, "They are over there, and we are over here." Stark concrete of brute force, slicing and slamming Zionist statist imperatives through Palestine, the wall is utterly without adornment, without subtlety, containing nothing but its own impetus to do the violence of absolute difference. This is a Jewish wall reserved for Palestinians; for that matter, it is hardly intended for civilian Jewish eyes. At a distance from the Jewish city, the wall even appears abstract and pastoral as it meanders and curves up and down ridges. Up close, it is a row of huge blunt teeth sunk into the earth, their bite savage and unyielding. Horizons of living are blocked, perspective severely foreshortened. One cannot look over, under, or around. For many Israeli Jews, the civilized world ends here. Were we speaking of a cartography of Israeli Jewish consciousness, the eastern side of the security wall might well be inscribed by the Israeli state with the warning "terra incognita" or "here there be monsters."

The security barrier may seem the termination of the vector I have laid out, but it is not. As it blocks movement, the barrier enfolds movement that may have been. By blocking movement, the barrier becomes different from the very block that it is. Put differently, in blocking movement the barrier does not repeat itself as just that which it was: it becomes different *in* itself even as it is identical *to* itself. Deleuze (1994: 57) argues provocatively, "It is always differences which resemble one another, which are analogous, opposed or identical: difference is behind everything, but behind difference there is nothing. Each difference passes through all the others; it must 'will' itself or find itself through all the others." As the barrier blocks movement, it is itself movement, a variation of itself. Sameness is a function of difference; without difference there is no sameness. Thus, sameness emerges through the *circulation* of difference—this is its repetition, its repetition through itself, its "willing" of itself that enables it to be that which it is and therefore other than it is. To wit, Deleuze (ibid.) quotes the American poet Benjamin Paul Blood: "[T]he same returns not, save to bring the different. The slow round of the engraver's lathe gains but the breadth of a hair, but the difference is distributed back over the whole curve, never an instant true—ever not quite."[16]

Thus, the separation barrier enfolds whatever, whomever it blocks as it blocks. And as it blocks, the barrier curves back, enfolding, in the direction of the pylon-parabola from where we began and which I called the beginning of this vector. Reaching its apparent limits, its outside, the vector bends back, the outside becoming inside, the vector enfolding itself, its interaction with itself augmented, becoming more complex, its power emerging further, effecting itself. The vector is a great folding, an ongoing folding and re-folding, forming a spheroid of forces and sites that, enfolded, interact. At this juncture, I can say that the sites themselves are not crucial in these dynamics; it is the dynamics of their vectorization that are crucial, their *Zeitgeist* diffusing through the spaces they organize as they do. In more topological terms, "the most distant point becomes interior, by being converted into the nearest: life within the folds" (Deleuze 1999: 101). It is in this sense that the separation barrier is the transmogrification of the pylon-parabola. The bridge is inviting, poetic, soaring, graceful, opening into the Jewish city, encouraging horizons, a site of cosmogenesis, the beginning of an enfolding, while the barrier is forbidding, massive in its squatting, brutal in its starkness, an altar of sacrificial violence blocking the horizon from earth to sky, a site of cosmic closure, a folding back through itself to constrain, own, and sacrifice the Palestinian city in its containing.

Aesthetics, Fold, Vector

To appreciate the role of an aesthetics of power and control in urban form, it is insufficient to consider particular or singular forms or even their comparisons based primarily on symbolic and architectural criteria. The most powerful aesthetics are those that are lived mundanely. Without the aesthetic experiencing of power as practice, there is no feel that this is how doing is doing, how doing is done, how done continues as doing. But I also can invert this to say that this is how surrounds naturalize us into the practices of power. Aesthetics—the synesthetic, sensuous feel of things fitting together (and not fitting together)—enable us to proceed formatively, coherently, perspectively, and prospectively in the nowness of here. The aesthetics of practice are the persuasive grounds of practice, persuading that practice is in the process of being done as the kind of practice it is (and is becoming). In this sense, aesthetics may be more of a *gestalt*, a "coherent entity" (Polanyi 1966), or an entity whose coherence is continuously coming into being, emerging, fitting itself together self-persuasively, even as that which it fits together erodes, ruptures, breaks. This is no less the aesthetics of the vector I have discussed. An aesthetics of power is distributed, circulated, transformed, and practiced throughout the vector rather than through connections between sites. In my terms, the aesthetics of control are those of an aesthetics continually practiced and augmented as a common-sense given.

More than five decades after the capture of Palestinian Jerusalem and the other Occupied Territories, despite two intifadas and numerous acts of resistance and protest, the conquest is fully naturalized in the most quotidian way for Israeli Jews. This is practiced into existence on a daily basis in ways far too numerous to enter into here—and likewise for the vector I have discussed. Beginning with the harmonic pylon-parabola as the entry to the historic and holy capital, gathering sacrificial empowerment through the museum-wall, its velocity becoming more directional, the vector accelerates through the mall-wall, gathering the power to own and fetishize, pinning Palestinians-as-objects against the security barrier with Holocaust history, squeezing, flattening, and sacrificing them with the power to consume against its unyielding, brute form. This form folds back toward the pylon-parabola, creating a multi-dimensional spheroid of forces to contain and imprison Palestinians' hopes and aspirations. Integral to this practice of power are the aesthetics that I call bureaucratic.

I argued at the outset that aesthetics enable the fitting together of people, things, places, worlds through practice. Aesthetics are crucial to all practice in mundane living. Historically, bureaucratic aesthetics are tied closely to the emergence of the modern state. This state-form (after Deleuze and Guattari 1988: 385), tree-like, is deeply rooted, centered stably around an *axis mundi* that opens in all directions and planes, vertical, tall, hierarchical, protective under the cover of its shading. Branching and reproducing clearly, exactly, this logic of forming expands by capture, by taking space, by reproducing its form in additional spaces, by making over these spaces into places. The state-form extends itself lineally, a design for quantitative growth of space and population (Patton 2000), giving especial regard to shaping and controlling its own interiority. Deleuze and Guattari (1988: 397) write: "The law of the State is . . . that of interior and exterior. The State is sovereignty. But sovereignty only reigns over what it is capable of internalizing, of appropriating locally." The aesthetics of doing this are in large measure the bureaucratic.

The bureaucratic aesthetics of what the state-form does are related to closing up space, dividing it into determinate intervals, establishing clear-cut breaks and absolutist boundaries. An integral component of this is monothetic classification (Bowker and Star 1999). This system demands that every classified item be put into a category with exact boundaries and explicit distinctions that set it apart from all other categories on the same level of classification, without fuzziness, overlap, confusion. This is the kind of classification that Foucault (1973) traced historically in Europe. This is how Western bureaucracy has desired to be practiced. This feels right aesthetically in the practice of bureaucracy, in its common-sensical self-persuasions. Everything is in its proper place, with concomitant consequences in the actualization of power. In practicing the imperatives of the state-form, bureaucratic aesthetics shape and control the social and spatial surfaces of expanding space by capturing new territory for the deployment of power. The aesthetics of bureaucratic classification enable the creation of space that simultaneously is captured, contained, and accounted for. Moreover, new classifications create their own *raison d'être* for expansion and self-totalization. Bureaucratic aesthetics enable the bureaucratic state to expand through a kind of cellular division of difference yet sameness.

In the modern state, the bureaucratic aesthetics of capture, containment, and taxonomic division are given the formidable impetus and coercion of law. Analyzing the mutual exclusiveness in law of categories such as lawful/unlawful and legal/illegal, King (1993: 223) argues that, through such social codes, wherever absolute categorical distinctions are made, they will be regarded as part of the legal system—and I emphasize that they will be *felt* aesthetically as part of the legal system. In my terms, phenomenal forms created through or enabled by an aesthetic of monothetic classification will have embedded in them something of the feel and force of legal mandate that stems from inclusion and exclusion. Through bureaucratic aesthetics, truth is a singular, not a multiple.[17]

Bureaucratic aesthetics are those of the making of walls, the walls of capture and containment, of lawfulness, the walls of an absolutist classification that strives to banish overlap, fuzziness, fluctuation, uncertainty—the walls discussed in this work. The wall that folds and enfolds (unlike so many other potentialities of folding) resonates with the lawful feel of bureaucratic aesthetics. The wall that folds and enfolds encloses by constraining access, perspective, exit, by striving to totalize everything it contains to make all of this homogeneous—in this way, whatever is within is self-fortifying and protected within itself. This is the vector that I have discussed, itself one of bureaucratic aesthetics. A vector connecting walls otherwise distant in topographical space from one another, in part through connectivities that resonate with bureaucratic aesthetics. A vector within which these folding and enfolding walls give through themselves a push, a *phusis* (Castoriades 1997: 331), toward the completion of the self-fortification of the city that they (and numerous other vectors) have helped set in motion.

Notes

First published in 2010 as "Folding and Enfolding Walls: Statist Imperatives and Bureaucratic Aesthetics in Divided Jerusalem," *Social Analysis* 54: 60–79. Reprinted with permission.

1. A classic modern exposition that reflects this perspective on the meaning of buildings is that of Goodman (1985).
2. Deleuze has influenced theorists of architecture in developing computer models of what they call "folding architecture," characterized by "a more fluid logic of connectivity" that integrates "unrelated elements within a new continuous mixture" (Greg Lynn, cited in Harris 2005: 37).
3. The term "haptic," according to Alois Riegl, refers to a kind of vision distinct from the optical, one in which the eye behaves as does the sense of touch (Deleuze 2003: 189). The haptic gaze

is tactile, reaching out, touching, even shaping the textures of another surface and penetrating the contours of its depth (Handelman 2006: 66). See also Gandelman (1991: 5).
4. This is what we are told. In fact, the bridge stands on its own; the pylon and cables are decoration. Since the bridge is not weight-bearing, this vector begins with an illusion. My thanks to Allen Weiss for this observation.
5. This is in relation to Deleuze's arguments regarding singularity coming-into-being from virtuality; virtuality creating, but the creation not quite yet created.
6. In Deleuzian terms, this point of cosmogenesis, a singularity, can also be understood as a point of catastrophe, with the consequences of the oscillation of its waves yet to be known fully.
7. In addition to high school students sent in droves to visit Auschwitz-Birkenau and other extermination camps (see Feldman 2008), during the past few years the Israeli Army has developed its "Witnesses in Uniform" program, which sends thousands of officers and soldiers annually to visit death camps.
8. In *The Feast of the Sorcerer*, Kapferer (1997) explicates this logic of sacrifice.
9. According to Meron Benvenisti, deputy mayor of Jerusalem at that time, "these plans were de facto a political tool, equal to government policy, in the light of the scarcity of symbolic land" (Nitzan-Shiftan 2005: 231).
10. This walkway, Alrov Mamilla Avenue, is named after the company developing the project, Alrov Properties and Lodgings, which is owned by the Israeli billionaire Alfred Akirov.
11. A recent advertisement aimed at foreign tourists describes the "shopping avenue" as overlooking the Old City—a "stretch of beautiful architecture, which *connects* the old and new city" (*International Herald Tribune*, 20 November 2008; emphasis added).
12. There is one angled turn in the mall walkway, about halfway along. It is here that the only steps leading up to the promenade alongside the Old City walls are located.
13. If we enter the Old City through the Jaffa Gate and continue straight on, downslope through markets and neighborhoods, we reach the ancient Israelite wall, the Western Wall, the last remnant of the outer walls of the Second Temple, which was destroyed in 70 CE. This is part of the wall that surrounds the Haram al-Sharif mosque complex, enclosing the Dome of the Rock and the al-Aqsa Mosque. After the 1967 war, the state religion officially turned the Western Wall, long a traditional place of Jewish worship, into the holiest place in Judaism, but also into the *ur*-wall, iconic of Israeli control of all of Jerusalem from its Judaic religious center.
14. The phrase "security needs" is stock-in-trade discourse for the military and security establishments and often should be understood as justification for undisguised statist and military interests. Apart from the Occupied Territories, Israel's military, defense, and security establishments have been estimated to control over half of the territory of the state (Oren 2008).
15. The original route of the barrier would have confiscated more than 20 percent of the occupied West Bank, but court-ordered alterations have reduced this to about 10 percent (Ben-Eliezer and Feinstein 2008: 178–79).
16. In this vein, Deleuze (1994: 57) argues: "The world is neither finite nor infinite as representation would have it: it is completed and unlimited. Eternal return is the unlimited of the finished itself.... Repetition is the formless being of all differences, the formless power of the ground which carries every object to that extreme 'form' in which its representation comes undone."
17. The above is discussed in Handelman (2004: 19–42) and elsewhere.

References

Asad, Maria. 1999. *Reading with Michel Serres: An Encounter with Time*. Albany: SUNY Press.
Ben-Eliezer, Uri, and Yuval Feinstein. 2008. "'The Battle over Our Homes': Reconstructing/Deconstructing Sovereign Practices around Israel's Separation Barrier on the West Bank." *Israel Studies* 12: 171–92.
Bennett, Barbara Horwitz. 2005. "For the Six Million." *Building Design & Construction* 46: 34–41.

Benvenisti, Meron. 1995. *Intimate Enemies: Jews and Arabs in a Shared Land*. Berkeley: University of California Press.
Bowker, Geoffrey C., and Susan Leigh Star. 1999. *Sorting Things Out: Classification and Its Consequences*. Cambridge, MA: MIT Press.
Castoriades, Cornelius. 1997. *World in Fragments*. Ed. and trans. David Ames Curtis. Stanford: Stanford University Press.
Dean, Andrea Oppenheimer. 2005. "Moshe Safdie Offers a Memorial Journey through the Depths of a Jerusalem Hillside with His Yad Vashem History Museum." *Architectural Record* 193: 112–19.
Deleuze, Gilles. 1993. *The Fold: Leibniz and the Baroque*. London: Athlone Press.
———. 1994. *Difference and Repetition*. London: Athlone Press.
———. 1999. *Foucault*. London: Continuum.
———. 2003. *Francis Bacon: The Logic of Sensation*. London: Continuum.
Deleuze, Gilles, and Felix Guattari. 1988. *A Thousand Plateaus*. London: Athlone Press.
Dufrenne, Mikel. 1973. *The Phenomenology of Aesthetic Experience*. Evanston: Northwestern University Press.
Feldman, Jackie. 2008. *Above the Death Pits, Beneath the Flag: Youth Voyages to Poland and the Performance of Israeli National Identity*. New York: Berghahn Books.
Foucault, Michel. 1973. *The Order of Things: An Archeology of the Human Sciences*. New York: Vintage.
Gandelman, Claude. 1991. *Reading Pictures, Viewing Texts*. Bloomington: Indiana University Press.
Goldman, Alan. 2001. "The Aesthetic." In *The Routledge Companion to Aesthetics*, ed. Berys Gant and Dominic M. Lopes, 181–92. London: Routledge.
Goodman, Nelson. 1985. "How Buildings Mean." *Critical Inquiry* 11: 642–53.
Handelman, Don. 2004. *Nationalism and the Israeli State: Bureaucratic Logic in Public Events*. Oxford: Berg.
———. 2005. "Introduction: Why Ritual in Its Own Right? How So?" In *Ritual in Its Own Right: Explorations in the Dynamics of Transformation*, ed. Don Handelman and Galina Lindquist, 1–32. New York: Berghahn Books.
———. 2006. "Death and the Mask." In *Behind the Mask: Dance, Healing, and Possession in South India*, ed. David Shulman and Deborah Thiagarajan, 59–71. South and Southeast Asian Series. Ann Arbor: University of Michigan.
Handelman, Don, and Lea Shamgar-Handelman. 1997. "The Presence of Absence: The Memorialism of National Death in Israel." In *Grasping Land: Space and Place in Contemporary Israeli Discourse and Experience*, ed. Eyal Ben-Ari and Yoram Bilu, 85–128. Albany: SUNY Press.
Harris, Paul A. 2005. "To See with the Mind and Think through the Eye: Deleuze, Folding Architecture and Simon Rodia's Watts Towers." In *Deleuze and Space*, ed. Ian Buchanan and Gregg Lambert, 36–60. Edinburgh: Edinburgh University Press.
Kane, Carolyn Lee. 2007. "*Aisthesis* and the Myth of Representation." *Minerva: An Internet Journal of Philosophy* 11: 83–100.
Kapferer, Bruce. 1997. *The Feast of the Sorcerer*. Chicago: University of Chicago Press.
Katz, Jack. 1999. *How Emotions Work*. Chicago: University of Chicago Press.
King, Michael. 1993. "The 'Truth' about Autopoiesis." *Journal of Law and Society* 20: 218–36.
Klein, Menachem. 2005. "Old and New Walls in Jerusalem." *Political Geography* 24: 53–76.
Nitzan-Shiftan, Alona. 2005. "Capital City or Spiritual Center? The Politics of Architecture in Post-1967 Jerusalem." *Cities* 22: 229–40.
Ockman, Joan. 2006a. "A Place in the World for a World Displaced." In *Yad Vashem: Moshe Safdie—The Architecture of Memory*, ed. Joan Ockman, 19–26. Baden: Lars Muller Verlag.
———, ed. 2006b. *Yad Vashem: Moshe Safdie—The Architecture of Memory*. Baden: Lars Muller Verlag.
Oren, Amiram. 2008. "Shadow Lands: The Use of Land Resources for Security Needs in Israel." *Israel Studies* 12: 149–70.

Patton, Paul. 2000. *Deleuze and the Political*. London: Routledge.
Polanyi, Michael. 1962. *Personal Knowledge: Towards a Post-Critical Philosophy*. New York: Harper Torchbooks.
———. 1966. *The Tacit Dimension*. London: Routledge & Kegan Paul.
Safdie, Moshe. 2006. "The Architecture of Memory." In *Yad Vashem: Moshe Safdie—The Architecture of Memory*, ed. Joan Ockman, 92–101. Baden: Lars Muller Verlag.
Sorkin, Michael. 2005. "Introduction: Up against the Wall." In *Against the Wall: Israel's Barrier to Peace*, ed. Michael Sorkin, vi–xx. New York: New Press.
Weizman, Eyal. 2007. *Hollow Land: Israel's Architecture of Occupation*. London: Verso.

Epilogue

Forming Form, Folding Time (Toward Dynamics through an Anthropology of Form)

> Listen O Lord of the Meeting Rivers
> Things standing shall fall
> But the moving ever shall stay.
> —Basavanna, twelfth-century CE Indian philosopher and poet

Part I: Forming Form

Thinking through my own anthropology of the past half-century I recognize an intermittent though abiding curiosity in the workings of phenomenal forms, formings of the social, some of which are more recognizable and identifiable by the people who shape and inhabit them for varying periods (for example, numerous "rituals" that I have discussed in detail elsewhere) while others, though less so, are discernible through analysis. In either instance and in their intermingling, phenomenal forms, social forms, are, paraphrasing Deleuze (1997: 91), those that show themselves in and through themselves. They *show themselves in and through themselves* as more or less distinct entities through their practice and through perceptions of their practice, though again these often cannot be distinguished and need not be. Clarity and fuzziness in worlds of practice coexist and often enable the existence of one another.

Nonetheless this is hardly sufficient to even begin theorizing about phenomenal forms. In the ways in which the thinking of anthropology is constituted, in order to theorize—social form, cultural form—the form in question is given a name that enters it into some regime of cultural contextualization, social relationships, rule-giving of some sort, ontological standing of some kind, and the like. Yet this kind of thinking says little about the form itself, the logics of form *qua* form, and issues of the order of, how does a form hold together as a form? Mainly from within itself, or mainly from outside itself? Is there something in, say, a particular form that in itself enables that form to continue for a while as it does, without turning for explanation in the first instance to some sort of stabilizing grounding that is external to this form—in my day this was grounding in culture, in tradition, values, norms, and now to multiple ontologies and to ethics? Such questions are hardly ever asked.

Yet it is questions like these that made me curious about whether something of a response might be found in the interiors of forms: in the ways these are put together, and in how these effect what it is that forms potentially can do within themselves and in relation to their external worlds—in other words, to search within their "own-ness." In thinking about such questions I found little aid in various anthropologies (nor in other of the social sciences). Anthropologists do not conceptualize social phenomena through such ideas as "form" and "forming." They still tend to move in the general directions of individual agency, social relationships, power, and collective activities and representations. The very idea that social forms may have degrees of autonomy from their social surrounds, and that this autonomy is related to how they come to be put together within themselves, is near to anathema within anthropologies where continuous connectedness and interdependencies are the rule, while their antinomies are perceived as destructive. This is even more so in the era of globalization, glocalization, and cosmopolitanism, producing anthropologies that emphasize expansiveness and the *inter*-relational rather than social interiority and the *intra*-relational.

Despite alterations of perspective in anthropology like the ontological turn that produces multiple ontologies, like actor-network theory (ANT), and others that produce multiple epistemologies, the foci and units used to discuss the social and the cultural remain more continuous than not with prior approaches. Claims to radical difference so often turn out to be academic exercises in hair-splitting that, following Freud and Lacan, can be called the narcissism of the minor difference. Put directly, intellectually I found myself quite alone in my attempts to discuss and theorize form, and have remained so.

From time to time I return to this problem that I am calling the interior organization of social or phenomenal forms. My intention in this Epilogue is to discuss how this recursiveness in my thinking developed, from the 1970s into the 2000s, beginning with my first monograph, *Work and Play Among the Aged* (1977), then turning to *Models and Mirrors* (1st ed. 1990, 2nd ed. 1998), followed by the introduction to *Ritual in Its Own Right* (Handelman and Lindquist 2005). I will give the most space to *Work and Play* for two reasons: it is the least known of my thoughts on form, and much of what I wrote in the other two works mentioned here was already embryonic in *Work and Play*. In looking through these materials, one major lacuna became evident: in my endeavors to discuss the interiority of social forms there is hardly any mention of time. For all of my fascination with movement within the forming of form I did not see the relevance of time as such. Previewing my current thinking on time, I will argue that time may be a dynamic, perhaps a dynamic in its own right. All forms, animate and inanimate, are time-full and, as time-full, they are full of movement, given that their interiors always are in motion within themselves even as their exteriors are no less moving with time; and, given that there often are differences of temporal movement between these time-full interior and exterior movements. Whatever else they are, these time-full movements are a given, even as this given is a multiplicity that varies greatly among forms. In other words, time should always be on the agenda of the study of the social-cultural and not necessarily shoved into the category of dimensionality that greatly restricts the multiplicity of the fullness of time's motion.

Whether time-as-incessant-movement qualifies time as dynamic is indeed an issue, and one not easily answered if at all. Time perhaps might be understood as an "enabler" of the movement of time-full forms, interiorly and exteriorly. In the second part of this Epilogue I will pursue this line of thinking, at least to raise the issue of time and the forming of form into view. To wit: if the movement of time is continuous (yet changing) then is time critical to the enabling of form? If all "solidities" in conceptions of social ordering (like "structure," "institution," "community," and the like) are time-full then is not their appearance of solidity due to the very movement of their interior times at different speeds and intensities, rather than to other qualities that position the appearance of solidness as chronological, yet outside of time-as-dynamic?

Before turning into my own work let me point to one kind of relatedness between form and time. All social, phenomenal forms have interiority. Have depth to differing degrees. Form without depth denies the very sociality of the social. Flatness of form speaks to the superficiality of the social. Degrees of depth, degrees of interiority, are critical to how forms come to be formed within themselves, and to how these formings relate to their external environments. Yet the opening and shaping of depth within the interiority of form should not be taken for granted. The phenomenologist, Merleau-Ponty, argued that Descartes understood space as an open, flat presence of measurable external relations, as a third dimension without depth. By contrast, Merleau-Ponty characterized depth as "both natal space and matrix of every other existing space," indeed, as the "first" dimension that is the very source of the Cartesian dimensions, yet that is "*self-containing*" (Rosen 2015: 263, my emphasis, to which I will return). Thus for Merleau-Ponty (1962: 298) depth became the originating and most "existential" of all dimensions (see Johnson 1993: 86). Existence emerges from the natality of depth. This is "where relationships between objects [and, I add, between persons] as differential processes are formed." (Somers-Hall 2009: 214).

Deleuze (in *Cinema Two: The Time-Image*) adds a significant moment of bridging to this opening of voluminosity, suggesting that Merleau-Ponty's idea of depth is not a spatial notion at all but is rather a temporal one—depth is a notion of *duration* that is not reducible to dimensions of space (Wambacq 2011: 327; see also Mazis 2010: 127–28). Time *is* depth so long as one does not reduce temporality to the shallow flatness of its linear, metric variant. Time and depth are inseparable. What could make more sense than this? If time were not depth-full then time would exist only as a metric of (chronological) passage; indeed time in its existential fullness would not exist (*pace* Julian Barbour [cf. Barbour 2009: 85–90]). In other words, existence is tightly braided into depth, time, and duration, and this is no less so for the existence of social forms in their own right. The existence of a social form is grounded intimately within its own depth(s) and duration, and duration-as-time is of course always moving, never fixed. Forms, time-full, are indeed *time-forms*: their own durations differ from one another, and these durations need not necessarily be linear. And depth, to whichever degree, is always created by the forming of form that itself becomes time-space folded into itself to varying degrees. As noted above, I will return to temporality and form in the second part of this Epilogue. For the moment it is sufficient to state this relationship so that the reader is aware of the tenor of that which is to come.

Evolving Thoughts on Emergence and the Forming of Form

Work and Play Among the Aged grew from intensive observations of interaction during a lengthy period in a number of workshops that employed the aged. As prosaic as this research sounds, it gave me insight into how human inter-action only sometimes could be reduced to individuals interacting through individual agency. Face-to-face interaction took the form of a sequence between beginning and ending. A simple point yet one with a powerful intimation: to wit, that I could treat an "interaction strip" (as Goffman sometimes called such sequences) as a unitary event in itself, however tiny this forming might be. Following Goffman (1961) I called such an occasion an "encounter." Encounters came and went. Given their speed and their short duration they frequently were momentary compared to the ongoing lengthy durations of the workshops within which they occurred. Nonetheless I called the encounter an ephemeral yet *natural form* (rather than an analytical kind) of social organization since, regardless of the substance of an encounter, all encounters took a sequential *form* between discontinuity (onset) and discontinuity (closure) (see also Goffman 1983: 6).

Furthermore, the form that an encounter developed was *emergent*, in that how an encounter developed could hardly be predicted from its onset—there was no straightforward linear, causal relationship in the interaction sequence. I recognized that the encounter could be studied "in terms of its own emergent sequential form" (Handelman 1977: 95)—the subtitle of the book is *Interaction, Replication and Emergence in a Jerusalem Setting*. In doing so I found that "the sequential unfolding of a particular encounter is very much a function of the organizational form which that encounter [itself] develops" (Handelman 1977: 95; see also Handelman 1973).[1] In other words, however an encounter developed, its properties, and so, too, its forming, were emergent. Moreover, these emerging properties were continually becoming part of the encounter, affecting the forming of its emergence in ongoing ways. As I wrote many years later, "Encounters are formed through the interaction of their creators, but they also shape this interaction as it is occurring. Therefore encounters are not reducible to the contributions—the particular life conditions, decisions, strategies, moves, emotions—of the participants. The forming of interaction cannot be reduced to versions of methodological individualism . . . interaction [that is] understood as the addition of discrete, individual acts, each with its own individual intention—without destroying the idea of the encounter," as a naturally existing, phenomenal, social form (Handelman 2006b).[2]

More than forty years ago I had not heard of complexity theory, yet influenced by Gregory Bateson's thinking at the Josiah Macy Jr. conferences, and by his brilliant Epilogue to the second edition of his monograph, *Naven* (1958), I called this interactional recursivity "feedback" (yet, strangely, not fully recognizing the implications of the curving movement of feedback). The quietening of methodological individualism in processes of emergence has its parallel in the subduing of the transcendent subjectivism of much of phenomenology, as Holland (2012: 21) puts this. In my terms, the "active self" as the ground, touchstone, and impetus for the shaping of the phenomenal becomes sucked or folded within the curving shaping of form to which self and selves contribute but that comes to form them, momentarily, lengthily. In extreme instances (for which many ritual forms qualify) the very forming of selves may become part of the form itself (see, for example, Harrison 1993).[3]

There was a powerful autopoietic moment here that I missed, and I was unable to name what it was that I was after in studying the social life of phenomenal forms. Not a systemics of the social (of which some two decades later Niklas Luhmann produced the most sophisticated version). Neither was I taken by systems theory as such, but rather by something that in cosmoses of multiplicity (to use Deleuze's fertile term) potentially could move in the direction of systemics yet so, too, toward many other alternatives. That something, in a Deleuzian vein, was the generation of *variation*. Not the occasional generation of variation, but rather its ongoing generation in social life. That is, the continuous generation of immanent potentiation that generated variation. I felt early on that anthropologists did not give enough attention to the epistemologies of how variation and change were generated (perhaps continuously) from *within* a social setup, given that the primary anthropological focus was on impetuses for change coming from some sort of contact with the external.[4]

Today the idea of emergence is a buzzword of complexity theory and the nonlinear (cf. Deacon 2006).[5] This was hardly so when I used the term in my own way decades ago. As Holland (2012: 18) notes, emergence refers to, "the spontaneous self-ordering of physical as well as social systems. Order emerges from chaos, without that order being imposed from above or pre-determined from before." The neatest description of emergence that I know of comes from the physicist, Murray Gell-Mann (Horgan 1998: 214), a Nobel laureate. Gell-Mann said that emergence occurs when, "We don't need something else in order to get something else." In the practice of the encounter when "something" else emerges into (phenomenal) existence the encounter re-organizes, in other words re-adapts (or doesn't) to enable itself to continue.[6] This is not order out of chaos but rather the ongoing generation of usually minor variation that has the potential to become difference. Generally speaking, interaction emerged from within itself and brought self-variations to the fore. This, in a simple sense, is *self-organization*.[7]

Variation often emerged during the interaction within an encounter. Exact repetition in the very practice of the everyday was rare, even though this might be summarized as sameness by participants. As Michael Fisch (2013: 336) puts this in his brilliant study of how the mechanics of the Tokyo underground were turned into a self-organizing, technological system (one perceived by the Japanese computer engineers to have organic properties of internal self-adaptation to changing conditions), "irregularity is regular." And the occurrence of "irregularity" is of course unpredictable. Moreover, the enabling of the self-organization of emergent properties seems to work most reliably and comprehensively when the "unit" producing these properties has relative autonomy (that can be termed "distributed autonomy" [Fisch 2013]). My guess is, and I will return to this when discussing "time," that this relative autonomy also involved a *multiplicity* of time; that is, a multiplicity of local incidents on the underground that had their own temporal existences yet that potentially effected one another. With regard to the encounters that I observed in *Work and Play*, some had this resiliency, while others did not; yet in so many of them the irregular, that is, variation, was quite common. Most likely one should understand the generation of variation as elemental to human social life (as it is to biological life more generally) and, so, to consider regularity in human existence as exceptional and as an ongoing struggle to attain some sort of steadiness (for an earlier statement relating social life to a premise of indeterminacy see Moore 1975: 221, 233).

Though interaction during encounters generated variation, this was not yet the emergence of difference. Emergence was immanent, though the great bulk of variation was ignored by workshop members and only some variants, a few, were disentangled, elaborated and made into the reality of difference. Gregory Bateson's maxim that a difference to be a difference has to make a difference was most relevant. In discussing encounters I realized that they varied in their capacities to sustain focused interaction, and that these capacities were no less emergent properties of encounters even as these themselves were emerging. This pointed toward ways of thinking that were within me though not yet with me, not for some years. To wit: that emergent forms of social existence differed in their capacity to sustain certain kinds of *life* and *living* within their forming; that this was related to the kinds of complexity that emergent forms developed within themselves; and that the more complex formings were greater than the sum of their parts and could not be reduced to these. In other words, encounters that developed more complex interiors were more sustainable in part because the interaction of participants was shaped by the emergent encounter. One could say that the encounter as it formed began to *enfold* the participants within itself, rather than their fully directing the encounter through individual choices and decisions.[8] Yet this too did not give me understanding of the ongoing formation of variation.

One of the few anthropologists at the time who for me exemplified a concern with questions of emergence and movement in social ordering was Victor Turner (another was Bruce Kapferer [see especially Kapferer 1972]). Yet Turner also exemplified difficulties that I had even with an anthropology that conceptualized movement yet that did not let go of points of rest and stability that often were (and are) called "structure" and the like. Doing a social structural kind of analysis amounts to a start . . . stop . . . start . . . stop anthropology. Stop: and set up the *hard* contrasts. Start: and activate the hard contrasts in relation to one another, calling processual that which moves *softly* amongst them. Stop: . . . and so forth. This kind of setup implies that the continual movement of the social within itself has to be frozen, has to be stilled in certain of its aspects so that the movement of other aspects can be attended to, an "all other things being equal" rendition of social ordering (that never exists in social life; see also Handelman 2007a). Simply put, the entirety is too complex and has to be simplified so that particular aspects can be isolated for analysis. Call this "methodological reductionism."[9] This entails a theorizing that rationalizes points or levels of rest as "structure," even as other points become vectors of "process." Turner, whom I cherished personally and professionally, was not radical enough in conceptualizing the very movement itself of emergence in dynamic terms, though at the time I did not phrase my reservations in this way. I should point out that what I am calling points of rest/structure are critical to our academic understandings of that which we call, in these and other terms, continuity *and* change, in which continuity is the expected and, even today, change is out of the ordinary if not necessarily problematic. However the critical positioning likely is that the generation of variation is continuous while the problematic is discovering how variation turns into change.

The quantum physicist and feminist, Karen Barad (2010: 249, see also 2007), asks: "How much of our understanding of the nature of change has been and continues to be caught up in the notion of continuity?" such that there is a "presumed radical disjuncture between continuity and discontinuity," a division that parallels that of the "stop-start" of movement between structure and process that I indicated above. This kind of distinction over-reifies both continuity and discontinuity, another phrasing of rapid change. From encounters, though so micro-scale, I began to understand a little that it is indeed the potential for change through the ongoing emergence of variation that is continuous, and that a good deal of this potential is generated *within* forms that emerge rather than from external impetuses. This pointed me toward emergence as continuous and to the within-ness of the emergence of form. This understanding of emergence differed from its general usage in complexity theory and the sciences as the appearance of an entirely new phenomenon that reorganizes any configuration that it appears within. That usage of emergence is closer to a singularity, as this is used in Chapter Three, this volume.

In 1977 Turner published a pathbreaking essay entitled, "Process, System, and Symbol: A New Anthropological Synthesis." There he argued that "culture has to be seen as processual because it emerges in interaction and imposes meaning on the ... systems (also dynamic) with which it interacts" (Turner 1977: 63). Turner understood culture as processual because "it" entailed "an endless series of negotiations among actors about the assignment of meaning ... ," and because these negotiations never were completed (ibid.). He added that, "social interaction generates an emergent social reality distinct from and external to that of the individuals who produce it" (ibid.). Turner's position here was not distant from that which I have outlined in earlier paragraphs. Yet he refused to part from "structure," arguing that, "process is intimately bound up with structure and that an adequate analysis of social life necessitates a rigorous consideration of the relation between them" (Turner 1977: 65). When discussing time I will suggest that this sense of "structure" is in itself the equivalent of the movement of slow time while "process" in itself is the equivalent of the movement of time faster. To put this more directly: "structure" is a constellation of slow-time movement, and "process" a constellation of fast-time movement, but *all* move *all* the time, though at different speeds through variable intensities, while speed and intensity of course also shift and change.[10] This is consequential for how long (if ever) we may have firm footing, as it were, through which to stand.

An emphasis on emergence in the forming of encounters raises the issue of whether this movement tends toward the linear or the nonlinear. One can question whether this issue is at all relevant to the organization of the social, belonging more to mathematics and to the physical sciences from whence it was taken. I think it is relevant. The historian, Alan Beyerchen (1992/93: 62) comments that: "Nonlinear phenomena are ... usually regarded as recalcitrant misfits in our catalogue of norms, although they are actually more prevalent than phenomena that conform to the rules of linearity. This can seriously distort perceptions of what is central and what is marginal ... ." Linear progression applies most when the reality of social ordering is *ultimately* (and *only* ultimately) stable (is there such a state of being?). The drive or pull to linearity (though rarely its full actualization) is evident wherever bureaucratic logic (see Chapter Four, this volume) is in use. Thus Michael King (1993) points to the strong *physis*,[11] the internal drive, in western (and other) legal systems to achieve juridical finality that is rendered as definitive, categorical decisions of "guilt" or "innocence" (rather than one of guilt *and* innocence, as may be the case in a variety of "nonwestern" judicial setups).[12] Yet in most everyday realities the irregular is regular, as the Japanese cybernetic engineers put this;[13] even though in American (and Israeli) social orderings (and elsewhere) Harold Garfinkel's (1967) "etc. clause" bridges the bottomless pit of interpretations of reality, enabling tacit knowledge (Polanyi 1958) to glide over many of the immanent, interpretive pitfalls of everyday life.

In the workshops, encounters that broke up quickly over some disagreement, over the expression of emotions that were painful, or over a history of rawness between the participants were closer to linearity in their emergent organization and progression. That is, these encounters lacked any self-correction as they proceeded. Ideas like self-correction again come from systems theory though here I am not referring to systems but rather to trajectories of emergence through which encounters embraced the participants within their emergent forms. Without any sort of self-correction the trajectory tended strongly toward the linear with a distinct lack of complexity as to how the encounter moved forward and crashed. When there was feedback, or, more accurately, degrees of curvature, complexity might have emerged and the encounter ramified, tending toward the nonlinear in the growth of its potential to sustain itself and to move in a multiplicity of trajectories.

In other terms, the contrast here between linear and nonlinear is that of the difference between a straight line (with minimal volume) and a curve (that is voluminous), as I put this in the introduction to *Ritual in Its Own Right*. Curvature and volume are critical to the interior growth of complexity and to its relative sustainability. Feedback *curves* back into the very trajectory of emergence through which it comes forth even as that trajectory moves forward.[14] Within the voluminosity of curving, the forming of form turns toward itself from within itself, opening time-space for activity that had not existed before the encounter began. This becomes even more salient if we recognize that as curving creates volume within itself this volume creates (or rather, *is*) depth, and depth is time-full. Within this depth forming may curl within itself opening to a form potentially developing its own time within itself—to wit, a local time, and indeed a local time that may be out of sync with time outside this particular folding (local time will be discussed in Part Two of this chapter).

Consider the following encounter in which the jazz vocalist, Nina Simone, meets her guitarist-to-be, Al Schackman, as Simone (1992) describes this in her memoir, *I Put a Spell on You*: "I called the title of the first song, 'Little Girl Blue.' What happened next was one of the most amazing moments in my entire life. Al was right there with me from the first moment, as if we had been playing together all our lives. It was more than that even; it was as if we were one instrument split in two. We played Bach-type tunes for hours, and all the way through we hardly dared look at each other for fear that the whole thing would come tumbling down and we wouldn't be able to pick it up again." The two interact, and Simone says this was as if one instrument split in two; though the emergent property of the encounter is that of two instruments becoming one, splitting into two related through synecdoche, without the mediation of symbol, indeed a relatedness that may be called unmediated immediateness.[15]

Playing improv the two are enfolded by their encounter as it is emerging; and the encounter curves them into itself, opening volume, opening depth. And what happens to time? The two enter into what Alfred Schutz called "concert time" (Schutz

1962–66), within which time becomes different without going away. Or, more accurately, linear, metric time turns into the "local time" of the Simone-Schackman encounter, perhaps through changing rhythms and intensities. Thus their local time became nonlinear, unpredictable, without border or direction, enabling the two artists to continue their playful improv "for hours." What comes first here, time or sociality? Is this a problem of the chicken and the egg? Without the change in the quality of time the encounter could not have emerged as it did. Without the budding sociality between the musicians, time would not have changed. The two cannot be separated, yet in my thinking the quality of time is at the very least an *enabler* here of the sociality that emerged.

In recasting my doctoral thesis on the workshops into *Work and Play* the significance of the confluence of curving, volume, depth, and (local) time in the emergence of form eluded me. Obviously, the encounter proceeded until it ceased to do so. Yet *how* did the emergent form hold itself together, to the extent that it did, while it existed? The usual understanding of this question was to phrase it in terms of a negotiated or constructed social order, of give-and-take, of exchange or transaction, interpreted by and managed by the participants mainly as individuals with agency, and/or as members of networks, and/or as representations of a cultural category or social unit. One way or another the phenomenological intentionality of social persons was at the forefront. By framing epistemological understanding of the question in this way the idea that form *qua* form, unless referenced in terms of highly embedded and repetitive forms such as "ritual" and the like, could have formative strength very rarely came to the fore.[16] In more or less accepting this I did not really catch the consequences of the potential in-turning of the emergence of form, and in not doing so I missed the critical consequences of this in-turning. In *Models and Mirrors* I started to address this problematic.

Models and Mirrors and *Ritual in Its Own Right*: The Nuances of Folding

Models and Mirrors was conceived as a critique of the elementary idea in the social sciences and in religious studies that a multitude of social and cultural forms, temporary though often recurring, are all placed theoretically under the same roof called "ritual," when in terms of the logics of their interior organization they are constituted in radically different ways that effect and affect what these events do and how they do this (Chapter One; see also Handelman 2006a). By grouping this multitude of forms under the same conceptual rubric and assuming that every social-cultural order has occasions that should be called "ritual," and that all these occasions across all societies have attributes in common that make these occasions "ritual," scholars continue to commit Whitehead's fallacy of misplaced concreteness. They concretize the *functions* these events are assumed to have for social orders, thereby *a priori* establishing the relationships these events have to the ordering of the social-cultural.

Instead, I suggested concretizing the phenomenal-ness—or, to use a more accurate neologism, the phenomenality—of the forms of such occasions, analyzing their interior workings in order to understand their relationships to the social orders in which they are found. In other words, I suggested reversing the usual anthropological presumption that the interiors of all "ritual" occasions reflected and represented the social-cultural orders within which they are found. Instead of this, I argued, begin with the phenomenal form of the event and, within this, discover its relationship to social-cultural ordering (and, so, too, the Peircean logic of abduction might be awakened). I have been accused of an implicit functionalism in these formulations, yet I find the premises regarding "ritual" mentioned above to be far more functionalist, and explicitly so, than those premises I used to study public events and other phenomenal forms.

In Chapter Two of *Models and Mirrors* I argued how logics of organization differ among "rituals," with profound consequences for the relationships between these events and the social orders that enable their existence. By beginning analysis with the phenomenal form I showed that certain forms do intentional transformation (i.e., make radical change) within themselves *through* the organization of their interior processes. These phenomenal forms may have degrees of self-correction shaped into their forms that enable them to adhere quite closely to the purposes for which they were activated. However other forms do little more than mirror or represent selected thematics of their socio-cultural surrounds. These latter forms are put together often using what I later called bureaucratic logic (this volume, Chapter Four), and usually have little or nothing in common with "ritual" events that do radical change within and through themselves.

In *Models and Mirrors* I did not use the conceptual language of emergence since most of the phenomenal forms I reanalyzed were based on the ethnography of others, and these studies were primarily synchronic. Nonetheless, in beginning with the interiors of forms, and thinking of how cultural and social forms may be held together from within themselves, I was able to argue in greater detail that forms with more complex interior organization are relatively more self-sustainable than are simpler forms. Moreover, I proposed that greater interior complexity goes together with degrees of separation from the social surround. By this I meant that interior complexity of phenomenal forms goes together with relatively greater autonomy from their social surrounds. Interior complexity endows these forms with greater resilience against external pressures. This idea of (always) temporary, relative autonomy from the social surround was heretical in anthropology (and I think still is) yet it enabled me to propose a different understanding of rituals that are organized intentionally and interiorly to directly accomplish particular outcomes within and through their own workings.[17] The capacity of such forms to activate controlled trajectories that may be causal is due in no small measure to their relative autonomy from their social surrounds. In archaic and tribal social orderings acts to influence cosmic ordering were largely limited to events precariously organized to control causality.[18]

The introduction to *Ritual in Its Own Right* was conceived when I was influenced by Deleuze's (1993) thinking on the fold in *The Fold: Leibniz and the Baroque*. Folding, as Deleuze (1995: 156–57) pointed out, is everywhere:

> Straight lines are all alike, but folds vary, and all folding proceeds by differentiation. No two things are folded in the same way . . . . Folds are in this sense everywhere, without the fold being universal. It's a "differentiator," a "differential" . . . . The concept of fold is always something *singular*, and can only get anywhere by varying, branching out, taking new forms. You've only . . . to see and touch mountains as formed by their folding, for them to lose their solidity, and for millennia to turn back into what they are, not something permanent but *time* in its pure state, pliability. There's nothing more unsettling than the continual movement of something that seems fixed. (My emphases, echoed at numerous junctures by Michel Serres; e.g., Serres 1998: 107–8)

I modified Deleuze's conception of the fold for my purposes by reflecting on forming form as the distance between the straight line and the curve.[19] As I wrote then, "The movement from the line to the curve is that of conditions of self-organization. Curving, the line becomes self-referential, opening space, acquiring depth. In relating to itself, the curve organizes itself in terms of itself, thereby enabling its existential and phenomenal self-organization as different from whatever exists outside the curve, while including this distinction within its self-referentiality" (Handelman 2005a: 14). Without the recursiveness of curvature, in other words of self-referentiality, phenomenal social forms cannot survive, as Bateson (1977: 242) implied.[20]

Through folding I furthered the argument on phenomenal form by expressly addressing what I called the forming of form, focusing now on the practice of form taking shape, folding in particular situations, and on the emergence of complexity within the folding itself. Interestingly, social form—as in the little encounter—is initiated by individual agency, yet if the form emerges complexly then the shaping it acquires contains to different degrees its own Castoriadian *physis* (Castoriades 1997: 331, see note 8), its own impetus toward a kind of completion (though this is not necessarily complete in any hermetic or hermeneutic sense). I suggested that while no social form "has the autonomous existence of absolute difference . . . without minimal self-propelling difference, no social form exists as it does . . . . This *propensity* to self-organization is present in the most mundane of everyday behavior and interaction" (Handelman 2005a: 13). One can say that the forming of *form-in-itself*, as I noted earlier, speaks to the degrees to which the form may hold itself together from within itself, and to the form's interior sustainability and so to its precarity; while as this form is activated within itself, doing whatever it does, it becomes *form-for-itself*, an active force within the world. Thus I am saying indirectly that some phenomenal forms may be endowed by their creators with their own intentionality; and if these forms are organized interiorly to accomplish this purposiveness then it may be more problematic for their practitioners to disrupt them.

In *Work and Play* I had thought that complexity developed through feedback, Norbert Weiner's cybernetic term. Later I recognized that feedback has the shallow thinness and flatness of a line turning back on its own linearity. Needed was a much fuller sense of form as volume potentially filling and fulfilling itself within itself. The idea of the "fold" supplied this sense of form curving into itself, folding into and enfolding itself as it emerges into fullness. Form curving into itself makes form self-referencing, self-reflexive. The self-referentiality of folding is critical to enabling the fold to contain itself, and so, too, to enabling the fold to open into volume within itself, and therefore critical to volume opening into depth within the fold. As noted, this depth is time. Put otherwise, the self-intersection of the fold demands *duration*. Folding can only occur through time, indeed *as time*, as time opens within the depth of the fold.[21]

Folding offered another improvement on "feedback." Through folding I could think in terms of *degrees of curving, degrees of interiority*, such that a fold can be understood in terms of degrees of closure, from the relatively open (and perhaps shallower) to the more fully self-intersecting, self-enclosing fold. By contrast, feedback requires the full return of a feedback loop into itself. Either there is feedback or there isn't. Although I did not go in this direction, folding better delineates the range of events and their interior complexities that I put forward in *Models and Mirrors* (Chapter Two). So, too, with regard to the resemblance of the interior of a fold to its social surround. In the instance of a more fully self-intersecting fold, the interior organization of the fold need have only a limited resemblance to the exterior environment (even as it folds elements or configurations of its surround into itself in order to affect these [Handelman 2005a: 11]). This is critical to my argument that certain events can be shaped as relatively autonomous from their exterior social surround, and that this self-enclosure enables these events to act on their exteriors in ways that are not simply representations of these surrounds. In other words, the interior of such a fold need not be reducible to the macro-order outside the fold. On the one hand the more fully self-intersecting a fold potentially is, the more relatively discontinuous is the fold from its social surround even as it acts on and through this, while on the other its self-referentiality as a more autonomous unit, one with greater own-ness, is heightened.

Dynamics of Form—Banana Time

I turn here to an instance of forming form through folding and self-organization that heads this discussion toward the movement of form that is time-full and dynamic. The ethnographic setting is a small industrial workshop within an American factory during the 1950s.[22] Three middle-aged men, George, Ike, and Sammy, worked in a room on separate machines that punched-out material used elsewhere in the factory.

In terms of the process of production there was no necessary contact amongst them, and they could have become social isolates without this interfering with their work. One can characterize this as three linear trajectories of activity that did not necessarily intersect. Nonetheless there was interaction and a good deal of this amongst the three. What is interesting is the form that emerged from their interaction and how this was put together.

George and Ike came to work before Sammy and the two shared a pot of coffee made on George's hotplate. The ethnographer, Donald Roy, called this occasion "coffee time." After Sammy arrived, he declared "peach time," took out two peaches from his bag and divided the two among the three workers (note the difficulty here of dividing two peaches into three equal portions). Sammy daily brought a banana to work. Following the sharing of peach time, Ike stole the banana, yelled, "banana time," and gulped down the fruit. Sammy remonstrated with Ike, as did George. As Sammy continued to dress down Ike, the latter retaliated by opening wide the window facing Sammy's machine, letting in the cold air. Sammy bitterly complained that he would "catch a cold," and closed the window. Yet now George encouraged Ike against Sammy. The ethnographer termed this incident, "window time." George's alarm clock kept the work schedule and the alarm rang when lunchtime came. Ike stealthily turned the clock ahead by some minutes so that the three would break for lunch earlier. George of course discovered this and remonstrated with Ike. The ethnographer called this incident, "lunch time." Every afternoon a worker came to collect the output done by the three during that day. They told him of that day's adventures and all three quarreled with one another. The ethnographer called this "pick-up time." Later in the afternoon George and Ike ate pickled fish together, provided by Ike. This was "fish time." The series of times ended in the late afternoon when the three took turns going to the Coca-Cola machine in another section of the factory to buy drinks for himself and the others. This was "coke time."

All of the "times" described by the ethnographer emerged from the practice of daily life—none were called for by the process of production in the workshop. Moreover, while the process of production was linear the emergent "times" were not. Through these "times" the workers curved the morning into the afternoon such that the curve enclosed them almost fully during the working day. Both ends of the curve—the early morning and late afternoon—were made of "times" that resonated amongst themselves. All were occasions of the sharing of sustenance, of drink and food—in the early morning coffee time and peach time; in the late afternoon fish time and coke time. The morning times of sharing were created to first include George and Ike who came to work earlier, and then to include all three when Sammy entered, so that the three cooperated in food-sharing with one another. At the close of the curve this was done in reverse. With fish-time George and Ike first shared food and then with coke time all three shared buying Coca-Colas for one another.

Parallel to the straight, linear trajectories of production the workers created a curve that intersected with itself and that enclosed the workers through the working

EPILOGUE | 303

day. As far as we know there was no reference to any factor in the social environment outside of this production space that would help explain the curvature that emerged within it. The curve opened volume within itself, one given to sociality. This volume was deep, containing eight distinct times that were repeated during every working day. And, so, this depth was organized through duration: the times were arranged temporally in a particular order of occurrence. With the depth of its interior volume this curve became a fold that enwrapped the three workers, opening a recursive timespace, that of sociality and the relational, that did not exist beforehand. It is no less important to emphasize that this phenomenon—the forming of form—emerged out of their practice and enfolded them reflexively within its emergent form. Reflexivity imbues whatever is enfolded with identity; in this instance reflexivity endowed the three workers with intense sociality toward one another.

The curving of this folding generated complexity in its organization. Inside the depth of this fold of sharing, solidarity, and strong relationships the three workers were in disharmony with one another. Within the curve of coffee time, peach time, fish time, and coke time the three shared sustenance and sociability; but the three argued and fought with one another during banana time, window time, lunch time, and pickup time. Daily recurring times of conflict were folded inside daily recurring times of sharing and solidarity—the increasing complexity of a fold within a fold. Thus the solidarity of the fold (that of times of sharing and reciprocity) contained the disharmony of the yet more interior fold (that of times of conflict).[23] One may argue that the very control of conflict encourages the generation of conflict that is controlled. Perhaps the fold acquires teleonomic properties as the fold regenerates itself over and again. In effect the three workers reflexively tested their relationships with one another over and over through the duration of times that curled into their sequencing and out again—times of sharing that curved into times of conflict that curled outward again into times of sharing.[24]

We have something of a test of that which I am arguing because of what happened when the folding of times frayed, and its curvature straightened wholly into parallel lines of production. Sammy went on vacation (the triad became a dyad) and the relationship between George and Ike collapsed after Ike accidentally insulted George. For the next two weeks George and Ike operated their machines with hardly a word passing between them. Then Sammy returned to work and the straight lines recurved and self-intersected, resurrecting the fold through the following order of events: One afternoon George and Ike ate George's pickled fish together. Later that same afternoon Ike and Sammy began to kid one another, and Ike began to sing. In the following days the times of disharmony returned, folded into those of shared sustenance and cooperation. The resurrected fold took the recursive form of its predecessor, returning as another version of itself since its times somewhat differed. In particular an entirely new "time" emerged, one that clearly indexed Ike's error that had led to the collapse of the fold. Donald Roy describes this new time as follows: "Ike broke wind [farted], and put his head in his hands on the [work] block as Sammy grabbed a rod and made a mock rush to open the window. He beat Ike on the head, and George threw some water on him [Ike], playfully."

What happened here? The folding curvedness of the working day broke down; the curve straightening, becoming nonreflexive. This difference indeed made a difference. Without reflexivity sociality disappeared. Then Sammy returned and some sort of reorganization occurred. Yet I would speak of this as a still existing residue of self-organizing qualities in the workshop. Why self-organization? Because the original fold was highly self-reflexive for the three participants—they belonged together, had a togetherness of identity, and were aware of their joint mutuality. So that when, after the rupture, they were together again their reflexiveness of themselves as a unit of some kind again came to the fore. Through the three the patterning of the fold self-organized anew. Self-organization followed a change in form, as it often seems to do. The reflexiveness of the refolding curve comes through clearly in the addition of the new "time" to the self-organization of times—the new time undoubtedly self-references the breakdown of the folding curve (Ike farts, committing a faux pas) and includes its own self-correction (the chastising of Ike by George and Sammy, accompanied by Ike's apologetic demeanor).

During this case, linearity turns into nonlinearity turns into linearity turns into nonlinearity . . . and each of these shifts is of great significance for the forming of form that holds the three participants together (and doesn't) in their sociality and social relationships. Just because we as anthropologists are unaccustomed to thinking in such terms certainly (with all of the qualifications that indeed attend to certainty) suggests that we must not exclude them if they demonstrate just how dynamic is the human (always). In discussing time further on I will point to how important nonlinearity is to the human and that it enables movement that is so human.

There is a very delicate trajectory here during the forming of form that follows where agency is situated and how it is redistributed. It is a near given in Western social science (including anthropology) that agency is first and foremost located in the consciousness of the individual, and that it is active individuals who make choices and decisions. In this regard what I am calling the forming of form would be understood as the outcome of the choices and decisions of individuals. So, too, a near-standard social critique of self-organization in complexity theory is that it does not relate to human consciousness and, so, not to human agency. Thus, as Forbes-Pitt (2013: 107) comments on the "self" in self-organization, "'self' makes no reference to *individual* system elements, or to any kind of consciousness, it refers to the *system* under investigation" and to the dynamics of the interiority of the system—this is its *self*-organization. This in contrast to the "self" as it is used in social science—the embodied self of phenomenology and culture, the "self" whose human qualities emerge through that which Sheets-Johnstone (1999) calls "the primacy of movement." These and other perspectives position the location of "self" within the embodied individual, a self expressed through interaction amongst individuals. Even as anthropologists have modified this to refer to "cultural selves," to how selves in a certain cultural milieu are constituted with different ontologies and qualities thereof than those in other milieus, nonetheless the location of qualities of "self" are entirely located in the acting individual. It is first and foremost the individual who has and who is responsible for agency.

In order to propose a modification of agency as the always primary prerogative of the individual self during the forming of form I make a brief detour here. Bialecki and Daswani (2015: 274) point to the importance of questioning "the Western assumptions of the bounded, singular, individual self, as the main form of [culturally] imagining the person." Then, are there other ways in the world of inhabiting embodiment in relation to other embodiments that are unlike (or overlap with) the dominant Western assumption of the self-person? McKim Marriott's shaping of the "dividual" in South India was foundational in this respect (see Marriott 1989 for an overview of thinking on this and related subjects).[25] No less significant was Valentine Daniels's (1984) research in Tamil Nadu, demonstrating just how much of Marriott's argument on the exchange of elements and qualities of life among persons, among persons and their natal earth, among persons and their homes, and so forth, occurs through the relatedness of interiorities that in my terms are intra-connected rather than interconnected. All domains in which life inheres—including the human, the deities, the apparently inanimate (soft matter, hard matter), and the moving (flora, water, wind)—exchange the elements and qualities through which life is constituted. This is that which enables the living cosmos.

In the logic of the Western conception of one self per individual interaction between individuals leaves from the interior of one individual to his exterior, passes over to the exterior of the other, enters the interior of this other where it is interpreted and responded to in the reverse order of its arrival. These inter-actional passages between the interiors and exteriors of persons are somewhat alien to South Indian self-personhood. The implications potentially are profound: for example, the elementary flows of life-substances and qualities in South India are in the first instance inherently *social*—cosmos must be social in its very existence, and any blockage of these (social) flows is fundamentally anti-social, indeed the extermination of the social in its worst, destructive sense. The South Indian social is not socially *constructed*, is not a social contract like the Western Hobbesian separation of individual and social order in order to put the latter together through the former; nor is it likely learned through childhood in quite the way suggested by the process philosophy of G. H. Mead and others, in terms of the development of self through taking the role of the other and seeing oneself through the eyes of the other, and so forth.[26] Given its intense intra-actions and intra-changes the South Indian cosmos is, one can say, naturally social.

To take an example of the blockage of flow mentioned above, South Indian sorcery results not merely from possession that shuts in and cuts off the individual from the sociality of her or his fellow human beings, resulting in extreme isolation. Rather, South Indian sorcery blocks the elementary intra-actional flows of living among persons and among all aspects of their total environments, and these flows like the cosmos they enliven are inherently social. The result is utterly destructive stasis for the ensorcelled selfness yet, more than this, the damage of stasis for all those who were in continuous intra-actional flow with the afflicted. (For an outline of this argument see Handelman and Shulman 2004: 210–14.)

Where is agency, or more to the point *when* is agency, as the curve straightens and the fold implodes in the workshop? The three did not consciously design and plan the curve, the order of its contents, nor the symmetry and significance of its self-referential intersection. One can say that as the curve emerged through practice the three endowed direction, impetus, and intensities to its folding. Their curve of sociality had direction, moving into self-intersection near the end of the working day. Folding, their curve opened time-space that had not existed beforehand. Within its enfolding each daily "time" or event of the curve indexed its impetus toward the next. Curving moved through moments of rising and lessening intensity of activity that gave to it an unnamed yet definite self-identity. Thus once a logic of curving and folding emerged in the shop, the way through which folding shaped the activities within it, the impulses and pulsations it gave to these activities, continued without the always active and ongoing need for human agency.

I surmise that in some way and to some degree the moving, folding curve existed in its own right as a fragile form, a transient phenomenon. One should not forget that form is force. That form is a line or trajectory of force, of forcefulness. And that, though neither concretized nor materialized in any common-sense way, when the force of form is absent after it has been present this absence is felt. This is to say that in the workshop the folding of form had some kind of agency—though only local agency—that self-organized *the lives of the three workers in the workshop who were enfolded within it*; and, moreover, that the force of the form could not be obtained by totaling together the various activities of the three. Put simply, the three created a social form that was vaster and deeper than themselves and their social relationships with one another in the shop. Form-in-itself, form existing, became form-for-itself, form-as-force in action through duration.

Yet what is concreteness? Anthropology has consistently concretized the physically invisible in order to presume the existence of the social and of cultural beliefs, ideas, norms, values, social relationships, community, social network, exchange, cosmologies, and on and on. It is these concretizations that largely enable social-cultural anthropology to exist as the kind of academic discipline that it is. Moreover, once concretized all of the above are assumed to exist even as particular concretizations are critiqued, and some fall out of favor as others rise in fashion. Concretizations have solidity, positions of rest, points of anchorage. They may even be felt as material. However, the sense of forming form that I am suggesting is anything but a point of rest or an anchorage. The forms I wrote of in *Work and Play*, in portions of *Models and Mirrors*, and in the introduction to *Ritual in Its Own Right*, are emergent and self-organizing movements, and often ones of force and duration.

Thus consider the following three examples of forming and folding in relation to concreteness. Diana Espirito Santo (2015) offers an alternative to the usual emphasis on concreteness in anthropology in her discussion of "knowledge" among practitioners of Cuban *espiritismo*. Knowledge is fluid (*fluido*), independent of cognition, existing outside of persons, including practitioners of *espiritismo*. Perhaps knowledge is ontogenic potentiality. Using words, practitioners give thingness to *fluido*, to latent knowledge. Interacting with this flow of potentiality through words, mediums instigate "the self-organization and emergence of knowledge as new cosmology comes to the fore" (2015: 588). *Fluido* emerges as form that self-organizes as knowledge. Moreover, knowledge-form is substantive and is *seen* by the medium but *not* as a representation of knowledge nor as a metaphor; but rather, that "knowledge [itself] is . . . a moving, mutable, and emergent form of *seeing* itself" (2015: 589).

Bar-On Cohen (2009) writes of the *kibadachi* (rider's stance) exercise in Japanese Shotokan karate. To enter the rider's stance the participants stand in a circle, bend and flex their knees as a rider would atop a horse, and hold this position without moving. After no more than a few minutes the stance becomes grueling, torturous and painful. Yet the experienced participants hold the rider position for even ninety minutes. This strongly implies that some sort of forming of form emerges within the bodies of the participants and that this forming nonverbally intra-connects and relates together all the bodies in the participatory circle, enabling them to withstand the agony of the exercise. Yet this forming is not set, is not a "structure," for it seems to continuously circulate through the participants. In a sense this forming is that of a loop whose moving through the participants is ongoing and recursive. One can say that this emergent forming enables the bodies of the participants to become folded *into* one another, or perhaps even folded *through* one another; and that this is their intra-connectedness, their intimate, simultaneous sharing of painful interior exertion that gives them the steadiness and steadfastness to endure as more than particular individuals and as more than a group of individuals. Yet by saying that these persons are folded into one another I am insisting that this process is one of a joining through involution and not one of encompassment.[27]

Deborah Bird Rose discusses dance in ritual among the Aboriginal peoples of the Victoria River District in Australia. Bird Rose (2000: 292–93) writes,

> Thus I learned that the body connects earth and air when you dance. The call comes from deep within and is propelled by the impact of your feet on the ground. It comes to feel as if the ground itself propels your voice into the night sky. That call starts somewhere below your feet and ends somewhere out in the world. The call is a motion, a sound wave of connection. You are dancing the earth, and the earth is dancing you, and so perhaps you are motion . . . a wave of connection . . . who is the dancer and who is the dance? . . . I find that [recursively] both are the dancer and the danced.

In my terms, the dancer's feet are folding into the ground, the ground folding into the feet, perhaps folding through each other, perhaps becoming a single folding moving with oneness, perhaps in Barad's terms entangling, creating greater complexity, as does the forming of intra-folding among participants during *kibadachi*, and through the self-organizing of fluid knowledge-forming in Cuban *espiritismo*. All are concrete, all are not. The distinction is a red herring. The cleavage between objective and subjective loses its presumed distinctiveness once we recognize that motion and movement are continuously folding and shaping human beings, while points of rest and anchorage are kinds of motion in themselves and, so, related to duration and, so, to time.

An additional word on the workshop. After the fall the three workers re-created their enfolding self-intersecting sociality with its emotional rhythmic pulsation of rising and falling intensities and dense moments (of Times and time). This reformed fold bore a strong resemblance to the previous one. One could ascribe this to memory, habit, micro-culture and the like, yet all of these are merely summarizing thoughts and weak explanations. Something more actively creative had happened. I am tempted to call this a moment of self-creation, of autopoiesis, of the unspoken synchronization of acts that index the emergence of form, now the three recreating the folding logic of their initial creation while using different materials for a similar forming. Here the three have a sense of selfness together, one of (unspoken) self-referentiality, of identity.[28]

Within the workshop, production time continued as before, linear, shallow, even in tone, moving from the beginning of the working day to its end. Yet, within the forming of the fold, time shifted from the linear toward the recursive, the working day beginning and ending in the spirit of reflexive reciprocity and good fellowship. The usual way of dealing with this kind of shift in anthropology would be to say that the structuring of interaction in the workshop changed; that the workers positioned "times" throughout the workday, and that this gave to the time and the timing of "times" a subjective, experiential circularity even as objective, linear time dominated the length and substance of the workday.

However my sense is that the change is not structural, not a matter of the fixing of positions, of "times," but one of changing movement, of a different kind of temporal motion that *enables* dynamically the arrangement of "times"; temporal motion that is recursive and, so, is self-reflexive. I entertain the likelihood that time curved around the workers as they began to practice sociality and its reciprocalness, a folding opened the depth of time-space for the "times" that the workers created, endowing recursive time within the folding with rhythmic pulsation through the intensities of the "times." If so, then it is time as such that makes or enables the folding of local motion, thereby playing a significant role in the forming of local phenomenal forms.

Thus one can argue for the *multiplicity* of local phenomenal forms through the *multiplicity* of temporal movements without necessarily beginning from the premise that different cultures are likely to have different interpretations and understandings of time as a single dimension. Both the relativism of Nancy Munn's (1992) review of the cultural anthropology of time and Alfred Gell's (1992) use of the A-Series and B-Series time of analytic philosophy are premised on the one foundational movement of time, indeed on time as a dimension, varied in terms of interpretations of time in different cultures and distinguished by objective and subjective perceptions of time. However if we take seriously at least some of the claims put forward by scholars of multiple ontologies then these may apply as well to time. In other words, instead of assuming (indeed, being able to assume) that there is always a single foundational movement of time, whether that of time measured metrically or time that is culturally perceived and subjectively felt, we should entertain the potentiality of a multiplicity of time movements that become more dominant or fade toward latency depending upon what manner of time movement enables certain kinds of actions and endeavors to become active. My guess is that the multiplicity of temporal movements will enable or will produce a multiplicity of phenomenal forms.

All of this requires discussion of temporality in the forming and folding of form. And this raises the question once more of whether time is a passive passage or a dynamic force, and what this says about the understanding of dynamics as time, through time. I think a beginning can be sought in the physical sciences, and I emphasize once more that I am not concerned with the science and its validity as such but rather with how the way its logics can give us an inkling into the relationship between time and organic life, including the human.

Part II: Folding Time

> If the known laws of physics are extrapolated beyond where they are valid, [then] where they are valid there is a singularity.
> —Graffiti on a bus stop sign, Mivtza Kadesh Street, Jerusalem, 29 July 2015

The Physical Time of the Universe Is Linear and Irreversible

Here the perspective on time of Ilya Prigogine—a Nobel laureate for his research on non-equilibrium thermodynamics and conditions far from equilibrium—is illuminating. Prigogine's theorizing is especially persuasive to me because he links the evolution of the physical universe to the emergence of organic life, aligning the time of the organic with the time of the physical universe. I will suggest that it is with the existence of organic life and its dynamics of reproduction that the folding of temporal movement within phenomenal forms becomes especially salient. Furthermore, with the emergence of the social as the primary human form of organization the dynamics of social reproduction are tied intimately to generational, biological reproduction. Folding is integral both to biological time and to social time, especially as the movements of the biological and the social—perhaps most prominently through different sorts of reproduction—diverge from that of physical time. This difference is critical to an understanding of social ordering as always out of sync with itself even as it tries to reproduce itself, an ongoing breach within social ordering that may be irreparable.

Prigogine argues that "time precedes the universe" (Grana 2016: 231), and thus precedes any and all matter, inorganic and organic. In his theory there was no singularity like the Big Bang that created the universe. Instead there was a primordial, empty (quantum), unstable universe in which time was latent yet irreversible. In a sense this was a virtual universe that contained, or perhaps was, pure potentiality, the potential existence of matter, yet without matter. This unstable void broke down and substance, matter, came into existence, and with matter, so, too, did entropy. Matter moved within itself and within the universe as the bearer of entropy (Magnani 2016: 250). Time actualized with the entropic movement of matter and time moved like an arrow, *linearly* and *irreversibly* (Prigogine and Stengers 1984). As Magnani (ibid.) comments: "The meaning of irreversibility [in physics] undergoes a radical change, since irreversibility should no longer be linked to an evolution that leads inexorably toward an inert state of the universe (thermic death), but to its birth, or perhaps to an eternal succession of universes that are born everywhere and that head toward the infinite." In other words, rather than moving temporally toward increasing disorder and thermal death the universe moves toward increasing complexity and its concomitant issues of organization.

For our purposes here it is sufficient to emphasize that it is precisely the irreversibility of the arrow of time that makes futurity open-ended, indeterminable, unknown. Irreversible time gives to the universe a changing, historical existence. As the sociologist, Barbara Adam (1998: 214) states succinctly, Prigogine established this conception of time "as a law of nature; and with it he changed the very meaning of the nature of a scientific law . . . laws themselves come to be understood as developing; and reversibility, far from being the most fundamental aspect of nature, comes to be recognized as a product of the consciousness of the human observer."

The evolving, entropic complexity of the universe through lengthy durations produces that which Prigogine terms conditions-far-from-equilibrium. Through these conditions the universe is in continuous emergence, the dynamics of which amplify fluctuations while ordering their disordering. Through these fluctuations time no less may develop different trajectories though continuing linearly. Nonetheless, the existence of temporal fluctuations can be considered as potential multiplicities of the movement of time. It is important to emphasize that with Prigogine's arrow of time the multiplicities that emerge from the indeterminacy of conditions-far-from-equilibrium are not undone or corrected. Were time subjective then, hypothetically, time could be shaped as circular; and so could correct or eliminate unstable complexities that are integral to the dynamics of emergence. Instead, developments must work out the consequences of their emergence that in turn contribute to increasing complexity. Prigogine (1997: 27) stated this as follows: "Irreversible processes [associated with the arrow of time] are as real as reversible processes described by the fundamental laws of physics; they do not correspond to approximations added to the basic laws. Irreversible processes play a fundamental constructive role in nature."[29]

In Prigogine's thinking, organic life emerged in conditions-far-from-equilibrium. As he put this (Prigogine 1997: 26–27): "Life is possible only in a nonequilibrium universe." To look ahead for a moment, organic life is always a fluctuation since it must reproduce and repeat itself in order to continue to exist. That is, organic life fluctuates through time that is far-from-equilibrium. Prigogine's theorizing aligns the time of the evolving universe with the time through which the organic evolves. In my understanding this implies that all forms in the universe are time-full, yet indeterministic. Nothing exists outside of or beyond time. There is no point in saying that the social and the biological are entirely removed from the physical because they are alive and not inert matter. As noted, not only does everything inorganic and organic move through time but time no less moves through everything. Yet, in "moving through" different forms of the organization of substance, time is shaped by their interiors even as forms move through time together. This implies that forms inorganic and organic have their own interior time trajectories that are, or that are synchronized with the interior movement of these forms.

In my terms, Prigogine's theorizing posits time as an ontological movement of the universe, and I emphasize here the status of the ontological. The point being that if time is ontological rather than dimensional then the status of time is likely not to change when this is considered in the world of organic life, including the human. If Prigogine's arguments have value we then can ask whether the universe would exist without time. Does the existence of the universe depend in some way on the existence of time? Or is time a passive passage? Passive in the sense that we move through time, though that which we are as human beings is not made or shaped by time as such; in other words not by time of itself. If time is merely a passive passage then we and everything else are shaped by other forces and configurations—biological, social, cultural—and we use time simply as a measure to evaluate these forces and their changes. Time then indeed is a passive, pliant medium through which interaction occurs, yet time is not accountable for interaction that itself depends on forces understood as independent of time. The physicist, Lee Smolin (2007: 256–57), in calling for physics to return to the study of time, states that physics treated time as a frozen, measurable dimension of space.

The philosopher Elizabeth Grosz (1999a: 3) calls such time a "neutral medium" in which matter and life are framed, rather than time as a dynamic force in their framing. As a neutral medium time again is cast as a dimension that is a measure of movement rather than a mover of movement. Or, *is* time perhaps a dynamic movement, indeed a mover of movement that is more than or different from thinking of time as a dimension? As the fourth dimension? Grosz (1999a: 3) points out that thinkers as disparate as Darwin, Nietzsche, Bergson, and Deleuze all understood time as a *force* of chance, randomness, open-ended-ness, becoming; and that each "conceives of *time* as *difference*."[30] These emphases fit well with the fluctuations of time that emerge through conditions-far-from-equilibrium, the conditions through which organic life exists.

Newton's and Einstein's conception of time as the fourth dimension continues to dominate anthropological thinking on time. This is present in such common-sense phrasings as "the flow of time" and "time unfolding," both of which are associated with that which is called "processual anthropology" in which "process" is critical to the (historical) temporality of anthropological analysis (Hodges 2014). Anthropologists in their research seem to accept that time is the fourth dimension; and therefore that this kind of time is an absolute baseline with which to compare and contrast cultural conceptions of time among other peoples with Western objective knowledge about time. In other words, that ideas of time among other peoples, while they may have powerful effects, are culturally subjective knowledge when compared with the objective knowledge gained by Western science. Yet as the historian, H. W. Brands (1992: 506), commented: Einstein did not say that space-time "*really* had four dimensions. What he said was that it was for human beings to think of space and time as being a four-dimensional continuum. The universe does not have four dimensions, or three dimensions, or eleven dimensions . . . . The dimensions are simply scaffolding erected by humans trying to measure the universe."[31]

So, too, it is practical for anthropologists to assume (and likely believe) that time as the fourth dimension is no less the objective undergirding of other cultures, while they, like ourselves, may well have different, subjective, experiential realities of time. In this sense the anthropological understanding of the living of time in other cultures often is categorized as belonging to the subjective realities of those moral and social orderings rather than to the scientific, objective reality of time as a linear medium of passive passage. So, say, an event to renew the cosmos, one intimately related to the movement of time, may well have culturally meaningful experiences for the people involved, yet does this objectively re-energize cosmos?

The philosopher, Jean Gebser (quoted in Simeonov 2015: 271–72), argued that time "is not a 'di-mension,' i.e., a dividing measure, but an *a-mension*, i.e., an element free from division and measurement . . . a basic phenomenon without spatial character. It is a *quality*, whereas the measurability of the spatial dimensions lets them appear as quantities."[32] As commented on in note 4, following this line of thinking the Greek preposition "a-" can liberate us from slipping over and again into incipient dualisms like that of the linear/nonlinear (see Gebser 1984: 2). Perhaps "local times" should be referred to as a-linear, enabling time potentially to move into a variety of relationships with space within different social and cultural forms. This fits with Bergson's use of the mathematician G. B. Riemann's distinction between "quantitative," or discrete, and "qualitative," or continuous, multiplicities. "Quantitative multiplicities are numerical in nature, and take the form of the one and the many: their differences are homogeneous differences of *degree*, and such multiplicities therefore can be divided without occasioning a difference in kind. By contrast, qualitative multiplicities on division create heterogenous differences" (Hodges 2008: 409). Hodges here quotes Deleuze (1991: 38) to wit that qualitative multiplicities are "of *differences in kind* . . . that cannot be reduced to numbers."[33]

Duration and the Curving of Organic Time

Prigogine's understanding of cosmic time fits well with an important proposition of Henri Bergson. After Einstein's utter disparagement of Bergson's thinking during their so-called debate of 1922 (see Canales 2015) the philosopher's theorizing was ignored until quite recently. Bergson (1992: 93) argued that: "Time is something. *Therefore it acts.* Time is what hinders everything from being given at once. It retards, or rather it is retardation. It must, therefore, be elaboration. Would it not then be a vehicle of creation and of choice? Would not the existence of time prove that there is indetermination in things? Would not time be that indetermination itself?" [my emphasis]. To paraphrase: Time exists to stop everything from happening at once. By banishing simultaneity Bergson banished all relations, all forms, from existing outside of time. So, too, from this perspective time enables the separate existence of every "thing." Existing through time, all relations, all forms, have *duration*, and, moreover, their durations differ. The social anthropologist, Max Gluckman, argued something like this fifty years ago with regard to social life, and I will turn to this further on.

Duration too in the first instance is a qualitative multiplicity. This is saying that forms—biological, social, cultural—have their own durations, their own interior times, their own "local times." Further on I will argue that this is critical to understanding how time is folded within form yet no less shapes form from within its depths, recalling Deleuze's comment on Merleau-Ponty in Part One that depth is time.

If Prigogine posits time as an ontological movement of the universe then this is complemented by Merleau-Ponty's radical shift from the acceptance of Husserl's theory of a phenomenology of time—one that depends upon structures of human consciousness, upon our perception of time-consciousness that depends from and is experienced by ourselves as subject—to his apparent rejection of this. In Merleau-Ponty's final but unfinished work, *The Visible and the Invisible* (1968) he

> expressly rejects his [own] *Phenomenology of Perception* for having retained the Husserlian philosophy of consciousness . . . . To say that he moves from phenomenology to ontology is to say that he rejects any privileging of the subject or consciousness as constituting time either as a perceptual object or through a lived experience . . . . Time now is characterized as an ontologically independent entity and not a construct disclosed by consciousness . . . this time is no longer an archetype of the self's non-objectivating self-awareness." (Kelly 2015).

Thus Merleau-Ponty (1968) stated bluntly, "The subject is time." Now in his thinking it is time that constitutes the subject, rather than the other way round. Time no longer provides any neat division between the human consciousness of the subject and the time of organism, or of any nonhuman living creature or, for that matter, the time of the object. Human Being did not invent time. The character of time as weaving together being, the organic, and the inanimate through its movement is rendered profoundly by Borges (1964: 205) in his celebrated philosophical essay, "A New Refutation of Time." After arguing, relentlessly so, that time does not exist, Borges concludes: "*And yet, and yet* . . . Time is the substance I am made of. Time is a river which sweeps me along, but I am the river; it is a tiger which destroys me, but I am the tiger; it is a fire which consumes me, but I am the fire. The world unfortunately is real; I unfortunately, am Borges."

Nonetheless there are critical differences between multiplicities of physical time and the multiplicities of time of living organisms, and this is related to that which Bergson called duration. Grosz (2005: 10) comments that for Bergson duration is a *force*, "the force of temporality." When Bergson banished simultaneity and insisted that every thing existed only through time he gave to duration the force to open time, in a sense to "stretch" time, and, so, to drive that which I called in Part One ongoing emergence, and the ongoing emergence of difference. Organic life of any kind in its existence and behavior is never in equilibrium and is always entropic through both physical time and biological time. Yet the life of biological time seeks negentropy, the reduction of entropy, the "turn" into itself, as it were, in order to accomplish the renewal of itself, keeping itself alive as a species of organism. In turning inward to accomplish negentropy, the organism or organisms (depending on the particular dynamic of reproduction) seek to reproduce and to repeat themselves.

In his *Difference and Repetition*, Deleuze argues intensively that repetition generates difference.[34] Discussing Deleuze on repetition, Bar-On Cohen (2014: 532) writes: "For Deleuze, a philosopher of difference, repetition is opposed to identity: identity is a tyrant who imposes external categories as a measurement of difference, but 'difference' as a concept emanating from repetition is not lodged between two distinctive states but rather *occurs from within itself* to become a condition of the emergent new" [my emphasis]. In my view, one signal impetus for the emergence of difference depends from duration. With Merleau-Ponty's recanting of the time-consciousness of the subject as the foundation of human time, duration comes to the fore as ever-present in the interior and exterior movements of organic life.

Thus duration disrupts the possibility of exact repetition and makes this indeterminate. The ongoing physical time of duration moves a repetition toward a future time. Everything is with-time-through-time and there is always a duration between repetition and repetition regardless of whether this is the briefest of moments or the expectation of a repetition far into the future. Duration ruptures the continuousness or even the continuity of repetition. Once said, this is obvious. Yet apparently it first must be said. Thus no organism can close itself fully and entirely into itself, not externally, not internally. That the organism exists with-time-through-time makes it interactional and vulnerable to the entry of factors, internal, external, that potentially may alter its life and modify the next round of repetition throughout its lifetime. Therefore time in its moving enables, and perhaps is critical to, the emergence of difference; and, so, difference is inherent in repetition. In Part One, I wrote that the forming of encounters in the workshop continually generated variations, yet that very few of these were taken up and elaborated by the workers. Whatever these elements, they entered the durational gap between one encounter and the next, and met their fate there. Repetitive human actions, repetitive human events, are all *time-forms* that will produce difference within themselves through the very actions of their mundane existence; and some of these, in Bateson's phrasing, will make a difference.

My sense is that human beings strive to live through the present continuous, holding to the continuity of their existence (see Handelman 2013). Yet our well-being depends on there being gaps in the continuousness of living consciously awake. We must sleep and sleep ruptures the linearity of the present continuous. So we live through the gaps in linear duration. We escape consciousness to experience the fluctuations of time through our own personal conditions-far-from-equilibrium away from the durations we experience consciously. We turn within our own "local" times folded within us when we sleep and when we daydream and, during these periods, these times organize our experience. Through these a-linear fluctuations of our "local" times we also avoid the precarity of tending to seek the shortest distances between two points, thereby avoiding losing the potentially valuable cognitive and emotional information of the scenic routes along the way (Bateson 1972).

The poet, Raymond McDaniel, offers himself as a case in point of what may happen if one cannot rupture the continuousness of the time of the organic, if one cannot escape fully for a period from the incessant movement of physical time. McDaniel is always aware and conscious. McDaniel sleeps normally and dreams and, simultaneously, is aware. Always aware, he knows what his sleeping-self dreams but the latter, asleep, is not aware of the former's awareness. As he says (2013: 211), "No, I am not sleepy. Were I failing to sleep I would be dead. I sleep perfectly well. What I cannot do is cease being aware, and so what I am is tired." McDaniel's awareness lives fully in the present continuous, through duration without rupture, which is saying he is aware (almost?) without duration. Thus,

> the concept of a long time no longer makes any personal sense, for all its prior conceptual validity. In some immeasurable [qualitative] way, I am having one day. Not the same day repeatedly, not a day of exceptional duration, because nothing ever truly repeats and a day is only as long as whatever not-day allows . . . [yet] I no longer feel if any sliver of time is any longer than any other . . . it isn't as if I don't know how long it has been since I have seen a friend . . . it's just that I register ten minutes and ten years as having the same aspect, which is that of having occurred today. I would rather not dwell on that . . . . If there's an afterlife I am going to be very, very upset. (Ibid.)

McDaniel lives in his own "local" time that is folded within him, and that in various ways affects how he experiences his life and how he synchronizes himself with durational time outside of himself.

In my own knowing, and somewhat apposite to McDaniel's, there was a brief period when I became out of sync with time external to myself. A conundrum emerged that for me became one of, not "where was I" but rather "when was I?" It happened like this. In the late spring of 1994 I brought my slowly dying wife, Lea, to the United States for a second cycle of stereotactic radiosurgery. While there I picked up a book by N. E. Thing Enterprises entitled, *Magic Eye: A New Way of Looking at the World* (1993). The book consisted of two-dimensional illustrations that, when looked at in certain ways, suddenly acquired depth, becoming three-dimensional. Back in Jerusalem, curious, I learned to shift perspective from the two-dimensional to the deeper three-dimensional and back again. And then I slid deliberately into trying to shift from one perspective to the other as quickly as possible. The duration of a shift from two-dimensionality to three was about a second, and I repeated this shifting many, many times.

Then, abruptly, out of this activity something weird emerged. I suddenly was out of sync with moving time outside of myself. No matter where, I was perhaps a second more or less behind time in the temporal surround. And I could not catch up, could not erase this disjunction. I should add that I felt this disjunction primarily when my eyes were open. This may sound absurd, but with this teeny durational gap I immediately became disorientated, discombobulated. Disconcertingly, the very when-ness of my presence became an issue for me. I did not feel that I was behind nor that I was late in relation to the surround. I was in the same space inhabited by others yet not quite simultaneously present together with them and with everything else in the surround. In other words, I was not fully "there," or perhaps I should say, "here." And I was not fully myself since this depended on my relationships with the world that immediately were integral to my self-embodiment.

What may have happened here? Perhaps an extremely concentrated in-turning that excluded all other external stimuli and that created depth for this repetitive in-curving. This repetition shaped a local time within myself that differed from external linear time; and this, even though I wanted to emerge from within myself and synchronize with time external to myself. I was caught within a personal, local time of my own making and could not escape. This local time apparently emerged from the concentrated shifting between the two-dimensional and the three-dimensional through repetitive durations of approximately one second that obsessively reversed themselves. In manipulating my vision with the Magic Eye illustrations I was playing with the chiasm, the (partial) crossover of the optic nerve. In mammals the optic chiasm enables stimuli to reach each eye simultaneously. This simultaneity enables stereoscopic, three-dimensional vision. Perhaps I was turning this on and off until this repetition of one-second durations somehow became autonomous and I became disjointed with external time. By the way, this went on for about three weeks. I then went to my friend, Su Schachter who practices a technique called "reflex balance." Su re-balanced me and suddenly I was back in sync with the movement of time outside of myself. I never fiddled again with Magic Eye though at this moment the book is in front of me (and is speedily going back into its cupboard).

For all the complexities involved, the prime difference between the inorganic and the organic is that the organic must reproduce in order to continue to exist. The organic is not only intra-entropic through time but in some way all organisms are aware of this. Entropy excites organic life to seek its own renewal. And, reproduction would not occur without one general movement—I will call this again a kind of in-turning, the organism or organisms recursively turning within, into itself or themselves and to others of its kind, the organism into its own-ness. In order to reproduce an organism relates to itself. This often is referred to as the organism referencing itself. That is, the organism is reflexive. Reflexivity too has duration. One can say that this in-turning is the curving of time—the organism referencing its own local time. Reflexivity curves time. If I phrase this as the organism going back into itself, relating to its own-ness, then I am implying that the organism seeks through reproduction to return itself to an earlier moment of reduced entropy, even as the organism moves forward with the movement of physical, linear time.[35] Organic life accomplishes the *repetition* of itself with whatever alterations that accrue between one reproductive round and the next. In the simplest sense an organism is constituted so as to reconstitute itself and adapt itself internally and externally.

Yet in-turning requires duration and, in doing so, organic life curves away from the movement of physical, linear time, indeed from its own ongoing, inevitable, forward movement through time. A conundrum results. On the one hand, organic time curves into itself to accomplish the negentropy of reproduction and renewal; while on the other, entropic, linear movement through time never ceases.[36] Thus, under conditions that are far-from-equilibrium, the time of the organism both separates from yet remains in physical time; and in-turning organic time lags behind the movement of the organism through physical time. Moreover, this is no less so for efforts by human beings to search for negentropy to renew and revitalize their social orderings through ritual and numerous other sociocultural formings. As I will argue, given the durations required, the regenerative time of negentropy sought by human beings in concert through participation in cultural and social formings never catches up with itself. The durational movement of negentropy lags behind the entropic movement of physical time through which the efforts of renewal occur. This endemic lag signifies, for example, why the full (social) regeneration of a sociocultural ordering through, say, ritual, is virtually impossible.[37] In simpler terms, why ritual never can be fully effective. Yet more than this, since in my terms all sustained interaction generates degrees of emergent folding (see Part One), the time-lag is always present. One can say that persons are (almost?) always out-of-sync with themselves as well as with others.

Max Gluckman's Idea of Structural Duration

In anthropology ideas are few concerning the significance of duration in social life that potentially could open into the perspective I am thinking here. One such instance is that of Max Gluckman's thoughts on what he called "structural duration."

In 1966, Gluckman, the founder of the Manchester School of social anthropology (Evens and Handelman 2006) was invited to give a plenary address to the American Anthropological Association. Then fifty-five years of age, this was a highlight of his illustrious career. Gluckman and the Manchester School anthropologists had pioneered ideas of the analysis of social situations and the extended case method, both of which contributed substantially to the understanding of social ordering as ongoing, processual movement. A second plenary lecture was delivered by the social anthropologist, Fredrik Barth, then thirty-eight years of age, and the founder of the Department of Social Anthropology at the University of Bergen. For over a decade Barth had dazzled anthropology with his sophisticated joining together and modeling of social organization, transactionalism, and individual agency. Barth lectured on the study of social change as the outgrowth of the cumulative, strategic choices persons made vis a vis one another. Gluckman too lectured on the study of social change, relating this to what he called "the utility of the equilibrium model" in the study of institutions undergoing change. Gluckman's lecture received polite applause.

Barth's lecture was treated to a standing ovation. "Transaction" and "individual agency" turned on the middle-class audience; while "equilibrium" and "institution" turned them off. The audience's reaction demonstrated that Barth was at the cutting edge of anthropology, addressing agency in decision-making and everyday life; while Gluckman was a passé structural-functionalist, a brontosaurus of an intellectual who insisted on holding onto outmoded theoretical ideas of systemic equilibrium. Gluckman returned to Manchester in deep gloom and, as far as I know, never referred again in print to the idea of structural duration.[38]

Gluckman's use of "equilibrium model" emphasized the modeling of reality and *not* reality as such, as a way of gauging the disruption of social order through conflict and its return to some sort of ordering. This was a strongly processual approach that in his perspective required the modeling of process since movement was continual. Yet beyond Gluckman's defense of the equilibrium model as a heuristic device with which to compare and contrast change through time there is a fascinating idea embedded in his lecture that he called the "structural duration" of institutions. An idea quite ignored and forgotten, tangled up with the equilibrium model and caught in the web of misidentification of Gluckman with structural-functionalism. Google Gluckman and "structural duration" and you will come up with a bare handful of references, most of them derogating his "static" anthropology, which could hardly be further from his actual labors (for a striking exception, see Crawford 2007).

What is the idea of "structural duration"? I prefer to drop the language of "institution" and continue to use that of form and phenomenon, or of assemblages that seem to hold together during time with varying degrees of self-integrity. Gluckman (1968: 220) wrote that, "The problem of time is critical for all studies of social and cultural systems." He (not so unlike Bergson) was saying that no phenomenon exists outside of time. Furthermore, that every phenomenon existing in the human world (and, I add, in the organic, more generally) "has its own time-scale built into it" (ibid.). Moreover, that "we cannot understand [a phenomenon, an organization] unless we do so in that [very] scale." The particular time-scale of a social form is its structural duration. The duration is the period through which the phenomenon lives fully, so that one can perceive this or, if its duration is lengthy, one can project the entirety of its existence forward through time. No form, no phenomenon or assemblage, whether tiny or huge, exists in such a simple manner that one can perceive its existence in the temporal flatness of the immediate present. Yet neither can we assign arbitrarily a period of time which we will declare as "sufficient time" to know the form through time.

In my terms one must discover through itself the "structural duration" during which a form may be said to exist fully. Then one can think with acumen on the in-turning of the form and how it is assembled as itself, as its own integrity that enables its phenomenal existence. How can one know, or project, the length and complexity of a structural duration, and whether this may be cyclical, oscillatory, periodic, or indeed open-ended? In the best of ethnographic worlds we do this by living and following what *seems* to be the phenomenal folding or assemblage of foldings, thereby learning what happens in what *seems* to be the nature of the organization. In fact one cannot know a structural duration without following what seems to be, is assumed to be, a folding of form, yet without knowing whether this is indeed the case. And without comprehending its structural duration one will not know in the fuller sense the nature of the phenomenon and how it changes (and as I have argued, changes during the duration of the very reproduction of itself). In discussing his idea of structural duration, Gluckman was not referring to historical time in the usual sense, but rather to time that is integral to a phenomenon, to that which I am calling a folding of form; the time within its folding that enables the form to be or to become fully its own; the time to go through the phases, alterations or changes that make the phenomenon as it is and/or how it will be. Structural duration indexes form through the temporalities of its own interior dynamics that are activated by the movement of time.[39] This enables us to comprehend how phenomena are constituted through their own temporalities—their own rhythms, tempos, disturbances, and chaotics.

There is no shortage of examples of structural duration in the anthropological literature. A few of small scale come to mind. In her study of family, community, and industry in an American town, June Nash (1989: 265) concluded that the researcher needs to account for four generations of family in order "to see the biological processes of mating, reproduction, maturity, and death worked out in a complete cycle." In his, *Fluid Signs: Being a Person the Tamil Way*, Valentine Daniels (1984) discovered unexpectedly that in participating in his third pilgrimage to the same shrine of a particular deity he actually was completing a full cycle of pilgrimage, and that this cycle is the critical mass of devotion of the devotee of this deity. Had he not gone on his third pilgrimage he may well not have acquired this knowledge. In her *Inuit Morality Play*, Jean Briggs (1998) watched numerous episodes of adults trying to play with three year-old Chubby Matta in ways that Jean came to think of as failed game-playing, only to discover that this Inuit play actually ended just when we would expect it to begin; so Jean was thinking entirely in the wrong direction through a mistaken duration.

Gluckman (1968: 223) understood "all social life as a *process* in time" [my emphasis], yet less as a *dynamic* that operated through time in a double sense—as moving only with time and as being moved by time moving. He argued for abstracting the structuring of the duration of an institution so that duration became the period through which the institution would show itself more fully; that perhaps in a sense, would tend to reproduce itself (including whatever alterations had accrued during this period). Yet in this he did not consider time as a force of movement in itself, one that is folded into a "structural duration" in certain ways and not in others; and so that helps organize the very movement of the duration from within itself. Gluckman's idea of duration acquires greater value when its "structuring" is understood as the forming of form that never loses its potential for emergence even as it is predisposed to in-turn and to fold in particular ways. Rather than duration becoming more of a skeleton of time (as it does in Gluckman's schema) time instead opens into that which I have called "prospective history" (Handelman 2005b). Prospective history begins with presentness always moving through future. Prospective history is a history of becoming, of the potential of duration to open into emergence. Even as time-moving is shaped by the durational forming of form so, too, moving-time enables social life to actualize its formings and foldings.

Reflexivity, Negentropy, and the Recursive In-Turning of Organic Time

For human beings, reflexivity is key in attempting to accomplish negentropy. However this kind of reflexivity is more basic and much broader in scope than that initiated by the "reflexive turn" in anthropology during the 1980s (see Handelman 1994, for a critique of *that* reflexive turn). Like phenomenology in general, the reflexive turn in anthropology focused on individual experience and referred to the relating of self to other as they mutually influence one another's perceptions and actions. So, this sort of reflexivity is the act of referencing oneself to oneself through the mediation of an external perspective on oneself, a perspective whose location may be through other persons or through other sources of stimuli. This version of reflexivity often is applied to the anthropologist as fieldworker in relation to a native other through a variety of media, producing, enhancing, and doubting perception, thought, feeling, and knowledge-making (Handelman 2016).

Here I depend from a different perspective on reflexivity. Evens, Handelman, and Roberts (2016: 1–20) argue that reflexivity-as-action is critical to the very becoming and being of the human condition.[40] To this I add that reflexivity is a movement that turns back on itself, a movement that is durational but not linear. Yet even as a time-trajectory curves into itself, re-entering itself with the experience and knowledge accumulated as it moves forward indeterminately, it re-enters later than when it began its curving. Put otherwise, curving time re-enters its own physical, time past. The self-intersection of reflexivity in its manifold planes is critical to consciousness in human beings. The self-awareness of consciousness does not exist without the reflexive curve. The self-awareness of consciousness depends on curving, in-turning duration.[41]

I suggested earlier that organic life is temporally out-of-sync with itself. Thus there is almost no way for life in general and human beings in particular to accomplish the full negation of the effects of entropy, either personally or in terms of the social. Nonetheless, the striving for this goal continues, today especially through the biology of gene editing, cloning, and the transplantation of organs. An historical example of such striving is that of (the rare instances of) self-mummification (*sokushimbutsu*) in Japan and elsewhere in Buddhist Asia. Pure Buddhist practice would concentrate on the perfection of the self as a way to Nirvana. Yet according to one Japanese Buddhist sect, a believer, through the practice of especially severe austerities, could perfect the self and become a Buddha in his own body (Hori 1962: 234). These austerities would produce a being of emptiness unaffected by the passage of time, escaping the entropic deterioration of selfness and biological death and attaining a kind of negentropy of the living soul.

In the process of self-mummification dietary restrictions were prominent: abstention from meat, the cereals, salt, and cooked foods. The ascetic did tree-eating (*mokujiki*), substituting only on parts of the tree. The ascetic dedicated to becoming a self-mummified Buddha in his own body would take a vow to perform the tree-eating austerities for periods of one thousand days, two thousand days and even lengthier periods. Blacker (1975: 88) comments that: "During the first part of the discipline their diet consisted of nuts, bark, fruit, berries, grass, and sometimes soy in fair abundance. The quantity of these things was then reduced, until by the end of their allotted period they had undergone a total fast of many days. Ideally . . . the man should die from starvation, upright in the lotus posture . . . . His body should have been reduced to skin and bone, all flesh and visceral contents having long disappeared." The body then was placed in a wooden coffin inside a stone sarcophagus, buried for three years, and then exhumed. By then the body should have mummified. Blacker adds that (1975: 89), "It was alleged . . . that such people did not suffer death. What appeared to be death is in fact the state of suspended animation known as *nyujo*, in which condition the soul may await the coming, millions of years hence, of the future Buddha Maitreya." In recognition of the tremendous powers acquired through the terrible suffering of self-mummification, each mummified Buddha was dressed in the robes of a Buddhist abbot and placed in the position usually kept for the Buddha image in a local temple. The self-mummified Buddha would then be supplicated and prayed to, as one would have done before the usual Buddha image.

Self-mummification is an instance of extreme in-turning, of folding and self-reflexivity that completely enclosed the individual deeply within himself in order to seek self-perfection that was perceived as suspended animation; that is, a condition of time whose movement is extremely slow or non-existent. To accomplish this, time within the individual folded into himself, becoming entirely local, separated from temporal movement outside the fold. Through his austerities the seeker comes to separate his own organic, temporal movement from those of the physical and sociocultural worlds beyond his self-folding. Within his self-folding the seeker becomes profoundly, actively, and continuously self-reflexive. He cannot be separated from this engrossing reflexivity. This self-folding is profoundly deep, with the practitioner discovering in this depth (in Deleuze's terms) how to alter the movement of time. In my terms the seeker creates a different time within the fold, and through this synchronizes his interior, organic time with this local time. The seeker within his self-folding moves time in two ways. Initially, through self-starvation he speeds up time to reach his early death in an emaciated condition. Then, once his body is mummified, the movement of organic time becomes minimal, extremely slow, perhaps eliminated, as his now selfless soul awaits Maitreya in the far distant future. If a kind of negentropy then is attained within the fold this enables the now minimalistic organic time to move through physical time without being (or hardly being) effected by the latter. Here, what is left of the selfless organic is not out-of-sync with itself as it moves through physical time. I emphasize that both Raymond McDaniel and the self-mummifiers (at their outset) are and were enfolded within their own local times, each out-of-sync with time outside their foldings. Without these changes in the movement of time, and, so, of the durations of time, neither would become what they are and were.

What are these folded durations that I am calling local times? How do they relate to the distinction that I drew between physical time and organic time? To the question of whether time is a force in itself or whether its movement can be relegated comfortably to the passive passage of the fourth dimension? And, so, whether anthropologists can continue to rely safely on different movements of time as the products of varying cultural interpretations of the same dimensionality that at least since Newton has provided the scientific foundation for theories of time. The existence of time apparently is not provable except through measuring its movement; yet this, in turn, locks time into dimensionality and avoids what the bio-mathematician, Plamen Simeonov (2015: 271), calls the true nature of time that is ineffable, eluding science and mathematics. And, as I noted earlier, no less eluding for anthropologists as they accept the dimensionality of time as basic to ontological premises regarding the constitution of the very movement of everything within itself and in relation to everything else. The ways in which time moves seem to be critical to questions of ontology.

Cultural orderings have different, though sometimes overlapping basic premises that permeate living through their worlds, their cosmologies. These are premises that are not deterministic, yet they enable certain formations of existence rather than others. The patternings of these premises are ontological for the peoples who live them and epistemological for their practice. To my knowledge there are no human ontologies whose premises are static, without the movement of time. Premises of time-as-movement likely are embedded in some way in all human ontologies. If there are different human ontologies, then are there different human realities? Most likely there are. Moreover, different realities may not be predicated on a distinction between subjective perception and experience and objective knowledge. If there are thoroughly different realities then do these realities have their own qualities of time (see, for example, Rosaldo 1980)? We know that a myriad of groupings live time, feel time, think time, and organize time differently from one another, thereby inducing the variable experiencing of time among their members.

If there is a multiplicity of cultural ontologies then perhaps time too is not a singular medium of passive passage that is always the same, though interpreted differently? Perhaps time is a multiplicity? Not a multiplicity of distinctions between objective, scientific time and subjective, native time, but as temporalities that work differently through the realities of cultural ontologies that themselves are no less real than is our unquestioned reliance on time as the fourth dimension. In my view, how ontological temporalities work differently to endow the reality of the movement of time may be one of the most difficult questions that an anthropology of time can take up; and, moreover, one to which there may well be no answers. Nonetheless this question should be asked and pondered.

Henry Rupert and the Dynamic Force of Time

I wish to address the above questions through fieldwork I did over fifty years ago with a Native American shaman in Nevada (see Chapter One). When I met the Washo shaman, Henry Moses Rupert, he was just about the same age as I am now. The ways in which Henry came to organize his healing practices may tell us something about how time and reality are irreducibly interwoven and perhaps suggest that the issue of the potential existence of ontological multiplicities of time is indubitably real.

The Washo people lived in the Great Basin, an arid plateau with relatively few natural foodstuffs. The traditional Washo cosmos was of a world continually in movement, in flux. This continuous movement was that of "power" (*wegeleyu*) which filled cosmos (perhaps one could say that this power *was* the very existence of cosmos) and had an intimate affinity to life-energy. Life-energy energized a vast array of beings. Cosmos was fluid within itself. The fluidity of the Washo cosmos was associated movingly with water, while power, life-energy, was intrinsically attracted to water and flowed along waterways (though also along trails) (Miller 1983). This was a living cosmos that can be characterized as organic, with all its elements and beings intimately interrelated and interactive. The ontology of such a cosmos has hardly an opening for an Archimedean perspective, one that is external to cosmos, a perspective that considers itself all-seeing and objective, since any move toward perceiving the exterior of cosmos disrupts its interior relatedness. Without an Archimedean point of observation this sort of cosmos is comprehended from within itself.

Over a period of years Henry had formulated for himself an ethic of living that he called the Law of Nature. This ethic was composed of three primary ways of relating to the cosmos of which he was a part. These were: be honest; be discreet; do no harm (Handelman 1967, 1972). Henry's ethic of existence was a way of entering and fitting directly into the interacting forms of the organic cosmos. In Henry's Law of Nature all beings, all flora and fauna, require water in order to continue to exist. Water flows with life, life flows with water. Water is the duration of life. To which I add the following: *water is time*. If the duration of water is disrupted, then life falls ill. Duration is disrupted when life is dried out and life-energy fails before the conclusion of its natural life span, its natural range of time. This usually occurs when a person inadvertently fails to provide water to the life-force of another organic entity, whether human or not, one for which he or she is responsible. In response the dried-out entity seeks and takes the water it needs from the person responsible, desiccating this person who then falls ill. To put this a little differently, life falters when its own time, its water, is taken from it. Henry's healing solution often was to ensure that water (and, so, time) would return to both of the afflicted.

Henry worked with entropy. This is to say that *he healed with time*. The reduction of water in an organic being increased its entropy and reduced the duration of its internal time. Thus the interior time of an organic being, its local time, was disrupted and faltered. Without the ongoing progression of time the condition of the afflicted became increasingly indeterminate. Healing involved restoring the life-force of the person by replenishing her or his water, that is, his or her internal time. In order to heal these conditions Henry had to make the ill person self-reflexive about her or his responsibility for the condition of illness. Here self-reflexivity again was a turning into oneself, a returning to a time when the person actually was making the error of desiccating another being, thereby triggering the loss of life-energy and time. Self-reflexivity had the potential to become an act of renewal just as the reflexive in-turning of the organism through reproduction is an act of renewal.

To call this in-turning "memory" is to obfuscate the necessity in self-reflexivity of re-experiencing what one has done. Let me reemphasize that which I have argued: it is more productive to say that in an indeterminate world of multiplicities (organic) self-reflexivity curves back through time even as physical time moves forward. The two are never fully synced, and the time of the organic never catches up with the movement of physical time.[42] Organic reproduction is the movement of time that is negentropic, in-turning, moving into dynamics that will re-energize and re-create the organism. Yet during this movement toward repetition the organism continues to move forward through time as a physical, linear progression. This suggests that there always is a time-gap, however tiny this may be, between the progression of physical time and the regeneration that is organic time. Yet I also am saying that the in-turning's reflexive regeneration of organic time is a hallmark of social ordering, an ordering that continually seeks to repeat and reproduce itself even as this movement makes this reproduction out-of-sync with its own movement through physical time, opening ordering to continuing potential ongoing impetuses for change.

I have suggested that in Henry Rupert's healing the replenishment of life-energy and the replenishment of time were one and the same. Yet, was time simply malleable, simply passive, thus to be manipulated by the healer? Or was time dynamic, *enabling* or even *making* something happen in the healing process? Let me note at this point that the first spirit helper whom Henry acquired was that of *water* itself. In Henry's healing he would pray for water for the well-being of the patient, asking that the aggrieved being, dried-out and disintegrating, agree to stop dehydrating the patient in return for receiving water from the patient. In other words, the time that is water acted to help replenish the time-duration of the patient's life. Here time is hardly a passive passage that healer and patient pass through. Time is life-giving, indeed time in itself is a force (as it may be in the reproducing and re-energizing of the organic).

Initially Henry Rupert did what was understood as traditional Washo healing. A healing ritual required the shaman to work for three consecutive nights from dusk until midnight, and a fourth night from dusk until dawn. The same ritual acts were repeated during each night. Night after night the ritual had a rhythmic pulsation of repetition with each lengthy repetition augmenting, magnifying, and deepening the ritual folding and its intentionality and intensity; and then into the dawn of the fourth day when the shaman would have a better idea of whether difference had been accomplished—whether or not the victim agreed to stop dehydrating the patient.

Later on Henry acquired a second spirit helper, a young Hindu whose skeleton stood in the local high school. Henry continued doing the traditional healing ritual; though during healing he now saw himself as a skeleton wearing a turban, moving quickly around the patient's body. His own being during the ritual had changed. Though Henry continued practicing the repetitive, pulsating velocity of four nights of healing, he had introduced into his practice the potential of *speedier* time. His own interior velocity became faster with the augmenting life-energy that the Hindu brought him.

Many years later, when Henry was seventy years old, he healed a Hawaiian curer who lived in California. In return the Hawaiian gifted Henry with some of his own power in the form of a Hawaiian spirit helper named George who lived in a volcano on one of the islands, but whose power was at its maximum in the vicinity of Henry's home. George brought Henry new healing techniques together with the maxims that, "everything comes quick and goes away quick" and "we help nature and nature does the rest." For ailments easier to cure Henry now dispensed with visions of diagnosis and prognosis, with chants, and with many other of the elements of the four-night healing rituals. The healing ritual now took between approximately ten minutes to four hours, and involved Henry praying to George and the placing of hands on the patient to remove pain from the body.

With the Hawaiian spirit helper the healing ritual changed radically. The rhythm of repetition and pulsation was omitted in many instances, while the speed and velocity of the ritual increased greatly, now perhaps matching the speed of Henry's interior after he acquired the Hindu spirit helper. Washo cosmology and Henry's development of the energy of time-as-water were largely excised. Moreover in these instances the patient was depersonalized since there was no need to establish causation through errors of omission and commission on the part of the patient. Through the emphasis on speed and velocity, time came more fully to the forefront as the dynamic that enabled "Hawaiian" healing. Yet, too, it was the sense and feel of the organic that Henry sought to heal. Today I think of Henry's healing as experimenting, albeit not deliberately, with the potentialities of time within his ritual (although he did not mention them as such). Nonetheless he was drawn to the dynamic potentiality of the movement of time as he folded this within his ritual. Initially, in his healing practice, time was contextualized through the movement of water as life-energy. Time in his healing ritual was repetitive, pulsating and, at the end of the fourth night at dawn, often climactic. Eventually, through the Hawaiian healing of George, contextualization disappeared and non-pulsating time—closer perhaps to the pure movement of time—came to the fore.

Interestingly, this change resonates to no small degree with how Deleuze, borrowing from the Stoic philosophers, understood the shift from pulsed time (Chronos) to non-pulsed time (Aion). Deleuze argued first that pulsed time is territorialized time, time marking territory. Second, that "pulsed time marks the temporality of a form in development." And third, that pulsed time "marks, or measures, or scans the formation of a subject"; thus education and the German idea of *bildung*, of character-formation, occur through pulsed time. Yet if de-territorialization occurs then non-pulsed time appears. So, too, if time moves primarily through speed and slowness then non-pulsed time is present. Furthermore, through non-pulsed time there is no formation of a subject.[43]

When Henry took on George's epistemology of intensity—the movement of speedier time—then time was de-territorialized, and non-pulsating time became the dynamic of movement. Furthermore, in this way of healing Henry gave little or no regard as to whom the patient-as-subject was. Henry was disinterested in the cause of pain, the errors made by the patient, and so forth. In Henry's world time was not a passive passage but an active force. The message seems to be clear: Change time, change the dynamic of time; thus, without changing time there is no change in the dynamic of time.

After Henry and I began talking about his shamanism he told me flatly, "What is real for me is not real for you." I was unsurprised yet nonetheless nonplussed. What was the significance of his statement? It did not single out one of our realities as objective and true and the other as subjective and, if not untrue, then misguided or deluded. Indeed he never did so. He seemed to be telling me that we lived in different worlds, and that different worlds existed and moved through themselves differently. He understood multiplicity much more comprehensively than did I. But then he practiced this as I did not. Well, so what? Couldn't I learn about his world and come to understand it without embracing it? Probably not. Not without living a world through premises of existence and movement distinctly different from my own, even though sometimes these premises *seemed,* and I emphasize this, to overlap one another. We lived through different ontologies, different cosmologies. I lived time more as the fourth dimension, time more as a passive passage. This too is what I had studied in anthropology. He frequently lived time as Gebser's a-dimensional time, time as a force for dynamic movement. My thought through the present moment is that without ontologies of time there may well be no ontology at all, and no epistemological difference that makes a difference. And this should be a sobering thought.

A Cosmic Macro-Folding: Jewish Cultural Time

I said earlier that how temporal ontologies move differently to endow the realities of the movement of time may be one of the most difficult questions that an anthropology of time can take up. In closing I would like to take up aspects of one ontology of cultural time that effected and affected those who lived with and through it and that continues to do so. My discussion here is necessarily sketchy.[44] Though here construed loosely and schematically, this ontology is basic to moving time in the Jewish religio-cultural cosmos. This time-moving is rhythmic, a moving-ness that thereby folds in on itself.

Writing of the Jewish week, Zerubavel (1985: 115) comments that this unit of duration is characterized by a peak day, the Sabbath, that imparts a "beat" to the week. He continues, "The experience of beat is essentially a sensation of a throbbing pulsation." The Jewish week is a unit of cultural time pulsating in accordance with a certain beat, or impulsion. This a deceptively simple yet profound observation, for this rhythm of temporal pulsing is critical to the forming of numerous units or durations of time in Jewish culture. This pulsing may be described as an impulsing from lower to higher, from ordinary to extraordinary. The rhythm is climactic, yet more so, for this impulsing implies movement from the less valued to the highly valued. For reasons not dwelt on here, this selfsame impulsing also may be found within the dynamic moving from fragmenting to integrating, to unity and holism. Time moving with Jewish culture is, generally, speaking, that of directional emerging and that of collective becoming. In the distant past this climactic impulsing of time was divorced in part from rhythms of nature, and therefore from ideas of the eternal character of dynamics of "becoming." As Zerubavel (1985: 11) notes of the Jewish week, it had to be based on an "entirely artificial mathematical rhythm."

Within this macro-folding of time, time-moving was imbued with the moral valuation of the human condition (Kauffman 1972: 73). Moving time that is a cultural becoming is then in the first instance (and in the last) a moral problem. Time is necessarily the moral ordering of existence. Put more emphatically, the dynamic movement of impulsing and pulsating time enables the coming into existence of Jewish moral ordering, through different durations. Should one need reminding, in the biblical myth of cosmogenesis the creation of time, the separation of light from darkness, day from night (Genesis 1: 3–5), is almost isomorphic with the onset of cosmic creation, while the entire creating movement is marked by consecutively numbered days, climaxing on the seventh, which God blessed and made holy. As the medieval philosopher Maimonides (1956: 171) commented, "Even time itself is among the things created." Whereupon he added (albeit for purposes of his own argument) that the "true and essential condition" of time "is not to remain in the same state for two consecutive moments." In other words, time is moving continuously, always.

That time has a special status in Jewish thought is not in question. Heschel (1951: 8) writes that, "Judaism is a religion of time. The main themes of faith lie in the realm of time." The nineteenth-century Orthodox thinker Hirsch (1985: 41) stated that, "The catechism of the Jew consists of his calendar." Once time is created, everything else (with the exception of the Creator) happens within and during continuous time. Heschel (1951: 100) argues that, "it is within time that we are able to sense the unity of all beings." One can say that moving time holds everything together in the Jewish phenomenal world. During (rather than in) the Judaic cosmos time never falters, never loses its continuous coherence, integrity, unity, even as Jewish human beings are falling, threatened, fragmenting.[45] Impulsing and pulsing time lifts them toward the potentiality of reintegration. Time never loses its rhythmic, impulsing and pulsating movement from low to high. The existence of the cultural logic that is this impulsing-pulsating rhythm enables moving time to become the template, as it were, for the moral ordering of becoming, of progressing, one that enables the forming of strivings for utopian perfection and for the unifying of people and place. The eschatological visions of traditional Judaism (that are growing steadily in Jewish Israel during the past fifty years, since the 1967 war and the occupation of Palestine), of God intervening in time to end time, and so to begin an eternity of perfection, point precisely to the essential integrity of the dynamic of moving time.

The rhythmic pulsing of time enables the forming of form that is climactic. It does not index the content of this forming; for example, it does not refer to the ways in which a messianic thrust takes form, nor to how the present-day forming of religious-political-territorial messianism in Israel compares with previous thrusts of the messianic potential of Judaism. To understand such phenomena one need do analyses of the social, the political, the economic, and so forth. Yet, in this respect, one can say that in the above perspective time ends when it is no longer necessary—when its dynamic of Becoming is completed and the impregnable boundary between God and the Jewish human being is dissolved.[46]

The rhythm of pulsation—from low to high, from morally inferior to morally superior —is evident through different durations of Jewish time, from the short to the lengthy. The Jewish cosmos folds moving time within its own depths, shaping a particular rhythmic relationship between different durational, calendrical units of time moving. As noted below, these durations differ in scale, yet these durations are self-similar to one another in the pulsing rhythm that organizes their moving times. Thus the relationship between these different durations of time-moving appears to be *fractal-like*. Fractal form was conceptualized mathematically by Benoit Mandelbrot, yet has a multiplicity of parallels and resonances in the organizing of form in the natural world.[47] Fractal organization refers to recurring patterns of similarity and difference on different planes or levels of scale (see Kreinath 2019, 2012). That is, regardless of their scale of organization, certain patterns maintain the same proportions in their internal constitution.[48]

The fractal is holographic. All the information of the three-dimensional hologram is contained and is present in any of its (arbitrarily selected) parts. Cut any piece arbitrarily from a visual hologram and this part contains the entire hologram. So, too, with fractal organization. As in the hologram, information in the fractal is distributed non-locally—the whole is in every part. A fractal contains all its information on any scale on which it is organizing or organized. Put otherwise, as in the hologram, "information is embedded . . . so densely and recursively that everything is connected simultaneously to everything else. Moreover, this information is actually embedded within embedments (that are embedded within other embedments, and so on)" (Handelman and Shulman 1997: 194; see Bohm 1981: 143–47). The fractal, like the holograph, is characterized by ongoing self-similarity (Grossing 1993: 80).

In this regard consider moving time within the following durations of Jewish time. Thus, the pulsing of the Jewish twenty-four hour "day": in the phrasing of Genesis (I: 5), "And the evening and the morning were the first day." The moving time of the Jewish day begins in darkness and emerges into light. Light rather than darkness implies the value of morality. In a simple yet ever-ongoing way this night-day, as Hirsch (1985: 42) calls it, is no less the recapitulation of cosmogonic and existential movement.

Consider the pulsing of the Jewish week. It moves through six ordinary days to peak at the extraordinary seventh, that Heschel calls "the climax of living," and that has its own superior character (Zerubavel 1985: 113). In the biblical text, at least, "the Sabbath commemorates the creation" (Kaufmann 1972: 117); and, so, one may surmise, again implicates that elementary momentum.

Consider the yearly pulsing of holidays like *Purim*, Passover, and *Hannukah*. Purim is preceded by a fast day that commemorates the period of trepidation and repentance when the lives of the Jews of Persia were under dire threat. On the eve of the holiday the story of their salvation is read. The following day is one of celebration and jubilation. Passover is preceded by a fast day that commemorates the time of trial when God slew the firstborn of the Egyptians, whilst those of the Israelites were spared. On the eve of the holiday the story of the exodus from Egypt is read. Hannukah, too, is a sequence of trial and triumph. The pulsing of all the holidays moves through the low of tribulation to the high of triumph. But the peak of these occasions, like that of the Sabbath, is always celebrated during their eves, in darkness. Again, in these instances darkness is eclipsed, turning into the heights of light and the moral, collective good of the Jewish people.

Consider rhythms pulsing through longer durations. Every Sabbath service includes a reading from the *Torah* (the *Pentateuch*) that concludes with a reading called *haftarah* (literally, "Conclusion"), usually from the books of the Prophets. Exegeses tend to link the meanings of these sets of readings. Consider the rhythmic pulsing of these Sabbath readings in Ashkenazic tradition, for six Sabbaths that fall in sequence between the end of the Hebrew month of *Shevat* (February–March) and Passover (March–April) plus one additional haftarah reading on the last day of Passover.[49] Here this implicit rhythm is discussed in brief (texts and commentaries are available easily in Hertz 1938). The first of these Sabbaths is called *Shekalim*. The Torah reading tells of the obligation of every Israelite to contribute a half-shekel toward the upkeep of the Temple. This has been interpreted as an annual renewal of collective membership (Hirsch 1985: 323; Vainstein 1953: 139). The associated haftarah tells of revolt against foreign idolaters, of the enemy within, and of their destruction (Hertz 1938: 954). The second, called *Zakhor* ("remember"), precedes the holiday of *Purim*. The Torah reading recalls the unprovoked and vicious attack of Amalek on the Israelites, following the exodus from Egypt. The haftarah tells of Saul's extermination of the Amalekites. Both readings relate to the destruction of the enemy without. Haman, the arch-enemy of the Jews of Persia who is destroyed at *Purim*, commonly is assimilated as a descendant of Amalek.

The third of these Sabbaths is called *Para* ("heifer"). Its readings are on themes of purification, bodily and moral, and of renewal of the nation from within, as preparation for the fruition of the desolate land (Hertz 1938: 961). The fourth is *Hahodesh* ("the month"). Its Torah reading describes preparations for Passover, the holiday of the exodus. The haftarah is part of a prophecy of the New Jerusalem, to arise when exile is ended. The fifth, *Shabbat Hagadol* (The Great Sabbath), is the Sabbath prior to Passover. The haftarah concludes with a vision of the coming of the Prophet Elijah, in religious tradition the herald of redemption who would appear at Passover-time (Hertz 1938: 967). The sixth of these Sabbaths occurs during Passover itself. Its haftarah is Ezekiel's great vision of the dry bones returning to life, of resurrection and redemption: "I will open your graves, and cause you to come up out of your graves, and bring you into the land of Israel" (Ezekiel 37: 12). The seventh reading is not on the following Sabbath but on the last day of Passover, and continues the upward impulsing of time moving. This haftarah from Isaiah (Isaiah 11) contains the vision of a perfected cosmos, one in which wolf and lamb, leopard and kid, and so forth, will dwell together in harmony—a vision of peaceful, cosmic holism. This last haftarah is also read during the special prayer service of Israeli Independence Day (Vainstein 1953: 159), and I will return to this detail.

Time-moving carries the sequence of these Sabbath texts plus one toward crescendo, one that includes the peaks of Purim and Passover. This sequence of impulsing begins with the corruption within, the expulsion of interior corruption, and the renewal of collective identity. The impulsing continues through the collective response to evil from without, and then through themes of purification and cleansing from within. Time-moving then raises visions of the end of fragmentation and exile, into the onset of reunification and perfection, climaxing during Passover, that itself is forming the primordial coalescence of the Israelites into a rudimentary collectivity emerging through their collective deliverance from oppression.

Consider the duration of fifty days (seven weeks of seven days plus one; in other words, the whole completion of this duration) called "Counting the Omer" (*Sefirat Ha'omer*). This begins on Passover and moves until the holiday of *Shavu'ot* (Weeks), identified with first fruits and often with the giving of the Torah by God to Moses on Mount Sinai. During this period, time moves from Passover, the struggling for collective freedom, to Shavu'ot, the contractual surrendering to God and God's laws by the Israelite collectivity. Again through this duration time is moving toward climactic impulsion. Consider the lengthiest of durations of Jewish time, the eschatological. Whether conceived of as progressive (moving slowly toward completion, toward endtime redemption) or as apocalyptic (God intervening abruptly in human life to end time) moving time is pulsating toward the climactic and utopic, toward the moral unifying and perfecting of the Jewish cosmos.

So, what happened when Israeli Jews were given a choice as to what manner of time-moving to adopt as their moving time? The founding of the State of Israel in 1948 is the case in point. Consider that the first Israeli government—orientated toward socialism, secularism, and nationalism—chose to adopt officially the Hebrew calendar with its significant holy days and holidays. In other words, Israel adopted the religious calendar with its fractal-like impulsing of time outlined above. Even though most of the populace organized their daily life in terms of the Gregorian calendar, the durations of cosmic Jewish time, with its rhythm of time folded within, surfaced continuously. The secular antidote to this (beginning even earlier, during the British Mandate) was to secularize the contents of holiday observances and celebrations, yet nonetheless to observe their occurrence on the dates of the religious calendar (Shavit and Sitton 2004). This was done as if it were the now secular contents themselves of time-moving that had the power to move persons rather than the pulsating rhythms of time folded into the religious calendar.

Consider that the State also invented three new days of state commemoration and celebration: Independence Day, Remembrance Day for the fallen soldiers, and Holocaust Remembrance Day. These three Days were scheduled soon after the end of Passover and were quickly arranged in the sequence of Holocaust Remembrance Day, Remembrance Day, and Independence Day. These Days move from the lowest depths of destruction that is the Holocaust, to the upward-moving fight for national independence and freedom commemorated by Remembrance Day for the fallen, to the heights of celebrating the founding and ongoing existence of the Jewish State, that is Independence Day. The sequencing of the three Days immediately picked up the impulsing, recursive, pulsating rhythm of cosmic Jewish time: moving from low to high, from darkness into light (see Handelman and Katz 1998).

Consider that in 1948 the State organized a competition to choose the design for the national emblem of Israel. A variety of designs were submitted, both secular and traditional in their shaping and thematics. The winning design was that of the seven-branched lampstand, the *menorah*, sculpted in relief and frozen for posterity in 81 CE on the triumphal Arch of the Emperor Titus in Rome. The menorah was one of the ritual implements that had stood in the Temple in Jerusalem, destroyed by the Roman armies in 70 CE, and that was carted off to Rome. The choice was understood to recuperate the ancient loss of Jewish sovereignty, returning the ancient symbol of independence to the newly founded Jewish state (Handelman and Shamgar-Handelman 1990, 1993). Again that pulsating rhythm of time from low to high that dominates the Jewish cosmic folding.

Consider that the two great all-out wars that Israel has fought since the 1948 War were the war of 1967 and that of 1973. That of 1967 speedily came to be called the Six-Day War, even though it had lasted seven days, and that of 1973 was termed the Yom Kippur War since it began on the Jewish Day of Atonement (according to the religious calendar). The Six-Day War immediately bore connotations of God's creation of cosmos: he labored for six days to create cosmos and rested on the holy seventh. So, too, the Israeli Army fought three Arab states for six days and rested victoriously on the seventh, having also recaptured the Old City of Jerusalem and, most significantly, the Western Wall, that sole remnant of the ancient Temple destroyed by the armies of Titus; the remainder that quite quickly became the most holy relic of the State (and of much of its Jewish population), tying together that ancient time of fragmentation and the present-day of unifying victory (and all Jewish historical moments in-between). In messianic terms the ownership of the Wall brought the State and Judaism, its official state religion, to the very verge of the Temple Mount (the Muslim *Haram al-Sharif*, the Noble Sanctuary) where the Temple destroyed by Titus's armies had stood. That which is ensuing at that site since 1967 is a story in itself.

During the 1973 War, Israel sustained severe losses of life and armament in desperate battles before regaining the upper hand against the Egyptian and Syrian armies. Not a few responses in Israel attributed Israel's trials in this war to the overweening pride of its leaders since the Six-Day War, and of their neglect of the ongoing training of the armed forces and the upkeep of their equipment. In other words, Israel had to struggle mightily to overcome its own weaknesses and the strengths of its enemies in order to move from the darkness of near defeat into the light of victory and salvation. These wars (and other actions) easily assimilate into the Jewish rhythmic pulsating of time.

Consider that two months after the Six-Day War a new social movement arose, called the Greater Land of Israel. Its founding signatories, primarily secular and primarily from the center-left of the political spectrum, were among the most senior and respected Jewish intelligentsia in the country. They included the revered poet and guru, Natan Alterman, and the author, S. Y. Agnon, who had been awarded the Nobel Prize for literature. It is worth quoting here from the document (in Hebrew) that they signed: "The Land of Israel is now in the hands of the Jewish people. Just as we are not permitted to relinquish the State of Israel, so we are commanded to maintain what we have received from its hands: the Land of Israel. We are hereby loyally committed to the *wholeness of our land*, with respect both to the people's past and to its future, and *no government in Israel is entitled to relinquish this wholeness*" [my emphases].⁵⁰

I am not saying that the simple temporal, fractal-like pulsating rhythm I am describing is causal. Not at all. Or, more accurately, I don't know. I am not relating to the "contents" of cultural classifications and social actions, nor to their contextual meanings, nor to their consequences grounded in the social, the geopolitical, and so forth. Nor am I saying that there is some distinction here between "ritual time" and mundane time, as Bloch (1974) argued long ago in criticizing Geertz's conception of Balinese time as cyclical. Please forgive my repetition. I must emphasize this: I am saying that within the macro-folding that is Jewish creation and its existing that is ongoing, time-moving often is organized through a pulsating rhythm that moves from low to high, from darkness to light; that this is integral to Jewish cosmology; that this is a common-sensical understanding within Jewish culture; that this organizes numerous occurrences of social existence; and that this naturalness is used both without and with intention.

Time here is dynamic because at the very least it enables movement, because it was shaped to move as it does, and because it has fractal-like qualities of self-similarity of scale on a host of planes and levels, micro and macro. Zionism carried this macro-folding of Jewish time to Palestine, first within the state-in-the-making during the British Mandate and then within the Jewish state, despite claims of secularization, socialism, liberalism, modernization, and, too, of course, of the creation of the post-Holocaust new Jewish person, heroic, strong, and unbending. The rhythmic impulsing and pulsating of Jewish time with its fractal-like self-similarity moves powerfully within and through the messianic wave that has been building in Israel at least since the 1967 War, a wave whose future heights and duration no one can predict, nor can one know what will be left after it breaks. The State of Israel is caught (perhaps trapped) within Jewish cosmic time. Can it break free of this?

Notes

1. However "unfolding" was used there more in a micro-historical sense, of occurrences following one another.
2. For a powerful critique of methodological individualism, see Evens (1977).
3. In what I call events of modeling (Handelman 1990) or rituals of transformation we can say something like, the ritual creates the persons who will produce the ritual as that ritual that created them during *n* number of generations.
4. A path-breaking yet quite ignored exception was John M. (Jack) Roberts's (1951) monograph on cultural variation in three closely-related Navaho households. Roberts (1951: 3) argued that anthropologists had neglected the study of small groups "as discrete cultural entities lying between the individual and the larger groups . . ." While small groups were not neglected, they nonetheless "have been treated as parts of larger entities and their cultures as segments or divisions of larger group-ordered cultures" (1951: 4). Roberts's radical hypothesis was that "every small group, like groups of other sizes, defines an independent and unique culture" (1951:

3). Thus, small groups "sometimes constitute entities which cannot be fully encompassed by some larger group-ordered culture . . ." (1951: 5). Moreover, in a later essay Roberts (1964) recognized the small-group culture as a medium of information-processing, one with greater capacity to do this than the small-group as such. Tom McFeat (1974) took up and developed Roberts's ideas in an intriguing and creative book that in turn anthropologists ignored. See also Handelman (1989).

5. The neologism of a-linear gives to movement a very different potentiality than does the nonlinear. Nonlinearity has linearity as its ground. The nonlinear is not-linear yet includes the referent of the linear. The nonlinear departs from the linear. However the Greek prefix /a-/ liberates movement from linearity. A-linearity locates movement (and time) away from and unconnected to linearity and nonlinearity, without any referent to the linear and without any commitment to an either-or arrangement of linearity *or* nonlinearity. See Gebser (1984: 2) for the significance of using the Greek prefix /a-/.
6. This also opens to the logic of abduction of C. S. Peirce through which surprise generates questioning and analysis, rather than the prediction of induction or the reductionism of deduction. The logic of abduction in fact is critical in anthropological fieldwork though hardly recognized by anthropologists even as they use it in common-sensical ways.
7. The sociologist, Keith Sawyer (2005: 104) argues that ideas of emergence were widespread in French nineteenth-century intellectual life. Durkheim made "emergence" central to his theorizing on the "social emergence" of social facts and collective representations from the interaction of individuals, and that: "social structure then becomes autonomous and external to individuals and exerts causal power over those individuals." In other words, society emerges from individuals in concert but then becomes *sui generis*. Sawyer suggests that Durkheim's place as a primary theoretician of social emergence was obscured by the emphasis he placed on the reproduction of society rather than on further social change. Though one should note that Durkheim's concern with social reproduction was likely related to his pondering on how the France of that period could be held together through the creation of social solidarity.

 Interestingly, the idea of the autopoietic moment is joined to the *sui generis* when linearity (suddenly?) begins to curl into itself, toward folding and the beginning of self-organizing. It is then, during emergence, that the interaction of individuals is becoming the intra-action of folding.
8. Compare what I have said on my early thinking on the encounter in the preceding pages with the following passage (Di Paolo 2009: 58), separated by some three decades from the latter: "Even though normal social encounters, for instance conversations, may only last a few minutes, our point is that during that period they may organize themselves [as follows] . . . the agents sustain the encounter, and the encounter itself influences the agents and invests them with the role of interactors. The interaction process emerges as an entity when social encounters acquire this operationally closed precarious organization. It constitutes a level of analysis not reducible to individual behaviors." The tenor of resemblance to that which I argued a generation before is remarkable.
9. This is one reason why in anthropology the journal article has become more prevalent in citation recording and evaluation. Much less can be accomplished through the article when compared with the monograph. The latter tries much harder to embody the complexity and richness of time, space, and person (see Handelman 2009). The length and character of the journal article in practice almost automatically invokes and legitimates the premise of "all other things being equal."
10. The historian of science Michel Serres (2015) argues for example, that "solidity" is slow speed.
11. The philosopher, Cornelius Castoriades, influenced by Francisco Varela's use of autopoiesis in cell biology, re-introduced and radicalized Aristotle's concept of *physis* (or *phusis*) as purposively "pushing-toward-giving-itself-a-form." See Adams (2008: 390; 2014).
12. For critiques of and support for the usefulness of autopoiesis in law see, for example, Zolo 1992; Bankowski 1994; Paterson 1995.

13. Fully supported by the Inuit households that the late Jean Briggs studied in the 1960s and 1970s. See Briggs (1970, 1998).
14. That might be worth thinking about, for example, in relation to Mircea Eliade's (1964) myth of the eternal return.
15. This thought builds on the philosopher Helmuth Plessner's conception of "mediated immediateness," in which the immediacy of human experience becomes mediated perception in order to shape the world (Lerch 2014: 208). Also cited in Soeffner (1997).
16. So neither Peter Blau (1964), the most prominent proponent of exchange theory at the time, nor Fredrik Barth (1981: 14–76), the innovator of transaction theory, related to the profound formative confluence of the conjunction of curving, volume, depth, and time. This kind of thinking was foreign to them, as it continues to be in anthropology and sociology. I am not discussing Gestalt Theory here though it is relevant to the stability of visual forms and, according to Gandelman (1982), to Husserl's phenomenology. However Gestalt Theory seems to say little about the problematic of time in social forms.
17. Here is one example of responses at the time to these ideas. In 2004 I lectured on ritual in its own right at the Institute for Indian Studies at the University of Heidelberg. When I began to discuss the step of taking a "ritual" out of context in order to study the phenomenality of its interior form the senior anthropologist at the Institute half stood up and loudly called out to me, "You can't do that!" My response was, "I'm doing it."
18. Present-day state and other official orderings largely downgrade "ritual" to mirroring and representing social orders. Yet oft forgotten in relation to "ritual" is that these orderings use the most powerful organ of making controlled change ever invented by human beings—bureaucratic logic and the ongoing, routine, making and changing of taxonomic bureaucratic classification (Handelman 1998: xxiv–xliii; this volume, Chapter Four). So it is not surprising that official "rituals" are often as lacking in interior dynamics as they are. In thinking like this I can be accused (once more) of implicit functionalism through lengthy durations. Yet to me this way of thinking is more akin to that of Michel Serres's use of the logic of "crumpled time," of times that—chronologically, linearly—are distant from one another yet that bring together, even join together, a logic in each that is akin to the other (See Serres's thinking on turbulence in Lucretius and in modern physics). In its crumpling, time is nonlinear or, more accurately, a-linear, such that there is no linear baseline to time, as the nonlinear (the "not-linear") implies. Then, why necessarily separate points of time chronologically distant from one another when the logic of what happens during each of these points in time is akin to that of the other? To what extent is such separation a product of an ontology that demands linearity in thinking, planning, and intellectualizing in order to conceal recursivity?
19. For example, look at the dynamism of curving and folding in paintings (Elasticity [1922], The Dynamism of a Football Player [1913], and The Dynamism of a Cyclist) by the Italian futurist, Umberto Boccioni.
20. Among those who have responded to the idea that it is worthwhile studying ritual in its own right are Clark-Deces (2007: 11–12), Espirito Santo (2016), and Shapiro (2015).
21. The mathematician, George Spencer Brown (1969), called this self-intersection, re-entry. His calculus shows how logical form emerges from the making of distinctions—how space comes into existence from nothing (Robertson 1999). In doing so he discovered that, contrary to his original intention to have space emerge only from space, his calculus could not continue indefinitely to develop space synchronically. In a sense the calculus demanded that form exit itself and re-enter itself in order to enable the calculus to make its creation of form just that—whole. Form, in order to become form, had to become self-referential. This is what the re-entry of form did in re-entering itself and thereby necessarily referring to itself. Yet, what is especially interesting here is that to have form make itself self-referential Spencer Brown had to introduce what he called "time" in order to deal with re-entry—of going outside in order to return inside. This operation could not be performed without *duration*, that is, time. As Schiltz (2007: 27) put this: "The reader must realize that time has thus been created as a consequence of a type of

space, namely space in which form can relate to itself [through self-intersection], and, as such, change . . . ." But here in my terms something no less intriguing occurred. By making time critical to the creation of form Spencer Brown had to take into account just what it is that time does. Time moves. As form durationally re-enters itself time continues to move forward, and therefore form, creating itself through its re-entering, can never catch up with itself, and is always out of sync with itself (see Schiltz 2007: 22). *Form therefore can never be whole*; holism is always just out of reach. Furthermore, again in my terms, if the re-entry of form into itself is understand as the repetition of form in a Deleuzian sense then repetition necessarily generates difference. Form therefore is ontogenetic (i.e., morphogenetic) rather than ontological (see Schiltz and Verschraegen 2002). For a similar argument on why holistic theories in physics—theories of everything (theory of relativity, quantum mechanics, string theory)—ultimately fail, see Rosen 2008.

22. The ethnographer was Donald Roy, an industrial sociologist whose orientation derived from the Chicago School of Sociology (see Roy 1959–60). In *Models and Mirrors* (Handelman 1998: 104–12) I offered an earlier interpretation, one related to dialectics, though I am more satisfied with my present-day understanding.

23. One might argue that the idea of framing is no less effective than that of folding and that framing has been an accepted term for many years. Yet note that "frame" is a linear idea that promotes the spatial and its interior shallowness, while "fold" accentuates depth, the temporal, and interior complexity.

24. This is similar to phenomena that Max Gluckman (1963) called "rituals of rebellion," in which recurrent, ritualized opposition to the social order is contained by that order, thereby demonstrated the strength and resilience of that order that then encourages further "rituals" of opposition to the social order. Myron Aronoff (2015) used Gluckman's idea to analyze the operations of the Central Committee of the Mapai (Labor) party in Israel during the 1970s.

25. Marilyn Strathern (1988) took the "dividual" to Melanesia, arguing that Melanesian persons are themselves composites of the substances and qualities of other persons so that in a sense each person contains a multiplicity of persons and is able to shift through aspects of these others as parts of oneself. The Melanesian person, she argues, is partible. In this regard, see the distinction drawn by Busby (1997) between partible and permeable personhood.

26. So, too, with regard to certain aspects of gender in South India. In Western perception categories of gender are monothetic, and as a new gender is "officially" recognized it is added to the string of others, each an encapsulated difference, hence the string of LGBTQ that is actually L+G+B+T+Q. South Indian gender may be more similar to a continuum or, more accurately, to the skins of an onion that overlap with one another more and more in deeper and deeper depth (see Handelman 2014: 109–10).

27. I must emphasize that the idea of folding is not the recourse to a more abstract metalevel understanding of the forming of form. Folding is *not* encompassment. Encompassment refers to a holding together from their exteriors of all the elements that hold together. The logics of this kind of assemblage are those of some kinds of forcefulness that tries to prevent the elements of the assemblage from falling apart or escaping. Encompassment is a top-down idea that dictates the organization of motion and movement. Folding is closer to a bottom-up idea, describing the emergence and self-organization of assemblages *through* their own motion and movement. Folding resonates in some ways with a qualitative use of the construct of the Klein Bottle with its self-intersecting involution that, according to Steven Rose in one of his works, is time as the fourth dimension; in other words, is the duration that necessarily enables movement through, within, and outside the Bottle. Of course the distinction between encompassment and folding may well be fuzzy, perhaps with shifts back-and-forth, in and out. This does not obviate the significance of the distinction; indeed folding and encompassment may grow out of one another, and then the conditions for the formation of each become critical.

What I deny is the simplistic ease with which we reach for higher-order metalevel concepts and arguments in order to enable order that then, again too easily, becomes the baseline for thinking on stability *and* change. I am in full agreement with the philosopher of science, Isabelle Stengers (2008: 107), when she argues about the problematic way "in which we accept the domination of abstractions; that is, the way in which we consent to forget or neglect what we are aware of when it cannot be formulated in a clear, self-contained way." The macro does not necessarily encompass and organize the micro. Phenomenal forms on their ways to folding self-intersection (to whatever degrees) have their own lives that thread through the lives of their participants. In order to perceive this we must avoid the condition of explanation in which, as the historian Siegfried Kracauer (1969: 126) commented, events (and social phenomena) arrive at macro altitudes in a "damaged state." Kracauer (1969: 130) accurately and wisely summarizes the problem of metalevel explanation in noting that, "The belief that the widening of the range of *intelligibility* involves an increase of *significance* is one of the basic tenets of Western thought. Throughout the history of philosophy it has been held that the highest principle, the highest abstractions, not only define all the principles they formally encompass but also contain the essences of all that exists in the lower depths. They are imagined as the 'highest things' in terms of both generality and substance" [italics in original]. As I (Handelman 2006b: 112) commented elsewhere, "The history of field-research anthropology in the twentieth and now the twenty-first century may be understood as an unresolved struggle with this premise [of Kracauer's]."

28. Another example of an autopoietic moment is what in Jewish Israel is called "crystallization" (*gibush*), the sudden formation of group-ness, of folded-ness, within a collection of loosely connected or disparate individuals (see Handelman 2007b: 132–34). See also the invention of an (unspoken) game, the Donkey Game, in one of the workshops I studied (Handelman 1990: 86–101).

29. Physics had long discounted time as a dynamic in the workings of the cosmos. As Stengers (1977: 40.1) states: "to affirm that time is nothing else than the geometrical parameter [i.e., a fourth dimension] that allows calculation from the exterior, and as such, negates the becoming of all natural beings, has been almost a constant of the tradition of physics for the last three centuries . . . . In our time it is Einstein who embodies with the greatest force the ambition of eliminating time," that was powerfully in evidence in his 1922 debate with Bergson during which Einstein dismissed the "[subjective] time of philosophers" as "incompetent" (ibid.). Yet according to Canales (2015: 346) later in life Einstein "admitted that he did not think that the division between the subjective and objective could be established once and for all, or even that between physics and metaphysics."

Interestingly, the historian, Kofi Campbell, in a blog post in 2008, wrote, "I was rereading some of the writings of Albert Einstein, and one sentence in particular struck me again: 'The only reason for time is so everything doesn't happen at once.'" This phrasing, here attributed to Einstein, is simply a paraphrase of Bergson's, "Time is what hinders everything from being given at once" (Bergson 1992: 93). Regrettably, Campbell does not give a reference for his reading, and apparently the other historian contributing to the blog did not ask him for one. I emailed Campbell at the University of Waterloo (4 April 2018) asking if perhaps he still had the reference even though a decade had passed but received no reply. Campbell's post was cited in Eileen Joy, "Signaling to Each Other From Inscrutable Depths: A Response to Gabrielle Spiegel's '"Getting Medieval": History and the Torture Memos'" (http://www.inthemedievalmiddle.com/2009/03/signaling-to-each-other-from.html; accessed 5 February 2017).

30. Thus Grosz (1999a: 4): "each [of these thinkers] in his own way affirms time as an open-ended and fundamentally active force—a materializing if not material—force whose movements and operations have an inherent element of surprise, unpredictability, or newness . . . and chance . . . is of the essence of a time that is not regulated by causality and determination but unfolds with its own rhythms and logic, its own enigmas and impetus." See also Grosz (1999b: 28).

31. Later on, Einstein was convinced the universe had four dimensions, and still later on he wondered about this. See note 29.

32. See note 4 in Simeonov 2015 for the translation.

33. Michel Serres's (1998: 81–122) exposition of "the birth of time" gives to time something of the qualities of the a-linear. Serres suggests that, in relation to space, time can shift to become less spatial (and closer to pure time in its own right) or more spatial, enabling a multiplicity of relationships between forms and time.
34. Bateson (1972) argued this through his theory of schismogenesis. See the modifications of Simonse (n.d.) and Thomassen (2010).
35. By using the neologism, own-ness, I do not have to assume the existence of self in relation to reflexivity. I assume instead that an organism of any variety has its own "own-ness," whatever this is that holds the organism together as a unit or units, without assuming that it necessarily has a self.
36. Organic matter, even at the molecular level (see Schweber 2016: 130–31; Torday 2018: 5) may be said to possess memory and hence to process information. This suggests that in-turning is no less the organic referencing itself through information-processing. In evolutionary terms, according to the cell biologist, J. S. Torday, such memory is genetic and, importantly, epigenetic, the cellular organism learning through time from its changing environments and passing this information from generation to generation. See also the discussions on the Neuroskeptic Blog ("Slug Life: About that Injectable Memory Study," <http://blogs.discovermagazine.com/neuroskeptic/2018/05/18/epic-snail-about-that-injectable-memory-study/#more-9517> accessed 4 June 2018) regarding experiments to transfer a component of memory from one sea slug to another. As Landecker and Panofsky (2013: 339) say, "With epigenetics, the formerly immutable genome is acquiring a life span." In my terms, life span is durational and the organism is a time-form contending with reproduction and change through the organism's in-turning, into itself. For a wise, cautionary note on epigenetics, society, and culture, see Lock (2015).
37. Once the movement of time is factored in, even the potentialities of Deleuzian virtuality (see Handelman 2013) cannot enable organic time to catch up with physical time.
38. I saw this first-hand and up close. At the time I was in Manchester and Gluckman was my PhD supervisor.
39. As Crawford (2007: 11) points out, "Gluckman's material example of structural duration was a chair, in which the molecules are always moving but the structure . . . remains the same. This is perhaps more telling than Gluckman realized. The significant distinction is not between 'the' structure of the chair and the constant movement of the many particles within it, but the multiple structures involved in a chair and their corresponding multiple timeframes. . . . Max Gluckman's chair contains a radical plurality of temporalities . . . The chair-in-itself is a sort of membrane, or what some have termed a 'moment,' where (when!?) a set of temporal processes of very different periodicities come together."
40. Thus the process philosopher, G. H. Mead, used a version of this kind of reflexivity to discuss the emergence and functioning of selfhood through taking the role of the other.
41. Without speaking of selfhood, self-identity may be embedded in a variety of organic forms. Some, like the body and flesh more generally, are clearly sentient in their own, active ways that are undoubtedly sensually cognitive. For example, the reactions of immune responses to the presence of foreign bodies that are felt as threatening to the organism, and the mistakes of immune responses in recognizing the surface disguises that some of these foreign bodies may take on, all depend on recognizing difference from the common identity that characterizes cellular membership in the organism (cf. Tauber 1997, Wilce 2003, Napier 2003).
42. Perhaps time, in opening to the potentiality of multiplicity, moves toward what Michel Serres called "crumpled time," a heterogeneous, polymorphic sense of time through which moments separated chronologically in linear time come into contact with one another because both use the same logic of thought and affect. Therefore these moments or events should not be thought of as separated by the duration between present and past, however distant. (For that matter, these moments could be thought of as existing on parallel time-lines in an indeterminate universe). Serres's most well-known example is the resonance (one can say the time-resonance) between the thinking on turbulence of the Roman, Epicurean poet, Lucretius (in his *De Rerum Natura*) and the twentieth-century thinking of physicists).

43. See Gilles Deleuze speaking with Richard Pinhas, "On Music," 03/05/1977, translated by Timothy S. Murphy, in Les Cours de Gilles Deleuze <www.webdeleuze.com>.
44. Much of this discussion is taken from Handelman and Katz (1998), though my understanding of this ontology today is radically different in certain respects from that previous version.
45. By contrast, space is alienated (by expulsion), and fragmented (by destruction); while desired space is often at best the promise of time: *elsewhen*, and attainable only through the coherent continuity and integrity of time.
46. Elsewhere (Handelman and Lindquist 2011) I have argued that the Jewish God holds together the cosmos of His creation from its outside rather than from its inside. The existence of God does not depend upon the survival of His cosmos (unlike, for example the South Indian cosmos of the deity, Shiva, whose very survival depends upon his cosmos holding itself together from its inside [Handelman and Shulman 2004]). One can say that the existence of His cosmos depends upon the capacity of Jews to perfect themselves morally in accordance with God's instructions through actions whose primary rhythm and pulsation is that of time moving from low to high; and that every striving for such moral perfection throughout Jewish history has failed, yet the rhythm of striving for moral perfection begins all over again. At times I think that the Jewish God placed his standards at such a height that Jews could only fail in their strivings to reach them, thereby ensuring that the rhythm and pulsation would begin over again.
47. Mandelbrot's geometry of the fractal refers to structures that in terms of classical mathematics of Euclid and Newton were perceived as pathological: "By definition, fractal objects have fractal dimension. According to Mandelbrot, they are *broken, irregular, fragmented, grainy, ramified, strange, tangled, wrinkled*. These wrinkled structures may extend over space, over time, or over both: fractal space-time patterns" (Abraham 1993: 53). Time, as discussed in this chapter, is neither objective nor subjective. Nor is time a structure that extends over time. Rather, time is moving and folding within form, enabling or aiding form to move through time within itself and through time exterior to itself. Thus I am saying that the organizing of Jewish cosmic time, its self-similar pulsation on different scales, is fractal-like in this respect.
48. The idea of the fractal was introduced into anthropology by Roy Wagner in the first instance to discuss Marilyn Strathern's "concept of the person who is neither singular nor plural" (Wagner 1991: 162), though Wagner demonstrates the relevance of its organization to a number of New Guinea cultural orderings.
49. The first four Sabbaths of this sequence are explicitly accorded a special status in traditional Judaism. Their temporal rhythm is accentuated if one adds to this sequencing the readings from Prophets of the two subsequent Sabbaths.
50. Meron Rapaport, "One Day, Two Declarations," *Haaretz* (English edition), 7 June 2007.

References

Abraham, Ralph H. 1993. "Human Fractals: The Arabesque in Our Mind." *Visual Anthropology Review* 9: 52–55.
Adam, Barbara. 1998. "Social Versus Natural Time, A Traditional Distinction Re-examined." In *The Rhythms of Society*, ed. Michael Young and Tom Schuller, 198–226. London: Routledge.
Adams, Suzi. 2008. "Towards a Post-Phenomenology of Life: Castoriades' Critical Naturphilosophie." *Cosmos and History* 4: 387–400.
———. 2014. "The Living Being." In *Cornelius Castoriades: Key Concepts*, ed. S. Adams, 135–41. London: Bloomsbury Academic.
Aronoff, Myron J. 2015. *Power and Ritual in the Israel Labor Party*. London: Routledge.
Bankowski, Zenon. 1994. "How does it feel to be on your own? The Person in the Sight of Autopoiesis." *Ratio Juris* 7: 254–66.

Barad, Karen. 2007. *Meeting the Universe Halfway: Quantum Physics and the Entanglement of Matter and Meaning*. Durham, NC: Duke University Press.

———. 2010. "Quantum Entanglements and Hauntological Relations of Inheritance: Dis/continuities, Space/Time Enfoldings, and Justice-to-come." *Derrida Today* 3: 240–68.

Barbour, Julian. 2009. "The View from Nowhen (Interview)." *Collapse* V: 75–118.

Bar-On Cohen, Einat. 2009. "*Kibadachi* in Karate: Pain and Crossing Boundaries within the 'Lived Body' and within Sociality." *JRAI* n.s.: 610–29.

———. 2014. "Kyudo—Resonance Involuted and the Folding of Time in Japanese Archery." *Anthropos* 109: 525–37.

Barth, Fredrik. 1981. *Process and Form in Social Life: Selected Essays of Fredrik Barth, Volume I*. London: Routledge & Kegan Paul.

Bateson, Gregory. 1958. *Naven*, 2nd ed. Stanford: Stanford University Press.

———. 1972. *Steps to an Ecology of Mind*. New York: Ballantine.

———. 1977. "Afterword." In *About Bateson*, ed. John Brockman, 235–47. New York: E. P. Dutton.

Bergson, Henri. 1992. *The Creative Mind: An Introduction to Metaphysics*. New York: Citadel Press.

Beyerchen, Alan. 1992/93. "Clausewitz, Nonlinearity, and the Unpredictability of War." *International Security* 17: 59–90.

Bialecki, Jon, and Girish Daswani. 2015. "What is an individual? The View from Christianity." *HAU* 5: 271–94.

Blacker, Carmen. 1975. *The Catalpa Bow: A Study of Shamanistic Practices in Japan*. London: Allen & Unwin.

Blau, Peter. 1964. *Exchange and Power in Social Life*. New York: John Wiley.

Bloch, Maurice. 1974. "Symbols, Song, Dance and Features of Articulation." *European Journal of Sociology* 15: 55–81.

Bohm, David. 1981. *Wholeness and the Implicate Order*. London: Routledge & Kegan Paul.

Borges, Jorge Luis. 1964. "A New Refutation of Time." In *Labyrinths*, 190–205. New York: New Directions.

Brands, Henry W. 1992. "Fractal History, or Clio and the Chaotics." *Diplomatic History* 16: 495–510.

Briggs, Jean. 1970. *Never in Anger: Portrait of an Eskimo Family*. Cambridge, MA: Harvard University Press.

———. 1998. *Inuit Morality Play: The Emotional Education of a Three-Year-Old*. New Haven: Yale University Press.

Busby, Cecilia. 1997. "Permeable and Partible Person: A Comparative Analysis of Gender and the Body in South India and Melanesia." *JRAI* n.s.: 261–78.

Canales, Jimena. 2015. *The Physicist and the Philosopher: Einstein, Bergson, and the Debate that Changed Our Understanding of Time*. Princeton: Princeton University Press.

Castoriades, Cornelius. 1997. *The Imaginary Institutions of Society*. Oxford: Blackwell.

Clark-Deces, Isabelle. 2007. *The Encounter Never Ends: A Return to the Field of Tamil Rituals*. Albany: SUNY Press.

Crawford, David L. 2007. "The Temporality of Resistance." In *Beyond Resistance: The Future of Freedom*, ed. Robert Fletcher, 3–20. Nova Science Publishers.

Daniel, Valentine. 1984. *Fluid Signs: Being a Person the Tamil Way*. Berkeley: University of California Press.

Deacon, Terrence W. 2006. "Emergence: The hole at the wheel's hub." In *The Re-Emergence of Emergence*, ed. Philip Clayton and Paul Sheldon Davies, 111–50. New York: Oxford University Press.

Deleuze, Gilles. 1991. *Bergsonism*. New York: Zone Books.

———. 1993. *The Fold: Leibniz and the Baroque*. London: Athlone Press.

———. 1995. "On Leibniz." In *Negotiations 1972–1990*, 156–63. New York: Columbia University Press.

———. 1997. "An Unrecognized Precursor to Heidegger: Alfred Jarry." In *Essays Critical and Clinical*, 91–98. Minneapolis: University of Minnesota Press.
Di Paolo, Ezequiel. 2009. "Overcoming Autopoiesis: An Enactive detour on the Way from Life to Society." In *Autopoiesis in Organizations and Information Systems*, ed. R. Magalhaes and R. Sanchez, 43–68. Amsterdam: Elsevier.
Eliade, Mircea. 1964. *Cosmos and History: The Myth of the Eternal Return*. New York: Harper Torchbooks.
Espirito Santo, Diana. 2015. "Liquid Sight, Thing-like Words, and the Precipitation of Knowledge in Cuban Espiritismo." *JRAI* n.s.: 579–96.
———. 2016. "Clothes for Spirits: Opening and Closing the Cosmos in Brazilian Umbanda." *HAU* 6: 85–106.
Evens, Terence M. S. 1977. "The Predication of the Individual in Anthropological Interactionism." *American Anthropologist* 79: 579–97.
Evens, T. M. S., and Don Handelman, eds. 2006. *The Manchester School: Practice and Ethnographic Praxis in Anthropology*. New York: Berghahn Books.
Evens, Terry, Don Handelman, and Christopher Roberts, eds. 2016. *Reflecting on Reflexivity: The Human Condition as an Ontological Surprise*. New York: Berghahn Books.
Fisch, Michael. 2013. "Tokyo's Commuter Train Suicides and the Society of Emergence." *Cultural Anthropology* 28: 320–43.
Forbes-Pitt, Kate. 2013. "Self-organization: What is it, what isn't it and what's it got to do with morphogenesis?" In *Social Morphogenesis*, ed. M. S. Archer, 105–24. Dordrecht: Springer Science+Business Media.
Gandelman, Claude. 1982. "Philosophy as a Sign-producing Activity: The Metastable Gestalt of Intentionality." *Semiotica* 39: 45–54.
Garfinkel, Harold. 1967. *Studies in Ethnomethodology*. Englewood Cliffs: Prentice-Hall.
Gebser, Jean. 1984. *The Ever-Present Origin*. Athens: Ohio University Press.
Gell, Alfred. 1992. *The Anthropology of Time*. Oxford: Berg.
Gluckman, Max. 1963. *Order and Rebellion in Tribal Africa*. New York: Free Press of Glencoe. (The chapter titled "Rituals of Rebellion in South-East Africa" was originally the Frazer Lecture of 1952.)
———. 1968. "The Utility of the Equilibrium Model in the Study of Social Change." *American Anthropologist* 70: 219–37.
Goffman, Erving. 1961. *Encounters: Two Studies in the Sociology of Interaction*. Indianapolis: Bobbs-Merrill.
———. 1983. "The Interaction Order." *American Sociological Review* 48: 1–17.
Grana, Nicola. 2016. "The Concept of Time in Prigogine." In *The Concept of Time in Early Twentieth-Century Philosophy*, ed. F. Santoianni, 229–37. Cham, Switzerland: Springer International Publishing.
Grossing, Gerhard. 1993. "Atomism at the End of the Twentieth Century." *Diogenes* 163: 71–88.
Grosz, Elizabeth. 1999a. "Becoming . . . An Introduction." In *Becomings: Explorations in Time, Memory and Futures*, ed. E. Grosz, 1–14. Ithaca: Cornell University Press.
———. 1999b. "Thinking the New: Of Futures Yet Unthought." In *Becomings: Explorations in Time, Memory and Futures*, ed. E. Grosz, 15–28. Ithaca: Cornell University Press.
———. 2005. "Bergson, Deleuze and the Becoming of Unbecoming." *Parallax* 11: 4–13.
Handelman, Don. 1967. "The Development of a Washo Shaman." *Ethnology* 4: 444–64.
———. 1972. "Aspects of the Moral Compact of a Washo Shaman." *Anthropological Quarterly* 45: 84–101.
———. 1973. "Gossip in Encounters: The Transmission of Information in a Bounded Social Setting." *Man* 8: 210–27.
———. 1977. *Work and Play Among the Aged: Interaction, Replication, and Emergence in a Jerusalem Setting*. Assen: Van Gorcum.

———. 1989. "Toward Small-group Culture: Intermediate Phases of Microstructure and Microprocess." In *The Content of Culture: Constants and Variants. Studies in Honor of John M. Roberts*, ed. Ralph Bolton, 407–23. New Haven: HRAF Press.

———. 1990. *Models and Mirrors: Towards an Anthropology of Public Events*. 1st ed. Cambridge, UK: Cambridge University Press.

———. 1994. "Critiques of Anthropology: Literary Turns, Slippery Bends." *Poetics Today* 15: 341–81.

———. 1998. *Models and Mirrors: Towards an Anthropology of Public Events*. 2nd ed. New York: Berghahn Books.

———. 2005a. "Introduction: Why Ritual in Its Own Right? How so?" In *Ritual in Its Own Right*, ed. Don Handelman and Galina Lindquist, 1–32. New York: Berghahn Books.

———. 2005b. "Microhistorical Anthropology: Towards a Prospective Perspective." In *Critical Junctions: Pathways Beyond the Cultural Turn*, ed. Don Kalb and Herman Tak, 29–52. New York: Berghahn Books.

———. 2006a. "Conceptual alternatives to ritual." In *Theorizing Ritual*, ed. Jens Kreinath, Jan Snoek, and Michael Stausberg, 37–49. Leiden: Brill.

———. 2006b. "The Extended Case: Interactional Foundations and Prospective Dimensions." In *The Manchester School: Practice and Ethnographic Praxis in Anthropology*, ed. T. M. S. Evens and Don Handelman, 94–117. New York: Berghahn Books.

———. 2007a. "How dynamic is the anthropology of chaos?" *Focaal: European Journal of Anthropology* 50: 155–65.

———. 2007b. "The Cartesian Divide of the Nation-state: Emotion and Bureaucratic Logic." In *The Emotions: A Cultural Reader*, ed. Helena Wulff, 119–40. Oxford: Berg.

———. 2009. "What is happening to the anthropological monograph? (The onslaught of the journal article)." *Social Anthropology* 17: 218–23.

———. 2013. "Bruce Kapferer, Deleuzian Virtuality, and the Making of a Ritual Masterstroke." *Religion and Society* 4: 32–40.

———. 2014. "The Guises of the Goddess and the Transformation of the Male: Gangamma's Visit to Tirupati and the Continuum of Gender." In *One God, Two Goddesses, Three Studies of South Indian Cosmology*, 63–113. Leiden: Brill.

Handelman, Don, and Elihu Katz. 1998. "State Ceremonies of Israel—Remembrance Day and Independence Day." In *Models and Mirrors: Towards an Anthropology of Public Events* by Don Handelman, 2nd ed., 191–233. New York: Berghahn Books.

Handelman, Don, and Galina Lindquist, eds. 2005. *Ritual in Its Own Right: Exploring the Dynamics of Transformation*. New York: Berghahn Books.

Handelman, Don, and Galina Lindquist. 2011. "Religion, Politics, and Globalization: The Long Past Foregrounding the Short Present—Prologue and Introduction." In *Religion, Politics & Globalization: Anthropological Approaches*, ed. Galina Lindquist and Don Handelman, 1–66. New York: Berghahn Books.

Handelman, Don, and Lea Shamgar-Handelman. 1990. "Shaping Time: The Choice of the National Emblem of Israel." In *Culture Through Time: Anthropological Approaches*, ed. Emiko Ohnuki-Tierney, 193–226. Stanford: Stanford University Press.

———. 1993. "Aesthetics Versus Ideology in National Symbolism: The Creation of the Emblem of Israel." *Public Culture* 5: 431–49.

Handelman, Don, and David Shulman. 1997. *God Inside Out: Siva's Game of Dice*. New York: Oxford University Press.

———. 2004. *Siva in the Forest of Pines: An Essay on Sorcery and Self-Knowledge*. New Delhi: Oxford University Press.

Harrison, Simon. 1993. *The Mask of War: Violence, Ritual and the Self in Melanesia*. Manchester: Manchester University Press.

Hertz, Joseph H. 1938. *The Pentateuch and the Haftorahs*. London: Soncino.

Heschel, Abraham Joshua. 1951. *The Sabbath: Its Meaning for Modern Man.* New York: Farrar, Straus, and Young.
Hirsch, Samson Rafael. 1985. *The Collected Writings, Vol. II.* New York and Jerusalem: Feldheim.
Hodges, Matt. 2008. "Rethinking Time's Arrow: Bergson, Deleuze and the Anthropology of Time." *Anthropological Theory* 8: 399–429.
———. 2014. "Immanent Anthropology: A Comparative Study of 'Process' in Contemporary France." *Journal of the Royal Anthropological Institute* 20: 33–51.
Holland, Eugene. 2012. "Non-linear Historical Materialism: Or, What is Revolutionary in Deleuze & Guattari's Philosophy of History." In *Time and History in Deleuze and Serres*, ed. Bernd Herzogenrath, 17–30. New York: Continuum.
Horgan, John. 1998. *The End of Science.* London: Abacus.
Hori, Ichiro. 1962. "Self-Mummified Buddhas in Japan. An Aspect of the Shugen-Do ('Mountain Asceticism') Sect." *History of Religions* 1: 222–42.
Johnson, Galen A. 1993. "Desire and invisibility in 'Eye and Mind': Some remarks on Merleau-Ponty's spirituality." In *Merleau-Ponty in Contemporary Perspective*, ed. P. Burke and J. Van der Veken, 85–96. Amsterdam: Kluwer Academic Publishers.
Kapferer, Bruce. 1972. *Strategy and Transaction in an African Factory.* Manchester: Manchester University Press.
Kauffman, Yehezkel. 1972. *The Religion of Israel.* New York: Schocken.
Kelly, Michael R. 2015. "Phenomenology and Time-Consciousness." *Internet Encyclopedia of Philosophy*, 1–28. Retrieved 23 March 2015 from http://www.iep.utm.edu/phe-time/.
King, Michael. 1993. "The 'Truth' about Autopoiesis." *Journal of Law and Society* 20: 218–36.
Kracauer, Siegfried. 1969. *History, the Last Things Before the Last.* New York: Oxford University Press.
Kreinath, Jens. 2012. "Naven, Moebius Strip, and Random Fractal Dynamics: Reframing Bateson's Play Frame and the Use of Mathematical Models for the Study of Ritual." *Journal of Ritual Studies* 26: 38–64.
———. 2019. "Playing with Frames of Reference in Veneration Rituals: Random Fractals in Encounters with a Muslim Saint." *Anthropological Theory* 19. https://doi.org/10.1177/1463499 619841212.
Landecker, Hannah, and Aaron Panofsky. 2013. "From Social Structure to Gene Regulation, and Back: A Critical Introduction to Environmental Epigenetics for Sociology." *Annual Review of Sociology* 39: 333–57.
Lerch, Henrike. 2014. "Anthropology as a Foundation of Cultural Philosophy: The Connection Between Human Nature and Culture by Helmuth Plessner and Ernst Cassirer." In *Plessner's Philosophical Anthropology: Perspectives and Prospects*, ed. Jos de Mul, 195–210. Amsterdam: Amsterdam University Press.
Lock, Margaret. 2015. "Comprehending the Body in the Era of the Epigenome." *Current Anthropology* 56: 151–77.
Magnani, Lorenzo. 2016. "Commentary: Einstein, Prigogine, Barbour, and Their Philosophical Refractions." In *The Concept of Time in Early Twentieth-Century Philosophy*, ed. F. Santoianni, 249–51. Cham, Switzerland: Springer International Publishing.
Maimonides, Moses. 1956. *The Guide for the Perplexed.* New York: Dover.
Marriott, McKim. 1989. "Constructing an Indian Ethnosociology." *Contributions to Indian Sociology* 23: 1–39.
Mazis, Glen A. 2010. "Time at the Depth of the World." In *Merleau-Ponty at the Limits of Art, Religion, and Perception*, ed. K. Semonovich and N. D. Rao, 120–44. New York: Continuum.
McDaniel, Raymond. 2013. "Ever Present: Attention and Alertness in the Unawake." *Anthropology of Consciousness* 24: 208–13.
McFeat, Tom. 1974. *Small-Group Cultures.* New York: Pergamon.
Merleau-Ponty, Maurice. 1962. *The Phenomenology of Perception.* London: Routledge & Kegan Paul.

———. 1968. *The Visible and the Invisible*. Evanston: Northwestern University Press.
Miller, Jay. 1983. "Basin Religion and Theology: A Comparative Study of Power (*Puha*)." *Journal of California and Great Basin Anthropology* 5: 66–86.
Moore, Sally Falk. 1975. "Uncertainties in Situations, Indeterminacies in Culture." In *Symbol and Politics in Communal Ideology*, ed. Sally Falk Moore and Barbara Myerhoff, 210–39. Ithaca: Cornell University Press.
Munn, Nancy. 1992. "The Cultural Anthropology of Time: A Critical Essay." *Annual Review of Anthropology* 21: 93–123.
Napier, A. David. 2003. *The Age of Immunology: Conceiving a Future in an Alienating World*. Chicago: University of Chicago Press.
Nash, June. 1989. *From Tank Town to High Tech*. Albany: SUNY Press.
Paterson, John. 1995. "Who is Zenon Bankowski talking to? The Person in the Sight of Autopoiesis." *Ratio Juris* 8: 212–29.
Polanyi, Michael. 1958. *Personal Knowledge: Toward a Post-Critical Philosophy*. London: Routledge & Kegan Paul.
Prigogine, Ilya. 1997. *The End of Certainty*. New York: Free Press.
Prigogine, Ilya, and Isabelle Stengers. 1984. *Order Out of Chaos: Man's New Dialogue With Nature*. New York: Bantam.
Roberts, John M. 1951. "Three Navajo Households: A Comparative Study in Small Group Culture." *Papers of the Peabody Museum of American Archeology and Ethnology* XL: 1–88.
———. 1964. "The Self-management of Cultures." In *Explorations in Cultural Anthropology: Essays in Honor of George Peter Murdock*, ed. Ward Goodenough, 433–54. New York: McGraw-Hill.
Robertson, Robin. 1999. "Some-thing from No-thing: G. Spencer-Brown's Laws of Form." *Cybernetics & Human Knowing* 6: 43–55.
Rosaldo, Renato. 1980. *Ilongot Headhunting*. Stanford: Stanford University Press.
Rose, Deborah Bird. 2000. "To Dance with Time: A Victoria River Aboriginal Study." *Australian Journal of Anthropology* 11: 287–96.
Rosen, Steven M. 2008. *The Self-Evolving Cosmos: A Phenomenological Approach to Nature's Unity-in-Diversity*. Singapore: World Scientific Publishing Company.
———. 2015. "Why Natural Science Needs Phenomenological Philosophy." *Progress in Biophysics and Molecular Biology* 119: 257–69.
Roy, Donald. 1959–60. "'Banana Time': Job Satisfaction and Informal Interaction." *Human Organization* 18: 158–68.
Sawyer, R. Keith. 2005. *Social Emergence: Societies as Complex Systems*. New York: Cambridge University Press.
Schiltz, Michael. 2007. "Space is the Place: The *Laws of Form* and Social Systems." *Thesis Eleven* 88: 8–30.
Schiltz, Michael, and Gert Verschraegen. 2002. "Spencer-Brown, Luhmann and Autology." *Cybernetics & Human Knowing* 9: 55–78.
Schutz, Alfred. 1962–66. "Making Music Together." In *Collected Papers*. Vol. 2, 159–76. The Hague: Martinus Nijhoff.
Schweber, Sam. 2016. "Some Comments on Emergence." In *What Reason Promises*, ed. Wendy Doniger et al., 124–35. Berlin: De Gruyter.
Serres, Michel. 1998. *Genesis*. Ann Arbor: University of Michigan Press.
———. 2015. *Statues*. London: Bloomsbury.
Shapiro, Matan. 2015. "Curving the Social, or, Why Antagonistic Rituals in Brazil are Variations on a Theme." *JRAI* 22: 47–66.
Shavit, Yaacov, and Shoshana Sitton. 2004. *Staging and Stagers in Modern Jewish Palestine: The Creation of Festive Lore in a New Culture, 1882–1948*. Detroit: Wayne State University Press.
Sheets-Johnstone, Maxine. 1999. *The Primacy of Movement*. Amsterdam: John Benjamins.
Simeonov, Plamen L. 2015. "Yet Another Time About Time . . . Part I: An Essay on the Phenomenology of Physical Time." *Progress in Biophysics and Molecular Biology* 119: 271–87.

Simone, Nina (with Stephen Cleary). 1992. *I Put a Spell on You: The Autobiography of Nina Simone*. New York: Pantheon.
Simonse, Simon. n.d. "Mimesis, Schismogenesis, and Catastrophe Theory: Gregory Bateson as a Forerunner of Mimetic Theory; With a Demonstration of His Theory on Nilotic Regicide." Unpublished Manuscript.
Smolin, Lee. 2007. *The Trouble with Physics*. New York: Houghton Mifflin.
Soeffner, Hans-Georg. 1997. *The Order of Rituals: The Interpretation of Everyday Life*. New Brunswick: Transaction Publishers.
Somers-Hall, Henry. 2009. "Deleuze and Merleau-Ponty: The Aesthetics of Difference." In *Gilles Deleuze: the Intensive Reduction*, ed. C. Boundas, 213–21. London: Continuum.
Spencer Brown, George. 1969. *Laws of Form*. London: Allen & Unwin.
Stengers, Isabelle. 1997. "The Reenchantment of the World (with Ilya Prigogine)." In *Power and Invention* by Isabelle Stengers, trans. Paul Bains, 34.3–58.9. Minneapolis: University of Minnesota Press.
———. 2008. "A Constructivist Reading of *Process and Reality*." *Theory, Culture & Society* 25: 91–110.
Strathern, Marilyn. 1988. *The Gender of the Gift: Problems with Women and Problems with Society in Melanesia*. Berkeley: University of California Press.
Tauber, Alfred I. 1997. *The Immune Self: Theory or Metaphor?* Cambridge, UK: Cambridge University Press.
Thomassen, Bjorn. 2010. "Schismogenesis and Schismogenetic Processes: Gregory Bateson Reconsidered." Conference on Social Pathologies of Contemporary Civilization. Aalborg, 28–29 October.
Torday, John S. 2018. "Reflections on Evolution Theory." New Year Essay for Foundations of Information Science, fis.sciforum.net.
Turner, Victor. 1977. "Process, System, and Symbol: A New Anthropological Synthesis." *Daedalus* 106: 61–80.
Vainstein, Yaacov. 1953. *The Cycle of the Jewish Year*. Jerusalem: World Zionist Organization.
Wagner, Roy. 1991. "The Fractal Person." In *Big Men and Great Men: Personifications of Power in Melanesia*, ed. Maurice Godelier and Marilyn Strathern, 159–73. Cambridge, UK: Cambridge University Press.
Wambacq, Judith. 2011. "Depth and time in Merleau-Ponty and Deleuze." *Chiasmi International* 13: 327–48.
Wilce, James M. Jr., ed. 2003. *Social and Cultural Lives of Immune Systems*. London: Routledge.
Zerubavel, Eviatar. 1985. *The Seven Day Circle: The History and Meaning of the Week*. New York: The Free Press.
Zolo, N. 1992. "The Epistemological Status of the Theory of Autopoiesis and its Application to the Social Sciences." In *European Law Book in the Sociology of Law: State, Law, Economy as Autopoietic Systems: Regulation and Autonomy in a New Perspective*, ed. A. Febrajo and G. Tuebner, 67–124. Milan: Giuffré.

INDEX

abduction, logic of, 40–58, 299, 334n6. *See also* mindful feeling
aesthetics: aesthetic feel of practice, 127–129, 271–272, 283–285; of the event of presentation, 129–131; of experience, 128; of mundane living, 127–129, 145n2, 272, 283; of performance, 130–131, 141, 145n2; of power, 283–285. *See also* bureaucratic aesthetics
autopoiesis (self-making), 68–69, 128, 187n3, 308, 334n11, 337n28
Axial Age. *See* First Great Rupture of Cosmos

banana time, 301–304. *See also* curving; folding; forming of form; self-organization
Bar-On Cohen, Einat, 307, 314
Barth, Fredrik, 318, 335n16
Bateson, Gregory, 44, 58n2, 69, 71, 90n18, 151–168, 172–187; schismogenesis, 58n2, 18; "A Theory of Play and Fantasy" (publication), 153. *See also* play, and fantasy theory; recursiveness
Beck, Ulrich, 233–234
Bentham, Jeremy. *See* Panopticon
Bergson, Henri, 128, 272, 312, 313–314
Black, Donald, 217
border, between interior and environment, 41, 80, 82–84, 111–112. *See also* Luhmann, Niklas
Borges, Jorge Luis, *Borges and I* (publication), 243–244, 314. *See also* curving
boundary: between humans and the divine, 10, 48, 194–195; between inside and outside, 171, 177–179 (*see also* framing, theory of; Kreinath, Jens); between play and not-play, 151–158, 160 (*see also* play, theory of; Bateson, Gregory). *See also* border
bureaucratic aesthetics: of the Israeli State, 126–146, 269–272, 283–285; of legal system, 110, 145, 285 (*see also* King, Michael); of power, 283–285; of ritual, 126–146; of temporality, 137–138
bureaucratic logic, 9, 40–58, 93–120, 126–146; of the Israeli State, 9, 49–52, 54–58, 110–116, 119nn18–19, 120n24, 126–146; of legal system (system of capture), 110, 145; of power, 101–103, 118n11, 142 (*see also* Panopticon); of ritual, 53–58, 126–146; of temporality, 138. *See also* lineal classification; Weber, Max

Calatrava Pylon-Parabola, 272–279. *See also* Impenetrable Block; Mall-Wall
Calvin and Hobbes, 64–65
Cartesian divide, 12
chaos theory, 177
complexity (interior), theory of, 64–70, 84–86, 293–301, 303–304, 310. *See also* self-organization
cosmology (*also* cosmos): ancient Indo-European, 165–166; filmic microcosmos of *Mulholland Drive*, 253–254, 259–260 (see also *Mulholland Drive*); intra-grated (*see* intra-gration); of Henry Rupert, 47–48, 53; of Hua-yen buddhism, 193–194; Jewish, 327–333, 339n46; monotheistic (*also* monothetic), 10, 175–176; of play, 152–153, 158–165; South Indian, 4–5, 158–163, 196–206, 305–306; Washo, 1, 29–30, 323–324; Zionist, 9, 333

curving (dynamic), 69–88, 89n13, 243, 244, 256–257, 262, 273–274, 297–298, 300–306, 316–317, 320–321. *See also* Borges, Jorge Luis; Deleuze, Gilles; dynamics, moebius; folding

Dancing Regiment, The, 76–78. *See also* autopoiesis; curving; rite
Daniels, Valentine, 305, 319. *See also* fluidity
Deleuze, Gilles, 10, 44, 253–256, 260–262, 292; cosmogenesis, 253–254, 264, 286n6 (*see also* Klee, Paul); fold, 71, 300 (*see also* folding); rhizome, 213–214, 223–225 (*see also* Guattari, Felix; rhizome [dynamic]); state-form, 97, 108–113, 131–134, 223, 234, 236n18, 283–285 (*see also* bureaucratic logic; forming of form; topology); territorialization (i.e., making place from space), 111–112, 326; *Thousand Plateaus, A*, 213–214
Devji, Faisal, 225, 228–232, 238n37
Dumont, Louis, 167n17, 192–194. *See also* holism
Durkheim, Emile, 166n14; altruistic suicide, egoistic suicide, 216, 226, 234 (*see also* self-exploding; self-sacrifice); effervescence, 85, 208; emergence, 334n7 (*see also* emergence)
dynamics: as cosmic process, 203–206 (*see also* Turner, Victor); filmic dynamics, 245–247; of folding place and space, 270–272, 278 (*see also* folding); interior dynamics of ritual, 55, 66, 68, 74, 84–85 (*see also* ritual); interval, 260–264 (*see also* liminality); moebius as alternative dynamics of framing, 175–179 (*see also* framing; moebius); moebius dynamics of the forming of form, 244–245 (*see also* forming of form); of rhizomic forming and movement, 223–228 (*see also* Deleuze, Gilles); theory of social, 2, 5, 8–11; time-full dynamics of movement and form, 289–337 (*see also* time)

Eisenstein, Sergei, 260
emergence, 3–5, 181, 293–300, 309–310, 320, 334n7; of bureaucratic logic, 42, 94, 105, 111 (*see also* bureaucratic logic; Foucault, Michel); of difference, 314; of monotheisms, 192, 194–195 (*see also* First Great Rupture of Cosmos); of play, 164, 167n19; of boundaries, 223–224 (*see also* boundary); of self-organization, 274, 307–308 (*see also* autopoiesis). *See also* Durkheim, Emile
Engler, Steven, 179, 184–185. *See also* Gardiner, Mark
entropy, 163, 310; as destruction of cosmos, 205 (*see also* cosmology, South Indian); and negentropy, 314, 317, 320–323
ethnography, 4, 43–44

First Great Rupture of Cosmos, 192, 194–195. *See also* Lindquist, Galina
fluidity, in South Indian cosmology, 4–5, 160–162, 166n10, 196–200, 203–206
folding, 10–11; fold, 71, 300–301 (*see also* Deleuze, Gilles); folding and enfolding as vector of control, 269–286; moebius dynamics as, 244–245, 253–254, 262; in monothetic classification, 95 (*see also* lineal classification); in ritual, 72–73, 77–84 (*see also* Turner, Victor); as self-organization, 301–309, 336n27 (*see also* self-organizing); of temporal movement, 309–320, 322, 326, 327, 331–333 (*see also* time)
forming of form: bureaucratic aesthetics of, 126–146 (*see also* aesthetics; framing); through bureaucratic logic, 93–120 (*see also* lineal classification; state-form); interior and exterior forming of cosmos, 191–208 (*see also* cosmology, South Indian; First Great Rupture of Cosmos); logic of the, 1–13; moebius qualities and dynamics of, 171–187, 243–266 (*see also* Bateson, Gregory; moebius; ritual); through play, paradox of, 151–168 (*see also* Bateson, Gregory; boundary between play and not-play; play, theory of); through ritual, 63–90 (*see also* curving; folding); through self-exploding, 213–238 (*see also* rhizomic organization;

terrorism); through the state, 269–286 (*see also* aesthetics; folding; vector)
Foucault, Michel, 93, 97–101, 103–108; *The Order of Things*, 93, 97. *See also* bureaucratic logic; lineal classification
fractal (dynamics), 329, 339nn47–48; in *naven* ritual, 177, 179–181, 182–183 (see also *naven*). *See also* Wagner, Roy
framing: paradox of framing play, 154–160 (*see also* play, and fantasy theory); theory of, 9, 141–142, 151–152, 171–187, 311, 336n22. *See also* Bateson, Gregory
Furez, 78–85. *See also* recursiveness; border; folding, fold; rite

Gardiner, Mark, 179, 184–185. *See also* Engler, Steven
Geertz, Clifford, 64–65
Gemeinschaft (community), 103–106. *See also* holism
gestalt (coherent entity), 129, 283–284. *See also* Polanyi, Michael
Gluckman, Max: on ritual as social relations, 88, 187n9, 336n24; on structural duration, 317–320
Goffman, Erving, on encounter, 50, 70, 89n11, 165n1, 184, 292
Guattari, Felix, *Thousand Plateaus, A*, 213–214. *See also* Deleuze, Gilles

Handelman, Don, 1–13, 47–58; "Administrative Frameworks and Clients" (special issue of *Social Analysis*, with Jeff Collmann), 93; *God Inside Out*, 152 (*see also* Shulman, David); *Models and Mirrors*, 63–64, 93, 173, 186, 298–301; *Nationalism and the Israeli State*, 93; *Ritual in Its Own Right* (publication), 300 (*see also* Lindquist, Galina); *Work and Play Among the Aged*, 290–294, 298–301
holism, 177, 192–203, 207n2. *See also* Dumont, Louis
Holocaust, 116, 136–137, 141–143, 274–279; Holocaust Martyrs and Heroes Remembrance Day (Israel), 9, 126–146,

331; memorial authority (*see* Yad Vashem). *See also* time
hologram, 329. *See also* fractal
Horwitz, Jonathan (shaman), 1, 17–18
Houseman, Michael, 181–182, 187n9

Impenetrable Block, 281–283. *See also* Calatrava Pylon-Parabola; Mall-Wall
inter-gration (i.e., exterior organization of cosmos), 192–208
interval, 246, 260–264
intra-gration (i.e., interior organization of cosmos), 9–10, 176–177, 192–208
Islam (*also* Muslim world), individuation of, 218, 225–227, 228–229, 238n37. *See also* Devji, Faisal; Mahmood, Saba; rhizome
Israel (*also* Palestine), bureaucratic logic in: the forming of pre-state Palestine, 93–94, 107, 109, 111–116; the memorialization of the Holocaust, 119nn18–19, 126–146; mundane life, 9, 42, 49–58; the topology of Jerusalem, 269–286. *See also* aesthetics; bureaucratic aesthetics; cosmology, Zionist; Deleuze, Gilles; folding; forming of form; Holocaust; Jerusalem; lineal classification; social ordering; state-form

Kapferer, Bruce, 54, 88; *Feast of the Sorcerer, The*, 179, 213; on Sinhalese Suniyama exorcism, 68–69, 179, 226–227, 262. *See also* emergence
Katz, Jack, 128–129
King, Michael, 56–57, 110–111, 145, 285, 296
Klee, Paul, 253, 264n1, 274. *See also* Deleuze, Gilles
Kreinath, Jens, 177–181, 187n5

Leach, Edmund, 183–184
Levi-Strauss, Claude, 65
lila and maya, 158–163. *See also* boundary; cosmology, South Indian; play, and self-transformation; play, and top-down cosmos

liminality, as a time/space of curvature, 72, 261–262. *See also* curving; Turner, Victor
Lindquist, Galina, 13, 17, 176, 192, 242; *Ritual in Its Own Right* (publication), 300 (*see also* Handelman, Don)
lineal classification (*also* linear classification, lineal logic of classification, lineal taxonomy, taxonomic classification), 9, 42, 52–58, 130; bureaucratic classification, 53–56; military classification, 131–134; monothetic classification, 94–103, 110–111, 117n3. *See also* forming of form
Luhmann, Niklas, 68, 70–71, 187n3. *See also* border
Lynch, David. See *Mulholland Drive*

Mahmood, Saba, 228–229
Mall-Wall, 279–281. *See also* Calatrava Pylon-Parabola; Impenetrable Block
Marie Antoinette (Maria Antonia) crossing the Rhine, 74–76. *See also* curving; rite
Marriott, McKim, 180–181, 207n9, 305
Maturana, Humberto. *See* autopoiesis
Merleau-Ponty, Maurice, 291–292, 313–314
mindful feeling (*also* feeling-thinking), 5, 41, 43, 46, 50, 57; knowing and feeling, paradox of, 1–2, 5–7, 11–12, 43; "Know through your feelings, but know!," 1, 12, 18 (*see also* Rupert, Henry Moses)
moebius: framing, 175, 177–179 (*see also* framing); paradoxical surface of, 6–7, 178; rhizomic movement of, 10; as self-entering form, 171, 176–177, 243–245, 262, 264n2 (*see also* folding; recursiveness; self-organization)
Mulholland Drive, 242–266
myth, 65. *See also* Levi-Strauss, Claude; Paiditalli

naven (Iatmul ritual), 90n18, 173, 177, 179–183; fractal *wau* in, 179–181; *Naven* (book), 173. 293. *See also* Bateson, Gregory
Neuman, Yair. *See* moebius, framing

ontology, 290, 322–323; temporal ontologies (*also* time as ontological movement), 311, 313, 327. *See also* time; Prigogine, Ilya
organization, exterior logics of (*also* hierarchical organization, symmetrical organization, systemic organization). *See* bureaucratic logic; lineal classification
organization, interior logics of (*also* self-organization), 63–64, 187n3, 304–305; complexity and self-organization, 84–85, 89n14; as emergence, 294; as folding, 298–301, 307–308, 336n27 (*see also* folding, fold); through moebius dynamics, 244 (*see also* dynamics, moebius); self-organization as ritual, 55, 58n7, 67–73, 74–84; of terrorism, 214–215, 219–225 (*see also* rhizome). *See also* autopoiesis; curving; forming of form; recursiveness

Paiditalli (the Golden Lady), 4–5, 196–206. *See also* autopoiesis; cosmology, South Indian; Durkheim, effervescence; entropy; fluidity; intra-gration; recursiveness; ritual
Panopticon, 100–101, 117–118n6
Peirce, C. S. *See* abduction, logic of
phenomena, 66–68; formation of phenomenal worlds, 108; phenomenal cosmos, 158–165 (*see also* play); phenomenality of phenomena, 85–88; phenomenology of time, 313, 318–319 (*see also* Prigogine, Ilya); phenomenon as boundary, 177–179 (*see also* boundary; moebius); self-organizing phenomenal form, 70–73, 289–298, 299–301. *See also* forming of form; ritual
physis (*phusis*, the internal drive), 70, 285, 296, 300, 334n11
play: and bottom-up cosmos, 163–165 (*see also* cosmology, monotheistic; self-ordering); boundary between play and not-play, paradox of, 153–160 (*see also* boundary); and fantasy theory, 9, 152–153 (*see also* Bateson, Gregory); and

Indian cosmologies (*see* lila and maya); and self-transformation, 158–163, 166n14, 167n16, 167n19, 167–168n21; theory of, 151–168; and top-down cosmos, 163–164
poetism, 40, 58
presentation, the event of, 129–131
Prigogine, Ilya: linear physical time (*contrast with* curving organic time), 309–311, 313; "time as arrow," 11
process: culture as processual, 296 (*see also* Turner, Victor); play as, 151–168 (*see also* Bateson, Gregory); social ordering as processual, 318 (*see also* Barth, Fredrik; Gluckman, Max). *See also* dynamics; emergence; play, theory of

recursiveness (*also* recursivity), 42–44, 58n2, 206; in framing cosmos, 176, 187n3; in framing ritual, 70–72, 74–84, 174, 177–179; in the moebius dynamic, 244, 253–255 (*see also* dynamics, moebius); phenomenal form (i.e., recursiveness of curvature), 300; recursive time-space, 303, 307–308, 320. *See also* Bateson, Gregory; Deleuze, Gilles
rhizome (dynamic), 10, 109; lines of flight (i.e., rhizomic movement), 223–225; rhizomic organization of terrorism, 213–215, 219–225, 233–234, 236n17, 237n23. *See also* Deleuze, Giles; singularity
rite: *rites de passage*, 72 (*see also* liminality; Turner, Victor; Van Gennep, Arnold); self-closure of, 74–88, 90n18 (*see also* folding; self-organization); study of, 65 (*see also* Black, Max)
ritual: and bureaucratic logic, 53–58, 126–146 (*see also* lineal classification); and cosmic logic, 191–208; through filmic dynamics, 245–248; and folding, 298–301; forms that form forms, 8; framing ritual, 171–187 (*see also* self-closure); in its own right, 8–9, 63–90, 335n17; moebius dynamics of, 244–245; play-within-ritual, 51, 165n3, 167n16; ritual plays, 262–264; and sacrifice, 228–233; as self-organization, 67–74, 81, 84–85, 86, 89n14; transformative ritual, 261–262 (*see also* process; Turner, Victor)
Rupert, Henry Moses (shaman), 1–2, 11–12, 17–38, 44–45, 47–48, 52–54, 88, 323–327. *See also* abduction, logic of; mindful feeling
Russell, Bertrand: set theory, 184; theory of logical types, 153, 175 (*see also* Bateson, Gregory)

self-exploding (i.e., destruction of one's interior existential being-ness), 10, 213–238; as social act, 214 (*see also* self-sacrifice). *See also* rhizome (dynamic); self-organization; terrorism
self-sacrifice (i.e., self-exploding as altruistic), 214–215, 226–228; altruistic suicide and egoistic suicide, 226 (*see also* Durkheim, Emile); shaping the ritual of, 228–234 (*see also* forming of form; rhizomic organization)
shaman: ethic of healing, 26–35; spirit helper, 23–27, 32–35, 36, 325–326; Washo, 1–2, 17–38, 45, 88, 323–327 (*see also* Rupert, Henry Moses)
Shamgar-Handelman, Lea (*also* Lea Shamgar), 13, 54, 57, 58n6, 316
Shulman, David, 18, 54, 166n13, 173; *God Inside Out*, 152 (*see also* Handelman, Don). *See also* cosmology, South Indian
Simmel, Georg, 129; on "social forms," 7, 105
singularity, 254–256, 257–259, 262–264. *See also* Deleuze, Gilles; rhizome
Siva, 117n3 152, 204–205. *See also* cosmology, South Indian; Handelman and Shulman, *God Inside Out*; hologram; Wagner, Roy
social ordering, 41–44, 55–58, 63–66, 294–299, 305, 309, 317–318, 335n18. *See also* folding; ritual organization
surprise, 40–48, 334n6. *See also* abduction, logic of

terrorism, 10, 213–238; rhizomic organization of (*also* rhizomic terrorism),

223–225, 233–234; terrorism in modernity, 219. *See also* Black, Donald
time: bureaucratic aesthetics of, 133–134, 139–141; bureaucratic logic of, 113; Jewish cultural time, 327–333; moebius movement of, 257–259, 262–263; perception of time as dimension, 11, 291–292, 295–298, 301–333; the splitting of time, 255 (*see also* Deleuze, Gilles). *See also* folding, fold; recursiveness
topology, 6, 69, 100; topological vector, 269–285 (*see also* folding; Israel; state-form); topology of homotopy, 183. *See also* forming of form; moebius, paradoxical surface of
Turner, Victor, 72, 187n9, 261, 295–296. *See also* emergence; ritual, transformative

Van Gennep, Arnold, 72. *See also* ritual
Vishnu (*also* Krishna), 160–161, 182, 262–263

Wagner, Roy, 339n48. *See also* fractal
Washo (people), 18–19; healing ritual, 25, 37n3, 325–327. *See also* ritual
Weber, Max, 93, 101–102, 118n10. *See also* bureaucratic logic
Wyschogrod, Edith, 102, 217

Yad Vashem, (Holocaust Memorial Authority), 131–136, 138, 142, 146n11, 274–276

Zionist narrative, 9, 49, 107, 114–116. *See also* cosmology, Zionist

www.ingramcontent.com/pod-product-compliance
Lightning Source LLC
Chambersburg PA
CBHW051524020426
42333CB00016B/1773